GUIDE TO YOUR CAREER

GUIDE TO
YOUR CAREER

6TH EDITION

By Alan B. Bernstein, CSW, PC
and the Editors of The Princeton Review

Random House, Inc., New York
www.PrincetonReview.com

The Princeton Review, Inc.
2315 Broadway
New York, NY 10024
E-mail: bookeditor@review.com

ISBN 0-375-76561-1
ISBN-13 978-0-375-76561-2

Publisher: Robert Franek
Designed by Sophie Ye Chin
Editor: Suzanne J. Podhurst
Production Editor: Christine LaRubio
Production Manager: Scott Harris
Contributing authors for 6th edition: Andrew Baker, Frank C. Napolitano, Andrea Kornstein, Erik Olson, and Kerry Dexter

Manufactured in the United States of America
10 9 8 7 6 5 4 3 2 1
6th Edition

DEDICATION

To my mother and father, who gave me just enough rope not to hang myself.

—ALAN BERNSTEIN

CONTENTS

INTRODUCTION

You hold in your hands a book dedicated to action. Most of us have moments of clarity during which we see vivid images of what our future careers will be like, but lack a method to make these ideas a reality. *Guide to Your Career* is designed to build on years of thought and experience, to move you from impulse to deed, thought to action, anxious planning to specific goal setting. We have put forth a plan to help you implement your goals, while anticipating some of the places you may get stuck or let down in your efforts. Our method focuses on two types of information gathering—intuitive and objective—as we lead you toward assembling the information you need to make a creative and informed decision about your life.

We believe in the creative style of career searching. This means getting to know thoroughly what *interests* you have, the *style* in which you enjoy pursuing those interests, and the personal *needs* that should be met for you to operate at your highest potential. After developing a strong and precise vocabulary with which to describe yourself to potential employers (you will be practicing extensively with friends and fellow enthusiasts first), you will develop a thorough working knowledge of the potential fields, careers, and professions that interest you. What do people do every day? How did they reach their positions? How do they think? How do they dress? Our goal at The Princeton Review is to help you present yourself as a resource to the industry or profession you have chosen— not in an empty, self-aggrandizing manner, but as someone who demonstrates a working knowledge of challenges and opportunities in that field. We will help you make yourself indispensable to an employer's future. This metamorphosis from career-seeker to industry resource requires extensive preparatory interviewing, professional or trade journal reading, and persistent information gathering.

To help develop your E.Q.* , we have included a custom-designed, self-scoring version of the Birkman Personality Profile. This will give you a way to understand and describe your interests and style. In addition, we have developed a second method for heightening self-awareness through selected memories. We call this "poetry for engineers" because intuitive ideas are explored through reasoned analysis. You can be guided to gain insight by using our suggested questions and techniques.

* From Daniel Goleman's evocative book *Emotional Intelligence*. E.Q. is a derivative equivalent of the intellect's IQ. It refers to a person's ability to perceive emotions and establish intimacy.

PART I

CAREER CREATION

FINDING A CAREER YOU LOVE

WHAT DO YOU LIKE TO DO?
HOW DO YOU LIKE TO DO IT?

To this day I remember the panic I felt when I graduated from college more than thirty years ago and realized I didn't have a clue about how to make my way in the world. I did what many of you have done or might do—I took a year off from my prescribed education to wander the world and try to discover what I needed by poking about in "life." Although I had a great year, this approach prepared me for only one option—more school. While this isn't so bad on its own, I ended up simply returning to the subjects in which I earned the best grades. The truth is, I was afraid to lose the structure I already knew how to negotiate in: pleasing teachers and getting good (enough) grades. In effect, I was condemned to perpetuate the system, enrolling in a PhD program at Rutgers. I stayed there long enough to be sure that I did not want to teach English literature as a career. But, like many of the people I now work with as a counselor— lawyers who do not want to practice law, physicians who do not want to participate in managed care—I had to face the frustrating prospect of giving up time I had invested in my career and the money and status it afforded me. Worse, I had to enter another program for more schooling. I had never really researched any careers outside of school, where I was safe, where I had mastered the rules.

I fell into my first profession, college teaching, by default. Realizing after a few years that I preferred a profession that brought me more intense emotional contact with people, I discovered psychotherapy, a profession I didn't know existed. By then I was nearly thirty, married with a child, and I had to take on the challenge of a new degree in a different graduate program. Believe it or not, I consider myself lucky. I was able to complete my education (those were the days of National Institute of Mental Health Fellowships), and I entered my career with only a decade of lost time.

A generation later, my daughter graduated from college and went through exactly the same process I had. Nothing had changed. Preparation for graduating from college is as necessary as any science or economics course. Students need a program to help them determine what their interests are, evaluate their options, and research those options thoroughly enough to make intelligent career choices. Unfortunately, few colleges offer such guidance. That's why we wrote this book.

You might think of *Guide to Your Career* as a point of entry to a job. That is only one of its potential uses. It's something else as well, a way to fill in parts of your education that school—high school, college, or graduate education—may never have addressed. We'll help you answer the following questions:

- Who am I? What makes me tick?

- What do I really enjoy? What gives me genuine satisfaction?

- Is there a way to convert what I most enjoy doing, my skills, my personal needs, and the ways in which I like doing things, into a moneymaking career?

Guide to Your Career has been developed to give you the opportunity and methods for answering these questions.

The first part of the book will help you figure out how you like to do things. You'll learn not only what interests you—you are probably already familiar with—but also the personal style in which you like to pursue your interests. You'll learn to work with preconscious* as well as conscious knowledge to interpret yourself and to understand your own needs and interests the same way you would an interesting work of art or poetry. We'll show you how to recognize aspects of yourself, frequently your greatest gifts, which you take for granted because they are so natural.

* Preconscious ideas are available to the conscious mind with disciplined attention; subconscious material requires skilled interpretation and is frequently coded as symbolic language.

WHAT CAN WE PROVIDE?

The most frequently asked question in my office is "How do I know what I really love compared to what I've been told I should do?" It is useful to have interest inventories, such as the Birkman Career Style Summar, to help us select and narrow down our interests, or even just to corroborate what we've always known. We'll help you hone your sense of personal style and clarify the unique ways in which you enjoy pursuing your interests. The Birkman Method, from which the Career Style Summary is derived, is a program used by major corporations to assess the strengths of individuals. The Birkman Career Style Summary allows you to gain access to broad information about yourself. The questions use the Birkman Method research material to clarify both your interests and your style. This will be a major asset in defining not only what you are drawn to, but how you like to achieve. The Birkman Group has created The Princeton Review's self-scoring test specifically for *Guide to Your Career* to enable you to develop a sense of the style in which you like to pursue your interests. For example, if you were to say, "I love working out at the gym," you would be establishing an interest. But some people might mean they love the team effort of a pickup basketball game, or working with a group in an organized aerobics class, while others might be referring to the solitude and concentration of weight lifting or a rowing machine. The interest (working out) is the same, but the style determines the ways in which a person feels happiest and most productive.

Next, we'll show you how to use selected memories to learn more about which types of professions would satisfy you the most. As a psychotherapist, my interests include not only conscious life but, as I mentioned, the vast territory we call the preconscious. I would like to show you how to use your memory to activate important material from your preconscious that we can explore to establish what might satisfy you in the future. Reading your memory complements the research studies and information we will be sharing with you in the career profiles. I call this technique "poetry for engineers" because we combine intuitive skills with precise methods for understanding and applying our history. By utilizing this method, we can help you confirm

- your chief interests
- how you enjoy using these interests
- what environments, both physical and emotional, produce the greatest satisfaction for you

Using your memories and the Birkman Career Style Summary together, we will be balancing intuitive and subjective information with objective data based on the millions of people who have taken the full Birkman Method.*

> Recognizing and understanding intuitive and precognitive needs will largely determine how satisfied you will feel in your career.

* The Princeton Review Seminar has used the computer-scored, extended version of the Birkman Method, but this version must be interpreted by a certified Birkman provider.

CREATING YOUR CAREER

Next, we'll show you how to create your new career. We encourage you to undertake the *career creation* process with at least one other person, preferably a group such as the ones we put together at The Princeton Review. To create your own group, find at least one person (but preferably a few other people) committed to generating information and career development skills. Agree on a date and time to meet weekly. Use the meetings to review the first three chapters in this book. Make a commitment to be active observers of one another's progress. Having this contract with a friend or small group will help you maintain your pace.

Guide to Your Career will help you set up a schedule for your career search and take you step-by-step through the process. After you define your goals, we'll show you how to pursue your new career interests through interviews and original research in the field you have chosen so that you can comfortably converse with prospective employers. You'll become a creative researcher, developing the skills to find the best uses for your interests and abilities. Accompanying each career profile are addresses that will give you starting points for your exploration. We'll tell you how long you should expect to spend at each stage of your career search. Finding the right job may take longer than you'd like it to; but methodical, steady application will eventually land you where you want to go.

And that's only the beginning.

BROADENING YOUR HORIZONS

The Princeton Review researchers have surveyed and interviewed hundreds of professionals in 240 careers so you can get some idea of where your skills and methods of working would be best applied. We'll answer your questions about scores of professions, some of which you might never have thought to consider.

What does a social worker, a carpenter, or an actuary do all day? What do you have to do to become an artist, an astronomer, a chef, or an editor? What personal qualities are necessary to thrive in each of these professions?

We have isolated key issues that may affect your sense of success or failure in your chosen field based on how well they serve your needs as an individual. We've outlined the issues facing significant professions and industries so you'll know how your life might change in a particular field. We've surveyed professionals to find out what a day is like in their careers, at the beginning, after five years, and after ten years. *Guide to Your Career* will help you select a career option that taps into your creative resources.

Good luck on your career creation journey, and *bon voyage!*

THE BIRKMAN METHOD

|WHAT IS THE BIRKMAN METHOD?

The Birkman Method is an effective instrument for personal and organizational development. It is not a psychological clinical assessment; rather, it profiles the behavior of normal, functioning people. Many other professional aptitude assessment instruments in the marketplace today began as psychological assessment tools for use in diagnosing problems (MMPI, 16PF). Others rephrase your answers in their terminologies (Strong Campbell, DISC) or label you in off-the-shelf-categories (Myers-Briggs). No other assessment instrument offers the depth of the Birkman Method.

The Birkman Method, endowed by the National Foundation for Science, has been in existence for more than forty years. The database used for generating the results of the Method, featuring individuals from almost every walk of life and nationality, is one of the most comprehensive ever created. Birkman is nonjudgmental. No one person's style is considered better than any other's—the various results merely bring to light your unique combination of interests and behavior that will help you in your career choice.

This version of the Birkman Profile is a simple way to visualize your overall behavior. The following questions are a condensed and self-scored version of the Birkman Method that was created especially for this book. As I mentioned in Chapter 1, the Birkman Career Style Summary allows you to gain access to a broad range of information about yourself. The questions presented here use the Birkman Method research material and enable you to apply it to clarify both your interests (symbolized by "I") and your style (symbolized by "S"). This will be a major asset in defining not only what you are drawn to, but also *how* you like to achieve.

THE GRID

The Birkman Career Style Summary plots aspects of your personality and behavior on a grid with four quadrants, each identified by a color name.

The Lifestyle Grid is based on a model of how people behave in general, and this particular model has been used for thousands of years. The first person to use it was probably Hippocrates, who is thought to be the father of medicine. Hippocrates claimed that he could take all the people in the world, divide them into four categories, and accurately describe how they would act or behave. Sometimes the Grid is called the Hippocratic Model. According to Hippocrates, there are four basic temperaments. He describes people as Implementors, Communicators, Planners, and Administrators, and bases his model on this idea. Models or pictures are not perfect; they are only generalizations. This one, however, is a very good generalization of how most people behave most of the time.

THE LIFESTYLE GRID

Outgoing
Exerts Direct Authority

Factual / **Objective**	**RED** IMPLEMENTORS	**GREEN** COMMUNICATORS	*Feelings* / **Subjective**
	Task–oriented	People–oriented	
	Organizer	Director	
	Delegates to get results	Works with people to get results	
	Acts direct	Acts direct	
	Feels direct	Feels sensitive	
	YELLOW ADMINISTRATORS	**BLUE** PLANNERS	
	System–oriented	Idea–oriented	
	Controller	Planner	
	Uses system to get results	Uses ideas to get results	
	Acts sensitive	Acts sensitive	
	Feels direct	Feels sensitive	

Reserved
Exerts Indirect Authority

THE GRID SYMBOLS

There are two aspects of your personality and behavior that appear on this Grid:

(I) An "I" indicates your *interests*, what you want to do—that is, your work preferences, as indicated by your interest patterns; the type of results you want, and the kind of activities that will give you the most satisfaction. *This does not measure skill or ability around those interests*; it only indicates preference. The color location of your "I" suggests what you like to do.

(S) An "S" indicates your *style*, how you like to do things, or what your usual behavior is. The "S" describes your style, or active behavior, for pursuing your interests. This is your preferred mode of achieving your personal goals and is descriptive of the way in which you like to operate when all your needs are met. It is how other people see you acting most of the time. It is how you do things when everything is going your way. If your style color results feel antithetical to your real-life style, consider whether you are operating under stress on a day-to-day basis, and remember that when considering your score.

The way someone behaves—style—does not necessarily relate to the way someone wants to be treated—needs. Thus, your style does not indicate that you need others to exhibit a similar style.

Now, please take the Birkman Career Style Summary. After the Summary you will want to put your interest symbol (I) and your style symbol (S) in your Lifestyle Grid.

YOUR LIFESTYLE GRID

RED	GREEN
YELLOW	BLUE

BIRKMAN CAREER STYLE SUMMARY

INSTRUCTIONS:

In order to develop an estimate of your "Birkman Colors" for your interests and style, you will need to complete and self-score the items below. To do this, read each pair of phrases and decide which side of the pair is most descriptive of you, then put a check mark by that phrase. As you make your choices, assume that all jobs are of equal pay and prestige.

COLUMN A	COLUMN B
1. ○ I would rather be a wildlife expert.	○ I would rather be a public relations professional.
2. ○ I would rather be a company controller.	○ I would rather be a TV news anchor.
3. ○ I would rather be a tax lawyer.	○ I would rather be a newspaper editor.

COLUMN A	COLUMN B
4. ○ I would rather be an auditor.	○ I would rather be a musician.
5. ○ I would rather be a production manager.	○ I would rather be an advertising manager.
6. ○ I would rather be an accounting manager.	○ I would rather be a history professor.
7. ○ I would rather be a bookkeeper.	○ I would rather be an electrician.
8. ○ I would rather be a writer.	○ I would rather be an elected official.
9. ○ I would rather be a clerical worker.	○ I would rather be a carpenter.
10. ○ I would rather be a payroll manager.	○ I would rather be a manager of engineering.
11. ○ I would rather be an audit manager.	○ I would rather be a safety manager.
12. ○ I would rather be an artist.	○ I would rather be a salesperson.
13. ○ I am usually patient when I have to wait on an appointment.	○ I get restless when I have to wait on an appointment.
14. ○ It is easy to laugh at one's little social errors or "faux pas."	○ It is hard to laugh at one's little social errors or "faux pas."
15. ○ It is wise to make it known if someone is doing something that bothers you.	○ It is wise to remain silent if someone is doing something that bothers you.

COLUMN A	COLUMN B
16. ○ It's not really okay to argue with others even when you know you are right.	○ It's okay to argue with others when you know you are right.
17. ○ I like to bargain to get a good price.	○ I don't like to have to bargain to get a good price.
18. ○ It is easy to be outgoing and sociable at a party with strangers.	○ It is hard to be outgoing and sociable at a party with strangers.
19. ○ I would read the instructions first when putting a new toy together for a child.	○ I would just "jump in" and start putting a new toy together for a child.
20. ○ It is usually best to be pleasant and let others decide if your ideas are worth accepting.	○ It is usually best to be forceful and "sell" your ideas to others.
21. ○ I usually like to work cautiously.	○ I usually like to work fast.
22. ○ Generally I prefer to work quietly with a minimum of wasted movement.	○ Generally I prefer to move around and burn some energy while I work.
23. ○ I don't like to have to persuade others to accept my ideas when there is strong forceful opposition or argument from others.	○ I like to sell and promote my ideas with others even when it takes some argument.
24. ○ It is better to listen carefully and be sure you understand when topics are being discussed.	○ It is better to speak up quickly and be heard when topics are being discussed.

SCORING YOUR ANSWERS:

Now that you have made your choices, you can score them to determine the "color" of your interests and style. To accomplish this, you will need to count the number of items you marked in **Column B** and enter these counts in the four spaces below.

- First, count the number of items checked in **Column B** for the first six (1-6) items and place that count in this space: _____ (Interest H)

- Second, count the number of items checked in **Column B** for the second six (7-12) items and place that count in this space: _____ (Interest V)

- Third, count the number of items checked in **Column B** for the third six (13-18) items and place that count in this space: _____ (Interest H)

- Fourth, count the number of items checked in **Column B** for the last six (19-24) items and place that count in this space: _____ (Interest V)

Now that you have these four counts, estimate your Interest and Style Colors.

YOUR INTEREST COLOR:

To *estimate* your Interest Color, simply read the four statements below and see which one describes your counts for Interest. The color associated with the statement that is correct for your counts is the best estimate of your Interest Color that you can make from this exercise.

- **BLUE**—If your **Interest H** count is 4 or greater (4, 5, or 6) and your **Interest V** count is 3 or fewer (1, 2, or 3), then your Interest Color is probably BLUE. You like creative, humanistic, thoughtful, quiet types of job responsibilities and professions.

- **GREEN**—If your **Interest H** count is 4 or greater (4, 5, or 6) and your **Interest V** count is 4 or greater (4, 5, or 6), then your Interest Color is probably GREEN. You like persuasive, selling, promotional, and group-contact types of job responsibilities and professions.

- **RED**—If your **Interest H** count is 3 or fewer (1, 2, or 3) and your **Interest V** count is 4 or greater (4, 5, or 6), then your Interest Color is probably RED. You like practical, technical, objective, and hands-on, problem-solving types of job responsibilities and professions.

- **YELLOW**—If your **Interest H** count is 3 or fewer (1, 2, or 3) and your **Interest V** count is 3 or fewer (1, 2, or 3), then your Interest Color is probably YELLOW. You like organized, detail-oriented, predictable, and objective types of job responsibilities and professions.

Now place an "I," indicating your interest, in the appropriate color square of the blank grid earlier in the chapter.

YOUR STYLE COLOR:

To estimate your Style Color, simply read the four statements below and see which one describes your counts for Style. The color associated with the statement that is correct for your counts is the best estimate of your Style Color that you can make from this exercise.

- **BLUE**—If your **Style H** count is 4 or greater (4, 5, or 6) and your **Style V** count is 3 or fewer (1, 2, or 3), then your Style Color is probably BLUE. You prefer to perform your job responsibilities in a manner that is supportive and helpful to others with a minimum of confrontation. You prefer to work where you and others have time to think things through before acting.

- **GREEN**—If your **Style H** count is 4 or greater (4, 5, or 6) and your **Style V** count is 4 or greater (4, 5, or 6), then your Style Color is probably GREEN. You prefer to perform your job responsibilities in a manner that is outgoing and even forceful. You prefer to work where things get done with a minimum of thought and where persuasion is well received by others.

- **RED**—If your **Style H** count is 3 or fewer (1, 2, or 3) and your **Style V** count is 4 or greater (4, 5, or 6), then your Style Color is probably RED. You prefer to perform your job responsibilities in a manner that is action-oriented and practical. You prefer to work where things happen quickly and results are seen immediately.

- **YELLOW**—If your **Style H** count is 3 or fewer (1, 2, or 3) and your **Style V** count is 3 or fewer (1, 2, or 3), then your Style Color is probably RED. You prefer to perform your job responsibilities in a manner that is orderly and planned to meet a known schedule. You prefer to work where things get done with a minimum of interpretation and unexpected change.

Now place an "S," indicating your Style Color, in the appropriate quadrant of the grid that appears earlier in the chapter.

APPLYING YOUR SYMBOLS

Now that you have a color for Interest and a color for Style, what do they mean?

YOUR INTEREST COLOR:

If your Interest Color suggests the same activities as the other techniques, then you will want to pay special attention to exploring the career options from this book that are described as consistent with your Interest Color.

Birkman organizes the "I" symbol, occupational interests, as:

OCCUPATIONAL INTERESTS

RED LIKES TO:	GREEN LIKES TO:
Build	Sell and promote
Organize	Persuade
See a finished product	Motivate people
Solve a practical problem	Counsel or teach
Work through people	Work with people
YELLOW LIKES TO:	**BLUE LIKES TO:**
Schedule activities	Plan activities
Do detailed work	Deal with abstraction
Keep close control	Think of new approaches
Work with numbers	Innovate
Work with systems	Work with ideas

As you begin to reflect on the career or profession you are drawn to, you will want to consider whether it contains aspects of the interests you are likely to wish to use. If your occupational interest is GREEN, for example, you will likely feel content in an environment that calls for promotion or persuasion.

YOUR STYLE COLOR:

Your Style Color (S) characterizes how others might describe you. It shows how you like to act, indicating your active behavior. Knowing the style in which you tend to pursue your interests is the first step toward describing the way in which you would like to pursue your interests. Your Style Color adds extra insight for possible career choices. It is not uncommon for a person's Interest and Style Colors to be different. Some may like the types of job responsibilities associated with their Interests, but prefer to practice these responsibilities in a manner and within an environment that is consistent with their Styles. For example, a GREEN Interest and BLUE Style combination suggests a career option that involves persuasive interest performed in a humanistic, creative, and supportive manner. Someone with this combination likes selling, promoting, persuading, and group contact responsibilities, but will still be most comfortable with a cause or product in which he holds conviction. A RED Interest would likely be drawn to an active career or profession, say, a visible leadership role in a company. If her Style is BLUE, however, she will likely need some downtime to withdraw and reflect on the *meaning* of proposals; while a RED Interest, RED Style might maintain an entirely proactive work style. A RED Interest with a YELLOW Style may be drawn to a leadership role, but is likely to operate conservatively with a close eye on the bottom line.

Birkman divides the style, or active behavior, as follows:

ACTIVE BEHAVIOR

RED APPEARS:	GREEN APPEARS:
Objective about people	Personable
Commanding	Directive
Competitive	Outspoken
Practical	Independent
Forceful	Enthusiastic about new things

YELLOW APPEARS:	BLUE APPEARS:
Sociable	Perceptive
Orderly	Agreeable
Cooperative	Conscientious
Consistent	Reflective and creative
Cautious	Cautious

When we have used the Birkman model in the career seminars at The Princeton Review, we have separated the colors, and then divided a page into two columns as follows: In the left-hand column, we have defined some characteristics that people associate with a specific color, for example RED interests, and on the right, we have listed the tasks and fields to which these interests might correspond in a work environment.

RED INTERESTS	RED FIELDS
doing	manufacturing
building	managing
implementing	directing
organizing	small-business owning
producing	surgery
delegating	
leading	

Similarly, we might list adjectives describing RED Style in the left-hand column and translate them on the right.

RED STYLE TENDS TOWARD BEING	. . . AND MIGHT THRIVE IN AN ENVIRONMENT THAT IS
straightforward	self-structured
assertive	high-pressured
logical	hierarchical
personable	production-oriented
authoritative	competitive
friendly	
direct	
resourceful	

GREEN INTERESTS	GREEN FIELDS
motivating	marketing
mediating	advertising
selling	training
influencing	therapy
consensus-building	consulting
persuading	teaching
debating	counseling
delegating authority	public relations
	law
	entertainment
	lobbying

GREEN STYLE TENDS TOWARD BEING

spontaneous
talkative
personal
enthusiastic
convincing
risk-taking

. . . AND MIGHT THRIVE IN AN ENVIRONMENT THAT IS

team-oriented
adventurous
informal
innovative
big picture-oriented
varied
competitive

YELLOW INTERESTS

ordering
numbering
scheduling
systematizing
preserving
maintaining
measuring
specifying details

YELLOW FIELDS

research
banking
accounting
systems analysis
tax law
finance
government work
engineering
archives
office management

YELLOW STYLE TENDS TOWARD BEING

cautious
structured
loyal
systematic
solitary
methodical
organized

. . . AND MIGHT THRIVE IN AN ENVIRONMENT THAT IS

predictable
established
controlled
measurable
orderly

BLUE INTERESTS

abstracting
theorizing
designing
writing
reflecting
originating

BLUE FIELDS

editing
teaching
composing
inventing
mediating
clergy
writing

BLUE STYLE TENDS TOWARD BEING	. . . AND MIGHT THRIVE IN AN ENVIRONMENT THAT IS
insightful	cutting-edge
reflective	informally paced
selectively sociable	organized in private offices
creative	low-key
thoughtful	future-oriented
emotional	
imaginative	
sensitive	

These lists come directly from the students at a Princeton Review seminar. For your purposes, it is best for you to make your own set of associations.

CHARACTERISTICS OF YOUR INTEREST COLOR

Describe your interests.

_____

_____

_____

How would these apply on a day-to-day basis in a career setting?

_____

_____

_____

What are some potential occupations?

_____

_____

_____

CHARACTERISTICS OF YOUR STYLE GROUP

How do you act and what style do you exhibit when things are going well?

_____

_____

_____

How would this apply on a day-to-day basis on the job?

_____

_____

_____

What are some potential occupations?

_____

_____

_____

As you isolate your interests and style and reflect on how they may be translated into specific, on-the-job applications, you might want to ask yourself the following questions:

What constructive action should I take?

_____

_____

_____

What strengths would I like to develop, based on my Interest and Style Colors?

_____

_____

_____

How will I seek opportunities to do this?

_____

_____

_____

You are now developing a vocabulary to describe yourself to a potential employer: what interests you, and how you have applied these interests; what your style is at its best; and how you might apply it. As you isolate your major interests and style, what further developmental work may be required?

USING YOUR INTEREST COLOR AND STYLE COLOR ESTIMATES

Now that you have an *estimate* of your Interest and Style Colors, you are ready to use them to begin exploring possible career options. As you use your Interest and Style Colors, please remember that they are just estimates and, as such, you should not make significant life choices based solely on them. These estimates are to be used as guides to help you explore possibilities. You will want to compare and work in conjunction with the other methods in *Guide to Your Career*, the "memories" you will recall in Chapter 3 and your informational interviewing (Chapter 4), to develop a full picture of your *interests*, *style*, and *needs*.

You are now prepared for Chapter 3, where you will have the opportunity to associate your *interests* and *style* with your *needs*, and to analyze how in your life to date these have come together to promote your most creative activity.

APPLYING YOUR MEMORIES

| REMEMBRANCE OF THINGS PAST

This is the most tantalizing part of the career creation process. You can train yourself to be an educated reader of your own preconscious mind through close observation and careful thought. This will require intense concentration, the kind you needed when you first analyzed a poem or when you put together your first stereo system. It's strange and unfamiliar, but not difficult. This kind of scrutiny helps you to interpret what you *really* want. We assign you a simple task with complex meanings: asking you to remember "stories" from your past. We define stories as isolated snapshots of incidents from your past that had the following characteristic:

> You were asked, or asked yourself, to accomplish a task, something you
> were not sure you could do. In doing this project you found not only that
> you could complete it, but that time had slipped away. You were in a
> state of "flow," and ordinary linear time disappeared.

In connection with the Birkman Career Style Summary, these snapshots give us information about what conditions are necessary for you to do your most creative work.

We find at The Princeton Review that it is best to work either with a friend or a group of people who are also trying to establish their career goals. Fresh insights help to solidify your sense of your interests and style. As you write your memories, reading them aloud to objective and interested listeners will help you free your preformed associations and enhance creative understanding of yourself and others. One of your goals is to expand your E.Q. (emotional intelligence), your capacity to empathize with and express interest in others. Later on, in Chapter 4, you will find this a significant skill when you begin your informational interviewing.

Try to remember those environments in which you've been most creative. They can be school, work, Boy Scouts or Girl Scouts, camp—wherever you've felt that you were completely satisfied to be doing what you were doing in the way you were doing it. See if you can isolate some common themes.

What I Was Doing When I Felt Happiest?

1. _____
2. _____
3. _____
4. _____
5. _____

For some of you critical thinkers, this may be a rough task, so we've developed a reverse twist to jog your memories:

Places Where I've Felt My Worst

1. _____
2. _____
3. _____
4. _____
5. _____

The purpose of this second list is to examine what absences created the bad feeling, whether physical or psychological. You may then be able to work backward to create your list of what conditions encourage you to feel happy and creative.

After you've finished your lists, select at least five specific memories in which *timelessness* was a key ingredient, when you were so involved in a project that you can recall the sense of ordinary linear time slipping away so that you couldn't tell how long you'd been working. Choose memories in which there was a challenge and that in facing that challenge, at some point you were so caught up that you felt, as the ancient Greeks distinguished, not *Chronos*, or clock time, but *Kairos*, or timeless time.* When you recall these specific occasions, jot them down, because they will be core events about which you will construct key stories.

* I am indebted to the group analyst Dr. Malcolm Pines for pointing out this verbal distinction in the original Greek.

Selected Memories

1. _____

2. _____

3. _____

4. _____

5. _____

Following this, I would like you to order these memories subjectively, placing the ones you remember with most pride or pleasure at the top. Select one memory and write a 250- to 350-word story telling your reader (your friend or group) what happened. Be specific; appeal to their senses. What did it feel like to be there? Were there colors, odors, textures? Really bring your audience in. What were you doing? What were you trying to accomplish? Did you expect to be able to do it? Who were you with? Was it necessary for them to be there? How long did you expect it to take? How good did you think it would be when you were done? Your memory-story should answer these questions in detail. Imagine yourself reading the story to a group of your peers, say, at a Princeton Review seminar. They want to know what happened next. What were the results?

In going through your remembered stories, we will take you through a checklist of questions you can ask yourself to determine the most needed motivators, the ones that make you ask, "Why this memory?" What qualities make it seem so highlighted, so clearly remembered by you? What elements of your personality were heightened by the experience of the memory?

| MEMORY AS LANGUAGE

It may be useful at this point to go over my first "story," the first memory that I selected out of a group of memory options that occurred to me.

> When I first bought a car, a used Peugeot 403, I was totally intimidated by the task of having to care for it. In my high school years I had secretly borrowed the family car one night and blown its engine as, unknown to me, it had an oil leak. Needless to say, the idea of caring for a foreign car (this was 1964) seemed both overwhelming and exotic. I had a friend who was an engineer and a creative type, a rare combination in those days, and he agreed to help me rebuild the head of the engine, as the valves had to be ground. One late afternoon we started the project, continuing well into the evening by the glow of flashlight and oil lamp. I was exhilarated to be actually working on a technical, mechanical project and not ruining or breaking it, but fixing it. I was the only one in my immediate family with any interest in or inclination toward mechanics, and I felt I had transcended some inherited, even genetic, barrier by loosening screws in an orderly manner, and uncoupling things from one another in such a way that they could be healed.

Now you might imagine, upon first hearing this story, that I wanted to be a mechanic. Well, you'd be partially right. It might help you to know that I worked in a bicycle shop during my junior and senior years of college, but my passion isn't really for being a mechanic.

What were my interests here? What kinds of things was I drawn to? Well, clearly there was a car; there was the support of friendship; and there was the negotiating and purchasing of items, and the organizing of the project.

What did I learn from this memory? One of the ways that we find meaning in this is by orienting ourselves to see what active behaviors we're actually drawn to, and what style we have when we are working at our best. In this case, what were the actions that made the experience so meaningful to me? I enjoyed

- Working with my hands
- Creating a solution to a problem
- Sharing the experience
- Completing the project
- Being my own boss
- Taking a risk; knowing that the project could fail, but that I could make it succeed

Perhaps the most subtle and yet most important elements of the story; what needs of mine were being met? It seems to me, in retrospect, that I was making up for my high school failure to understand how an engine worked and that it needed oil. I needed to take on a project that was bigger than I was comfortable with and then complete it. I also wanted to explore an area with which I was totally unfamiliar. My family lived in a rented apartment in New York City; we called the handyman to change the light-bulb. So, to me, the notion of mechanically caring for something as complex as an automobile was tremendously exciting and almost frightening. Additionally, and perhaps more subtly, I was beginning a career in which I would take things apart and try to put them back together so that they came out better than when I started. Now, this may seem to be an inflated reading of a story about fixing an engine, but bear in mind that I have selected this story out of perhaps thousands, even millions, of incidents that have taken place over the course of my life. So I have to assume that it has more than ordinary significance for me, that some special ideas, some germs of real passion, made this moment especially exciting to me.

When I told this story to my career group, they isolated the following skills:

- Negotiating to buy the car	- Researching the project
- Learning to maintain the car	- Organizing the project
- Selecting a mentor	- Taking risks
- Persisting in figuring out how to care for the car	- Developing physical dexterity to use the tools
- Dedicating myself to a project	- Venturing outside my comfort zone

- Freeing myself from preconceived notions

- Not being discouraged by my previous error

- Presuming that I could do better than I feared

READING MEMORIES

Now we have the basics of how preconscious memories function, how a special moment contains information for us about what our favorite interests are, in what environment or style we enjoy doing them, and what inner experiences or needs are being met. And yet, if we choose, we can go even further as we become more comfortable in our self-analysis. For example, it may interest you to know that my father was a surgeon, and that I considered medicine as a career. However, I found myself far more comfortable with literary and psychological ideas than with science courses and so became an English major. But, an intuitive reader may speculate, was I not in some controlled way introducing myself to surgery, finding a unique and personal integration of entering a closed body (a car engine), opening it, and replacing bad parts with good ones? Can you imagine my beginning search for a form of work in which I too could heal people in a way that met my needs? Can you see me motivating others to use their unique strengths in an environment of intellectual curiosity and emotional readiness? I certainly can. When you reconsider my initial story in which two friends worked on a car, you may see how such a memory can be understood or explored in this way.

You will want to think about and apply the results of your Birkman Grid from Chapter 2 to what you learn from your story. In my Birkman Career Style Summary, my Interest is GREEN and my Style is BLUE. My GREEN Interests were totally fulfilled; I had promoted a project that grabbed my friend's attention. This project required concentrated time and energy and some creative planning, characteristically appealing to my BLUE Style. My needs are more subtle: I was partially relieved at not failing, not making anything worse. But even more deeply I enjoyed creating solutions to problems, whether mechanical or human. The environment was one in which I felt like an explorer and my friend felt like an expert, so that together we had defined exciting roles. Furthermore, we were working on a mechanical project, something with a beginning and an end, yet in an atmosphere in which we could take as long as we needed.

| SETTING OUT ON YOUR INNER JOURNEY

How can you isolate the motivators, the needs, the key intangibles that gave you a feeling of deep satisfaction? Look over your selected memories and ask yourself: Are there related links between them? What is different at the end of each story from the beginning? What has changed? When you think of movies you have loved, or plays, or even sporting events that thrilled you, can you identify similarities that link them? Do you like reversals, come-from-behind situations? Or consistent smooth teamwork? In movies or plays, what is the quality of change that grips you? Do you prefer dramas in which good triumphs over evil? Or in which people are ennobled and enlightened by internal changes?

You have by now selected five memories in which you were attempting to accomplish something, and you've written about one of them; ideally, over the course of this task, you felt a loss of ordinary time, a sense of excitement or urgency that altered your sense of time. If you have not selected your memories and written your story yet, do it now!

INTERPRETING YOUR STORY

Now read your story to your group or friend. Remember that your contract with your group includes frank and open commentary. The object is to help one another maintain momentum. Be careful not to be merely critical, as that could possibly slow down the process. First, note what you did—what you are drawn to, what the action or subject is, in short, your *interests*. In my story, for example, it was fixing a car. Then observe your *style*—in what manner you were operating in this memory. Were you alone, with one other person, or in a group? If you were in a group, were you leading or following?

We might ask you to consider, for your *style*, which of the following are the most important?

- Having plenty to do
- Having to make clear-cut decisions
- Having others be direct and logical
- Having objective supervision
- Knowing exactly what to do
- Being able to work without interruption
- Having low-key direction
- Being trusted
- Having others be democratic
- Utilizing a variety of skills

- Having others encourage competition
- Having novelty and variety of work
- Having others encourage expression of feelings
- Having freedom from unnecessary rules or guidelines
- Having personal respect
- Having freedom from constant social demands
- Having a self-determined schedule
- Having individualized rewards
- Knowing who is in charge

Now make your own "style" notes of what modes of activity are important to you. Refer to my story about the car if you wish.

_____

_____

_____

_____

_____

Next, we might ask what needs were being met. In these memories you are operating with all your needs being met, so if we find similar styles of activity in your memories, we may surmise that operating in this manner is important to your success and sense of well-being. Sometimes asking backward is a useful entry point. For example, what parts of the story, if changed, would have taken away the feeling of achievement in your memory?

What _needs_ did you find gratified or satisfied from your memory?

- Did you demonstrate independence?
- Did you contribute to a feeling of community?
- Were you working alone? With one other person? With a group?
- Were you working for self-gain?
- Were you working to be important to others?
- Were you working for philosophical or altruistic purposes?
- Were you working for yourself? For someone else? For an organization?

- Were you directing and controlling the situation?
- Were you playing an indispensable role?
- Were you carrying out orders?
- Were you directing others?
- Were you helping others?
- Were you learning something new?
- Were you utilizing creativity?
- Were you influencing others?

Now make your own "needs" notes about what conditions are present when you feel fulfilled.

_____

_____

_____

_____

STRESS REACTIONS

For those who work best critically or negatively, you may find that operating from *stress* the absence of needs being met is easier.

How do you behave when many of your needs are not being met?

_____

In which environment (people, place, stress levels) are you least productive?

- People I work worst with:

_____

- Places I can't stand:

_____

- Stress level—I do my worst work when I am:

_____

- Summarize—I work best in the following circumstances:

_____

_____

_____

After you have defined your favorite *interests*, the *style* in which you prefer to pursue them, and the *needs* that you must meet to operate at your most creative level, we ask you to isolate the *skills* you used over the course of your story. Are they consistent with the level you would need to operate in your style? For example, had I wished to become a car mechanic, I would have had to go to school or apprentice myself at a garage. Assess the compatibility of your skills to your interests, needs, and style. You will have to consider, both by using the careers section of the book and in your informational interviewing (see Chapter 4), whether you can upgrade your skills, and if so, whether you can do so on the job, at school, or in some other way, such as by mentoring or in an internship.

TERMINOLOGY

Analyzing Your Story

Let's review some of the terminology that we've been throwing around. In this way, you will be able to incorporate some of the information from your Birkman Life Style Grid.

Interests

These are things you are drawn to, what you like to do. They also tell you what your goals are, or what you are trying to achieve. They are not an indication of your ability or skill.

Style

This is how you like to behave or act when you are doing the things you like to do. Your usual style of behavior assumes that all your personal and psychological needs are being met. Your story is about a time when you were working at your best, and you felt charged because all your needs were being met. How you behaved during that time is an indication of your preferred behavioral style. Your style is very important because it will be one of your greatest selling points when you are interviewing for a job. Your skills emerge in your behavioral style. Your actions are ways of reading your style, that is, what other people would see if they described what you were actually doing.

Needs

Environment is critical for us to operate at our best. For the same sense of satisfaction that you had in your story, your needs should be met. When they are met, you feel a sense of self-approval. You like yourself as you are doing what you're doing; it's the right thing at the right time. Ideally, your bosses and colleagues give you the same sense of approval.

Skills

These are the abilities and resources that you would bring to an employment situation. There is something to the old adage that "people enjoy doing what they are good at," but in this specialized age it is becoming more and more important to know exactly what those skills are.

STORY ANALYSIS

1. What interests were revealed in your story?

_____

_____

_____

2. What was your style? How did you carry out the actions in your story?

_____

_____

_____

3. Why was the situation satisfying? What needs were being met?

_____

_____

_____

4. What skills were revealed?

_____

_____

_____

5. Why did you choose this story?

_____

_____

_____

APPLYING MEMORIES

Now I would like to take you through another story, this one written by a woman in a Career Creation group.

AMELIA'S COAT

It was not a good year for George and me, and at this moment—August—I did not realize how bad it would get. We had started the year with the news that Amelia would need open-heart surgery, then a second pregnancy that we had not planned, and finally George not making partner at Coopers. At this moment, George had left for a three-week life planning course. In his admirable way, he had marshaled unbelievable energy and organizational skills in his job search. It was hot and muggy and I was lonely. I should have gone away to visit my family but George's departure was last minute and I was gripped in a torpid moment. Amelia was one and a half, and typically in August I began to lust for cooler, autumnal weather. I decided to make Amelia a plaid car coat and took out a lovely plaid woolen fabric I had been saving since my days at Pemberton Woolens. I settled on a hooded double-breasted style and decided to make the coat reversible in a matching navy blue wool I also had. Years ago I had made a plaid coat for myself which I thought came out well, though not perfect because the lining did not sit well in the lower hem and I never could bring myself to add buttons and buttonholes. So I'd had some practice but still went slowly, carefully following instructions as I have now learned to do in sewing and not cutting corners to save time. (Basting and ironing are the two most important aspects of sewing!) I purposely made the coat big so it would last several years and also made a matching skirt. It is my finest work to date with perfect matching at all the seams. When Amelia wears it, it makes her look unique—which she is—and I feel so proud to say I made it. I took this picture and sent it to my mother, who had taught me to sew, so she could enjoy my success also. Even George has told others that I made it.

The group started by exploring her interests—what drew her to this project?

- A sense of fashion ("I settled on a hooded double-breasted . . .")
- Her enjoyment in self-education ("carefully following instructions and not cutting corners to save time")
- Her desire to complete unfinished projects ("years ago I had made . . . came out well, though not perfect . . .")

These are their observations about her style

- She enjoyed converting feelings into artistry.
- She liked working with her hands.
- She tended toward meticulousness.
- She showed perseverance.
- She demonstrated an ability to express and transmit her experience.

As you read the story and think about the person in it, ask yourself, "What changes came about for her in the course of this memory; what could be the source of this memory?"

What can we say about the writer of this story and what does she want to express about herself? We have outlined her general style but have not covered the elements that make her and her story unique. Let us go over other kinds of observations from her story that may help you create working material

- Challenged, she eventually becomes active ("in a torpid moment . . . I decided to make").
- Though her feelings impel her toward paralyzing responses ("I should have gone away . . . I was gripped"), her aesthetic and pragmatic responses are her deeper needs ("I decided to make . . . carefully following instructions . . . and not cutting corners").
- She generates self-respect through her achievements ("It is my finest work . . . I feel so proud . . .").

How could you use this in-depth information about yourself? At our Princeton Review seminar, we would note the following about her:

- Hand/eye skills (sewing, ironing, etc.)

- Ability to learn ("... carefully following instructions ...")

And then we would examine more subtle but nevertheless significant parts of her memory, such as

- Her capacity to file and remember details ("a lovely plaid woolen fabric I had been saving ...")

We might ask, In what ways did she feel rewarded? What needs of hers were met?

- Her self-esteem ("I feel so proud to say I made it ...")

- Others' praise and appreciation ("my mother ... could enjoy my success ... even George has told others ...")

Are there other aspects of the story we note that we can develop as we imagine a career that responds to the needs of this creative person?

- She found an active way to feel close to her mother, her daughter, and her husband through an achievement.

- She is able to transform strong feeling into an aesthetic shape ("I was gripped," "I began to lust for," became the creative wellspring for "I decided," "I had been saving," "I settled on,"; these are eventually transformed into "a reversible coat" with "perfect matching at all the seams").

We might then further ask, "How do you think someone who was present might have described the writer's *actions;* in other words, what style of activity does she use?" We have already noted how methodical and skilled in using resources she is, following instructions and saving fabric. Have we noted, though, her response to her "bad ... year" (her daughter's surgery, an unplanned pregnancy, and George's three-week absence and uncertain professional future)? We might note that this is a person who in an uncertain and depressing period becomes focused, decisive, resourceful, and self-challenging. The form of her challenge is aesthetic and filled with meticulous detail; she reminds us that earlier, "the lining did not sit well ... and I never could bring myself to add buttons ... ."

We could then compare the writer's memory to her Birkman Career Style Summary and see what correspondences there might be

...this ...are GREEN, suggesting the promotional elements found ... Her style is ... d her desire ... Vhat doesn't ... ion with her ... marketer of ... ae wanted to ... ired as pres- ... quality work- ... er part.

... can explore ... e and in what ... depository of ... reveal. The ... o personality

... ote them, but ... describe what ... my strengths, ... I can (usually)

... ds in life, and ... o write a letter ... loose, and pre- ... day and how it ... hallenges, and ... ating at length ... t you will have ... our profession ... to your future.

BUSINESS REPLY MAIL
FIRST-CLASS MAIL   PERMIT NO. 21714   CHICAGO IL
POSTAGE WILL BE PAID BY ADDRESSEE

THE GRADUATE LOAN CENTER
1436 WEST RANDOLPH STREET
CHICAGO IL 60607-9850

NO POSTAGE NECESSARY IF MAILED IN THE UNITED STATES

RED   GREEN
S   I
YELLOW   BLUE

INTERVIEWING AS AN ART FORM

CAREER CREATION

Now that you have a working vocabulary to describe your favorite interests, the style or manner in which you prefer to pursue them, and some of your needs that should be met to give you a feeling of satisfaction and creativity, how will you go about putting your new knowledge, and yourself, to work? *Guide to Your Career* provides original research into 240 professions that you can use as a starting point for your own exploration. Now that you've conducted some self-research using memories and the Birkman Career Style Summary, it's time for you to begin researching careers.

If you don't already have a group with whom you discuss your memories, ask a friend or group of friends to form a career creation group now. Even if everybody you know has a job, many of them may be wondering how to develop a career they love. Your friends can give you objective feedback about your skills; you can help one another stay on schedule; and you can boost one another's morale when the searching seems fruitless. Not all parts of looking for a job will be easy; disappointment, frustration, canceled interviews, and other unknowns will surely show up along the way. In Princeton Review seminars, we work in small groups to provide an environment of multiple points of view all oriented toward a similar goal. Setting up a support system will help you complete each task in your career search.

Concentrate on defining benefits mutual to both you and your potential employer. In-depth research is required. Rather than thinking, "Please, anyone, offer me a job; I'll take anything," you should be thinking, "Here's what I have to offer an employer, and I *know* he/she needs these skills." And believe it or not, the employer prefers to fulfill your interests and needs. The better utilized you are, the more creatively you will work. We'll show you how to develop your research techniques so that you feel like a naturally inquisitive person—not like a hustler—when looking for a career.

KEEPING YOURSELF ON TRACK

Your career creation group or friend will be there to support you in this sometimes difficult search, but the following exercise will help you keep yourself on track, as well.

Before you get too far into the career creation process, list how you're likely to get yourself to fail. Tax those old brain cells; given your unique style, how might you falter? Answers that have come up in other groups I have led include some tried-and-true beauties, such as:

- Forgetting to do assignments
- Blaming others (mother/father/teacher) for not having prepared you for these assignments
- Trivializing the work
- Quitting
- Taking the first job offered
- Not setting objectives
- Rationalizing that the current job is really not that bad
- Becoming overwhelmed by too many ideas

You get the idea; become familiar with the ways you're likely to undermine yourself. Then, when obstacles arise, you'll know how you might trip yourself up so that you can avoid doing any of the things that are likely to make you quit. Formulate your list *now*, based on how you've managed to short-circuit in the past.

Ways that I Sometimes Fail

1. _____
2. _____
3. _____
4. _____
5. _____
6. _____
7. _____
8. _____
9. _____
10. _____

Now, knowing how you're likely to fail is a big help in starting out. You'll be able to go back to this list along the way. I'd like you to develop a second list now. You can be as funny as you want, but remember, this list may save your behind when you don't feel like making a call one day, and you recognize that you've anticipated that problem.

What to Do When I Feel Like Failing

1. _____
2. _____
3. _____
4. _____
5. _____
6. _____
7. _____
8. _____
9. _____
10. _____

Now that you have your failure prevention lists, let's get down to the business of career creation.

PIE INTERVIEWING

In Career Creation, we follow the PIE (Pleasure/Practice, Information, Employment) interview formula first developed by Daniel Porot, a career expert in Europe. In PIE development, each interview develops skills needed in the following stage. For example, the practice interviews develop skills in establishing emotional contact with a stranger. At best, this becomes second nature during the information-gathering phase, so that you establish contact automatically while gaining information. In doing so, you are cueing your interviewer, and encouraging him to be interested in your well-being. This can elicit important help, such as making calls to help set up other informational contacts for you. Finally, by the time you feel prepared for employment, speaking the language of a new field should feel as comfortable as if you had mastered the subject matter at school. You will also be adept at attuning yourself to the emotional flow of the interview environment, so that you minimize the feelings of being a novice or a potential liability to this person. Be persistent. The worst that can happen is that you'll feel like a pest. But people are often hired for their persistence. Employers believe that if they want the position so much, they will do a great job once hired.

The following chart outlines the PIE process.

	P **Pleasure/Practice**	**I** **Information**	**E** **Employment**
Kind of interview	Practice field survey	Informational interviewing or researching	Employment or hiring interview
Purpose	To get used to and learn to enjoy talking with people: to penetrate networks	To find out if you'd like a particular field before you try to get into it	To get hired for the work you have decided you would most like to do
How You Go to the Interview	You can take somebody with you	By yourself or you can take somebody with you (not into the interview itself, though)	By yourself
Whom You Talk to	Anyone who shares your enthusiasm about a non-job-related subject (for you)	A worker who has a job similar to what you are thinking about doing	An employer who has the power to hire you for the job you have decided you would most like to do
How Much Time You Ask for	Ten minutes (and DON'T run over—making an 11:50 appointment may help, since some employers have lunch at noon)		Not your option as an interviewee

What You Discuss	Any questions about your shared interest or enthusiasm
	
	Suggested questions:
	1. How did you start with this hobby, interest, etc.?
	2. What excites or interests you the most about it?
	3. What do you find is the thing you least like about it?
	4. Who else do you know who shares this interest, hobby, or enthusiasm, or could tell me more about my curiosity?
	
	  a. Can I go and see them?
	  b. May I mention that it was you who suggested I see them?
	  c. May I say that you recommended them?
	
	Get interviewer's name and address
		Any questions you have about this job or this kind of work
		
		Suggested questions:
		1. How did you get interested in this work, and how did you get hired?
		2. What excites or interests you the most about it?
		3. What do you find is the thing you like the least about it?
		4. What kinds of challenges or problems do you have to deal with in this job?
		5. What skills do you need in order to meet those challenges or problems?
		6. Who else do you know who does this kind of work but with this difference:_____
		
		Get interviewer's name and address
			Tell them what it is you like about their organization and what kind of work you are looking for.
			
			Discuss:
			1. The kinds of challenges you like to deal with
			2. What skills you have to help you deal with those challenges
			3. What experience you have had in dealing with those challenges in the past

Afterward: The Same Day	Send a thank-you note	Send a thank-you note	Send a thank-you note

PLEASURE

The "P" stands for pleasure or practice. Get used to talking with people you don't know (strangers!) about a subject about which you are knowledgeable and enthusiastic. Having practice conversations will help you learn how to talk to people who are older or more successful and will enable you to feel comfortable talking to people even if you are shy or feel you have nothing to contribute. Spend ten minutes with someone you haven't talked to before discussing a subject you know he or she enjoys or has a vested interest in (shop owners are perfect for this). Send a thank-you note; he or she will appreciate your thoughtfulness. You want your conversation to have a shared enthusiasm, much as you would if you were speaking to an interviewer about a career you both liked. You are training yourself to be as confident as you can be. This may take a few interviews, but DON'T SKIP IT. You want shared enthusiasm to be your second nature. You'll find that you make mental notes as you're talking together: Is the other person speaking enough? Am I giving signs of encouragement? These are significant parts of the interview process. For many of you, this will be a rare foray outside your generational boundary where you encounter an older person in order to share an interest, rather than as an authority. Make sure you're comfortable with this! To start this exercise, fill out the following:

"P" Exercise

Please list up to ten subjects that you thoroughly enjoy talking about.

1. _____
2. _____
3. _____
4. _____
5. _____
6. _____
7. _____
8. _____
9. _____
10. _____

Choose one of these subjects for your first interview.

Your Goal

Establish a connection with the person you are "interviewing" while discussing:

     1. How he became interested or involved in this subject

     2. What she likes most about it

     3. What, if anything, frustrates him about the subject

     4. Who else she knows who shares your interest

(Write the questions on a card and take it to the interview if you want.)

What did it feel like to "interview" someone about a subject in which you share an interest?

1. Did you both enjoy it?

2. Did it feel like you were juggling time, attention, and interest?

3. Were you both alert and involved?

_____

_____

_____

_____

INFORMATION-GATHERING

The "I" or information-gathering phase of career creation is when you start to learn more about the fields that interest you. In this phase, you want to have enthusiastic conversations (or informational interviews) with people in the industry that interests you. The people you encounter at these types of interviews will not have a job to offer, but they can give you information about their field, their job, and how they became a successful professional. Informational interviewing is perhaps the most critical phase of this process. You will be gathering the knowledge that separates you from the "job beggars," people who take what's available whether it suits them or not, and the resourceful person you aspire to be. Having clarified your interests and the style in which you like to pursue them, you are now ready to attach these interests to fields in which you might like to use them. As you narrow your search to include your interests, style, and needs, you may wish to consider the fields in which you might like to pursue them. Look through the careers corresponding to your interest color to get a sense of where you may wish to begin your own informational interviewing.

What do you hope to accomplish in the "I" interview stage of PIE? Remember that in addition to being a fact-finding mission, an "I" interview is a sales event. An informational interview is a two-way process. You want to learn as much about the industry as you want the interviewer to learn about you. You wish to

- Enlist the person as an ally in your job search

- Find out

    1. How to enter the industry

    2. The future of the industry

    3. How the person recommends you proceed in your search

    4. If the person were starting out again, would he enter this industry? If not, why?

    5. If you match up well with this industry

6. What skills are used in the field

7. What challenges are present in the industry

- Try to obtain three new names of contacts

PREPARATION FOR YOUR INFORMATIONAL INTERVIEWS

Let's revisit my story from Chapter 3. Taking into account some of the information we extracted from my story, I would want to answer the following questions in an informational interview that I would conduct:

- Do I make my own schedule?
- Can I work with others, or am I always on my own?
- Is there recognition for individual achievement?
- Can I be innovative, or is there a procedure manual?
- Are there learning opportunities in the job?
- Is advancement based on merit or seniority?

What are the key questions for you in a work environment?

_____

_____

_____

What interests do you want to see present in the career area for which you are interviewing?

_____

_____

_____

What kinds of career satisfactions in this industry or profession are you noting as you gather information in the interview?

_____

_____

No matter how comfortable you become with the social side of interviewing, it is important that you get specific information when conducting your interviews. The following seven questions, which can be phrased in a variety of ways, tend to elicit the essentials:

- How did you get started in your profession?

- What do you like most about your profession?

- What frustrates you most?

- What skills do you make use of?

- What challenges or obstacles are facing you now? (And do you anticipate facing in the future?)

- We could you refer me to anyone else in your field who would be as excellent a source of information as you have been?

- May I stay in touch with you as I continue this process?

The Thank-You Note

Immediately following your interview you will want to write the thank– you note. You might be thinking, "What a pain," but this note is more important than you can believe. It should

- At best be handwritten

- If it must be sent via e-mail, DO NOT use informal emoticons (i.e. ;-) or :-p), or colloquialisms

- Have the individual's name and title spelled correctly

- Make specific reference to subjects discussed

- Make reference to any personal knowledge you learned in the course of the interview

- Ask the question: "May I stay in touch with you?"

The information you discover will help you plan your transformation into a resource person for the industry or profession you are exploring. At this point, you might want to start using a binder to store your (growing) list of interviewers. Here is an example of a contact sheet from a career creation group:

CONTACT SHEET

Recap of Meeting

_____   Date _____

_____   Name _____

_____   _____

_____   Title _____

_____   _____

_____   Phone _____

_____   _____

_____   Company _____

_____   _____

_____   Fax _____

Personal Information   _____

_____   Address _____

_____   _____

_____   _____

Next step   _____

_____   E-mail _____

_____   _____

_____   Website _____

Follow-up   _____

_____   Referred by _____

_____   _____

_____

Additional contacts

1. _____

2. _____

3. _____   ❏ Follow-up letter sent

EMPLOYMENT

Finally (and none too soon), the "E," or employment phase. Where and for whom do you wish to work? How can you help them? How can your skills help meet the challenges in their industry? How have you used your skills in similar situations (not necessarily moneymaking) to help solve similar challenges to the ones in their field? Your critical task in this phase is to develop your "pitch," a clear and concise representation of how your research has demonstrated the way in which your skills can be a resource to this company. You must clearly articulate beforehand what you see as a challenge, and how your background and experience would make you a resource in helping to meet this challenge. You must be familiar with the language and thinking in the industry and have done your research. If you do not have paid experience, use examples from other areas, from work as an intern, volunteer, or member of a community. Develop a history of experience whether you have worked or not. Why do you wish to work for this person? By now, you can convincingly state this. If you must, would you work for free for two months to show them what you can do? Wilder offers have been made and accepted. This is your pitch, and you should practice, practice, practice.

Assuming that you have spent some quality time in the "I" phase, you

- Are extremely comfortable with interview situations

- Have built a network of contacts through which you have located the industries/jobs in which you are likely to succeed

- Know how to enter the industry

- Have identified a potential career or job that matches your ideal work environment

- Know the challenges facing the industry

- Can present yourself and your achievements in a manner that addresses these challenges

By the way, it's the last one that gets you the job!

"E" Checklist

Here are some suggestions to follow as you begin setting up your employment interviews

- Avoid personnel offices in scheduling employment interviews.

- Hold back your resume for as long as possible so you can tailor it to a specific position.

- Meet with the person who has the power to hire you as early as possible.

- When asked about salary, be prepared to answer with a range.

- If possible, have the employer mention salary numbers first.

Don't forget to send a thank-you note as you did in the information-gathering phase, and keep using the contact sheets to keep your career creation process organized.

SCHEDULING GUIDELINES

You and your friend/group should complete the first stories within a week. You will want to have your list of prioritized favorite interests and skills within a month of starting, including a working knowledge of the style in which you like to use them and the needs that are vital to your sense of creativity and well-being. You can then begin the practice interviews. Schedule at least three in the following week. They shouldn't be anything elaborate, just ten-minute conversations. Do these until you actually enjoy them, or at least until you aren't staring at your feet most of the time. The next step, informational interviewing, may take a good deal of time, at least three or four months, but you should aim to schedule informational interviews regularly—three a week if possible. This is where you develop knowledge, confidence, and the opportunity to decide if this is a good field for you. Do it! Don't walk through this phase and take the first job offered to you (unless it happens to be exactly what you want).

GETTING YOUR SHOW ON THE ROAD

The following pages on careers can help you select areas of interest or specific careers. Keep your interests and needs in mind as you do your research. The descriptions we've provided will leverage your career creation process. The purpose of our research is to cut down the grunt work in yours. Take advantage of it.

Good luck (which, as we all know, favors the prepared mind!).

PART II
CAREER OPTIONS

KEY TO THE CAREERS

| A NOTE ON SIDEBAR STATISTICS

The statistical information in this book came from a variety of sources, including government publications, published reports, broadcast news reports, industry self-reporting statistics, professional associations, telephone interviews, and Internet resources. They should all be used as guidelines; individual statistics vary within each industry. A summary of how to interpret each statistic is included below.

PEOPLE IN PROFESSION

The number of people in the specific profession in the United States. This does not include cross-career statistics, for example, the human resource manager who is also an accountant will appear as one or the other, not both, depending on how they choose to self-report. Some independent-type professions do not keep track of these statistics and therefore will be marked as N/A.

HOURS

The average number of hours a professional in this field works each week. Individual reports vary based on company need, additional responsibilities, personal initiative, and projects involving travel.

SALARY

Salary One

Average entry-level salary. For industries in which entry-level salaries vary with experience, Salary One is comparable for the people in the bottom 25 percent of the entry-level salary pool. N/A is listed for Salary One when salaries are not meaningful for the career, one in which any pay is insignificant relative to potential future income (see Entrepreneur for an example), or one in which pay varies greatly or is especially difficult to quantify.

Salary Two

Average five-year salary as reported for each profession. For industries in which two-to five-year salaries vary with pace of promotion, experience, and starting salary, Salary Two is comparable for the people in the middle 50 percent of the five-year salary pool. N/A is listed for Salary Two when salaries are not meaningful for the career, one in which any pay is insignificant relative to potential future income (see Entrepreneur for an example), or one in which pay varies greatly or is especially difficult to quantify.

Salary Three

Average ten- to fifteen-year salary as reported for each profession. For industries in which the ten- to fifteen-year salaries vary with pace of promotion, bonus levels, experience, competitive bidding, starting salary and rising industry salary base, Salary Three is comparable for the people in the top 25 percent of the ten- to fifteen-year salary pool. N/A is listed for Salary Three when salaries are not meaningful for the career, one in which any pay varies too greatly to report accurately, or one in which pay is especially difficult to quantify.

MAJOR ASSOCIATIONS

These are major associations recommended by government sources, professionals in their industry, and major employers in the field. They are not intended to be comprehensive listings of associations. Candidates are encouraged to use them as springboards for further research.

MAJOR EMPLOYERS

These are large employers of professionals in their associated career. Wherever possible, we have tried to list employers that would provide professionals with a range of work, style, geographic choices, and schedules. In some industries, professionals are often the only representative from their fields on their employers' staffs. In these cases, we listed the types of companies and organizations that hire those professionals. In other cases, we indicated that professionals in a given industry are primarily employed as single practitioners, in partnerships, or at small companies. Listing companies does not constitute an endorsement of them or their practices. These listings are provided for informational purposes only.

Note: Not all fields for each career profile are reported. For example, some careers had no widely recognized major associations at the time we went to print. In these cases, the field has simply been omitted. For omitted fields, you are advised to either perform focused Internet searches for the information you are seeking (a new association may incorporate at any time), or contact your local chamber of commerce to ask for the names and contact information of companies that may have positions corresponding to the career in which you are interested. A quick call to these companies should yield helpful insight for your career search.

Any insight you have into careers would be appreciated for future volumes of this book. Our challenge is to keep it relevant to the people who are searching for the right place for themselves in the workforce. With your comments and your suggestions, we can continue to make this book a valuable resource to professionals like yourself.

Please send any comments to:

Books Division
The Princeton Review
2315 Broadway
New York, NY 10024

| INTERPRETING THE SCORES

Salary

Average salary level in the industry as it relates to other fields:

●   Generally low salary

● ●   Generally middle salary

● ● ● Generally high salary

Hours

Average number of hours worked weekly compared with other fields:

●   Generally low hours

● ●   Generally medium hours

● ● ● Generally long hours

Education

The level of academic education generally needed to enter the profession:

●   High school diploma

● ●   College undergraduate degree

● ● ● Graduate or professional degree

TOP TEN LISTS

THE TOP TEN JOBS FOR PEOPLE WHO LIKE TO KEEP LEARNING

1. Software Developer
2. Physicist
3. Diplomat
4. Journalist
5. Architect
6. Benefits Administrator
7. Physician
8. Computer Programmer
9. Teacher
10. Writer

THE TOP TEN JOBS FOR PEOPLE WHO NEED TO PAY OFF STUDENT LOANS RIGHT AWAY

1. Investment Banker
2. Financial Analyst
3. Management Consultant
4. Construction Manager
5. Trader
6. Service Sales Representative (potentially)
7. Stockbroker
8. Court Reporter
9. Carpenter
10. Marketing Executive

THE TOP TEN JOBS FOR PEOPLE WHO CAN'T STAND TIES OR PANTYHOSE

1. Farmer
2. Artist
3. Firefighter
4. Actor
5. Writer
6. Coach
7. Computer Programmer
8. Zoologist
9. Anthropologist
10. Child Care Worker

THE TOP TEN JOBS FOR TYPE-A PERSONALITIES

1. Attorney
2. Investment Banker
3. Astronaut
4. Management Consultant
5. Pilot
6. Military Officer
7. Architect
8. Systems Analyst
9. Accountant/Auditor
10. Stockbroker

THE TOP TEN JOBS FOR PEOPLE WHO LONG FOR UNPREDICTABLE DAYS

1. Small Business Owner
2. FBI Agent
3. Police Officer
4. Restaurateur
5. Firefighter
6. Musician
7. Advertising Executive
8. Auto Salesperson
9. Promoter
10. Agent

THE TOP TEN JOBS FOR PEOPLE PEOPLE

1. Teacher
2. Human Resources Manager
3. Guidance Counselor
4. Career Counselor
5. Psychologist
6. Social Worker
7. Child Care Worker
8. Physical Therapist
9. Fund-raiser/Institutional Solicitor
10. Hotel Manager

THE TOP TEN JOBS FOR PEOPLE WHO LIKE TO WORK WITH THEIR HANDS

1. Carpenter
2. Auto Mechanic
3. Dentist
4. Artist
5. Farmer
6. Veterinarian
7. Set Designer
8. Physician
9. Avionics Technician
10. Chef

THE RED CAREERS

AEROSPACE ENGINEER

A DAY IN THE LIFE

"I'm a rocket scientist; who wants anything more?" one of our survey respondents wrote, with a sentiment echoed by many others. Aerospace engineers examine, analyze, design, produce, and occasionally install components that make up aircraft, spacecraft, high-altitude vehicles, and high-altitude delivery systems (missiles). Satisfaction with the romantic image of rocket building can buoy many engineers amidst the highly anonymous work environments that many of them face. Individuals don't assemble rockets; teams do—dozens of teams working in highly supervised coordination. An aerospace engineer plays some part on one of the teams, spending more of his or her time (roughly 70 percent) in a lab, at a computer, and assembling reports than

{ Individuals don't assemble rockets; teams do. }

doing anything else. Not being able to see the "big picture" frustrates some professionals. "What do I do? I don't know," wrote one engineer, who later claimed to be a victim of this "moon shot myopia." Due to the complexity of the final product, an intricate and rigid organizational structure for production has to be maintained, and this severely curtails any single engineer's ability to understand his or her role as it relates to the final project. It is not unusual to be pulled off one project without explanation and thrown into the midst of another already in progress. As one person explained, "This is not referred to as disorganization; it carries the name 'prioritization.'"

PAYING YOUR DUES

The path to becoming an aerospace engineer is a rigorous one, but those who manage to survive the difficult liftoff emerge with an above-average degree of career satisfaction.

The demands may be intense, but if you've ever yearned to respond, "Well, actually . . ." to the retort, "you're no rocket scientist," then this is just the career for you. Academic requirements are strict and wide-ranging: Physics, chemistry, computer science, mathematics, materials science, statistics, and engineering courses provide the base for any aspiring rocket scientist. Some colleges offer a degree in aerospace engineering; others offer a more generalized engineering degree with some course work in aerospace engineering. These courses might include aerospace guidance systems, extreme-altitude material science, and the physics of high-altitude radiation. Internships, summer jobs, and any experience in the field are helpful, as entry into this industry is highly competitive. Many aspirants may need to relocate to California, Washington State, or Texas, where the majority of defense industry aerospace work is done.

ASSOCIATED CAREERS

Aerospace engineers end up teaching far more frequently than do members of most other professions. This isn't surprising due to the dual nature of the discipline; professionals love what they do in exploring concepts and building them; and in academia, they avoid the anonymity the profession fosters. Most people who leave the profession do so because of lack of work, lack of responsibility, or lack of control. Jobs are highly responsive to defense industry spending and anticipated aerospace orders. Those who leave tend to find themselves satisfied in other scientific or manufacturing positions.

PAST AND FUTURE

Flying has been a human aspiration since we first watched birds swoop across the air and navigate the highest reaches with ease. The first plane flight, in 1903, by Wilbur and Orville Wright at Kitty Hawk, North Carolina, was the initial major step in making that dream a reality.

In the present and future, the dream extends into space and beyond. Aerospace engineers who currently design shuttles, military aircraft, rockets, and missiles will design craft that can land on and take off from the surfaces of other planets. The occupation would have a potentially limitless future except for its dependence on military funding. As budget issues come more and more to the forefront, uncertainties in funding, cutbacks, and layoffs render the potentially crucial and exotic future of aerospace engineers always uncertain.

QUALITY OF LIFE

2 YEARS Junior members of research staff are swamped with work, both in the lab and in offices, places in which they crunch data and organize research. More like "lab assistants," their early years are marked by relatively menial tasks (testing equipment, tracking results, etc.) with little input into the testing or recommendation processes. Average hours and pay characterize these environments, but education continues apace. Few people leave the profession during these years; the hours already devoted to school make it easier to tolerate these few extra workplace indignities.

5 YEARS Five-year veterans lead research teams and develop into people managers as well as project managers. This is an unanticipated turn of events for some, as it removes them from the challenging, intellectually rarefied environment they enjoy and places them in a more administrative role. Most significant design and production work is done in these years. More than 25 percent leave, frustrated with the anonymity of the profession and limited opportunity to pursue what they believe to be promising and interesting ideas.

10 YEARS About 5 percent start their own aerospace research and development firms, based on patents, contacts, and access to adequate financing. Those who become project and personnel managers have significant input on the direction of research but little contact with the actual day-to-day functioning of these research and development teams. Budgeting, oversight, and intracompany contacts all become important parts of the 10-year survivor's life. Hours remain about the same, and satisfaction tends to level off. Salary increases occur; but after this point, without equity interest in smaller, private companies, administrators can only expect cost-of-living salary increases. The attrition rate has slowed, but those who leave from this point go back into academia, training programs, or private consulting.

MAJOR EMPLOYERS

THE AEROSPACE CORPORATION
2350 East El Segundo Boulevard
El Segundo, CA 90245-4691
Mail: PO Box 92957
Los Angeles, CA 90009-2957
Tel: 310-336-5000
Fax: 310-336-7055
www.aero.org

THE BOEING COMPANY
PO Box 3707
Seattle, WA 98124-2207
Tel: 206-655-2121
www.boeing.com

MAJOR ASSOCIATIONS

AIR FORCE ASSOCIATION
1501 Lee Highway
Arlington, VA 22209
Tel: 800-727-3337 or
703-247-5800
Fax: 703-247-5853
www.afa.org

AMERICAN INSTITUTE OF AERONAUTICS AND ASTRONAUTICS
1801 Alexander Bell Drive, Suite 500
Reston, VA 20191-4344
Tel: 800-639-2422 or 703-264-7500
Fax: 703-264-7551
www.aiaa.org

AIR FORCE—ENLISTEE, OFFICER

BOOKS, FILMS, AND TV SHOWS
FEATURING THE PROFESSION
- Air Force
- God is My Co-Pilot
- Iron Eagle

YOU'LL HAVE CONTACT WITH
- Engineers
- High-ranking officials
- Maintenance crews
- Pilots

PROFESSIONALS READ
- Air Force Journal of Logistics
- Air Force Magazine
- Air Force Times

A DAY IN THE LIFE

There are several technical, scientific, and specialized job opportunities available in the Air Force. Enlistees and officers alike have to be up to speed with the newest tactics, weapons, and countermeasures. Many enlist with the hope of becoming a fighter pilot. With job responsibilities like planning missions, gathering intelligence, and operating state-of-the-art and sometimes top-secret planes, there's hardly a more alluring career in the military. In addition to fighter pilots, there are bomber pilots, test pilots, helicopter pilots, and covert special operations pilots. A lot of time must be spent planning, briefing, and fine-tuning plans before a pilot can even step into the cockpit. And for every pilot in the sky, there are hundreds of people on the ground working to ensure { **The job is not limited to the confines of Earth.** } his or her safety. These individuals include aircraft maintenance specialists, radar specialists, communications officers, and morale officers. The Air Force divides AFSCs (Air Force Specialty Codes, a.k.a. enlisted jobs) into the following overall categories: Operations, Maintenance & Logistics, Support, Medical & Dental, Legal & Chaplain, Finance & Contracting, and Special Investigations. The Air Force classifies and assigns people worldwide to ensure a high state of readiness. Depending on your job and duty assignment, you may find yourself spending up to seven months of the year deployed to such destinations as Kosovo, Saudi Arabia, Kuwait, Afghanistan, Iraq, and Turkey. Oh, and the job is not just limited to the confines of Earth—astronauts get their start in the Air Force, as well.

PAYING YOUR DUES

High school students who wish to enlist in the Air Force have two options. Those already in possession of a high school diploma or GED may take the Armed Services Vocational Aptitude Battery (ASVAB) to test their fitness for duty. Those who are certified as fit for duty can enter Basic Military Training (BMT). There is also a 12-month Delayed Entry Program (DEP), for which students who do not yet have diplomas may join in a legal contract to enlist in the Air Force and to enter active duty on a specified date. Applicants take the oath of enlistment to the Air Force Reserve but receive no military training, pay, or benefits before the actual date of enlistment. The time spent in the DEP does, however, count toward fulfillment of the military service term obligation.

Officers are required to obtain a four-year college degree, and candidates may follow one of three available paths: ROTC training, the Air Force Academy, or Officer Training School. Students may enter the ROTC training program during college. The Air Force Academy is a highly selective four-year college that prepares cadets to become officers. The OTS is divided into three categories to cover students with different backgrounds: pilot/navigator, technical, and non-technical. In order to obtain a spot in this program, students must pass the Air Force Officer Qualifying Test.

ASSOCIATED CAREERS

Air Force enlistees and officers spend time with pilots, electricians, engineers, fellow officers, doctors, and administrators; and they also work with other branches of the United States Armed Forces. For those who have left the military after their service requirements have been met or who are in reserve, the incredible technical and professional training background they have opens doors in many civilian fields, including those of engineering and flight instruction.

PAST AND FUTURE

In December 1906, the U.S. military authorized Army Specification #486, which called for the creation of an aircraft for military use. Just three years earlier, the Wright brothers had taken their first flight, and they signed a contract with the Army on February 10, 1908. In 1917, upon United States entry into World War I, the U.S. Army Air Service was formed; this body provided tactical support for the Army. In 1926, the Air Service was reorganized as a branch of the Army and became the U.S. Army Air Corps (USAAC). During this period, the USAAC began experimenting with new techniques, including air-to-air refueling and the development of new fighter planes. The United States Department of the Air Force was created when President Harry S. Truman signed the National Security Act of 1947. The chain of command goes directly from the President to the Secretary of Defense to the Secretary of the Air Force. The Air Force played a key role in both world wars. After World War II, the Air Force quickly grew in importance and became the foundation for President Eisenhower's defense policy.

In 2004, the Air Force issued its U.S. Air Force Transformation Flight Plan, a major document that specifically addressed important issues of transformation, including how to expand the military forces into space operations for the purpose of protecting the nation from chemical, biological, radiological, nuclear, and high-explosive attack. In this regard, a career in the Air Force promises to bring with it opportunities to take part in cutting-edge research, operations, and defense strategies.

QUALITY OF LIFE

2 YEARS Enlistees typically sign enlistment contracts that involve a commitment to eight years of service. Depending on the terms of the contract, two to six years are typically spent on active duty, and the rest is spent in the Air Force Reserves. After two years, the enlistee is probably completing his or her term of active duty. Commissioned officers are recommended for promotion by their commanders and are selected by centralized promotion boards. The two most significant factors in an officer's promotion records are fitness reports and level of responsibility in current and past assignments. All officers (including Academy graduates) are initially commissioned as Reserve Officers and compete for regular officer appointments at the time they are considered for promotion.

5 YEARS Enlistees at this point are probably serving on the Air Force Reserves, unless they have decided to stay on and rise up the ranks. Air Force officers are initially considered for promotion to the grades of captain through major general by Central Selection Boards, which select officers based on their potential to serve in the next-higher grade and in positions of greater responsibility. Promotion involves a number of considerations, including the time served in one's rank, time spent in service, job rating, and amount of professional training the officer has acquired. The Air Force is the only service that gives accelerated promotion for those who agree to enlist for six years.

10 YEARS Generally, the first few promotions for both enlisted and officer personnel come relatively easily; subsequent promotions are much more competitive. Being an Air Force officer comes with a benefit package that's hard to beat: regular pay raises, tax-free housing, tuition assistance, health care at no cost, and full retirement benefits after twenty years of service.

MAJOR EMPLOYERS
U.S. AIR FORCE
www.airforce.com

MAJOR ASSOCIATIONS
AIR FORCE SERGEANTS ASSOCIATION
www.afsahq.org

ASSOCIATION OF AIR FORCE MISSILEERS
PO Box 5693
Breckenridge, CO 80424
www.afmissileers.org

RESERVE OFFICERS ASSOCIATION
One Constitution Avenue, NE
Washington, DC 20002
Tel: 202-479-2200 or 800-809-9448
Fax: 202-479-0416
E-mail: info@roa.org
www.roa.org

ARCHITECT

A DAY IN THE LIFE

Most people enter architecture with a desire to build and a pre-discovered engineering ability; unfortunately, most architects don't get to utilize any of these skills when they first enter the profession. Beginning architects research zoning, building codes, and legal filings; draft plans from others' designs; and build models at the side of a more experienced architect. The accomplished architect doesn't spend as much time as he would like designing, either; he spends it on the phone, in meetings, and consulting closely with his clients. Of the people we surveyed, each person was surprised by the amount of time he or she had to spend "selling" or "explaining" his or her ideas. The most financially successful architects seemed to be the ones best at communicating their unique vision. { **unique vision** }

Becoming an architect is a long process; spending years as a draftsperson or researcher leads those without patience to grow frustrated and dissatisfied with their choice of career. Even after the grueling "weeding out" period, surviving as a working architect is difficult. Most architecture firms employ five or fewer people, and the work firms do mostly commercial or pre-planned residential housing with strict budgets and practical limitations. Only a select few architects get to "design" in the way that most budding architects imagine they will. Perpetual revision of plans based on client needs, contractor inefficiency, and budget strictures are daily features of the architect's life. Plans and priorities have to be reevaluated daily and revised accordingly. One architect said, "Practically every plan you draft will look something like what you build, but don't count on it." A successful architect needs talent; practical, interpersonal, and organizational skills; and most of all, patience.

PAYING YOUR DUES

The requirements for becoming an architect are stringent because, like an attorney or a physician, an architect must take all legal responsibility for his work. A prospective architect must complete an academic degree specifically focused on architecture. This can be a five-year bachelor of architecture program, an affiliated two-year master of architecture program, or, for those whose undergraduate degrees were in a field unassociated with architecture, a three- to four-year master of architecture program (one architect we surveyed received a bachelor's degree in animal behavior). Nearly all states require three years of practice in the field as a junior associate, draftsperson, or researcher before you are eligible for accreditation. Aspiring architects must also have an accredited sponsor. Lastly, each candidate must pass all sections of the Architect Registration Exam (ARE), a rigorous multipart test. Greater emphasis is now placed by employers on those applicants who have mastered computer-assisted design (CAD) programs, which promise to become required knowledge for any architect as technology continues to develop.

ASSOCIATED CAREERS

Architects move into a variety of careers and often delve into different careers while handling their architectural duties. Architects who have reached a level of professional achievement may go on to teach at universities. Some members of the field move to private design firms or focus on other aspects of design, including furniture, housewares, and product design. Architects frequently work as consultants on projects already under way, advising on such details as materials, construction, and scheduling.

PAST AND FUTURE

Architecture reflects the time period and culture in which the architect lives. Cultural signature is often found in structures built by humans. Ancient Greek societies focused on aesthetic and mathematical harmonies, as displayed in their architecture. Renaissance Italy created ornate public buildings and palaces reflecting the country's wealth.

Modern architecture as a profession seems to be heading in two directions at once. First, advancements in the technology of computer aides should improve the productivity and creative capabilities of architects. Some believe this computerized "equalizing" of the tables (small and large firms alike will use the same software) will lead to a great democratization of architecture, with many more architects being able to handle and coordinate massive construction projects. Others believe that since job prospects are driven by local construction cycles, the future of architecture is tied to the future of local economies. In the future, architects must be willing to relocate for periods of time to find work, must become involved in electronic communications where design and theory meet, and will work under less generous conditions than those currently enjoyed by the profession.

QUALITY OF LIFE

2 YEARS In the first two years, prospective architects work as interns or research assistants for established architects, with salaries in the low $30,000 range. Duties include researching zoning regulations, working with subcontractors (electricians, plumbers, et al.), and drafting plans, either manually or with computer assistance. Long hours and little responsibility characterize these first few years, during which many study for the ARE. Nearly 25 percent leave the profession during this period.

5 YEARS Responsibility and areas of control have increased. Finally, candidates get a chance to design parts of a building (a bathroom, a closet). Others are given areas of responsibility (lighting, heating, air conditioning). Many work with partners or senior associates and learn the practical end of turning plans into production. These five-year survivors get their first taste of client contact and, in many cases, become the primary contacts for smaller jobs. Most work with contractors and inspect work to make sure it matches up with plans. Some are involved in planning and pitching new contracts, depending on their interpersonal skills. Hours increase with responsibility, and another 20 percent decide to leave the occupation during this period, based on either their frustration with the slow degree of advancement or difficulty with the ARE. Those people who remain in the industry become accredited between years three and seven.

10 YEARS Professionals who last ten years in this field are competent designers and coordinators who are able to recruit business, successfully communicate with clients, and distinguish themselves professionally. Architects at this stage of their careers are more involved in designing and creative planning and less involved in implementation, construction, and detail work. They've become supervisors and teachers to newer entrants to the profession. Some reenter academia either to pursue graduate work or teach basic architectural studies. But self-employed architects always remember that they have only as much work as their clients give them: recruiting business is an integral part of the successful architect's life.

MAJOR EMPLOYERS

HOK
211 North Broadway, Suite 700
St. Louis, MO 63102
Tel: 314-421-2000
Fax: 314-421-6073
www.hok.com

GENSLER
2 Harrison Street
San Francisco, CA 94105
Tel: 415-433-3700
Fax: 415-836-4599
www.gensler.com
Contact: info@gensler.com

NBBJ
111 South Jackson Street
Seattle, WA 98104
Tel: 206-223-5555
Fax: 206-621-2300
www.nbbj.com

MAJOR ASSOCIATIONS

AMERICAN INSTITUTE OF ARCHITECTS
1735 New York Avenue, NW
Washington, DC 20006
Tel: 800-242-3837
Fax: 202-626-7547
www.aia.org
Contact: infocentral@aia.org

ARMY—ENLISTEE, OFFICER

BOOKS, FILMS, AND TV SHOWS
FEATURING THE PROFESSION

- Hogan's Heroes
- Saving Private Ryan
- The Thin Red Line
- A Walk in the Sun

YOU'LL HAVE CONTACT WITH

- Engineers
- Firefighters
- Law enforcement officials
- Medical personnel
- Translators

PROFESSIONALS READ

- Global Defense Review
- Guns and Ammo
- Journal of Military History
- Military Review
- National Defense
- Popular Mechanics
- Soldiers
- Stars and Stripes
- U.N. & Conflict Monitor

A DAY IN THE LIFE

It is difficult to describe in detail all of the things one might do during a typical day in the U.S. Army, since the range of specialties is broad. One could be a driver or the pilot of a combat vehicle, a mechanic, field artillery person, firefighter, translator, code breaker, or medic. Or one could be a journalist, accountant, lawyer, or engineer. Men also have the option of becoming combat infantrymen (a functional area still closed to women). There are numerous other area specializations, many of which have civilian counterparts, as well. Life as a soldier can be difficult, but one soldier we spoke with described his career choice as one of the "most challenging and rewarding" professions he could have imagined.

{ challenging and rewarding }

During peacetime, a soldier's life consists mainly of training, planning, and drilling. Training involves learning new skills relevant either to the general role of being a soldier or to a particular area of specialization. Planning entails organizing the tasks that need to be accomplished during a specified period of time. For example, a lieutenant who commands an infantry platoon might plan a field exercise for that platoon to measure the preparedness both of individuals and the group as a unit. Drilling involves practicing over and over again all of the functions to be employed in a time of war. An infantryman will appreciate all the time spent breaking down and reassembling his weapon many times in succession if ever he has to clear a jam in it during a combat situation. Translators will similarly value all of the language drills they have under their belts when captured documents come in that describe plans of an imminent attack against comrades in the field. During wartime, all of this training, planning, and drilling is put to the test. Each soldier does his or her part to accomplish national goals as quickly and at as low a cost—in terms of lives and money—as possible.

PAYING YOUR DUES

All soldiers, regardless of specialization area, begin in the same place: basic combat training. This lasts nine weeks and consists of intense physical conditioning, weapons training, and combat skills development. After basic training, enlistees go to one of the various Advanced Individual Training schools, while prospective officers go to Officer Candidate School. (Students at the United States Military Academy at West Point or in ROTC—the Reserve Officers' Training Corps—are exempt from Officer Candidate School.) Advanced Individual Training programs vary in duration and provide enlistees with the necessary technical expertise for their areas of specialization. Base pay is very low for enlistees and only slightly higher for officers; but the Army augments base pay with various bonuses (for signing specified length of commitment contracts, for example) and allowances for different needs (like clothing and housing as well as dental and medical care). Beyond this, soldiers may receive educational subsidies after they have completed their service.

ASSOCIATED CAREERS

The skills learned in all of areas of Army specialization transfer well into counterpart jobs in the civilian world. For example, Army firefighters can become civilian firefighters; just as Army engineers can become civilian engineers. All soldiers learn how to lead and function in a team. This skill, of course, is helpful in just about any career.

PAST AND FUTURE

Since the time of Cain and Abel, human beings have fought one another and sought to defend themselves. Organized military branches in countries across the globe have been in existence for thousands of years. A brief, very incomplete history of the American Army would have to include the semi-organized force of colonists in the French and Indian Wars. The colonists formed an army as a tool to free themselves from England during the Revolutionary War. The Army defeated Mexico in the era of Manifest Destiny. In the 1860s, the Federal Army fought the Confederate Army over the Confederacy's attempt to secede from the Union in what became the Civil War, the only extended conflict in American history in which Americans have fought and killed fellow Americans. Spain was defeated in 1898. Germany was defeated by America and her allies not once but twice in the two World Wars. The latter half of the twentieth century saw the Army challenged by forces in Korea, Vietnam, and Iraq; although these conflicts were technically police actions and not wars (Congress never declared war), they were nevertheless important parts of American military history.

Although the most publicized military action in recent years has been Operation Iraqi Freedom, the U.S. Army is constantly engaged in lower-profile peacekeeping and humanitarian missions throughout the world. Because of the global presence of the U.S. Army, opportunities for soldiers continue to be promising.

QUALITY OF LIFE

2 YEARS After two years, enlistees and officers have both completed their initial training. They have most likely been serving at a permanent post for several months, and have become accustomed to Army life. Responsibilities remain limited in this initial acclimation phase. Unless they have committed infractions, enlistees should have been promoted at least once.

5 YEARS At the five-year mark, talented and motivated enlisted personnel are sergeants; officers with the same characteristics are captains. Responsibility increases with rank. Captains may command a company of troops, that is, 60 to 190 soldiers. Sergeants may be in charge of a squad (about ten soldiers), or serve as a principle NCO assistant to a platoon or company commander. Pay increases over time and with rank.

10 YEARS Many Army personnel do not stay on active duty for ten years or longer. Those who do often expect to make a lifelong career out of it. Enlisted personnel who have remained motivated may have achieved the rank of Sergeant First Class, a title that identifies them as model soldiers. There are only two more promotions one can receive in the enlisted ranks after being made Sergeant First Class: Master Sergeant, and then Sergeant Major. As soldiers advance further up the enlisted ranks, they become increasingly likely to serve in a planning capacity as an assistant to a battalion (which consists of about 1,000 soldiers) or commander of a brigade (which has about 4,000 soldiers). A motivated officer may become a major after ten years, with command of up to a battalion. There are several more promotions a major could potentially receive, but one internal criticism of the Army promotion system is that it becomes increasingly political the further one makes it up the ladder, especially in trying to break into the ranks of general officers. Less than 1 percent of career officers will ever be promoted to general.

MAJOR EMPLOYERS
UNITED STATES ARMY
www.goarmy.com
www.army.mil

MAJOR ASSOCIATIONS
NATIONAL ASSOCIATION FOR UNIFORMED SERVICES
5535 Hempstead Way
Springfield, VA 22151
Tel: 703-750-1342
www.naus.org

VETERANS OF FOREIGN WARS
406 West 34th Street
Kansas City, MO 64111
Tel: 816-756-3390
Fax: 816-968-1149
E-mail: info@vfw.org
www.vfw.org

ASTRONAUT

A DAY IN THE LIFE

Astronauts command high-altitude vehicles that venture into space. Astronauts typically come from a variety of fields, train for a year or two with the chance of being chosen as a member of a shuttle crew, and then return to their original jobs. They rise early and work late into the night, training for potential space missions during which as many hours as possible will be utilized for intensive experimentation. Stamina is crucial, since most astronauts only sleep for five hours at a time on their missions. Astronauts-in-training participate in scenarios that simulate weightlessness and heavy gravity (excessive g-forces), and navigate nature's call in an unbroachable interstellar suit. Intensive psychological screening, required of all applicants, is supposed to weed out those with claustrophobia, but one or two are discovered

{ interstellar suit }

annually in the program and dismissed. Other unusual skills astronauts learn include eating and drinking through straws, washing their entire bodies with a hand cloth, and sleeping in a noisy environment, buckled to a bed so they don't float around the craft uncontrollably. Nearly every basic task taken for granted on Earth offers unusual difficulties in space and must be relearned. This retraining of basic skills is a difficult coming-down for those scientists—many of whom have PhDs—who are used to navigating more intellectual and ostensibly more difficult tasks. Roughly ten candidates per year are asked to leave because they cannot master these basic maneuvers. The ability to focus is the most important feature of the successful astronaut, but the ability to make choices under pressured and limited-option situations is also important. In only rare circumstances does an *Apollo 13*-type crisis situation come to pass; more often, the most difficult decision an astronaut faces is how to juggle a variety of experiments in a limited time. Members of shuttle launches overbook their time in the event that their mission is delayed; since this is often the case, every potential free moment is scheduled. The ability to work as part of a team is enormously important, and much of the training associated with becoming an astronaut focuses on developing this team mentality and working together in a cramped environment. The rigorous training fosters a strong sense of camaraderie. While only a few make the final cut to be members of a spacebound crew (the constituency is based on the needs of the mission), more than 100 people train at any given time at the Johnson Space Center, in Houston, Texas. They live, train, eat, and exercise together, many of them working in concert on research projects with components that can only be completed in space. The environment is said to be supportive and mutually encouraging, partly because each astronaut has no idea who will be picked to be a crew member on the next mission, and who they might be paired with.

PAYING YOUR DUES

Nearly every child dreams, at one time or another, of becoming an astronaut, but few carry this dream through to adulthood and for a good reason: It's damn tough to become an astronaut. Requirements include an excellent academic record (undergraduate and graduate) in any of a number of scientific fields, including aerospace engineering, medicine, biology, chemistry, physics, astronomy, optics, and computer science. Candidates are usually very accomplished in another field before they apply to become astronauts. They must be in excellent shape physically and mentally, between 5'4" and 6'4" tall, and be willing to spend a full year of training for a space mission. They must also be willing to brave the odds, because in any given year, the greatest number of NASA astronauts that has been assigned to a flight was sixteen. Their year of rigorous training offers no guarantee of being assigned as a crew member on a mission. Most importantly, applicants must pass the NASA standards for astronauts, which include jet-pilot qualifications and flight experience, a rigorous security check, and an in-depth personality profile. The average shuttle launch costs 1 billion—that's right, 1 billion dollars. Since NASA is footing the bill, they tend to be quite selective about who they offer seats to. Of the 11 to 12 thousand people each year who apply to become astronauts, only between 100 and 200 make it through the difficult screening.

ASSOCIATED CAREERS

Most return to research, teaching, flying, or the military, whatever their occupations were prior to becoming an astronaut; a few, like Senator John Glenn, enter politics. The major difference between becoming an astronaut and going into other professions is that the former is an end in and of itself. One does not progress or advance from being an astronaut; one returns to normal life. Astronauts occasionally become celebrities due to their unusual status, and a few parlay their fame into media-supported careers.

PAST AND FUTURE

The career of astronaut began in fiction in the 1800s and as an intellectual exercise in 1923, with the publication of the book The Rocket into Interplanetary Space, which described the potential problems with space travel. In October 1957, the Cold War between the United States and the U.S.S.R. heated up with the Russian launch of Sputnik I, the first orbiting satellite. Just twelve years later, American Neil Armstrong became the first human to set foot on the moon. Beginning in 1981, the space shuttle became the vehicle of choice for cross-atmosphere travel.

The duties of an astronaut should change with increasing technology, but because future opportunities for the improvement of existing systems depend on more flights, and because these flights are extremely expensive, any anticipated increase in the number of astronauts would be optimistic. Budget restrictions tend to cut back on the most immediately unprofitable segments first. NASA has never shown a direct profit, but their unique ability to place satellites into orbit and do unusual zero-gravity scientific experiments will probably continue to draw funding.

QUALITY OF LIFE

2 YEARS An astronaut's first few years are spent in candidate training at the Johnson Space Center near Houston, TX. During this period, they attend classes in a variety of subjects, including shuttle systems, guidance and navigation, orbital dynamics, oceanography, and geology meteorology. Additionally, candidates undergo rigorous physical tests including altitude chambers and military water survival training. Those wishing to become pilots will also log considerable flying time in NASA's fleet of T-38 jets.

5 YEARS Five years into their careers, astronauts have established their roles within the space program; they may be pilots, mission specialists, or payload specialists, for example. At this juncture, an astronaut is considered active and eligible for flight assignment. A fair number are assigned to crews.

10 YEARS Astronauts who stay with NASA for ten years have clearly garnered significant experience. Some are promoted to management astronaut and take on new roles within the space program. Many are appointed to special-duty assignments, while others may opt to go on sabbatical.

MAJOR EMPLOYERS
NASA JOHNSON SPACE CENTER
Space Center Houston
Houston, TX 77058

NASA HEADQUARTERS
Suite 1M32
Washington, DC 20546-0001
Tel: 202-358-0001
Fax: 202-358-3469
www.nasa.gov

MAJOR ASSOCIATIONS
AMERICAN INSTITUTE OF AERONAUTICS AND ASTRONAUTICS
1801 Alexander Bell Drive, Suite 500
Reston, VA 20191-4344
Tel: 800-639-2422 or 703-264-7500
Fax: 703-264-7551
www.aiaa.org

ATHLETIC TRAINER

SALARY ● ● ●
HOURS ● ● ●
EDUCATION ● ● ●

BOOKS, FILMS, AND TV SHOWS
FEATURING THE PROFESSION

- Chariots of Fire
- Evening Shade

YOU'LL HAVE CONTACT WITH

- Athletes
- Clients
- Coaches
- Dancers
- Doctors
- Nurses
- Nutritionists

PROFESSIONALS READ

- Advance for Directors in Rehabilitation
- Biomechanics
- Journal of Athletic Training
- Occupational Hazards
- Occupational Health and Safety
- Rehab Management

A DAY IN THE LIFE

Athletic trainers work with recreational, professional, student, and amateur athletes to assist them in recovering from injury and to instruct them in good practices that will benefit their current and future physical health. Trainers also work with other professionals (such as nutritionists) to design health and fitness programs for those who are involved in sports or maintain active lifestyles. The ability to apply scientific and medical knowledge to the varied needs and concerns of professional and recreational athletes, as well as the capacity to listen and communicate clearly with a range of personalities are both essential for success in the profession. A trainer may spend part of a typical day reviewing records and data and conducting research relevant to the { current and future physical health } needs and goals of individual clients. He or she will very likely meet with individuals one-on-one, gather information, and devise a fitness plan. In a school or team situation, part of the trainer's day may be spent attending practices, at which he or she may observe and offer suggestions to coaches and players. In a business environment, he or she may observe workers at their tasks or counsel individuals on lifestyle and work-related issues. Trainers may also give group presentations or teach classes and will probably spend a portion of each day consulting with other professionals such as coaches, teachers, work supervisors, and parents. Those who work with sports teams may find they are required to work long hours and to travel often. Whatever the environment, though, trainers may find themselves working with individuals who are under stress, in pain, and concerned for their health.

PAYING YOUR DUES

A bachelor's degree and subsequent certification are required of aspiring athletic trainers. Trainers often also undertake graduate study to increase their opportunities. Typical subjects studied on both the undergraduate and graduate levels include biomechanics, human anatomy, nutrition, physiology, psychology, and related subjects. Health care administration, interpersonal communication, and business or education subjects are also often useful to a trainer, as is the ability to speak more than one language. Possible career paths include moving from junior- or assistant-level positions to a job as head trainer or even, ultimately, to a private practice. Employment in school systems tends to offer regular hours but less income potential, while work with sports teams or in health clubs often requires irregular hours but may add potential for higher levels of income. Each field offers the potential to gain satisfaction from helping individual athletes overcome obstacles and attain their goals.

ASSOCIATED CAREERS

The knowledge of health sciences and sports may lead athletic trainers into careers in teaching or coaching. Some may choose to combine a teaching career with continued work as a trainer. Athletic trainers may also go into sales of sports-related products or seek management positions in health clubs or medical practices. Trainers may also opt to move into other health-related careers as nurses or paramedics.

PAST AND FUTURE

The athletes of ancient Greece had helpers to assist them, and they also consulted with experts about their progress. As team sports developed in the nineteenth century, the trainer sometimes took on the role of administrative assistant. As interest in sports and knowledge of science and medicine grew, so too did the role of athletic trainers—complete with training standards and certification requirements that emerged around 1950.

Use of athletic trainers as allied health professionals in situations beyond the sports arena is a potential area for growth in the profession, as both businesses and schools recognize the importance of preventing injury and of integrating out-of-work and out-of-classroom activities with the physical demands of daily office and school settings. Increased participation in recreational sports and the aging of the baby boomer generation offer additional opportunities to help individuals maintain active lifestyles. Knowledge of health sciences and psychology as well as understanding issues concerning older athletes will probably be essential for trainers in upcoming years.

QUALITY OF LIFE

2 YEARS At the early stages of this career, an athletic trainer may work as an assistant to an experienced trainer or as a member of the junior staff in a large business or sports facility. Athletic trainers may also be employed at smaller businesses or schools—or, with the proper credentials, they may combine part-time work as a trainer with part-time teaching responsibilities. Trainers may, alternatively, find part- and full-time employment at recreational facilities and health clubs. Learning to apply academic knowledge and training to real-world situations is the chief challenge for the new athletic trainer.

5 YEARS At this point in his or her career, the trainer may be in charge of operations at a moderate-sized school, business, or club; alternatively, he or she may have taken on a more senior role in a larger organization. This is also a point at which many trainers seek a master's degree in a health-related field and/or pursue teaching credentials.

10 YEARS Ten years into their careers, trainers are well-positioned to work in supervisory roles, if they are not already doing so. Trainers may also choose to start their own private practices at this point. A handful may opt to seek academic training in scientific fields or business areas.

MAJOR EMPLOYERS

Athletic trainers find employment in health clubs or in high schools and colleges.

They are also employed by professional sports teams and professional dance companies. Some practice with doctors in sports medicine clinics.

MAJOR ASSOCIATIONS

NATIONAL ATHLETIC TRAINERS' ASSOCIATION

2952 Stemmons Freeway
Dallas, TX 75247
Tel: 800-879-6282
www.nata.org/careercenter

AUTO MECHANIC

A DAY IN THE LIFE

Auto mechanics repair and maintain cars. Some mechanics work on all parts of any car, while others specialize in one area or one type of car. The most challenging aspect of car repair is often the mechanic's favorite part: diagnosing the problem. Speed and accuracy in diagnosis and quoting prices to the customer are crucial, if the mechanic intends to keep long-term clients. The mechanic examines the engine while it is running (if possible) to see if his or her initial assumptions are correct. The use of the latest electronic diagnostic equipment is combined with a mechanic's sensory skills to search for problems and potential hazards. Sometimes a mechanic repairs parts; but if a part is worn or damaged, he replaces it. Some mechanics compare their field to that of the physician. Like clients of physicians, { speed and accuracy } most come in only when their car is in dire straits, not when regular preventive maintenance could have avoided the problems all together. When people come in for an automotive check-up, mechanics often replace worn parts before they become hazardous to the driver, even though drivers can be suspicious of mechanics who recommend the replacement of parts that haven't stopped functioning. Concerned about your technician's qualifications? Check for a certificate from the ASE—the National Institute for Automotive Service Excellence.

The best mechanics have considerable knowledge concerning specific aspects of cars: electrical systems (a car's wiring and computer systems are more complicated than those in an average home); and fuel systems and refrigeration (a car's "plumbing" is a maze of tubes). Because car designs change every year, the job requires more preparation than ever before. More and more, cars are controlled by electronic instruments, so mechanics are using computers constantly. "Computers have become as much a part of the toolbox as wrenches," said one mechanic. Most auto mechanics intern while still in automotive repair school, then work full-time at the same dealerships. They read trade papers daily to keep abreast of changes and trends in their industry. As they gain experience they can move into higher-paying, specialized positions. They can also rise to the ranks of supervisor or manager, particularly if they have strong interpersonal skills to calm cranky customers who are displeased by expensive service bills and inconvenience.

PAYING YOUR DUES

Aspiring auto mechanics must have increasingly sophisticated vocational skills and must constantly adapt to changing technology. The integration of computers in automobiles means mechanics must be familiar with complicated new systems. While this emphasis on ongoing training intimidates some, most mechanics soon find that motivation and an enthusiastic instructor can help. Students begin their training by studying car processes in manuals and then work on older cars. Most mechanics find themselves in technical educational programs after graduating high school, but there are a few high schools that offer four-year automotive programs that culminate in certification. All auto mechanics are required to be certified not by law but by employers. Few will hire uncertified personnel. To obtain certification, students spend more than a thousand hours working on cars and must pass a written exam. There are test-preparation guides for all certifying exams. Community college programs encourage students to complete an applied-science degree and then acquire an automotive technology certificate. A number of training programs work with local shops to place students in internships with car dealerships or service centers during their studies. Most mechanics are responsible for obtaining their own sets of tools, but employers are responsible for supplying large power tools and electronic testing equipment. Some auto repair shops require union membership.

ASSOCIATED CAREERS

Teaching auto repair is a growing field. Many older instructors do not possess the sophisticated computer knowledge required to teach today's aspiring auto mechanics. Those mechanics who do possess the computer knowledge can easily obtain employment. If you enjoy cars but don't want to get your hands dirty, perhaps auto body repair is for you. Auto body repair personnel do cosmetic repairs on cars or custom-paint them. Salespeople in dealerships also need sophisticated knowledge of cars. The glamorous world of professional racing is another option for the exceptionally gifted mechanic. Being a part of a pit crew involves anticipating problems and making repairs with perfect accuracy under pressure. Pit crew positions, however, are extremely difficult to come by.

PAST AND FUTURE

Automobiles were first produced in the 1890s, when they were little more than novelties for the very rich. As cars entered mass production and the manufacturing process grew more complex, owners came to rely increasingly on specialized auto mechanics. By the 1980s, the computer had become an integral part of automotive design and troubleshooting. Currently, there is a shortage of auto mechanics. One community college instructor said that every one of his students who completes his program gets a job. The field is anticipated to grow, since the trends are for people to keep their cars longer and replace them with increasingly complex models. The profession is relatively immune to fluctuations in the economy as a car is a necessity, not a luxury, for many people. Given rising gasoline costs, the use of hybrids and other alternative-energy models is likely to open up new dimensions of the field.

QUALITY OF LIFE

2 YEARS Mechanics generally enter the field after a lifetime fascination with cars, so it is rare that they jump ship to another profession within the first two years. Many enjoy the challenge of making cars safer and more useful. This, when coupled with the fact that auto mechanics have extremely low levels of unemployment, leads to high levels of satisfaction for the novice. The money is good, but the hours can be long.

5 YEARS Mechanics are earning their reputations and exposing themselves to a variety of automotive problems. Many of them have gained enough experience to become specialists. Those who are dissatisfied with the long hours go into nonautomotive repair jobs. Well-trained technicians are more efficient, even using fewer expensive gadgets than their untrained counterparts—so proper and continuous training is imperative.

10 YEARS Experienced and ambitious mechanics often open their own shops and hire other mechanics. Those mechanics working for big dealerships and shops should by now have risen to supervisory positions. Others who have not updated their skills may be forced into lesser-paying jobs. The majority of people in the field remain automotive mechanics for the rest of their careers.

MAJOR EMPLOYERS
Auto mechanics are employed by car dealerships, specialized repair facilities, and general service stations.

MAJOR ASSOCIATIONS
AUTOMOTIVE SERVICE ASSOCIATION, INC.
PO Box 929
Bedford, TX 76095
Tel: 800-272-7467 or 817-283-6205
Fax: 817-685-0225
www.asashop.org

AVIONICS TECHNICIAN

A DAY IN THE LIFE

Without avionics technicians, most military and high-tech planes would be unsafe. Avionics technicians test, maintain, and produce aviation electronics, including missile-guidance systems, jet engines, and flight-control circuitry. Much of an avionics job is preventative. Technicians work unusual hours, providing maintenance and support to private research concerns, aerospace companies, the military, and other government agencies. Levels of satisfaction in the industry are high mainly because it provides intellectual curiosity with a very close attention to detail. The installation of electronics devices, their calibration, and their testing are critical to the success of any aviation endeavor.

{ military and high-tech planes }

Many avionics technicians specialize in one area of expertise, such as microcircuit television microscopy, oscilloscope review, or computerized guidance systems. Since the field is evolving, many people's specialties change over time. Because of rapid changes in technology, continuing education through professional reading and attending company-sponsored seminars, industry events, and conferences is the norm in this field. Most technicians are also educated through interaction with their colleagues; while each member has an assigned responsibility, the majority of technicians work as part of a team. Communication skills and the ability to write comprehensive and complete reports are as important as technical skills.

Two discrete professional categories exist for those in the industry. The first is in the research and development (design and testing stages) of new electronic equipment. These technicians must have curious minds that can take into account potential factors that may cause problems, including atmospheric conditions, magnetic field interference, and weight limitations. The second category is involvement in direct installation and maintenance. These people must be extremely attentive to detail, organized, and interested in high degrees of responsibility and long hours. The two fields do cross over at a variety of points, but in general, the fields are separate.

PAYING YOUR DUES

Most people attend a specialty school or community college that specializes in electronics engineering for one to three years. Major aerospace employers run their own schools and training centers; but corporate-run schools teach only about each company's own product line. General course work at these schools includes electronics, the physics of electricity, circuit design, and computer science. Familiarity with math (calculus-level studies are preferred) and a degree of manual dexterity are both helpful. If communications equipment is part of your job, you will need a Federal Communications Commission (FCC) license as a restricted radio-telephone operator. Most specific skills, such as use of an oscilloscope or a circuit analyzer, are part of on-the-job training.

ASSOCIATED CAREERS

Some avionics technicians continue their education and become aviation engineers, electrical engineers (specializing in circuit design and testing), or communications engineers. Others become repair consultants, in-house electronics designers, or join research groups that test and rate developed products. But few avionics technicians leave the field due to the interesting work and competitive salaries the profession offers.

PAST AND FUTURE

Avionics developed with the rise of modern warfare. The number of electronic devices used in navigation, control, maintenance, and flight multiplied by a factor of a hundred between the World War II B-29 bomber and the current B-58 supersonic bomber. Missile technology, including the development of SCUDS, ICBMs, and other "smart" missiles, has also matured. The current demand for aviation technicians is significant.

While strong demand exists for technicians now, much of the direction of avionics technicians relies on defense spending, and with budget slashing looming on the horizon, this career faces an uncertain financial future. Aerospace work will continue to be done at some level, but to what degree and by how many people is the question. Research project support and government funding sway from supporting laser-based missile defense systems to backing propulsion-based systems, from encouraging the development of stealth weapons and high-altitude aircraft to supporting nothing at all.

QUALITY OF LIFE

2 YEARS Avionics technicians make the transition from school to the practical work environment during these early, busy years. Many participate in one- to two-month on-the-job training programs sponsored by their aerospace employers. Beginners join research teams as "junior" members, and their work is carefully scrutinized by more experienced members. Duties include calibration and installation of communication and other, less complicated, electronics systems. Salaries are reasonable, as are the hours, but many professionals entering the field mentioned that reading technical journals, a feature of most evolving professions, is one unexpected time-stealer.

5 YEARS Five-year survivors are now the senior members of research teams, and, in rare cases, leading them. Those involved in the design and research stages of products now have significant input into the testing protocols and installation procedures. Those involved in maintenance have regular schedules and may have some oversight responsibility for newer entrants to the field. The majority of avionics technicians—more than 70 percent—remain with their original employer through their first five years, possibly due to the paucity of aerospace companies.

10 YEARS Ten-year avionics technicians spend their time running research projects, working with designers and producers, and managing less-experienced avionics technicians. Those veterans who have advanced not only understand the technical specifications and the electronic requirements of what they do, but also realize the spirit of cooperation that must take place for teams in this industry to function efficiently. The majority of ten-year veterans are employed by the major aerospace companies, with the government employing the second largest number. Satisfaction is high, and the hours increase.

MAJOR EMPLOYERS
THE BOEING COMPANY
PO Box 3707
Seattle, WA 98124
Tel: 206-655-2121
www.boeing.com

CESSNA AIRCRAFT COMPANY
PO Box 7704
Wichita, KS 67277-7704
Tel: 316-517-6157
Fax: 316-517-7865
www.cessna.com
Contact: Employment/Human Resources
E-mail: CessnaJobs@cessna.textron.com

MAJOR ASSOCIATIONS
AMERICAN INSTITUTE OF AERONAUTICS AND ASTRONAUTICS
1801 Alexander Bell Drive, Suite 500
Reston, VA 20191-4344
Tel: 800-639-2422 or 703-264-7500
Fax: 703-264-7551
www.aiaa.org

PROFESSIONAL AVIATION MAINTENANCE ASSOCIATION
717 Princess Street
Alexandria, VA 22314
Tel: 703-683-3171
Fax: 703-683-0018
www.pama.org

BIOCHEMIST

A DAY IN THE LIFE

It would be wrong to call it a niche, since the science of biochemistry spans the study of all living things and provides the foundation for all of the life sciences. It would be right, however, to say that most biochemists are neck-deep in research. About 75 percent work in either basic or applied research; those who work in applied research take the fruits of basic research and employ them for the benefit of medicine, agriculture, veterinary science, environmental science, and manufacturing. Each of these fields offers safe harbor for the biochemist in search of a specialty, with clinical biochemists, for one example, working in hospital laboratories and studying various tissues and body fluids to help them understand and treat diseases; and industrial biochemists, for another example, are involved in analytical research work, such as checking the purity of food and beverages.

{ chemical reactions }

Research biochemists find work in the labs of biotechnology companies; agricultural, medical, and veterinary institutes; and, in the case of half of all biochemists, universities. They study chemical reactions in metabolism, growth, reproduction, and heredity and apply techniques drawn from biotechnology and genetic engineering to help them in their research. The workday usually includes some laboratory duties, such as culturing, filtering, purifying, drying, weighing, and measuring substances using special instruments. Research includes the effects of foods, drugs, allergens, and other substances on living tissues. Many biochemists are also interested in molecular biology: the study of life at the molecular level and the study of genes and gene expression.

PAYING YOUR DUES

Unlike chemists, who can find opportunities to enter the field upon completion of a bachelor's degree, biochemists traditionally hold a doctoral degree. Therefore, aspiring biochemists have to complete an additional two to four years of study to earn their PhD, MD, or other doctoral degree on top of their BS. After finishing school, most biochemists embark on their career in the laboratory as research technicians. Biochemists usually work forty to fifty hours per week, with occasional weekend and evening work to meet deadlines or to attend and observe experiments.

ASSOCIATED CAREERS

A biochemistry degree can be put to use in a wide array of related medical, industrial, governmental, and environmental fields. The field of medicine offers related careers such as nutrition, genetics, biophysics, and pharmacology; industrial needs include everything from beverage and food technology to toxicology and vaccine production; while governmental and environmental fields require biochemists to work on everything from forensic science and wildlife management to marine biology and viticulture. This incredibly wide range makes biochemistry an extremely flexible career choice.

PAST AND FUTURE

Rapid advancements in research and technology are enabling the pace of discovery in biochemistry to stay as exciting as ever. Today's biochemists are working to attain the levels of contribution reached by forefathers such as the early twentieth century's Sir Frederick Gowland Hopkins, who won the Nobel Prize for his discovery of vitamins, and Marshall W. Nirenberg, whose work in protein synthesis and later genetics earned him a Nobel Prize in 1968. Since the pioneering work of Mr. Nirenberg and his colleagues to crack the human genome, biochemists are now working with other scientists to unlock its secrets fully. Employment opportunities in biochemistry can be expected to increase well into the second decade of the twenty-first century as demand grows for expertise in everything from lawn-care technology to the detection of chemical weapons. Projects related to health issues, such as AIDS, cancer, and the human genome project, will continue to need biochemists with advanced degrees, a trend that will be helped if the federal government continues to fund research.

QUALITY OF LIFE

2 YEARS While the level of work may resemble an apprenticeship in its early stages, most biochemists receive paid holidays and vacations, health insurance, and a retirement plan when they become full-time employees. In the early stages, a biochemist's experience can define whether the future holds government, educational, or private-sector work.

5 YEARS Large private companies may give employees bonuses, stock options, paid travel, and expense accounts; university and government posts can attract sizable grants to fund research.

10 YEARS By the tenth year, biochemists have felt the satisfaction of finding out new things and making new discoveries that make a difference to fellow human beings. They are very unlikely to lose their jobs during periods of recession, and most are employed on long-term research projects. And since biochemistry is an interdisciplinary science, biochemists can take their skills laterally to jobs in other biological sciences.

MAJOR EMPLOYERS

Biochemists work at biotechnology and pharmaceutical firms, as well as universities, colleges, and government laboratories.

MAJOR ASSOCIATIONS

FEDERATION OF AMERICAN SOCIETIES FOR EXPERIMENTAL BIOLOGY
9650 Rockville Pike
Bethesda, MD 20814
Tel: 301-634-7000
www.faseb.org

THE BIOCHEMICAL SOCIETY
16 Procter Street
London, England
WC1V 6NX
Tel: 020-7280-4100
Fax: 020-7280-4170
www.biochemistry.org

BIOLOGIST

A DAY IN THE LIFE

Biologists study humans, plants, animals, and the environments in which they live. They may conduct their studies—human medical research, plant research, animal research, or environmental system research—at the cellular level, the ecosystem level, or anywhere in between. Biologists are students of the world and are interested in learning from every facet of life. Although this scope may seem overwhelming, in practice, biologists tend to specialize in discrete areas.

Biologists' daily activities are driven by their area of specialization. Marine biologists study marine populations and physiology, working off boats, at oceanography centers, aquariums, and at a variety of coastal sites.

{ the world's largest laboratory }

Biochemists spend most of their day in a laboratory analyzing tissue samples and designing and carrying out research projects to test new hypotheses. Agricultural scientists analyze crop yields produced from different soils, fertilizers, or chemicals. Biologists study life to uncover its secrets and to find ways to solve problems, such as finding a cure for a disease. Much research is done in ecologically diverse areas such as the Brazilian rain forest, where nature—the world's largest laboratory—has produced biological compounds scientists cannot yet create on their own.

Biologists generally love what they do. Many put in long hours, compelled by their dedication to work beyond the requirements of their jobs. Significant time at the lab, in the field, and at lectures and conferences contributes to many biologists' lack of a personal life outside the discipline. Within the field, colleagues are aware of and sensitive to others' research progress and philosophical approaches. Relationships with colleagues can be intense and often are substitutes for average social interaction. The rarefied knowledge and dedication required to analyze the basic stuff of life may be one reason why biologists choose to spend even more time with other biologists: they understand one another's devotion to their work. From anatomy to zoology, biologists are engaged in a demanding and creative scientific endeavor. One biologist described it as "assembling the pieces of nature's puzzle."

PAYING YOUR DUES

Academic requirements are strict in this discipline. Most individuals in positions of authority have extensive post-graduate degrees, but entry-level positions are available for people with only a bachelor's degree in a biological science. Most researchers have a master's degree; they direct research and perform out-of-lab functions, such as on-site sampling and interviewing about medication side effects. Those who wish to direct research functions must obtain a PhD in a biological science. The largest employer of biologists is the federal government, particularly the Environmental Protection Agency (EPA), the National Institutes of Health (NIH), the Center for Disease Control (CDC), and the Department of Agriculture. Biologists at these organizations conduct practical research on existing biological compounds. Pharmaceutical companies employ the next largest block of biologists in their research labs. Certification is available from certain professional organizations, but it is not required.

ASSOCIATED CAREERS

Biologists who leave the field generally look for careers that will satisfy both their scientific and social interests. They become doctors, veterinarians, laboratory managers, statisticians, and even dentists at a higher salary than do those who leave most other professions.

PAST AND FUTURE

Research on biological systems and their relationships is thought to have begun in ancient Greece, but little of this work was recorded. Early physicians explored the microbiological elements, looking for the causes and effects of disease, malnutrition, and deformity. In the fourteenth century, the Catholic Church began keeping comprehensive records of public activities and health. The data provided by the Catholic Church began with the study of large systems and their methods of interaction. A combination of the church data and the data of the early physicians forms the foundation of the biological sciences.

The prospects for biologists depend not only on the demand for their services—which will probably increase in the coming years—but also on the availability of funding. Pharmaceutical companies will continue to fund potentially lucrative pharmaceutical projects. The U.S. government will continue to fund the testing of health products for release to the public; but universities, private research concerns, and foundations will face strict budgetary limitations. Therefore, it's uncertain how biologists will fare in the next ten years. Those who succeed will most likely be strong academically in a specific area of specialization and will have excellent technical skills.

QUALITY OF LIFE

2 YEARS Biologists are primarily technicians who operate equipment, conduct tests, and record data for senior researchers. They spend significant time performing routine tasks regardless of their experience prior to hire. The hours can be long, and most of their time is spent in the lab. Although others may scoff at this "internship" of sorts, technicians generally expect to pay these dues in their first few years and satisfaction remains high. A number of aspiring researchers ally themselves with more experienced and well-known researchers to position themselves to become future researchers in their fields of interest.

5 YEARS Fieldwork arrives and satisfaction generally increases. Those who are not promoted to research positions either gravitate to other fields or return to school to earn additional credentials that will make them more attractive candidates in their chosen fields. The hours can be long and the work environment unpredictable but responsibilities and salary increase. Some seek to publish their research and theories to make their ideas known and to distinguish themselves from their contemporaries.

10 YEARS Many researchers have assumed positions as assistant directors of research or have limited control of disbursement of funds and distribution of personnel. Some researchers are still finishing their PhDs and are having a difficult time juggling work and academics. Some researchers join professional organizations or advisory committees to add another feather to their cap. A number of researchers enter academia. The hours flatten out and ambitions remain high.

MAJOR EMPLOYERS

AMGEN
One Amgen Center Drive
Thousand Oaks, CA 91320-1799
Tel: 805-447-1000 or 800-77-AMGEN
Fax: 805-447-1010
www.amgen.com

CENTER FOR DISEASE CONTROL AND PREVENTION
1600 Clifton Road
Atlanta, GA 30333
Tel: 404-639-3534 or 800-311-3435
www.cdc.gov
Contact: Human Resources

DOW CHEMICAL COMPANY
2030 Dow Center
Midland, MI 48674
Tel: 989-636-1000
www.dow.com

MAJOR ASSOCIATIONS

AMERICAN INSTITUTION OF BIOLOGICAL SCIENCES
1441 I Street, NW, Suite 200
Washington, DC 20005
Tel: 202-628-1500
Fax: 202-628-1509
www.aibs.org
admin@aibs.org

AMERICAN SOCIETY FOR MICROBIOLOGY
1752 N Street, NW
Washington, DC 20036-2804
Tel: 202-737-3600
Fax: 202-942-9346
www.asm.org

BOTANICAL SOCIETY OF AMERICA
PO Box 299
St. Louis, MO 63166
Tel: 314-577-9566
Fax: 314-577-9515
www.botany.org

CARPENTER

A DAY IN THE LIFE

Carpenters are skilled workers who make, finish, and repair objects and structures. The occupation rewards people who can combine precise detail work with strenuous manual labor. Carpenters construct two categories of items: those used in the erection, maintenance, and aesthetic mix of structures and those used as furniture, art, or framing. Similar skills are important in each category: the ability to turn blueprints and plans into finished objects, to pick good wood, and to use all woodworking tools. But structural carpenters enjoy a larger market for their services and a more consistent demand than piecework carpenters do. The satisfaction levels in both fields are high, but the lifestyle in each is quite different. "The best thing about building things is that you know you can do a good job that will last for years. It's great to walk by a place ten years after you built it and say, 'Oh, you know, I put up those walls and put in those floors.'" This sense of pride came through in the majority of structural carpenter surveys we received. Structural carpenters work with supervisors and construction managers on the production of multi-material products. They work with fiberglass, drywall, and plastic as well as wood, and they use saws, tape measures, drills, and sanders in their jobs. They shape and join material to the specifications of blueprints or at the direction of their contractor. This can entail long hours of physical labor, sometimes in unpleasant circumstances. "Putting up a house in November isn't fun at all," said one carpenter from the Northeast. Structural carpenters also spend a significant amount of time checking their work with plumb bobs, rules, and levels. The injury rate among structural carpenters is above average.

{ building things }

Detail carpenters usually work indoors: Some are involved in maintenance and refinishing, and others are involved in creation. The majority of detail carpenters work as furniture restorers and repairmen. They fix, sand, even, and stain used furniture. Detail work requires a good eye for prior construction methods, an understanding of restoration techniques, and patience. Other detail carpenters fashion and create their own pieces of furniture, choosing the wood, designing the final product, then shaping and assembling the parts. Many of them then sell these pieces to retail houses and private buyers. Detail carpenters work directly with clients more often than structural carpenters, so interpersonal skills are much more significant.

PAYING YOUR DUES

Carpenters learn their trade on the job and through apprenticeships. Many of the apprentice programs are administered by the Associated Builders and Contractors and the Associated General Contractors, Inc., as well as by unions such as the United Brotherhood of Carpenters and Joiners of America and the National Association of Home Builders. You have to be at least seventeen years old and demonstrate the following: a capacity to learn; the ability to do sustained, difficult, physical work; manual dexterity; some mathematical aptitude; and a willingness to take direction. Most apprenticeships last from three to four years. The market for carpenters is tied to local construction markets, and while the education gained by being a carpenter is invaluable for someone who wants to be involved in the construction industry, the unpredictability of the work is something applicants should be familiar with before entering this profession. Applicants may also need to relocate at times to find work.

ASSOCIATED CAREERS

Structural carpenters have a broad base of exposure to the different areas of construction, so it is not surprising that many who leave the profession go into plumbing, electrical wiring, or contracting. Detail carpenters go into graphic design, sculpture, and glasswork. Professionals who leave the field usually do so because of lack of opportunity rather than dissatisfaction with the profession.

PAST AND FUTURE

Carpentry has been around since human beings first built structures, but methodologies and powerful construction tools have been developed through the ages. In particular, the development of the flexible nail made construction of objects that could survive shipping, stress, and settling possible.

Carpenters will be in strong demand for the next ten years, subject to normal considerations of real estate construction cycles and local economies. In general, the field has a relatively high turnover rate, due to retirement and injury. The potential increased use of prefabricated components in the construction industry means that fewer carpenters will be needed to build the same number of structures; but even this will not be enough to dam the growth of job prospects through the end of the century. Carpenter unions continue to take creative steps to ensure occupations for many of their members.

QUALITY OF LIFE

2 YEARS — Many carpenters are in training programs or are assistants to established carpenters. Long hours working in the field on construction sites are complemented by extra hours in the classroom learning blueprint reading skills, techniques of construction, and instruction in safety and first aid. Minor injuries during these first two years are common, mainly from overexertion and lack of experience. The pay is low, but many carpenters find that these years pass quickly, as each day brings new experiences.

5 YEARS — Five-year carpenters have chosen an area of specialty, completed their training programs, joined a union, and established their reputations among regular employers. The hours are long, and the work is plentiful. Many carpenters become involved in their unions, which provide powerful contacts. Satisfaction is high during these years, and many of our respondents went out of their way to say they socialized with their coworkers and felt they were "supportive."

10 YEARS — Carpenters are subject to injury less often than their younger and older counterparts, having found that safe balance between expediency and experience. Those carpenters who go into contracting use their union connections to employ efficient, hardworking carpentry crews. People who remain in the field often become heads of carpentry teams or work as managers under general contractors. Detail carpenters have established reputations with retailers, taken work on contract, and even work closely with architects in the design and aesthetic configuration of houses and their furniture at the ten-year mark. The salaries increase, but beyond this, only true stars earn extraordinary incomes.

MAJOR EMPLOYERS

ASSOCIATED GENERAL CONTRACTORS OF AMERICA
333 John Carlyle Street, Suite 200
Alexandria, VA 22314
Tel: 703-548-3118
Fax: 703-548-3119
www.agc.org
Contact: Human Resources

HABITAT FOR HUMANITY INTERNATIONAL
322 Lamar Street
Americus, GA 31709
Tel: 229-924-6935
Fax: 229-924-0641
www.habitat.org
Contact: Human Resources

MAJOR ASSOCIATIONS

UNITED BROTHERHOOD OF CARPENTERS AND JOINERS OF AMERICA
Visit www.carpenters.org to find a UBC office in your area.

CATERER

A DAY IN THE LIFE

A caterer works closely with clients to design, prepare, and serve menus for events, including wedding dinners, charity balls, holiday brunches, office lunches, and any other occasions at which people gather and consume food. A caterer must understand how dishes work together; have strong interpersonal, particularly listening, skills; and possess the ability to manage a cooking and serving staff. More than 70 percent of all catering services are owner-run, so many caterers must also have sharp business acumen. Most people are drawn to the industry because of their love of cooking or preparing elegant meals for special events. In their first few years in catering, many people find that talent only gets you so far. "You can have dozens of clients, great reviews, and the best products—and you can still lose money," reported one ten-year veteran. Management and organizational skills are critical for those caterers who wish to keep their business concerns solvent. Caterers spend considerable amounts of time developing their menus, unique styles, and business plans.

{ **sharp business acumen** }

"You have to oversee everything," one caterer noted. "That's why catering services never get too large." While some catering services do employ hundreds of full- and part-time staff, a large majority have fewer than six full-time employees and hire temporary staff on an as-needed basis. Business is driven by season. A caterer may have three to five meetings with prospective clients to work out the details of an event. The caterer provides menus; the clients choose their favorite dishes and work with the caterer to assemble a meal in which each dish complements the others. Successful caterers are able to guide people to decisions that will benefit the event.

PAYING YOUR DUES

There are no educational requirements for becoming a caterer, though many people choose to attend a culinary academy to learn the basics of certain schools of cooking. Other caterers attend restaurant management school or at least take course work that addresses some of the concerns of the business, such as finance, management, and organization. Those caterers who do not attend any special schools should have some type of professional food preparation experience; cooking food for large numbers of people in a limited time frame is a crucial (and not necessarily intuitive) skill. Caterers also have to be certified for sanitary cooking conditions and safe equipment. Most boards of health offer two- or three-day courses in health laws for prospective caterers and restaurants.

ASSOCIATED CAREERS

Caterers are chefs of a sort, and many of them become chefs when catering concerns fold (and they do at a significant rate). Other caterers get involved in the service end of the industry and become event coordinators, party planners, and waiting staff managers. A small number go into the mass-produced food industry; many people view that life as "selling out." Most frequently, caterers who leave the industry take some time away, review their situations, and then enter the field again with more knowledge and experience.

PAST AND FUTURE

Catering used to be the prerogative of wealthy, mannered families who would have their in-house cooks or chefs prepare meals for large events or parties. In the late 1800s, as the tap-room gave way to the fine restaurant, these families began to expect the same quality and service they received at restaurants at their private events. Deals were initially struck with those restaurants to provide service, and restaurateurs began to see a market. In the mid-twentieth century, catering concerns blossomed, and they continue to do so today.

Caterers will still face the roller coaster of success that has marked the industry for the past twenty-five years. Greater specialization seems to be taking place, with caterers choosing their territory more carefully in terms of cuisine and products.

QUALITY OF LIFE

2 YEARS In the early years, caterers develop their identities, define menus, learn to manage events successfully, and network. Many caterers introduce their services to local restaurant owners who do not cater themselves to persuade the owners to recommend them to clients who need catering services. Earnings are generally low; and the hours are long and strenuous. Fewer than half of the people who start out as caterers remain after two years in the profession. The majority go out of business in fewer than eighteen months because of their failure to manage costs, market successfully, or establish a positive reputation.

5 YEARS Caterers who have lasted five years in the business have built local reputations, established specialties, and cultivated records of performance. Many caterers attempt to expand during these years; but overexposure, lack of centralized quality control, and rising costs can make expansion a mixed blessing at best. The hours are long, but many caterers have established areas of responsibility for each of their full-time employees and have by now learned how to delegate authority. Satisfaction is high, and the earnings have probably become livable.

10 YEARS Caterers who last ten years now have considerable experience running a business, an established expertise in an area of cuisine, and a reliable client base. Efforts at reinvention, though numerous during this period, are generally not well received by the client base. Reputations for service have also brought with them an expectation of menu selections, but many caterers find that their satisfaction wanes after ten years of preparing the same dishes. Earnings are consistent and strong. Many caterers pass their businesses to newer entrants in the field during the course of the next ten years and teach them the skills and responsibilities of the job while gradually passing on greater and greater client responsibility. When most people sell their catering businesses, it is usually to a long-term partner.

MAJOR EMPLOYERS
FOUR SEASONS HOTEL
57 East 57th Street
New York, NY 10022
Tel: 800-819-5053
Fax: 212-758-5711
www.fshr.com
Contact: Human Resources

GLORIOUS FOODS
504 East 74th Street
New York, NY 10021
Tel: 212-628-2320
Fax: 212-988-8136

TAVERN ON THE GREEN
Central Park West at 67th Street
New York, NY 10023
Tel: 212-873-3200
Fax: 212-580-4265
www.tavernonthegreen.com

MAJOR ASSOCIATIONS
MOBILE INDUSTRIAL CATERERS ASSOCIATION
304 West Liberty Street, Suite 201
Louisville, KY 40202
Tel: 800-620-6422 or 502-583-3783
Fax: 502-589-3602
www.mobilecaterers.com

CHEF

BOOKS, FILMS, AND TV SHOWS
FEATURING THE PROFESSION

- **Big Night**
- **Eat, Drink, Man, Woman**
- **If You Can Stand the Heat**
- **The Iron Chef (and anything else on The Food Network)**
- **Kitchen Confidential**
- **Like Water for Chocolate**
- **The Making of a Chef**
- **Mostly Martha**
- **The Restaurant**

YOU'LL HAVE CONTACT WITH

- **Assistant chefs**
- **Restaurateurs**
- **Sommeliers**
- **Suppliers**

PROFESSIONALS READ

- **Food and Wine**
- **Gourmet**
- **Nation's Restaurant News**
- **Restaurant Business**
- **Restaurant Hospitality**
- **Restaurants and Institutions**

A DAY IN THE LIFE

Chefs have earned a celebrity status in society that transcends the column of epicuriousness, from the banquettes of the world's finest restaurants to rural backyard barbecues everywhere. Although the glitz and glamour enjoyed by recognizable faces may overshadow the thankless toil many career kitchen-dwellers experience, people who become chefs tend to have very high levels of satisfaction with their professions. One chef said that his career "is only for the very crazy. It is hard work, it is grueling work, it is important work, and still, I would do nothing else." Many chefs mentioned the long hours, the painstaking attention to detail, and being constantly surrounded by food as keystones of a job they love. The profession rewards the talented and the daring who can see opportunity and grab it.

{ career kitchen-dwellers }

In urban centers, chefs were quick to mention that a supportive camaraderie exists within the community of chefs. "You start out knowing absolutely nothing, and these experienced, exciting chefs you've idolized all your life will show you how to run your kitchen. It's like having a living library at your disposal." Rural chefs, by comparison, reported experiencing the sense of isolation that can be discouraging. Chefs work long and unusual hours; this makes it difficult for them to socialize outside of working hours. One mentioned that "only doctors and truck drivers work the 4:00 P.M. to 2:00 A.M. shift." This leaves limited opportunity for meeting others, particularly if they are in a part of the country with few chefs.

The first few years are education. Few chefs survive cooking school; many don't understand the physical requirements of the profession: lifting heavy pots, being on your feet for eight hours, stirring vats of sauces, rolling pounds of dough. Many chefs specialize in a certain type of cuisine. It is difficult for new chefs to have their skills recognized without an established history of success in a variety of workplaces. Chefs who leave the profession do so with heavy hearts; they genuinely enjoy the companionship of fellow chefs, the creativity involved in working with food, and the aesthetic beauty and gustatory delights of the profession. But they sometimes leave anyway due to the lack of opportunity, the daily pressures (which can be considerable), and the low wages for those who do not advance immediately to positions of authority.

PAYING YOUR DUES

While the profession used to offer a direct progression for new entrants—begin as a preparation chef, move on to assistant chef, then get a chance at becoming your own chef—it is becoming more difficult to become a head chef unless you demonstrate exceptional talent, an extremely creative mind, and can also inspire financing. There are more than 550 cooking schools in the country, and employers are beginning to impose higher culinary academic standards on their prospective employees. Some employers are even turning to organizations such as the American Culinary Federation, which has certified a mere 70 of these 550 schools, for recommendations. Most training programs are practical; cooking, preparation, working as part of a team, instrument maintenance, and personal hygiene (yes, that is a course) are taught by example and as part of basic cooking principles. Programs last up to four years. Specialization is important in this industry for people looking to work at swankier restaurants, people interested in entree preparation (the most sought-after work), aspiring pastry chefs, and chefs specializing in a geographically distinctive type of cuisine.

ASSOCIATED CAREERS

While most chefs view their profession as a job for life, many become restaurateurs or enter some related food-industry position. A few chefs move into catering.

PAST AND FUTURE

Chefs were once under the sole command of nobility because they were the only people who could afford to pay professionals to prepare their food. The rise of commercial eating establishments in Europe allowed others to benefit from chefs' skills. Restaurants trained young chefs, often under the supervision of head chefs. Head chefs who achieved international fame, such as Auguste Escoffier, began their own cooking schools.

Opportunities for chefs are expected to rise by more than 20 percent over the next ten years, as the restaurant industry is experiencing a period of growth.

QUALITY OF LIFE

2 YEARS Many chefs start out as cooks, assistant chefs, preparatory chefs, and unpaid interns, sacrificing long hours for low wages to gain the practical experience necessary in a number of fields before they can assume positions of responsibility in a professional kitchen. Some people gain these positions while finishing up their second, third, or fourth years at culinary academies. Those chefs who are successful cite being able to listen carefully, work hard, and seize any opportunity to demonstrate skills as factors in their advancement.

5 YEARS Five years into the profession, many chefs have moved from cook to assistant chef, or from assistant chef to chef with a special area of responsibility, such as vegetable chef or saucier. Years four to nine are the most active portion of prospective chefs' careers, both in terms of the amount of work and that of job movement. Many chefs manage staffs of assistant chefs and preparatory chefs. Salaries, responsibilities, and hours all increase. Many people find their fates tied to those at the head of the kitchen; if the head chef is fired from his job, entire staffs may go too.

10 YEARS Professionals who have attained the position of chef have had experience in a number of different areas and have held a variety of positions managing and overseeing sub-chefs and prep workers at the ten-year point. Many chefs have found positions that offer them significant satisfaction, although the majority attempt to open their own establishments during years ten through fifteen. A chef must have a unique and clearly explainable vision of what his or her restaurant should be to work well with a financial restaurateur. Networking both with chefs and patrons is at its peak, and a significant number of professionals spend their free time away from their chef duties researching other restaurants' menus, prices, and service. For most, wages rise appreciably.

MAJOR EMPLOYERS

FOUR SEASONS HOTELS AND RESORTS
1165 Leslie Street
Toronto, CN MC3 2K2
Tel: 416-449-1750
Fax: 416-441-4374
www.fshr.com
Contact: Human Resources

LE DOME RESTAURANT
8720 West Sunset Boulevard
West Hollywood, CA 90069
Tel: 310-659-6919

TAVERN ON THE GREEN
Central Park West at 67th Street
New York, NY 10023
Tel: 212-873-3200 x229
Fax: 212-580-4265
www.tavernonthegreen.com

MAJOR ASSOCIATIONS

CHEFS DE CUISINE ASSOCIATION OF AMERICA
155 East 55th Street
New York, NY 10022
Tel: 212-832-4939

NATIONAL RESTAURANT ASSOCIATION EDUCATIONAL FOUNDATION
175 West Jackson Boulevard, Suite 1500
Chicago, IL 60604
Tel: 800-765-2122 or 312-715-5397
Fax: 312-566-9737
www.nraef.org

NATIONAL RESTAURANT ASSOCIATION
1200 17th Street, NW
Washington, DC 20036-3097
Tel: 202-331-5900
Fax: 202-331-2429
www.restaurant.org
jobs@dineout.org

CHEMICAL ENGINEER

A DAY IN THE LIFE

The headline of the brochure for the American Institute of Chemical Engineers states that chemical engineers are responsible for the production of items "from microchips to potato chips." Chemical engineers work in the chemical, fuel, aerospace, environmental, food, and pulp and paper industries, among many others. Responsibilities include research, design, development, production, technical sales, and—for people with good communication skills—management. Chemical engineering is a problem-solving profession with a practical bias; chemical engineers should expect to answer the question of "how" more than any other. Chemical engineers translate the discoveries of chemists and make them into real-world products. If a chemist invents a better fertilizer, for example, a $\{$ *intellectual challenge* $\}$ chemical engineer might design the method to make mass production of that fertilizer possible. Much of this work involves planning, theoretical "modeling" of production processes, and analysis that takes place on computer or in preliminary reports. Chemical engineers work with chemists, accountants, human resources personnel, and regulators to create efficient, safe, and cost-effective methods of reproducing valuable items. Chemical engineers work in teams, mostly for large corporations. Engineers thrive on the intellectual challenge they get from their work. Good chemical engineers are always trying to refine, improve, and make their systems safer and more efficient.

PAYING YOUR DUES

Like all engineers, the would-be chemical engineer must pass a rigorous set of academic requirements. Course work must include a full spectrum of chemistry courses, some physics, electrical engineering, mathematics, computer science, and biology, as well as some applied-materials science courses for people who want to go into manufacturing industries. English courses are extremely helpful, as many chemical engineers must write and review reports. More than 140 colleges and universities offer accredited chemical engineering curricula. Master's and doctoral degrees are preferred for people who hope to achieve any supervisory or directed research positions.

The most difficult aspect of becoming a chemical engineer is applying theoretical knowledge to a practical discipline. Many engineers find it helpful to attend professional seminars and subscribe to publications, such as Chemical Engineering, which explore industry breakthroughs in their area of responsibility. Others enjoy the support of professional organizations, such as the American Institute of Chemical Engineers (AIChE). Employers, for the most part, view chemical engineering as a practical discipline and look for experience in production, manufacturing, or management to verify these traits in potential employees. Also, each state has its own written exam for chemical engineers who wish to work in the public sector.

ASSOCIATED CAREERS

Chemical engineers use their skills to become entrepreneurs and managers in a number of fields, ranging from patent law to microbrewing. A notable few become astronauts. The majority of chemical engineers rotate within the profession rather than leave it.

PAST AND FUTURE

Chemical engineers have been around since the first distilling process took place. Chemical engineering became a science in the Renaissance, with the codification of experiments and results. This organization was coupled with achievements in pure (not applied) chemistry. Chemical engineering began to be taught as a discipline in 1888 at the Massachusetts Institute of Technology.

Forty percent of all chemical engineers are employed by the chemical industry, which followed distantly by environmental organizations, the food industry, biotechnology companies, and electronics. The level of employment is expected to remain static, with the notable exception that many employed in the chemicals industry, which includes the petroleum industry, will migrate to the emerging bio and electronic technology fields. While the number of jobs is expected to remain stable for the next ten years, fewer applicants are expected to vie for these jobs, leading to a potentially bright future for the aspiring chemical engineer.

QUALITY OF LIFE

2 YEARS Chemical engineers work in teams as data collectors and computer modelers. Many of them have limited input and low levels of responsibility during these early years. The hours are unremarkable, but professional associations, professional reading, and additional research may eat up the free time of the ambitious chemical engineer. People who leave get the yearnings to do so in these early years, but few follow through until later. Satisfaction is average.

5 YEARS Five years into the profession, many chemical engineers have specialized in research, design, production, development, or technical sales. The number of responsibilities has increased, and many engineers get their first taste of managerial status. Significant input is expected from the five-year engineer. People skills become more important. Five-year veterans are judged on the success of their track records. People who leave to start their own companies most often do so between years seven and nine.

10 YEARS Ten-year chemical engineers are senior engineers, and many of them have been promoted to levels of personnel and project management. Many engineers are involved in the coordination and development phase of projects (the initial planning stages) and offer experienced direction without having to do any of the more mundane modeling that more junior chemical engineers undertake. Private firm employees earn higher wages than do those in the public sector, but many of the engineers in the public sector choose to work for the EPA or the Department of Agriculture, citing more regular hours and less corporate politics.

MAJOR EMPLOYERS
ADVANCE INTERNATIONAL
1200 Zerega Avenue
Bronx, NY 10462
Tel: 718-892-3460
Fax: 718-409-2385

AIR PRODUCTS AND CHEMICALS
7201 Hamilton Boulevard
Allentown, PA 18195-1501
Tel: 610-481-4911
Fax: 610-481-5900
www.airproducts.com
Contact: University Relations

NORPLEX-MICARTA
665 Lybrand Street
PO Box 977
Postville, IA 52162-8910
Tel: 800-848-4431 or 319-864-7321
Fax: 563-864-4231
www.norplex.com
Contact: Personnel

MAJOR ASSOCIATIONS
AMERICAN CHEMICAL SOCIETY
1115 16th Street, NW
Washington, DC 20036
Tel: 800-227-5558 or 202-872-4600
Fax: 202-872-8258
www.acs.org

CHEMIST

BOOKS, FILMS, AND TV SHOWS
FEATURING THE PROFESSION
- **The Biography of Linus Pauling**
- **Dr. Jekyll and Mr. Hyde**
- **The Elixer**
- **Lorenzo's Oil**

YOU'LL HAVE CONTACT WITH
- **Chemical engineers**
- **Lab technicians**
- **Pharmaceutical executives**
- **Researchers**

PROFESSIONALS READ
- **Chemical & Engineering News**
- **Chemical Engineering Progress**
- **The Chemist**
- **The Journal of the American Chemical Society**
- **Science, Next Wave**
- **Today's Chemist at Work**

A DAY IN THE LIFE

Chemists "are paid to be creative, careful, and productive," said one of our survey respondents, a description with which the rest agreed. "It's a career for people who think about the future," mentioned another. Everything in the world, whether naturally occurring or man-made, is made of chemicals. Professionals in the chemistry industry analyze the most basic components of the environment. In the commercial sector, they find new uses and applications for the materials they study. In the academic sector, they study the implications of newly discovered chemical properties. Chemists spend more than 60 percent of their time in the lab or in front of their computers analyzing data. Most work is done in teams, and more than one respondent pointed out that teamwork skills are "essential" to success in this field. Specific duties may include modeling, analysis, synthesis, research, limited fieldwork, or even sales and information management. There are as many specialties—such as quality-control chemistry or organic chemistry—as there are areas of application of chemical principles. A chemist's specialty depends on his or her style of working; but the desire to search for the ability to manipulate matter and make useful materials is common to all chemists.

> creative, careful, and productive

Chemists work closely with other experts, including chemical engineers, who plan the production and development of discoveries made by chemists; sales forces, who explain their products; and academic chemists, who share cutting edge information. This aspect of the job requires strong interpersonal skills and an ability to keep end goals in mind. "You don't spend a lot of time hanging out with other chemists, but you do spend a lot of time reading about them." Professional reading can be significant, as discoveries can change the understanding of the physical systems that are critical to this profession. Chemists are challenged, excited, and satisfied with the profession in which the majority of them spend their entire careers.

PAYING YOUR DUES

About 600 colleges and universities offer undergraduate degrees in chemistry, and 300 offer graduate degrees. Those in the industry warn, however, that not all colleges have ample facilities for research, so aspiring chemists should research and choose their school wisely. While a bachelor's degree in chemistry is the minimum requirement for entry-level jobs in the field—mostly quality control, assistant, and production chemist positions—many research positions require a PhD. Chemists are increasingly expected to work on interdisciplinary teams, and many employers look for people who have taken a wide variety of courses, including biology, physics, materials science, English, and business. Chemists with strong interpersonal skills—"the ability to play well in the sandbox," as one of our survey respondents put it—are also sought out. Intelligence, historically the single factor in determining job opportunities in the field of chemistry, is no longer the only consideration.

ASSOCIATED CAREERS

Chemists become chemical engineers more often than anything else, but their analytical skills are suitable to many professions. Material scientists, agricultural and food scientists, physicists, and science technicians conduct research similar to the work done by chemists. Any field that rewards a curious, organized mind is open to an emigrant from the field of chemistry.

PAST AND FUTURE

Chemistry has been around as a learned discipline since people started to rely on the medicinal value of herbs and plants. While an understanding of the reasons behind the curative effects of these plants was lacking, the original cause-and-effect study of them established the foundation for modern chemistry. Notable luminaries in the development of chemistry include Mendeleyev and Meyer, who developed the periodic table of elements in the nineteenth century, and Niels Bohr, who correctly postulated the structure of the atom early in the twentieth century.

Today the chemistry industry is looking toward a relatively stable period. While some companies are downsizing, growth in the industry is expected among the pharmaceutical and biotechnology firms, which are augmenting their research teams to meet the demands of an aging population. Environmental research will offer many new opportunities to experienced chemists. A master's degree or PhD will become increasingly important in the field.

QUALITY OF LIFE

2 YEARS Chemists work as general assistants, performing experiments and recording data under the direction of more experienced, more senior chemists. Many chemists are placed in areas that they did not anticipate, such as quality control or information management. These early years are marked by average hours and reasonable levels of satisfaction. Few chemists have any illusions about the mundane duties that will be their responsibilities.

5 YEARS Five-year veterans have chosen an area of specialization that matches their style, and many have been put in charge of research, production, or development teams. Tasks include the assembly and analysis of data based on computer models. Many chemists have managerial duties as well as hands-on tasks to complete. People who wish to rise above this project managing level should note that personnel management skills are important beyond this point.

10 YEARS Ten-year chemists have had their responsibilities extend more in terms of direction, budgeting, and planning than actual research and development. Many chemists use management skills more than research abilities. Significant connections help those chemists who start their own research companies. The hours increase; the salaries grow; and satisfaction remains level. Many chemists find it helpful to join a professional organization such as the American Chemical Society (ACS).

MAJOR EMPLOYERS

DUPONT
Corporate Information Center
Chestnut Run Plaza
705/GS38
Wilmington, DE 19880-0705
Tel: 302-774-1000
E-mail: info@dupont.com
www.dupont.com

ELI LILLY AND COMPANY
Lilly Corporate Center
Indianapolis, IN 46285
Tel: 317-276-2000
www.lilly.com

MAJOR ASSOCIATIONS

AMERICAN CHEMICAL SOCIETY
1115 16th Street, NW
Washington, DC 20036
Tel: 800-227-5558 or 202-872-4600
Fax: 202-872-8068
www.acs.org

AMERICAN CHEMISTRY COUNCIL
1300 Wilson Boulevard
Arlington, VA 22209
Tel: 703-741-5000
Fax: 703-741-6000

CIVIL ENGINEER

SALARY   ● ● ●

HOURS   ● ● ○

EDUCATION   ● ● ○

BOOKS, FILMS, AND TV SHOWS
FEATURING THE PROFESSION
- **Bridge over the River Kwai**
- **The Brooklyn Bridge**
- **The Dresden Project**
- **Making Manhattan**
- **Modern Marvels**

YOU'LL HAVE CONTACT WITH
- **Architects**
- **Construction managers**
- **Structural engineers**
- **Urban planners**

PROFESSIONALS READ
- **Journal of Materials Engineering**
- **Structural Engineering**

A DAY IN THE LIFE

"If you're the type of kid who built whole cities out of blocks in his bedroom, look into civil engineering," advised one respondent. Civil engineers build real cities, from roads and bridges to tunnels, public buildings, and sewer systems. Projects have three phases: precon-struction planning, implementation, and infrastructure maintenance. The preconstruction phase involves surveying land, reviewing plans, assessing funding and needs, and then making decisions about schedule, materials, and staffing. Most work is done indoors during this phase. Implementation is the stage during which construction begins, and many civil engineers spend considerable amounts of time on-site reviewing progress and coordinating all construction. One engineer noted, "Sometimes you live out there for two or three days at a time." Problems must be

$\{$ ingenuity $\}$

solved on the spot, and civil engineers are the only ones with the knowledge and responsibil-ity to do so. Infrastructure maintenance, which includes stress tests, evaluations, and ongoing support, takes place after construction is finished. Civil engineers move back to their offices to wrap up paperwork and make final adjustments to the project. Then it is time to start the entire process again.

Civil engineers work hard. The hours can be long; government funding cuts can destroy a project; deadlines are firm; and weather can throw projects off schedule. If the timetable degenerates, an engineer has to overcome scheduling obstacles with ingenuity. Nearly all of our survey respondents mentioned creativity as the first or second most important trait a civil engineer should have. About half of all civil engineers are employed by federal, state, or local governments. This group must be prepared to face bureaucratic delays, political stalls, and mounds of paperwork. Though civil engineers don't know where or when their next project will be, this doesn't seem to faze them. "Projects can last up to ten years, so it's not exactly like you're moving every week," said one engineer. Satisfaction is strong; most engineers would-n't trade their occupation for any other.

PAYING YOUR DUES

Civil engineers must have an engineering degree from a school accredited by the Accreditation Board for Engineering and Technology and three to four years of work experi-ence. They also must pass a state-sponsored professional engineer examination. Many civil engineers find it helpful to join a professional association, such as the American Society of Civil Engineers (ASCE).

ASSOCIATED CAREERS

Civil engineers are planners by nature, and many of them may pursue managerial jobs that allow them to use this skill. They are particularly good at estimating labor and materials needs, and many engineers become professional staffers and materials buyers. Some become materials researchers, while others become inspectors, checking the work of other civil engi-neers and receiving more regular hours for less pay.

PAST AND FUTURE

Civil engineers built pyramids in Egypt at the time of the pharaohs; civil engineers in ancient Greece and Rome built temples, aqueducts, and great public buildings; civil engineers in China built the Forbidden City. Cities could not have been built without civil engineers; they designed every major infrastructure system in the United States today.

Civil engineering work over the next decade is likely to lie in rebuilding, as opposed to constructing, America's crumbling infrastructure. Most of this rebuilding will take place in urban areas in which budgets are tight, and only projects that are in a state of crisis will be funded. Civil engineers will also be building water treatment plants and hazardous-waste processing sites. Demand for civil engineers is expected to remain strong, but applicants should be willing to relocate to areas of need to pursue these opportunities.

QUALITY OF LIFE

2 YEARS Two years into the profession, civil engineers are still cutting their teeth and earning the work experience that will allow them to take the state-sponsored engineering exam. Many engineers do routine construction or administrative assistant work. Many professionals are "junior" engineers directed by more experienced, licensed professionals. The hours are long, but satisfaction is high.

5 YEARS People who have remained five years in the field have achieved "assistant"—or "grade one"—level civil engineering status. Many engineers put in their hardest work in years three through eight in trying to distinguish themselves from other applicants. Fifteen-hour days are not unusual for those working on-site. Valuable experience is gained. Many of them must relocate to find positions of responsibility. Satisfaction remains high; the hours increase.

10 YEARS Civil engineers who've lasted ten years are in supervisory or management roles. Many of them are heavily involved in the preconstruction stages of development and spend less time at the site during the construction phase than they did in earlier years. Some engineers become research engineers and use their practical experience to explore new materials, methods, and ways of building infrastructures. Satisfaction remains high; the hours decrease; the salary rises.

MAJOR EMPLOYERS

TENNESSEE VALLEY AUTHORITY
400 West Summit Hill Drive
Mailstop WTCP
Knoxville, TN 37902-1499
Tel: 865-632-2101
www.tva.gov

UNITED STATES ARMY CORPS OF ENGINEERS
441 G Street, NW
Washington, DC 20314
www.usace.army.mil

MAJOR ASSOCIATIONS

AMERICAN SOCIETY OF CIVIL ENGINEERS
1801 Alexander Bell Drive
Reston, VA 20191-4400
Tel: 800-548-2723
www.asce.org

INSTITUTE OF TRANSPORTATION ENGINEERS
1099 14th Street, NW, Suite 300 West
Washington, DC 20005
Tel: 202-289-0222
Fax: 202-289-7722
www.ite.org

COAST GUARD—ENLISTEE, OFFICER

PROFESSIONAL PROFILE

# of people in profession	38,000
Avg. hours per week	40
Avg. starting salary	$13,800 (enlistee)
	$26,196 (officer)
Avg. salary after 5 years	$47,000
Avg. salary after 10 to 15 years	$60,000

SALARY ● ● ●
HOURS ● ● ●
EDUCATION ● ● ●

BOOKS, FILMS, AND TV SHOWS
FEATURING THE PROFESSION
- **Bad Boys II**
- **Captain Ron**
- **Clear and Present Danger**
- **Double Jeopardy**
- **The Hunt for Red October**
- **Lethal Weapon 4**
- **The Perfect Storm**
- **White Squall**

YOU'LL HAVE CONTACT WITH
- **Electricians**
- **Engineers**
- **FBI agents**
- **Law enforcement officials**
- **Physicians**
- **Scientists**
- **Shipping agents**

PROFESSIONALS READ
- **The Defense Monitor**
- **Global Defense Review**
- **Military Review**
- **National Defense**
- **Newsweek**
- **Popular Mechanics**
- **Time**
- **U.N. & Conflict Monitor**

A DAY IN THE LIFE

The United States Coast Guard is one of the nation's five Armed Services. (The other four are the Army, Marine Corps, Navy, and Air Force.) Currently under the jurisdiction of the U.S. Department of Homeland Security, the Coast Guard has become increasingly important as a counter-terrorism agency in the post-September 11 world. As a military personnel member of the Coast Guard, you may be involved in search and rescue, maritime law enforcement, navigation aid, icebreaking, environmental protection, port security, and military readiness operations. Because of the variety of responsibilities you will have, it might be best to think of the Coast Guard as a law-enforcement, environmental, and military agency. One member summed up the job as follows: "[The Coast Guard] prevents spills, clears waterways, and keeps narcotics off our shores."

{ search and rescue }

The Coast Guard has at its disposal 38,000 active-duty men and women, 8,000 Reservists, and 35,000 Auxiliarists. When considering a position with the Coast Guard, you will have to decide between entering as an enlisted member or as an officer. Each career path has different requirements and offers a unique set of advancement options. In general, enlisted members work in—but are not limited to—office, transportation, mechanical, human service, and seaman positions. In the entire military, enlistees comprise about 85 percent of personnel; officers make up about 15 percent of service personnel and count among their ranks doctors, nurses, lawyers, engineers, pilots, and others.

As government employees, members of the Coast Guard are entitled to a number of benefits. These include the following: opportunities for advancement, 30 days of paid vacation per year, free medical and dental care while on active duty, life insurance, and the benefits of the Montgomery GI Bill, which helps pay for college or vocational training. Additionally, the Coast Guard is the only branch of military service in which all specialties are open to women (this includes combat roles). There are, however, also limitations placed on individuals interested in a career with the Coast Guard. To be eligible for an officer position, for example, you must be a U.S. citizen or national; if you wish to enlist, you must be either a citizen or resident alien. Anyone interested in serving with the U.S. military must pass the Armed Services Vocational Aptitude Battery (ASVAB) test as well as a military entrance medical exam. The Coast Guard also requires that any non-U.S. citizen be able to speak, write, and read English fluently.

PAYING YOUR DUES

As is also the case for the other armed service branches, the Coast Guard requires an intensive training session called boot camp. The boot camp training for all potential Coast Guard personnel takes place in Cape May, New Jersey. The eight-week training includes exercises that are both physically and mentally grueling, among which are swim tests, fitness tests, and several academic tests. Individuals wishing to become Officers have several options: they may attend (and graduate from) the Coast Guard Academy; complete Officer Candidate School (OCS); or participate in one of several Direct Commissioning Programs, which are special four-week programs available only to lawyers, engineers, maritime graduates, and environmental managers.

The Coast Guard places minimal obstacles in the way of potential recruits. The egalitarian advancement process is truly merit-based. Although it may take a lot of blood, sweat, and tears to persevere through boot camp, the good news is that if you can prove yourself and perform well at your job, you will be given many fair opportunities for advancement.

ASSOCIATED CAREERS

The skills required to excel in the Coast Guard are considered characteristic of those needed for any career in the U.S. military. Teamwork, dependability, and determination are all qualities upon which the U.S. government armed forces leadership looks favorably. And with more than 4,100 military jobs available, you will almost certainly be able to find the opportunities you're seeking.

Coast Guardians often cooperate with law enforcement agencies like the Federal Bureau of Investigation and the DEA (Drug Enforcement Agency) and work in conjunction with other branches of the armed forces, particularly the Navy. Coast Guardians also interact with civilian and commercial boating interest groups, local and federal law enforcement officials, engineers, electricians, medical personnel, and administrators.

PAST AND FUTURE

The origins of the United States Coast Guard can be traced back to 1790, the year in which Congress first authorized the construction of ten ships for the purpose of protecting tariff and trade laws and preventing smuggling. The service came to be known by its present name in 1915, when an act of Congress merged the Revenue Cutter Service with the Life-Saving Service. Since then, the Coast Guard has been responsible for saving lives at sea and enforcing the United State's maritime laws.

Opportunities for qualified individuals will be promising at least through the year 2012, if not beyond. The U.S. government currently relies heavily on military personnel, including members of the Coast Guard. One continuing trend in military recruitment is increasingly higher educational requirements, brought about by the growing complexity of military jobs.

QUALITY OF LIFE

2 YEARS After enlistees have finished boot camp, they are assigned to a base (either domestic or overseas), or to a ship of some kind. On average, an enlistee will spend between one and four years at a given station. After completing their initial training, two-year coast guard officers are commissioned as ensigns with an initial three-year active-duty obligation.

5 YEARS A career as an enlistee requires moving around as the Coast Guard deems necessary. Standard tours of duty can be supplemented with college or vocational training, depending on eligibility. The Coast Guard decides after the third year whether or not to allow officers to extend active duty, if they so desire.

10 YEARS After ten years in the Coast Guard, enlistees have had the opportunity to gain valuable on-the-job experience and possibly some education, as well. They are probably earning relatively high salaries, and with any luck, working in the duty station of their choice. By now, officers will probably have been promoted several times and may be eligible for as high as a position as lieutenant commander. In general, if one is continually passed up for promotion, that person should leave the military.

MAJOR EMPLOYERS

COAST GUARD RECRUITING
4200 Wilson Boulevard, Suite 450
Arlington, VA 22203
Tel: 877-NOW-USCG
www.uscg.mil

MAJOR ASSOCIATIONS

ASSOCIATION OF NAVAL SERVICES OFFICERS
www.ansomil.org

COAST GUARD WOMEN'S LEADERSHIP ASSOCIATION
PO Box 3440
235 Glebe Road
Arlington, VA 22203
Tel: 202-493-1280
Fax: 202-493-1269
E-mail: info@ballston.uscg.mil
www.cgwla.org

COMPUTER ENGINEER

BOOKS, FILMS, AND TV SHOWS FEATURING THE PROFESSION
- Disclosure
- Galatea 2.2
- The Net
- War Games

YOU'LL HAVE CONTACT WITH
- Computer programmers
- Information managers
- Office managers
- Telecommunication specialists

PROFESSIONALS READ
- LAN Times
- Novell Networker
- PC World
- Windows Sources

A DAY IN THE LIFE

"Expect the unexpected," one computer engineer wrote about her profession, and this statement was reflected on all the surveys we received. Computer engineers coordinate the construction, maintenance, and future growth of company computer systems. They work with all departments, deciphering each one's computer needs, and then make suggestions about the technical direction in which the company should proceed. While this occupation sounds organized and logical, most computer engineers enter the profession at companies that have already made uncertain steps into the technical world. Faced with uncertain budget restrictions, presented with old or misapplied systems, and expected to know the nuances of each department's needs, systems analysts must rapidly

{ expect the unexpected }

become experts in the company's and each department's functions and learn how to use second-best systems to satisfy rather specific needs. "Getting people to tell you up front all the things they want to do is like pulling teeth," one engineer wrote. Flexibility, strong interpersonal skills, and a friendly disposition are highly valued traits in this industry.

The bottom line is performance, and engineers without strong technical skills find themselves quickly outpaced by the expertise their job demands. More than 30 percent of systems analysts had not intended to become full-time systems analysts. In most smaller companies, the position develops as an ancillary responsibility for the most technically savvy of the current employees. As the company realizes the benefits of a full-time computer representative, the position becomes permanent and exclusive. "I was hired as a researcher," one analyst noted, "and now all I use is my screwdriver." Many engineers who have fallen into the profession point to continuing education as an attractive part of the job. Others find themselves hamstrung by the decisions of their predecessors and the technical limitations of the systems they inherit.

The high level of satisfaction these high-tech tinkerers feel might be related to the creative-thinking and problem-solving aspects of their job. "It's like having the most expensive Tinkertoy set in the world—I love it!" one systems analyst exclaimed. Few occupations allow the physical construction of an object and the intellectual challenge offered by computer engineering. For those people who can make the most of limited resources and listen carefully for the distinction between what people want and what people need from their computer systems, computer engineering is an excellent profession.

PAYING YOUR DUES

Computer engineers come from virtually all walks of life and professional fields: accountants, researchers, inventory-managers, programmers, and others who found the technology with which they worked fascinating, who assumed responsibility for those systems and who continued their education in the field. All computer engineers must be good with details and know how to approach structural problems logically. But practical experience is the most important credential. Nearly all the surveys returned to us from computer engineers emphasized that experience is significantly more important than education in this field. "I don't even look at the education portion of the resume," one candid senior analyst mentioned. "Just tell me what problems you've encountered and what you've done about them." Technology changes rapidly in this field, so continuous study and learning are part of any professional's life. Certain certifications are gaining credence in the field such as the Certified Systems Professional (CSP) credential and the Certified Quality Analyst (CQA) designation, but for the most part, none are required.

ASSOCIATED CAREERS

For engineers who enjoy their profession and want to pursue it on a more structured and ground-up level, the position of systems architect is responsible for the same structural decision-making and maintenance, but for systems not yet in place. About 60 percent of computer engineers leave after ten years to pursue other opportunities. Ten percent of those who leave follow their more technical leanings by becoming computer repair personnel. Another 35 percent become programmers, librarians, information managers, or online service producers or specialists, and around 15 percent enter the world of Local Area Network (LAN) companies.

PAST AND FUTURE

Computer engineers have been around since the early 1970s, when computers became more widespread in the business sector. Many companies purchased computers individually without considering how they could use them to work together. Out of incompatibility rose LAN systems, which promised to link individual users in each office to a central software, database, and routing computer.

The profession of computer engineering is likely to continue growing very quickly and attain a significant position within many large and small corporations. It is fast becoming a unique and distinct occupation that people study in school and pursue as a career. Certain firms have emerged that act solely as systems analysts or "hired guns" that handle all computer issues at a company. Computer consulting businesses are expected to grow much faster than other types of consulting firms.

QUALITY OF LIFE

2 YEARS These first years are marked by a hectic pace, limited input, and a high degree of personal accountability. Computer engineers find these first years frustrating, as many have inherited awkwardly created systems and are asked to make them run smoothly. The pay is slightly above average; the hours can be long.

5 YEARS Five-year engineers maintain and upgrade existing information systems and have significant input on future purchases and system architecture. Responsibilities and salaries increase. Professional connections become more important, as more than 20 percent of five-year engineers change jobs. Satisfaction is high; the hours are long. Many engineers who have been taking professional courses officially enroll in degree programs.

10 YEARS Many ten-year computer engineers open their own consulting firms, which examine and analyze systems and then propose methods of information flow. Veteran engineers are very valuable assets to any company, and their salaries reflect this. The hours remain more static, and many engineers are put in charge of managing two or three other engineers instead of doing installations and maintenance themselves. People who remain at the ten-year mark are likely to be computer engineers for life.

MAJOR EMPLOYERS
ADVANCED MICRO DEVICES, INC.
One AMD Place
PO Box 3453
Sunnyvale, CA 94088-3453
Tel: 408-749-4000 or 800-538-9450
Fax: 408-774-7023
www.amd.com
E-mail: jobs@amd.com

INTEL CORPORATION
705-2 East Bidwell Street, Suite 246
Folsom, CA 95630
Tel: 916-356-8080
Fax: 916-356-5427
E-mail: jobs2@intel.com
www.intel.com
Contact: Human Resources

MICROSOFT CORPORATION
One Microsoft Way
Redmond, WA 98052-6399
www.microsoft.com/careers
Telecordia Technologies
6 Corporate Place
Piscataway, NJ 08854-4157
Tel: 732-699-2000
Fax: 732-336-2945
www.bellcore.com

MAJOR ASSOCIATIONS
IEEE COMPUTER SOCIETY
1730 Massachusetts Avenue, NW
Washington, DC 20036-1992
Tel: 202-371-0101
Fax: 202-728-9614
www.computer.org

COMPUTER PROGRAMMER

A DAY IN THE LIFE

Programmers write the code that tells computers what to do. System code tells a computer how to interact with its hardware; applications code tells a computer how to accomplish a specific task, such as word processing or spreadsheet calculating. Systems programmers must be familiar with hardware specifications, design, memory management, and structure; while applications programmers must know standard user interface protocols, data structure, program architecture, and response speed. Most programmers specialize in one of these two areas.

At the start of projects, applications programmers meet with the designers, artists, and financiers to determine the expected scope and capabilities of the intend- { technically fluent }

ed final product. Next, they map out a strategy for the program, finding the most potentially difficult features and working out ways to avoid troublesome patches. Programmers present different methods to the producer of the project, who then chooses one direction. Then the programmer writes the code. The final stages of the project are marked by intense, isolated coding, extensive error-checking, and testing for quality control. The programmer is expected to address all issues that arise during this testing. Systems programmers may be hired on a Monday, handed the technical specifications to a piece of hardware, then told to write an interface, or a patch, or some small, discrete project that takes only a few hours. Then on Tuesday, they might be moved to a different project, working on code inherited from previous projects. Systems programmers must prove themselves as technically fluent: "If you can't code, get off the keyboard and make room for someone who can," one programmer wrote. Both arenas accommodate a wide range of work styles, but communication skills, technical expertise, and the ability to work with others are important in general.

Programmers work together respectfully, but there are no significant professional organizations that transform this group of people into a community. The best features of this profession are the creative outlet it provides for curious and technical minds, the pay, which can skyrocket if a product you coded is a major success, and the continuing education. A few programmers we surveyed indicated that an aesthetic sensibility emerges at the highest levels of the profession, saying that "reading good code is like reading a well-written book. You're left with wonder and admiration for the person who wrote it."

PAYING YOUR DUES

Academic qualifications are important for entry-level positions in the field of programming. Course work should include basic and advanced programming, some technical computer science courses, and some logic or systems architecture classes. The complexity of what first-time programmers are asked to code is growing, as is the variety of applications used. Long hours and a variety of programming languages—PERL, FORTRAN, COBOL, C, C++—can make the initial programmer's life a whirlwind of numbers, terms, and variables. Programmers who are not comfortable working in many modes at once may find it difficult to complete tasks. The programmer must remain detail-oriented amidst this maelstrom of acronyms. For mobility within the field, programmers should concentrate on developing a portfolio of working programs that show competence, style, and ability.

ASSOCIATED CAREERS

A number of programmers take on additional duties to become systems architects, software producers, or technical writers. Others apply their programming expertise to a related profession, such as graphic design or animation. People who go into government work can become computer security consultants, encryption specialists, or federal agents specializing in computer science. A few of them who enter the business world become Management Information Systems Specialists (MISSs) who analyze, improve, and maintain corporate information systems for (usually) large, multinational corporations.

PAST AND FUTURE

In the 1960s, all software was originally known as "freeware" and was distributed among the few technically-savvy people who built their own computers. During this period, one young Harvard student sent a letter to his fellow programmers saying that he thought freeware was a destructive concept and people should trademark and copyright all their programs in order to receive the value of what these programs would eventually be worth. Most scoffed at this impudent young man for his arrogant vision of the future of the personal computer and his denial of the 1960s sentiment of sharing and community. Young Bill Gates decided to stick to his opinions, and after his earning so many billions of dollars, it is hard to argue with his success.

Programming right now is understaffed and the field will continue to grow at a fast pace for the next five years. Many industries are realizing the benefit of having tailored and modular code written to address their specific needs. Staffing levels at many major programming corporations are expected to increase, and individual freelancers or "hackers for hire" are expected to become valuable outsourcing resources for these companies.

QUALITY OF LIFE

2 YEARS Two-year professionals work under the supervision of established programmers, handling sections of code or modular pieces of programs. Little responsibility is offered to new hires in terms of defining program architecture and creating new methods of handling data or graphics. They are, however, given reasonable autonomy on their own sections of code. Satisfaction is high. The pay is slightly above average. Many programmers work for one to two years at a given firm, then move to another with greater challenges and salaries.

5 YEARS Salaries rise, and the hours increase significantly. Duties include defining programming architecture, coding, and debugging more junior programmers' codes. Many programmers have contact with executives and clients. People who progress tend to possess strong communication skills and understand what the client wants and needs. Travel may be a feature of the five-year programmer's life, as he or she may need to go on-site to address client needs. Some programmers begin their own businesses.

10 YEARS Ten-year professionals have either begun their own businesses as independent programmers or consolidated their positions as experienced programmers at large concerns. The hours may increase, but the position becomes one more of defining program architecture, working with staffs of programmers, and managing a variety of projects. Few ten-year professionals do basic coding; a number of people who love it do some but delegate the detail work to less-experienced junior programmers. Satisfaction is high; the salaries can become significant.

MAJOR EMPLOYERS

ADVANCED MICRO DEVICES
One AMD Place
PO Box 3453
Sunnyvale, CA 94088-3453
Tel: 800-538-9450
Fax: 408-774-7023
E-mail: jobs@amd.com
www.amd.com

TELECORDIA TECHNOLOGIES
6 Corporate Place
Piscataway, NJ 08854-4157
Tel: 732-699-2000
Fax: 732-336-2945
www.bellcore.com

INTEL CORPORATION
705-2 East Bidwell Street, Suite 246
Folsom, CA 95630
Tel: 916-356-8080
Fax: 916-356-5427
E-mail: jobs2@intel.com
www.intel.com
Contact: Human Resources

MICROSOFT CORPORATION
One Microsoft Way
Redmond, WA 98052-6399
www.microsoft.com/careers
Telecordia Technologies
6 Corporate Place
Piscataway, NJ 08854-4157
Tel: 732-699-2000
Fax: 732-336-2945
www.bellcore.com

MAJOR ASSOCIATIONS

AMERICAN ELECTRONICS ASSOCIATION
5210 Great American Parkway, Suite 520
Santa Clara, CA 95054
Tel: 800-284-4232 or 408-987-4200
Fax: 408-970-8565
www.aeanet.org

CONSTRUCTION MANAGER/CONSTRUCTOR

A DAY IN THE LIFE

Being a construction manager or constructor demands organization, attention to detail, an ability to see the "big picture," and an understanding of all facets of the construction process. This last is acquired through years of schooling and experience. Both construction managers and constructors are expected to regulate the time, cost, and quality of the projects they oversee. On construction projects too large for one person to manage—housing projects and skyscrapers, for example—a construction manager or constructor may oversee one or two aspects of the project, such as site preparation, sewage systems, landscaping and road construction, building construction, and building systems (which includes electricity, plumbing, air-conditioning, and heating).

{ wide range of responsibilities }

Though similar in many ways—enough so to be described in the same profile—there are key differences between construction managers and constructors. Construction managers represent the owner or developer during the course of a project, and use their design, construction, engineering, and management expertise to make sure the project is completed successfully. They schedule and coordinate work done by everyone from architects to construction supervisors; hire contractors to complete specialized aspects of the project; and try to make optimum use of available funds and resources. Constructors are responsible for more day-to-day administrative duties, though they also organize the people, materials, and equipment necessary to get a construction project done. The safety of their crew and of the general public is also their responsibility.

The wide range of responsibilities that construction managers and constructors face makes it necessary for those in these positions to know the construction process inside and out. A construction manager or constructor may have to convince a client that a last-minute change suggested by the architect will bring about innumerable delays or cost increases. "You can always do your job better, if you can make other people do their jobs better," one manager said.

Today, cell phones and laptops allow professionals in the field to spend the majority of their day at the job site. When they're not on duty, construction managers and constructors are on call 24 hours a day to deal with any emergencies that arise at the project site. The high level of stress notwithstanding, the sense of satisfaction among people in the industry is high.

PAYING YOUR DUES

The construction management industry requires a solid background in building science, business, and management. A bachelor's degree in construction science, construction management, building construction, or civil engineering, along with construction industry work experience, will give you a good start in the field. People looking to break into the field soak up any and all information about contracts and building plans; and they familiarize themselves with construction methods, materials, and regulations. They also start to learn computer programs for online communications, job costing, and estimating.

Though entry-level positions in construction management usually only require a bachelor's degree, advancement is difficult without further education. Graduate degrees in business, law, construction, engineering, or architecture are common among construction managers; while most constructors hold an advanced degree in construction. Continued work experience is vital to finding a job as either.

Prospective employers seeking to ensure that the construction manager or constructor they hire has a specific canon of knowledge employ those with the certified construction manager (CMC), associate constructor (AC), or certified professional constructor (CPC) designation. The CMC designation may be obtained through a voluntary certification program offered by the Construction Management Association of America, and the AC and CPC designations may be obtained through a similar program offered by the American Institute of Constructors.

ASSOCIATED CAREERS

It is not unusual for veteran construction managers or constructors to become independent consultants in the field. Some highly experienced individuals move on to serve as arbitrators in disputes, and others serve as expert witnesses in court cases involving construction projects. Many professionals in the field become architects, civil engineers, cost estimators, or engineers, depending on their schooling.

PAST AND FUTURE

Construction managers and constructors have been part of all large-scale building projects throughout history (sometimes under various and differing titles). Current professionals in the field require a savvy set of skills.

Because construction in any region of the country is tied to local economies and residential preferences, construction markets are difficult to predict on a basis of more than eighteen months (the length of time in which people apply for financing to start new projects). The role of the construction manager and constructor is secure. No technical innovations, labor restructuring, or consumer advocacy can replace the need for a person who can coordinate all the elements of raising a building.

QUALITY OF LIFE

2 YEARS The aspiring construction manager or constructor works on-site as an assistant to an established professional. They apply what they learned in the classroom to real-world situations. The responsibilities are few; the hours are long.

5 YEARS "Busy" is an understatement for construction managers and constructors at this stage. Professionals begin to supervise all stages of the construction process. The stress is significant; more than 60 percent of respondents cited it as a major element of their job. Client communication skills are learned most fully in years four through eight, and professionals can find themselves spending what they believe to be too much time in meetings and too little time supervising on-site.

10 YEARS Ten-year veterans have established reputations. They spend long hours at the construction site but are able to delegate so their professional life is less hectic. Client contact is critical at this stage. Many people find work through connections and word of mouth. Ten-year construction managers and constructors less frequently manage people on a daily basis; but they oversee all work and sign off on it before crews are relocated. Within large firms, professionals may become top-level executives. People with the necessary funds may establish their own construction management or contracting firms. Satisfaction is high at this stage, but so is stress; the incidence of heart attacks among contractors rises by 50 percent after ten years in the profession.

MAJOR EMPLOYERS
STETON CONSTRUCTION GROUP
451 West Lambert Road, Suite 210
Brea, CA 92821-3920
Tel: 714-255-7080
Fax: 714-255-7086
E-mail: info@stetoncg.com
www.stetoncg.com

MONADNOCK CONSTRUCTION, INC.
155 3rd Street
Brooklyn, NY 11231
Tel: 718-875-8160
Fax: 718-802-1109
www.moncon.com

JANSSEN BUILDERS, INC.
7855 Enterprise Drive
Newark, CA 94560
Tel: 408-499-7383
Fax: 408-297-7383
E-mail: inquiries@jbuilders.com
www.jbuilders.com

MAJOR ASSOCIATIONS
AMERICAN INSTITUTE OF CONSTRUCTORS
PO Box 26334
Alexandria, VA 22314
Tel: 703-683-4999
Fax: 703-683-5480
E-mail: admin@aicnet.org
www.aicnet.org

CONSTRUCTION MANAGEMENT ASSOCIATION OF AMERICA
7918 Jones Branch Drive, Suite 540
McLean, VA 22102
Tel: 703-356-2622
Fax: 703-356-6388
www.cmaanet.org

CORRECTIONS OFFICER

A DAY IN THE LIFE

Corrections officers serve as a combination of police officers, social workers, counselors, security specialists, managers, and teachers. A corrections officer oversees individuals who have been arrested, are awaiting trial, or who have been convicted and sentenced to jail. While many think that all corrections officers do is observe inmate behavior to prevent fights or escapes, their responsibilities reach far beyond this. A corrections officer in a small county jail or precinct station house may also serve as deputy sheriff or police officer; whereas an officer in a large state and federal prison will have highly specialized duties, such as overseeing prisoner transfers. Working conditions vary immensely, as do the hours. Corrections officers tend to work a five-day week in eight-hour shifts, but because prison security must be provided around the clock, shifts aren't always Monday through Friday, 8:00 A.M. to 5:00 P.M. Officers may be expected to work overtime as well as on weekends and holidays.

{ inspect security measures }

Most corrections officers attend to their duties unarmed, while a few officers (mostly those with military backgrounds) hold positions in lookout towers and have high-powered rifles. Duties such as checking cells and other areas for unsanitary conditions, weapons, drugs, fire hazards, and any evidence of infractions of rules are part of a normal day on the job. Officers also check locks, window bars, and gates for any signs of tampering. They also inspect mail for contraband and monitor visitors. Even the most senior officers may perform any and all of these tasks. Officers are responsible for escorting inmates to and from cells and recreation, visiting, and dining areas.

Beyond these duties, corrections officers aid in the rehabilitation of inmates. They arrange daily schedules that include library visits, work assignments, family visits, and counseling appointments. Some institutions give officers specialized training so that they may engage in more formal counseling roles. "The hardest part to this job," one corrections officer says, "is being able to separate yourself from some of the inhumanities that you see inside of the prison. Like for instance . . . there was this young guy of about nineteen that had been raped . . . . The trauma you could see in his face . . . just being able to deal with it . . . [and] separate yourself from it . . . when you go home."

PAYING YOUR DUES

To be a corrections officer most institutions require that you have a high school education or its equivalent, be at least eighteen or twenty-one years of age, be a United States citizen, and have no felony convictions. As the trend moves toward having corrections officers function in a wider range of capacities, many institutions are seeking applicants with postsecondary education in the fields of psychology, criminal justice, police science, and criminology. More than 1,000 schools of higher learning in the United States offer degrees in criminal justice and criminology, and all jail officers are encouraged to pursue a concentration in those areas in the attainment of their bachelor's degrees. A potential corrections officer must also be in excellent health and meet formal standards of physical fitness, eyesight, and hearing. Drug testing and background checks of applicants are the norm.

ASSOCIATED CAREERS

The most obvious alternate law enforcement career choice is the police force, but courtroom bailiffs supervise offenders in a way quite similar to that of corrections officers. Probation and parole officers monitor and counsel offenders following their reintegration into society; this can be equally satisfying and frustrating. Corrections officers also perform investigative work within the prison walls, assisting police in investigation of inmates or dissecting the events of crimes that have occurred within the walls of the institution. For this reason, some corrections officers find careers as in-house or store detectives rewarding. Other popular alternative careers are private security officers and recreational leaders.

PAST AND FUTURE

Corrections officers today have many more responsibilities than they did even 30 years ago, with counseling and mentoring roles becoming more common in institutions. It is sad to say, but this is a growth industry. Prison populations have climbed steadily in the past ten years, and the number of new prisons built to accommodate the burgeoning populations is increasing.

The trend toward "direct supervision" jails, in which officers are in "the pods" with inmates during their entire shifts, has made interpersonal communication skills the number one goal in the training of new officers. It is a fast-growing career, and job opportunities are expected to be plentiful in the next few years to come. Finding qualified applicants is also tough, so the field has highly favorable job prospects.

QUALITY OF LIFE

2 YEARS "I distinctly remember the first day I went into the unit, and they slammed the door behind me. And it was a feeling that just raised all the hairs on your person," a corrections officer from Texas says. Just getting used to one's surroundings can be the hardest part of the first years in this profession. Experienced officers spend a lot of time with new officers, showing them the ropes. All state and local departments provide on-the-job training at the conclusion of formal instruction that can last anywhere from a period of weeks to months in the actual job setting. Training includes instruction in the following areas: institutional policies, regulations, and operations; constitutional law and cultural awareness; crisis intervention; contraband control; custody and security protocol; self-defense and firearms training; fire and safety; and administrative training for dealing with institutional paperwork. There is a lot to learn, and salaries are relatively low at the outset.

5 YEARS Experienced corrections officers have the opportunity to join prison tactical response teams and train to respond to riots, hostage situations, forced cell moves, and other dangerous situations. Tactical and weapons training comes with this terrain. Officers who have both experience and this kind of training can expect to see their salaries increase notably as they become instructors themselves and valuable assets to their (or any other) institution. Officers sometimes transfer to related jobs at this point in their career, such as probation and parole officers.

10 YEARS Education, experience, and training can allow qualified officers to advance to correctional sergeant and other supervisory and administrative positions. Ambitious correctional officers can be promoted to assistant warden, a high-paying job in the field of corrections.

MAJOR EMPLOYERS
Corrections officers are hired by prison systems nationwide.

MAJOR ASSOCIATIONS
AMERICAN CORRECTIONAL ASSOCIATION
4380 Forbes Boulevard
Lanham, MD 20706-4322
Tel: 800-222-5646 or 301-918-1886
www.aca.org

THE AMERICAN JAIL ASSOCIATION
1135 Professional Court
Hagerstown, MD 21740
Tel: 301-790-3930
E-mail: jails@worldnet.att.net
www.corrections.com

CRIMINOLOGIST

PROFESSIONAL PROFILE

# of people in profession	17,420
Avg. hours per week	40
Avg. starting salary	$21,400
Avg. salary after 5 years	$33,200
Avg. salary 10 to 15 years	$47,100

SALARY ● ● ●
HOURS ● ● ●
EDUCATION ● ● ●

BOOKS, FILMS, AND TV SHOWS
FEATURING THE PROFESSION
- **Manhunter**
- **Quincy**
- **Silence of the Lambs**
- **The Usual Suspects**

YOU'LL HAVE CONTACT WITH
- **Attorneys**
- **FBI agents**
- **Pathologists**
- **Police officers**

PROFESSIONALS READ
- **Criminology and Public Policy**
- **Criminology: An Interdisciplinary Journal**
- **The Criminologist**

A DAY IN THE LIFE

"Being a criminologist is exciting," one respondent wrote. "It's interesting," another said. "It's unpredictable," a third ventured. The number of adjectives that describe the world of a criminologist would fill more than a page, but one thing is certain: few occupations require that people be as skilled on both a detail level and a large-picture level as does that of criminologist. A criminologist studies normal social behaviors and how certain factors influence deviation from the norms. Criminologists work with and often for law enforcement offices (both local and federal), analyzing the behavior and methods of criminals for a variety of reasons: to increase the chances of apprehending criminals; predict patterns and motives for behaviors in certain groups; and assess the responsiveness of crime to various methods of law enforcement. These duties border on the territory of the statistician, and many of the same skills are required of the criminologist, but the additional components of psychological insight and analysis of sociological patterns of behavior make this profession unique.

{ unpredictable }

Criminologists' duties can be as distant from police work as reviewing a pattern of behavior among a certain demographic group and writing a profile of the pressures that increase that behavior. They may, alternatively, involve going to crime scenes, attending autopsies, and questioning potential suspects to see if they fit the general psychological profile constructed of the suspect for that crime. One criminologist reported that the work can be "gruesome," but the type of personality that likes the intellectual task of understanding patterns and deviations from patterns is well challenged in this profession; a number of respondents included the word "fascinating" in their description.

Many criminologists cited the intellectual challenge and their fellow law enforcement officers as the two best aspects of their profession. The opportunity for advancement in this career is, however, limited to the sphere of employment; in other words, if you are hired by a state law enforcement agency, you can rise within that agency, but few move from state agencies to federal agencies, or vice versa. Some members of the profession feel that criminologists are removed from the actual process of law enforcement. "Sometimes it feels that I write reports that no one ever reads," one frustrated three-year criminologist mentioned. For the most part, though, enthusiasm for the profession is high, and most criminologists enjoy the hard and varied work this profession brings.

PAYING YOUR DUES

There are comprehensive and rigorous academic requirements to become a criminologist. The job is, after all, academic in nature: much of criminology rests on evaluating and predicting the foundations of behavior based on incomplete information. The overwhelming majority of criminologists are sociology and psychology majors. Course work should include statistics, writing, computer science, and logic. While many enter the profession with only a bachelor's degree, a significant number pursue graduate work in the behavioral sciences, and people who wish to teach are expected to pursue a doctorate in psychology or sociology. Since most criminologists are employed by law enforcement agencies, background and security checks are standard. Employers look for candidates who have demonstrated responsibility, creativity, and logical thinking. Criminologists must know how to design and construct sound research projects. Written examinations are required in a number of states for licensure, so check with your local law enforcement agency for requirements in your state and county.

ASSOCIATED CAREERS

Criminologists work closely with many law enforcement officers, and the few people who leave often pursue a variety of law enforcement careers. Criminologists become police officers, FBI agents, and state medical examiners. A number use their psychological training as springboards to careers as therapists, psychologists, and counselors.

PAST AND FUTURE

Criminology is a relatively modern science and emerged on two levels simultaneously. National interest in the causes and effects of criminal behavior sparked the FBI to commission a number of studies of federal crimes and criminals in the late 1960s and early 1970s. At the same time, economic and political pressure led urban police departments to commission studies on a much smaller level. The successes of these two endeavors in preventing crime became evident immediately.

Criminologists face much of the same demand as sociologists in general. Police departments are less likely to lay off street officers compared to easily replaceable criminologists. Currently, applicants face a competitive market. This bottleneck of qualified candidates for limited positions is expected to continue into the foreseeable future.

QUALITY OF LIFE

2 YEARS "Junior" or "assistant" criminologists are in charge of data collection, report proofing, and computer work. These years are marked by low responsibility, average hours, and average levels of pay. Much of the time is spent learning the specific methods, protocols, and procedures involved in law enforcement.

5 YEARS Five-year veterans may have earned the title "criminologist," depending on the size of the department and the opportunities for advancement. Most criminologists work as part of a team, assembling the data collected by more junior members and providing analysis. Their work is overseen by head or chief criminologists, but responsibilities (compared with the first two years) have skyrocketed. Satisfaction levels have increased but so have hours. Fieldwork is more common than in the early years, and many criminologists are now involved in discussions of policy and procedure, though few have any direct influence. The pay increases. Most people who were going to leave the profession—a mere 15 percent—have already left by this point.

10 YEARS Professionals have, for the most part, become the chief or head of criminology at their agencies. Many criminologists are project developers and manage staffs of junior criminologists, overseeing their research and directing projects through the final report status. This position, while more financially rewarding, removes criminologists from one of the most attractive features of their profession: analysis. Many people merely review what associates have written and offer advice and guidance. Satisfaction levels dip, but as members of law enforcement agencies, many criminologists benefit from liberal retirement policies.

MAJOR EMPLOYERS

ABT ASSOCIATES
55 Wheeler Street
Cambridge, MA 02138-1168
Tel: 617-492-7100
Fax: 617-492-5219
www.abtassoc.com
Contact: Human Resources Department

FEDERAL BUREAU OF INVESTIGATION
J. Edgar Hoover Building
935 Pennsylvania Avenue, NW
Washington, DC 20535-0001
Tel: 202-324-3000
www.fbi.gov

MAJOR ASSOCIATIONS

AMERICAN SOCIETY OF CRIMINOLOGY
1314 Kinnear Road, Suite 214
Columbus, OH 43212-1156
Tel: 614-292-9207
Fax: 614-292-6767
www.asc41.com

AMERICAN SOCIOLOGICAL ASSOCIATION
1307 New York Avenue, NW, Suite 700
Washington, DC 20005
Tel: 202-383-9005
Fax: 202-638-0882
E-mail: eb@asanet.org
www.asanet.org

DETECTIVE/PRIVATE INVESTIGATOR

BOOKS, FILMS, AND TV SHOWS
FEATURING THE PROFESSION
- **Ace Ventura: Pet Detective**
- **The Big Sleep**
- **Law and Order**
- **The Maltese Falcon**
- **The Rockford Files**

YOU'LL HAVE CONTACT WITH
- **Credit agents**
- **Government record clerks**
- **Police officers**
- **Researchers**

PROFESSIONALS READ
- **NCISS Report**
- **P.I. Magazine**
- **World Association of Detectives Newsletter**

A DAY IN THE LIFE

The Raymond Chandler-spawned image of the hard-boiled detective who sips scotch, fights in dark alleys, and is pursued by rich, beautiful women gave way to detectives more like James Garner as Jim Rockford, on the entertainment circuit. On The Rockford Files, a scrappy street-smart ex-con eschewed violence and ducked moral stands in favor of maintaining personal safety. For the first time, detectives were portrayed doing what they really do: "Mostly it's just background checks and finding lost people," one detective from Dallas said. Detectives fulfill client requests for research and surveillance; more than 40 percent of their work has to do with divorces. Most detectives spend a lot of time using computer-searching resources. Familiarity with credit checks and Lexis/Nexis searches is crucial. Detectives frequently search credit reports, birth and death records, marriage licenses, tax filings, news reports, and legal filings. Involvement with legal issues and lawyers is cited as one of the most prominent features of daily life. Usually, only the final stages of searches for lost or missing people involve significant travel.

{ **research and surveillance** }

Detective work for smaller agencies involves a high quotient of solitude and isolation. A solo practitioner must have solid budgeting and client-relations skills, a strong work ethic, and an independent style. Most detectives are paid per project; there are usually limitations on the time that any fee will cover. People who join larger agencies must be skilled at prioritizing, writing reports, using a variety of institutionalized resources, and working with teams of other detectives. Large agencies sometimes have annual contracts with corporations to investigate internal problems and provide security. Maintaining contacts and personal recommendations is critical. Private investigators often work long hours, including nights and weekends. Depending on their current project, they can be on call twenty-four hours a day.

PAYING YOUR DUES

The skills acquired during an academic career aren't the skills that a detective uses, so degrees are relatively unimportant. At larger agencies, a degree in criminal behavior, psychology, or law enforcement may be a plus on a resume, but the primary traits employers look for are experience in related fields and an appropriate temperament. More than 75 percent of all private detectives learn the investigative skills required for the profession and make contacts with other future private detectives in the military, local law enforcement, federal law enforcement, or private security firms. Others attend private detective schools, which teach students how to fingerprint, take samples, write reports, and use firearms. More than 25 percent of all private investigators have experience as bodyguards, and more than 80 percent have licenses for firearms. Few use firearms, however: "If you want to be a gunslinger, rent a movie. Private detectives investigate and report. That's all," one said. Specific computer search skills are usually taught by any hiring firm.

An investigator should be able to work alone, think logically, react quickly to changing circumstances, use sound judgment, and keep a professional distance from his or her work. Maturity is essential. Some states require private detectives to pass certain exams and post a bond to ensure their compliance with state regulations; check with local authorities for the laws in your area.

ASSOCIATED CAREERS

Investigators who leave the profession often return to the law enforcement, security work, or military setting from which they came. The uncertainty of detective work seems the most significant reason for people leaving; a few cite burnout as the hours are long and the pay is uneven. Detectives also often go to law school when they want to switch careers.

PAST AND FUTURE

Most law enforcement between the Revolutionary and Civil Wars was primarily work for hire by bounty hunters and so-called "thief takers." They walked on the border of the law to achieve their goals. The Pinkerton Detective Agency, founded in the 1850s by Allan Pinkerton, was the first private detective firm to promise integrity and trustworthiness for a daily wage (as opposed to bounty-based pay).

Private detective agencies are expected to grow rapidly and increase in size over the next five to ten years. Private detective firms are more in demand than ever. As local governments continue to downsize their police forces, communities, companies, and individuals need to hire private detectives. Economies of scale make it likely that larger, more technologically advanced firms will begin to consolidate many of the smaller firms.

QUALITY OF LIFE

2 YEARS

Private investigators in large firms work with more experienced mentors and learn the methods and protocols that the firm employs. Many detectives spend significant amounts of time doing research based in libraries, court houses, and city halls. They also review reports written by their colleagues. Most detectives work purely behind the scenes. People who wish to advance aggressively pursue additional duties and responsibilities, such as late-night and weekend projects. Small-firm or solo investigators have many of the same problems that small-business owners face: client recruitment, instability of income, and unpredictable staffing needs. Satisfaction is average; the hours can be long.

5 YEARS

Five-year survivors are experienced private investigators. Many investigators have learned valuable computer-searching skills, established contacts in a variety of record-keeping industries (such as credit-reporting companies, city hall, and the police department), and brought a number of cases from inception to completion. Members of large firms have contact with clients. Many of the investigators have supervisory roles. Small-firm practitioners add bodyguard and security duties to their investigative roles in order to attract more clients and to ensure a more steady stream of income. Satisfaction is, again, average; the hours are still long.

10 YEARS

Private investigators who have lasted ten years in the profession have strong reputations and valuable experience. The majority of people who leave the profession do so between years four and eight, dissatisfied with the limited range of their responsibilities. Investigators who are going to launch their own firms have done so by this point, and many of them supervise instead of doing field investigative work. A number of ten-year veterans find this transition jarring, as the skills that make one a good investigator do not necessarily make a good supervisor. Salaries increase, the hours decrease, and satisfaction goes up for those who like the new job role but down for those who dislike it.

MAJOR EMPLOYERS

Most private investigators are employed by small, local firms. Contact agencies in your area for employment opportunities.

MAJOR ASSOCIATIONS

NATIONAL ASSOCIATION OF INVESTIGATIVE SPECIALISTS
PO Box 33244
Austin, TX 78764
Tel: 512-719-3595
Fax: 512-420-3594
E-mail: RThomas007@aol.com
www.pimall.com/nais

WORLD ASSOCIATION OF DETECTIVES
PO Box 333
Brough, England
HU15 1XL
Tel: +44 (0)1482 665577
Fax: +44 (0)870 831 0957
E-mail: info@world-detectives.com
www.wad.net

DEVELOPER

A DAY IN THE LIFE

Developers find undeveloped property, or what they believe to be improperly developed property, and build on it or convert it for optimal use. A typical day moves at a frenzied pace. Successful developers love the pace and feel that without it the job would be "just another paper shuffle." To get a deal together, developers need to quickly coordinate the financial side, the production side, and the end-sales side. Few properties are developed these days without tenants already lined up for post-construction. This reality places an added burden on the developer, who must give the tenants a reliable date on which they can move in.

Developers' responsibilities depend on which of three areas they call their specialty: finance, construction, or recruitment. Developers involved in the finance end are busiest at the initial stages of projects, when they research, explore, and negotiate the terms of new deals. They work with banks, government agencies, and financial consultants, calculating the feasibility of projects, reviewing sites, and planning for contingencies. Deals are very risky—they seem to earn either a continuing 18–22 percent return or a 35–44 percent loss. Financial developers oversee all payments, rates of production, and negotiations with banks during and after the development of a site.

{ Deals are very risky. }

Construction liaisons work with construction managers and local agencies to ensure that the structure meets local building codes, all necessary permits are obtained, and production moves along on schedule. An understanding of basic engineering and construction principles is helpful, as are strong communication skills. Within development, professionals in this area seemed least satisfied with their positions. Eighty percent of respondents cited the role of "policeman" on the job as the least enjoyable, and several of them said they felt isolated. Developers who supervise construction can be caught between financial oversights of the financial developer and the mistrust of the general contractor. This position, nevertheless, records the highest intellectual satisfaction among the three.

A recruiter puts together statistics, models, and plans for the site and then sells rental space to tenants. Recruiters must have strong selling skills, excellent negotiating instincts, and a grasp of construction scheduling. They must be comfortable working with numbers. Construction delays, labor holdups, or permit problems are not considered valid excuses for delays of occupancy, as so many clients insist on penalties for missing the date of completion. Successful recruiters rely to a large extent on their expertise in construction scheduling.

While some thrive on the pace, the pressure gets to others. A staggering 18 percent of developers leave per year within their first five years in the profession. Most aspiring developers have to travel to be able to work on a variety of projects, or they risk facing long periods of time during which their expertise is of little or no use. The ultimate goal for most people in development is working on their own projects. To do this, one must have expertise, access to capital, and a strong stomach for high-risk stakes against unfavorable odds.

PAYING YOUR DUES

The aspiring developer needs an academic background with an emphasis on real estate, finance, managerial skills, psychology, or accounting. Many developers work for a few years and then return to school for an MBA—the degree of choice. Work experience in real estate or finance is important too. Some employers require new employees to have real estate licenses or accounting accreditations prior to starting work. As specialization occurs within the industry, such accreditations as CPA and CFA become significant. Unlike many other fields in which applicants are exposed to the entire process, then slotted to their specific skill set, employees are hired for a specialization within a development company and immersed in the details of the occupation right away. Many developers spend extra hours and free time learning about the other parts of the process.

ASSOCIATED CAREERS

Developers who leave the field often move on to banking, investment banking, construction financing, and real estate sales, all of which are less lucrative professions, but ones that carry less potential downsides and more steady incomes.

PAST AND FUTURE

The United States Pre-Emption Act of 1841 encouraged people to go west and settle on unused government land, then claim it as their own. (This program was so successful that the act was abolished in 1891.) Speculation ran high during these years, and many made fortunes. This speculative instinct continues on an institutional level for the modern developer.

Developers are subject to the caprice of many independent variables, such as interest rates, general economic optimism, urban-rural migration rates, cost of equipment, new construction projects, and local permit restrictions. In general, the market for developers should remain at its current level for the next few years, and a number of developers believe that a balanced budget will improve long-term interest rates and encourage large-scale development projects that will not be sensitive to short-term interest rate fluctuation. Even without a balanced budget, though, the developer's role is secure for the foreseeable future.

QUALITY OF LIFE

2 YEARS Two-year developers are assistants who do anything and everything senior developers need, including preparing reports, researching topics, and coordinating meetings between parties. A number of developers are on-site representatives who monitor construction progress, double-check figures, and keep track of files for prospective clients. Aggressive opportunity seeking and long hours of careful work mark those people who advance beyond this stage. Many developers, dissatisfied with the low levels of responsibility and recognition, leave between years two and three.

5 YEARS Developers of this stage have attained "associate" status and have been given responsibility for more junior members in the profession. Positions are marked by long hours, average pay, and hard work. Client and contractor contact and sales responsibility are significant. Developers dream of working on their own projects, and many spend their free time socializing with financial, construction, and property managing contacts.

10 YEARS Ten-year developers have worked on many projects (perhaps a number of them simultaneously) and have seen the best and worst that the industry has to offer. Many veteran developers consult on running one specific area of development: the construction end, the financing end, or the sales end. The hours increase but financial rewards do as well. Most developers try to attain some percentage of a deal in exchange for a low base pay. Experience is valuable, and most employers recognize this fact.

MAJOR EMPLOYERS
CARRAMERICA
1850 K Street, NW
Washington, DC 20006
Tel: 202-729-7500
Fax: 202-729-1150

TRUMP ORGANIZATION
Trump Tower
725 Fifth Avenue
New York, NY 10022
Tel: 212-715-7200
Fax: 212-935-0141
Contact: Human Resources

MAJOR ASSOCIATIONS
INSTITUTE OF REAL ESTATE MANAGEMENT
430 North Michigan Avenue
Chicago, IL 60611-4090
Tel: 800-837-0706
Fax: 800-338-4736
www.irem.org

ECOLOGIST

SALARY   ● ● ●

HOURS   ● ● ●

EDUCATION   ● ● ●

BOOKS, FILMS, AND TV SHOWS
FEATURING THE PROFESSION
- **Arctic Wolves**
- **Ecoconservatism**
- **Losing Ground**

YOU'LL HAVE CONTACT WITH
- **Biologists**
- **Environmentalists**
- **Researchers**
- **Waste managers**

PROFESSIONALS READ
- **Ecoverse**
- **Nature**
- **Natural History**

A DAY IN THE LIFE

Ecologists examine the relationship between the environment and actions and events that affect it, including rainfall, pollution, temperature shifts, and industrialization. People envision ecologists as being bearded, outdoorsy mountaineers standing on piles of litter. This is only true for about one out of every 100 ecologists. "We're not all Grizzly Adams!" wrote one ecological scientist, and she is right; the most accurate picture of an ecologist would be of one in a lab coat or one reading volumes of collected data. Some ecologists work for not-for-profit environmental groups; others work for large corporations or for the government. Ecologists work with scientific and mathematical models to analyze and interpret correlations between actions and effects on the environment.  { keen analytic mind } These responsibilities entail spending a significant amount of time examining data. "You've got to be able to find the assumptions [that] underlie every study, or you're history," one ecologist cautioned. More than 40 percent of those ecologists we surveyed used the phrase "keen analytic mind" to describe a trait of the most successful members of their profession. Some fieldwork is required—at most, three to six months per year but more often two to four weeks per year.

Individuals who enter the profession with strong academic training have no difficulty finding a job; more than 80 percent of environmental science majors who enter the field stay ecologists for at least five years. For people who come to the career via other routes, the path is less certain: Only 55 percent remain in the profession after five years. People with strong essay-writing and report-writing skills last longer than those without them. "I had to learn to think all over again, and once I had done that, I had to learn how to write all over again," one professional reported. A solid majority of respondents ranked writing the second or third most important skill in this profession. An ecologist can make a difference in how the general population treats the environment with rigorous scientific research and a presentation of ideas in well-written reports and articles that educate others.

One ecologist described her colleagues as "smart people who love looking at big systems and, if possible, saving them." Many researchers review others' articles and papers before they are sent out to publishers. The strong sense of community often sustains ecologists in their careers even when little, if anything, is done with their recommendations. Aspiring ecologists should be aware of the institutional difficulties in making headway in the initiative to prevent environmental degradation. A sense of frustration can be significant for those entering this profession.

PAYING YOUR DUES

Most ecologists are scientists with backgrounds in chemistry, environmental science, geology, biology, climatology, statistics, and, in many cases, economics. The depth of knowledge in each field determines the specialty area in which each candidate works; a master's degree in a science or ecology itself is becoming increasingly common as the minimum requirement. Nearly all aspiring ecologists are expected to have some field experience.

ASSOCIATED CAREERS

Because of their exposure to the growing mountain of numbers that indicate that we are ravaging our own planet, ecologists often become environmentalists, using their scientific and statistics-based background as a resource for their educational and lobbying efforts. They also often become teachers and address the problem of environmental degradation in that forum.

PAST AND FUTURE

Ecological issues came to the forefront during the industrialization of Europe. Coal, the main fuel, had blackened the sky of many pristine countries and led to public health problems. Unsafe mining practices resulted to the contamination of otherwise arable land. In the United States, ecology became a public issue in the early 1970s. In the early 1990s, recycling bins appeared in almost every home and office.

Ecology is one of the fastest-growing professions surveyed in this book. Ecological concerns across the globe are becoming more widespread, giving rise to the need for more experts. The number of impact studies undertaken by private employers, governments, and developers who need global ecological information is expected to double over the next twenty years. Opportunities are emerging that will make the profession more visible, significant, and rewarding.

QUALITY OF LIFE

2 YEARS Ecologists have done field research, collected and assembled data, and produced reports. All of their work is supervised, and many of them are assigned to specific tasks by senior ecologists. Nonscience majors spend these early years learning about ecological science topics, while science majors brush up on their writing skills. The hours are average, but satisfaction (particularly among science-friendly personnel) is high. Wages are low.

5 YEARS Ecologists are promoted from assistants to associate ecologists, positions that have greater responsibility for data collection, report presentation, and supervising junior ecologists in their daily tasks. Many ecologists pursue advanced degrees in materials science, chemistry, ecology, and economics. Satisfaction is average; individuals unsuited for the lifestyle leave the profession between years four and nine.

10 YEARS Ten-year ecologists direct research, allocate funds, and manage personnel. They are involved in independent research, publishing, and lecturing. Ecologists who teach classes begin to do so during these years. Fieldwork drops significantly after year six in the profession. Many professionals become involved in high-profile debates concerning the effects that certain behaviors have on the environment.

MAJOR EMPLOYERS

ENVIRONMENTAL PROTECTION AGENCY
Ariel Rios Building
1200 Pennsylvania Avenue, NW
Washington, DC 20460
Tel: 202-272-0167
www.epa.gov
Contact: Personnel Officer

NATURAL RESOURCES DEFENSE COUNCIL
40 West 20th Street
New York, NY 10011
Tel: 212-727-2700
Fax: 212-727-1773
www.nrdc.org
Contact: Human Resources

TEXAS A&M UNIVERSITY
809 University Drive East, Suite 101A
College Station, TX 77843
Tel: 979-845-5154
www.tamu.edu
Contact: Employment Office

MAJOR ASSOCIATIONS

AMERICAN INSTITUTION OF BIOLOGICAL SCIENCES
1441 I Street, NW, Suite 200
Washington, DC 20005
Tel: 202-628-1500
Fax: 202-628-1509
E-mail: admin@aibs.org
www.aibs.org

ELECTRICAL ENGINEER

A DAY IN THE LIFE

From radar to motors, electrical engineers design, implement, maintain, and improve all the electronics that people use every day. "Most electrical engineers love to talk about technology," one mentioned, "and that is a wonderful thing." Many engineers enter the profession for the intellectual stimulation and are generally driven people who aim to strike a balance between competition with and mutual support of their peers. More than 85 percent of the electrical engineers we surveyed cited interaction with their colleagues as the most positive aspect of the profession.

Daily activities include studying technical manuals, articles, and other publications; designing, testing, and assembling devices; writing reports; and keeping track of various assignments. Computer skills are a must. More than 40 percent of the time of an electrical engineer is spent attending meetings, working on strategic planning, and tracking projects. The amount of interpersonal communication can be disconcerting to many project-oriented engineers; more than 15 percent of newly hired electrical engineers take in-house management organization or writing skills courses. Contact between engineers and clients is infrequent. This sense of "project vs. product" isolation actually seems to be valuable.

{ project vs. product }

Beyond designing and creating new circuits for televisions, VCRs, slot machines, or stereo equipment, engineers with creative instincts usually flock to more esoteric areas such as cutting-edge medical technology and HDTV. Choosing a specialty is important and happens quickly, with engineers moving into such areas as quantum electronics, acoustics, signal processing, and ferroelectrics. Electrical engineers must have patience; the average span of time from the design of a product to placement on a shelf is two years.

PAYING YOUR DUES

An undergraduate degree in electrical engineering will suffice for most entry-level positions, such as tester and data collector, but a master's degree or PhD will be necessary for those who intend to progress further. Necessary course work includes physics, chemistry, some biology, heavy mathematics, and statistics. A large segment of the job market for aspiring electrical engineers is in the defense industry, so passing a security check may be required. The aviation industry encompasses another sizable segment of jobs. Candidates should be familiar with the production, testing, and assembly of electronics components, the general methods and means of power transference, and, if possible, computer electronic modeling. Aspiring electrical engineers who want to work for large corporations should be willing to follow established procedures and protocols. Some of the most exciting and revolutionary innovations come out of smaller companies.

ASSOCIATED CAREERS

Individuals who choose to become electrical engineers usually stay with the position for life. The few people who leave the field mostly become physicists, electricians, aviation engineers, or computer scientists. A number of former electrical engineers head to Wall Street, where intellectual acuity can be rewarded on a higher salary scale.

PAST AND FUTURE

The current information age is made possible in large part by electrical engineers. The science as we now think of it essentially began with the invention of the microchip in the 1960s. This in turn gave rise to the modern personal computer. Through the 1970s, most major EE advances emerged out of defense-industry-sponsored research, but in more recent years, that trend seems to have reversed, with the most significant advances coming from the consumer electronics industry, particularly the computer sector. Product development is becoming more and more closely tied to the use of the microchip.

QUALITY OF LIFE

2 YEARS "Out of the frying pan and into the fire," two of our respondents said about their initial years in electrical engineering. The pay is reasonable, but recent graduates who are used to flexible deadlines and accommodating professors find the transition jarring. Some 20 percent of them change jobs in their first three years, trying to find the match for their own personal working style. Work is highly supervised and highly compartmentalized; expect to be unable to distinguish yourself for the first two years, since you will be buried in the details of modeling, computer analysis, and drafting.

5 YEARS The development of a specialty takes place between years three and five. Many engineers move from "assistant" to "designer" or "quality control" areas. The amount of pay and responsibility increase. Playing the corporate game is crucial for engineers at large firms. Contacts made early on are very important for people wishing to form startup companies of their own. Just 10 percent of all electrical engineers change occupations within the industry, if even a remote chance of advancement exists in the current firm.

10 YEARS Almost 35 percent of electrical engineers control equity stakes in their firms; have filed for their own patents; or have started their own companies. A significant number of ten-year veterans become a part of the upper management team within their company. Electrical engineers spend more time forming budgets, allocating resources, and overseeing production than designing, drafting, modeling, and testing. Ten years is regarded by some as an enormously significant time frame in this profession; at this point, your academic education has been exploited to its fullest, and the rapidly changing electronics industry requires that you change with it or be left behind.

MAJOR EMPLOYERS

ADEMCO
165 Eileen Way
Syosset, NY 11791
Tel: 516-921-6704
Fax: 516-364-0746
www.honeywell.com

ANACOMP INC.
15378 Avenue of Science
San Diego, CA 92128
Tel: 858-716-3400
Fax: 858-716-3775
www.anacomp.com

MAJOR ASSOCIATIONS

AMERICAN ELECTRONICS ASSOCIATION
5210 Great American Parkway, Suite 520
Santa Clara, CA 95054
Tel: 800-284-4232 or 408-987-4200
www.aeanet.org

ELECTRONIC INDUSTRIES ALLIANCE
2500 Wilson Boulevard
Arlington, VA 22201-3834
Tel: 703-907-7500
Fax: 703-907-7966
www.eia.org

INSTITUTE OF ELECTRICAL AND ELECTRONICS ENGINEERS
3 Park Avenue, 17th Floor
New York, NY 10016-5997
Tel: 212-419-7900
Fax: 212-752-4929
www.ieee.org

ELECTRICIAN

A DAY IN THE LIFE

Many of our survey respondents reported that they had been fascinated by electricity ever since they were small, and only a few of them were disappointed with their choice of career. There are two general types of electrical work: construction work, which includes reading blueprints, wiring, installing, and testing electrical systems; and maintenance work, which involves troubleshooting, testing, and fixing already–installed, improperly functioning electrical systems. Most construction electricians are employed by contractors during the secondary phases of building. Maintenance electricians work as freelancers or for large factories, office buildings, or hospitals.

$\left\{ \text{troubleshooting, testing, and fixing} \right\}$

"If you make it through the training and spend a little time with someone good, you'll be all right," one electrician commented. Almost all electricians go through an academically rigorous apprenticeship program. Only people with a careful eye for detail, responsible work habits, and sound on-the-spot judgment should consider becoming electricians. Electricians must know how to read blueprints and specifications and install, connect, and test electrical devices and power sources. They must be familiar with local and federal electrical codes and regulations. Individuals who succeed in this field have a sound theoretical understanding of electrical systems, good manual dexterity, and patience. While on-the-job injuries are not uncommon, electricians are seriously injured by electricity at half the rate of the general population, while assuming ten times the risk. Most on-the-job injuries occur at the end of long hours, when being rushed to complete a task, or when blueprints have been incorrectly drawn. An important part of becoming a good electrician is knowing when it would be dangerous to proceed.

Electricians are finding that their profession is becoming increasingly linked with that of computer and telecommunications wiring. The systems are installed at the same time, and more often than not, new structures are wired for networks and telecommunications immediately. More than 20 percent of electricians take additional classes in telecommunications systems, wiring, and electrical interfaces to be able to undertake this work themselves.

PAYING YOUR DUES

Electricians work indoors and out, under both difficult and ordinary pressures, and are subjected to daily tests of mental acuity and physical dexterity. Though most in the field have only a high school diploma, electricians are paid well and look toward a solid future, as America becomes more dependent on consistent and well-maintained supplies of electricity. Most people become electricians by entering an apprenticeship program with the sponsorship of an established electrician. These programs are run by such unions as the International Brotherhood of Electrical Workers and the National Electrical Contractors Association. Most programs take four to five years to complete. Candidates must attend a minimum of 144 hours of classroom instruction per year, but the emphasis is on practical experience, with at least 2,000 hours of paid, on-the-job training annually. About a third of electricians become union members. Aspiring electricians should be mature and responsible and have strong mathematical skills and good physical dexterity and stamina. Most states have their own licensing exams that test an electrician's knowledge of local regulations as well as information contained in the National Electrical Code, the national register of electrical regulations.

ASSOCIATED CAREERS

Few electricians leave the field. They tend to do so only when work in a particular region becomes unavailable. Some of the 10 percent of electricians who do leave the profession each year are retirees. Some become electrical inspectors, enter teaching programs, or work as construction consultants specializing in secondary building systems. A few of them enter training programs to become contractors.

PAST AND FUTURE

In the 1900s, when electricity was developed, electricians were responsible for the wiring, testing, and constructing of every electrical system, groundline, and socket in the United States.

Electricians are in high demand these days, both for maintenance and construction. Outdated electrical systems need upgrading. As sources of electricity change over time, methods of delivery and capacity differentiation will require that the electrician engage in continuing education. With the population growing and the power usage rising, the demand for electricians should be steady for the next ten years. Current population trends indicate that more work is likely to be available in the South and Southwest than in the North and Northeast.

QUALITY OF LIFE

2 YEARS Most training programs have progressed nearly halfway, and those who couldn't hack the academic rigor of these programs have probably already left them. At the two-year mark, training involves a blend of classroom and on-the-job training, with a transition from raw learning to analysis and problem-solving. Work is still highly supervised, and tasks are limited to basic installation, testing, and maintenance. Blueprint-reading skills are developing. Wages are low for the industry, but many electricians report that this is not a problem, "as you are learning a career."

5 YEARS Nearly everyone has finished the training program and is a certified electrician. People who haven't yet passed state and federal requirements work as "electricians' assistants" while they study for them. Those people who have passed these tests pursue work through local sponsoring guilds and unions; already-employed electricians or general contractors who are hiring subcontractors, a process that also goes through the local guild or union; or on-site maintenance contractors that may or may not go through the union. Often, the decision to join a union is made based on the choice of company for which an electrician works, and whether that company is signatory to a union contract.

10 YEARS After ten years, an electrician has established himself as a valuable and capable player in the industry. The electrician's skills are excellent; a variety of unusual situations—such as remodeling entire buildings that have outdated wiring or meeting the demands of companies with unusual power needs—have been encountered and handled. Most electricians have formed relationships in the industry. These often replace formalized partnerships. While in many other industries a significant number of ten-year veterans form their own consulting companies, only about 20 percent of ten-year electricians do this. The hassles for private electrical contractors are numerous—insurance, liability, unhappy clients—and the pay as a freelance electrician working for individual contractors is good. A few of the teaching-inclined have gone back to the apprenticeship programs as instructors who work for slightly less pay but with more consistent and less taxing hours.

MAJOR EMPLOYERS
Electricians are hired by utility companies, schools and colleges, hospitals, private electrical service providers, manufacturers, and communications companies.

MAJOR ASSOCIATIONS
ASSOCIATED BUILDERS AND CONTRACTORS
4250 N. Fairfax Drive, 9th Floor
Arlington, VA 22203

INDEPENDENT ELECTRICAL CONTRACTORS
4401 Ford Avenue, Suite 1100
Alexandria, VA 22302
Tel: 703-549-7351
Fax: 703-549-7448
www.ieci.org

NATIONAL ELECTRICAL CONTRACTORS ASSOCIATION
3 Bethesda Metro Center, Suite 1100
Bethesda, MD 20814
Tel: 301-657-3110
Fax: 301-215-4500
www.necanet.org

ENTREPRENEUR

BOOKS, FILMS, AND TV SHOWS FEATURING THE PROFESSION
- **The Art of the Deal**
- **The Entrepreneurs**
- **Forrest Gump**
- **The Jerk**
- **Risking It All**

YOU'LL HAVE CONTACT WITH
- **Accountants**
- **Attorneys**
- **Bankers**
- **Suppliers**

PROFESSIONALS READ
- **Black Enterprise**
- **Forbes**
- **Fortune**
- **Money**

A DAY IN THE LIFE

An entrepreneur risks his or her own capital, services, and skills in a company (or in several companies). Entrepreneurs exemplify the American dream—working without a boss and using their own hands, hearts, and intellects to build a livelihood. Successful entrepreneurs seem to have a number of similar qualities. First, they know business, either from their own experience or through extensive research. Second, they are extremely motivated. The average number of working hours per week of a successful starting entrepreneur is seventy. This may catch the typical American dreamer by surprise. Third, successful entrepreneurs become obsessed with—or at least fascinated by—all parts of their chosen area of expertise. No aspect of the business is too large or too small

> { Entrepreneurs exemplify the American dream. }

to consider. The best aspect of this career is that entrepreneurs control their own destinies to a greater extent than if they were working for someone else. Unlike working for someone else who judges their work and assigns a value to their services, every stitch of work they do goes toward their betterment. This not only puts intense pressure on entrepreneurs, but it can also be the source of immense pleasure.

The most important entrepreneurial concerns should be thought about long before someone starts his or her own business. He or she must know how to run the company and when to reassess management strategies. He or she must be on top of cash flow, expansion (or consolidation), liquidity, and corporate governance. More than three-fifths of new businesses and franchises fail within their first eighteen months. Many of the factors leading to failure are uncontrollable by the entrepreneur. If he or she is trying to sell widgets and a widgets superstore opens down the street, the new venture may fail. Being an entrepreneur means thinking about the business all the time and accepting its responsibilities and its failures. But being one's own boss, owning a business, and reaping all the rewards are powerful enough forces to attract people in droves.

PAYING YOUR DUES

If you feel capable of running a business and you have the capital, initiative, money, creativity, and nerves of steel, you may want to become an entrepreneur. A background in finance helps; people who don't have one often take on a (trustworthy) partner who does. Entrepreneurs should also know their product, their market, and their competitors. Research in the field is a must. Access to capital is crucial to the fledgling entrepreneur. Some can go to a bank and use their knowledge of the field with a solid business plan to request a loan. Certain loan programs are available through the federal government for small businesses. Municipalities, small business associations, and private organizations also offer financial assistance and planning. Contact your local chamber of commerce for information.

ASSOCIATED CAREERS

Although most entrepreneurs run into difficulty, few people think to arrange a backup plan in case of failure. Many entrepreneurs return to the industries in which they initiated their careers. Others venture into the field again and again. Take heart—many great industrialists failed four, five, and six times before they succeeded in their speculative ventures. The most important lesson is to learn from the mistakes made in the past and address them when planning a new entrepreneurial venture.

PAST AND FUTURE

Private ownership and personal control is more than just an American phenomenon, but American history has been linked closely with this ideal. The notion that the United States has no entrenched class system but operates purely on a merit-based system is the foundation for the Horatio Alger story, in which anyone can move from "rags to riches"—the notion that opportunity is available to all. Any observer of American life knows that this American dream is largely a myth, but successful entrepreneurs prove that the basis for the myth is not entirely groundless.

Entrepreneurs make their own opportunities, and they will continue to do so. The franchising trend—people purchasing the exclusive rights to one of a nationally recognized chain of stores—peaked in the late 1980s and early 1990s. Franchises are in decline, and more and more people are choosing to undertake only one part of an entrepreneurial venture: providing expertise, financing, or managing. With three or more individuals involved in the same project, issues of corporate governance are more complicated, but areas of responsibility become more clearly delineated.

QUALITY OF LIFE

2 YEARS Entrepreneurs are most likely to fail during the first two years, but their failure generally doesn't come about from lack of effort. Many people spend the majority of their waking hours working, trying to promote and support their ventures. Still, there is no substitute for experience and reputation—not to mention adequate demand. Entrepreneurs who've lasted two years have learned an enormous amount about how to run a business. Even many of the successful ones earn just enough to support themselves in these early years.

5 YEARS Five-year entrepreneurial survivors have established business plans, expanded as necessary, and restructured according to common sense. Many of them engage in long-term financing relationships at this point, as they have established a track record of being able to maintain a financially viable company. Many entrepreneurs are earning significant incomes from their businesses, and they must make a key decision: Do they remain in the profession, or do they sell out and cease to be an entrepreneur? Perhaps they should seek out new businesses for profit? Most entrepreneurs begin their businesses to sell a chosen product, so they usually choose to stick with it.

10 YEARS Entrepreneurs who've remained in the same business for ten years cannot really be considered entrepreneurs anymore; they are truly businesspeople of their chosen field. Many of them still apply the mindset of expansion, growth, and profit to their corporations or partnerships, but this in no way distinguishes them from the CEOs of hundreds of other nonentrepreneurial companies. Hours worked per week remain high, but survivors have at this point probably gained immeasurable financial, managerial, and interpersonal expertise.

MAJOR EMPLOYERS
Entrepreneurs are self-employed.

MAJOR ASSOCIATIONS
CENTER FOR INTERNATIONAL PRIVATE ENTERPRISE
1155 15th Street, NW, Suite 700
Washington, DC 20005
Tel: 202-721-9200
Fax: 202-721-9250
www.cipe.org

CEO CLUB
47 West Street, Suite 5C
New York, NY 10006
Tel: 212-925-7911
Fax: 212-925-7463
www.ceoclubs.com

COMMITTEE OF 200
980 North Michigan Avenue, Suite 1575
Chicago, IL 60611
Tel: 312-255-0296
Fax: 312-255-0789
www.c200.org

ENVIRONMENTALIST/ENVIRONMENTAL SCIENTIST

BOOKS, FILMS, AND TV SHOWS
FEATURING THE PROFESSION
- **Green Card**
- **Planet Green**
- **Singles**
- **The Smog Epidemic**

YOU'LL HAVE CONTACT WITH
- **Ecologists**
- **Lobbyists**
- **Publicists**
- **Researchers**

PROFESSIONALS READ
- **Ecoverse**
- **Journal of Environmental Quality**
- **Journal of Natural Resources and Life Sciences Education**

A DAY IN THE LIFE

"I became an environmentalist because I wanted a profession that would let me sleep well at night," one respondent wrote. Nearly all of our respondents said their desire to better the world was key in their decisions to become environmentalists, and many of them also said that even if their jobs didn't pay, they would still do environmental work. Environmentalists help the public make informed decisions about the use of limited natural resources. They do research, produce reports, write articles, lecture, issue press releases, lobby Congress, raise funds, and campaign. The daily routine depends on the specialty. Environmental researchers measure decay and its pace and patterns, including the depletion of the ozone layer in space or contaminated groundwater in suburban communities. Policy-determining environmentalists figure out how behavior can be modified in the future to avoid these problems. Other environmental positions involve office work, policy analysis, lab work, or computer analysis.

{ policy-determining }

Some companies sell "environmentally friendly" goods and services such as recyclable products or products with recycled content. Not-for-profit environmentalist companies, which account for 70 percent of the industry, engage in more aggressive campaigns to educate the public about environmental causes and often work in education campaigns on college campuses, where much of the scientific work is done. In the private sector, at least 80 percent of the not-for-profit companies have ten or fewer employees. More than 50 percent of the companies in this field rely on nonguaranteed sources of income such as federal grants, private donations, or corporate sponsorship.

The occupation can entail long hours, difficult and sometimes severely underfunded work situations, and a sense of frustration that "no one listens, and even if they listen, no one does anything." But environmentalists are drawn to their work by a sense of satisfaction in doing something they really believe in—even if the warm feelings about their work rarely produce strong financial rewards.

PAYING YOUR DUES

Understanding the issues involved in environmentalism—degradation, conservation, recycling, and replenishment—is central to finding work in the environmental care and maintenance industry. An academic background is recommended but not required (some colleges now offer degrees in environmental science). Many entry-level positions are highly competitive and require a rigorous set of interviews. By letting representatives from a range of areas meet and talk with prospective candidates who have majored in anything from psychology to natural science to economics, these companies ensure they hire people who can fill a number of roles and who are dedicated to hard work. Entry-level employees use many skills, including interviewing and writing, organizing events or mailings, raising funds, and conducting scientific testing in a laboratory environment. Continuing education is the norm, because the work deals with a changing physical system.

ASSOCIATED CAREERS

Individuals who leave the profession are most likely to do so out of frustration with the slow pace of progress rather than a repudiation of the environmentalist agenda. They become high school teachers at a faster rate than do any other profession for which we have such statistics. Others become ecological scientists, policy analysts, lobbyists, campaign organizers, advertising executives (the art of persuasion is crucial in both industries), or graphic designers. Most of them continue environmental policy debates on a local, official, or personal level by encouraging recycling and promoting "green"—environmentally friendly—products.

PAST AND FUTURE

Environmental concerns arose with the land use changes brought about by urbanization and increasing population density. As early as 1300, London was thick with smoke from excessive coal use. Today, Los Angeles is one of many cities with a substantial smog problem. We are currently in a time of environmental reconsideration.

Air pollution control alone is now a substantial industry unto itself; hazardous waste management (see separate listing) is also a fast-growing industry. The biggest question is whether environmentalists' concerns will be addressed through legislation in the next few years. More regulation for a cleaner environment could dramatically increase the demand for people in the environmental sciences. Deregulation and a return to the laissez-faire attitude of the 1960s will result in a weakening of these prospects. But environmental crises are ongoing; the steady deforestation of the Brazilian rain forest will continue to pose challenges—and opportunities—for environmentalists for years to come.

QUALITY OF LIFE

2 YEARS At the beginning, this profession involves plenty of paperwork and phone calls. New environmentalists learn the specific concerns of their companies, acquire contacts needed to get information quickly and accurately, and assist in the ongoing educational process. Choosing a specialization happens right away; your company's concerns become yours immediately. Client contact, responsibility, and pay are limited. The hours tend to be reasonable. The burnout rate is very high (about 35 percent), perhaps due to unfulfilled expectations for immediate change in environmental attitudes.

5 YEARS Responsibilities increase; environmentalists oversee projects and write articles, reports, and press releases. Many of them organize conferences on specific topics, using contacts within the industry to bring together notable speakers and players. Salaries increase, but so do the hours. Some environmentalists earn the title of "senior environmentalist" between years four and seven. The attrition rate levels off at seven percent for the five-year veterans.

10 YEARS Most remaining environmentalists have attained the title of vice president or its equivalent at small companies or moved on to other industries, most often the private sector. Fifteen percent become freelance consultants to other industries, advising ways of improving their environmental education and environmental friendliness. Many environmentalists begin their own businesses. While more than 20 percent of these companies fail within the first year, ten-year survivors can trade on their reputations and experience to find other companies and begin again.

MAJOR EMPLOYERS

BROWN & CALDWELL CONSULTANTS
201 North Civic Drive
Walnut Creek, CA 94596
Tel: 925-937-9010 or 800-727-2224
Fax: 925-937-9026
www.brownandcaldwell.com

CLEAN HARBORS, INC.
1501 Washington Street
PO Box 859048
Braintree, MA 02185-9048
Tel: 781-849-1800
Fax: 781-356-1527
www.cleanharbors.com

MAJOR ASSOCIATIONS

NATIONAL RESOURCES DEFENSE COUNCIL
40 West 20th Street
New York, NY 10011
Tel: 212-727-2700
Fax: 212-727-1773
www.nrdc.org

FARMER

SALARY

HOURS

EDUCATION

BOOKS, FILMS, AND TV SHOWS
FEATURING THE PROFESSION
- **Country**
- **The Grapes of Wrath**
- **The Milagro Bean Field War**
- **Witness**

YOU'LL HAVE CONTACT WITH
- **Food buyers**
- **Ranchers**
- **Suppliers**

PROFESSIONALS READ
- **Farm Forum**
- **North American Seeds**
- **Progressive Farmer**
- **Successful Farming**

A DAY IN THE LIFE

Few other occupations provide the variety of physical work, productivity, and intangible rewards associated with farming. Part of the high return rate of family members to the profession of farming can be attributed to an emotional attachment to the lifestyle; people who choose it often wouldn't opt to do anything else. Most farms employ fewer than 30 workers, and a sense of family pervades many of these communities: "When you spend 15 hours a day with people working to exhaustion, you get to know each other really well." Even with modern advances in farming technology, the work can be grueling and may require critical decision-making skills and many long, thankless hours. Long-term planning of crop yields and profits is extremely difficult, as production and income are determined by a combination of { **self-motivation** } weather, disease, price fluctuation, and domestic and foreign subsidy and tariff policy. Farmers have a higher-than-average level of daily anxiety, but in general enjoy what they do and certainly enjoy what they produce. "I've never been more tired," one farmer said, "but I wouldn't trade it for the world." Farmers tend to specialize in one or a limited number of crops. The producer chooses his crop based on the climate, land, market, and history of growing in the region. Each crop utilizes different types of equipment, and each piece of equipment requires different maintenance and personnel decisions. Farmers make difficult decisions about how to allocate resources and deal with unanticipated problems, such as insect infestation, drought, and fire. Over the course of any year, regular equipment and land maintenance requirements must be made. Self-motivation is a must because those farmers who don't take advantage of downtime to take care of long-term projects can find themselves relying on unreliable machinery or storage facilities. Farmers also arrange for the storage, transportation, purchase, and sale of produced items and negotiate and coordinate all agreements relating to them.

PAYING YOUR DUES

For some people, owning or running a farm is a childhood dream, fostered in their high school Future Farmers of America (FFA) organizations or their neighborhood 4-H youth educational programs. For many, farming is the family business (nearly 35 percent of all farms are family-owned or employ multigenerational workers). Operating larger, less-centralized farms, however, requires more study. It is recommended (and sometimes required) that people who want to run their own farms attend a two- or four-year agricultural college located in the state in which they want to work. All states have land-grant colleges with agricultural programs whose course catalogs include dairy science, farm economics, horticulture, crop science, and animal science. Some people choose to gain certification as an Accredited Farm Manager (AFM) through the American Society of Farm Managers and Rural Appraisers, although these certifications are more encouraged than required. Work is rigorous and challenging and requires a variety of managerial, scientific, and practical skills.

ASSOCIATED CAREERS

Farmers usually choose the profession for life, and those individuals who leave the field are more hamstrung by the paucity of viable opportunities than by dissatisfaction with the lifestyle. A number of farming refugees become ranchers; others become businesspeople in the agricultural field (fertilizer suppliers, seed suppliers, etc.); a smaller number of them become commodities traders for goods such as cotton, soybeans, and frozen orange juice. People in this realm who have experience as producers are likely also to possess insight into how external events influence production.

PAST AND FUTURE

More than 90 percent of America's first settlers were farmers, and agriculture will always be a vital profession. The future of farming is tied to the future of agricultural science. As methods of crop breeding, land rotation, soil enrichment, and shortening growing periods develop, the farmer's job can be expected to become more specialized. Currently, farmers face difficult decisions; prices for produce and farm goods have been effectively flat, while mortgage rates, lines of credit, cost of machinery, and cost of labor have risen. Farming is consolidating, and the old family farm is rapidly giving way to large agribusiness, which trades on the commodities exchange to ensure the best price for its goods.

QUALITY OF LIFE

2 YEARS Duties of the beginning farmer include crop tilling, fertilizing, composting, and harvesting. The new farmer rotates among different jobs, all integral to the practical running of a farm; he may also supplement his income with nonfarm employment. Many take night classes at local agricultural colleges or rural community colleges with agricultural programs or take courses sponsored by large farming concerns. The variety of tasks undertaken in the first two years is the best part of the job; the physical hazard is the worst—farming ranks among the most dangerous professions, with some 40 percent of all workers losing at least one week during the first two years to injury. Pay is low; the work is taxing, especially during the spring (planting) and fall (harvesting) seasons.

5 YEARS Five years into the profession, farmers who have taken the requisite courses, shown ability in managing other workers, and demonstrate ambition and energy obtain management positions. Individuals who have found areas of specialization—such as harvesting, storage management, or soil analysis—continue their education through conferences and conventions. Pay rises to reasonable levels but continues to be influenced by meteorological and legislative whims.

10 YEARS A 10-year survivor of the agricultural production industry has faced growing, business, and distribution challenges. By now, many farmers have purchased or soon will purchase their own land, using their successful experience as an asset to secure financing. On average, 10-year veterans will remain farmers for another 35 years.

MAJOR EMPLOYERS
CARGILL INC.
Cargill Office Center
PO Box 9300
Minneapolis, MN 55440-9300
Tel: 800-227-4455
www.cargill.com

DOW AGROSCIENCES LLC
9330 Zionsville Road
Indianapolis, IN 46268
Tel: 317-337-3000
www.dowagro.com

ARCHER DANIELS MIDLAND COMPANY
4666 Faries Parkway
Decatur, IL 62526
Tel: 800-637-5843
E-mail: info@admworld.com
www.admworld.com

MAJOR ASSOCIATIONS
AMERICAN DAIRY SCIENCE ASSOCIATION
1111 North Dunlap Avenue
Savoy, IL 61874
Tel: 217-356-5146
Fax: 217-398-4119
www.adsa.org

AMERICAN FARM BUREAU
600 Maryland Avenue, SW
Suite 800
Washington, DC 20024
Tel: 202-406-3600
Fax: 202-406-3604
www.fb.com

FBI AGENT

A DAY IN THE LIFE

Do you see yourself as Clarice Starling (Jodie Foster) tracking Hannibal Lechter (Anthony Hopkins) in *Silence of the Lambs*? Do you want to fight for truth, justice, and the American way on American soil? FBI agents investigate people suspected of violating federal law, including serial killers, kidnappers, bank robbers, bombers, and perpetrators of mail fraud. Strong deductive reasoning skills, flexibility, and irreproachable moral character are key traits for people who want to succeed in the FBI. The sensitive nature of the work requires a person with sound judgment and discretion. The application process is one of the most rigorous and selective in the nation.

{ irreproachable moral character }

Agents research and gather evidence about suspected criminals. Duties include surveillance, transcription, research, coordination with local authorities, and report-writing. Individuals in the scientific division work in labs and in the field, collecting and analyzing evidence and working with private labs. Many agents in the profession feel that the variety of tasks keeps the job fresh and exciting. By themselves, FBI agents have limited power to arrest and no power to punish people suspected of violating federal law. An FBI agent investigates and reports, and when other government agencies make the arrest, they often invite the FBI agent or agents who were involved with the case but merely as a courtesy. It is common for the agent to move on to another case before any arrests are actually made.

The most difficult part of being an FBI agent is the sense of isolation it can foster. Most agents work by themselves or, if necessary, in pairs. They often travel for long periods of time. The project-based nature of this career may keep it exciting, but the uncertainty of it can lead to frustration. One agent from New York wrote, "My wife and I were married on May 25 of last year. I was assigned to a case two days later and couldn't tell her where I was or when I would be back or what was going on. I next saw her July 14." Even with all the pressures the work entails and the lifestyle limitations it demands, only 4 percent of agents leave each year (not including retirees). There must be something great about being an FBI agent—but of course it's a secret.

PAYING YOUR DUES

To become a member of the FBI, you must be a U.S. citizen between 23 and 37 years of age, meet stringent physical requirements, and hold at least a bachelor's degree, and in many cases, an even more advanced degree. The FBI has five entry programs: law, accounting, science, language, and diversified; and each program has its own specific academic requirements. The application process is renowned for its rigor and thoroughness. In addition to giving each applicant difficult written tests and interviews, the FBI conducts intensive background checks including criminal record checks; credit checks; interviews with associates, roommates, and landlords; professional references; and academic verifications. Each candidate takes a drug test, physical exam, and, at the discretion of the FBI, a polygraph (lie detector) test. After making it through this intense examination, new agents spend four months at the FBI Academy in Quantico, Virginia, studying investigative techniques, personal defense, and firearms. The FBI will disqualify any candidate who has physical or emotional handicaps that will not allow him or her to perform important and dangerous duties within acceptable parameters.

ASSOCIATED CAREERS

Since there is mandatory retirement of field agents after 20 years or at age 55, older ex-FBI agents are scattered throughout a number of fields in the United States. They usually find a career in their area of expertise when they leave the FBI. Local law enforcement and other federal agencies—the CIA; the Bureau of Alcohol, Tobacco, and Firearms; the Federal Marshals; and the NSA—hire many ex-agents. Others move into consulting at private laboratories, go into teaching, or become practicing attorneys. A few become private investigators.

PAST AND FUTURE

Founded in 1908 under the United States Department of Justice, the Federal Bureau of Investigation was meant to be the active investigative arm of federal law enforcement. The FBI wasn't particularly significant until J. Edgar Hoover took over in 1924 and increased its responsibilities, its scientific methods, and its efficacy. The modern FBI has one of the world's most advanced crime laboratories, and its fingerprint division contains the largest database of fingerprints in the world.

Like all government agencies, the future direction of the FBI is highly dependent on changing political climates and federal budget restrictions. The need for the FBI, however, continues to be readily apparent.

QUALITY OF LIFE

2 YEARS New FBI agents, known as "special agents," are usually paired with experienced agents in a specific division. Usually the work involves travel, investigation, surveillance, and report-writing. Techniques discussed in the classroom are used in real-life situations, and people who expected glamour are disappointed by the generally unexciting nature of the work. Satisfaction levels are low but rebound in the next few years as agents are rotated among a number of cases and gain valuable and varied experience.

5 YEARS Five-year veterans have worked with a number of other government agencies on cases, and their skill levels have risen dramatically. The hours decrease, the pay increases, and satisfaction levels are high. Field agents who wish to combine a more predictable lifestyle with a career in the FBI can apply for desk-bound coordination positions. Individuals who show talent become senior agents and take charge of investigations. Communication and analysis skills are at a premium in these years, when agents are involved in investigations in a hands-on fashion while also reporting to assistant directors.

10 YEARS Halfway to a pension, most agents are still driven by the same motivations that encouraged them to enter the profession in the first place. Pay and responsibilities have increased, and satisfaction levels are solid. Those who show talent in organization and management move into assistant directorship positions on a local level and, while emergencies still rule the day, can control their hours to some degree. Individuals who enjoy the life of a field agent remain on cases, liaise with other government departments, and work with newer employees. A very successful few return to Quantico at this point as instructors, trainers, and educators for the FBI training program.

MAJOR EMPLOYER

FEDERAL BUREAU OF INVESTIGATION
J. Edgar Hoover Building
935 Pennsylvania Avenue, NW
Washington, DC 20535-0001
Tel: 202-324-3000
www.fbi.gov

MAJOR ASSOCIATIONS

Federal Bureau of Investigation (FBI) agents have strict loyalty and confidentiality obligations that make participation in general professional associations difficult.

NATIONAL ASSOCIATION OF INVESTIGATIVE SPECIALISTS (NAIS)
PO Box 33244
Austin, TX 78764
Tel: 512-719-3595
Fax: 512-420-3594
www.pimall.com/nais

FILM PRODUCER

A DAY IN THE LIFE

The producer of a film is the administrative—and sometimes even artistic—maestro of the project. In other words, the producer manages most aspects of the filmmaking process, from the development of the script to the opening in theaters. In a word, the producer is an entrepreneur. He or she needs to have a creative eye for talent and a keen business sense. Studio producers (that is, ones who have signed a contract to produce solely for a single studio) have the power of the Hollywood machine behind them; as a result, they may have an easier time getting a script actualized into a movie. An independent film producer has to jump through a few more hoops to see that finished product.

{ searching for that great script }

The process work as follows: Once the producer selects a script (a producer will spend days, months, even years searching for that "great script"—the one that sets the stage for the rest of her career), she must arrange funding for the project. The producer whips out his or her Rolodex (which is filled with connections made over the years), and the race to get the film off the ground begins. A great producer knows how to sell the right script to the right people. Once a producer knows how much money he or she has to work with, the search for talent begins. The producer chooses the director, the principal cast, and the production staff. He or she also coordinates and negotiates the legal logistics, such as contracts, salaries, and other expenses. Throughout the making of the film, a good producer stays on the sidelines, interfering very little in the artistic process of the actors and directors. The producer is, however, very involved in ensuring that the writers, directors, managers, and agents are all in sync, on schedule, and within the budget. Successful producers understand the needs of both the artistic personnel working on the film and the financial backers supporting the film.

There are many different types of producers, from the executive producer (who gives the final say on important matters) to the line producer (who is the on-the-set person who ensures all filming expenses fall within budget). In general, the job of executive producer is the job all producers eventually hope to call their own.

PAYING YOUR DUES

There are many inroads to becoming a producer. If you are equipped with the right skills and talents, a sufficient supply of drive, and a brimming Rolodex, you are well on your way. The success of a producer, similar to that of the artists with whom he or she works, hinges on the proper combination of luck, timing, and talent. Formal training (when it is available) rarely proves as helpful as on-the-job experience.

Many producers start their careers in management settings. Producers sometimes begin their careers working in theatrical management offices or for press agents. Some have even begun by taking a job for a managing director or in business management. Others have worked for performing arts unions or behind-the-scenes with a successful director. And some are completely self-generated producers who begin by promoting their own projects. A handful of colleges and universities now offer degrees in arts management; this development will prove useful—both in providing experience and offering networking opportunities—to aspiring film producers.

ASSOCIATED CAREERS

Producers share many traits with those in top management positions in the business world. Careers in educational administration, financial management, food service management, sales, advertising, marketing, promotions, and public relations demand similar skill sets.

PAST AND FUTURE

Film production took off in the early part of the 1920s with the advent of silent films. Most film production took place on the West Coast, although Paramount Pictures was, at the time, still based in Astoria (in Queens, New York). In fewer than five years, movies became a big business. By the end of the decade, there were 20 Hollywood studios; and the need for producers was at an all-time high. The 1920s and 1930s saw the greatest output of feature films in U.S. history: 800 films were released on average per year. Film producers such as David O. Selznik and Darryl F. Zanuck helped define entire genres of film with the production of King Kong and the Shirley Temple movies. Now Hollywood struggles to produce just 500 films per year. In the early years of film, the producer took charge of both the business and creative aspects of a film. The decline of the studio system in the 1950s, however, resulted in a shift of control over artistic elements from the producer to the director. In the 1970s and '80s, with the introduction of the blockbuster film, creative power shifted once again (though to a lesser degree) back into the hands of producers.

Job opportunities for producers are expected to grow at the average rate for all occupations during the course of the next several years. The changing nature of entertainment media will also increase the need for producers—but as the need grows, so will the competition. To remain a competitor, aspiring producers must be able to learn and adapt to the new forms of technology and media outlets that continue to emerge. The film producer career is a difficult one to pursue, but it's highly rewarding for those who manage to break into the industry, and then stay there.

QUALITY OF LIFE

2 YEARS There is no set path to becoming a successful producer. As it is typically a freelance undertaking, a producer may take years to find success; or he or she may achieve it with the first film. During the course of a producer's first two years, the primary objective is to find and produce a small project that will catch the eye of Hollywood and provide a solid foundation for reputation building. At this point in their careers, producers can expect to earn very little money, or none at all.

5 YEARS After five years, a producer may still be working on the same projects. With a bit of luck, he or she has been able to produce one or two noteworthy films and is starting to become known in the filmmaking community. Even if it is not high, he or she at least has an income at this stage. After five years, however, it is unlikely that he or she has "arrived" as a producer—yet.

10 YEARS After 10 years, if he or she is still devoting a great deal of time to producing, he or she has probably attained a solid and favorable reputation. He or she has probably also produced a few profitable films. People are now beginning to come to this person with ideas for projects. He or she may even be able to form a production company and produce a film with his or her own money.

MAJOR EMPLOYERS
PARAMOUNT PICTURES (OWNED BY VIACOM)
Paramount Studios
5555 Melrose Avenue
Hollywood, CA 90038
Tel: 323-956-5000
www.paramount.com

PIXAR
Recruiting
Pixar Animation Studios
1200 Park Avenue
Emeryville, CA 94608
www.pixar.com/companyinfo/jobs/howto.html

MAJOR ASSOCIATIONS
PRODUCERS GUILD OF AMERICA INC.
8530 Wilshire Boulevard, Suite 450
Beverly Hills, CA 90211
Tel: 310-358-9020
Fax: 310-358-9520
E-mail: info@producersguild.org
www.producersguild.org

FIREFIGHTER

A DAY IN THE LIFE

"We try to save things and protect people," is how one New York City firefighter describes one of society's nobler professions. A firefighter protects people, their property, and their goods from destruction or damage due to fire. The successful firefighter is an approachable communicator with the ability to take decisive action under trying circumstances. Firefighters must be able to perform strenuous physical tasks, such as carrying unconscious people down flights of stairs, directing the flow of a hose that carries 2,000 gallons of water per minute, or breaking down doors locked from the inside. The profession is very dangerous—more than one in four firefighters have to take time off for work-related injuries, ranging from slipped disks to disfiguring { unique professional bond } burns—and requires a strong sense of commitment to public service. Firehouses are manned around the clock. Firefighters must be able to deal with brief bursts of intense activity, then long periods of "crushing boredom." "Get good at solitaire," one wrote, alluding to the amount of downtime he faces. The firefighters who responded to our survey were unanimous in their estimation of their colleagues: "The best people I've ever known," one 10-year veteran wrote. "I count on them to guard my life every day." This reliance on one another encourages close companionship among members of any firehouse, who can boast the unique professional bond of having "been through hell" together. Most firefighters are deeply proud of what they do. Aside from taking on extra responsibilities, such as becoming a company leader or training other firefighters, firefighters don't have any kind of "corporate ladder" to climb. They make sure they are educated about technological or technique-oriented changes in firefighting through seminars, conferences, and conventions. Retirement is usually available at half-pay at age 50 for 20-year veterans. Most firefighters enjoy structured raises based on seniority and job performance. The largest fire departments have many battalions and divisions, with lieutenants, captains, battalion chiefs, division chiefs, fire marshals, and investigators. In such cases, there are substantial pay hikes for individuals who obtain senior positions.

PAYING YOUR DUES

While many colleges offer courses in fire science, these classes are usually taken by firefighting professionals after they've been in the field for a while. To become a firefighter, you need to be between 18 and 31 years of age; you need a high school diploma; you must have corrected 20/20 vision; and you must pass the firefighters' examination, offered annually by local governments throughout the country. Applicants who earn high scores on the written portion of the test and demonstrate physical dexterity, strength, and mental alertness should be able to find employment. Many departments now require an Emergency Medical Technician (EMT) certificate as a condition of employment. The hours are long for firefighters on duty, and you should check with the firefighters' association in your area for details (some have 24 hours on, 48 or 72 hours off; most city departments require firefighters to work an average of 48–56 hours per week). Firefighters can become members of the firefighters' union (affiliated with the AFL-CIO) and the International Association of Firefighters.

ASSOCIATED CAREERS

Firefighters who leave the profession (14 percent annually, including those who are put on disability retirement) generally continue in public service. A number of them apply to become police officers, frustrated with the "reactive" nature of firefighting. Roughly 5 percent return to school to be trained in paramedic or medical duties. Others go into teaching or fire safety consulting. Individuals who wish to rise to positions of advice and influence, particularly on a national level, take high-profile political positions elsewhere or become private consultants or authors. Firefighters are, in general, very satisfied with their choice of career, and the majority of those firefighters who leave their jobs do so within the first few years. Those individuals who remain firefighters for the first six years tend to stay for 20.

PAST AND FUTURE

Fire departments began as locally organized groups of residents and merchants who would come to one another's aid in times of crisis. They formed unofficial "bucket brigades" that would make a human chain from the nearest water supply, passing buckets to one another to the mouth of the fire. At the turn of the century, municipalities formed professional fire departments of their own. Many smaller communities still rely on volunteers who keep their ears open for the alarm whistle or through pages on their beepers.

Although technology has improved considerably and safety records are set each year for the protection of firefighters, unforeseen circumstances and unique developments all require competent and experienced professionals to make snap decisions and take decisive action. The number of firefighters hired each year corresponds proportionally to population increases, so an awareness of shifting demographics can help the aspiring firefighter find a promising location.

QUALITY OF LIFE

2 YEARS At the beginning of their careers, firefighters are put through a rigorous three- to sixteen-week training program to learn firefighting techniques. Attrition rate is highest in these initial years—almost 25 percent. Many individuals who leave have found the lifestyle too uneven (high-pressure or excessively dull), and rookies are generally stuck with the late-night "graveyard" shifts, which may inhibit personal life at the beginning of their careers.

5 YEARS During these years, attrition declines to between 3 and 5 percent for those who leave the profession due to dissatisfaction. More than 20 percent of firefighters receive on-the-job injuries in years four through seven, as those people who have survived five years have battled a number of different types of fires and may become a touch overconfident in their abilities. Most of the injuries during this time only result in three to twelve weeks of missed time. Individuals who wish to progress in the field take additional courses during these years and begin to teach at local training academies or give fire-prevention lectures at schools. Some of them get promoted to chief or manager of a firehouse.

10 YEARS Ten-year veterans have more control over their hours and receive higher pay but do basically the same job they were initially hired to do: fight fires. Halfway to their pension, most firefighters who've lasted this long have enough experience in action to avoid disabling injuries. Of those individuals who have the option to retire at age 50, only about half of them accept. People who see themselves as firefighters enjoy the profession for as long as they can.

MAJOR EMPLOYERS
NEW JERSEY FOREST FIRE SERVICE
State Headquarters
501 East State Street
PO Box 404
Trenton, New Jersey 08625
Tel: 609-292-2977
Fax: 609-984-0378
www.state.nj.us/dep/parksandforests/fire

NEW YORK CITY FIRE DEPARTMENT
1 Chase Manhattan Plaza
New York, NY 10005
Tel: 212-809-4887
http://nyc.gov/html/fdny/html/home2.shtml

MAJOR ASSOCIATIONS
INTERNATIONAL ASSOCIATION OF FIRE CHIEFS
4025 Fair Ridge Drive, Suite 300
Fairfax, VA 22033
Tel: 703-273-0911
Fax: 703-273-9363
www.iafc.org

INTERNATIONAL ASSOCIATION OF FIRE FIGHTERS
1750 New York Avenue, NW
Washington, DC 20006
Tel: 202-737-8484
Fax: 202-737-8418
www.iaff.org

GEOLOGIST

BOOKS, FILMS, AND TV SHOWS
FEATURING THE PROFESSION

- Annals of the Former
- A Civil Action
- Evolution
- Journey to the Center of the Earth
- The Map that Changed the World

YOU'LL HAVE CONTACT WITH

- Developers
- Environmental scientists
- Geophysicists
- Hydrologists
- Petroleum engineers
- Surveyors

PROFESSIONALS READ

- Geology
- Geotimes
- GSA Today
- Journal of Geology and Geomorphology
- Journal of Structural Geology

A DAY IN THE LIFE

One geologist surveyed said she owns a bumper sticker that reads "I've got rocks in my head." Another's reads, "I brake for outcrops." A little levity may be appreciated in between analyzing and interpreting data. Geologists who are reviewing outcrops in the field or consulting on environmental issues can expect to spend five to fifteen hours a day outdoors, usually during the more pleasant months of the year. They take samples and measurements and explore underneath the upper layers of the earth. Once they've completed their fieldwork, most of them return to the lab and test their samples for content and composition. One geologist said, "You'll be asked simple questions, and you've got to come up with ways of answering them when no one method

{ work in a lab and outdoors }

is foolproof. Is there oil under here? If so, how much? How long will it take to get it out? Those questions can only be answered with probabilities, not certainties." It takes a person not only adept at approaching problems but also savvy in dealing with people to satisfy the requirements of this occupation.

Many geologists do prospective development for the potential value of land sites for the oil and gas industry. They write reports recommending whether or not to lease a particular plot of land. A good geologist can be worth millions to a venture-capital-based oil company. "Don't count on seeing any of the money you make for them," one semi-disgruntled geologist wrote. Pay is moderate in this academic industry. Many people who enter it cite the intellectual challenge and the ability to work both in a lab and outdoors as the most positive features of the profession. Geologists appreciate the supportive and involved community of geological scientists: "You learn every day from your peers and the world around you. It's a perfect combination." A geologist may find him or herself in the field from three to seven months per year. Those long periods abroad can make life not so predictable for people who value family life and a stable work environment. People who don't work in the private sector may find work under the auspices of the largest hirer of geologists—the federal government. Many individuals are employed by the Department of Agriculture, the Department of the Interior, and the Department of Defense.

PAYING YOUR DUES

A geologist must have at least a bachelor's degree in geology or geophysics. Individuals who wish to advance should consider a master's degree and, in certain cases, a PhD. Course work includes such scientific staples as math, physics, chemistry, and statistics, but should also include mineralogy, stratigraphy, and structural geology. Entry-level positions, characterized by a lack of responsibility and paltry remuneration, include field research assistants and lab assistants. Most people work in teams. "I've never heard of an occupation that depends more on how well you work with others," one geologist wrote, "and you'll never hear more jokes about rocks." Someone interested in this career should be good with numbers and people, interested in sciences and natural formations, and comfortable working both alone and in groups. This person should also be willing to work long hours under uncertain working conditions (indoors and outside) and be happy with a small to average paycheck.

ASSOCIATED CAREERS

Few geologists—about 10 percent—leave the profession, and when they do, they tend to migrate to other related sciences. Some of these other sciences, such as geophysics and statistics, have direct correlations to geology. Others, such as oceanography and petroleum engineering, are applied versions of geological knowledge in specific areas. Some geologists join the enforcement division of the Environmental Protection Agency or the National Parks Service as land surveyors. Others return to school to receive advanced degrees in related or geological sciences.

PAST AND FUTURE

At the end of the eighteenth century, literature on the beginning and history of rock formations first began to be published in England by A. Werner and J. Hutton. The field grew with information gathered during explorations of Europe and the New World.

In the near future, geological job opportunities should remain about the same as they are now. Over the course of the next few decades, however, the nature and the process of the job should change dramatically. Technological innovations will be important in innovating methods of ground exploration and analysis, and the number of undiscovered sites will diminish, shrinking the available job pool. Geologists may find their role more related to environmental questions than resting on issues of venture capital.

QUALITY OF LIFE

2 YEARS
Most geologists just do field exploration and lab testing in their first two years. Usually paired with a "mentor" or "senior geologist," entry-level employees visit sites and learn how to take, label, and store samples. Back at the office, duties include proofreading, summarizing professional articles, and learning specific lab techniques. While not glamorous, the education is important, and those people who rise in the profession cite these initial training years as important to their continued success.

5 YEARS
Most people who've decided to leave the profession have left by this point, although a few more will leave between years six and eight. Many people in the field are promoted to "senior geologist" positions that involve the supervision of newer geologists and have more supervisory responsibilities, moving away from the duties of a tester or field agent. The hours become more predictable and schedules become more flexible to allow for more family interaction and a personal life. Many write articles on their own explorations or projects that act as an introduction to the community of geologists. A number of respondents cite the discovery of this community as significant to their satisfaction.

10 YEARS
The majority (more than 60 percent) of 10-year geological survivors are employed by large companies, universities, or the federal government. The remaining 40 percent work as private consultants or for small firms with fewer than six employees. Salaries by this point have increased, but from here on out, geologists can only expect cost-of-living adjustments. Many PhDs who once worked in the private sector have returned to academia, relying on their experience to help them as teachers. Government geologists have settled in administrative positions and deal with people and direct issues of policy and administration rather than individual testing and report writing. People who leave the profession at this point typically do so for health reasons or retirement.

MAJOR EMPLOYERS
EXXONMOBIL EXPLORATION COMPANY
PO Box 4778
Houston, TX 77210-4778
Contact: Geoscience Recruiting Coordinator

KLEINFELDER, INC.
5015 Shoreham Place
San Diego, CA 92122
Tel: 858-320-2000
www.kleinfelder.com
United States Geological Survey
Department of the Interior
www.usgs.gov/ohr

MAJOR ASSOCIATIONS
AMERICAN ASSOCIATION OF PETROLEUM GEOLOGISTS
1444 South Boulder Avenue
Tulsa, OK 74101-0979
Tel: 918-584-2555
Fax: 918-560-2694
www.aapg.org

AMERICAN GEOLOGICAL INSTITUTE
4220 King Street
Alexandria, VA 22302-1502
Tel: 703-379-2480
Fax: 703-379-7563
www.agiweb.org

GEOLOGICAL SOCIETY OF AMERICA
PO Box 9140
Boulder, CO 80301
Tel: 303-447-2020
Fax: 303-357-1070
www.geosociety.org

GEOPHYSICIST

A DAY IN THE LIFE

A successful geophysicist must have a strong science background, a curious mind, and a fascination with natural phenomena. Geophysicists measure, examine, and explore the physical properties of Earth, from below the ground to the atmosphere, from the depths of the ocean to the tops of volcanoes. Their daily duties include studying readouts from measurement equipment, examining natural phenomena (such as tidal waves and electromagnetic fields), and writing reports that combine the two. Geophysics is an academic field that ventures into the practical arena in a number of areas.

Developing a specialty is significant early on in geophysics. For example, the work of a seismologist—studying seismic readings and trying to predict earthquakes—is like { specialization } that of the tectonic physicist, who studies the movement of tectonic plates, but very unlike the work of a volcanologist, who measures temperatures underneath the Earth's surface and examines other readings that might predict the formation or eruption of volcanoes. Some geophysicists study gravity; others study electronic fields. Most of the work of each of the specialties is done primarily in the lab, but there is also some fieldwork. Geophysicists often have to rush to examine an immediate phenomenon, despite the location in which the phenomenon takes place. Unlike geologists, who analyze fairly static systems, geophysicists usually examine systems in flux. Those individuals who succeed in geophysics seem to have the ability to be flexible and the willingness to challenge previously held assumptions if their data prove those assumptions untrue. Successful geophysicists are generally able to encompass the complexities of their profession.

Many geophysicists move through a number of areas of specialization in five-year blocks. Initial specialization is important because it leads to five years of learning that particular aspect of the field. Professionals tend to enjoy learning how geological systems interrelate, and they are interested in examining the systems that interact with the ones they already know. Learning about new specialties often happens gradually. Geophysicists take home the most out-of-work reading of any other profession in this book, with the possible exception of editors. The perpetual education that this occupation encourages seems to be a major reason geophysicists are so satisfied with their work.

PAYING YOUR DUES

Geophysicists study geology and physics; a bachelor's degree is required in the field, although more and more employers are requiring a master's degree, a PhD, and/or three years' experience. Course work should include a basic geological core curriculum—stratigraphy, structural geography, and mineralogy—and a basic physics curriculum—classical physics, quantum mechanics, electromagnetism, and gravity. It should also include logic, mathematics, and ecological science, a recent addition that is becoming increasingly important to employers. Many companies that use geophysicists, such as hydroelectric power plants and research institutions, put new hires through an intense two-day to two-week training course in internal protocols and responsibilities. A mature outlook and sense of professional obligation are helpful in this career. Much of the work that geophysicists do is unsupervised, and the only line of defense against sloppy research is the set of standards for integrity within the geophysics community.

ASSOCIATED CAREERS

Geophysicists leave the profession only when they retire, die, or find a scientific challenge more interesting. This happens about 5 percent of the time. Some of them venture into more obscure branches of physics. The most common reason people leave the profession is that they begin teaching in university settings.

PAST AND FUTURE

Amalgam professions, such as biochemistry and geophysics, are new entrants to the sciences as discrete areas of study. Geophysics grew out of geology and the realizations among geologists that it is different to study a living, moving system than the results of a historical system. It is like comparing the study of history to the study of current events; both studies are valuable, but they require different intellectual processes.

Geophysicists are limited by what they are able to see and examine. New opportunities aren't created, they just happen when the earth shows some activity. The job market should remain stable, with positions opening up and research duties still available.

QUALITY OF LIFE

2 YEARS A geophysicist's first years offer two distinct challenges. First, the transition from the shelter of the academic community to the working world seems to shock geophysicists more than many other professionals. While the sense of encouragement continues in the community of geophysicists, the daily tasks of taking readings, assembling large bodies of data, and finding patterns in that data are more monotonous and less challenging than the work students perform in college. Second, more often than not, the candidate has to relocate for work, often to remote places in which readings can be taken without significant man-made equipment interfering. The hours are reasonable, and pay is low to average.

5 YEARS Most geophysicists reach the limits of their current specialization (not the limits of knowledge in the profession, just their professional limits of their area), and begin to branch out into new areas of study. Many of them begin to write articles and circulate them among colleagues. Those geophysicists who have been successful as field researchers and lab analysts are given supervisory responsibilities over newer entrants to the profession; many of them teach elective courses at local universities. Geophysicists gain some control over the direction of their research, and many of them move into government service. Those individuals who leave the profession do so at critical junctures when they cease to be challenged by their activities for a time.

10 YEARS A large number of geophysicists return to academic circles as they reach the limits of their specialties, both in terms of responsibility and independence. Teaching, particularly at research institutions, allows greater leeway in investigation. Geophysicists can expect only cost-of-living adjustments to their salaries from this point forward.

MAJOR EMPLOYERS

BP AMOCO
200 East Randolph Drive
Chicago, IL 60601-7125
Tel: 312-856-5111
www.amoco.com
Contact: Human Resources

CHEVRONTEXACO CORPORATION
6001 Bollinger Canyon Road
San Ramon, CA 94583
Tel: 925-842-1000
www.chevrontexaco.com

UNITED STATES DEPARTMENT OF ENERGY
1000 Independence Avenue, SW
Washington, DC 20585
Tel: 800-342-5363
www.doe.gov

MAJOR ASSOCIATIONS

AMERICAN ASSOCIATION OF PETROLEUM GEOLOGISTS
1444 South Boulder Avenue
Tulsa, OK 74101-0979
Tel: 918-584-2555
Fax: 918-560-2694
www.aapg.org

GEOLOGICAL SOCIETY OF AMERICA
PO Box 9140
Boulder, CO 80301-9140
Tel: 303-447-2020
Fax: 303-357-1070
www.geosociety.org

HAZARDOUS WASTE MANAGER

A DAY IN THE LIFE

Many people are involved in the management of waste, from the local garbage collector to the analytical chemist, but no aspect of waste management presents challenges as great as those faced by hazardous waste professionals. Management of hazardous waste is perhaps the weakest link in America's dynamic industrial economy because of the dangers posed by toxic chemicals, nuclear by-products, and organic garbage.

A career in hazardous waste disposal and management may lead you to a lab, to a landfill, or to Washington, DC. Several federal agencies deal with hazardous waste, including the Environmental Protection Agency (EPA), the Occupational Health and Safety Administration (OSHA), the Department of Defense, and the Department of Energy. Private industrial enterprises, such as large corporations, employ their own teams of waste specialists or hire consultants to manage their hazardous waste output. A hazardous waste professional may be a geologist, chemist, biologist, environmental scientist, or nuclear physicist. Other hazardous waste professionals are engineers or managers, who work to develop systems that reduce waste in the production process or to protect the environment from dangerous substances that must be disposed of. Many specialists must work together to reduce the burden of hazardous waste.

{ control and clean up }

There are two approaches to hazardous waste management: remedial and removal. Remedial waste management specialists define the waste problem—for instance, a leaky landfill seeping dangerous chemicals into a drinking-water supply—and then explore various possible solutions. They have to consider the impact on the environment, design a solution, and finally implement that solution. Removal specialists control and clean up major hazardous waste accidents, such as oil spills, and ensure that wastes are properly packaged and documented for transport and disposal.

PAYING YOUR DUES

A bachelor's degree is necessary to enter this profession and, in today's competitive job market, a master's degree or even a doctorate is preferred. Highly sought-after hazardous waste professionals usually specialize in one or more sciences. Individuals interested in a career in waste management should major in biology, geology, chemistry, physics, ecology, or any combination of these sciences. If you want to specialize in a particular area, then you might wish to consider soil, air, or water ecology, or natural or environmental science. Since much of your job may require preparing environmental impact statements or proposing waste-management systems, it's a good idea to develop your speaking and writing skills.

Working for the government is rewarding, but it's not always easy. If you choose a job with the EPA or another federal agency, remember that you are joining a large bureaucracy whose commitment to waste management is occasionally diluted by political considerations. Big businesses that hire hazardous waste professionals are committed to keeping the air, earth, and water clean, but they must also keep their eyes on the bottom line. A committed hazardous waste specialist must be patient and resourceful to fulfill this twin agenda. Because of the growing emphasis on environmentalism, effective professionals are, nevertheless, always in demand.

ASSOCIATED CAREERS

If you're interested in this area, but toxic chemicals aren't for you, the natural sciences are still worth exploring. Agriculture, industry, and academia need qualified scientists. The skills that designing a remedial waste management system entails can also be applied to managing other systems and to general business management. These skills can also be applied to developing automated tracking systems, containment systems, monitoring devices for detecting releases, and designing processes that minimize the amount of hazardous waste produced.

PAST AND FUTURE

Improper disposal of hazardous waste has led to some of history's most vicious epidemics. The industrial revolution, symbolized by belching smokestacks, highlighted the problem. Nevertheless, it is only since World War II that the U.S. government has taken significant steps to control environmental hazards. The Superfund legislation of 1980, which earmarked billions of dollars to finance hazardous waste cleanups, set in motion what is now the thriving industry of hazardous waste disposal.

Waste management is a promising field. The negligence of environmental law enforcement of the 1980s has left a legacy of hazardous waste accidents waiting to happen. Changing priorities and mounting health concerns in the 1990s spurred a trend of more vigorous enforcement of environmental regulations, with a new wave of prevention and cleanup efforts. Nuclear waste disposal alone represents a multibillion-dollar industry (with the U.S. government likely to foot the bill for the most expensive projects, including burying waste deep within the earth's crust in what amounts to a monumental public works project). Chemicals, used car tires, medical (biological waste), and a range of other hazards will provide opportunities for hazardous waste management. As the number of available disposal sites shrinks and the challenges and costs of disposal continue to rise, industries and governments will be forced to join forces to help resolve ongoing crises in the years ahead.

QUALITY OF LIFE

2 YEARS Many professionals work part-time while working toward their master's degrees or doctorates in environmental science, and part-time jobs often lead to full-time positions when they graduate. Professionals collect and analyze samples and write summary reports. The hours are average to long; most professionals spend time reading professional journals and traveling for the job.

5 YEARS Professionals start to specialize in remedial or removal management, depending on their temperament, abilities, and available opportunities. Many of them publish articles in professional journals, which enhances their reputations and establishes professional networking contacts. Government employees often shift to the private sector in years four through six, citing better pay, more control over working conditions, and greater responsibilities. The hours remain stable and salary increases.

10 YEARS Hazardous waste removers lead teams and direct tests at this point, rather than spend time in the field or lab conducting them. Many of them are involved in policy discussions and environmental and business issues and engage in debates over technology and management strategies.

MAJOR EMPLOYERS
Hazardous waste managers are employed by universities, local and state governments, research laboratories, hospitals and health centers, and major corporations. Contact organizations in your area for employment opportunities.

MAJOR ASSOCIATIONS
AMERICAN WATER WORKS ASSOCIATION
6666 West Quincy Avenue
Denver, CO 80235
Tel: 303-794-7711
Fax: 303-347-0804
www.awwa.org

INSTITUTE OF HAZARDOUS MATERIALS MANAGEMENT
11900 Parklawn Drive, Suite 450
Rockville, MD 20852
Tel: 301-984-8969
Fax: 301-984-1516
www.ihmm.org

WATER ENVIRONMENT FEDERATION
601 Wythe Street
Alexandria, VA 22314-1994
Tel: 800-666-0206
Fax: 703-684-2492
www.wef.org

INDUSTRIAL ENGINEER

A DAY IN THE LIFE

Industrial engineers analyze and evaluate methods of production and ascertain ways to improve them. They decide how a company should allocate its limited tangible resources (equipment and labor) within the framework of existing physical constraints. Each company that hires an industrial engineer, either as a consultant or as an internal manager, has its own specific limitations. An industrial engineer must quickly become an expert not only in the manufacturing and production processes of the company's industry but also in the specific culture, problems, and challenges that the company faces. This may entail face-to-face meetings with executives, extensive stays on manufacturing floors, and reviews of historical production data.

{ intellectually challenging work }

Industrial engineers receive information from other employers about what occurs during the day-to-day work environment, but they must also make their own observations of these activities. Many employees are uncomfortable being "watched" by industrial engineers, and industrial engineers often walk a thin line between being an analyst and being a detective. An industrial engineer's most difficult task is communicating his or her observations and suggestions to company executives, many of whom are emotionally invested in their traditional way of doing business. Industrial engineers must be tactful in what they say and in how they say it. In addition to possessing tact, being a successful industrial engineer requires charm and the willingness to stand by one's recommendations even in the face of unresponsive management.

The large majority of industrial engineers—around 70 percent—work at manufacturing companies, and many of them have specific areas of specialization, such as assembly, raw-product processing, or administrative (paperwork) practices. Most industrial engineers have good working conditions, intellectually challenging work, and a high level of satisfaction. The hours can be long, but this tends to be outweighed by the satisfaction derived from the learning experiences that each unique project provides.

PAYING YOUR DUES

To become an industrial engineer, you must have a bachelor's degree in industrial engineering. Recommended course work includes statistics, computer skills, ergonomics, management science, quality control, sociology, psychology, organizational behavior, economics, finance, labor relations, and mathematics. People who plan to specialize in manufacturing areas find it useful to study shipping, billing, and automated systems, along with computer science. Graduate programs in industrial engineering are primarily for individuals who wish to enter the realm of academia. Employers consider production or manufacturing experience extremely useful; they also view favorably administrative experience in industries that involve large amounts of paperwork (such as the insurance, health care, or brokerage industries). Many industrial engineers find joining a professional organization helpful (some even join while still in school) because the organization keeps them on top of important topics and trends in industrial engineering.

ASSOCIATED CAREERS

Most industrial engineers are consultants in the manufacturing and administrative industries. The expertise they gain as consultants or internal managers leads many of them to accept management positions in these industries. Since the core of an industrial engineer's job entails properly allocating resources, industrial engineers are valuable to any organization with limited resources and many responsibilities.

PAST AND FUTURE

Industrial engineering began in the late nineteenth century with the development of time-and-motion study, which led to the standardization of steelworkers' motions and production processes and thereby increased their output. The field became known as "productivity management" in the early 1900s, and it flourished in America with Henry Ford's successful implementation of the assembly line. The industrial revolution galvanized support for productivity management, and academic institutions gave it the name "industrial engineering," which is what is studied today.

The future of industrial engineering is linked to the unpredictable future of American manufacturing. Manufacturing is affected by tariffs, employment levels, inflation, advertising, demand, public perception, inventory levels—the list is endless. Technology has improved job efficiency and will continue to do so in the future. Industrial engineers will continue to be in demand, but their numbers are expected to increase only as fast as manufacturing in the United States increases.

QUALITY OF LIFE

2 YEARS Two years into the profession, industrial engineers are most often working at a manufacturing or production company. They are supervised by more senior industrial engineers and have limited effect on implementing change. Daily duties include collecting data, putting it into a usable form, analyzing it, and writing reports. Often these reports are cowritten by a junior industrial engineer and a senior industrial engineer. Many young industrial engineers are asked to take an actual production position for three months to learn firsthand the daily challenges faced in that sector of production. Individuals who have gone directly into freelance consulting have been through training programs and work as part of teams. The hours are long for these consultants, and client contact during these first two years is limited. Computer skills are important for all industrial engineers during these early years.

5 YEARS After five years, industrial engineers have experienced a variety of problems and worked both on teams and by themselves to solve them. Many engineers meet with senior managers to discuss suggestions for improvement and budgetary decisions. About 10 percent of five-year veterans move out of the industrial engineering field and into management positions by this stage. Individuals with people-managing skills may achieve the title "senior industrial engineer" and manage other employees. Engineers in consulting firms lead teams instead of merely working on them. The hours increase; salaries increase as well but more for engineers in consulting than for engineers in manufacturing.

10 YEARS Ten-year veterans of industrial engineering fall into one of three categories: people who work for a single company and have moved into management positions; people who work for consulting firms, are at the senior associate or vice president level, and have extensive client contact and supervisory responsibilities; and people who have worked for a number of firms and continue to enjoy the day-to-day challenge that industrial engineering poses. The hours have decreased for all but the last group; salaries have risen across the board. Satisfaction levels are high for all three groups as well.

MAJOR EMPLOYERS
THE BOEING COMPANY
PO Box 3707, M/S 10-06
Seattle, WA 98124-2207
Tel: 206-655-2121
www.boeing.com

HONDA
R & D Americas, Inc.
21001 State Route 739
Raymond, OH 43067-9705
Tel: 937-644-0439
Fax: 937-645-6337
E-mail: emp@oh.hra.com
www.honda.com

MAJOR ASSOCIATIONS
INSTITUTE OF INDUSTRIAL ENGINEERS
3577 Parkway Lane, Suite 200
Norcross, GA 30092
Tel: 770-449-0460
Fax: 770-441-3295
www.iienet.org

MACHINIST

BOOKS, FILMS, AND TV SHOWS
FEATURING THE PROFESSION
- CNMs
- Junkyard Wars
- Latheworkers: A History
- Monster Garage
- Swing Shift

YOU'LL HAVE CONTACT WITH
- Production managers
- Quality control managers
- Safety inspectors
- Technicians

PROFESSIONALS READ
- American Machinist
- Modern Machine Shop
- Tooling and Production

A DAY IN THE LIFE

Machinists use both manual metalworking equipment—traditional lathes, shapers, grinders, and saws—and their CNC-driven ("computer numeric control") counterparts, to form either unique and carefully shaped individual pieces or multiple pieces of specifically tailored metal. Machinists work for large companies that use metal in their final products. These include heating-vent manufacturers or automobile factories, or they work for specialty shops that take specific orders for needed parts and equipment. Machinists must be able to read blueprints and must be familiar with laser and optical measuring devices that can test the degree of precision of their work. Some specifications call for shaping a piece of metal to within one-thousandth-of-an-inch accuracy. { high-viscosity lubricants }
Machine shops usually employ between four and fifteen machinists, so individuals who work in this part of the industry should be comfortable working in close quarters with one another. Machinists often know more about the metals they work with than do the clients who order pieces made from these metals. The machinist can and does act as an advisor, should the client make false or misleading assumptions about the materials being used or the finished product.

Successful machinists have good vision, endurance, an eye for detail, excellent hand-eye coordination, a love for quality and precision, and respect for the tools of their trade. Working with metals can be dangerous for someone who is careless or easily distracted. Indeed, the biggest concern with being a machinist is the daily threat of serious injury. Few professions place employees in such regular contact with high-powered and potentially destructive tools. Surprisingly, however, the average injury rate in this profession is only slightly above the national average. Machinists must wear protective safety goggles and earplugs, and they must carefully decontaminate themselves after working with high-viscosity lubricants, as many of these lubricants are quite toxic. These worries, however, only slightly diminish the satisfaction machinists derive from shaping something out of nothing in an expert and craftsman-like way every day.

PAYING YOUR DUES

There are no specific educational requirements to become a machinist, but many employers prefer to hire individuals with a high school diploma (or its equivalent) and some work experience (which demonstrates responsibility). Course work that employers value includes that in mathematics, machine shop, and computer science. Employers also view blueprint-reading skills favorably. The large majority of entrants to the profession are funneled through apprenticeship programs sponsored by unions in a specific area of machinist work, such as automotive machinery or agricultural machinery. These apprenticeships require hard work, with many machinists taking more than four years to complete them. Programs generally combine shop work (6,000-plus hours) with classwork (700-plus hours) and place an emphasis on practical results. Individuals who successfully complete these programs are eligible for union machinist positions. To enter an apprenticeship program, many unions require that candidates be sponsored by a union member. Contact the appropriate union in your field of interest for more information.

ASSOCIATED CAREERS

Most individuals who choose a career as a machinist remain machinists, as few careers combine the precise detail work with the strenuous physical activity in the way and to the degree that this one does. Other professions with similar characteristics to which machinists may migrate include carpentry, construction, and automobile manufacturing. Some machinists who have progressed to managerial status transfer to other personnel-management occupations, but this is more the exception than the rule.

PAST AND FUTURE

All complicated construction, engineering, and mass-production projects have employed skilled machinists. Robert Fulton's steamboats and Henry Ford's assembly line of automobiles would have been impossible without the help of skilled machinists. It is not an exaggeration to say that machinists were central to the industrial revolution. The foundations of the aerospace and aircraft industries depend upon the precision shaping of metals. One individual who influenced the development of machinists' tools is Henry Maudslay, who developed the lathe.

The future of machinists has both positive and negative aspects. On the one hand, more machinists are expected to be hired over the coming decade, as aircraft manufacturing orders are at an all-time high, automobile plants are operating at significant levels, and housing developments are increasing. On the other hand, traditionally metal-based equipment is also being replaced by parts made from plastics and fiberglass. Precision machining of metal may gradually become precision pressing of plastics in some fields and, unfortunately, these two careers are quite different.

QUALITY OF LIFE

2 YEARS After two years, many machinists are still in apprenticeship programs, working as machine operators and handling tasks that require little expertise. The hours are long, and pay is low because beginning machinists spend a good deal of time in unpaid classroom settings or in partially salaried on-the-job training positions. Satisfaction level is average. However, many machinists surveyed said the training programs teach new machinists a respect for their machines that contributes significantly to their Quality of Life as a machinist.

5 YEARS Five years into the profession, machinists are fully certified and are working in an area of specialization. Many of them are involved in their unions as professionals, having had extensive exposure to the unions while they were trainees. Machinists with ambition and interpersonal skills work additional shifts and begin to gain experience managing other employees. The shift to managerial work can be difficult for many machinists, since being a machinist and being a machinist manager require very different skills. Salaries increase. Additional hours are available for those who want them. Satisfaction is high.

10 YEARS About 80 percent of those who are machinists for ten years are likely to remain machinists for life. Many of them become managers or shop heads at this time, and an aggressive few begin their own machinist company—although high startup costs make this endeavor difficult. For most machinists, salaries increase, and the hours stabilize.

MAJOR ASSOCIATIONS
AMERICAN WELDING SOCIETY
550 NW LeJeune Road
Miami, FL 33126
Tel: 305-443-9353
Fax: 305-443-7559
www.aws.org

THE ASSOCIATION FOR MANUFACTURING TECHNOLOGY
7901 Westpark Drive
McLean, VA 22102
Tel: 703-893-2900
Fax: 703-827-1151
www.mfgtech.org

THE TOOLING AND MANUFACTURING ASSOCIATION
1177 South Dee Road
Park Ridge, IL 60068
Tel: 847-825-1120
Fax: 847-825-0041
www.tmanet.com

MANUFACTURING EXECUTIVE

BOOKS, FILMS, AND TV SHOWS
FEATURING THE PROFESSION
- **Atlas Shrugged**
- **Gung Ho**
- **Line Production**
- **Overtime**

YOU'LL HAVE CONTACT WITH
- **Inventory managers**
- **Production managers**
- **Quality control managers**
- **Service sales representatives**

PROFESSIONALS READ
- **Appliance Manufacturer**
- **Food Manufacturer**
- **Professional Manufacturing**
- **Shopfloor**

A DAY IN THE LIFE

Manufacturing executives come in two varieties: production line executives and wholesale sales representatives. Production line executives coordinate production on the factory floor. They supervise production employees, check inventory levels, ensure that sales representatives' orders are being filled, and oversee equipment maintenance and employee needs. They are based in manufacturing plants; work closely with employees; and have predictable hours. Wholesale sales representatives, who comprise more than 70 percent of manufacturing executives, are, first and foremost, salespeople. They spend most of their time on the road, meeting with clients, recruiting new business, and checking shipments and inventory levels. { time spent on the road } Wholesale sales representatives liaise with professional buyers, wholesale purchasing agents, and retail store representatives to make certain that goods get from the factory to the consumer.

Wholesale sales representatives are usually assigned a territory (which can range from a section of a large city to a number of states) and are given responsibility for maintaining and improving wholesale sales in that region. To be able to negotiate with clients, existing and prospective, and keep the sales commitments they make, wholesale sales representatives must have up-to-date information from their product line executive counterparts at the manufacturing facility. This information includes manufacturing costs, delivery costs, speed of production, inventory levels, and product line options. "You've got to have credibility in your region," one wholesale sales representative mentioned, "because all the buyers talk to each other, and if you don't follow through on what you tell them, you're finished. No one will buy from you again." This theme of "credibility" was echoed by a number of our survey respondents.

Wholesale sales representatives work long hours, but their salaries are higher than those of production line executives. Wholesale sales representatives also have more control over their schedules. They have to meet with their clients regularly, but they can determine when and in what order. For many sales representatives, the least attractive part of their job is the time spent on the road. Wholesale sales representatives lead a hard and varied life, but individuals who are successful salespeople reap large rewards.

PAYING YOUR DUES

It used to be that anyone with initiative, sales skills, and negotiating savvy could find a job as a manufacturing representative. More frequently, though, employers are requiring that new hires have college degrees. Marketing, business, psychology, or advertising majors have advantages in the applicant pool. Manufacturing executives also generate sales reports, analyze figures, and file expense reports, so any work experience that demonstrates comfort with numbers is welcomed. At larger companies, all new hires complete training programs in which they learn about the companies' product lines and manufacturing processes, their competitors' products, and general sales techniques. A wholesale sales representative may spend his or her first six months working as part of a team with a more experienced sales representative, particularly if the company manufactures a product with technical elements.

ASSOCIATED CAREERS

Former wholesale sales representatives hold most of the upper-level management positions at manufacturing companies. A significant number of wholesale sales representatives become professional buyers for retail and wholesale companies, using their product and manufacturing expertise to drive good bargains. A few enter marketing or advertising or do demographic studies in their industry. More than 20 percent of all wholesale sales representatives take up graduate studies; only 10 percent of this group return as manufacturing executives.

PAST AND FUTURE

Manufacturing executives used to be the owners of their companies—the ones who knew the production processes best, who handled all negotiations, and who knew their reputations were on the line with every item that came out of their factories. In the 1860s, the rapid growth of manufacturing in the United States made this owner-intensive approach unworkable and forced owners to delegate these responsibilities to trusted managers or "owner representatives." As internal competition intensified in these industries, formal training programs developed that led to the separation of manufacturing representatives' duties into those of the product line executive and those of the wholesale sales representative.

Product line executives can expect job prospects to hold steady, because it is impossible to replace the human element in production supervision. Wholesale sales representatives, however, will encounter pressure from two sides. General manufacturing downsizing in the United States, combined with the decline of small retail firms and the rise of larger bulk-sales and direct-sales houses, will decrease the need for wholesale sales representatives. In addition, the development of standardized-interface merchandise ordering systems, known as electronic data interchange (EDI) systems, is rendering some of the wholesale sales representative's functions obsolete. Some clients may view, price, and order merchandise or samples on demand.

QUALITY OF LIFE

2 YEARS Two years into the profession, manufacturing executives have become either production line executives on the manufacturing floor or wholesale sales representatives out in the field, trying to build a client base. Many wholesale sales representatives work 45 or more hours a week as they establish relationships with the clients who were assigned to them and find new clients all on their own. Satisfaction is average; salaries are low to average, depending on commissions.

5 YEARS Wholesale sales representatives have gone through whole product and business cycles and have at times had to work very hard to maintain their Quality of Life. Salaries have increased, but many individuals have exhausted the opportunities within their assigned region. Successful wholesale sales representatives have moved to more promising territories; others with managerial skills have been assigned to oversee large territories with a number of sales managers. The hours become fewer and more predictable and satisfaction rises.

10 YEARS Ten-year veterans begin to make decisions about their future direction. Those veterans who are excellent salespeople with good contacts often choose to remain salespeople, finally earning a sizable income from their hard work. Those individuals who are tired of the long hours on the road, the frequent complaints from clients, and the posturing of negotiations attempt to secure supervisory, managerial, or consultant positions in the industry. Salaries and satisfaction are above average.

MAJOR EMPLOYERS
BURLINGTON INDUSTRIES, INC.
3330 West Friendly Avenue
Greensboro, NC 27410
Tel: 336-379-2000
Fax: 336-379-3329
www.burlington.com

FORD MOTOR COMPANY
5111 Auto Club Drive
Dearborn, MI 48126
Tel: 313-322-0155
www.ford.com

REVLON
625 Madison Avenue
New York, NY 10022
Tel: 212-527-4000
Fax: 212-527-5588
E-mail: jobs.mail@revlon.com
www.revlon.com

MAJOR ASSOCIATIONS
NATIONAL ASSOCIATION OF MANUFACTURERS
1331 Pennsylvania Avenue, NW
Washington, DC 20004-1790
Tel: 202-637-3000
Fax: 202-637-3182
www.nam.org

THE ASSOCIATION FOR MANUFACTURING TECHNOLOGY
7901 Westpark Drive
McLean, VA 22102
Tel: 703-893-2900
Fax: 703-893-1151
www.mfgtech.org

MARINE CORPS—ENLISTEE, OFFICER

BOOKS, FILMS AND TV SHOWS FEATURING THE PROFESSION:

- A Few Good Men
- Full Metal Jacket
- Jarhead
- Rules of Engagement
- Sands of Iwo Jima

YOU'LL HAVE CONTACT WITH

- Engineers
- Firefighters
- Law enforcement officials
- Technical specialists
- Translators

PROFESSIONALS READ

- Global Defense Review
- Guns and Ammo
- Marine Corps Strategy
- Marines Magazine
- National Defense
- Popular Mechanics
- Stars and Stripes
- U.N. & Conflict Monitor

A DAY IN THE LIFE

The Marine Corps, despite being the second-smallest branch of the armed forces, is arguably the fiercest, the proudest, and the most motivated. You might be familiar with the slogan, "The Few, The Proud, The Marines." Marines possess a gung-ho attitude and a healthy respect for the chain of command and the Corps in general. As a rapid-response force, the Marines are able to deploy troops anywhere in the world on short notice. They are utilized for short-term strikes; whereas longer missions go to the larger, slower-moving Army. The Corps specializes in amphibious tactics and also maintains air capabilities. Marine tactics and doctrine emphasize aggressiveness and taking the offensive. The Marines maintain an operational and training culture that focuses on the infantry combat abilities of all enlisted persons. First and foremost, all marines receive training as basic riflemen and -women.

{ "Born to defend, built to conquer." }

You need not worry if driving an amphibious assault vehicle into battle isn't what you want to do on a daily basis. There are a number of noncombative roles within the Corps. As a self-sufficient organization, the Marine Corps is outfitted with its own engineers, computer programmers, lawyers, meteorologists, police officers, news reporters, and accountants. There is a focus on technical skills, and Marines work on everything from Web design to aircraft maintenance. The Marines can prepare a potential officer to serve in any one of 34 occupational fields, including Maintenance Management (the organization of military gear for field use and storage), Field Artillery Radar Fire (identification of targets), Data Systems (computer programming), and Avionics (a wide range of aircraft-care jobs). Marines acquire the proper training in the Corps and, importantly, gain skill sets that ultimately prove transferable to jobs in the civilian workforce. This is the only branch of the armed forces that utilizes the technology of all the others. Marines may even become pilots, for example. In fact, the only career options that are closed to Marines are positions within the medical and religious fields, as the services that these fields encompass are provided by the Navy.

PAYING YOUR DUES

Enlistees must sign a legal agreement known as an enlistment contract. This contract stipulates a commitment to eight years of service. Typically, two to six years are spent on active duty, with the remainder served in the reserves. The Marines require enlistees to be between the ages of 17 and 29. Recruits must also be U.S. citizens or aliens with permanent resident status. Anyone with a felony record is automatically prohibited from joining. Applicants need to pass a written examination known as the Armed Services Vocational Aptitude Battery (ASVAB) and meet minimum physical standards. Lastly, all divisions of the armed forces require a high school diploma or its equivalent for certain enlistment options.

The path to becoming an officer is somewhat different. Commissioned officers need to have earned a four-year college degree and attended Officer Candidate School (OCS). Upon completion of OCS, Marines earn the rank of Second Lieutenant. After both Officer Candidate School and commissioning, Marines attend The Basic School (TBS) for six months. Here, they learn the fundamental skills required of an officer and study such topics as land navigation, weapons, small-unit tactics, and communications. Interested candidates currently immersed in undergraduate studies can choose to enroll in Naval ROTC. The program pays for students' college tuition and grooms them for military commission as they earn their degrees. Qualified applicants must pass a physical exam, meet certain academic criteria, and be legally allowed to bear arms in the United States. Upon graduating from NROTC, students enter the Corps as Second Lieutenants. They are committed to eight years of service with the Marines, with at least four of those years served on active duty.

ASSOCIATED CAREERS

There is no typical career path for a former marine. They can be found in the classroom, in law firms, and on Wall Street. Employers in any industry respect their work ethic, their determination, and their ability to rise to a challenge. And given the broad range of training options available to Marines, they are likely to be able to transition to civilian life virtually seamlessly.

PAST AND FUTURE

The Marine Corps was founded on November 10, 1775, when the Continental Congress ordered two battalions to be created during the Revolutionary War. It was decided that this special force should be well-versed in maritime operations so that they would be able to serve aboard naval vessels. John Hancock, president of the Congress, appointed Captain Samuel Nicholas the first commandant of the Corps. Nicholas set up headquarters in Philadelphia at Tun Tavern and immediately began recruiting.

The Marine Corps is the only arm of the military to be expedition-centered. The Corps operates in a state of "forward deployment" at all times. Marines are, therefore, stationed across the globe, ready to act when the need arises.

QUALITY OF LIFE

2 YEARS Those Marines who enlist directly after high school will be serving as a specialist within any one of the 34 occupations available. Officers will have acquired a position with responsibility that includes leading and training soldiers. All Marines, regardless of status, face the possibility of being stationed anywhere in the world.

5 YEARS After five years, enlisted Marines are either finished or nearly finished with their term of active duty. Most likely, they have earned a promotion to a position with increased responsibility. At this juncture, Marines usually assess whether or not they want to remain with the Corps after their active duty term is complete. For those who decide to pursue options outside of the military, the Marines maintain several schools that train enlistees for a variety of civilian jobs. At the five-year mark, commissioned officers are likely to achieve the rank of First Lieutenant or above. Officers who thrive typically possess intelligence, strong interpersonal skills, and outstanding leadership capabilities.

10 YEARS At the 10-year point, enlistees have completed their contractual obligation, and many decide to move on. Those who become career Marines continue putting in their time. They will probably receive additional promotions until they qualify for retirement. Officers who have been with the Corps for 10 years have clearly demonstrated remarkable aptitude for leadership. By this point in their military careers, they've managed to work their way through the ranks, and their pay has increased significantly. Many officers retire at this point, and a fair number consider running for political office.

MAJOR EMPLOYERS
UNITED STATES MARINE CORPS
3250 Catlin Avenue
Quantico, VA 22134-5001
Tel: 703-784-2741
Fax: 703-784-0065
www.marines.com or www.usmc.mil

MAJOR ASSOCIATIONS
MARINE CORPS ASSOCIATION
715 Broadway Street
Quantico, VA 22134
Tel: 800-336-0291 or 703-640-6161
Fax: 703-640-0823
E-mail: mca@mca-marines.org
www.mca-marines.org

MARINE CORPS HERITAGE FOUNDATION
PO Box 998
Quantico, VA 22134-0998
Tel: 800-397-7585 or 703-640-7965
Fax: 703-640-9546
E-mail: info@marineheritage.org
www.marineheritage.org

NATIONAL ASSOCIATION FOR UNIFORMED SERVICES
5535 Hempstead Way
Springfield, VA 22151
Tel: 703-750-1342
www.naus.org

VETERANS OF FOREIGN WARS
406 West 34th Street
Kansas City, Missouri 64111
Tel: 816-756-3390
Fax: 816-968-1149
E-mail: info@vfw.org
www.vfw.org

MATHEMATICIAN

BOOKS, FILMS, AND TV SHOWS
FEATURING THE PROFESSION

- π
- A Beautiful Mind
- Good Will Hunting
- Jurassic Park
- Mr. Pi
- Ratner's Star

YOU'LL HAVE CONTACT WITH

- Actuaries
- Computer programmers
- Electrical engineers
- Statisticians

PROFESSIONALS READ

- American Journal of Mathematics
- American Mathematical Monthly
- Notices of the American Mathematical Society

A DAY IN THE LIFE

Mathematicians generally work in theoretical or applied mathematics, and their daily routine is determined by which of these specialties they've chosen. Theoretical mathematicians work with mathematical theory in research and academic settings, rarely with a practical application in mind. Applied mathematicians, not suprisingly, principles to practical problems, such as cryptography, economic analysis, and data-interference patterns. Both theoretical and applied mathematics are important in the real world; advances in both disciplines have led to breakthroughs.

Theoretical mathematicians are generally mathematics professors or graduate students, with stipends or grants to work on specific mathematical problems. The majority of { breakthroughs } them use computers in their analysis and work alone a large part of the time. "You don't really notice that you're alone," one respondent wrote about the solitude this profession maintains, "because you're focusing on the problem." Professional communication takes up the other large block of time in the theoretical mathematician's life; some theoretical mathematicians estimate that they spend more than 30 percent of their time reading professional journals, talking on the telephone with other mathematicians, and attending conferences on related topics. The applied mathematician works in a business setting and usually on a specific task. He or she is paid to use mathematical concepts to analyze behavior and improve existing systems. This can involve a lot of guesswork: "About 99 percent of the time you're wrong," one mathematician said, "so you try again. Every now and then you get something right." Individuals with low tolerance levels for failure should think long and hard before entering this end of the profession. Many applied mathematicians noted interpersonal skills are quite important in mathematics positions, and many of them wished they had taken more writing courses in college, as their jobs require regular reports on progress and development.

Mathematicians said the best feature of their profession is the intellectual challenge of struggling with these problems on a daily basis. No mathematician thought he could ever find all the solutions—most of our respondents would agree with the theoretical mathematician who wrote, "You can struggle with an equation for ages, trying to get it to tell you something, but if it doesn't want to, there's nothing you can do."

PAYING YOUR DUES

There are strict academic requirements for mathematicians. More than 180 schools offer PhD programs in mathematics. About 97 percent of theoretical mathematicians have a PhD. For entry-level positions in applied mathematics, most employers accept candidates with only a bachelor's degree in mathematics, but many employers ask that those candidates have cross-disciplinary experience, such as math/computer science or math/economics. These new hires input data, write simple analysis programs, and do basic mathematical modeling. To progress to a level of significant responsibility or leadership, many mathematicians find it helpful to earn an advanced degree not in mathematics, but in a related discipline, such as computer science, statistics, or materials engineering. A curious mind, sound deductive reasoning skills, and a willingness to approach difficult (and sometimes unsolvable) problems are all characteristics of the successful mathematician.

ASSOCIATED CAREERS

A number of areas are open to mathematicians who leave their profession. Computer programming, cryptology, teaching, financial analysis, business management, and economics provide sound homes for individuals with mathematical training. In the course of their work, many mathematicians come into contact with these professions and find one of them more appealing.

PAST AND FUTURE

The ancient Greeks, Romans, Arabs, and Egyptians made significant contributions to our knowledge of mathematics, including such discoveries as the decimal point, pi, and even the placeholder zero. Europeans made advances throughout the Renaissance, and the field truly began to blossom after the scientific revolution of the 1600s, which gave us Isaac Newton's invention of calculus and Rene Descartes's concept of analytical geometry. The use of computer programs has reduced the time it takes to do extremely complicated calculations.

The number of jobs in the profession is fairly evenly divided between theoretical and applied mathematics. The job market is, however, expected to be sluggish, at best, for both groups. Industry professionals are being selected for both their knowledge of mathematical theory and their proficiency in related areas. Mathematicians who are well versed in another area, such as computer science, environmental issues, medical technology, or aircraft design are likely to fare better than are other mathematicians. Positions for academic mathematicians are expected to increase more slowly than other jobs. Reductions in government spending and fierce competition for teaching positions are among the challenges that aspiring mathematicians face.

QUALITY OF LIFE

2 YEARS Theoretical mathematicians are still completing master's work, earning their doctorate in an academic setting; while applied mathematicians are doing semi-skilled work in the business world. Flexible academic deadlines give way to the pressure to solve practical business problems. Many new professionals spend long nights at the computer, trying to make the transition from school to work. Job mobility is high in these early years (nearly 20 percent leave the profession), as mathematicians look for an environment for which they are a good fit.

5 YEARS Mathematicians in academia have typically had a year or two of post-doctoral appointments and are working toward tenure. Applied mathematicians are heads or coheads of projects with significant responsibility for them. Many mathematicians have added managerial duties to their job and are mentors to new hires. Most of them welcome this new aspect of the job. Interpersonal skills become significant, with the ability to rise beyond this point determined not by intelligence but by effectiveness and leadership abilities.

10 YEARS Many 10-year veterans become experts in a chosen area of specialization. This sudden directional burst seems to be a result of diminishing career pressure as many mathematicians are in satisfying positions, and many mathematicians desire to continue their education. A number of mathematicians become involved in professional organizations and communities of mathematicians with similar interests. Individuals who have chosen the research path are now in their prime as they find their professional recognition expanding.

MAJOR EMPLOYERS
NATIONAL SECURITY AGENCY
9800 Savage Road, Suite 6779
Fort Meade, MD 20755-6779
Tel: 301-688-6311
E-mail: njobs@fggm.osis.gov
www.nsa.gov

NEW YORK STOCK EXCHANGE
11 Wall Street, 16th Floor
New York, NY 10005
Tel: 212-656-2050
Contact: Human Resources

WOLFRAM RESEARCH, INC.
100 Trade Center Drive
Champaign, IL 61820-7237
Tel: 217-398-0700
Fax: 217-398-0747
E-mail: resumes@wolfram.com
www.wolfram.com
Contact: Human Resources

MAJOR ASSOCIATIONS
AMERICAN MATHEMATICAL SOCIETY
201 Charles Street
Providence, RI 02904
Tel: 800-321-4267 or 401-455-4000
Fax: 401-331-3842
E-mail: ams@ams.org
www.ams.org

MATHEMATICAL ASSOCIATION OF AMERICA
1529 18th Street, NW
Washington, DC 20036
Tel: 800-741-9415
Fax: 202-265-2384
www.maa.org

MEDIA PLANNER

A DAY IN THE LIFE

Ever wonder why you don't see commercials for Depends during Disney's *One Saturday Morning* or commercials for tattoo parlors during *7th Heaven*? It has to do with demographics. You've got a lot of little kids watching television on Saturday morning. The commercials they'll see are filled with cool toys and sugar-coated chocolate cereals. *7th Heaven* has a more conservative audience that probably wouldn't be looking to get into body art or piercing. Businesses want to place their products and services in front of audiences they know are watching, listening, or even driving by on the road. How do they know? They turn to media planners. Media planners work in the media departments of advertising agencies. They are responsible for putting ads in the right place at the right time,

{ people's viewing and reading habits }

and for reaching the desired audience for the least amount of money. Media planners gather information on people's viewing and reading habits. They evaluate editorial content and programming to determine the potential use of media, such as newspapers, magazines, radio, television, billboards and electric displays, or the Internet, and areas such as buses, subways, taxis, airports, or bus terminals. Media planners have to know demographics and statistics and use extensive formulas to chart out the best way a business can spend its money to get its product in front of the public. Media planners also have to be proficient in math. They then turn their information over to media buyers, who track the media space and times available for purchase, negotiate and purchase time and space for ads, and make sure ads appear exactly as scheduled. Media planners work in the big cities: New York, Chicago, and Los Angeles. Other top cities in which they work include San Francisco, Minneapolis, and Dallas. They may work in small advertising firms that employ fewer than 10 people or in big firms that employee dozens. Other media planners may work in-house, that is, for a company that produces its own product and advertisements. No matter where they work, media planners can expect to put in a good 50 or more hours per week, as they strive to put together proposals for clients in very short periods of time. Advertising is a highly stressful business, but the monetary reward of seeing your work pay off for the client can be well worth it.

PAYING YOUR DUES

Most entry-level professional and managerial positions in the advertising industry require a bachelor's degree, preferably with broad liberal arts exposure. Assistant media planner or assistant media buyer are also good entry-level positions; these jobs require a bachelor's degree. Beginners in the advertising world usually enter the industry in the account management or media department. Most media planners don't stay in their positions for the duration of their careers, so training in marketing, psychology, accounting, and creative design allow media planners to move to other positions within an agency. Media planners possess good people skills, common sense, creativity, communication skills, and problem-solving abilities. There is also a need for additional training for individuals already employed. Knowing the newest technology and using it to your customer's advantage are fundamental to success. Media planners must also stay in tune with the culture as it ages and changes. Success in small projects will lead to bigger ones, and success in these endeavors can lead to supervisory positions.

ASSOCIATED CAREERS

Other careers that employ comparable skills to those of media planners are media buyers, advertising executives, and even statisticians. Media planners often move into the marketing part of advertising, working as copywriters and editors. Some of them with Internet experience move into Web design and marketing.

PAST AND FUTURE

Media planner positions are expected to grow faster than average over the next decade. With a greater number of media becoming available, the savvy media planner needs to know how to distinguish which are the best formats for his or her client. The Internet is a medium that's full of advertising opportunities. A media planner will be more marketable if he or she is skilled in deciphering the demographics of surfers on any given site.

With the advent of Tivo and DVR, media planners may find it harder to place advertisements in the most popular medium. Media planners may also find a shortage of jobs if government legislation restricts the advertising of specific products such as alcoholic beverages or on specific media such as billboards.

QUALITY OF LIFE

2 YEARS Most media planners start out as a junior media planner or media planner assistant. They assist on large projects or take on smaller tasks under the supervision of a senior-level planner. A lot of hard work and long hours can be expected for the first two years, as young media planners find themselves responsible for doing most of the legwork, especially if employed by a smaller firm.

5 YEARS Media planners with five years of experience take on bigger projects, and usually oversee one or more assistant planners. To make themselves more marketable, some media planners also assume the added responsibility of becoming media buyers. The ability to plan and buy media time and space from outlets such as television, radio, and the Internet makes the media planner/buyer more effective.

10 YEARS Senior media planners constantly reach for strategic marketing solutions beyond the traditional ones. With 10 years' experience, a senior media planner may be called upon to take on larger projects with prestigious national clients. Some media planners with this level of experience move to other positions in the advertising agency, while still others may start their own small firms.

MAJOR EMPLOYERS

THE CREATIVE GROUP
Robert Half International Inc.
2884 Sand Hill Road
Menlo Park, CA 94025
Tel: 650-234-6000
www.creativegroup.com

J. WALTER THOMPSON U.S.A., INC.
466 Lexington Avenue
New York, NY 10017-314
Tel: 212-210-7000
www.jwt.com

HAWORTH MARKETING & MEDIA COMPANY
121 South 8th Street, 10th Floor
TCF Tower
Minneapolis, MN 55402
Tel: 612-677-8900
Fax: 612-677-8901
www.haworthmedia.com

MAJOR ASSOCIATIONS

AMERICAN ADVERTISING FEDERATION
1101 Vermont Avenue, NW, Suite 500
Washington, DC 20005-6306
Tel: 202-898-0089
Fax: 202-898-0159
E-mail: aaf@aaf.org
www.aaf.org

AMERICAN ASSOCIATION OF ADVERTISING AGENCIES
405 Lexington Avenue, 18th Floor
New York, NY 10174
Tel: 212-682-2500
Fax: 212-682-8391
www.aaaa.org

NAVY—ENLISTEE, OFFICER

A DAY IN THE LIFE

Of all the branches of the armed forces, The Village People singled out the Navy as important enough to have their own song. What better endorsement could you ask for? The Navy is often viewed as the military branch most flavored with adventure. Who wouldn't want to travel around the world on an enormous ship; visit exotic locales such as Hawaii, Australia, and Japan; and get to wear those super-cool bellbottom sailor pants? So sign up, and get ready to sail the seven seas in the Navy. With more than 1,000 careers available to sailors and officers, the Navy offers a wide variety of options for the prospective recruit. Like all branches of the armed forces, members of the Navy are divided into two distinct categories: enlistees and officers. { shore and sea tours } Enlistees comprise the majority of individuals in the Navy. They serve as cooks, engineers, members of the clergy, medical doctors, SEALs, and even musicians. Enlistees need only a high school diploma or its equivalent. Officers are required to have completed a four-year BS or BA degree from an accredited university as well as Officer Candidate School (OCS). Some opt to participate in the Naval Reserve Officers Training Corps (NROTC) Scholarship Program during college—those who do receive impressive amounts of tuition assistance.

Usually alternating between shore and sea tours, officers serve for a minimum of four years. An officer is responsible for overseeing a ship and ensuring the well-being of his or her crew.

Life in the Navy is as diverse as the jobs available. Members of the Navy work on ships, submarines, and airplanes. Those on a shore-duty tour or working at a naval base spend no time at sea for a two- to three-year period, whereas those working on a ship get to see a lot of the water. A navy workday varies depending on the tour. Those working an on-land tour will have workdays comparable to those of civilian jobs, while those at sea often work longer days to operate and maintain the ship. How much one travels also varies greatly and depends on the person, the tour of duty, and how long he or she remains in the service.

PAYING YOUR DUES

To become one of the 373,612 members of Navy personnel on active duty, you must be a high school graduate, a U.S. citizen or resident alien, and pass the ASVAB (Armed Service Vocational Aptitude Battery), a test designed to determine your skills and placement. The Navy has three different sets of training: Primary (this focuses on fitness and is similar to boot camp or Basic), Intermediate (this trains personnel in the necessary skills aboard a ship), and Advanced (this provides more in-depth instruction than Intermediate).

To become an officer in the Navy compels you to test your physical strength, leadership abilities, and technological prowess. You can apply to enlist as an officer as early as your sophomore year in college. The NROTC (Naval Reserve Officers Training Corps) allows college students to become officers while attending school full-time. There is also the Naval Academy, which accepts potential officers right out of high school. Anyone who has already completed a four-year BS or BA degree and has a demonstrated history of leadership may be chosen for Officer Candidate School (OCS), a demanding 13-week program that prepares you for a career as an officer in the Navy.

|ASSOCIATED CAREERS

Naval personnel spend time working with pilots, electricians, engineers, fellow officers, doctors, and administrators. Joining the armed forces is like joining an enormous corporation, and all sections work in cooperation with one another. Enlistees gain valuable technical training and know-how, which often proves useful for entrance into the civilian workforce after the completion of their tours of duty. They may also choose to pursue further educational studies—which the Navy not only recommends but also subsidizes. Officers gain real-world leadership experience in the Navy and, if they decide to enter the civilian workforce, compete successfully for jobs in a variety of areas including management, finance, education, and government service, among others.

|PAST AND FUTURE

The United States Navy was created by an act of Congress on April 30, 1798 to fight the—you guessed it—Barbary pirates! Several battles between 1801 and 1805 involving fancy swords, cannons, and some well-choreographed song and dance numbers (well, maybe not that last one!) ended in victory for the United States, with the Barbary rulers agreeing to cease their attacks. Since that time, the Navy has played a pivotal role in every U.S. military conflict. One of most notable Americans ever to serve in the Navy was President John F. Kennedy, who won the Navy and Marine Corps Medal as well as the Purple Heart Medal for his service.

Opportunities for qualified individuals are promising through 2012. The number of active-duty personnel may even increase over time as the country struggles to maintain a sufficient force to fight major regional conflicts while maintaining sufficient resources to protect security on American shores. One continuing trend in military recruitment will be rising educational requirements in response to the increasing complexity of military jobs.

|QUALITY OF LIFE

2 YEARS As an enlistee, you have completed your primary training, job training, and have been assigned to your first duty assignment. As an officer, you will by this point be eligible for promotion to Lieutenant Junior Grade.

5 YEARS An enlistee has completed his or her first enlistment and has a few options available. He or she can stay in the Navy and sign up for another tour of duty, join the civilian workforce, or take advantage of a Navy Scholarship and go to college. An officer is eligible for promotion to the rank of Lieutenant after serving four years in the Navy, if he or she opts to stay.

10 YEARS You are making a career out of the Navy if you're in it for this long. Enlistees may have picked up more training by this point and broadened their horizons. Officers by this time are eligible for promotion to Lieutenant Commander. The possibilities really are limitless and vary from career to career.

MAJOR EMPLOYERS

U.S. NAVY
Chief of Information
1200 Navy Pentagon, Room 4B463
Washington, D.C. 20350-1200
www.navy.mil

MAJOR ASSOCIATIONS

FLEET RESERVE ASSOCIATION
125 N West Street
Alexandria, VA 22314
Tel: 703-683-1400
www.fra.org

NATIONAL ASSOCIATION FOR UNIFORMED SERVICES
5535 Hempstead Way
Springfield, VA 22151
Tel: 703-750-1342
www.naus.org

U.S. NAVAL ACADEMY ALUMNI ASSOCIATION AND FOUNDATION
247 King George Street
Annapolis, MD 21402
Tel: 410-295-4000
http://usna.com

VETERANS OF FOREIGN WARS
406 West 34th Street
Kansas City, Missouri 64111
Tel: 816-756-3390
Fax: 816-968-1149
E-mail: info@vfw.org
www.vfw.org

NETWORK ENGINEER

A DAY IN THE LIFE

A network engineer handles all of the "plumbing" for a company's computers: connecting offices with T1 lines, hooking the company up to the Internet, and configuring all internal systems, such as net routers and firewalls. The position usually spills over into some Unix systems administration work, but "basically, it's a plumbing job," one network engineer writes. Configuring a startup Web company is a pretty easy network design job; most of these companies have a small staff and only one location. On the other hand, if you work for a large corporation, you may find yourself dealing with an incredibly complicated network that requires tiers upon tiers of network engineers. If you're willing to wear a suit and tie every day, then you may opt to work for a bank, where you'll earn twice as much as anywhere else.

> { think your way through problems }

A network engineer needs to know how to use basic network devices like "packet sniffers," but the work itself doesn't utilize a lot of tools. "It's a 'noodly' job; you have to be able to think your way through problems and understand how stuff works," one professional says. You don't spend a lot of time typing but rather in front of white boards drawing pictures to visualize your solutions. A typical day demands atypical hours; network engineers usually work off-hours when they're tinkering with something. It's the earmark of techies to show up later, often around 10:00 or 11:00 A.M., but they're usually at work until 7:00, 8:00, or 9:00 P.M. and often stay on call 24/7. Networking has a culture unto itself. "Anyone in the general public would not be like, 'Cool, you're a network consultant,'" one insider remarks.

PAYING YOUR DUES

"I took one networking class in college, and everything I know about modern networking I learned on the job," one engineer reported. There are certifications, like CCIE (Cisco Certified Internet Engineers), and the classes are quite difficult. "But from a manager's perspective, it seems as though the people who are certified aren't actually very smart. They've spent two years studying for this test, but they've never actually set up a router before. I look for intelligence and enthusiasm because you're going to learn it all on the job anyway."

Routing and networking is a mindset—understanding how stuff flows from one place to another—so it does help if you studied math, computer science, or engineering as an undergraduate. "However, one of the best network engineers I know was a literature major in college. So your actual background really means nothing. It's all about tenacity—being able to sit in front of a problem that you have no idea why it's doing what it's doing until you solve it, which is usually at 2:00 or 3:00 A.M., because you have to do this stuff when no one else is around so you don't interrupt the company's work."

ASSOCIATED CAREERS

"I started out as a systems Unix administrator, then moved to network engineering, then switched to being a programmer, and now I'm managing a company and handling business development," one former network professional reported. The same thinking that makes for a talented network engineer applies well to programming, systems administration, and other sorts of fields employing logic, like engineering. The skills themselves are very specific, narrow, and vertical. "There aren't really any industries where parallel skills would be appropriate. It's not like you can say, 'Oh, I see how this could apply to being a chef,' for example."

PAST AND FUTURE

Networks evolved along with teletype in the early 1970s when businesses started to connect to one another with things other than the telephone line. As teletype went back and forth, the first network administrators were responsible for managing the exchange of data between two offices, such as law firms or large financial institutions. The first wired networks evolved in the late 1970s and early 1980s among very large companies. Most engineers in that era came out of the phone company, which required extensive networking of wires and switches. When the Internet hit in the early 1990s, many others became network engineers.

In the near future, networking is going to get more complicated because all the standards are new. There are so many advancements in hardware that companies upgrade their networks very frequently. "But in the next ten to fifteen years, I see network engineering becoming more similar to your basic plumbing job," one engineer speculated. "It's a high-paying job that's pretty well-defined and not particularly exciting or glamorous. But how often do you upgrade the plumbing system in your house? Hopefully only when it breaks. And you're going to see networking get to that level. As more home users have broadband, the network is going to become very static."

QUALITY OF LIFE

2 YEARS — In an entry-level position, you'll configure small routers at first, and then spend a lot of time tinkering. In dealing with hardware, you will be the one getting the plan to work after it has been designed by the group. The demand for network engineers is currently high but will probably correct itself in the near future as colleges churn out more computer science grads. Be prepared to work a lot in an entry-level position, and "tell your employer that you know how to do the work even if you don't know how and figure it out before they figure out that you don't know what you're doing," one engineer advises. "That's mostly what network engineering comes down to. You say, 'Yeah, sure I can set that up,' and then you're there all weekend getting it to work. Some of the technology is so new that there's no way you could actually know it unless you were on the design team that built it. It's all about being able to figure it out."

5 YEARS — As you grow into a networking position, you'll work on more core and central systems, and larger portions of the network will come under your responsibility over time. Someone who's a certified network engineer can earn about $80,000.

10 YEARS — A network engineer at the top of the field never touches a keyboard. After a point in this field, you either implement complex networks because you're very efficient, or you mentor others. In the next decade, network engineers will work for large Internet service providers. Today, very few people know how to do the hard stuff, like the complicated routing between Internet service providers, but "networking will become almost a position for a drone," one expert predicts.

MAJOR EMPLOYERS
Most are large companies with a large network of offices.

MAJOR ASSOCIATIONS
NETWORK PROFESSIONAL ASSOCIATION
17 South High Street Suite 200
Tel: 614-221-1900
Fax: 614-221-1989
www.npa.org

SYSTEM ADMINISTRATION, NETWORKING AND SECURITY SANS INSTITUTE
8120 Woodmont Avenue
Bethesda, MD 20814
E-mail: info@sans.org
www.sans.org

NUCLEAR ENGINEER

A DAY IN THE LIFE

Like most engineers, nuclear engineers spend their time working in large, high-tech environments. Employment in nuclear engineering is divided equally among the federal government, utilities companies, and the research and testing units of defense and engineering companies. The navy, with its fleet of nuclear-powered ships, is a large employer of nuclear engineers, as is the Nuclear Regulatory Commission. Nuclear engineers conduct research for utility companies to optimize the performance of existing plants, and they are employed in atomic research facilities like the Los Alamos National Laboratory and the Stanford Linear Accelerator Center. Nuclear engineering has become increasingly important in the development of new medical scanning technologies—one of the few growing segments of the field.

{ tightly-regulated environment }

These employers are all large, established operations. The research side of nuclear engineering can be extremely creative, but the field is best suited for individuals who won't feel confined in large, bureaucratic work environments. Nuclear engineers work in extended teams, and caution and risk control are the bywords of the industry—appropriately so, given the dangers of nuclear radiation. With the exception of radio-medical, nuclear waste, and theoretical atomic research, which make up a small percentage of areas in the field, nuclear engineering is not a field marked by breakthroughs. Most nuclear engineers face occasional engineering challenges among otherwise routine tasks in a tightly-regulated environment. The halt in new power plant construction has ended all but incremental, evolutionary nuclear power research. The field does, however, offer extremely stable, secure, and well-paying professional employment.

PAYING YOUR DUES

Graduate education is a prerequisite for employment as a design or research nuclear engineer. Engineers must at least have a master's degree that involved significant course work in math, physics, and engineering design. Both private and government research jobs often require that the applicant complete a doctorate degree program in nuclear engineering. Typically, the educational requirements for an operating engineer are less rigorous: A bachelor's degree in nuclear engineering is one qualification, while others with only high school diplomas get their training through the United States Navy Nuclear Power Plant Program.

ASSOCIATED CAREERS

The skills and training of a nuclear engineer are rather specialized, though there is mobility within the various employers in the field, and opportunities often arise in related energy fields. Military and civilian nuclear power engineers have similar skills, and the government frequently hires nuclear engineers with experience in the various nuclear fields it regulates. Engineers who have risen to positions of significant managerial authority acquire skills and credentials useful in the management of other large enterprises, though there is not significant turnover in the field.

PAST AND FUTURE

Nuclear physics dates back to the 1896 discovery of radiation in uranium by the French physicist Henri Bequerel, but the tools of the modern profession date back to the successful creation of a chain fission reaction by Enrico Fermi at the University of Chicago in 1942. During the 1940s and 1950s, nuclear progress was largely military, with the development of fusion bombs, ever-smaller atomic warheads, and nuclear-powered ships. The first nuclear power plant wasn't built until 1957, in Shippingport, Pennsylvania, but construction then boomed through the 1960s and early 1970s.

Nuclear energy is currently America's second-largest source of energy, only exceeded by coal; but concerns over its risks and over the environmental damage caused by radioactive waste have led to a complete halt in its expansion. While no new nuclear power plants have been built in the United States since 1978, improved operating performance has caused nuclear power to grow in importance and become one of the cheapest sources of electricity. This combined with concerns about greenhouse gas emissions from fossil fuels suggest that nuclear power plant construction may one day resume. Regardless, demand for nuclear engineers to operate, maintain, and improve existing plants is expected to remain steady.

With the advent of nuclear reduction treaties, demand for nuclear-weapons designers has also waned. The navy continues to employ nuclear engineers to operate its nuclear ships, however, and there is increased demand for engineers to dispose of military radioactive waste. Nuclear engineering is not a growing field, but the decreasing supply of trained engineers has made it relatively easy for qualified individuals to find work.

QUALITY OF LIFE

2 YEARS Nuclear engineers, whether their specializations are in design or operations, usually work in teams. At this early stage in their careers, nuclear engineers are generally the junior members of their working groups. They have supervisory authority over less-educated technicians in their labs, ships, or plants, but their work is in turn supervised by more experienced engineers, and they have little managerial responsibility.

5 YEARS By this stage, nuclear engineers have acquired some managerial authority for either responsibility for an element of a larger research project or supervisory control over a team of engineers and technicians in a power plant or military installation. Pay has increased, and these engineers have some responsibility for training other employees in their operations.

10 YEARS By now, nuclear engineers have a significant amount of authority and responsibility. In research, they are responsible, along with other senior engineers, for designing experiment plans and supervising them. As operations engineers, they will have a voice in setting operational and safety procedures for a military or civilian nuclear plant.

MAJOR EMPLOYERS

GENERAL ELECTRIC NUCLEAR COMPANY
175 Curtner Avenue
San Jose, CA 95125
Tel: 408-925-1000
Fax: 408-925-1422
www.ge.com
Contact: Human Resources Department

FRAMATOME
Corporate Headquarters
3315 Old Forest Road
Lynchburg, VA 24501
Tel: 434-832-3000
Fax: 434-832-2997
www.us.framatome-anp.com

WESTINGHOUSE ELECTRIC, INC.
Regional Activity Center
PO Box 355
Energy Center Complex
Pittsburgh, PA 15230-0355
Tel: 412-244-2000
Fax: 412-374-6611
www.westinghouse.com

MAJOR ASSOCIATIONS

AMERICAN NUCLEAR SOCIETY
555 North Kensington Avenue
La Grange Park, IL 60526
Tel: 708-352-6611
Fax: 708-352-0499
www.ans.org

AMERICAN SOCIETY FOR ENGINEERING EDUCATION
1818 N Street, NW, Suite 600
Washington, DC 20036-2479
Tel: 202-331-3500
Fax: 202-265-8504
www.asee.org

NUCLEAR ENGINEERING INSTITUTE
1818 N Street, NW, Suite 200
Washington, DC 20036
Tel: 202-331-3500
Fax: 202-265-8504
www.nei.org

ORGANIZATION DEVELOPMENT CONSULTANT

SALARY   ● ● ●

HOURS   ● ● ●

EDUCATION   ● ● ●

BOOKS, FILMS, AND TV SHOWS
FEATURING THE PROFESSION

- **Behavior and Management**
- **Feedback and Organization Development**
- **Intervention End Method**
- **Office Space**
- **Process Consultation**
- **Statistics for Gerbils**

YOU'LL HAVE CONTACT WITH

- **Accountants**
- **Employees**
- **Human resources personnel**
- **Production managers**
- **Researchers**

PROFESSIONALS READ

- **The International Registry of Organization Development Professionals and Organization Development Handbook**
- **OD Practitioner**
- **Organizations in Change Newsletter**
- **Organization Development Journal**

A DAY IN THE LIFE

An organization development consultant works with client corporations to streamline them and plan future development. Companies hire organization development consultants when they are suffering from internal inefficiency or need help identifying their potential growth points and personnel needs. The organization development consultant is brought in to provide information and a perspective on what a company needs. It is important for an organization development consultant to be open, inquiring, and analytical. Organization development falls into three areas of concern: structure, personnel, and procedure. Many second- or third-year consultants are assigned to specific areas of specialization and then follow those tracks for their entire careers. Organization development consultants usually work in teams.

{ *exchange information* }

Structural organization development consultants analyze corporate structures and responsibilities. They examine who is in charge of what areas of the business and how much time they spend on each duty. Many people have to look back to their original job descriptions to find out what they are supposed to be doing, and then they describe what they really do. An organization development consultant must be able to interview people in a nonconfrontational way and be able to tell when individuals are merely saying what they think they should say rather than telling the truth. Organization development consultants who are involved in personnel concerns often have a very hard time interviewing employees, who tend to be extremely reluctant to tell the truth around personnel developers out of fear for their own jobs. Since they must rely on information from data and records, personnel developers face the most number-intensive task of the three. Procedural organization development consultants observe employees. They track projects through the company, examine who comes into contact with them, and what their regular procedures are. Procedural developers don't make any recommendations until they have spent significant time meeting with the other organization development specialists; recommendations from any other field will affect procedural decisions immensely.

Organization development consultants said that the most exhausting part of their job is finalizing any project, at which point all three teams meet to exchange information and prepare recommendations. This can entail marathon meeting sessions in which each team makes a presentation to the other teams, and then all discuss the recommendations. Once they reach a consensus, sometimes after tremendous internal disagreement, they prepare a recommendation summary and make a presentation to the client. Recommendations may include restructuring, changing benefits, encouraging employee education, eliminating personnel, or changing the specific goals of business. They focus on internal recommendations rather than external development.

PAYING YOUR DUES

There have traditionally been no specific academic requirements for becoming an organization development consultant, but organization development has now been structured into the curriculum in more than a thousand programs that offer certificate, master's, and doctoral degrees in organization development. Employers consider people emerging from those specialized programs but also look favorably upon people who have majored in business, finance, economics, or psychology. Scientific survey methodology, which can be very interview-intensive, is important. A number of organization development consultants pursue graduate degrees in either organization behavior or business administration. There is intense competition for entry-level organization development positions, which entail long hours but only come with limited responsibility. Any experience demonstrating the ability to work in teams is valuable to employers. Organization development consultants can also register their credentials with the Organization Development Institute. The qualities that distinguish a successful candidate in this field are an inquisitive mind, the ability to assemble details into a coherent whole, and persistence.

ASSOCIATED CAREERS

Organization development consultants can use their analytical minds in a number of other business-related occupations, such as a management consultant or financial analyst. A number of them become efficiency experts or quality control personnel. An OD's specialization—structure, personnel, or production—generally determines which avenues are available.

PAST AND FUTURE

The idea that companies should reevaluate all their operations and methods of doing business every few years is fairly recent. Organization development led the charge to provide significant internal information from objective sources. The future of the organization development consultant looks bright, particularly as companies grow in size but are ill-equipped to handle the unanticipated problems that accompany expansion. Information, production, staffing, and structural decisions are all important to the financial health and welfare of a company. Job growth in this industry is expected to be greater than the average for the economy as a whole.

QUALITY OF LIFE

2 YEARS
The first two years in this profession can be difficult. Many consultants spend their first year on small projects in all three areas of specialization as they try to find matches between their skills and companies' needs. This can entail working at many low-responsibility jobs and performing such dull tasks as entering data into a computer, transcribing interviews into data files, or maintaining files on projects. Those individuals who show immediate promise in any area find that their responsibilities increase; those individuals who do not will find themselves rotating between or among departments swiftly. Satisfaction is low for those individuals who do not find a match right away. The hours are long as entrants to the field try to distinguish themselves through hard work.

5 YEARS
The first taste of client contact emerges in years three through seven, as many structural and procedural organization development consultants spend long hours conducting interviews. Relocation may be required, as some projects can require up to six weeks of on-site work. By year five, many organization development consultants have become contributing members of teams or team leaders. Extremely long hours are required for those individuals who wish to rise beyond this point. Satisfaction increases, but those individuals looking for greater salaries often enter other, more lucrative fields.

10 YEARS
Most 10-year members of the profession have positions of organization oversight and coordination. For those who are not interested in managing large projects and converting their analytic jobs to managerial ones, the profession becomes less satisfying than it used to be. Many developers who prefer a more "hands-on" approach to the career leave. Successful organization development consultants have a number of career options open to them.

MAJOR EMPLOYERS

Many organization development professionals work in conjunction with management consultant firms. Contact management consultant firms in your area for information on employment opportunities. Resources such as the Organization Development Institute list job opportunities in their monthly newsletters and on the Web.

ORGANIZATION RESOURCES COUNSELORS
500 Fifth Avenue
New York, NY 10110
Tel: 212-719-3400
Fax: 212-398-1358
www.orcinc.com

MAJOR ASSOCIATIONS

ORGANIZATION DEVELOPMENT INSTITUTE
11234 Walnut Ridge Road
Chesterland, OH 44026
Tel: 441-729-7419
www.odinstitute.org

ORGANIZATIONAL DEVELOPMENT NETWORK
71 Valley Street, Suite 301
South Orange, NJ 07079-2825
Tel: 973-763-7337
Fax: 973-763-7488
www.odnetwork.org

PARAMEDIC

A DAY IN THE LIFE

Are you familiar with the people running the stretchers through the door and shouting numbers at the doctors on *ER*? Those are paramedics and Emergency Medical Technicians (EMTs). Paramedics are the highest level of pre-hospital providers; EMTs are the basic-level personnel. Paramedics and EMTs are often the first medical people at the scene of an accident or sudden illness; they give immediate care to heart attack victims, car crash victims, gunshot victims, and poison victims. They even assist in childbirth. The sick or injured are then transported to health care facilities in specially equipped emergency vehicles. On arrival at a medical center, the paramedics transfer the patient to nursing personnel and report their observations and treatment procedure to the attending physician.

{ **physically and emotionally strong** }

The guidelines or procedures that EMTs follow are directly related to their level of training. The EMT-paramedic is at the upper rung of a three-level hierarchy. Paramedics administer sophisticated pre-hospital care. They are trained in the use of complex medical equipment, such as EKGs, and are capable of administering drugs both orally and intravenously. EMT-intermediates have more advanced training than EMT-basics, who bandage wounds, stabilize blood pressure, assist heart attack victims, and treat accident victims for shock. All three levels of EMTs can be talked through care procedures in the event that they are confronted with a difficult or complicated situation. For this reason EMTs maintain radio contact with a dispatcher and keep him or her aware of the situation. Should the need arise, senior medical personnel (physicians) will then take charge.

For EMTs and paramedics, helping people can be an athletic experience; you have to be where people need you at the time they need you. Like firefighters or other emergency response personnel, paramedics and EMTs are involved in life-and-death situations. Their work can be richly rewarding, as when a child is born despite difficulties, or terribly sad, as when, even after administering proper care, a patient dies. Conditions are tremendously stressful, the hours are long and irregular, and salaries are low. Paramedics must be physically and emotionally strong enough to do backbreaking and sometimes dangerous work; they also have to be ready to hustle on a moment's notice, as someone's life may be on the line. The paramedic never knows what conditions he or she might meet on any given day, so emotional stability is at a premium. "It's a lot of stress and anxiety," one EMT who has been on the job for three years says. "But some days you go home feeling like you really made a difference, and that's a real good feeling."

PAYING YOUR DUES

Training to become an EMT is offered by police, fire, and health departments, and also in some hospitals. Many colleges and universities offer non-degree courses and programs. Basic training to become a first-level EMT requires 100–120 hours of classroom sessions plus 10 hours of internship in a hospital emergency room and 20–50 hours on field rescue or ambulance companies. An additional 35–55 hours of instruction in patient assessment, intravenous fluids, antishock garments, and esophageal airways are required in intermediate training. Paramedics usually undergo between 750 and 2,000 hours of training. As is often the case, the *real* training comes with experience.

"Some days you go home feeling like you really made a difference, and that's a real good feeling."

Although registration is not generally required, it does enhance the possibility of advancement and employment opportunities. A certified EMT must renew his or her registration every two years. This requires remaining active in the field and meeting a continuing education requirement. A paramedic seeking advancement must leave fieldwork, however, if he or she is to move up to operations manager, administrative officer, or executive director of emergency services.

ASSOCIATED CAREERS

Because of the high-stress environment in which they work, many paramedics suffer from burnout. A lack of advancement opportunities and low salaries leads to a high turnover in this profession. Police, fire, and rescue squad departments, on the other hand, offer attractive salaries and benefits. For paramedics looking to switch careers, the health care profession offers several avenues. With a rapidly aging population and scientific breakthroughs that prolong life and the proliferation of residential retirement communities, nursing homes, adult day care centers, and health care agencies, the need for health care professionals promises to remain strong. With more schooling, paramedics can become registered nurses, occupational and physical therapists, doctors, or other health care workers. Closer to the field, paramedics can make the transition to EMT instructor, dispatcher, or firefighter.

PAST AND FUTURE

Doctors saving soldiers on battlefields are the forerunners of today's paramedics. Unfortunately, there will always be a need for people who can administer emergency treatment and rush the sick and injured to doctors' care. Employment opportunities in the emergency services industry will continue to expand with an aging population that will increasingly have a need for such services.

QUALITY OF LIFE

2 YEARS If the paramedic is already board certified, the two-year mark signals the time for recertification. Continuing education classes are an integral part of the paramedic's first two years on the job. On-the-job training has given him or her the confidence and ability to deal with a variety of situations. The paramedic is relatively new to the field and is likely to continue to approach his or her job with energy and idealism.

5 YEARS The registered paramedic is still updating his skills through classes and workshops. After five years, he or she is beginning to feel the stresses of the job. Long and irregular hours and being on call sometimes 24 hours a day are taking their toll. For those individuals who are still stress-free at the five-year level, advancement figures are prominently in their thoughts. Operations manager and administrative director are positions to which the five-year veteran would consider advancing. This is also the ideal time to consider pursuing further studies to become a registered nurse, physician's assistant, nurse practitioner, physician, or other health care professional.

10 YEARS After ten years, paramedics have usually left the field for middle- or top-level administrative positions. But even then, continuing education classes and refresher courses are still essential.

MAJOR EMPLOYERS
Paramedics are employed by local government agencies and by hospitals. Contact the paramedic department in your area for employment information.

MAJOR ASSOCIATIONS
NATIONAL ASSOCIATION OF EMERGENCY MEDICAL TECHNICIANS
PO Box 1400
Clinton, MS 39056-4210
Tel: 800-346-2368
Fax: 601-924-7325
www.naemt.org

NATIONAL REGISTRY OF EMERGENCY MEDICAL TECHNICIANS
Rocco V. Morando Building
6610 Busch Boulevard
PO Box 29233
Columbus, OH 43229
Tel: 614-888-4484
Fax: 614-888-8920
www.nremt.org

PARK RANGER

A DAY IN THE LIFE

If you love the beauty of misty mornings outlined by hazy sunshine and the smell of dew and new beginnings, then a park ranger's life might be ideal for you. With more than seventy-six million acres of national parks in its care, the United States National Park Service and the park rangers it employs educate and ensure the safety of the millions of visitors who hike, climb, ski, boat, fish, and explore these natural resources.

The primary responsibility of the park ranger is ensuring safety. Rangers must strictly enforce outdoor safety codes and ensure the compliance of campers, hikers, and picnickers. Seemingly small details such as accurately completing registration forms at park offices become crucial links, should a search-and-rescue mission  become necessary. As accidents will and often do happen in the great outdoors, park rangers are trained in first aid and rescue operations and are alert at all times to changing weather conditions, the progress and safe return of hiking or climbing groups, the condition of trails, the movement of wildlife, wind gusts, and forest fires. Besides the daily activities of communicating with visitors, answering questions, providing guided tours, rescuing park users who might have strayed too far, enforcing laws, and directing traffic, park rangers are often called upon to be conservationists, ecologists, environmentalists, and even botanists. Park rangers protect park's natural resources from vandals who destroy park property, use fallen trees for firewood, pollute lakes and rivers, harm wildlife, and leave campfires unattended. Should a forest fire start, rangers may also assume the roles of firefighters.

Park rangers are empowered to arrest and forcibly evict those individuals who violate park laws. If you shrink from confrontation and lack the confidence and authority of a strong leader, then you may want to consider a different profession. Park rangers must be flexible enough to wear many hats in the execution of their duties. Strong people skills, the ability to work under pressure, in groups or alone, sometimes for extraordinarily long hours, and the patience of Job are the hallmarks of a fine park ranger. If you have the requisite stamina, can handle the rigors of all kinds of climate and terrain, and are concerned about the earth's rapidly diminishing natural resources, then the life of a park ranger may indeed be the right choice for you.

PAYING YOUR DUES

A college degree and/or the right combination of education and experience in park recreation and management will possibly get you into this profession. Job openings are few, and competition is fierce, so college credits in forestry, geology, botany, conservation, wildlife management, and other relevant subjects will go a long way in preparing you for a career that offers a multitude of possibilities. In lieu of a college education, competitive candidates may alternatively have at least three years of experience in parks and conservation and demonstrate an overall understanding of park work. A working knowledge of law enforcement, management, and communication skills also enhances one's prospects. Higher-level management positions may require graduate degrees.

Part-time or seasonal work at national or state parks is an important stepping-stone to an entry-level park ranger position. Seasonal workers perform jobs such as information-desk manning, trash collection, fire services, trail maintenance, law enforcement, and other unskilled tasks that are the core of the park ranger's life. Perform these well and you may make it into an entry-level position in the big league. A vast majority of high-level park rangers start out as entry-level drones. Thus the trail to promotion and high executive office starts with successful and thorough completion of every step. A keen grasp of the overall mechanics of the business can make you a sharper, more competent administrator. Promotions occur largely from within the ranks; salary is commensurate with responsibility. Today's entry-level worker may be tomorrow's park manager or district ranger. But a virtual lack of new job openings coupled with state and federal budget cuts mean that job seekers will have to look for work outside of the federally funded National Park Service, in other federal land and resource management agencies, as well as in state and local agencies.

ASSOCIATED CAREERS

Park rangers are tenured professionals. Such are the rewards and enjoyment of this career that rangers do not readily relinquish their posts. Because much of a park ranger's duties involve policing, law enforcement offers a readily available career for the retired or out-of-work park ranger. For the ranger specializing in landscaping, conservation, wildlife management, and ecological studies, possible career alternatives abound in areas such as being a zookeeper, landscaping corporate/industrial parks, and containing pollution. The winning combination of communication, people, and management skills allows them to become successful customer and public relations managers.

PAST AND FUTURE

Once a park ranger's most significant qualification was a love of nature. Today that love must redefine itself within the expanding scope of technology and reduced budgets. Job openings will continue to be scarce, and the competition fierce. Specialization and diversification are the new buzzwords, as potential candidates have to demonstrate a number of skills in depth and across a broad scope of areas.

QUALITY OF LIFE

2 YEARS For those individuals entering this career via part-time or seasonal work, these are the critical years for developing strong contacts and establishing apprenticeships. If you are still in college and have not decided on an area of specialization, this is an ideal time to get a firsthand overview of the business and focus on a specialty. The more diverse the skills one has, the better the chances of getting in the door.

5 YEARS At the five-year level, the park ranger should have acquired enough hands-on experience to be qualified for a position in administration. Management and communication skills, the ability to work effectively in teams and to motivate others, plus clear leadership abilities will determine the level of success you will achieve.

10 YEARS By the tenth year, the park ranger has moved up to a high-level administrative post, such as director at the regional or national level. He or she is an experienced, motivated, and confident leader with a number of specialties.

MAJOR EMPLOYERS

GRAND CANYON NATIONAL PARK
PO Box 129
Grand Canyon, AZ 86023
Tel: 928-638-7888
www.nps.gov/grca/

U.S. DEPARTMENT OF THE INTERIOR NATIONAL PARK SERVICE
1849 C Street, NW
Washington, DC 20240
Tel: 202-208-6843
Fax: 202-219-0910
www.nps.gov

YELLOWSTONE NATIONAL PARK
PO Box 168
Yellowstone National Park,
WY 82190-0168
Tel: 307-344-7381
Fax: 307-344-2005
www.nps.gov/yell/

MAJOR ASSOCIATIONS

NATIONAL ASSOCIATION OF STATE PARK DIRECTORS
8829 Woodyhill Road
Raleigh, NC 27613
Tel: 919-971-9300
www.naspd.org

THE PARK LAW ENFORCEMENT ASSOCIATION
www.parkranger.com

PETROLEUM ENGINEER

BOOKS, FILMS, AND TV SHOWS
FEATURING THE PROFESSION
- **Black Gold**
- **The OPEC Builders**
- **A Year in Saudi Arabia**

YOU'LL HAVE CONTACT WITH
- **Drilling rig operators**
- **Geologists**
- **Geophysicists**
- **Lab technicians**

PROFESSIONALS READ
- **International Petrochemical Report**
- **Oil and Gas Journal**
- **Petroleum Engineering**

A DAY IN THE LIFE

The subtitle for Petroleum Engineering 101 at Stanford University reads "How to dig oil wells," and that is for the most part what a petroleum engineer does. He or she is involved in all phases of oil exploration, from choosing the prospective site through taking down the drilling rig after extracting the oil. This can entail travel, long stays in unusual (and sometimes inhospitable) locations, and uncertain working conditions. "It's a gambler's life," one petroleum engineer wrote, and others agreed. "If you're into engineering and gambling, petroleum engineering is for you," another wrote. Those individuals not attracted to both should steer clear of this high-risk field.

{ see problems before they happen }

A petroleum engineer usually works for a petroleum company in various capacities. The typical petroleum engineer works in the field. First, he or she scouts prospective sites that have a strong likelihood of containing oil or gas below. Then, he or she takes samples from the site and determines the amount and quality of oil, the depth at which these resources lie, and the equipment that will be needed to properly extract them. The petroleum engineer then supervises construction and operations at the site and adjusts plans accordingly. Finally, when the well or pocket is exhausted, he or she supervises the removal of the drilling equipment and the safe return of the land to structural stability, and he or she oversees the removal of any waste (hazardous or otherwise) left at the site. These stages of work can be quick three-month stints, or they can be extended to as long as two years.

Patience, sound judgment, and maturity are required for the successful petroleum engineer. "You've got to be able to see problems before they happen," one veteran Californian petroleum engineer wrote, "otherwise you're right in the middle of them." Self-confidence is also crucial, as on-site decisions have to be made quickly and surely. Another petroleum engineer said, "You have to be able to handle failure" if you want to survive in this industry. Speculative oil-well drilling is somewhere between a science and an art; expect to frequently plant rigs that prove barren or that only yield limited amounts of oil. But despite the frustrations that go with the turf, petroleum engineers seem to enjoy being out in the field, where they can get their hands dirty. One big satisfaction for many we surveyed was that they worked with both their minds and their hands.

Some petroleum engineers do work in offices, however, analyzing the reports and recommendations of field engineers and advising corporate decision-makers on whether to proceed. These positions are usually held by veteran personnel with experience as field engineers, drilling engineers, and reservoir estimators. While these people are crucial to the success of the industry as a whole, their levels of satisfaction were slightly lower than those of field engineers; the gambling lifestyle, it seems, is less exciting from behind a desk.

PAYING YOUR DUES

Petroleum engineers have rigorous academic requirements. They must hold an undergraduate degree in engineering or earth sciences (geology, geophysics, tectonics, mining, etc.), and the majority in the profession continue on to graduate study. For those individuals who wish to enter academia, a PhD is a must. Only a handful of universities in the United States offer programs that focus on petroleum engineering with course work in such subjects as geology, geophysics, chemistry, fluid dynamics, and physics. Most petroleum engineer programs are located in oil-producing states, as are, obviously, most petroleum engineer jobs. Petroleum engineers must often relocate within these oil-producing parts of the country (California, Texas, and Oklahoma are big ones) or the world. Many states require practicing petroleum engineers to pass a state licensing exam.

ASSOCIATED CAREERS

Petroleum engineers develop extensive knowledge about the world of oil production, and many of them become industry analysts. A number of them use their economics skills—all oil production is a cost-benefit analysis—to enter companies as in-house economists. The largest number of emigrants from this profession, however, enter environmental companies, are hired by the Environmental Protection Agency (EPA), or become consultants to professional oil organizations. Digging oil wells can be a dirty business, and some respondents mentioned that after a few years of seeing what actually goes on at a site they wanted to change the direction of their lives.

PAST AND FUTURE

Before 1860, oil was an anomaly that sometimes bubbled up through the ground and proved useful as a lubricant or for lighting lamps. In the late 1800s, Edwin Drake pumped the first oil well in Titusville, Pennsylvania, ushering in the age of oil production. The development and popularization of the automobile in this century provided a steady market of customers for one of oil's by-products—gasoline—and thus was born the world's richest industry. Oil wells now reach more than 20,000 feet below the ground to drain "black gold" from the earth.

The future of the petroleum engineer will be influenced by two factors: the short-term glut of oil (only seen 12 months into the future) and the long-term scramble that oil depletion necessarily brings. In the short term, the demand for petroleum engineers should be weak, due to cheap and plentiful on-hand oil inventories, consistently producing wells, and inexpensive foreign oil alternatives. By the year 2020, however, experts predict that the long-term demand for petroleum will greatly exceed the supply. This anticipated shortage will make it worthwhile for companies to hire many petroleum engineers in search of any valuable undiscovered pockets of oil. It will also, however, make it necessary to seek out alternative energy sources.

QUALITY OF LIFE

2 YEARS Two years into the profession, petroleum engineers are working as junior assistants, taking rock samples and sending them to labs for testing. They often collect data and assemble it for more senior researchers. Many of them take this opportunity to form mentor relationships with these project managers and are exposed to years of experience in short periods of time. Much time is spent on-site, and a number of junior members use these early years to gain foreign oil exploration experience. The hours are long, and the pay is average. In these first two years, it's important to get the state licensing exams out of the way because they become more difficult to pass the farther away you get from your course work.

5 YEARS The middle years of the profession are marked by significant responsibility and a lot of risk-taking. Many petroleum engineers are assigned lead roles in one phase of oil exploration or development. Future assignments rely on success in previous ones, so stress levels can be significant. The hours are long, particularly for field engineers. Those individuals who are likely to become back-office consultants begin cultivating connections during these years; many of them attempt to publish in academic journals as an additional credential. Satisfaction levels are high.

10 YEARS Ten-year veteran petroleum engineers have not only been through a number of diverse projects but have also seen the rapid fluctuation of the oil market affect their business. Those people who make the transition from the field to the office do so between years six and twelve. Many have changed employers at least once. Salaries rise; satisfaction dips, then levels off.

MAJOR EMPLOYERS
AMOCO CORPORATION
200 East Randol, Suite 3408
Chicago, IL 60601
Tel: 312-856-5111
www.amoco.com
Contact: Human Resources

CHEVRON
6001 Bollinger Canyon
San Ramon, CA 94583
Tel: 925-842-1000
E-mail: employ@chevron.com
www.chevron.com
Contact: Human Resources

DOMINION
Dominion Tower
625 Liberty Avenue
Pittsburgh, PA 15222-3199
Tel: 412-690-1000
www.cng.com
Contact: Human Resources

DUPONT
1007 Market Street, N12419
Wilmington, DE 19898
Tel: 332-774-1000
Fax: 800-978-9774
www.dupont.com
Contact: Human Resources Professional
    Staffing

MAJOR ASSOCIATIONS
AMERICAN PETROLEUM INSTITUTE
1229 L Street, NW
Washington, DC 20005
Tel: 202-682-8000
www.api.org

SOCIETY OF PETROLEUM ENGINEERS
PO Box 833836
Richardson, TX 75803-3836
Tel: 972-952-9393
Fax: 972-952-9435
www.spe.org

PHYSICIAN ASSISTANT

A DAY IN THE LIFE

Like the physicians with whom they work, physician assistants can find work in hospitals, private practices, and HMOs. Basically, wherever there are doctors, there are physician assistants. University hospital work entails working alongside doctors and other physician assistants and splitting time between treating patients and aiding in research and instruction (more experienced physician assistants often manage less experienced physician assistants). Depending on the size of the private practice, physician assistants are more likely to spend the majority of their time working directly with doctors, handling patients, lab tests, and paperwork. Physician assistants who work for an HMO are part of the large corporate medicine machine that not only provides for the patients but also most likely assigns physician assistants to the physicians they will assist.

{ intensive medical study }

Currently, about 50 percent of all physician assistants practice primary care medicine, that is, family medicine, internal medicine, pediatrics, and obstetrics and gynecology. Just more than 20 percent focus their talents in surgery or the surgical subspecialties. Although family medicine attracts the most physician assistants, many also specialize in dermatology, psychiatry, radiology, and pathology.

The physician assistant's license allows licensees to practice medicine only under supervision, while always working for at least one physician and handling a significant portion of the physician's massive workload. Work weeks tend to be at or near the 40-hour mark. Work in this profession is rewarding; but it can also be very demanding.

PAYING YOUR DUES

Competition can be intense: nurses, emergency medical technicians (EMTs), and paramedics most commonly apply to physician assistant certification programs. The typical applicant to a physical assistant program has a bachelor's degree (who has followed a pre-med track as an undergraduate) and approximately four years of health care experience. For those individuals interested in becoming physician assistants who haven't followed the traditional science route in college, a post-baccalaureate program may be the solution. Some universities have programs in which students can take all the undergraduate sciences courses in one post-baccalaureate program.

Because physician assistants are going to be in a close working relationship with physicians, they are educated in a medical model designed to complement physician training. Once candidates have been accepted to a physician assistant program, the average curriculum stretches into 111 weeks of intensive medical study. During that time physical assistant students will be sharing many classes and rotations in clinical medicine with medical students who are going for a medical doctor degree, and the work is stressful and intense. The education itself consists of classroom and laboratory instruction in basic medical and behavioral sciences (such as anatomy, pharmacology, and clinical medicine), followed by rotations in internal medicine, family medicine, surgery, pediatrics, obstetrics and gynecology, emergency medicine, and geriatric medicine. After completing the course work required in a physical assistant program, graduates still have to pass a national certification exam. Graduation from an accredited physician assistant program and passage of the certifying exam are required for state licensure.

All this work and they still aren't done. Physician assistants are required to take ongoing medical education classes (at least 100 hours of classroom time every two years) and must retake the certification test every six years to maintain their national certification.

ASSOCIATED CAREERS

Physician assistants are not full-fledged doctors, but in medicine there are plenty of careers that don't require a medical doctor degree. Some physician assistants consider nursing, working as paramedics or EMTs, lab technicians, pharmacologists, or biologists. All of these careers require long hours of study and come with a great deal of responsibility.

PAST AND FUTURE

In 1965 Eugene Stead, MD, of Duke University Medical Center, assembled the first class of physician assistants to address the shortage and uneven distribution of primary-care physicians. This first class was comprised of navy corpsmen who had received medical training during their military service. Physicians quickly warmed up to the new profession; physician assistants provided them with knowledgeable, efficient, and much-needed help. Since then, physician assistants have become a staple of the medical workforce. There are now 63,000 physician assistants working in the United States and practicing in every field of medicine.

Job growth in the field of physician assistants is expected to outpace total employment growth. Even now, the majority of physician assistants are concentrated in primary care areas, leaving a lot of room for physician assistants in other fields. Demand for physician assistants will only become greater in the years to come. Demand is greatest in rural areas and inner cities.

QUALITY OF LIFE

2 YEARS   In the early years of their careers, physician assistants will still be learning as they gain valuable experience in techniques for dealing with patients and the intricacies of applied medicine. They will also be discovering fields they might want to specialize in as their careers continue. As with most professions, incomes for physician assistants tend to increase with years of experience, but it is important to note that larger increases in income tend to come near the beginning of a physician assistant's career. Physician assistants won't have the same potentially immense debt that medical students will have accrued, making their dollars stretch further.

5 YEARS   Physician assistants will have had an ongoing medical education and will be approaching the time when they will have to take the recertification exam. At this point, many physician assistants have had hands-on experience. A physician assistant's specialty has a significant impact on earnings; currently, the highest-paid physician assistant specialists are in surgical subspecialties. Many of them may also find themselves managing other physician assistants.

10 YEARS   An experienced physician assistant, whether a specialist in emergency medicine or in general pediatrics, is valuable and income will reflect this. Without a doubt, veteran physician assistants can work in managerial positions for any health care organization or private practice. In short, physician assistants are a commodity in demand and will be in a good position to choose where to work.

MAJOR EMPLOYERS
Hospitals, HMOs, health centers, and physicians in private practice across the country employ physician assistants.

MAJOR ASSOCIATIONS
AMERICAN ACADEMY OF PHYSICIAN ASSISTANTS
950 North Washington Street
Alexandria, VA 22314-1552
Tel: 703-836-2272
Fax: 703-684-1924
www.aapa.org

SOCIETY OF EMERGENCY MEDICINE PHYSICIAN ASSISTANTS
950 North Washington Street
Alexandria, VA 22314-1552
Tel: 703-519-5334
Fax: 703-684-1924
www.sempa.org

PHYSICIST

BOOKS, FILMS, AND TV SHOWS
FEATURING THE PROFESSION
- The Core
- Fat Man and Little Boy
- Genius
- IQ

YOU'LL HAVE CONTACT WITH
- Chemists
- Lab technicians
- Mathematicians
- Researchers

PROFESSIONALS READ
- Journal of Applied Physics
- Physics News Update
- Physics Today

A DAY IN THE LIFE

Physicists deal with all aspects of matter and energy. Their work ranges from basic research of the most fundamental laws of nature to the practical development of devices and instruments. The study of physics falls into many categories. These categories include studies of the motion and properties of physical objects both large and small (classical and quantum mechanics and astrophysics), the properties of waves (optics, acoustics, and electromagnetics), the properties of states of matter (solid state and plasma physics), and the fundamental properties of matter and energy (atomic, nuclear, and particle physics). Because of the vast range of subject matter, physicists tend to specialize in one of these categories at the graduate level. Across most categories, physicists also tend to specialize either in theoretical and experimental work. Theoretical physicists use mathematical concepts to analyze and predict the behavior of the physical world. Experimental physicists use laboratory experiments to verify these theoretical predictions or develop devices and instruments.

{ Physics is not for the fainthearted. }

Physicists tend to be curious, creative, and dedicated. The majority of all physicists are employed by universities and divide their time between research, teaching, and writing scientific articles. Many physicists work independently on problems, while others work in laboratories as part of teams for the duration of particular projects. Many physicists working in industry not only work in traditional areas just like university physicists but also branch out into engineering fields and other scientific fields, working with engineers and other scientists in overlapping areas. Because of their broad scientific background, physicists in industry are known for their ability to work in many areas and have helped create many nontraditional fields. Physics is not for the fainthearted, but for those individuals with good mathematical skills who want a broad scientific education and the ability to branch out later into other fields, physics may be just the thing.

Like individuals in many other scientific fields, a physicist's career progresses from being a team member doing hands-on work to being a team leader, responsible for developing new projects, running existing ones, and raising money to fund projects. One Ivy League physicist complains that fund-raising is a necessary evil in his line of work. In both universities and industry, there have been cutbacks in research funding that have affected almost everyone in the field.

PAYING YOUR DUES

Excellent mathematical skills and statistical knowledge are required of the physicist, who will spend a large part of his or her academic life studying these subjects. The physicist must be as competent in these areas as any mathematician or statistician. Computer knowledge is also key to success in the profession, and the most successful physicists go beyond a bachelor's degree to earn a master's and then a doctorate. This entails a significant piece of original research. Without postgraduate degrees, it's generally difficult to find work as a physicist. Individuals who do land a job in this field with only a bachelor of science degree will find that they need to further their studies, if they want to progress beyond rudimentary lab duties.

ASSOCIATED CAREERS

A substantial number of nonpracticing physicists end up teaching. Depending on the degree he or she has, a physicist can teach science in high school or at the college level. A background in physics along with some writing talent can also help individuals procure jobs in scientific journalism. The field most closely related to physics is engineering. Engineers need to have a sophisticated knowledge of physics, but the course of study is often not as long. There are also fields that unite physics with other sciences. Biophysicists, for example, study the processes of life by bringing together physics, chemistry, and biology. Astrophysicists are involved in developing theories about the origin of the universe and the physical mechanisms that have generated the objects seen by astronomers. Astronomy is one of the laboratories for testing fundamental theories about the nature of matter and energy from relativity to particle physics.

PAST AND FUTURE

The origins of physics can be traced to Aristotle, who wrote at a time when physics was considered a philosophical science. It wasn't until 1,000 years later, with the work of Galileo, that physics was acknowledged to be a hard mathematical science. Galileo's discoveries in physics—the fact that matter of varying weights will always fall at the same speed in a vacuum, for instance—have earned him the label of "first modern scientist." Since then, physics has progressed rapidly—with many breakthroughs, such as the lightbulb and the motion picture.

Physicists agree that there is plenty of room for the field to grow as new discoveries are made concerning nuclear energy, communications, the ocean, and space. Unfortunately, the growth rate for this career is expected to be slower than average in the near future due to cuts in government funding, which will affect the field substantially. Eighty percent of employed physicists work for universities or the government. But as one prominent physicist consoles himself, "if you have a degree in physics, you have something very few people have."

QUALITY OF LIFE

2 Physicists report very high levels of satisfaction with their chosen profession at all levels. Very few people leave the field at this time. Physicists are a dedicated lot, and after having spent upwards of seven years preparing for this career, they rarely lose interest so soon. Within two years of completing their degrees, many physicists decide whether to compete for tenure at a university or pursue research interests.

5 Physicists may teach or obtain jobs in government or private laboratories to continue their careers. Many of them work in information technology, concentrating on chip design and hardware applications. Those individuals who leave the field at this time sometimes report feeling like failures for the first year or so in the broader job market. They do, however, find their educational backgrounds to be invaluable assets. A doctoral degree in physics can open a number of doors in other fields such as research in medical applications, space technology, and nuclear power.

10 Many physicists leave the profession at this time because they feel they have "topped out" in their field. They go on to seek employment that will allow them to use their scientific background in less scientific ventures as business-sector managers or as regulators and administrators in government agencies. A number of physicists who have left the field report, however, that they miss being physicists.

MAJOR EMPLOYERS
DUPONT
1007 Market Street, N12149
Wilmington, DE 19898
Tel: 332-774-1000
Fax: 800-978-9774
www.dupont.com
Contact: Human Resources Professional Staffing

INTEL
2200 Mission College Boulevard
Santa Clara, CA 95052
Tel: 408-765-8080
Fax: 408-765-9904
www.intel.com

LUCENT TECHNOLOGIES
Corporate Headquarters
600 Mountain Avenue
Murray Hill, NJ 07974-0636
Tel: 908-582-3000
www.lucent.com

MAJOR ASSOCIATIONS
AMERICAN GEOPHYSICAL UNION
2000 Florida Avenue, NW
Washington, DC 20009
Tel: 800-966-2481 or 202-462-6900
Fax: 202-328-0566
www.agu.org

AMERICAN NUCLEAR SOCIETY
555 North Kensington Avenue
La Grange Park, IL 60526
Tel: 708-352-6611
Fax: 708-352-0499
www.ans.org

AMERICAN PHYSICAL SOCIETY
1 Physics Ellipse
College Park, MD 20740-3843
Tel: 301-209-3200
Fax: 301-209-0865
E-mail: personnel@aps.org
www.aps.org

PILOT

A DAY IN THE LIFE

The job of an airplane pilot carries considerable prestige, responsibility, and risk. Airline pilots often find themselves in a different time zone, climate, and culture every day. As one pilot notes, "It's like a new and different expedition every time . . . a new and exciting world to discover and journey through." Pilots literally have the lives of their passengers in their hands. The physical and mental demands are rigorous. The ability to remain calm under pressure and having perfect vision, hearing, and coordination are crucial requirements.

Roughly 60 percent of all pilots are employed by airlines, the most visible and widely known job available to pilots. Of those pilots employed by airlines, about 60

{ the ability to remain calm under pressure }

percent have civilian flight training, and 40 percent come from military aviation backgrounds. Such professional visibility and prestige come with significantly more responsibility and a better pay scale. Airline pilots fly passenger planes that often carry 200 or more people onboard. There are several important safety steps that a pilot must take before every flight: checking and filing flight plans, ensuring that there is enough fuel, securing the approval of the air traffic control personnel of the Federal Aviation Administration (FAA), and checking weather and flight conditions. The airline pilot, or captain, is assisted in his or her job by a crew consisting of a copilot or a flight engineer and an appropriate number of flight attendants for the size of the aircraft. Sometimes the crew is extended to include additional pilots for extremely long flights. Another important "member" of the crew is the automatic pilot, an electronic device that is programmed to fly the plane. Even when the automatic pilot is on, it is the pilot-in-command's responsibility to remain alert to problems that may affect the flight. During the flight, the pilot and copilot maintain radio contact with ground control stations to report on altitude, speed, weather conditions, and a host of flight details.

With minimal retraining, the airline pilot can make the transition to other areas of aviation. Helicopter pilots are used by television networks and radio stations to deliver traffic and accident reports. They also work for air taxi services, sightseeing operations, mail delivery, and rescue services. Agricultural pilots are involved in farm maintenance techniques such as crop dusting, fertilization, and insect and weed control. To make such a transition, the pilot would have to learn about the proper use and transportation of chemicals. Pilot instructors teach company airline pilots regulations and procedures. Chief pilots supervise the training of new pilots and handle other administrative work; test pilots test new planes; executive pilots are employed by large corporations that own or lease planes for company use.

PAYING YOUR DUES

At least four years of college are preferred for individuals seeking entry to this profession. FAA-certified military and civilian flying schools provide adequate practical and classroom training, and some colleges and universities offer degree credit for pilot training. Prospective pilots must work long and hard at accumulating required flying time. They must be focused and determined to complete the various stages of what is a rigorous routine to an ultimately satisfying career. In the long run, seniority counts in this profession, so young pilots are advised to buckle their seat belts, enjoy the ride, and keep racking up those hours.

Applicants for the commercial airplane pilot's license must have 250 hours of flying time and successfully complete rigorous testing, including a physical examination, a written test given by the FAA, and a practical test. Before receiving an FAA license, pilots must be rated according to the kind of plane they can fly—single-engine, multi-engine, or seaplane—and for the type—Boeing 707 or 747. Airline pilots must also have an airline transport pilot's license, for which a minimum of 1,500 hours of flight time, including night flying and instrument time, are required. Most airline pilots start out as flight instructors and move to "feeder" airlines before becoming major airline pilots. Many airline pilots begin their careers with military aviation training.

ASSOCIATED CAREERS

Pilots tend to be very satisfied with their jobs and remain in them until forced to retire. Under current regulations in the United States, airline pilots must retire at age 60. When they do stop flying airliners, though, possible career moves include working as executives for airlines, going into private enterprise, opening flying schools, operating charter services, or delivering cargo.

PAST AND FUTURE

Orville and Wilbur Wright became the first airplane pilots when their craft stayed up for 12 seconds at Kitty Hawk, North Carolina, in 1903. The field has expanded considerably since then. The Lockheed brothers built early commercial planes in 1913. Charles Lindbergh became the first American to cross the Atlantic by plane in 1927, and TWA's regular transatlantic service was inaugurated 20 years later.

Now, more than half of all pilots are employed by commercial airlines and, as commerce steadily expands, an even greater number will be able to secure employment. Competition will decrease and a possible shortage will develop as aging pilots retire and new openings are created. Business or executive pilots, on the other hand, will face fewer job prospects, as more companies under tighter budget controls opt to travel commercially rather than operate their own planes.

QUALITY OF LIFE

2 YEARS The pilot, who has probably started out as a first officer on a small airline, is ready to move up to a larger aircraft, though his or her company may not be ready for the move. His or her main professional concern is amassing flying hours, including pilot-in-command, night flying, and instrument time, to make it to the next position.

5 YEARS Airline pilots are now close to being promoted. Their salary levels will begin to increase at significant rates. They will begin to be able to bid for better aircraft, routes, or flight schedules. Pilots rarely switch companies or careers at this point if they want to become captains.

10 YEARS Pilots with 10 years of experience and thousands of miles of flying time will likely be captains by now or be within five years of becoming captains. They have seniority. Should they seek employment elsewhere, they will lose this seniority and have to work their way up from the bottom again. Pilots must be tenacious if captaincy is their goal.

MAJOR EMPLOYERS

U.S. AIR FORCE ACADEMY
2304 Cadet Drive
USAF Academy, CO 80841
Tel: 719-333-1100
www.usafa.af.mil

FEDEX CORPORATION
942 South Shady Grove Road
Memphis, TN 38120
Tel: 901-369-3600
www.fedex.com/us/careers

JETBLUE AIRWAYS
118-29 Queens Boulevard
Forest Hills, NY 11375
Tel: 801-365-2514
www.jetblue.com
Contact: Job Hotline

MAJOR ASSOCIATIONS

AIR LINE PILOTS ASSOCIATION, INTERNATIONAL
1625 Massachusetts, NW
Washington, DC 20036
Tel: 703-689-2270
Fax: 703-481-4446
www.alpa.org

AIR TRANSPORT ASSOCIATION OF AMERICA
1301 Pennsylvania Avenue, NW, Suite 1100
Washington, DC 20004
Tel: 202-626-4000
Fax: 202-626-4066
www.airlines.org

PLASTICS MANUFACTURER

PROFESSIONAL PROFILE

# of people in profession	26,000
Avg. hours per week	40
Avg. starting salary	$24,600
Avg. salary after 5 years:	$34,200
Avg. salary after 10 to 15 years:	$47,100

SALARY

HOURS

EDUCATION

BOOKS, FILMS, AND TV SHOWS
FEATURING THE PROFESSION

- The Art of Milling
- The Graduate

YOU'LL HAVE CONTACT WITH

- Quality control managers
- Safety inspectors
- Technicians

PROFESSIONALS READ

- Modern Plastics
- Plastics Engineering
- Plastics Technology
- Plastics World
- Polymer Composite

A DAY IN THE LIFE

"You'll never get rich doing this," the supervisor of one injection-molding floor wrote, "but you're sure as hell going to have fun." Satisfaction levels were high among most respondents in this industry, who cited the regular work schedule, the production of a useful (and often recyclable) product, and the camaraderie between machine operators and supervisors as advantages of the profession. Even those individuals who supervise workers must understand the nuances of their precise machinery, so many supervisors have been known to take a shift themselves at various stages of the process. Without this fluid line between boss and employee that supports many departments through work crunches and technical crises, plastics manufacturing would be just another { putting out fires before they begin } hard production job. There are four main types of plastics manufacturing: injection molding, blow molding, extrusion, and thermoflowing. Injection molding equipment is used for precision parts, such as appliances. Blow molding equipment is used to make circular, volume-oriented items such as two-liter soda bottles and shampoo containers. Extrusion molding melts, forms, and cools plastics into cut-to-size sheets or rolls for custom orders. Thermoforming uses mechanical or pneumatic means to shape heated plastic around a mold. The original press of a mold is critical for future replicas, so supervisors have to take exquisite care in the preparation and casting of that initial mold. Production pressures can be intense, but manufacturers are usually responsible only for their own shifts, from the melting of the powdered plastic (or pellet plastic) to the cooling and testing of the final product. Manufacturers may dash from production area to production area "putting out fires before they begin" and making certain that their shifts run smoothly.

According to many respondents, the most unexpected part of being a plastics manufacturer is the socializing and friendships between bosses and employees. The production work can be difficult—working with molten plastic, handling equipment at temperatures that can reach 2,000 degrees Fahrenheit or more, testing plastic for tensile strength—and this shared stress seems to encourage mutual respect. "The workers are good people who work hard. You take care of them, and they'll take care of you," one manufacturer said. Plastics manufacturing is a busy, friendly world where one's reward isn't necessarily determined by the size of one's paycheck.

PAYING YOUR DUES

A college degree isn't required in the plastics manufacturing profession. Many manufacturing executives are chosen from manufacturing operator pools, which make long periods of job-specific education unnecessary. Many individuals do attend college, and some of them come into the profession with no relevant experience, but employers look for other qualities—scientific skills, leadership abilities, and manufacturing experience—from candidates. All applicants should be familiar with math and basic science, have good communication skills, and be able to take direction. Successful candidates seem to have one other quality that can't be learned: They inspire respect in the people around them.

ASSOCIATED CAREERS

The plastics manufacturing profession boasts one of the lowest attrition rates—less than 80 percent per year. High levels of satisfaction contribute to this phenomenon. Many plastics manufacturers go back to school for materials engineering classes, mechanical design, and blueprint reading. Individuals who leave the profession usually take industrial engineering positions.

PAST AND FUTURE

Plastics are so common in contemporary life that it's hard to imagine a time when plastic products didn't exist. Yet there were no plastic products until the early 1900s, when Leo Baekeland developed a practical, synthetic plastic. The flexibility and durability of this new, lightweight (and inexpensive) product revolutionized manufacturing, packaging, bottling, storage, and transportation. Recent efforts at expanding America's recycling base have given rise to the used plastics industry, which may still experience financial uncertainty, but which has reduced landfill waste by more than 5 percent in the last seven years. Plastics manufacturing jobs that require less skill are slowly becoming automated; new entrants to the field must meet increased computer and technical skill requirements. The impact of the trend toward automation is still mild in this industry, but over time it could significantly change the plastics industry. So much of the operation of the plastics industry is founded on and guided by the personal loyalties and associations that develop among the employees that automation of the work processes could have a seriously negative effect on the productivity of the remaining workers. Automation through computer numerically controlled (CNC) production is proceeding at a fairly slow pace in this industry; nevertheless, eventual automation is virtually inevitable because of its promise of still greater efficiency.

QUALITY OF LIFE

2 YEARS Many aspiring plastics manufacturers are line technicians, machine operators, or assistants learning how to be good injection molders or extruder operators. People new to the profession are often surprised at how helpful their fellow employees are in this early stage of their careers. The hours are regular and salaries are low, but satisfaction is high. Many people in these beginning jobs learn the front-line lessons that will make them effective managers.

5 YEARS Five-year plastics executives have been pulled from the line and put in charge of one area of operation such as plastic bead molding, casting, striping, or shaping. Although initially this switch from operator to supervisor is unsettling, many individuals quickly see the advantages—particularly in the 60 percent decrease in the likelihood of injury. The hours can increase as administrative duties are added to production duties. Salaries rise, and satisfaction is high.

10 YEARS Ten-year veterans become involved in such areas as inventory control, client contact, and long-term planning but expect input to be limited for another five years or so. Many of them are encouraged to take additional courses in finance or to try their hand at sales (because they are intimately familiar with the production process). Many individuals turn down these options and remain manufacturing supervisors, keeping close to the people they care about and doing the job they love.

MAJOR EMPLOYERS

DUPONT
http://plastics.dupont.com

EXXONMOBIL
http://exxonmobil.com

NOVA CHEMICALS
U.S. Operating Center
1550 Coraopolis Heights Road
Moon Township, PA 15108
Tel: 412-490-4000
www.novachem.com

PARAGON PLASTICS, INC.
PO Box 1395
Discovery Bay, CA 94514
Tel: 925-516-1839 or 866-784-6953
E-mail: info@paragonplastics.com
http://paragonplastics.com

MAJOR ASSOCIATIONS

NATIONAL ASSOCIATION OF MANUFACTURERS
1331 Pennsylvania Avenue, NW
Washington, DC 20004-1790
Tel: 202-637-3000
Fax: 202-637-3182
www.nam.org

SOCIETY OF PLASTICS ENGINEERS
PO Box 403
Brookfield, CT 06804-0403
Tel: 203-775-0471
Fax: 203-775-8490
E-mail: info@4spe.orgwww.4spe.org

THE ASSOCIATION FOR MANUFACTURING TECHNOLOGY
7901 Westpark Drive
McLean, VA 22102
Tel: 703-893-2900
Fax: 703-893-1151
www.mfgtech.org

THE SOCIETY OF THE PLASTICS INDUSTRY, INC.
1667 K Street, NW, Suite 1000
Washington, DC 20006
Tel: 202-974-5200
Fax: 202-296-7005
www.socplas.org

PLUMBER

BOOKS, FILMS, AND TV SHOWS
FEATURING THE PROFESSION

- **Desperate Housewives**
- **Super Mario Brothers**

YOU'LL HAVE CONTACT WITH

- **Contractors**
- **Landlords**
- **Manufacturers**
- **Pipelayers**
- **Pipefitters**
- **Plumbing engineers**
- **Steamfitters**

PROFESSIONALS READ

- **Builder: The Magazine of the National Association for Home Builders**
- **Engineering News Record**
- **Plumbers Handbook Revised**
- **Plumbing and Mechanical**
- **Plumbing Engineer**
- **PM Engineer**

A DAY IN THE LIFE

Plumbers are responsible for a number of tasks. Among these are repairs and installations of water, waste, drainage, and gas systems. Plumbers also install fixtures, such as bathtubs, showers, sinks, and toilets, as well as appliances, including dishwashers and water heaters. They work on both residential and municipal sewage systems. In completing a residential job, plumbers may have to cut holes in the walls, ceilings, and floors of a house. Complex systems sometimes require plumbers to assemble steel supports to hold plumbing systems in place. Plumbers often must work with potentially dangerous tools, namely, saws, pipe cutters, and pipe-bending machines to complete a project.

{ involved in the design process }

Think you have what it takes? The physical nature of the work and the placement of most plumbing systems require some strength and flexibility on the plumber's part. Some jobs even necessitate working outside amidst inclement weather. Plumbers are subject to falls from ladders, cuts from tools, and burns from hot pipes. They must also be able to work from building plans or blueprints. Knowledge of codes and proficiency in the operation of plumbing systems are both essential. In recent years, plumbers have become more involved in the design process. The ability of a plumber to design, plan, and execute a job on his or her own saves clients money—and in turn, makes him or her more marketable.

Plumbers involved in construction generally work a standard 40-hour workweek. Those who work in maintenance often work evening and/or weekend shifts and may have to be on call, as well. Maintenance workers may spend a lot of time traveling to work sites. Plumbing and its related fields—pipelaying, pipefitting, and steamfitting—are sometimes considered a single trade; and workers tend to specialize in one of these four areas. Together, plumbers are in one of the largest and highest-paid construction occupations.

PAYING YOUR DUES

A college education is not required for the position. There are no national licensing requirements; instead, requirements vary from place to place and employer to employer. Most plumbers undergo some type of apprenticeship training. Some programs are administered under the auspices of a local union-management committee and members of one of several major unions, including the Mechanical Contractors Association of America, the National Association of Plumbing-Heating-Cooling Contractors, and the National Fire Sprinkler Association. Typical apprenticeship programs include four to five years of on-the-job training supplemented by courses in drafting, blueprint reading, and plumbing codes and regulations. Armed forces training is considered valuable in the profession. Some former military personnel can even receive credit for previous work toward a civilian apprenticeship program. Also, secondary or postsecondary courses in fields such as plumbing, mathematics, drafting, AutoCAD, etc., can provide solid preparation.

Those interested in advancing in the field can, with additional training, become supervisors for mechanical and plumbing contractors. Moreover, many plumbers go into business for themselves. Still others migrate into related fields, such as construction management or building inspection.

ASSOCIATED CAREERS

Plumbers are closely related, professionally speaking, to pipelayers, pipefitters, and steamfitters. Because of the similarity among them, it is fairly easy to move from one of these occupations to another. Other related fields involve construction supervision, including construction management and building maintenance.

PAST AND FUTURE

Although hot and cold water systems were actually developed first by the Greeks, public baths and sewage systems reached their height with the Romans. The job description of the ancient Roman plumber lasted well into the twentieth century. This plumber installed and repaired lead (*plumbus* is Latin for "lead") pipes, worked on roofs, gutters, sewers, drains, basically anything involving supply and waste. With the advances of plumbing systems in the last century, plumbers now require more knowledge than before to succeed in their trade. The profession has also become more specialized over time.

The outlook for the plumbing industry is very good. Demand for work is expected to exceed the supply of workers in the field. A multiplicity of factors will contribute to the increasing demand of plumbers, including building renovations and maintenance of existing residential and municipal systems. One of the advantages of being a plumber is that, even when construction activities decline, maintenance for (or replacement of) existing piping systems continues to serve as a source of work. For this reason, the plumbing industry is generally not as adversely affected as other construction industries during periods of economic decline.

QUALITY OF LIFE

2 YEARS During the first several years in the profession, new plumbers will be trained in local apprenticeship programs or in the Armed Forces. They work closely with full-time (and in all likelihood, licensed) plumbing professionals and learn about the installation, function, repair, and maintenance of plumbing systems. Each year of training is supplemented by at least 144 hours of relevant classroom instruction, which familiarizes new plumbers with the specifics of blueprint reading, building codes, construction, and other essential plumbing-related topics.

5 YEARS At this point in their careers, plumbers have finished their apprenticeships and are ready to enter the workforce. They may take a full-time position with a construction or maintenance company, work on a per-project basis, or—if they are especially motivated—start their own businesses. Self-employed plumbers usually begin working from home. If they are successful, they may one day be the owners of small businesses or work as managers who oversee teams of plumbers.

10 YEARS Depending on their specific goals, plumbers may have taken any number of career paths. They may have gone into business for themselves. Some plumbers seek out additional training and move into supervisor positions for mechanical and plumbing contractors. Still others venture into related areas, such as construction management or building inspection.

MAJOR EMPLOYERS

AMERICAN PLUMBING AND MECHANICAL, INC.
1950 Louis Henna Boulevard
Round Rock, TX 78664
Tel: 512-246-5260
Fax: 512-246-5290

GEM PLUMBING AND HEATING COMPANY
1 Wellington Road
Lincoln, RI 02865
Tel: 401-831-7000
Fax: 401-528-1976
www.gemplumbing.com

MCGRAW-HILL CONSTRUCTION
E-mail: contactus_cc@constructioncustomer-care.com
www.construction.com

Note: Many plumbers are either self-employed or work for small operations.

MAJOR ASSOCIATIONS

NATIONAL ASSOCIATION OF PLUMBING, COOLING AND HEATING CONTRACTORS
180 South Washington Street
Falls Church, VA 22046
Tel: 703-273-8100 or 800-533-7694
Fax: 703-237-7442
www.phccweb.org

THE NATIONAL FIRE SPRINKLER ASSOCIATION
PO Box 1000
Patterson, New York 12563
Tel: 845-878-4200
Fax: 845-878-4215
www.nfsa.org

UNITED ASSOCIATION OF JOURNEYMEN AND APPRENTICES OF THE PLUMBING AND PIPEFITTING INDUSTRY OF THE U.S. AND CANADA
United Association Building
901 Massachusetts Avenue, NW
Washington, DC 20001-4397
Tel: 202-628-5823
Fax: 202-628-5024
www.ua.org

POLICE OFFICER/MANAGER

SALARY • • •

HOURS • • •

EDUCATION • • •

BOOKS, FILMS, AND TV SHOWS
FEATURING THE PROFESSION

- **The Choirboys**
- **Cop Land**
- **Law & Order**
- **Narc**
- **NYPD Blue**

YOU'LL HAVE CONTACT WITH

- **Attorneys**
- **Criminals**
- **Criminologists**
- **Federal agents**
- **Paramedics**

PROFESSIONALS READ

- **Best Practices Review**
- **Biosecurity and Bioterrorism**
- **Community Policing Exchange**
- **Crime & Justice International**
- **Forensic Examiner**
- **Police Journal Online**

A DAY IN THE LIFE

Of the many Hollywood portrayals of police officers, only a few of them have provided an accurate picture of the demands and rewards a career on a police force offers. Police work comes in many forms. Sheriffs, state troopers, bailiffs, detectives, and cops on the beat are all part of the local law enforcement community. (If you're interested in federal law enforcement, see the "FBI Agent" profile.) A police officer's basic responsibilities include maintaining public order and protecting lives and property. A police officer must be alert to any and all impending threats. Once a crime has been committed, detectives seize the reins and engage in sleuthing that ranges from routine questioning to DNA analysis. Sheriffs and state troopers maintain order in bigger bailiwicks: large, thinly populated districts and major highways. Once selected for the force, many officers specialize in a particular aspect of law enforcement or investigation. Most officers are assigned to patrol a specific area. As police officers rise up the ranks, their duties become more specialized. All police officers, because of their unique role in society, are responsible for maintaining the trust of the public they serve.

> The pressure on officers can be enormous.

Because of the responsibilities and prerogatives that come with doing police work, the pressure on officers can be enormous. "As a police officer, you're called on to do everything. You need to be a social worker, a psychologist, an officer of the peace, and a soldier," one officer reported. Being the first line of defense between criminals and their victims can be very stressful. Nevertheless, police work is mostly a series of routines: patrols, investigations, and paperwork. Even in America's biggest and most violent cities, police officers seldom have occasion to draw their guns, much less fire them. Perhaps the most common burdens of police work are filling out forms in triplicate and enduring long, uneventful hours walking a beat or riding around in a patrol car. Local law enforcement is a demanding job, but one that most police officers find worthwhile. As one officer commented, "It's interesting to map out strategies to solve community problems."

PAYING YOUR DUES

Police officers are expected to be in good physical shape. If a candidate's height, weight, strength, or vision do not meet the standards that the police department requires, the candidate's application for employment may be rejected. Most police forces require only a high school diploma, although some of them expect their officers to have taken college courses or encourage them to pursue higher education while serving on the force. Character is also an important consideration. Some applicants to law enforcement jobs undergo psychological evaluation. All applicants are tested for drug use.

Because law enforcement is a local concern, the path to the police force differs from community to community and state to state, but as the world becomes more complicated, so does the training required to become a police officer. Smaller communities may require new officers to complete an apprenticeship program. Large cities maintain police academies where aspiring officers are trained in the various aspects of police work, including investigative procedures, self-defense, and the law, while fulfilling more minor duties such as directing traffic. Officers can pursue a managerial track and advance to become a sergeant, lieutenant, captain, or even a police chief or commissioner. Generally speaking, you must serve on the force for five years before you are eligible to take the lieutenant's exam, and after two years as a lieutenant, you can take the captain's test. Each post requires increased education as well. You must have a two-year associate's degree to advance to sergeant status, 96 credits toward a bachelor's degree to be considered for a lieutenant position, and a bachelor's degree to become a captain.

ASSOCIATED CAREERS

There are many law enforcement tasks that the police leave to civilian personnel. Psychologists, chemists, biologists, photographers, and many other specialists can find employment with larger police departments. Although none of these specialties is essential to police work all the time, in some situations, expertise can be the key to cracking a case.

Since police officers can and often do retire at an early age, many former police officers find good work providing private security for corporations or individuals.

PAST AND FUTURE

Many law enforcement duties were once left to the military. By 1829, the city of London had established a metropolitan police force separate from the military. America's first state police force was the Texas Rangers (established in 1853). Much of America's frontier law enforcement was voluntary, which made obedience to the law equally voluntary.

Police officers note that their job changes dramatically under different political administrations. The agenda of the administration, whether they want to focus on reducing theft, cutting down on white-collar crime, or pursuing drug dealers, affects the kinds of criminals police target. The overall strategies police officers then have to employ changes their daily routine. Larger cities have expanded their police forces, but the occupation as a whole is expected to undergo slower growth than other professions through the turn of the century.

QUALITY OF LIFE

2 YEARS
The routine duties of a beginning police officer may be disappointing, or they may be terrifying. Nevertheless, few officers leave the profession at this stage. Opportunities for advancement in a police department are tied to seniority, so dedicated police officers stick out the tedious times as they move up on the list of men and women eligible for promotion. Long, uneventful days are punctuated by moments of danger and occasional moments of triumphs.

5 YEARS
Around this time, command positions become available. At this point, an officer is usually eligible to take the sergeant's exam if he or she has at least a two-year associate's degree. Other officers specialize in investigating particular crimes (murder, fraud, drug trafficking). As police work becomes more scientific, many officers find it necessary to return to school in order to move up the ranks.

10 YEARS
Police officers can usually retire with a pension after 20 years on the force, so 10 years marks the halfway point. Many seasoned officers choose to stay in uniform on the beat. These officers serve as examples for their younger colleagues and provide what may be the rookies' most important training. Officers who have already made captain are eligible for consideration to become inspectors, police chiefs, or commissioners. These positions are obtained through political appointments. Upon retirement, police officers can expect a pension (usually at half pay), an opportunity to pursue a second career, and the appreciation of a safer society.

POLITICAL CAMPAIGN WORKER

A DAY IN THE LIFE

Political campaign workers specialize in the art of winning elections. The profession includes many subspecialties: press and public relations, polling, opposition research, fund-raising, logistical organizing, and a wide range of other skills to deal with the crises of a campaign. In large campaigns, specialists representing all of these skills work together to develop integrated campaign strategies; in smaller, local elections, one or two professionals will serve as jacks-of-all-trades, putting to use this entire range of skills and developing their expertise. Technical and tactical skills are extremely important in campaign management, but the ultimate emphasis in the profession is on winning. Campaign professionals with a reputation for victory can have lucrative, prominent careers; individuals who participate in too many losing campaigns will have trouble finding work.

{ highly public }

This is a career for people who love the thrill of the chase. Many individuals get into the profession by volunteering for a particular candidate they support and falling in love with the excitement of campaigns. In the weeks preceding elections, campaign professionals work full-time, 24 hours a day, seven days a week, as they plan and coordinate down-to-the-wire campaign strategies. Deadline pressure is intense, as election day provides a final test of the staff's campaign work. Many people in the profession thrive on the pressure; others burn out and find other work.

Campaign management is also highly public work. Pollsters and researchers may work behind the scenes; but the press and public relations specialists and those who wish to rise to the position of campaign manager must feel comfortable working with the media. At the highest level of political campaigns, statements and actions of senior campaign aides are as important as those of the candidate. Some relish being in the public eye; others are more comfortable working behind the scenes.

PAYING YOUR DUES

The career campaign professional's first exposure to politics is usually as a volunteer for a campaign, perhaps over summer vacation while still a student. Volunteers perform the bulk of the low-level jobs in every campaign, but they are often found in positions of substantial responsibility in smaller, local campaigns. A bright, hardworking volunteer can rise rapidly in a reelection staff, and this is often the best way to acquire the credentials that can lead to a career working on major political campaigns.

In some of the profession's disciplines, educational or career background is also extremely important. Training in statistics is a prerequisite to polling and voter analysis; many influential pollsters have doctorates in statistics. Many political workers begin as journalists and then put their knowledge of the media to use as press aides and campaign spokespeople. A degree in political science can also be useful. Some universities offer master's degrees in political management. This can also be an effective route into the profession.

ASSOCIATED CAREERS

Campaign workers often depart to fields where the skills they have developed will be valuable, such as advertising, public relations, and journalism. Some of them go to law school, often with an eye toward developing their own political careers. The more senior and victorious campaign workers often take jobs as press secretaries, political and policy consultants, or general staff workers in the administrations of their successful candidates.

PAST AND FUTURE

United States campaign politics have changed significantly since the days of political machines like New York's Tammany Hall at the turn of the century, when Thanksgiving turkeys were exchanged for votes. Ward captains who can mobilize small armies of volunteers to man phones and hand out leaflets still play an important role in political campaigns, but campaign management has become a sophisticated science. Demographic studies, focus groups, and advertising consultants have become the field's stock-in-trade and management of these resources has demanded increasing professionalization in the field.

The trend has been toward increasing budgets and technological sophistication—mass mailings, tightly choreographed press conferences, and photo opportunities are now supplemented by websites and chat rooms on the Internet. The cost of political campaigning has risen with every election in recent years. With the increased resources expended on campaigns have come increased opportunities for professionals with the ability to make effective use of them, and this pattern seems likely to continue.

QUALITY OF LIFE

2 YEARS Young campaign managers build reputations by managing local campaigns or by signing on in junior positions under a known manager running a large, well-staffed election effort. Often, young campaign professionals move back and forth between these options as job opportunities arise. Developing personal contacts in the field is vital, as managers with the prestige to get hired to run major campaigns have core groups of favored aides whom they take with them from campaign to campaign, and it is these favored few who have the best chance for a shot at running a large campaign of their own.

5 YEARS Individuals who remain in the field have worked through two or three campaigns and have begun to establish themselves. Some of them remain on the campaign circuit, moving from race to race as opportunities appear. Many campaign workers move into more permanent positions in state and national party organizations, providing support to party campaigns and coordinating cooperative campaign efforts at different election levels. Others move into political consulting firms, which offer expert polling, media, or financial services to a number of campaigns in any given election year.

10 YEARS By now, campaign workers have established themselves as managers. Individuals who have left for the private sector, perhaps as consultants, exploit their contacts in the political world. Party officials have considerable authority over the allocation of their organization's resources, and they have a voice in the setting of party priorities and platforms. Independent campaign managers have reached the point where they can count on senior campaign positions—as managers, spokespersons, pollsters—in each election year. There is significant job mobility at this level: Successful campaign officials often become senior political aides, and managers move back and forth between party and campaign positions.

MAJOR EMPLOYERS
DEMOCRATIC NATIONAL COMMITTEE
430 South Capital Street, SE
Washington, DC 20003
Tel: 202-863-8000
Fax: 202-488-5043

LIBERTARIAN PARTY
2600 Virginia Avenue, NW, Suite 100
Washington, DC 20037
Tel: 202-333-0008
Fax: 202-333-0072
E-mail: hq@lp.org
www.lp.org

REPUBLICAN NATIONAL COMMITTEE
310 First Street, SE
Washington, DC 20003
Tel: 202-863-8500
Fax: 202-863-8820

MAJOR ASSOCIATIONS
AMERICAN ASSOCIATION OF POLITICAL CONSULTANTS
600 Pennsylvania Avenue, SE, Suite 330
Washington, DC 20003
Tel: 202-544-9815
Fax: 202-544-9816
www.theaapc.com

POWER PLANT MANAGER

BOOKS, FILMS, AND TV SHOWS
FEATURING THE PROFESSION
- **Keeping Time**
- **Listen to Your Workers**
- **McCaughen**

YOU'LL HAVE CONTACT WITH
- **Computer engineers**
- **Electrical engineers**
- **Production managers**
- **Technicians**

PROFESSIONALS READ
- **Power and Light**

A DAY IN THE LIFE

Most power plant managers supervise the production of one specific good: electricity. Power plants operate 24 hours a day, seven days a week, turbines churning out megawatt after megawatt of powerful, invisible current. Plant managers soon learn that the technical aspects of the job notwithstanding—managing power loads, controlling production and inventory, and handling the continuous maintenance chores—the heart of managing a power plant is managing people. Plant managers who embrace both these aspects of the job tend to be the most successful at this career. Power plant managers can work during the day or night, and many of them come to know their plants as well as they know their own homes. They must be on top of everything, so many of them make rounds themselves, greeting workers on their shift and personally inspecting any problem areas. This hands-on managing is one of the reasons that power plant managers have such a high level of satisfaction; the job provides opportunities for intellectual stimulation, social interaction, and physical activity. Some power plant managers added that the sterile environment and rotating shifts make personal connections very important. A power plant manager must know the basic rules of electrical safety. The first rule of the profession is, "When in doubt, shut it down." Power grids of entire countries are under the watch of power plant managers. Supplying too little or too much electricity could have grave consequences, like medical equipment ceasing to function or main power trunks burning out (these can take days to fix). A power plant is maintained and operated by hundreds of workers, and the manager coordinates all activities. One manager told us, "You're like a cruise director, telling people where they need to go and who they have to meet up with." Successful power plant managers are adept at distributing their human resources and combining seriousness and a dedicated work effort with a personal approach that fosters quality work and loyalty. They are able to think before they act, to act when they need to, and to inspire others to follow them on ordinary days and in times of crisis.

> { You're like a cruise director. }

PAYING YOUR DUES

Employers seek out candidates with a college degree in any major that demonstrates quantitative skills and attention to detail, as well as courses in mathematics, physics, electrical engineering, or computer science. Some power plant managers begin as technicians and work up to supervisory and managerial positions; this can mean extra shifts and long days for beginners in the profession. Individuals who want to work in nuclear power plants have to satisfy additional academic and professional requirements. The Nuclear Regulatory Commission (NRC) administers tests each year for professionals to earn licenses to operate these special power plants. Many employers look for candidates who have experience in the navy nuclear submarine program. Although not a requirement, individuals in any part of the profession (nuclear or otherwise) often find it helpful to join a professional union, such as the International Brotherhood of Electrical Workers.

ASSOCIATED CAREERS

The personality traits of power plant managers allow them to adapt well to any managerial position. Some of them become production managers, quality control managers, and inventory control managers. Some of them continue with their education and become electricians, electrical engineers, and power plant inspectors.

PAST AND FUTURE

Power plant managers became a necessary part of the workforce with the growth of the use of electricity in the early 1900s. Cities, which used to be lit by gas lamps, found they could provide safe, consistent streetlamp light by harnessing this electrical power. Once cities began to be wired for electricity, the demand for the product spread rapidly, and power became part of nearly every household in America after the middle of the century. Power, understood as a great benefit, was also recognized as a potential danger. The power industry continues to be one of the most heavily regulated industries in the country.

The future of power plant managers is tied to the expansion of power facilities in the United States. Currently, there are no production plans for extensive power plants on the slate of any state government construction programs. Demand for electricity is on the rise, but instead of building new plants, existing facilities are being refitted to handle the increased capacity, and power is being purchased from other sources.

QUALITY OF LIFE

2 YEARS Two-year managers are usually technicians. Many of them are in technical managerial positions, but only a few of them have reached the level of power plant manager. Most of them are involved in meetings and coordination with the power plant manager and learn more technical skills in their free time. Two-year managers said the lessons they learned as technicians helped them become more sensitive and capable managers. The hours are reasonable; satisfaction is average.

5 YEARS Individuals in the profession for five years know whether they are on a power plant manager track or not. Many of them have moved from technical positions to administrative positions to familiarize themselves with the other requirements of the job. Individuals working at nuclear facilities regularly pass their licensing exams; a single failing grade can ruin the best candidate's chances for a power plant managerial position. Promotions at this point are driven by the availability of openings, as the number of qualified candidates exceeds the number of available power plant managerial positions.

10 YEARS Many individuals are now power plant managers, although some of them have had to relocate to pursue opportunities. Many power facilities are designed in a very standard fashion (and strict regulations encourage that), so mobility doesn't require an extraordinary amount of reeducation. The biggest problem that power plant managers face in new plants is earning the loyalty, trust, and respect of their fellow workers. Ex-power plant managers usually have a strong following, and stepping into someone else's well-respected shoes requires skill and perseverance.

MAJOR EMPLOYERS
HONDA
R & D Americas, Inc.
21001 State Route 739
Raymond, OH 43067-9705
Tel: 937-644-0439
Fax: 937-645-6337
E-mail: emp@oh.hra.com
www.honda.com

LONG ISLAND POWER ASSOCIATION
333 Earle Ovington Boulevard
Uniondale, NY 11553
Tel: 631-755-6000
Fax: 516-222-9137
www.lipower.org

MAJOR ASSOCIATIONS
INTERNATIONAL BROTHERHOOD OF ELECTRICAL WORKERS
900 Seventh Street, NW
Washington, DC 20001
Tel: 202-833-7000
Fax: 202-728-7676
www.ibew.org

PRINTER

A DAY IN THE LIFE

Do you want to design and produce books, newspapers, magazines, posters, or brochures? Have you ever wondered who gets to print "All the News That's Fit to Print"? And how it gets to the newsstand? Many positions in this field serve what is known as the graphic communications industry—the third-largest employer in the United States. Being a printer can be very gratifying because you can touch and see your final product. Printers have an obvious, clearly definable and useful skill. The printing industry offers positions for individuals with a variety of skills, needs, and work styles. With computers aiding the process to turn facilities that once offered particular types of printing into full-service operations offering every type of print matter, today's print shop is staffed by an army of specialists who perfect their step in the process using a wide range of graphic, software, and factory-floor skills.

{ intense deadlines }

Printers usually work under intense deadlines. While almost everybody involved in the printing field works 40 hours a week, many printers work nights and holidays to meet deadlines. All printing jobs follow a similarly structured order. To start, sales representatives and brokers get clients. They pass the job onto the production manager, who then estimates how much the job will cost, oversees other workers, and maintains deadlines. The production manager depends on the plant manager, who oversees aspects of the printing process and handles all technical emergencies. Plant engineers, who maintain and improve the equipment, are also in contact with the manager. In the first step of the physical process, compositors read the copy and arrange the type, which requires extraordinary patience. Typesetting is done by computer to make plates; color separators render digital and printed art into layers of film separated into four or more colors. Printing press operators yield the final result, generally through the use of computers. Finally, the binder completes the process. He or she puts the printed matter together to create books, pamphlets, newspapers, journals, or magazines.

PAYING YOUR DUES

Each aspect of the field has different education and training requirements. Some of the aspects can be learned in under a year; others require years of training for total fluency. High school diplomas are required for all workers. Both two- and four-year colleges offer associate and bachelor's degrees in graphics arts, degrees that have become necessary for supervisory and some entry-level positions in this field. Applicants should study math, electronics, and computers to widen their options for specialization in the field.

Normally, the printer begins his or her career as a helper and receives on-the-job training. New printers move forward in their careers as they master each skill or technique. They should expect to learn new skills whenever advancements are made in the technology of their specialty. Sometimes printers enter the field through four- to six-year apprenticeships. Openings for these are decreasing in number, but they are still valuable in every position in printing. Due to increased automation, some specializations are requiring increased technical ability (rather than craft skills). Traditionally, plant managers have risen from the ranks of the physical careers. Today, though, companies are looking for applicants with degrees in fields like engineering. Employers also want applicants who display creativity yet can work under time constraints and have good eyesight. The most likely candidates are people who are analytical and outgoing and have an eye for color and graphics.

ASSOCIATED CAREERS

Printers who tire of printing can transfer their skills to another part of the process of creating books and newspapers. Many people, such as copyeditors (see "Copyeditor" profile), are involved with the product before it reaches the printer. Jewelers, sign painters, and graphic artists create models that give the printer a prototype for what they would like. Their work is slightly more artistic than that of the printer. Printers' skills can be valuable in publishers' production departments.

PAST AND FUTURE

When Johannes Gutenberg invented movable type, the printing industry was born. His first book was the *Gutenberg Bible*, printed in 1456 by applying ink to raised metal and pressing the letters onto paper. Later his methods evolved into the revolving cylinder that is still used today, along with many other new technologies.

Computers have changed printing drastically. They have made some jobs, such as photo engraving and composition, almost obsolete, but have created new opportunities for lithographers and those involved in computer technology. The advents of direct marketing and desktop publishing have been boons for the printer. Desktop publishing is anticipated to become the most prolific area in printing. The printer's environment is changing, too. More printers find themselves working for small desktop publishing companies rather than for large presses.

QUALITY OF LIFE

2 YEARS During the first two years, printers usually work in apprenticeships as production or sales assistants. One printer advises novices to "learn computers, have fun, and pick the area that you enjoy the most." Many of the newest printers are computer-controlled and learning the "art" of working the software so as to produce the desired effects requires working with an experienced operator—especially with color presses. Often beginners are stuck with the "graveyard shift" and are working on press at odd hours under heavy deadline pressure.

5 YEARS By this point in their careers, most printers have established positions in the company. They are working full-time with fairly regular hours and are afforded greater independence in operating and maintaining the machinery.

10 YEARS Ten-year printers tend to be happy with their professions. Most have moved into managerial positions, supervising pressmen and perhaps dealing with clients on the more complicated jobs. They are consulted on major capital investments such as new presses and thus take on a crucial role within their company.

MAJOR EMPLOYERS

BANTA CORPORATION
225 Main Street, Box 8003
Menasha, WI 54952-8003
Tel: 920-751-7777
Fax 920-751-7790
E-mail: info@banta.com
www.banta.com

CONSOLIDATED GRAPHICS, INC.
Corporate Headquarters
5858 Westheimer, Suite 200
Houston, TX 77057
Tel: 713-787-0977
Fax: 713-787-5013
www.consolidatedgraphics.com

DARBY PRINTING COMPANY
6215 Perdue Drive
Atlanta, GA 30336
Tel: 800-241-5292
Fax: 404-346-3332
www.darbyprinting.com
Contact: Human Resources

PLYMOUTH PRINTING COMPANY, INC.
450 North Avenue
Cranford, NJ 07016
Tel: 908-276-8100
Fax: 908-276-6566
www.plymouthprinting.com
Contact: Human Resources

QUAD GRAPHICS
Corporate Headquarters
W224 N3322 Duplainville Road
Pewaukee, WI 53072
Tel: 414-566-6000
www.qg.com

MAJOR ASSOCIATIONS

NATIONAL ASSOCIATION FOR PRINTING LEADERSHIP
75 West Century Road
Paramus, NJ 07652
Tel: 800-642-6275 or 201-634-9600
Fax: 201-986-2976
www.napl.org

THE ASSOCIATION FOR SUPPLIERS OF PRINTING, PUBLISHING, AND CONVERTING TECHNOLOGIES
1899 Preston White Drives
Reston, VA 22091-4367
Tel: 703-264-7200
Fax: 703-620-0994
E-mail: npes@npes.org
www.npes.org

PRODUCTION MANAGER

BOOKS, FILMS, AND TV SHOWS
FEATURING THE PROFESSION
- **Gung Ho**
- **Take This Job and Shove It**

YOU'LL HAVE CONTACT WITH
- **Industrial engineers**
- **Line workers**
- **Product designers**
- **Quality control managers**

PROFESSIONALS READ
- **Industry Week**

A DAY IN THE LIFE

A few production managers we surveyed added "traffic controller" to their title parenthetically. The clarification is apt, since their job is not to produce but to make sure that production runs smoothly. Production managers are primarily administrators or supervisors; they determine the allocation of labor resources, track production scheduling and costs, make any on-the-fly adjustments to the process, and coordinate any receiving of raw materials or shipping of final goods. A production manager is very busy most days. "The job [entails] a lot of coordination. You should be able to juggle a lot of different jobs at the same time and deal with any emergencies that come up," explained one. The variety of the work on a day-to-day basis recommends this job to people with strong work ethics, curious minds, and organizational abilities.

{ flexibility }

Many production managers are asked to implement systems of production tracking and quality control, so the first step for product managers is to become informed about existing systems of production, past cost estimates, and company policies. "You've got to be careful not to make recommendations until you've gathered enough information to make intelligent ones," offered a five-year production manager. Also, production managers need to gain the trust of the people who work for them. "If you're not credible, you're not effective," said one production manager. A good production manager will also react to situations as they occur. "Flexibility is the key to success," as one respondent noted. Priorities, backlogs, breakdowns, and strikes can alter intricately planned scheduling, and the production manager has to be flexible enough to adjust to these situations without reducing overall efficiency.

It's not unusual for the production manager to be located on the production floor so that he or she can see firsthand the running of the production process. But while production managers are involved in each stage of production, few micromanage the day-to-day details of each department's work. A production manager spends some time working alone on reports, but most of his or her time (more than 60 percent) is spent meeting with representatives from different levels of the production process. When production facilities are spread over large areas, a production manager typically spends a significant amount of time on the telephone.

The visible, tangible results they produce are a source of satisfaction for most production managers. Many of the managers surveyed noted that it was good to be able to point to shipments going out and coming in, to quality products produced cheaply and efficiently, and to the increase companies see in their bottom line. One summarized his feelings simply by saying, "It feels great because people at first resent what you do, and when they see the results, they come around. Everybody wins."

PAYING YOUR DUES

Production managers have no specific academic requirements, but coursework that proves helpful includes economics, accounting, finance, production and manufacturing systems, organizational behavior, psychology, sociology, and English. Production managers have to be well organized and creative—a combination of talents that many of them find difficult to demonstrate through ordinary work experience. Production experience can be a big plus on a resume. No licensing requirements exist, and professional organizations are significant only in areas of specialization, such as for quality control managers or human resource managers.

ASSOCIATED CAREERS

Production managers who decide to leave the profession search out challenges that excite both the creative and the detail-oriented sides of their personalities. Many of them become entrepreneurs, efficiency experts, and strategic marketers. Their intimacy with the production process makes a transition to general administrative management easy, but relatively few managers take this option. It seems that the profession provides a challenge that few people are in a hurry to forsake.

PAST AND FUTURE

Production managers can trace their origins back to the time-efficiency experts who first analyzed modern industrial society at the turn of the century. Today, production managers are essential to a variety of industries and will likely remain so for at least the next decade. Opportunities for production managers are expected to grow at a healthy pace as industries recognize the benefits the centralization of production responsibilities bring.

QUALITY OF LIFE

2 YEARS Two years into the profession, production managers have made some headway in improving production efficiency, but many of them are still educating themselves on the production process, familiarizing themselves with client needs and concerns, and working as assistants to more experienced managers. Many of them have proposed changes, and most often a few of these proposals have been adopted as test cases to see how they will affect production. The hours are long but interesting; salaries are low in relation to the hours.

5 YEARS Five-year survivors have earned the trust of their coworkers, proposed significant changes, seen these proposals implemented, and achieved production results. They also look for new challenges. Many of them decide during these middle years whether to pursue higher-level managerial responsibility; a significant number of them, however, choose to stay as production managers. Important contacts are made with suppliers and shippers; these contacts can become significant if one changes jobs.

10 YEARS Individuals who have survived 10 years in the profession face a big question: should they stay, or should they go? A fair number of them switch firms at this point, opting for newer challenges rather than resting on their laurels. The hours decrease as many of them choose instead to remain at their current positions and fine-tune existing operations. Salaries rise, and most people who leave the profession at this point only do so to retire.

MAJOR EMPLOYERS

NATIONAL SEMICONDUCTOR CORPORATION
2900 Semiconductor Drive
PO Box 58090
Santa Clara, CA 95052
Tel: 408-721-5000
Fax: 800-413-3467
www.nsc.com
Contact: Professional Staffing

PROCTER & GAMBLE
1 P&G Plaza
Cincinnati, OH 45202
Tel: 513-983-1100
www.pg.com
Contact: Personnel

MAJOR ASSOCIATIONS

THE ASSOCIATION FOR MANUFACTURING TECHNOLOGY
7901 Westpark Drive
McLean, VA 22102
Tel: 703-893-2900
Fax: 703-893-1151
www.mfgtech.org

QUALITY ASSURANCE ENGINEER

BOOKS, FILMS, AND TV SHOWS FEATURING THE PROFESSION
- Hackers

YOU'LL HAVE CONTACT WITH
- Production staff
- Programmers

PROFESSIONALS READ
- Information Week
- Wired

A DAY IN THE LIFE

Quality assurance departments exist in large companies that produce software or are involved in Web development. The quality assurance engineer makes sure that all of the programs work properly and that everything on a website functions properly. Software testing is diverse and involves examining the Web server, which the user never sees.

The goal of the quality assurance engineer is to try and make things not work so the programmer can catch errors before they occur. "If it works, we're not interested in it. It's our job to anticipate a problem and think of any bone-headed thing that a user can do to a program or Web page. We play devil's advocate, troubleshooting any combination of errors that a user could potentially make," says one engineer.

> { "If it works, we're not interested in it." }

Quality assurance professionals come from a variety of backgrounds, and they are generally freethinkers who don't have a preconceived notion of how things are supposed to work. They are problem solvers who like a good puzzle. They are often thorough and detail-oriented and enjoy tinkering. "Persistence is also key [to success]," notes one tennis pro turned computer pro. "If you can't make something not work, keep on trying."

PAYING YOUR DUES

Quality assurance engineers are the bridge between end-users and programmers, so they must understand the problems that users can encounter. Early on, an entry-level quality assurance position involves simple testing. For example, a user may need to input a password, which must be between 5 and 10 characters, into a website. The quality assurance engineer must then test how this will work if the user types a space, a dot, a dash, or a comma.

ASSOCIATED CAREERS

Depending on their technical skills, quality assurance engineers could move into programming or production, which deals with creating Web pages that are displayed on-screen.

Every company that produces a product has a need for quality assurance engineers, from chemical engineering to auto manufacturing. While major specialization is obviously required within various industries, there are some overarching paradigms, including understanding user behavior and being familiar with pattern recognition. With further training, a quality assurance professional could also move into another field.

PAST AND FUTURE

The quality assurance model is a concept that originated with manufacturing and crossed over into other industries, such as agriculture. Because programmers tend to lack the disciplined eye needed to see flaws, computer companies employ quality assurance engineers to catch potential bugs before their products go to market.

Computer programming used to place a heavy emphasis on testing, and there was no room for error. If you look at how the computer field has evolved, programming has become more complicated and difficult, while the end product has become much easier to use. Quality assurance engineers deal with the finished product without any care for the code that goes into it. Ease of use and functionality are their only concerns, so the future of quality assurance remains to be seen.

QUALITY OF LIFE

2 YEARS An entry-level quality assurance engineer will test simple applications and basic user interaction, such as opening a Web page, trying different menu options, and clicking on links.

5 YEARS After five years, a good quality assurance professional handles larger projects or more complicated software and is adept at minimizing the number of steps needed to identify an error, an art akin to programming. The fewer steps there are, the simpler it is to figure out where something went wrong, and the easier it is for the programmer to fix.

10 YEARS At this level, most quality assurance engineers are managing a staff of quality assurance engineers, and they are often responsible for large, important projects. Alternate career paths at this stage include a position in programming or a job as a technical sales representative with a software company.

MAJOR EMPLOYERS

Large companies (usually 100+ people) that produce Web development or software typically hire QA engineers.

MAJOR ASSOCIATIONS

INFORMATION TECHNOLOGY ASSOCIATION OF AMERICA
1401 Wilson Boulevard, Suite 1100
Arlington, VA 22209
Tel: 703-522-5055
Fax: 703-525-2279
www.itaa.org

QUALITY ASSURANCE INSTITUTE WORLDWIDE
2101 Park Center Drive, Suite 200
Orlando, FL 32835
Tel: 407-363-1111
www.qaiusa.com

QUALITY CONTROL MANAGER

SALARY ● ●
HOURS ● ●
EDUCATION ● ●

BOOKS, FILMS, AND TV SHOWS
FEATURING THE PROFESSION
- Listen to Your Workers

YOU'LL HAVE CONTACT WITH
- Industrial engineers
- Inventory managers
- Management consultants
- Production managers

PROFESSIONALS READ
- Industry Week
- Journal of Quality Issues
- Quality Control

A DAY IN THE LIFE

Quality control managers work in every type of production environment imaginable, from producing dictionaries to dowel-cutting for boat plugs. A quality control manager samples products, analyzes them, and then makes recommendations about how to better the quality of the goods. It takes a firm grasp of scientific as well as managerial concepts to be a successful quality control expert; quality control managers work hard inspecting, analyzing, and writing reports about production. These people are the last line of defense between quality goods that the public respects and shoddy work that can harm a company's reputation.

Does this mean they are appreciated by coworkers? Quality control managers answered us with a resounding one-word answer: "No." If you absolutely need approbation from your colleagues, be warned: Quality control is not the field for you. "People see you as the policeman, criticizing people's work and telling them that they're not doing their job right," reported one quality control inspector. The best quality control professionals act as educators as well, letting people know that they are only there to help everyone keep product quality high. "I spend more time talking with people than examining objects," wrote one eight-year veteran of the quality control field, "because the object can't change."

{ last line of defense }

Meeting with workers, executives, and supervisors takes up about 30 percent of the quality control manager's day; another 30 percent is spent testing and analyzing materials. Scientific methodologies are important; individuals who do not properly conduct their tests are going to make recommendations based on faulty data. The remainder of the quality control manager's time is spent writing reports, making recommendations, and doing professional reading. Quality control experts must keep up with current materials used, statistical studies, and technological advances that affect the field of quality control. For example, stress-testing of construction materials can be done using high-pressured pistons to compress them to the point of breakage; a recent advance lets the quality control expert analyze the molecular composition of a small sample to get nearly as precise an estimate of its tensile strength.

PAYING YOUR DUES

No specific academic requirements exist for quality control experts, but the many positions in the field that involve scientific analysis require a bachelor's degree. Candidates who majored in chemistry, physics, and engineering are at an advantage during the job hunt; at a minimum, coursework should include mathematics, statistics, and computer modeling. Some candidates who have only high school degrees are sponsored to take two- or three-year post-high-school courses that train them in a particular industry. Many of these industries (i.e., the automobile, aerospace, and glassmaking industries) have requirements that can only be satisfied through specific training. Quality control trainees may also have to spend a significant amount of time on a production floor analyzing behavior that affects quality control.

ASSOCIATED CAREERS

Quality control managers find a number of detail-oriented jobs open to them. People with financial backgrounds become bookkeepers, accountants, and loan officers more than anything else. A number of individuals with strong interpersonal skills become production supervisors and inventory managers—fields well-suited to their organizational abilities and analytic natures.

PAST AND FUTURE

Quality control managers first became important with the industrial revolution and the mass production of similar items. Large-scale production initially brought with it high levels of variation between goods from the same plant, and consumers were wary. Craftsmen were no longer attending to their individual concerns; the consumers were dealing now with a faceless organization in which there was no personal accountability. The need for consistent customer satisfaction inspired the creation of quality control managers. The position has been a central feature of industrialized production ever since.

Quality control managers can expect to find job openings in many industries in the next decade, but positions should grow at a slightly slower pace than that of the economy in general. As standardized systems that predict levels of quality are developed, and as larger companies dominate production environments, fewer quality control experts will be needed to maintain the same level of excellence. Still, a significant number of quality control managers will reach retirement age in the next decade, and positions should be available at a rate only slightly below the current one.

QUALITY OF LIFE

2 YEARS Quality control managers have developed systems of testing that accurately describe the quality levels of their company's products. Many managers spend their first three months merely familiarizing themselves with their company's product line, reviewing past quality statistics, and analyzing methods of production. Quality control managers work closely with production managers, raw material suppliers, and production line workers during these initial years to make solid and sensible recommendations.

5 YEARS After five years, most quality control managers have seen their programs implemented and have had to manage and resolve many unforeseen complications. Many individuals have been rotated between different production facilities and different product lines and are required to rapidly become experts in each item's production process. A number of them are asked to relocate for two to nine months or longer. Satisfaction is extremely high in these middle years; salaries are average.

10 YEARS Quality control managers who have remained in the position for 10 years are familiar with their company's product lines and production processes. They have a strong understanding of raw material suppliers' costs and quality. Few shift jobs in these later years, as much of the knowledge they absorbed throughout their career is only useful with respect to one company—the one for which they currently work. The hours are average, and travel becomes less likely as salaries rise.

MAJOR EMPLOYERS
BURLINGTON INDUSTRIES INC.
3330 West Friendly Avenue
Greensboro, NC 27410
Tel: 336-379-2855
www.burlington.com

FORD MOTOR COMPANY
5111 Auto Club Drive
Dearborn, MI 48126
Tel: 313-322-0155
www.ford.com

REVLON
237 Park Avenue
New York, NY 10017
Tel: 212-527-4000
Fax: 212-527-5588
www.revlon.com

MAJOR ASSOCIATIONS
AMERICAN SOCIETY FOR QUALITY CONTROL
600 North Plankinton Avenue
Milwaukee, WI 53203
Tel: 800-248-1946 or 414-272-8575
Fax: 414-272-1734
www.asq.org

RADIO PRODUCER

SALARY   ● ● ●

HOURS   ● ● ●

EDUCATION   ● ● ●

BOOKS, FILMS, AND TV SHOWS
FEATURING THE PROFESSION
- Frasier
- News Radio

YOU'LL HAVE CONTACT WITH
- Radio announcers
- Reporters
- Sound technicians
- Station managers

PROFESSIONALS READ
- Historical Journal of Film, Radio and Television

A DAY IN THE LIFE

This medium of communication was around long before television and the Internet. In fact, families used to gather around their radios to listen to the news, sports games, and entertaining programs. Radio stations provide an important function in society: They relay news, sports, discussions concerning current events, and music to the general public. Someone must be responsible for the on-air programming, and that someone is the radio producer. For stations that play music, radio producers decide what type of music will be played and supervise on-air personnel. Most of these radio producers come to the profession after years working as a disc jockey. Radio producers for stations that have all news formats are sometimes called on to edit and write the news stories from information collected by reporters. Radio producers often hire station employees, work with sales associates, and act as intermediaries between upper management and the on-air talent. At smaller stations, radio producers take on many different roles, including bookkeeper, administrative assistant, and marketing manager. Some radio producers plan, develop, and create live or taped productions. A touch of artistic talent is needed when writing scripts, helping sound technicians, and developing other production elements. Radio producers deal with station managers, accountants, the community, and the FCC.

{ artistic talent }

PAYING YOUR DUES

Want to get a job in the radio business? You'll need a degree. More than 450 colleges offer programs in journalism and mass communications, including programs in radio and television broadcasting. Some trade schools offer six-month courses in radio and television announcing, writing, and production. Most people who want a career in broadcasting begin to gain experience by working at college radio stations or through internships at professional stations. Interns are often unpaid, but the hands-on training they earn can be invaluable, often leading to higher-paying jobs. Some individuals start out as production assistants, helping the producer create the programming. They also provide clerical and research assistance. Radio producers just starting out usually find a job in smaller stations serving smaller markets. Competition for positions in large metropolitan areas is strong. The chance for advancement is small unless employees change employers. Relocation to communities in other parts of the country is frequently necessary.

ASSOCIATED CAREERS

The skills needed to run a radio station translate well into various other professions in the broadcasting arts, including video editors, announcers, disc jockeys, reporters, correspondents, newscasters, technical directors, station managers, and account executives. Any experience managing large groups of diverse people lends itself well to business world positions such as managers.

PAST AND FUTURE

Radio stations have been around since the early 1920s. Even with the advent of television and the Internet, radio isn't going away any time soon. With streaming audio and satellite radio, no matter where you are, you can listen to radio broadcasts from stations all over the world. This doesn't mean that radio producers are able to find more job openings, though. For every new station being made, another two are consolidated to cut costs. New technologies that allow greater use of prepared programming will require fewer management duties in most large radio stations.

QUALITY OF LIFE

2 YEARS Most radio producers with two years of experience come from internships or college radio station jobs. Some have worked as assistants in larger markets. With two years of experience, radio producers can find jobs in small radio stations in small to midsize markets.

5 YEARS If a radio producer is willing to move, then breaking into a larger market even at a smaller station is possible for radio producers with five years of experience. The move can bring with it more money and fewer overall responsibilities. Moving to a larger radio station means there are more employees to take care of bookkeeping, marketing, and other duties a radio producer may have had to take on in a smaller station.

10 YEARS Radio producers with 10 years of experience are in high demand. If you're already in a large metropolitan area, the move to a more popular radio station is easier with so much experience. Radio producers who have been around this long usually have an assistant who deals with the minutiae of everyday work (clerical work, small production design, and so forth), freeing up the radio producer to work on guiding his or her on-air talent and programming to bring in more and more listeners.

MAJOR EMPLOYERS

Positions are available nationwide. Visit the websites of local radio stations to find out about positions in your area.

MAJOR ASSOCIATIONS

NATIONAL ASSOCIATION OF BROADCAST EMPLOYEES AND TECHNICIANS, COMMUNICATIONS WORKERS OF AMERICA, INTERNATIONAL
501 Third Street, NW
Washington, DC 20001
www.nabetcwa.org

NATIONAL ASSOCIATION OF BROADCASTERS
1771 N Street, NW
Washington, DC 20036
Tel: 202-429-5300
Fax: 202-429-3520
www.nab.org

ROBOTICS ENGINEER

A DAY IN THE LIFE

Robotics engineers design robots, maintain them, develop new applications for them, and conduct research to expand the potential of robotics. This is a rapidly developing field, with advances in computing constantly opening up new possibilities for robotics applications. Manufacturing, the first industry to invest heavily in robotics, remains the primary employer in the area, but recent years have seen rapid expansion of research and engineering in robots for such applications as agriculture, mining, and nuclear power plant maintenance.

The profession offers jobs for a wide range of temperaments. Visionary robotics engineers can design experimental mobile robots, with applications ranging from medical and military

{ rapidly developing field }

uses to designs aimed at creating vehicles capable of piloting themselves on other planets. More down-to-earth jobs involve designing new production line robots, often with programmable arms, and maintaining and upgrading older production line installations. Somewhere in between are those engineers designing and producing robots for expanding but tested fields, such as self-piloting crop harvesters and automated nuclear-safety equipment. Robotics engineers must have the same disciplined attention to detail required of all engineers, but the relative novelty of the field puts an additional premium on creativity. The engineers who can best anticipate needs that can be successfully filled by robots and who can work effectively in engineering teams to develop them will be extremely successful in the field.

PAYING YOUR DUES

Graduate education is usually a necessity for advancement in robotics engineering. This can range from one to two years of additional graduate-level coursework in electrical and/or mechanical engineering for an operating engineer to several years for a doctorate degree, which gives candidates a better opportunity of obtaining positions in design and research. The most-sought-after jobs go to engineers with academic backgrounds that allow them to combine knowledge in computer science with applied physical sciences. As automated systems must be designed to optimally integrate into the production line, knowledge of the manufacturing environment in which the robot will operate is invaluable.

ASSOCIATED CAREERS

Robotics engineers tend to stay in the field. Professional mobility largely occurs between robotics manufacturing firms and their clients, with engineers leaving to oversee the robot operations of major clients. In addition, as new applications for robots appear, opportunities arise for engineers to move into these new branches of the field.

"The relative novelty of the field puts an additional premium on creativity."

PAST AND FUTURE

Robotics dates back to the Renaissance, when machines capable of accurately performing repetitive tasks were designed. Later, in 1804, Joseph-Marie Jacquard designed a machine capable of following instructions on a punched paper tape. Modern robotics dates from this invention, though the field did not truly develop until later, when computers capable of guiding a programmable machine through a series of complex tasks were created. Today, robotics is a booming field, with an expanding role in manufacturing, mining, agriculture, and a wide range of other fields, including jobs too hazardous to be performed by people.

QUALITY OF LIFE

2 YEARS At this point in their career, robotics engineers function as professional apprentices, working on elements of larger design or programming problems under more experienced engineers who manage the overall progress of projects.

5 YEARS Robotics engineers with 5–10 years of experience are the middle managers of the profession. With sufficient expertise to oversee the work of their junior colleagues, they have substantial oversight responsibilities in the design and development of robotics projects, and, as they gain experience, they begin to become involved in the generation of project concepts. Some engineers will leave to join clients' manufacturing firms to manage their robotic operations.

10 YEARS Robotics engineers now have significant responsibilities. In design and manufacturing companies, they may be responsible for managing the development and/or manufacture of new robots. They likely spend a significant amount of time with potential clients, analyzing their needs, and developing proposals for robotics applications to meet them. If they have gone to work in a client industry, they are responsible for managing robotics operations and working with robotics manufacturing firms as problems or new needs arise. Alternatively, they may have struck out on their own, manufacturing robots in their specific areas of engineering expertise.

MAJOR EMPLOYERS
AMERICAN ROBOT CORPORATION
303 Robinson Road
Imperial, PA 15126
Tel: 724-695-9000
Fax: 724-695-9001
www.americanrobot.com

FORD MOTOR COMPANY
5111 Auto Club Drive
Dearborn, MI 48126
Tel: 313-322-0155
www.ford.com

GSMA-PARISH
2730 Kirby Avenue, NE Building 5
Palm Bay, FL 32905
Tel: 321-728-3800
Fax: 321-728-5555
www.gsma.com

MAJOR ASSOCIATIONS
INSTITUTE OF ELECTRICAL AND ELECTRONICS ENGINEERS
3 Park Avenue, 17th Floor
New York, NY 10016-5997
Tel: 212-419-7900
Fax: 212-752-4929
www.ieee.org

ROBOTIC INDUSTRIES ASSOCIATION
900 Victors Way, Suite 140
PO Box 3724
Ann Arbor, MI 48106
Tel: 734-994-6088
Fax: 734-994-3338
www.robotics.org

SOCIETY OF MANUFACTURING ENGINEERS
1 SME Drive
Dearborn, MI 48121
Tel: 800-733-4763 or 313-271-1500
Fax: 313-271-2861
www.sme.org

SOFTWARE DEVELOPER

A DAY IN THE LIFE

Software and Internet developers produce computer-based goods and services for individual consumers and companies. Software developers coordinate the production of software products, from choosing content providers, assembling graphics creators, and working with programmers to the actual assembling, pressing, and distribution of the final product. Internet producers go through much of the same process, except instead of pressing a final product, they set up and maintain an Internet site that provides services to the user.

Developers spend most of the day on the telephone coordinating production with the members of the team. One developer wrote that she sees herself as a chef: "The parts I have to put together are the ingredients, and I have to decide how and when to put them together to make a beautiful dish." As pleasant as this sounds, developers are not strangers to hard work. Late nights are not unusual; unforeseen problems are standard. "Build in an extra two weeks to any project," cautioned one five-year software developer, "then you'll only be two weeks late." Software developers should be organized but flexible and have strong technical and interpersonal skills. A high tolerance for frustration is equally important. Software and Internet producers are self-starters by nature and tend to tackle problems head-on. Individuals who can combine all these talents will find themselves well-suited for the industry.

{ unique product }

Developers told us the most exciting thing about the work is being able to produce a unique product that takes advantage of an unexploited medium. The final product each developer produces acts as a living resume, and many point with pride to the projects they are involved in. Also, because the software and Internet industries are so young, the field is wide open to those with talent. Talented developers are extremely mobile in this industry; ability sells, and many companies are willing to pay top dollar to have ability on their team.

PAYING YOUR DUES

There are no specific academic criteria for software developers and Internet producers, although many employers consider a college degree desirable. Individuals involved in coordinating all phases of projects are likely to benefit from courses or a degree in computer science, finance, English, psychology, sociology, and graphics design. Individuals who expect to specialize in a limited area of production responsibility (such as programming or graphic design) should focus on developing skills in that area and assembling a portfolio that demonstrates those skills.

ASSOCIATED CAREERS

Software developers with technical expertise can become managers or programmers. Software and Internet developers also go into a number of project-related fields that involve managerial decision-making, budgeting, and scheduling. Some of them go into publishing (hard copy and electronic); others go into manufacturing and product development. A few developers become consultants to firms, advising them on their Internet presence and providing such abilities as translation services for annual reports (i.e., turning them into interactive media).

> "The parts I have to put together are the ingredients, and I have to decide how and when to put them together to make a beautiful dish."

PAST AND FUTURE

Software development and Internet production began in the early 1980s when personal computers started to become widespread in America. Few individuals realized then the impact these machines would have on every American's life.

Job growth has slowed considerably since the initial industry boom. Software and Internet development is a maturing industry, and the growth rate will slow as that maturation continues. That said, the industry continues to expand, and many companies invest heavily in the Internet. Much of this money will be used toward hiring Internet site developers.

QUALITY OF LIFE

2 YEARS Software developers have important responsibilities from the start. While the atmosphere is less "Wild West" than the early days—newcomers won't get their feet wet managing real products until they've proven themselves—the pace can still be frantic. Projects must be coordinated, deadlines must be met, and budgets must be complied with. Many individuals use these early years to learn by making mistakes, which they may spend long hours in the office correcting. The pressure is high, but so is the level of satisfaction.

5 YEARS Developers begin to address the gaps in their knowledge; experience has honed their managerial skills. Many individuals take classes in programming, software, aesthetics, or other areas related to their profession. Job mobility is high. Salaries increase, and the hours stabilize. Satisfaction is above average.

10 YEARS Ten-year veterans of the field have been in charge of a number of projects and seen them through from idea to revision. Many individuals have given up their day-to-day managerial duties and either supervise other developers or move into strategic planning areas of the company. A number of them start their own companies using connections made in the industry. Quality of life improves, salaries increase, and the hours decrease.

MAJOR EMPLOYERS
MICROSOFT CORPORATION
One Microsoft Way
Redmond, WA 98052-6399
Tel: 425-882-8080
Fax: 425-936-7329
www.microsoft.com

RIVERDEEP, INC.
100 Pine Street, Suite 1900
San Francisco, CA
Tel: 415-659-2000
Fax: 415-659-2020
www.riverdeep.net
Contact: Human Resources

IBM CORPORATION
1133 Westchester Avenue
White Plains, NY 10604
Tel: 404-238-1234
Fax: 404-238-6628
www.ibm.com

MAJOR ASSOCIATIONS
AMERICAN ELECTRONICS ASSOCIATION
5210 Great American Parkway, Suite 520
Santa Clara, CA 95054
Tel: 800-284-4323
Fax: 408-970-8565
www.aeanet.org

SOFTWARE & INFORMATION INDUSTRY ASSOCIATION
1090 Vermont Avenue, 6th Floor
Washington, DC 20005
Tel: 202-289-7442
Fax: 202-289-7097
E-mail: Jkim@siia.net
www.siia.net

SPORTS MANAGER

A DAY IN THE LIFE

Sports managers spend their time behind the scenes coordinating all business-related activities for the team that employs them. During the playing season, they may work seven days a week. When they work for college or professional teams, they stay behind in their office at the team's home facility while the team travels to away games. A few managers who have been in the business for many years travel with the team from city to city, but they are the exception.

During the off-season, the manager is busy negotiating trades and signing free agents. The sports manager or general manager, as he or she is sometimes called, signs all players to the pro-

{ drafting college players }

fessional team. According to one successful manager, "It is more important to know which deals not to make than which deals you should make." This is often the most delicate aspect of the job, as a manager must make deals that satisfy the owners without alienating any of the players. Managers who work for a professional sports team are involved in the yearly ritual of drafting college players. They work closely with the coach and scouts to determine which players are the most talented, request salaries that are economically feasible, and play positions the team needs. Managers must do this while keeping an eye on the team's budget. They are in charge of everyone's salary, from the coach and players down to the assistants. They also make financial arrangements for travel, equipment, and uniform purchases and must factor into their budgets player injury and the possible team success that leads to additional playing and travel costs.

Sports managers have to participate in press conferences and explain the reasons for their decisions to the media, without giving away their intentions for the future. They may be the subject of both complimentary and critical press reports. When they sign a great player, they are considered heroes. When a respected player leaves the team or slides into a losing streak, managers are often seen as contributing to the team's downfall. Managers should expect to be fired and forced to relocate a number of times during their careers. For all of these reasons, this is a highly stressful job.

PAYING YOUR DUES

There is no one ideal background for a sports manager. Sports managers should, of course, love the game they are managing and should have experience playing or coaching it. Most managers have spent time as an assistant to a manager or coach while in high school and college. Most managers begin managing local school teams, work their way up to the college level, and eventually work with professional athletes. Sport management is increasingly found as a college minor or major in the United States and around the world. Students gain an upper hand for advancement in the profession by graduating with standards established by national associations that serve as a quality control mechanism for the development of professional sports managers. For managers of professional teams, a business degree is recommended. The manager should be familiar with contract laws, economics, and accounting. There are no licensing requirements for managers. They may belong to an organization or association of managers in their particular sport.

ASSOCIATED CAREERS

The general manager is usually promoted from the position of head coach or head of scouting. A coach organizes practice schedules and develops playing strategies for the team. The scout visits teams in lower divisions of the sport to find new talent; for example, college team scouts attend high school events. They meet with exceptional players and watch them play. When they find a player who they think would be an asset to their team, they generally work out a scholarship plan to entice the player to attend their employer's school.

PAST AND FUTURE

Sports have been a part of all societies for so long that no one is sure which sport was developed first. The first organized sporting event was the Olympic Games in 776 B.C. Modern sports developed primarily over the last two centuries, with the greatest advances being made in the last 50 years. The difference between sports in this century and sports in earlier years is the level of organization. Just before World War I, a number of people realized what a profitable business organized sports could be. Teams began to receive increasing press coverage, people realized that the players needed support staff, and the sports manager was born. The number of positions is small, although the growing popularity of such areas as gymnastics and women's sports is opening up the field somewhat. The competition is fierce; the position of sports manager is a coveted one.

QUALITY OF LIFE

2 YEARS Satisfaction is high in this field. The manager receives a very large paycheck and is participating in one of his or her favorite pastimes. Working in the glamorous field of professional and college sports has been a lifetime dream for many.

5 YEARS Most managers are still involved with the sport, although they may no longer be working with their first team. Many individuals make lateral moves to other teams, which often brings them new challenges and greater financial rewards. Satisfaction remains high.

10 YEARS Some managers earn huge sums of money at this point, as they have earned the trust of the team owners and coaches, if not always the general public. A few of them have their eye on the presidency of the club or a partial ownership, which are the only advancements open to them at this point.

MAJOR EMPLOYERS

NCAA
PO Box 6222,
Indianapolis, IN 46206-6222
Fax: 317-917-6888
www.ncaa.org/mailbox/human_resources.html

NATIONAL INTRAMURAL RECREATIONAL ASSOCIATION
4185 Southwest Research Way
Corvallis, OR 97333-1067
Tel: 541-766-8211
Fax: 541-766-8284
E-mail: nirsa@nirsa.org
www.nirsa.org

NATIONAL RECREATION AND PARK ASSOCIATION
22377 Belmont Ridge Road
Ashburn, VA 20148-4501
Tel: 703-858-0784
Fax: 703-858-0794
E-mail: info@nrpa.org
www.nrpa.org

LOS ANGELES ATHLETIC CLUB
431 West 7th Street
Los Angeles, CA 90014
Tel: 213-625-2211
Fax: 213-625-0128
www.laac.com
Contact: Human Resources

SUGAR LOAF/USA
5092 Access Road
Carrabassett Valley, ME 04947
Tel: 207-237-2000
Fax: 207-237-2718
www.sugarloaf.com
Contact: Human Resources

VAIL RESORTS
PO Box 7
Vail, CO 81658
Tel: 970-845-2460
Fax: 970-845-2465
www.vail.com
Contact: Human Resources
Jobline: 888-SKI-JOBS

MAJOR ASSOCIATIONS

AMERICAN ALLIANCE FOR HEALTH, PHYSICAL EDUCATION, RECREATION, AND DANCE
1900 Association Drive
Reston, VA 20191
Tel: 703-476-3400 or 800-213-7193
www.aahperd.org

STAGE TECHNICIAN

SALARY   ● ● ●

HOURS   ● ● ●

EDUCATION   ● ● ●

BOOKS, FILMS, AND TV SHOWS
FEATURING THE PROFESSION
- **Stage Crafts**
- **Waiting for Guffman**

YOU'LL HAVE CONTACT WITH
- **Actors**
- **Directors**
- **Lighting designers**
- **Producers**

PROFESSIONALS READ
- **Stage Directions Magazine**

A DAY IN THE LIFE

If you enjoy the theater but haven't been bitten by the acting bug or if you enjoy working with your hands, you may want to look into a career in theater production. Stage technicians fill a variety of jobs in the theater—they are light- and sound-board operators, carpenters, prop handlers, production assistants, wardrobe supervisors, and stage managers. The stage manager is perhaps the most visible and versatile of the production crew. The stage manager's job requires an understanding of all of the elements of stage production, as well as some familiarity with a director's duties. He or she coordinates the production once the run is under way, often managing the actors themselves and seeing to it that the director's instructions are not forgot-  { understanding of all of the elements of stage production } ten. Stage carpenters build and repair sets. Once the show is running, they place and move sets and scenery during the performance. Prop handlers maintain the various objects used on stage. They work with the production designers in selecting props and with the carpenters in repairing props when they break. Wardrobe supervisors keep costumes clean and mended. Although designers and directors make the final decisions about what the sets and actors should look like, they often rely on a technician for practical advice.

During preproduction, technicians typically work from 9:00 A.M. to 6:00 P.M., bringing to life the images and sounds that a play's directors, authors, and designers propose. When the show is up and running, these same hands work nights, starting about two hours before showtime, maintaining the machinery of the theater, cleaning and fixing stages, lights, and sets and, as one technician said, "moving whatever needs to be moved." Post-show cleanup and preparation for the next evening's performance can last well into the night.

Good stage technicians can translate the plans of others into finished products, are committed to the theater, and can handle the frustrations and problems that come with the job. A stagehand's job is not a terribly secure one. Your job lasts for the duration of each show, so a flop can really wreck your finances. Pay scales start low and don't really provide a comfortable living until after a couple of years. The competition for higher-paying and more secure union jobs can be fierce. Nevertheless, most stage technicians value a life in the theater and relish the opportunity to make a hands-on contribution to the creative process.

PAYING YOUR DUES

While not mandatory, a high school diploma is recommended, and high school is where many technicians gain their first experiences. A number of colleges and universities across the nation also have programs for aspiring stage technicians. Most employers look for experienced technicians, so technicians often work at regional theaters or in summer stock before heading to the nation's biggest labor markets: the East and West Coasts. A general understanding of stagecraft and the theater is desirable. A good technician is handy with tools and knows the ins and outs of constructing and lighting sets. "It isn't like building a house," said one stagehand.

If you choose to join a union, you'll probably have to take a written test (depending on the specific profession) and participate in a three-year apprenticeship. Unions are selective about their members, and only well-reputed technicians can expect to be invited to join. Unionized stage managers belong to the ultra-competitive Actors' Equity Association, so opportunities to join are few.

ASSOCIATED CAREERS

If live theater isn't what excites you, you may want to pursue a career in film or television, although competition there is even more intense than in the theater. Another option for stagehands is a career in stage or lighting design, which requires an undergraduate or even a graduate degree.

PAST AND FUTURE

Even dating back to ancient times, there were people responsible for the creation, maintenance, and improvement of the theater. Some large Greek amphitheaters could hold audiences of more than 5,000, and writings from the Hellenic age mention elaborate sets and costumes that added to the theater experience.

The modern theater is marked by technical specialists, such as lighting designers, prop managers, and set designers. The role of these specialists is important, and opportunities will continue to be available for newcomers to the profession. Individuals with electrical or artistic skills will have an advantage in finding jobs; individuals who perform more menial tasks (e.g., stage cleanup) will find opportunities harder to come by.

QUALITY OF LIFE

2 YEARS Many aspiring technicians spend their first two years establishing a reputation and adding credits to their resume. Since employment is show by show, thorough networking is essential to job security. Many individuals make barely enough money to live on but gain a valuable understanding of the craft from the seasoned professionals with whom they work. After two years, many technicians choose to follow the union track, while others apply to college or graduate school to pursue a degree in production or design. Technical theater production can be tiring; many individuals cite professional fatigue in these early years that few anticipated when they began.

5 YEARS By this time, members have decided to join the technical theater union or to remain independent laborers. The competition among stage technicians drives many people out of the profession, which means that those individuals who stick it out, establish contacts, and earn a good name for themselves will find greater opportunities available to them. Satisfaction is average, as many people experience a "mid-career lull" where their responsibilities stay the same and their hours increase. Salaries rise, but not tremendously.

10 YEARS Ten-year veterans have most likely established their reputations, made significant professional contacts, and developed a long resume that allows them to choose their own jobs. Veterans supervise less experienced technicians, and many technicians start their own training companies and freelance technical theatrical agencies. Union members can expect to enjoy relative job security and a decent living.

MAJOR EMPLOYERS
ARENA STAGE
1101 6th Street, SW
Washington, DC 20024
Tel: 202-554-9066
Fax: 202-488-4056
www.arenastage.org
Contact: Jane Casamajor

DENVER CENTER
1101 13th Street
Denver, CO 80204
Tel: 303-893-4000
www.denvercenter.org

THE DISNEY CORPORATION
Attn: Artist Recruitment
500 South Buena Vista Street
Burbank, CA 91521-3020
Tel: 818-558-2868
Fax: 818-556-6969
http://disney.go.com

MAJOR ASSOCIATIONS
NEW YORK FOUNDATION FOR THE ARTS
155 Avenue of the Americas, 14th Floor
New York, NY 10013
Tel: 212-366-6900
Fax: 212-366-1778
www.nyfa.org

THEATER ARTS COMMUNICATIONS GROUP INC.
520 8th Avenue, 24th Floor
New York, NY 10018
Tel: 212-609-5900
Fax: 212-609-5901
www.tcg.org

STATISTICIAN

A DAY IN THE LIFE

Statisticians collect data and analyze it, looking for patterns that explain behavior or describe the world. A good statistician is involved in survey development and data collection from the beginning, ensuring the validity and usefulness of the data. Statisticians are employed by private and public concerns and apply their skills to specific industry issues, such as economic analysis, inventory control problems, health problems, and even television demographics. Statisticians must be familiar with valid scientific protocol and be able to quickly familiarize themselves with baselines and historical industry figures to structure an uncompromised analysis.

Statisticians spend over half their day in front of a computer,

{ Statistics is a science of trends and probabilities, not certainties. }

setting up models, manipulating data, analyzing data, or writing reports. "You don't just crunch numbers. You explain them," wrote one veteran statistician, who said that writing skills are important for individuals hoping to advance in the field. They spend the rest of their day in meetings, in planning sessions, or on the telephone exchanging ideas with colleagues. Respondents said, "Statistics is a visual science. You have to be able to picture the data and how it fits in with other known data shapes. It is not a numbers-only job." Most statisticians are applied statisticians, tailoring studies to real-life problems. It takes mathematical, visual, and practical skills to excel in this occupation as well as flexibility, curiosity, and a rigorous mind.

Statisticians said the most difficult part of their job is explaining the implications of their studies to nonstatisticians. Many said that statistics are best used as a starting point for investigation, not as a conclusion, and upper-level managers find this concept difficult to grasp. One wrote, "Statistics is a science of trends and probabilities, not certainties. We can tell what things happened and suggest why they might have happened, but they're only suggestions." Many statisticians cited the support of the statistician community as important to their satisfaction in the field. Statisticians feel challenged, involved, and invigorated by their work, and this is evidenced by the small number (fewer than 11 percent) of statisticians who leave the field each year.

PAYING YOUR DUES

There are strict academic requirements for becoming a statistician. Entry-level positions require a bachelor's degree in mathematics or statistics. Individuals who wish to rise in the profession should consider obtaining a master's degree or a PhD. About 100 universities offer graduate degrees in statistics. Suggested coursework includes mathematics (calculus and linear algebra), probability, logic, psychology, and computer science. Candidates who combine statistical skills with another major that reflects their professional direction—such as economics and econometrics, computer and material science, or biology—have a distinct competitive advantage when seeking employment. Membership in professional organizations is not required, but many individuals choose to join the ones affiliated with their occupation, such as organizations for economists or manufacturers.

ASSOCIATED CAREERS

With their strong mathematical aptitude, many careers are open to statisticians. Wall Street is the most common employer of mathematical statisticians who leave their field, followed closely by the government, which regularly hires statisticians as "area analysts." A number of individuals become accountants, insurance analysts, and actuarial analysts when they want to improve their quality of life. A few statisticians enter computer science and become programmers and systems analysts.

PAST AND FUTURE

Statisticians first became noteworthy in the study of infectious disease outbreaks. In the 1800s, they were able to trace an outbreak of cholera to a single water supply. The growth of actuarial science increased the need for statisticians, and the demand has surged again with the development of computer science. Almost 90 percent of America's industries use statistics in their daily operations.

The opportunities available to statisticians are expected to grow in the future, due to an increasing reliance on expert analysis, growth in industries that use statisticians (entertainment, advertising, computer science, etc.); and general growth in the economy. Statisticians with interdisciplinary skills, such as biology, economics, and chemistry, should find it easier to obtain positions than statisticians without these specialized backgrounds. Employers often expect statisticians to obtain a graduate degree not in statistics, but in the related discipline of their choice.

QUALITY OF LIFE

2 YEARS Individuals with only undergraduate degrees enter data, perform simple analysis, and summarize internal reports. These tasks involve limited responsibility and are done under rigorous supervision. Satisfaction is lowest in the early years, and the hours can be long for individuals who keep up with professional reading and continue to educate themselves about their field. Individuals with graduate degrees are more likely to be assigned interesting tasks, but these first two years can be a time of menial tasks for all.

5 YEARS Many statisticians spend five or more years at a single firm learning their profession. By this time, they usually have graduate degrees, and many of them plan and supervise projects. The majority of statisticians supervise researchers, analyze data, and write reports. They concentrate on producing quality work and getting published in professional or academic journals. Professional education is important during this period and includes attending conferences or lectures during people's free time. Satisfaction is high; salaries increase significantly.

10 YEARS Ten-year veterans have a good deal of job mobility and begin seeking new positions that make use of their now-substantial skills. Many statisticians move from smaller companies to larger ones or from statistician to executive positions. Many of them plan and direct research projects. Satisfaction is high, and salaries increase, particularly in the private sector.

MAJOR EMPLOYERS
AETNA
151 Farmington Avenue
Hartford, CT 06156
Tel: 860-273-0123
www.aetna.com
Contact: Staffing

ALLSTATE INSURANCE COMPANIES
Allstate Plaza
North Brook, IL 60062
Tel: 847-402-5000
Contact: Recruiting and Selection Team

BLUE CROSS & BLUE SHIELD OF NORTH CAROLINA
1 Copley Parkway
Durham, NC 27701
Tel: 919-481-0283
www.bluecross.com
Contact: Human Resources

MAJOR ASSOCIATIONS
AMERICAN STATISTICAL ASSOCIATION
1429 Duke Street
Alexandria, VA 22314
Tel: 888-231-3473
Fax: 703-684-2037
www.amstat.org

STRUCTURAL ENGINEER

DAY IN THE LIFE

Structural engineers (SEs) deal with the frameworks and skeletons of buildings, bridges, towers, stadiums, tunnels, roller coasters, and monuments—in short, virtually every aspect of the world's built environment. SEs work with other engineers—mechanical, geotechnical, electrical, and civil—as well as urban planners and architects on projects as varied as the Louisiana Superdome, Channel Tunnel, Hoover Dam, and Sunshine Skyway Bridge. The primary duty of a structural engineer is to ensure public safety and to serve the client's interests while abiding by the appropriate standards and legal codes. SEs design the components of a structure that hold its contents—"contents" being people, vehicles, and property. In buildings, SEs design roof framing (beams, rafters, joists, trusses),

{ random inspections }

floor framing (floor decks, joists, beams, trusses, girders), arches, columns, braces, frames, foundations, and walls. For bridges, they design the deck surface, girders or stringers, and piers. They work with a broad range of materials, including steel, concrete, wood, masonry, and aluminum.

SEs must design structures to resist forces from gravity, earthquakes, high winds, water, collisions, and explosions. They develop their designs by performing a complex series of calculations and by utilizing computer programs. They then draw their results on a set of plans, and those drawings are used by contractors to price and build the structures in question. The job is challenging but also highly rewarding; one SE notes, "One of the greatest joys is seeing a project under construction and then walking into or driving on the finished product." Within the field of structural engineering, there are many specialties. SEs may opt to specialize in working with certain types of buildings or bridges, or even certain types that are made of a particular material. One may specialize in long-span bridges or even amusement park roller coasters, for example. Established SEs advise that it is a good idea for engineers to become involved in the design and analysis of as many different structure types as possible early in their careers. That way, young SEs may have a broad range of options open to them later on.

PAYING YOUR DUES

SEs typically hold a college degree in structural engineering, civil engineering with an emphasis on structures, or architectural engineering. Many even hold a master's degree, and some have PhDs. Course work typically includes physics, mechanics, blueprint reading, architecture, mathematics, and materials science. A structural engineer must be familiar with all components and methods of construction. Many states require that structural engineers have at least two years of experience in the construction industry and pass a written test that assesses their analytical skills and their knowledge of stress levels as well as local and federal construction codes. Usually, just prior to or shortly after completing their bachelor's degrees, engineering majors take an exam that, once passed, affords the test taker the designation of engineer-in-training. Early in their careers, SEs are mentored by senior staff. They then seek to obtain professional licensure; this usually occurs four years after college graduation.

ASSOCIATED CAREERS

Many structural engineers have a construction background, and they may opt to return to this field and become construction managers, materials purchasers, architectural assistants, and consultants to worksites. SEs possess analytical abilities that make them well-suited to many professions, though.

PAST AND FUTURE

Originally, engineering was a military activity. Over time, though, the benefit of engineering in nonmilitary activities became recognized. Engineering came to be divided into two subdisciplines: military engineering and civil engineering. From the latter, other subdisciplines soon emerged: mechanical engineering, electrical engineering, chemical and petroleum engineering, and of course, structural engineering, among others. Some particularly well-known structural engineers include Washington Roebling (the Brooklyn Bridge), Gustave Eiffel (the Eiffel Tower), and William Le Baron Jenney (the Home Insurance Building in Chicago).

The demand for structural engineers is driven largely by the demand for construction. As new innovations in software, construction, and materials arise, the demand for trained SEs is expected to remain strong.

QUALITY OF LIFE

2 YEARS
Structural engineers probably still have the designation of engineers-in-training at this point. Many continue to be supervised and mentored by veteran SEs. The hours can become longer as SEs begin to make the transition from doing planning to doing planning as well as on-site work.

5 YEARS
At five years into the profession, many SEs have become licensed and operate independently. They are beginning to work on larger-scale projects. The hours and salaries increase, and satisfaction is high.

10 YEARS
At this point, the veteran SE is likely mentoring young as-yet-unlicensed engineers. He or she has developed a specialty and built a solid reputation. SEs at this stage of their careers have a lot of autonomy in determining which projects to assume. Some of them work long hours because they are dedicated to their work. Salaries increase while required hours decrease; satisfaction is high.

The Princeton Review is grateful to Jonathan C. Mallard, PE, and Gerard Madden, SE, PE, for providing the information upon which this profile is based.

MAJOR EMPLOYERS

DEGENKOLB ENGINEERS
225 Bush Street, Suite 1000
San Francisco, CA 94104-4207
Tel: 415-392-6952
Fax: 415-981-3157
www.degenkolb.com

STANTEC
2810 North Parham Road, Suite 242
Richmond, VA 23294
Tel: 804-346-0317
Fax: 804-527-0895
www.stantec.com

WEIDLINGER ASSOCIATES, INC.
375 Hudson Street, 12th Floor
New York, NY 10014-3658
Tel: 212-367-3000
Fax: 212-367-3030
www.weidlinger.com

MAJOR ASSOCIATIONS

AMERICAN COUNCIL OF ENGINEERING COMPANIES
1015 15th Street, NW, Suite 802
Washington, DC 20005
Tel: 202-347-7474
Fax: 202-989-0068
www.acec.org

NATIONAL COUNCIL OF STRUCTURAL ENGINEERING ASSOCIATIONS
645 North Michigan Avenue, Suite 540
Chicago, IL 60611
Tel: 312-649-4600
Fax: 312-649-5840
E-mail: office@ncsea.com
www.ncsea.com

NATIONAL SOCIETY OF PROFESSIONAL ENGINEERS
1420 King Street
Alexandria, VA 22341-2794
Tel: 703-684-2800
Fax: 703-836-4875
E-mail: salbaugh@nspe.org
www.nspe.org

STRUCTURAL ENGINEERING INSTITUTE
American Society of Civil Engineers
1801 Alexander Bell Drive
Reston, VA 20191
Tel: 800-548-2723
E-mail: sei@asce.org
www.seinstitute.org

SYSTEMS ADMINISTRATOR

A DAY IN THE LIFE

A systems administrator installs computers and their operating systems, as well as the software that relates to the Internet, including Web servers—the heart of the system that delivers information to the Internet. There are lots of pieces of software that run in conjunction with Web servers that need to be installed, maintained, and configured to deliver different kinds of content to Web pages. There are, among other delights, Java applets, programs that run in conjunction with Web servers, and advertising servers that deliver ads to Web pages—all of these pieces of software demand the attention of the systems administrator. Even after all of these pieces are installed and running, the components require maintenance. Maintenance issues, upgrade issues, and compatibility issues sometimes arise.

{ a tinkerer at heart }

The Internet was essentially invented by UNIX professionals, and much of the Internet is run on UNIX (an operating system like Windows). Versions of UNIX are free (like Linux) or commercial (like Sun Microsystems, Hewlett Packard, IBM, and Silicon Graphics). Though there are websites that run on other systems, a systems administrator generally utilizes a UNIX-based system.

It takes years to learn and master UNIX. "I don't know every nuance of the program. I know as much as I need to know to keep things running, and I learn all the time. Once you have a feel for UNIX, you can make your way around other versions," says one systems administrator. There's a favorite saying among the UNIX crowd: "You can't create UNIX administrators; you have to grow them." "It's really an organic process, and you learn from doing. You can't just teach someone a bunch of UNIX commands. You have to be using it in an environment. You can go to Sun Microsystems' training school and learn UNIX that way, but you won't actually know how to maintain a system."

Depending on the systems administrator job, an eight-hour day is fairly typical. The stress level varies, depending on the number of Web servers running. When one is down, revenue runs out the door, so the job can be stressful at times.

If you're interested in systems administration, get a really cheap computer, obtain Linux or UNIX shareware like BSD, and install it. Get a manual and learn how to use it. "You'll spend many frustrating hours banging your head against the wall, but if you're the kind of person who likes to solve puzzles, you'll like this job. It's extremely rewarding when you figure out a problem and see how it all makes sense. This field is all about problem solving. You need to be a tinkerer at heart," says one systems administrator.

PAYING YOUR DUES

If you're constantly messing with your computer at home—fixing it, upgrading it, and reinstalling things on it, then systems administration may be a good career opportunity for you. You can probably land an interview simply because you fool around with your computer at home and are able to speak intelligently about how to fix problems.

A systems administration position is not a first step; it's a second step, and without any training or knowledge of UNIX, technical support is the best place to start. "At the beginning stage, a large part of desktop support is personality—people skills, being able to hand-hold, patience, confidence, an avid interest in technology, and a willingness to learn are qualities that go a long way," reports one systems administrator.

Even before you learn the practical applications, it's good to learn the theory. Go to a search engine, type TCP/IP, and start reading about how it works. "You're [going to] be knee-deep in the nitty-gritty, and it's essential to understand how computers work and how networks talk to each other in order to debug problems," recommends one systems administrator.

ASSOCIATED CAREERS

Database and UNIX administration opportunities are available in other sectors, such as the financial industry. Though this route offers high pay, many people choose a Web atmosphere for its less corporate and less stressful environment. Most large companies using any kind of enterprise software rely on UNIX. For example, human resource companies utilize People Soft, which relies on the UNIX platform.

Many people enter systems administration from varied backgrounds, and some leave to return to fields that use the same abilities to manipulate within systems, whether they work with notes of a symphony or blueprints of an office building.

PAST AND FUTURE

The Internet was started by the military to create a network of computers that could withstand a nuclear holocaust and still fire off missiles if the phone network went down. A set of networking protocols was developed to enable computers to talk to one another. Though most of the older ones are no longer used, they have led to what is the most common group of networking protocols on the Internet today: TCP/IP.

According to systems administrators, "all businesses are focused on getting their legacy systems open to their websites. Programmers are leaning toward 'systems integration'—getting different computers to talk to each other, exchange data, and operate in tandem."

QUALITY OF LIFE

2 YEARS During your first two years, you may not do anything directly related to the smooth running of the system; you may be just reading up on new developments. Part of your job is to expand your knowledge base and figure out how to improve the system you're working on. It's a constant learning process; you build on your foundation of knowledge. "For the first year, you're not going to know what you're doing," says one systems administrator.

At this level, "Try to get into a company that is pre-IPO where you can get stock options," recommends one technical professional. "People make millions that way, and you can rack up some serious cash."

5 YEARS Once you can say that you know UNIX, you've configured a Netscape Web server, you've worked with Apache, and you understand Perl, every job you take will pay more money. Professionals earn about a 20 percent raise moving from one company to another. After five years of doing nothing but UNIX, you can easily command a six-figure salary.

10 YEARS At this stage, you're at the top of the UNIX administration game, and you can move on to chief technical officer as the head of a group. These professionals earn big money. You can also consult and earn $125 per hour (or more!).

MAJOR EMPLOYERS

Most companies, large or small, employ systems administrators to keep their systems running smoothly.

MAJOR ASSOCIATIONS

THE SYSTEMS ADMINISTRATION GUILD (USENIX)
2560 9th Street, Suite 215
Berkeley, CA 94710
Tel: 510-528-8649
Fax: 510-548-5738
www.usenix.org

SYSTEMS ANALYST

A DAY IN THE LIFE

Someone on your left speaks French, and someone on your right speaks English; both individuals need to speak to each other. The systems analyst is the intermediary who assesses the needs of the end-user and translates them into programming or turning over the programming responsibility to the development department. What are the business requirements? Who will be a part of the user community? How large is the application going to be? Will it be internal or external? These are questions facing the systems analyst, who spends much of the day in front of the computer poring over these issues. With a new product, other elements come into play, such as network location, user community, type of machine, and portability. If the analyst is reviewing an established product, the user community will dictate its changes and enhancements.

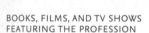
{ Take the ball and run with it. }

"One of the biggest surprises in my [25] years of technology work is that people who have a creative background as opposed to a degree in computer science tend to make better systems analysts," remarks one seasoned professional. "The best analysts I've come across came from backgrounds in theater, art, and filmmaking. But they were all able to see and grasp big-picture concepts very quickly and break them down into subcomponents. People who have a computer science or math background tend to be very technical, and sometimes that can be a hindrance."

Systems analysts need to be independent thinkers—people who can "think out of the box" by grasping concepts quickly and seeing the big picture as opposed to the small details. "I also look for someone who is self-motivated. Here, take the ball and run with it and come back if you have any issues," says one employer who heads up a technology group.

PAYING YOUR DUES

Few companies are willing to spend money on someone who doesn't have some kind of programming background. There is not much difference between an analyst and a programmer, though the programmer needs to be versed in a programming language. As far as dealing with the functional requirements, these are the same position. There are junior-level analyst positions, which is almost like being a junior programmer. Any of the Java applets and the visual basic C++ programs are applicable to today's market. Without experience, a supporting role at the help desk with internal training is a good way to start out.

ASSOCIATED CAREERS

Financial companies and most of the Fortune 100 companies have systems analysts who may also have programming responsibilities. Many systems analysts come from creative backgrounds; some individuals return to those fields, while others combine their artistic passions with Internet opportunities. "If I left my position and were able to do anything, I would go back to photography or painting or apply those talents to Web design," says one systems analyst.

PAST AND FUTURE

In the 1970s, systems analysts worked on mainframes, which were very different from the UNIX world. Mainframes were more structured, and codes had to be written a particular way because of the memory and hardware limitations. Mainframes were rigid in terms of what the system could do, the applications you could run, and the number of users you could have. UNIX, however, is an open platform with a different mentality, giving systems analysts and programmers unlimited ability to create.

The Web began as a commercial enterprise around 1994. In the pre-Internet era, the environment was only open to the techies. Before Web browsers were invented, going from one Web page to another was like pulling teeth. You had to generate a ridiculously long command chain just to get to another server, and the Internet was only available to a very small community. This changed with the release of the first version of Netscape®, the first commercial browser.

"Today the field is open to the entire world, and anything that's Internet-based will provide good job opportunities," says one systems analyst. "Right now the market is extremely hot, and I think it will be this way for many years to come."

QUALITY OF LIFE

2 YEARS When starting out, you will be allowed to make certain mistakes, and you won't suffer the consequences, since you are in a learning and growth position. As you become more experienced in the environment, your role in the big picture changes, and you will learn to break that big picture down into its component smaller details. A systems analyst with moderate experience can demand a hefty salary. "I have a position available for someone with two years' experience. I can't get anyone for less than $80,000, and the position is still open," laments one employer.

5 YEARS At this stage, you will be given more responsibility in tying a project together; whereas you might have been given one application to look at as a beginner, you will now manage an entire project that encompasses the application, the machinery, the network, and the user community. A systems analyst with a UNIX background should understand the network aspect of UNIX and be able to perform systems administration and Perl programming.

10 YEARS After 10 years in the field, a systems analyst is in a position to run a technology department as chief technical officer. These professionals earn salaries well into the six figures. At this level, you can also consult and earn $125 per hour or more.

MAJOR EMPLOYERS

Systems analysts may work for any company with an Intranet or website.

MAJOR ASSOCIATIONS

THE SYSTEMS ADMINISTRATION GUILD (USENIX)
2560 9th Street, Suite 215
Berkeley, CA 94710
Tel: 510-528-8649
Fax: 510-548-5738
www.usenix.org

TECHNICAL SUPPORT SPECIALIST

A DAY IN THE LIFE

The technical support specialist deals with the nitty-gritty of troubleshooting and problem solving, using specialized technical knowledge to provide computer support. Help desk support serves as the middleman, acting as the administrator to answer the phone and route the call to the proper specialist. The most common problems that technical specialists address are connectivity—the user cannot reach data or gain access to it, missing data—data cannot be found, slow performance—excessive amounts of users are slowing down the system, overload—lack of space on a machine for data, or program problems—the program is not running efficiently.

{ adaptable }

While some companies have an internal group to support their technical needs, many large businesses outsource their technical help to other firms. Companies will often pay someone else to supply their hardware and equipment and to provide support for their system and all the technology needed to run it. Database management plays a large part in administering a company's or client's data, and Sybase® is one of the most popular applications to create and manage databases. Many companies are heading toward certifying employees in database management. Sybase databases are supported by UNIX and operating platforms such as Windows. A technical support specialist with a background in both Sybase and UNIX is more valuable. Knowledge of Oracle®, a more fine-tuned database program, is also in demand, as are Microsoft applications, particularly Sequel Server®.

A technical support specialist should be adaptable and able to work flexible shifts and hours in this round-the-clock business. "The hours are demanding, and there is no such thing as nine to five. Your pager is on you at all times, even outside of the office. We have 24-hour, seven-day-a-week coverage to deal with clients, and I often work a 12-hour day," says one professional. In addition, stress levels run fairly high, since all problems are considered urgent. "The client doesn't have any technical savvy or understanding of the problem. All they see is a screen where they can type something in and click on a button to make something happen. We can't resolve everything immediately, and my job becomes stressful because I'm dealing with people who are often irate."

PAYING YOUR DUES

In your first job, you probably will get stuck with the night shift, particularly at a large company. After a few years, you may be eligible to work during the day, though on a less desirable shift, such as 3:00 P.M. to 11:00 P.M. You can also expect to spend at least seven and a half hours of a nine-hour day in front of the computer.

ASSOCIATED CAREERS

Many technical support specialists are hired by companies to maintain their websites. Consulting firms hire tech support people who are sent out to companies for a period of time. With further training in UNIX, a technical support specialist could also move into systems analysis and administration. There is also a need for specialized industry knowledge, such as a background in finance.

PAST AND FUTURE

Tech support specialists came about the instant people wanted their systems to be up and running 24 hours a day, seven days a week. Early on, when the Internet was accessed by a select few, if a site was down, it wasn't a big deal. Today, this means not only egg on your face, but lost revenue as the Web runs on a global, round-the-clock schedule. As more complicated applications are developed, they need to be tested more thoroughly and monitored more carefully. As a result, some companies hire people whose job it is to perform only those tasks. Constructing a corporate network is quite distinct from being plug-and-play, and technical support specialists will continue to be in high demand.

QUALITY OF LIFE

2 YEARS
It is desirable to gain desktop support experience before moving into technical support; and the best way to gain this experience is to start with an administrative position at a help desk. If you boast enough experience to dig into technical support right after school, your pay will increase dramatically.

5 YEARS
At this point, it is common for technical support specialists to switch companies relatively frequently in search of higher pay. One professional we surveyed joked that tech guys change jobs more often than people change underwear. After five years in this field, professionals occupy a senior role in their departments.

10 YEARS
After 10 years in the industry, a technical support specialist is eligible to head up a tech support department. At this level, you are delegating troubleshooting responsibilities and are ultimately overseeing the overall function of the system.

MAJOR EMPLOYERS

Most large corporations and Internet companies hire technical support specialists.

MAJOR ASSOCIATIONS

HELP DESK INSTITUTE
102 South Tejon, Suite 1200
Colorado Springs, CO 80903
Tel: 800-248-5667 or 719-268-0174
Fax: 719-268-0174
www.thinkhdi.com

SUPPORT PROFESSIONALS ASSOCIATION
11031 Via Frontera, Suite A
San Diego, CA 92127
Tel: 858-674-5491
Fax: 858-674-6794
www.thesspa.org

THE ASSOCIATION OF SUPPORT PROFESSIONALS
122 Barnard Avenue
Watertown, 02472
Tel: 617-924-3944
Fax: 647-924-7288
www.asponline.com

TECHNICIAN

A DAY IN THE LIFE

Technicians are typically repair people. "You fix things. You make them do what they're designed to do. I repair televisions, and everyone who comes to my shop needs me to be able to do my job," wrote one New York repairman. Technicians handle faulty electrical and electronic equipment. They analyze problems, run tests, and then, where possible, repair the item. They are "gadget doctors," as one put it, who understand the principles of electronics, equipment testing, and tools.

Good technicians elicit as much information about the problem from the client as possible before attempting a solution. "Sometimes the fax or copier works just fine—you only need to clean

{ Technicians work with their hands. }

the glass or replace the toner," said one technician, who remarked that people cause their equipment to malfunction more often than the equipment itself fails. Service representatives for manufacturers and technicians who maintain large equipment spend a good deal of time in the field. After each trip, they complete extensive paperwork to satisfy corporate requirements. Many of them described this mountain of forms as formidable and unpleasant. Technicians generally work regular hours, except the ones who handle infrastructure equipment or vital-life equipment, such as mainframe computer technicians or hospital equipment repair personnel.

The independent technician has a less paper-heavy life, but must be a generalist within a loose area of specialization to have enough clients to stay in business. Technicians may specialize in television and VCR repair, personal computer and financial calculator repair, or audio equipment maintenance. Some of them choose refrigerator or air-conditioner maintenance and repair. Since air-conditioner repair is seasonal, some technicians learn to repair heating equipment, as well. Sole practitioners enjoy being their own bosses, but it's not necessarily an easy life. "When two or three days go by and nobody comes into your store—you've got problems," said one independent technician, who added that he avoids off-site repairs or schedules them after his regular business hours so potential clients won't think he's not available at his store. Still, satisfaction in this profession is significant. Technicians work with their hands; they solve problems; and they rarely take their work home with them. For people with the technical and interpersonal skills, this job brings a lot of positive feedback and repeat business.

PAYING YOUR DUES

Technicians do not need a college degree; instead, most of them attend a technical or vocational school that offers general training and elective courses in various specializations. Standard coursework includes circuit analysis, electrical testing, wiring and capacity, and audio/video repair. A number of states have licensing exams for technicians in fields that affect daily life, such as microwave, medical equipment, and heating system repair, so check with the local authorities in the region in which you wish to practice. Technicians who want to work for a large service corporation may have to relocate, at least for the initial training program, which can last up to two months.

ASSOCIATED CAREERS

Technicians often discover that they have an interest in designing and creating electronic products. A number of them are amateur inventors, but more pursue further education and become designers, blueprint drafters, programmers, and salespeople. Those individuals who become salespeople know which products are well constructed and which are not from their years of experience in the field.

PAST AND FUTURE

The need for technicians grew with the popularization of electronic products in the 1950s and 1960s. Nearly everything imaginable—toasters, blenders, microwaves, and washers—was designed for and purchased by the American consumer. In the rush to offer all these options, many companies failed to test their products properly or educate consumers on how to keep their equipment functioning. Technicians experienced unparalleled demand for their services during these decades.

The future looks good for technicians, given the seemingly endless variety of electronic, computer-based, and sophisticated products. Every year, new records are set for the number of electronic devices introduced into the market, from parlor games to research equipment. In addition, the profession is getting older, and a significant number of technicians are expected to retire over the next decade. Both of these factors should keep the demand for aspiring technicians high.

QUALITY OF LIFE

2 YEARS New technicians usually either work for large companies that provide consumer support or practice independently. The hours are longer than average for both groups, but the satisfaction levels of in-house technicians are higher because their jobs are more secure and their work is more regular. Salaries are average, and many individuals use these first years to learn how to apply their technical-school skills to real-life repair situations.

5 YEARS Satisfaction levels begin to pivot for both careers. On the one hand, in-house technicians find that supervisory jobs—the most common step up—are in great demand and limited supply. On the other hand, the independent technician who has been in business for five years has begun to build a reputation in his or her community and the work has become steadier. Both work average yet intense hours in an effort to accomplish their goals. Salaries increase.

10 YEARS Most 10-year veteran technicians have become independent technicians. Individuals who are in-house technicians are generally supervisors, managers, or senior technicians, but these positions are far less plentiful than basic technician positions. Independent practitioners have seen their growth flatten, as they realize that one person can do only so much work. Many of them form partnerships with other established technicians (although some of these partnerships do not work out) or hire and train less experienced technicians to handle the less difficult repairs and allow the business to expand.

MAJOR EMPLOYERS
ADVANCED MICRO DEVICES, INC.
One AMD Place, PO Box 3453
Sunnyvale, CA 91088-3453
Tel: 408-732-2400 or 800-538-9450
Fax: 408-774-7023
E-mail: jobs@amd.com
www.amd.com

INTEL CORPORATION
705-2 East Bidwell Street, Suite 246
Folsom, CA 95630
Tel: 916-356-8080
Fax: 916-356-5427
E-mail: jobs2@intel.com
www.intel.com
Contact: Human Resources

MICROSOFT CORPORATION
One Microsoft Way
Redmond, WA 98052-6399
Tel: 425-882-8080
Fax: 425-936-7329
www.microsoft.com

MAJOR ASSOCIATIONS
ELECTRONICS TECHNICIANS ASSOCIATION, INTERNATIONAL
5 Depot Street
Greencastle, IN 46135
Tel: 800-288-3824
Fax: 765-653-4287
E-mail: eta@eta-i.org
www.eta-i.org

TELEVISION PRODUCER

BOOKS, FILMS, AND TV SHOWS
FEATURING THE PROFESSION

- **Broadcast News**
- **The Mary Tyler Moore Show**
- **Scrooged**

YOU'LL HAVE CONTACT WITH

- **Camera operators**
- **Censors**
- **Editors**
- **On-air personalities**

PROFESSIONALS READ

- **Demographics**
- **Entertainment Weekly**
- **Nielsen Today**
- **TV Guide**

A DAY IN THE LIFE

Television producers make sure that television shows run smoothly and take responsibility for everything from coordinating writers and performers/correspondents to overseeing the fact-checking of credit names and titles. "You're always scrambling up to airtime, checking information, and making sure [the show] goes right," wrote one producer. Having complete responsibility for all facets of on-air production can be a very stressful job, and the successful television producer has to be organized; able to communicate clearly and succinctly with everyone on and off the set, from actors to directors to writers to technical crew; and have a gift for thinking on his or her feet to come up with creative ideas fast under extraordinary time pressure. Television producers report high excitement and job satisfaction— $\{$ last-minute job $\}$ these are implementers and problem-solvers who are project-oriented and love to see tangible results—despite the physical toll of the work (all report being tired a lot).

The public perception of the television industry is one of high-profile personalities, and while it helps for the television producer to act as a dynamic, motivating force, nearly everything a producer does is known only to individuals involved with the show itself. "Only other producers can tell a really well-produced show. You never get any fan mail," said one 15-year veteran producer. Another was quick to add, "It's not as glamorous as it seems on television," saying that even the smallest detail must be checked and rechecked before a show goes on the air. A good producer should have enough of an ego to make important decisions and defend them, but should not be afraid of drudge work. Even writing text may be a part of the television producer's last-minute job. Most producers rise in the ranks from production assistant positions, so they know what it takes to get a show from concept to broadcast. Producers ultimately take credit for a successful broadcast but also have to take the blame for anything that goes wrong on their watch.

Between fellow producers, there is respect but little camaraderie. A number of respondents mentioned that fierce competition—even "backstabbing" behavior—was not only common but virtually expected in the industry. A final word of advice, offered by a producer at a major network: "Work hard and look out for yourself." For individuals who can master it, television production is an exciting, difficult job that can be quite financially rewarding.

PAYING YOUR DUES

College coursework should include English, journalism, history, political science, and American studies for individuals interested in going into television news production, and classes in other areas such as drama, meteorology, or business for individuals who wish to enter a specialized area of television production. A few producers attend graduate school in journalism or film, but it is not expected. Competition for entry-level positions is intense, and many aspiring producers take any available job. In general, candidates should have a wide range of knowledge and a willingness to work hard. Any prior work experience that demonstrates an ability to juggle multiple tasks under stressful circumstances is looked on favorably by employers. Most dues are actually paid in the form of entry-level positions, such as in production assistant jobs, where duties may be as mundane as proofreading copy for typos and making sure lunch reservations are made. College internships are heavily sought-after because they provide an appreciable advantage in securing that first job as production assistant. Aggressive pursuit and completion of more and more demanding tasks distinguishes the production assistant who rises in rank from one who does not.

ASSOCIATED CAREERS

Many producers have extensive writing experience at their jobs, and a number of them decide to employ those skills as managing editors, editors, and writers in other occupations. Some people break into the profession from (or, in some cases, escape to) magazine and newspaper journalism. A few producers use their industry contacts and become public relations personnel for major studios or agents for major stars.

PAST AND FUTURE

Ever since television became a sizable industry in the late 1950s, the position of television producer has been critical to its success. In the past decade, he creation of new television networks has spurred competition. Cable is the newest force, particularly those specialized channels devoted exclusively to subjects such as news, sports, nature, cooking, etc. Collectively, these reflect a trend toward "narrowcasting" across the media. This growing market has created opportunities for smart, aggressive, hardworking applicants in production assistant and assistant producer roles. Understand, however, that this is only an expansion of opportunity for entry-level positions. Competition for producers' positions will continue to be fierce.

QUALITY OF LIFE

2 The life of the production assistant is (to recontextualize a remark by Thomas Hobbes) "nasty, brutish, and, as often as not, short." Fierce competition by glamour-seeking upstarts with dreams of high-level schmoozing and long limousines results in low starting salaries and high burnout rates in the first two years. Long hours of grunt work test a person's tenacity, and even talented workers are forced to wait for years on end without rewards. Work shifts can last sixteen hours or more, and when an emergency arises, production assistants are expected to stay and cope until it is resolved. Some individuals may be assigned graveyard shifts, working from 12:00 A.M. to 8:00 A.M., assembling data for morning newscasts and entering Associated Press wire feeds into computers. Production assistants rise when positions open. Some of them can jump two or three steps up the ladder with an exceptional performance; others experience only a rise in salary and no added responsibilities.

5 Individuals who've lasted five years have moved from production assistant jobs to assistant producer positions. A number of them have regular contacts with celebrities or at least on-air personalities, and many of them use their writing skills extensively. The first tests of managerial skills generally occur in years four through seven, when assistant producers start to supervise production assistants and interns. Many of them still do research and proofread copy, but more to ensure they keep their areas of responsibility under control rather than give another potential producer who is working harder an advantage for promotion. The hours can be extremely long, but salaries have risen significantly.

10 Many 10-year veterans have become full-fledged producers, and a few "shooting stars" have worked on several shows. The most difficult feature of the producer's life now is instability—constantly worrying about who is gunning for their position, "who's up and who's down" in the ratings race, what changes may take place in the network's programming philosophy, and the demands of on-air talent. Responsibilities rise with salaries, and time commitments remain tremendous.

MAJOR EMPLOYERS
CAPITAL CITIES/ABC INC.
77 West 66th Street
New York, NY 10023
Tel: 212-456-1000
Fax: 212-456-7112
www.abc.com
Contact: Employee Relations Department

NATIONAL BROADCASTING COMPANY
30 Rockefeller Plaza
New York, NY 10112
Tel: 212-664-4444/7870
www.nbc.com

VIACOM INTERNATIONAL
1515 Broadway
New York, NY 10036
Tel: 212-258-6000
www.viacom.com
Contact: Human Resources

MAJOR ASSOCIATIONS
NATIONAL ASSOCIATION OF TELEVISION PROGRAM EXECUTIVES
5757 Wilshire Boulevard, Penthouse 10
Los Angeles, California 90036-3681
Tel: 310-453-4440
Fax: 310-453-5258
www.natpe.org

PRODUCERS GUILD OF AMERICA
8530 Wilshire Boulevard, Suite 450
Beverly Hills, CA 90211
Tel: 310-358-9020
Fax: 310-358-9520
www.producersguild.com

TEXTILE MANUFACTURER

A DAY IN THE LIFE

A textile manufacturer supervises workers who make products that contain fibers, such as fabrics, tires, yarn, and insulation. Whatever the industry, the task of a textiles manufacturer is the same: to oversee the conversion of a raw product (either natural or man-made fibers) into usable goods. Successful textile manufacturers plan multistage projects, work with widely varying batches of raw material, maintain high-quality levels, and get optimal output from workers. One textile manufacturer described himself as "one-third scientist, one-third problem-solver, and one-third quarterback." Another described how he found this career: "I was looking for a job that would push me on a lot of levels—intellectually, physically, emotionally—and I've found it." Individuals who { uneven lots of raw materials } can juggle the innumerable duties this job entails will find a comfortable home in textile manufacturing.

Some fibers are manufactured or milled from plants, spun into yarn, and then, depending on the end product, further altered through tufting, weaving, or knitting. Others have to be pulped, washed, and spun-dry. Fibers must also be blended, wound, and stored before the dyeing, matching, or finishing takes place. At each stage in the process, textile manufacturers have to oversee a group of workers who specialize in that area of production. "Each section thinks they're the most important to the process, and if you try to tell them otherwise, you've got trouble," said one New Jersey manufacturer. A number of respondents noted that the people skills they use on the job every day are their most critical asset. "I thought I was a manufacturer, not a babysitter," quipped one executive. Still, only those individuals who can manage people effectively make it in this field.

Many respondents remarked that the best part of the job is the challenge; they cited dealing with uneven lots of raw materials and final products, meeting tight deadlines, coordinating production (sometimes a 24-hour-a-day staff), and shipping final goods. Others said they liked having a tangible product of their labor. "I drive down a stretch of road I supplied with threaded tarbase," said one happy executive, "and I point it out to my kid." This satisfaction is common among those individuals who thrive amid the multiple-task demands of this profession.

PAYING YOUR DUES

Textiles manufacturers don't need any specific academic degree, but many employers value a college education that emphasizes competency dealing with numbers and an ability to plan. Experience that demonstrates an ability to lead production teams is also highly valued. The scientific aspects of the job—understanding the nuances of creating a finished textile product from raw, unpredictable materials—are nearly always learned on the job. Textile manufacturers have to know their machines, which are fast-moving, dangerous, and subject to frequent breakdown. Individuals who wish to have job mobility should gain broad experience; exposure to different methods of production increases a person's chances of being able to jump into a new job.

ASSOCIATED CAREERS

Few textile manufacturers find satisfaction outside of their profession. Some of them work in nontextile production manufacturing, such as finished products or crafted woods. Others become salespeople, representatives, or managers in the textile industry. Their knowledge of the production process helps them understand pricing and the pace of production in the industry. Fewer than 4 percent of all textile manufacturers return to school.

PAST AND FUTURE

Wool, linen, and silk fabrics dating as far back as 2,500 B.C. have been found. Many people milled their own clothes until the industrial revolution, when Eli Whitney's cotton gin made the mass production of cotton-based cloth an economic reality in the southern United States. Man-made fibers, either wrinkle-resistant, fire-resistant, or shrink-resistant, were the next breakthrough in the industry. The modern use of fibers in nonclothing products is important because these fibers increase flexibility and durability while reducing weight.

The future of textile manufacturing is uncertain. Automation is eliminating many of the jobs of unskilled textile machinists. Managers will continue to be hired at the same or even a slightly increased pace, yet their responsibilities will become more technical and more clerical. Many important skills will become less important: communication skills and motivation skills, for example. For the textile manufacturer of the future, computer skills, mechanical aptitude, and inventory control skills will be the hallmark of success.

QUALITY OF LIFE

2 YEARS Many manufacturers are assistant supervisors or assistant manufacturers, learning about the elements of the manufacturing process and how they interact. Many of them watch their supervisors not only to learn technical skills but also to learn how they manage people. The hours are regular; salaries are low; satisfaction is high. The majority of individuals who leave the profession—20 percent—leave in the first two years.

5 YEARS Five-year veterans are manufacturing executives, in charge of a shift or an area of production. Many individuals are in charge of one discrete part of the process, such as quality control. Others' duties are more wide-ranging, such as shepherding shipments from mill to cloth. The hours increase, salaries increase, and the percentage of people who leave the profession drops to 10 percent. Satisfaction is high.

10 YEARS Ten-year professionals see the scope of their responsibilities increase. Many of them run large plants or coordinate entire shifts of workers. Individuals who make the transition to sales or management usually do so between years 11 and 15, when the loud sound of the weaving floor starts to get to them. The hours stabilize; satisfaction is high. Many manufacturers take pleasure in teaching their skills to new hires.

MAJOR EMPLOYERS

COATS NORTH AMERICA
Two Lakepointe Plaza
4135 South Stream Boulevard
Charlotte, NC 28217
Tel: 800-631-0965
Fax: 704-329-5829
www.coatscna.com

HARTMAXX
101 North Wacker Drive
Chicago, IL 60606
Tel: 312-372-6300
Fax: 312-444-2679

UNIFI, INC.
Corporate Human Resources
7201 West Friendly Avenue
Greensboro, NC 27410
Tel: 336-294-4410
Fax: 336-316-5422
E-mail: careers@unifi-inc.com or
humanresources@unifi-inc.com

MAJOR ASSOCIATIONS

**AMERICAN TEXTILE
MANUFACTURERS INSTITUTE**
1130 Connecticut Avenue, NW, Suite 1200
Washington, DC 20036
Tel: 202-286-2050
Fax: 202-862-0590
www.atmi.org

**INSTITUTE OF TEXTILE
TECHNOLOGY**
2401 Research Drive
Box 8301
Raleigh, NC 27695
Tel: 919-513-7704
Fax: 919-882-9410
www.itt.edu

NATIONAL TEXTILE ASSOCIATION
6 Beacon Street, Suite 1125
Boston, MA 02108
Tel: 617-542-8220
Fax: 617-542-2199
www.nationaltextile.org

TRAINING SPECIALIST

A DAY IN THE LIFE

Training is one of many specialized subdivisions in the field of human resources. While human resource managers typically deal with things like staffing and personnel issues, total quality management, recruiting, and hiring and firing of employees, a training specialist's job is much more defined within the field. A training specialist is a person who offers training in a job-specific area. While training in new technologies is understandably popular, training specialists don't just teach people how to post and download files to their LAN and understand their computer networks. Currently, companies are having training specialists focus on specific areas of technical knowledge or on-the-job capabilities needed for particular positions. These skills include computer applications, phone systems, product assembly, policies and procedures, and inventory planning. Training specialists present information, direct structured learning experiences, and manage group discussions and group services. They are teachers for professionals. Like anyone in the field of human resources, a training specialist is required to possess excellent interpersonal and communications skills and is expected to increase the skills, productivity, and quality of work of trainees.

{ plan, organize, and implement }

To achieve these goals, training specialists plan, organize, and implement a wide range of training activities for both new hires and veteran employees. They conduct orientation sessions and arrange on-the-job training for new hires. They conduct workshops and arrange training for veteran employees, targeting skills that need improving or helping them prepare for jobs requiring greater skill. Some companies have training specialists devise programs that develop executive potential in lower-level employees, "grooming" them for a higher-profile job.

To come up with development programs and plans that address the needs of the company, training specialists must identify and assess the training needs within the company. To do so, trainers meet with managers and supervisors and even conduct surveys. They also have to evaluate training effectiveness and be ready with alternative ideas if they are not seeing the necessary improvement.

The methods a trainer uses depend on the size and nature of the organization's goals. For the most part, training methods include on-the-job training, classroom training, apprenticeship training, monitored simulations or problem-solving scenarios, and programmed instruction that can involve interactive, multimedia instructional technologies. According to the American Society for Training and Development, some traditional workshop and classroom work is being replaced by modular training in short, flexible courses focused on specific needs. It is becoming increasingly common for training specialists to be involved in developing and providing training online.

PAYING YOUR DUES

Applicants for jobs in the field of human resources must hold bachelor's degrees. If trainers are seeking managerial spots or consulting practice, a master's degree is beneficial, if not required. It is a good idea to have both academic expertise and experience in your field if you want to be a training specialist. For instance, a trainer in charge of computer literacy would have an advantage with a degree in computer science, but since strong communications and interpersonal skills are also required, degrees in English, psychology, and business are also highly regarded. Professional education is also a benchmark for trainers since they are going to be responsible for the professional education of numerous employees over the course of their careers.

ASSOCIATED CAREERS

Since training specialists often fall under the umbrella of human resources, all personnel, training, and labor-relations occupations are closely related. Many of the people in this field also find success in careers that require expertise in interpersonal skills—college and career planning, placement counseling, law, psychology, social work, public relations, and teaching.

PAST AND FUTURE

Thirty years ago, an employee might have thought of a training specialist as the person who teaches you how to use the phone system on your first day of work. That has changed a lot, especially in an era in which almost all jobs require a constant updating of knowledge and skill. Today, trainers provide instruction in all areas of business, and to do so, they should have a functional comprehension of workplace technology. Training specialists are in demand even as corporate downsizing eliminates many other human resource positions.

QUALITY OF LIFE

2 YEARS Training specialists will be expected to understand their organization's business goals and how their work contributes to achieving them. They must also learn company protocols and the intricacies of their human resources or training department so that they may apply them to their training and developmental plans. The integration of a specific corporate philosophy into a developmental plan can be difficult for new trainers, but they are usually supervised by a human resources director who provides assistance. Education and degree level make a difference early, and individuals without a bachelor's degree will find themselves starting at a salary below $30,000, whereas individuals with a doctorate in their specific field can expect to start at or above $34,000. Early involvement in a professional association can help a new trainer make valuable connections and keep up with new practices in the field.

5 YEARS Five years of experience will definitely help not only your bank account but also your choice of career track. A training specialist who, through professional education and experience, has established expertise in developing successful training programs can become a training material development specialist commanding anywhere from a $42,000 salary to a $50,000 salary. It is important to note that with the rapid pace of changing technologies in the workplace, any training specialist is going to have to keep up his or her expertise and anticipate what trends he or she will need to address in the workplace to secure employment.

10 YEARS Some training specialists go on to become training directors for all sorts of companies, attaining even higher annual incomes. Many other trainers have moved on to related careers in the human resources field. Still others have established private practices, working as consultants to large corporations that don't have full-time training specialists. Training specialists who have become consultants depend on a good track record of success, connections, and cutting-edge development programs that attract fast-track companies.

MAJOR EMPLOYERS
EASTMAN KODAK COMPANY
343 State Street
Rochester, NY 14603
Tel: 585-724-4000
www.kodak.com
Contact: Staffing

SALOMON SMITH BARNEY
388 Greenwich Street
New York, NY 10013
Tel: 212-816-6000
www.smithbarney.com
Contact: Human Resources

MAJOR ASSOCIATIONS
AMERICAN SOCIETY FOR TRAINING AND DEVELOPMENT
1640 King Street, Box 1443
Alexandria, VA 22313-2043
Tel: 703-683-8100
Fax: 703-683-8103
www.astd.org

WORLDATWORK
14040 North Northsight Boulevard.
Scottsdale, AZ 85260
Tel: 480-951-9191
Fax: 480-483-8352
www.worldatwork.org

VETERINARIAN

A DAY IN THE LIFE

Veterinarians provide medical services for animals. They also give advice to pet owners about the care and breeding of their pets. What many people don't consider is that veterinarians also protect humans from diseases that animals carry. Most veterinarians treat sick pets and provide routine checkups and shots for pets in private offices. Veterinarians must be tuned in to an animal's discomfort. They must be able to calm and reassure frightened animals. Since animals cannot communicate their symptoms, veterinarians must depend on their own and the owners' observations to make their diagnoses. Vets in private practice have to handle the business end of the practice, including scheduling appointments, sending

> { Veterinarians also protect humans from diseases that animals carry. }

specimens to labs, and taking payments from pet owners. They generally enjoy a 40-hour workweek, but this does include some evening and weekend hours (to accommodate their clients' schedules).

Some veterinarians work with large animals, such as cattle, racehorses, or zoo animals. These doctors often spend a substantial amount of time on the road commuting to ranches and farms. They also work outdoors in all weather conditions. More frequently, however, they work in laboratory conditions very much like those of any hospital.

Some vets work in the food industry, for the government, or both. They inspect meat-packing plants and check the livestock for disease. Occasionally, they perform autopsies on dead animals to determine what caused the animal's death and how to prevent the problem from spreading to or afflicting other animals. The information obtained from an autopsy often helps them determine which medications, if any, the other animals should receive. Some vets research what diseases animals are susceptible to, and others explore what medicines can treat them.

PAYING YOUR DUES

Veterinarians must have a Doctor of Veterinary Medicine degree and be licensed by the state. It takes six to eight years to complete a DVM. During the first two years of the program, candidates complete general science studies at the college level. Most aspiring vets complete a four-year degree in biological or physiological science. A minor in business is useful for vets who plan to go into private practice. In their senior year of college, aspiring vets apply to four-year veterinary programs. Vet schools require a GPA of 3.0 or higher and high scores on the Veterinary Aptitude Test, GRE, or MCAT. Most of the 27 veterinarian schools in the United States are state funded, so applicants stand the best chance of being admitted to the school in their home state. Competition for a spot in a vet school is intense, and only half of those who apply are admitted. In the veterinary program, students acquire practical experience by working in clinics and assisting in surgeries. During the last two years of school, students do clinical rounds and go on to complete a three-year residency. Only then are they eligible to sit for the licensing exam. About 85 percent of those who take the exam pass it at some point. Some veterinarians who pass the licensing exam continue their studies in a specialized area of veterinary medicine, such as ophthalmology or surgery.

ASSOCIATED CAREERS

Veterinarians can employ their skills in a vast number of areas. Kennel owners run facilities to care for pets while their owners are away. They feed, exercise, and bathe the animals. Groomers bathe animals, brush them, and trim their coats and nails. Ranch hands are responsible for the day-to-day care of farm animals. Zookeepers care for and monitor the behavior of zoo animals; curators manage the animals.

PAST AND FUTURE

The first school of veterinary medicine opened in 1762. Its founder, Alexandre Francois, sought to make veterinary medicine a respected science. The field grew and became organized, and the American Veterinary Medical Association was established in 1863. Unfortunately, most of the schools that were established in the following years closed because they were so expensive. However, the field of veterinary medicine continued, and the prospects are brighter today. More people are buying pets, and they are increasingly willing to pay for their care. Technology for the care and treatment of livestock is creating more opportunities for vets. The demand for other vet specialists, like ophthalmologists, exists primarily in urban areas. Most veterinarians prefer working in urban locations. The field for farm animal vets, as a result, is relatively open.

QUALITY OF LIFE

2 YEARS Very few vets leave the field at this time, as most are still completing their residencies. Their biggest decision is whether to specialize in a particular area. Although many vets decide to specialize in something right away, one experienced vet said it is much better to get your feet wet first before choosing a specialty.

5 YEARS Veterinary medicine is a career in which most people remain until they retire. Few vets leave the field entirely. Vets report high levels of satisfaction in diagnosing animals' problems and caring for them, not to mention in earning the gratitude of the animals' owners.

10 YEARS Occasionally, experienced vets take on assistants or begin teaching aspiring vets. Many vets find this the most rewarding time in their careers.

MAJOR EMPLOYERS

ANIMAL MEDICAL CENTER
510 East 62nd Street
New York, NY 10021
Tel: 212-758-8157
Fax: 212-832-9630

ASPCA
424 East 92nd Street
New York, NY 10128-6804
Tel: 212-876-7700
Fax: 212-876-0014
www.aspca.org

COLORADO STATE UNIVERSITY
Department of Animal Sciences
Fort Collins, CO 80523-1171
Tel: 970-491-1442
http://ansci.colostate.edu

MAJOR ASSOCIATIONS

AMERICAN VETERINARY MEDICAL ASSOCIATION
1931 North Meacham Road, Suite 100
Schaumburg, IL 60173-4360
Tel: 847-925-8070
Fax: 847-925-1329
www.avma.org

WEBMASTER

A DAY IN THE LIFE

The Internet grew exponentially through the 1990s, and now in the twenty-first century, everyone is online. Webmasters, like the website designers with whom they work, may be the authors of the Web pages they tend. Webmasters also need to share the basic technical skills and knowledge of their designing cohorts. They must be competent in HTML and other extensions, browser compatibility issues, and Common Gateway Interface (CGI) scripting devices such as Java and UNIX. In fact, the more technical knowledge Webmasters have, the better off they are, especially since scripting languages and HTML protocols continue to upgrade and change at a rapid pace. Though Webmasters are not often responsible for creating the programs a site needs, they must, in any case, keep on top of these changes in software.

{ rapid pace }

The majority of a Webmaster's work consists of maintenance, augmentation, and improvement of existing sites and pages. Much of this takes the form of an on-screen editor responsible for presenting a uniform visual quality to a site through font selection, formatting, and icons—essentially streamlining a designer's work. The Webmaster also checks for consistency across a site and creates and installs tools for updating Web content. To accomplish these tasks, Webmasters are usually the liaisons among designers, systems administrators, and Internet/Intranet managers. As such, they ensure that HTML validity and active links are upheld for the administrators, and that content, function, quality, and presentation are meeting the goals of the managers. Webmasters are also responsible for optimizing navigability of Web browsers, promoting proper use of URLs (Uniform Resource Locators), establishing efficient Web architecture, enforcing the house style, creating liaisons with graphic artists, and providing first-level user support by creating and maintaining FAQ (frequently asked questions) pages for the sites they oversee.

PAYING YOUR DUES

Both creativity and straightforward technical skills are necessary. Strong writing skills are valued, as is knowledge of computer science, programming, and advertising. A Bachelor's Degree in Computer Science and/or English is useful. In terms of learning the skills needed for Web maintenance itself, anything you study today could quite possibly be outdated tomorrow; on-the-job learning is an intrinsic part of being a Webmaster.

ASSOCIATED CAREERS

Webmasters have much in common with copywriters, computer systems analysts, website designers, and workers in other multimedia fields. Since a unique variety of skills is required of Webmasters, any of these other careers offer the chance to use some or all of those skills. It is also an attractive option for many Webmasters to stick it out and gain the necessary years of experience to gun for a promotion to Web/Intranet manager. Why? Salaries in this area tend to be higher.

PAST AND FUTURE

During the Internet's initial wave of popularity, the desire to be on the forefront of the Web wave created a feeding frenzy among major companies. Even companies that couldn't afford large expenditures for their net presence hired designers and Webmasters.

Since then, though, employers have become more knowledgeable and discriminating. The ever-increasing demand for quality websites means that Webmasters should be technically proficient in computer graphics and their marketing applications. Currently, Web developers are in highest demand in major urban markets such as Los Angeles, San Francisco, New York, and Boston.

QUALITY OF LIFE

2 YEARS A self-employed Webmaster can work as many as 70 hours a week; whereas Webmasters who work on company time come closer to the standard 40-hour week. Individuals in the field of entertainment report the highest salaries, even with only two years of experience. Salaries in general have stabilized, and overall career expectations are high.

5 YEARS People who have been in the field for five years can pull in high salaries, but six-figure salaries are rarely the norm at this point. By now, many Webmasters are self-employed and work on a consulting basis, handling up to five different sites at any one time.

10 YEARS Ten years ago, Webmasters were a rare breed; those young go-getters are now industry veterans. They either do contract work or launch their own design companies.

MAJOR EMPLOYERS
Webmasters may work for any company with an Intranet or website.

MAJOR ASSOCIATIONS
INFORMATION TECHNOLOGY ASSOCIATION OF AMERICA
1401 Wilson Boulevard, Suite 1100
Arlington, VA 22209
Tel: 703-522-5055
Fax: 703-525-2279
www.itaa.org

INSTITUTE FOR THE CERTIFICATION OF COMPUTER PROFESSIONALS
2350 East Devon Avenue, Suite 115
Des Plaines, IL 60018
Tel: 800-843-8227 or 847-299-4227
Fax: 847-299-4280
www.iccp.org

WORLD ORGANIZATION OF WEBMASTERS
9580 Oak Avenue Parkway, Suite 7-177
Folsom, CA 95630
Tel: 916-989-2933
Fax: 916-987-3022
www.joinwow.org
info@joinwow.org

WEB PROGRAMMER

A DAY IN THE LIFE

A Web programmer translates the requirements of end-users and internal clients into a functional product. In other words, a programmer knows how to make a computer do what people want it to do. Usually, that product is an application that allows an end-user to do something on the Web, such as ordering a pizza, trading stocks, or buying an airline ticket. The programmer assesses the technical parameters of a project, decides how to approach the work, and then carries it out. The terms for this job often vary from one Web company to the next, taking Internet changes into account; sometimes this job is also known by the titles of software engineer, developer, or programmer.

On a daily basis, a programmer will modify preexisting code, design new products and applications, create and test { *virtually endless* } those products, and discuss how a design is going to flow. "There is never only one way to get a project done; we are involved with a team of people who have different factions and can never agree on how to get something done," reports one programmer.

The number of applications that a programmer can develop is virtually endless; basically, anything that can be done in real life can be translated into an application for the Web. Moreover, a programmer will often work on two very diverse projects simultaneously.

Programming requires highly creative, perceptual thinking and an ability to visualize what people want so a conceptual solution can be generated. There is nothing physical for the programmer to look at since he or she has to create it first.

PAYING YOUR DUES

The potential knowledge base of computer programmers is virtually unlimited. If it's out there, someone is using it, and you can learn it. Some programmers need to know Unix, which is an operating system and scripting language; others need to know SQL, which manages databases. Learning C, a general programming language, is the basis for finding a first job. "As long as you have some idea of how to program and understand how logic flows, you can apply and translate that knowledge," says one programmer. "You can always pick up other languages, or even learn new languages that haven't yet been invented."

"Solid communication skills are the most important asset that will make you valuable," notes one programmer. "Lack of communication is a big barrier and a serious problem. This leads to errors, confusion, and ultimately, missed deadlines. Know how to understand and interact with people."

ASSOCIATED CAREERS

Outside of a Web environment, general programmers can apply their skills to any industry. One Web programmer formerly worked on an application to generate monthly billing for AT&T. There are even specialty programmers, such as those whose design applications for recording the chemicals used in paint. This would require more specialized knowledge, and an appropriate candidate for this should have a degree in chemical engineering and a certificate in programming.

Programmers have a common subset of skills with engineers: the ability to create and design within a framework. Some establish crossover between these two realms.

PAST AND FUTURE

Before the Internet, programming had a very strict methodology. There was a lengthy manual that programmers had to follow that included detailed documentation for each application. Today, programmers are focused on system integration, which entails getting different computers to talk to one another, exchange data, and operate in tandem.

Regardless of the ways the Web changes, companies are constantly looking in new directions and developing new applications that require programmers. There will also be a need for maintenance; even when a company has an application in existence for several years, it needs fairly frequent attention. Currently, there are more jobs open than there have been in the past, and industry analysts expect this trend to continue. "I think this will be a high-demand position for at least the next 10 years," posits one programmer. "There is a wide open horizon of jobs on the Web representing every industry. You're in the driver's seat; you have your choice of company and salary."

QUALITY OF LIFE

2 YEARS While a large project may take anywhere from eight months to a year to complete, a junior programmer unused to managing time and juggling work will often be assigned smaller tasks. These can include fixing errors in a code or changing the appearance of a client's existing websites; these are jobs that can take can take anywhere from one hour to one week.

5 YEARS As Web programmers become more proficient with various languages, their work will steer more toward designing applications, and away from the actual implementation. Senior programmers are more involved in meetings that discuss the technical aspects of projects and will spend 25 percent or less of their day in front of computers.

10 YEARS Your experience in programming, your facility with using various programming languages, and the number of people that you manage all add up to a higher salary at this level. A senior programmer can even earn a salary of $150,000. At this stage, some programmers become independent contractors and charge their clients up to $150 per hour, and can bring in as much as $250,000 per year.

MAJOR EMPLOYERS
Web programmers are employed by most Web-based companies.

MAJOR ASSOCIATIONS
WEB PROGRAMMER WORLD ORGANIZATION OF WEBMASTERS
9580 Oak Avenue Parkway, Suite 7-177
Folsom, CA 95630
Tel: 916-989-2933
Fax: 916-987-3022
www.joinwow.org
info@joinwow.org

ZOOLOGIST

PROFESSIONAL PROFILE

# of people in profession	13,000
Avg. hours per week	40
Avg. starting salary	$37,100
Avg. salary after 5 years	$47,740
Avg. salary 10 to 15 years	$58,040

SALARY ● ●
HOURS ●
EDUCATION ● ●

BOOKS, FILMS, AND TV SHOWS FEATURING THE PROFESSION
- **Cat People**
- **Life of Pi**
- **Project X**

YOU'LL HAVE CONTACT WITH
- **Animal trainers**
- **Biologists**
- **Ecologists**
- **Nutritionists**

PROFESSIONALS READ
- **American Zoologist**
- **Journal of Mammalogy**
- **Journal of Primatology**

A DAY IN THE LIFE

Zoologists typically work in one of three fields: curating, directing, or zookeeping. The curator oversees the care and distribution of animals in the zoo, while the director does not work directly with the animals but rather performs more administrative duties, such as fundraising and public relations. Curators and directors work closely together to determine the best way to contain the animals, maintain their habitats, and manage the facility. They are far more active in the matter of running a zoo, though, and need to have additional business background. The zookeeper provides the daily care of feeding, cleaning, and monitoring the animals and their habitats.

{ good working relationship with colleagues }

Curators design the budget for the zoo, remaining mindful of the goals at the zoo. The educational programs they design for the zoo and the animals they procure for exhibition reflect these goals. The curator leads the zoo staff and delegates assignments to them. Often curators write articles for scientific journals and provide information to reporters for stories. Zoos often loan animals to other zoos, so a good working relationship with colleagues around the country is vital to the curator. Traveling to conferences and other zoos is part of the curator's long workweek, too. Often animals are bred in captivity, and it is the curator who locates potential mates for his or her zoo's animals. A curator also makes the arrangements for an animal's transport to a museum when it dies. Larger zoos employ a number of curators who specialize in specific areas.

The health of the animals is in the hands of the zookeeper, who prepares the food according to each animal's specialized diet. A zookeeper makes sure that they have enough water, feeds and grooms them, and cleans both the animals and their grounds. When animals transfer locations, the zookeeper attends to them and arranges their new environment. The zookeeper supervises the animals and records their activities continuously, so a zookeeper must understand nuances in animal behavior to keep accurate records. If the keeper notices any change in the animal's behavior, he or she brings it to the attention of the veterinarian. The zookeeper often trains the animals to move in ways that can help veterinarians examine them. All of these responsibilities mean that zookeepers have ample opportunity to venture into the noisy and smelly animal cages, but they are hardly confined to the cages. They must answer the patrons' questions and tactfully keep them from feeding or teasing the animals. Zookeepers in small zoos work with all the animals, while those individuals employed at larger zoos specialize in certain species. Because animals must be cared for around the clock, zookeepers work a variety of schedules. When emergencies arise, like illness, the keeper may work extremely long hours. Most importantly, the keeper must be able to develop a rapport with his or her charges and be infinitely cautious to avoid being injured by the animals.

PAYING YOUR DUES

Every zoo employee must first and foremost love animals. Beyond this requirement, a Bachelor's Degree in a Biological Science is the best way to prepare to work in a zoo. Courses in subjects like zoology, anatomy, and virology are a good idea. More often than not, a curator must have a master's or doctorate degree. Don't underestimate the value of English classes, either—writing articles provides a significant boost to the zoologist's income. Since no zoo hires a curator without practical experience, it's important to gain some practical knowledge and training while you work toward your degree. Most zoos and animal-care facilities have volunteer programs and internships; some zoos even offer paid part-time positions.

A zookeeper also needs to have a college degree: Most hold degrees in biology or zoology and a master's degree if they want to advance in the field. Experience working with large populations of animals is also advisable, for example as a ranch worker or in a veterinary hospital. Many people in the volunteer and paid training programs at zoos are specifically aimed at aspiring zookeepers. Some zoos require that their keepers pass written or oral exams, and all zoos have strict physical requirements for their zookeepers, since the work is usually physically demanding. There are two levels of advancement in this profession: Senior keeper and head keeper, though these positions usually exist only in large zoos. Beyond this, if zookeepers want to advance further they should look to curating.

Animals may stay the same, but the technology used to assist in their care and study is rapidly advancing, so whatever their particular position, the zoologists' education is never completed. Zoo-related industries are highly competitive, and zookeepers, curators, and directors must stay up-to-date in their fields throughout their careers.

ASSOCIATED CAREERS

Veterinarians work with animals and their keepers to maintain the animals' health and care for them when they are sick.

PAST AND FUTURE

No one is quite sure when people began keeping animals in enclosed areas. Prehistoric humans did not keep animals, but hunted them. Later, people began keeping animals to assist them in hunting. The earliest recordings of primitive zoos are in Asia, where emperors kept fish and animals to enjoy their beauty. Between 1750 and 1850, many zoos, as we think of them today, opened in Europe. Today, zoos serve largely to educate the public.

There are only about 200 zoos in North America, and that number is not expected to grow. Few zoologists leave the profession, and as a result, entry-level positions are increasingly scarce, whether for keepers, curators, or directors. Well-educated zookeepers stand the greatest chance of finding employment in this highly competitive field.

QUALITY OF LIFE

2 YEARS People fortunate enough to find a job in this field report incredible satisfaction with their jobs. Even zookeepers find that the monotony of their tasks is tolerable because of the enjoyment they receive from working with the animals.

5 YEARS Most zoologists remain in their field at this time. Zookeepers are happily moving forward in their careers and enjoy the more stable hours that come with seniority.

10 YEARS Many zookeepers have reached head zookeeper status by this time and a few have their eyes on the position of curator. Zookeepers who have become curators report missing the constant physical contact with the animals. Individuals with a decade of curator experience enjoy continually updating the zoo's facilities.

MAJOR EMPLOYERS
BRONX ZOO
2300 Southern Boulevard
Bronx, NY 10460
Tel: 718-220-5100
www.bronxzoo.org

MILWAUKEE ZOO
10001 West Bluemound Road
Milwaukee, WI 53226
Tel: 414-771-3040
Fax: 414-256-5410

SAN DIEGO ZOO
PO Box 120551
San Diego, CA 92112-0551
Tel: 619-231-1575
Fax: 619-557-3937
www.sandiegozoo.org
Contact: Human Resources

MAJOR ASSOCIATIONS
AMERICAN ZOO AND AQUARIUM ASSOCIATION
8403 Colesville Road, Suite 710
Silver Spring, MD 20910-3314
Tel: 301-562-0777
Fax: 301-562-0888
www.aza.org

SOCIETY FOR INTEGRATIVE AND COMPARATIVE BIOLOGY
1313 Dolley Madison Boulevard, Suite 402
Chicago, IL 60611
Tel: 800-955-1236 or 703-790-1745
Fax: 703-790-2672
www.sicb.org

THE GREEN CAREERS

ADMISSIONS OFFICER

SALARY   ● ●

HOURS   ● ●

EDUCATION   ● ●

BOOKS, FILMS, AND TV SHOWS FEATURING THE PROFESSION

- **How I Got into College**
- **Legally Blonde**
- **Soul Man**

YOU'LL HAVE CONTACT WITH

- **Deans**
- **Financial aid officers**
- **Parents**
- **Professors**
- **Students**

PROFESSIONALS READ

- **Chronicle of Higher Education**
- **The College Recruiter's Quick Guide (AACRAO)**
- **Journal of College Admission**
- **NACAC Bulletin**
- **The Work of the Registrar: A Summary of Principles and Practices in American Universities and Colleges (AACRA)**

A DAY IN THE LIFE

A college admissions officer is involved in the recruitment, evaluation, and—you guessed it—admission of students. Admissions officers also sometimes help calculate and estimate the fees and costs for potential students, a task that entails working closely with financial aid officers who manage scholarship, fellowship, and loan programs. Admissions officers also serve as the public representatives of the colleges for which they work, a function that involves overseeing information sessions and coordinating campus tours for prospective students and their parents. The job entails a significant knowledge of the college in general as well as the admissions process in particular; as admissions officers must be able to answer questions relating to college programs and services as well as admissions criteria and statistics. $\{$ multitasking $\}$ During the peak season, this job is no cake walk. One veteran admissions officer remarks that he doesn't have "free weekends from December to May"—not that he seems to mind; he notes, "I like to learn the history and background of the applicant."

Communication skills are essential, as the position involves constant contact with students, parents, colleagues, members of other college offices, and sometimes even donors. Admissions officers, hence, need to be able to work effectively as members of a team, and to have the capacity to manage multiple tasks simultaneously. Several officers typically report to an admissions director, who works closely with program directors, faculty, and deans of to ensure an efficient and effective admissions process. Proficiency with computers, particularly with word processing and database programs, is crucial. Interacting with faculty, students, parents, and other university employees can be an exhilarating experience. One drawback, however, is that the job can also be stressful and demanding. As many colleges and universities face budget cuts, admissions officers often find themselves taking on additional responsibilities in a position that already requires a lot of multitasking. Nevertheless, most who are drawn to this position find that the rewards of working with students more than compensate for the stress and relatively low salary with respect to comparable office jobs.

PAYING YOUR DUES

Admissions officers typically hold bachelor's degrees. Often, institutions like for their admissions officers to have degrees in the field of specialty of the school (if there is one). A requirement of two to four years of experience within that field or in a related area is also standard. Priority is usually given to applicants who have experience working in postsecondary education, particularly those who may have previously worked in the area of admissions. If you plan on moving up the ranks, either to become a chief admissions officer or an admissions director, you should seek to get to know as many members of the administration as you can.

ASSOCIATED CAREERS

Admissions officers are well-positioned to move into other realms of the administration of the institutions they serve. They may opt to take positions as financial aid officers, for example. Financial aid officers put together and manage the financial aid packages of students; they handle work-study, scholarships, fellowships, and loan programs. If, however, you like working in postsecondary education administration but aren't a fan of the whirlwind admissions season, you may seek to take on another type of administrative position at the college. Those who work in the Registrar's office, for example, manage students' records, oversee student registration, assess and collect tuition and fees, and record grades. Because of the seasonal nature of education in general, any administrator will experience busy periods and lulls; but some positions (that of admissions or financial aid officer, for example) have more ebbs and flows than others.

PAST AND FUTURE

Since there have been colleges, there have been college admissions—and hence, admissions officers. As increasing numbers of students in recent decades have opted to attend college, the position has become more systematized and more widespread. As college admissions have become ever more competitive over the past few years, admissions officers have faced the increasingly difficult task of attracting students to their college—and of determining which applicants to admit. Compounding this problem is the increasing cost of tuition as well as budget shortfalls both for private and federal colleges alike.

Still, the employment of education administrators should grow faster than average due to the increasing emphasis placed on education in American society. Although their decisions may become more trying with time, that prospect only further secures the promise of their profession.

QUALITY OF LIFE

2 YEARS
By now, you should feel comfortable with most of the policies and procedures of the school at which you work. Your job will have required you to deal with a number of faculty and other officers of the university with whom you should now have a healthy working relationship. The stress of juggling your tasks should also be decreasing as you become accustomed to the academic calendar of the university you represent.

5 YEARS
If you have demonstrated yourself capable of juggling all of your responsibilities, you may expect a promotion within the office to the level of associate admissions director or even that of head admissions office position. At this point, you are likely to have been given the opportunity to oversee several admissions officers.

10 YEARS
By now, you have should have established yourself as a presence within the office. If you have done your job well, you are connected with deans and faculty within the university, have a comfortable working relationship with the many other offices on campus, and have developed an intricate knowledge of the university and its operation. You may be a candidate under consideration for the position of admissions director, although this position usually requires you to have a master's degree and sometimes even a PhD.

MAJOR EMPLOYERS

Admissions officers may find work at colleges and universities across the nation.

MAJOR ASSOCIATIONS

AMERICAN ASSOCIATION OF COLLEGIATE REGISTRARS AND ADMISSIONS OFFICERS (AACRAO)
One Dupont Circle, NW, Suite 520
Washington, DC 20036
Tel: 202-293-9161
Fax: 202-872-8857

ASSOCIATION OF AMERICAN COLLEGES AND UNIVERSITIES
1818 R Street, NW
Washington, DC 20009
Tel: 202-387-3760
Fax: 202-265-9532

NATIONAL ACADEMIC ADVISING ASSOCIATION (NACADA)
Kansas State University
2323 Anderson Avenue, Suite 225
Manhattan, KS 66502-2912
Tel: 785-532-5717
Fax: 785-532-7732

NATIONAL ASSOCIATION FOR COLLEGE ADMISSION COUNSELING (NACAC)
1631 Prince Street
Alexandria, VA 22314
Tel: 703-836-2222
Fax: 703-836-8015

NATIONAL ASSOCIATION OF GRADUATE ADMISSIONS PROFESSIONALS
www.nagap.org

ADVERTISING EXECUTIVE

A DAY IN THE LIFE

Advertising professionals combine creativity with sound business sense to market a product based on financial, sociological, and psychological research. To ensure that this complicated process works smoothly (and many we surveyed mentioned that you have to be prepared when it doesn't), you'll spend a lot of time in the office (a six-day week is not unusual). Most of your time is spent brainstorming, creative blockbusting, and sifting through demographic research; less time is spent meeting with clients or pitching advertising campaigns. Fluidity of daily activity marks the life of the advertising executive who jumps from project to project, but it can't happen at the expense of attention to detail. It takes an extremely disciplined person to handle both the creative end and the detail-oriented side.

> "You get recognized when you have a good idea."

Advertising executives work on projects in teams, so working with others is crucial; those who are successful have the ability to add to other people's ideas and help them grow. "You can't have an ego in this business, but be aware that everybody has one," mentioned one executive. The need to be flexible cannot be emphasized enough. As a number of large players in the industry move toward "computer-based brainstorming"—a way in which creative ideas are kept in a fluid database without regard to account specificity—computer skills will become more valuable. Like most project-oriented careers, you can expect periods of intense activity during which you have little, if any, free time. At other times, the work load is light and mundane. A number of people interviewed said their favorite part of the profession is that "you get recognized when you have a good idea." They also mentioned that failure is always recognized. The ability to work on a team is one of the most important skills a successful advertising executive has; however, camaraderie and a sense of community beyond any given project is not why people enter advertising. Many of the advertising surveys we received mentioned that in the industry, the word "friend" has the effect of a four-letter word.

PAYING YOUR DUES

In general, an outgoing, well-spoken, well-informed person with confidence and common sense is a typical advertising candidate. However, a degree in communications, graphic design, English, psychology, or any medium of expression does not hurt amidst the competitive rush for advertising jobs. The requirements for an advertising executive differ depending on whether you work in an advertising firm or within a large manufacturing company. If you are working for a manufacturer, you should have a degree or previous work experience that relates to their product line and/or their demographic profile. Advancement is based mainly on achievement at all levels of the industry, not on academic achievement, course of study, connections, or professional associations (although the last two of these factors are growing in stature).

"You can't have an ego in this business, but be aware that everybody has one."

ASSOCIATED CAREERS

The skills you obtain in the advertising industry are transferable to any business-oriented setting, and many executives choose to leave the profession after obtaining their masters of business administration. Other advertising professionals stay in the field for the financial rewards, creative environment, and constant challenge of "reinventing" themselves for every new campaign. Those who have specialized in a particular area sometimes move in-house at a particular company to direct marketing efforts or review which advertising firms to hire. It is important to note that this career has a significant rate of burnout and that nearly 35 percent of people who reach the level of executive vice president or higher leave the profession.

PAST AND FUTURE

Ancient Romans advertised by placing large painted signs on walls, much like the billboards found today along any highway in the United States. Commercial progress, both individually and collectively, has been encouraged by advertising. It is not unusual for products you use in your home to have had significant advertising budgets and for your tastes or interests to have been unconsciously influenced by modern advertising.

The future of advertising is expanding around you today, particularly with respect to electronic media. Smaller, more focused companies are emerging from the gargantuan players of the 1980s and 1990s (although they still are major forces). These use new technologies and response-based, personalized advertising as creative marketing strategies. The Internet continues to broaden the market for advertising while allowing advertisers to zero in on their target audiences.

QUALITY OF LIFE

2 YEARS Entry-level positions, mostly "assistantships," can mean answering mail, entering computer data, returning phone calls, and proofreading copy text. Responsibilities can increase, but only with persistence, luck, and the help of someone currently in a position of responsibility. The lack of complicated tasks during these first two years is actually a blessing; much is learned by observing, following, and listening to experienced advertising executives. The attrition rate is around 20 percent.

5 YEARS Rising young executives move into "account representative" positions, with the responsibility of coordinating the variety of parts involved in a campaign, but no client contact. Salaries rise by around 50 percent—to about $60,000. The number of hours becomes deadly, and many young professionals—frustrated with the small amount of creative input allowed, long hours, and limited pay—leave the profession (25 percent). The few professionals who have the opportunity to make creative input to a campaign see the results of their input and feel the ramifications of that responsibility.

10 YEARS After 10 years, the average industry professional has changed jobs three times, seen about 60 percent of his or her contemporaries leave the profession, and hopefully, developed some specialty in an industry, demographic, or a medium of expression. Many professionals have risen to "account executive" level or higher. About 20 percent more have entered other industries as consultants, managers, or executives. Pay can skyrocket—but it can also plummet to zero. The reason it can fall so dramatically is that advertising holds the particular belief that experience, while important, runs second to "freshness." Advertising executives over the age of 52 are rare.

MAJOR EMPLOYERS
LEO BURNETT COMPANY
35 West Wacker Drive
Chicago, IL 60601
Tel: 312-220-5959
Fax: 312-220-3299
www.leoburnett.com

NW AYER & PARTNERS
825 Eighth Avenue
New York, NY 10019
Tel: 212-474-5000
Fax: 212-474-5353

OGILVY & MATHER
Worldwide Plaza
309 West 49th Street
New York, NY 10019-7399
Tel: 212-237-5627
Fax: 212-237-5123
www.ogilvy.com

MAJOR ASSOCIATIONS
AMERICAN ADVERTISING FEDERATION
1101 Vermont Avenue, NW, Suite 500
Washington, DC 20005-6306
Tel: 202-898-0089
Fax: 202-898-0159
E-mail: aaf@aaf.org
www.aaf.org

AMERICAN ASSOCIATION OF ADVERTISING AGENCIES
405 Lexington Avenue, 18th Floor
New York, NY 10174
Tel: 212-682-2500
Fax: 212-682-8391
www.aaaa.org

ASSOCIATION OF NATIONAL ADVERTISERS, INC.
708 Third Avenue
New York, NY 10017-4270
Tel: 212-697-5950
Fax: 212-661-8057
www.ana.net

AGENT

A DAY IN THE LIFE

The public's perception of agents, largely based on their portrayal in film, ranges from nurturing to nefarious. While almost everyone who has ever needed representation seems to have an "I got screwed by an agent" story, in reality, agents need clients to succeed so that they can earn money.

An agent is a representative who advises clients in a certain area of expertise. Agents represent athletes, writers, models, actors, producers, performers, and other celebrities. They help make their clients' successes happen. If the client doesn't do well, the agent doesn't survive. But there's a significant paycheck for those whose clients strike it

> { If the client doesn't do well, the agent doesn't survive. }

rich; and in this era of multimedia feeding frenzies, skilled agents work diligently to monitor and maximize the impact of every media opportunity for their client. The fact that agents and publicists can decide which stars appear on which magazine covers doesn't sit well with too many editors, but it's how the game is often played.

An agent spends most of the day on the telephone arranging meetings, discussing prospects, networking connections, and keeping in touch with the industry trends and deals. Nearly one-third of all phone time is spent with clients, explaining what the agent is doing on their behalf and strategizing. Face-to-face meetings are also important. Negotiating skills are the agent's bread and butter. Some believe that "to get killed in a negotiation—you only get a little less than what you want." An agent has to be willing to find creative compromises and live with them. Those who are successful must have tenacity, the willingness to fight for their clients, and the ability to sell ideas effectively and communicate clearly. Agents must also have access to those able to make deals to be effective for their clients, so cocktail conversational skills and power-lunch political savvy are important as well.

It's important to know that other agents will not necessarily welcome prospective agents with open arms. Other agents will acknowledge you; they will even discuss their work with you, but they will not offer you their contacts, and they will not tell you any of their secrets. Much of the difficulty of being a successful agent is developing your own contacts, your own strategies, and your own techniques. Despite this arm's length relationship, agents record high levels of respect for one another.

PAYING YOUR DUES

No specific academic requirements exist to become an agent, although most agencies note that a college degree is "preferred." College major is relatively unimportant (although marketing and statistical analysis are looked on favorably), but candidates must show a knowledge of the field, an ability to work under pressure and difficult circumstances, and an ability to relate to their clients. Specialization occurs early on, as representation in different areas (film, literature, sports) requires unique sets of contacts and skills. Often beginning in a smaller, more hands-on firm provides many agents with exposure to the duties associated with the field. Jobs are marked by low wages (often with incentives), long hours, and significant "face time," when agents must entertain clients, reassure them of their advocacy, and keep in touch with their clients' needs.

ASSOCIATED CAREERS

The connections agents make in their careers come in handy if they decide to leave. Many enter the field of their clients, such as producing, editing, publishing, and in rare cases, writing or directing.

PAST AND FUTURE

Representation and negotiation by a third party has existed ever since people began to communicate with one another. In merry old England, the official "facilitator" would, for a fee, match up people who wanted audiences with important officials or royalty. In the United States, the profit-centric efforts of large, monopolistic movie studios in the early 1930s and 1940s demanded the rise of agents to protect the interests of stars. For example, in 1937 and 1938, Mickey Rooney's films outsold those of Clark Gable and any other Hollywood icon; he was paid (through a nonagent-negotiated deal) $2,000 a week. While good money at the time, the studios made nearly $240,000 a week from his films.

With the finances as scintillating to the public as the performances and performers themselves, agents are thrust into the spotlight and headlines alongside their clients as the dealmakers who negotiate the terms of all this wealth and fame. Ethical and lawmaking councils seek to maintain fairness and professionalism in the business. The role of the agent promises to remain secure for the forseeable future.

QUALITY OF LIFE

2 YEARS Administrative duties fill the first two years of aspiring agents' lives as they learn the stock-in-trade of the business. New agents familiarize themselves with contracts, the pace of negotiations, client interaction, and the means of pursuing new clients. Many new agents aggressively pursue unknown talent, taking risks that later would be unthinkable. A fair number of agents (30 percent by some measures) leave the profession because of dissatisfaction with the lack of glamour, the pace of progress, and the menial responsibilities the job offers. The hours are long, and the pay can be low.

5 YEARS Client contact has increased considerably, and those who began at large firms either become "senior agents" or leave to start their own firms (a solid 18 percent). Most agents who find their own firms do so within four to nine years after beginning in the profession. Satisfaction at this stage in the career depends on the person's suitability to their chosen field and their success in their chosen area of specialization. Fifteen percent leave, lured by promotional, publicity, or public relations departments, and the consistent and solid paychecks that these fields provide. Hours have increased, but pay has as well. A gulf in earnings may begin to form between agents with clients whose careers are taking off and those whose clients can't catch a break.

10 YEARS Many agents start their own business by this point (35 percent); those who remain at larger firms guide less experienced agents. Mentoring has been cited by a majority of 10-year survivors in the field as important to their sense of satisfaction. Agents now have scads of direct client contact and head up campaigns to recruit new clients. Interpersonal skills are supplanted by financial and directional decision-making abilities as the primary concern of 10-year veterans.

MAJOR EMPLOYERS

COLUMBIA ARTIST MANAGEMENT
165 West 57th Street
New York, NY 10019
Tel: 212-397-6900
Fax: 212-841-9744
Contact: Human Resources

INTERNATIONAL CREATIVE MANAGEMENT
40 West 57th Street
New York, NY 10019
Tel: 212-556-5600
Fax: 212-556-5665

INTERNATIONAL MANAGEMENT GROUP CENTER
1360 East 9th Street, Suite 100
Cleveland, OH 44114
Tel: 216-522-1200
Fax: 216-522-1145
Contact: Human Resources

MAJOR ASSOCIATIONS

ASSOCIATION OF AUTHORS REPRESENTATIVES
PO Box 237201
Ansonia Station
New York, NY 10003
Tel: 212-353-3709
www.aar-online.org

ASSOCIATION OF TALENT AGENTS
9255 Sunset Boulevard, Suite 930
Los Angeles, CA 90069
Tel: 310-274-0628
Fax: 310-274-5063
www.agentassociation.com

ART DEALER

PROFESSIONAL PROFILE

# of people in profession	6,000
Avg. hours per week	50
Avg. starting salary	$32,100
Avg. salary after 5 years	$74,900
Avg. salary 10 to 15 years	$187,000

SALARY   ● ● ●
HOURS   ● ●
EDUCATION   ● ●

**BOOKS, FILMS, AND TV SHOWS
FEATURING THE PROFESSION**
- 9 1/2 Weeks
- As Good As It Gets
- Legal Eagles

YOU'LL HAVE CONTACT WITH
- Artists
- Bankers
- Event planners
- Publicists

PROFESSIONALS READ
- American Art Review
- Art Direction
- Art Forum
- Journal of Contemporary Art

A DAY IN THE LIFE

In general, people become art dealers because they have a passion for art. The pleasure that comes with making a living from art, combined with the freedom of having one's own business can make this an extremely gratifying career. Successful art dealers have the ability to cultivate a network of artists while simultaneously establishing connections with collectors and museums interested in the work of their artists. The very best dealers develop reputations for anticipating swings in taste and value. Some seem to be able to create demand for an artist by simply agreeing to represent him or her. Most dealers specialize in a period, style, or type of art, such as eighteenth century painting, works of the New York School, or contemporary sculpture. All dealers must keep up with developments in the art world, particularly in their areas of specialty; their careers depend on maintaining a wide range of contacts among critics, curators, auction houses, artists, and collectors. This is a career for the social-minded person, since much of the business is conducted at openings and in sales proposals made to collectors and museum curators. Most successful art dealers enjoy spending time with people in the art world and cultivating contacts with people who are interested in art.

{ cultivating contacts }

Art markets are notoriously volatile, and the fortunes of gallery owners rise and fall with these markets. During the early 1990s art market crash, prices fell 30–50 percent, and 70 of New York City's 500 art galleries were forced to close. Galleries that develop reputations for representing specific styles see their fortunes rise and fall as tastes change, and anticipating these changes is difficult, even for the most experienced professionals. However, the pleasures and possibilities for huge profits in the profession seem to offer rewards that balance the risks in art dealing. Many dealers have long and successful careers, and there is a steady supply of those whose taste and talent in the art world leads them to establish galleries.

PAYING YOUR DUES

There are many paths to becoming an art dealer; almost all involve some participation in the art world. Many dealers begin with degrees in art history and work their way up as assistants in other galleries, developing contacts with clients and artists that enable them to strike out on their own. Others are former museum and auction house curators who decide to establish galleries specializing in the areas of art in which they are familiar. Some artists discover that they have the business and social skills necessary to sell art, and they use their contacts with other artists to develop a body of work to represent.

As with any entrepreneurial venture, strong business and sales skills are a must. Most of the revenue earned by a typical gallery is generated by personal sales pitches to prospective buyers. Access to capital is also vital; gallery cash flow is variable. To survive in the long run, a gallery must be able to withstand dry spells. Frequently, galleries are partnerships in which one partner contributes capital and the other contributes the connections and knowledge to successfully operate the business.

ASSOCIATED CAREERS

Gallery owners whose galleries don't succeed often remain in the art world. Some go to work for more successful galleries, while others pursue careers as museum or auction curators, art critics, academics, or practicing artists. Some who are hit by downturns in the art market use one or more of these options to weather the storm and then reestablish their galleries when economic times improve.

PAST AND FUTURE

For as long as there have been artists and buyers of art, there have been dealers, providing access to and information about the art world to those who wish to invest in or acquire art. The profession has existed in Europe since the Middle Ages; galleries are a more recent innovation providing a place for the public to come and view a dealer's stock. Many of the best known and longest lasting art galleries in the United States were originally founded in the 1920s, as American wealth in the world and greater post-war exposure to Europe created a wave of interest in art investment that caused the auction and gallery markets to grow significantly. Like all art booms, this one passed and was followed by other rises and falls. It is unlikely that the future will be any different. Galleries will persist as long as there is a demand for art.

QUALITY OF LIFE

2 YEARS Art dealers develop connections with the artists, collectors, and curators who will be crucial to their gallery's success. Much depends on decisions made at this point; the most successful dealers are those who can anticipate tidal swings in the world of artistic taste. Signing up artists who will be hot a decade hence is a sure-fire recipe for success. Of course, knowing which artists will be successful in the next decade is what distinguishes the talented and lucky dealers from the rest.

5 YEARS By now, dealers who have stayed in business have a network of buyers and artists. They have survived at least one swing in the art market and can start to look forward to the luxury of developing long-term dealer-buyer relationships. Their gallery is by no means mature, however, and the search for new talent that fits their buyers' tastes continues.

10 YEARS A gallery that lasts for 10 years has staying power: the ability to establish values that can weather the storms of the art market. In other words, the dealer who makes it this long has begun to establish a reputation, perhaps the most valuable commodity in the art world. The challenge is to maintain this network of buyers, which often includes museum curators by now, and to continue to anticipate the vagaries of the art market.

MAJOR EMPLOYERS

CHRISTIE'S
502 Park Avenue
New York, NY 10022
Tel: 212-546-1000 or 212-636-2000
Fax: 212-421-8722
www.christies.com
Contact: Human Resources

SOTHEBY'S
1334 York Avenue
New York, NY 10021
Tel: 212-606-7000
Fax: 847-236-5426
www.sothebys.com
Contact: Personnel

LEO CASTELLI GALLERY
59 East 79th Street
New York, NY 10021
Tel: 212-249-4470
Fax: 847-249-5220

MAJOR ASSOCIATIONS

ART DEALERS ASSOCIATION OF AMERICA
575 Madison Avenue
New York, NY 10022
Tel: 212-940-8590
Fax: 212-940-6484
E-mail: Adaa@artdealers.org
www.artdealers.org

NATIONAL ANTIQUE AND ART DEALERS ASSOCIATION OF AMERICA
220 East 57th Street
New York, NY 10022
Tel: 212-826-9707
Fax: 212-832-9493
www.naadaa.org

ATTORNEY

A DAY IN THE LIFE

Attorneys counsel their clients in legal matters. Law can be intellectually fascinating, and many take great satisfaction in the daily challenges. Detail mavens and big-picture thinkers alike find a friendly home in this profession. But not all were as gushing as this respondent: "You are paid to provide expert counsel to someone in a specific area of expertise, where usually the answers aren't black and white. This pushes you and makes you think harder than you ever have before." More than 30 percent of those who receive law degrees, however, are not practicing law (regularly) 10 years after graduation.

It is impossible to mention attorneys without mentioning the public perception of attorneys. One attorney reminds us of the joke, "What's the difference between a run-over snake and a run-over attorney? There are skid marks in front of the snake." Attorneys are blamed for a variety of social ills, from the litigious nature of our society, to hindering new inventions from reaching the marketplace, to getting guilty people set free due to technicalities or sloppy police work. While these labels speak to the excesses within the profession, many people apply them to the profession as a whole. "It's hard to work 14-hour days researching a case when you know that even your client thinks you're a bloodsucker," wrote a New York attorney.

{ public perception }

The work is hard. Attorneys can work 18-hour days and spend up to 3,000 hours per year on cases. "On some level you have to like what you do because you're doing it all day long," mentioned one attorney. Many lawyers are subordinate to senior associates and partners for the majority of their careers. Attorneys usually work at a number of firms before finding a position perfectly suited to them. Many spend their first few years finding out if they want to focus on transactional work (corporate law or real estate law) or litigation (criminal or civil cases). Some specialized lawyers have restricted areas of responsibility. For example, district attorneys prosecute accused criminals, and probate lawyers plan and settle estates. The quality of life is low during the early to mid-years, but many find the financial rewards too enticing to abandon. Those who wish to enter this field should have solid work habits, curious minds, and the ability to work with—and for—others.

PAYING YOUR DUES

Attorneys must have a law degree from an institution accredited by the American Bar Association. Many find that undergraduate majors with heavy reading and writing loads, such as history, English, philosophy, and logic, prepare them well for law school. In addition, students must take the Law School Admissions Test. Admission at accredited U.S. law schools is competitive. In law school, students first take general courses, which include such classes as torts, contracts, constitutional law, property, and trusts and estates. They then move on to specialized study in an area of expertise. Law students spend their summers working for potential employers, finding out what the working attorney's life is like, and discovering whether or not they want to work in a particular area. Before an attorney can practice in a given state, he must pass a state bar exam, a two-day written examination that tests the prospective attorney's knowledge of the specific laws of that state. Following passage of the written part of the test, many states require "character and fitness" oral examinations to test the ability of a person to practice law in a given state.

ASSOCIATED CAREERS

Many people become attorneys with the understanding that the career is an excellent springboard to other professions. Lawyers enter business, accounting, finance, entrepreneurship, and academia after being in the profession a number of years. Some become judges. Many enter politics, and a number have become presidents.

PAST AND FUTURE

The field of law has a long and storied history. The Sumerians wrote Hammurabi's Code, the first written laws of mankind. Ancient Greek civilization trained youths in logical thinking and rhetorical skills, a key part of legal training. Under Henry II, the English developed a system of common law, matching offenses with standard penalties. America operates under the general guidelines of statutory law, in which elected lawmakers enact statutes that can be reviewed by the judiciary. The number of lawyers grew exponentially in the 1980s when commercial activity was at a peak. When the economy slowed down, so did the need for attorneys. But people will always need attorneys to represent them, and the profession should remain the stable, lucrative field it is today.

QUALITY OF LIFE

2 YEARS Second-year attorneys work grueling hours, but they use their paychecks to buoy their spirits. Those who work in the field of public interest law and those who clerk for judges often find they work as hard, but they don't get the paycheck to show for it. However, their positions are prestigious and the experience they gain makes them all the more valuable if they choose to reenter the job market.

5 YEARS Many find it difficult to switch specializations beyond this point. Career paths diverge for those pursuing partner-track opportunities at large firms and those who choose to dedicate time to other aspects of their life. Partner-track associates can work thousands of hours a year, spending most of their time in the office. A number of attorneys pursue work at smaller firms or as in-house counsel at corporations, where the chances of advancement are greater and the hours are more palatable. Salary, however, declines for those who choose this work.

10 YEARS Those who have survived 10 years as attorneys have accrued valuable knowledge in their area of specialization and have established reputations. Attorneys pursuing partnership at a sizable firm try to recruit new business to prove that they can be valuable assets not just as attorneys, but as "rainmakers" who bring in business. Those who are passed up for partnership either migrate to smaller firms or take positions with corporate firms that need in-house counsel. Hours may have declined somewhat.

MAJOR EMPLOYERS

SIDLEY & AUSTIN
Bank One Plaza
10 South Dearborn
Chicago, IL 60603
Tel: 312-853-7000
Fax: 312-853-7036
www.sidley.com
Contact: Human Resources

SIMPSON, THATCHER & BARTLETT
425 Lexington Avenue
New York, NY 10017
Tel: 212-455-2000
Fax: 212-455-2502

WEIL, GOTSHAL & MANGES LLP
767 Fifth Avenue
New York, NY 10153
Tel: 212-310-8000
Fax: 212-310-8007
www.weil.com

MAJOR ASSOCIATIONS

AMERICAN BAR ASSOCIATION
740 15th Street, NW, 9th Floor
Washington, DC 20005-1022
Tel: 202-662-1000
Fax: 202-662-1032
E-mail: abasvcctr@aba.org
www.abanet.org

AMERICAN BAR FOUNDATION
750 North Lake Shore Drive, 4th Floor
Chicago, IL 60611
Tel: 312-988-6500
Fax: 312-988-6579
E-mail: info@abfn.org
www.abf-sociolegal.org

NATIONAL LAWYERS GUILD
143 Madison Avenue, 4th Floor
New York, NY 10016
Tel: 212-679-5100
Fax: 212-679-2811
www.nlg.org

AUCTIONEER

BOOKS, FILMS, AND TV SHOWS
FEATURING THE PROFESSION

- East/West
- The Flanders Panel
- Secrets of Fast Talkers
- Without Reserve

PROFESSIONALS READ

- American Antiques
- Art and Auction
- The Auctioneer

A DAY IN THE LIFE

Auctioneers manage public sales at which property or merchandise is sold to the highest bidder. These items can be anything from real estate or farm equipment to jewelry or exotic animals. Because knowledge of the value of such goods is important to the successful auctioneer, many auctioneers choose to specialize in just three or four types of auctions. Auctioneers not only represent sellers but also work with buyers. An auctioneer should have a strong voice, a good sense of humor, and an agile mind. Auctioneering is a fast-paced, unpredictable career that can bring financial rewards to those who show ability in all of these areas. Auctions can take place in large convention centers, barns, yards, and parking lots. Travel is often required. An auctioneer faces the crowd (usu-

{ unpredictable career }

ally between 50 and 10,000 people), introduces items, and calls out bids with the help of assistants or "ringmen." While many use public address systems, bid calling for four to six hours per day still puts considerable strain on the voice. More than 75 percent of auctioneers are independent contractors who work for a daily fee or a percentage of sales. As independent contractors, marketing and drumming up business are the auctioneer's responsibilities, so business skills are important. Auctioneers also render appraisal values in two realms: on the value of the asset itself and the price the asset is likely to command. Successful auctioneers have an understanding of the psychology of the auction. The range of value of sales at auctions can run from $2,000 all the way up to $300 million, so financial shrewdness is critical. The community of auctioneers is fairly supportive, and the majority of auctioneers belong to one of the major professional associations. Many entrants to the field work for (or with) more established members of the community. The old vision of the auctioneer as slick bid-chanter has changed with the scale of auctions in America. One auctioneer mentioned, "There . . . has been an improvement in the area of ethics in the auction industry" and was very positive about the future of auctioneering. Many auctions take place under the auspices of the federal government, so an understanding of federal regulations and the ability to work with federal agencies is important.

PAYING YOUR DUES

An auctioneer must have at least a high school education, and auctioneers often have college degrees, as well. Coursework should include finance, accounting, management, psychology, and public speaking. Many auctioneers have experience in marketing and a few cited acting as a helpful course of study. Many professionals spend a year or two learning about valuation in their intended area of specialization; other professionals work as assistants or ringmen in the industry first, then choose an area of specialization. An auctioneer should have a quick mind, an ability to speak clearly and honestly with prospective buyers and sellers, and strong organizational skills. Many states require licensing (particularly for those auctioneers who intend to preside over real estate auctions), and others require aspiring auctioneers to pass an examination and complete an apprenticeship. Check with local authorities to find out about the restrictions in your area.

ASSOCIATED CAREERS

Auctioneers' strong valuation skills and excellent communication skills transfer well into marketing and sales fields. Auctioneers may also become brokers, merchants, professional buyers, entrepreneurs, and salesmen. Those whose specialties focus on the psychological and financial aspects of auctioneering find employment in financial, marketing, and public relations institutions. A few go into public-speaking and negotiation skills teaching for private firms.

PAST AND FUTURE

The profession of auctioneer was first established so that rural families could sell their goods when no established store or market existed in their regions. These families would hire an auctioneer who presided over the sale of all the items to eliminate any semblance of unfair play and dispensed of them quickly. Auctions spread rapidly to urban centers. Now auctioneers work at auction houses, charitable events, and large-scale liquidations of assets, providing a means of sale that can be both fun and profitable. In terms of demand, the future of auctioneering looks very much like the present. Continuous turnover of estates, farm equipment changing hands, and charities' increased reliance on donations of goods and services to raise money as opposed to receiving straight capital provide a steady market for auctioneers. A new breed of auctioneer is developing on the Internet: a cyber-auctioneer, who sends out announcements of times and places for bidders to meet, then manages a forum based on people bidding for goods.

QUALITY OF LIFE

2 YEARS Many auctioneers begin as ringmen and -women: assistants who take bids and tend to the details at auction. New auctioneers learn the protocol and procedures for different auctions; the larger the scale of the auction, the more specific skills are required. Many learn about the computer software associated with auctions, as well as the intangible and people-oriented skills. Professional reviews are brutally honest in these first years; this may account for the 30 percent attrition rate.

5 YEARS Auctioneering skills improve, but many auctioneers move from ringmen positions to other specialized positions, particularly in the marketing department, and learn how to publicize, run, and make profitable auctioneering ventures. The pay doesn't necessarily increase, but the attrition rate shrinks to 10 percent—below average for professions during this period. Auctioneers split into two groups: those in the field who work for national auctioneering services for a salary and those who start their own businesses. The majority of auctioneers who start their own businesses do so between years four and six. Professionals in the field begin to develop specialties and regional reputations. Satisfaction is high, as many in the industry enjoy the freedom their profession brings.

10 YEARS Ten-year auctioneers are, for the most part, independent practitioners with established reputations. Many have regular clients, often including local law enforcement agencies and large banking establishments who hold foreclosure auctions regularly. Nearly all auctioneers have established specialty areas, such as livestock, restaurant equipment, aircraft, art, or firearms. Industry associations are significant for networking and finding new business. Salaries rise, but because private practitioners can only preside over as many auctions as days they are available, increases beyond this point are not considerable.

MAJOR EMPLOYERS

CHRISTIE'S
502 Park Avenue
New York, NY 10022
Tel: 212-546-1000 or 212-636-2000
Fax: 212-421-8722
www.christies.com
Contact: Human Resources

SOTHEBY'S
1334 York Avenue
New York, NY 10021
Tel: 212-606-7000
Fax: 847-236-5426
www.sothebys.com
Contact: Personnel

MAJOR ASSOCIATIONS

NATIONAL AUCTIONEERS ASSOCIATION
8880 Ballentine
Overland Park, KS 66214
Tel: 913-541-8084
Fax: 913-894-5281
www.auctioneers.org

NEW YORK STATE AUCTIONEERS ASSOCIATION
PO Box 69
Falconer, NY 14733
Tel: 716-665-6614
Fax: 716-665-6617
www.nyauctioneers.org

AUTO SALESPERSON

BOOKS, FILMS, AND TV SHOWS
FEATURING THE PROFESSION

- Brackensure
- Cadillac Man
- Showroom Models
- Used Cars

PROFESSIONALS READ

- AutoExec
- Automotive News
- AutoWeek
- Car and Driver
- Special Car Journal

A DAY IN THE LIFE

Car salespeople like the challenge of learning about autos and the unique features of each model and brand, as well as finding the appropriate match for a customer. "I don't know of another profession," mentioned one salesperson, "where there's so much excitement and uncertainty. Everyone who walks into your business wants to buy a car. You've got to find a way to make them want to buy your car. You've got to understand what they need." This psychological aspect to the profession cannot be minimized. People buy cars for a variety of reasons, and the automobile salesperson's job is to figure out what those reasons are. A successful salesperson is a combination of businessperson, advisor, and friend. The average automobile salesperson sells between 200 and 1,000

> { You've got to understand what they need. }

cars per year. Most average over one per day. Although many salespeople work partially for salary, many also receive "commission on sales" as a significant part of their compensation. This places them under some pressure to sell cars. Professional turnover, based primarily on production, is high. Those who can't sell cars aren't given long chances to prove themselves; dealers are under pressure to sell cars themselves. Automobile dealers follow their clients from the moment they walk into the dealership through their signing of the final paperwork. Successful salespeople exude honesty and interest, and integrity is respected. Car sales require someone who thrives on the excitement of the deal and has a strong degree of self-confidence. Other important qualities are the ability to listen, a thorough knowledge of product lines, and an understanding of financing options. The most significant schism in the industry is between those who work for initial dealerships and those who work for used car dealerships. Not only must the used car salesperson be aware of the features associated with a variety of models, but he or she must also be familiar with mileage, modifications, rebuilds, and the quirks of each car on the lot. Also, the used car salesperson works against a stereotype as a slick con artist looking to make a quick buck. Part of this may be due to the larger commissions used car salespeople make on each sale, thus encouraging them to complete as many sales as possible.

PAYING YOUR DUES

A high school education is required by the large employers. College coursework in such fields as marketing, finance, sales, psychology, and public speaking is becoming more common. Large employers have their own sales-training methods, and many new salespeople spend three or four weeks at a national training center, where they learn about the manufacturing process, each model's features, all available options, general negotiating strategies, and the culture of the company for which they work. Some new salespeople are trained by veteran salespeople and have an initial probationary period where all deals must be overseen and approved by a more experienced colleague. Voluntary certification through the National Automobile Dealers Association (NADA) and the Society of Automotive Sales Professionals (SASP) is gaining popularity, but is not required.

ASSOCIATED CAREERS

Automobile salespeople use their personal finesse and their deftness with numbers in a variety of professions as salespeople. Some move into real-estate sales, in which the same abilities are important. A few become supply-house salespeople and negotiate large scale contracts and long-term relationships between retail salespeople and suppliers. Others who are successful and can get financing start their own car dealerships where they hire other car salespeople. Most automobile salespeople continue to work, at least part-time, as automobile salespeople with increasing commissions, finding the excitement of the deal and the challenge of selling such a high-ticket item addictive.

QUALITY OF LIFE

2 YEARS The training period typically lasts between two and six weeks. The first three months may be considered a probationary period. By the end of the second year, salespeople have reasonable salaries, regular hours, and a professional ease in conducting sales. The majority of those unsuited for the profession leave within the first six months (40 percent).

5 YEARS At the five-year mark, automobile salespeople have managed to produce and sell at regular levels. Many salespeople have achieved bonus-triggering sales levels and some have renegotiated the amount of commission they receive. Fluidity of employer marks these years, as successful producers look for the best commissions deals they can cut and the most appropriate shop for their talents. A number of salespeople find themselves surprised by the difficulty of moving from one realm of car sales (for example, the $9,000–$14,000 range) to another (for example, the $20,000–$40,000 luxury car range). Professionals trying to increase sales work more hours; a few top salespeople sell near 1,000 cars per year.

10 YEARS Ten-year veterans are senior sales associates at large dealerships and have found the type of consumer they are good at selling cars to. Many supervise newer employees and administer dealership responsibilities. A few who truly enjoy the world of sales continue their dealership-floor or used-lot responsibilities, usually with success. Around half of the 10-year veterans stay in sales part-time and take on other dealership duties. Salaries level off, but quality of life improves with this choice. Satisfaction is average, as are the number of hours worked.

MAJOR EMPLOYERS
BMW OF MANHATTAN
555 West 57th Street
New York, NY 10019-2925
Tel: 212-586-2269
Fax: 212-262-8722
www.bmwnyc.com

SAM LINDER AUTOMOTIVE GROUP
333 North Main Street
Salinas, CA 93901
Tel: 831-424-1500
Fax: 831-422-2361
www.samlinder.com

MAJOR ASSOCIATIONS
AMERICAN INTERNATIONAL AUTOMOTIVE DEALERS ASSOCIATION
211 North Union Street, Suite 300
Alexandria, VA 22314
Tel: 703-519-7800
Fax: 703-236-6889
www.aiada.org

NATIONAL AUTOMOBILE DEALERS ASSOCIATION
8400 West Park Drive
McLean, VA 22102
Tel: 713-821-7000
Fax: 703-821-7025
www.nada.org

BANK OFFICER

A DAY IN THE LIFE

Bank officers are in charge of every aspect of retail banking (as distinguished from investment banking—see that listing), from making certain that accounting procedures are followed to approving loans to marketing the bank to potential customers. Bank trust officers act as trust and estate managers; loan officers manage, evaluate, and distribute loans; operations officers handle the interface between banking institutions and technology, such as computer systems; and marketing officers identify customer needs and evaluate service. They all work together to ensure the proper functioning of the bank on a day-to-day basis. The intricate networks of responsibility are internally reviewed and subject to the supervision of the United States government. Interaction is marked by a sense of { **enormous responsibility** } professionalism; while few bank officers cited "closeness" as a way of describing their relationships with their coworkers, many said that they could and did rely on them every day.

Each type of officership requires a different set of strengths. For example, those who become trust and estate managers must have a strong understanding of tax implications, an ability to anticipate future problems, and excellent communication skills as they will work closely with clients. Loan officers, however, must have an understanding of statistics and strong judgment skills, anticipating a potential borrower's future ability to repay a loan. Our respondents emphasized the enormous responsibility most banking officers face. "You have to make real decisions that have real responsibilities attached, and you've got to be smart [about them]" mentioned one. Beginning employees aren't thrown into the industry without training or supervision, but they are given a surprising amount of power for people with little work experience. Banking requires an agility with numbers, good organizational skills, sound interpersonal skills, and a strong fundamental work ethic. Those in the banking industry ranked the intensity of their day-to-day jobs in the top 10 percent of all professions; this career isn't for someone who pines for long vacations and sinecures.

PAYING YOUR DUES

While tellers and occasionally bank managers can find work with as little as a high school education, most senior bank officers have at least a bachelor's degree (most large employers look favorably on finance, banking, economics, accounting, and marketing majors), if not an MBA. International banks may request proof of language skills. Many request work experience that demonstrates a facility with numbers or the ability to handle a wide area of responsibility. Bank officers come in contact with confidential information every day, so new hires may be required to sign nondisclosure agreements. Upon hire, many bank officers spend three weeks to six months training for their positions. Officers must have a solid understanding of financial rules and regulations, and many firms require that new employees pass an in-house test that assesses their knowledge before they are allowed to begin their positions.

ASSOCIATED CAREERS

Retail bankers who yearn for higher risk and challenges (and higher rewards with success) become investment bankers. The less bold move to accounting fields where responsibilities are limited and tasks more discrete. A number of former bank officers enter the securities industry and become brokers, traders, and salesmen. A few operations officers move into the computer industry and become programmers, operations specialists, or hardware specialists.

PAST AND FUTURE

Banking in the United States began immediately following the American Revolution, but that bank failed, so the federal government formed a second bank of the United States, and that failed, too. States then took up the slack and formed large and powerful state banks, which issued their own currencies and proved very successful. The Federal Reserve was then formed, with 12 branches, and given the job of coordinating these large state banks. As banks grew and became less centralized, a bank officer position was developed for each area of responsibility.

Currently there are about 10,000 banks in operation, but most analysts believe that the industry will undergo a wave of consolidation and acquisition, and settle somewhere between the 4,000–6,000 bank range. A natural result of this consolidation is the reduction of jobs with overlapping functions, which means that many bank officers will face layoffs. The ascendancy of automatic teller machines (ATMs) has further contributed to displacement as workers are shunted from customer service to back-office functions (if they are lucky enough to stay employed at all). The banks that survive consolidation will be stronger, larger, and more efficient, with excellent prospects for growth. Bank officers who survive the next several years should thrive in well-positioned companies looking to expand in the years to come.

QUALITY OF LIFE

2 YEARS Bank officers spend the first two years at hectic on-the-job training sessions, learning their professions at the side of more experienced employees. Hours are long, and time spent doing professional reading or attending industry seminars can be significant. Responsibility levels are high for trust officers and marketing officers, but loan officers have significant departmental oversight. Duties include budgeting, scheduling, administrative work, and report writing. Communication skills are important during these early years, more to ensure that the education process progresses smoothly than to ensure that the duties of the job are managed.

5 YEARS Five-year officers are termed "senior" officers of the bank, and many head up staffs composed of less experienced colleagues. Relocation is a major issue during these years, as is fluidity of employer. Well-considered officers are important strengths in any bank; those with creative and effective strategies are in strong demand. Hours become even longer for those looking to rise to V.P. status or beyond: The ambitious take additional course work (many take time off to pursue MBAs after garnering a couple of years' on-the-job experience, which most business schools expect from candidates) and a few try to either achieve industry accreditation or assume significant roles within professional associations ("networking" is as important in banking as in any industry). Those who enjoy their current level of success work on honing managerial skills. Salaries and responsibilities increase; job satisfaction is average. Twenty percent will leave the field during these years, mainly to enter the related areas of corporate finance, investment banking, and accounting.

10 YEARS Ten-year survivors either have established areas of responsibility or are aggressively pursuing the title of vice president. Salaries have risen, and satisfaction is high; those who remain in the profession after 10 years are most likely to remain in it for life. The low attrition rate after this point—under 5 percent—is notable.

MAJOR EMPLOYERS
CITY NATIONAL CORPORATION
City National Center
400 North Roxbury Drive
Beverly Hills, CA 90210
Tel: 213-553-8272 or 800-281-5656
Fax: 213-553-8285
www.citynational.com
Contact: Human Resources

FEDERAL RESERVE BANK OF CHICAGO
230 South Lassie Street
Chicago, IL 60604
Tel: 312-322-5322
Fax: 312-322-5515
www.chicagofed.org
Contact: Staffing Manager

UBS
299 Park Avenue
New York, NY 10171
Tel: 212-821-3000
www.ubs.com

MAJOR ASSOCIATIONS
BANK ADMINISTRATION INSTITUTE
1 North Franklin, Suite 1000
Chicago, IL 60606-3421
Tel: 800-284-4078 or 312-683-2464
Fax: 312-683-2373
E-mail: info@bai.org
www.bai.org

BAR/CLUB MANAGER

PROFESSIONAL PROFILE

# of people in profession	15,000
Avg. hours per week	55
Avg. starting salary	$20,500
Avg. salary after 5 years	$33,900
Avg. salary 10 to 15 years	$56,800

SALARY ●
HOURS ● ● ●
EDUCATION ●

BOOKS, FILMS, AND TV SHOWS
FEATURING THE PROFESSION
- Cheers
- Cocktail
- Pug Trencher's House of Dreams
- Road House

YOU'LL HAVE CONTACT WITH
- Bartenders
- Bookkeepers
- Entertainers
- Suppliers
- Waiters

PROFESSIONALS READ
- Bar Supply Monthly Report
- Hype

A DAY IN THE LIFE

Managing a bar or club is a high-profile job, but don't let anyone tell you it is glamorous. "When you have to, you do everything from carrying kegs of beer up flights of stairs to mopping up spills," reported one bar manager. At the end of the night, the responsibility for the smooth functioning and, on some levels, the profitability of the bar or club rests with the manager. Club managers have a significant degree of input on the attitude and operation of the club and can impress their sensibility on the patrons' experiences. "You can give them the night they always wanted," said one manager, "and that feels great." The most enjoyable aspect about being a club or bar manager is the creativity the profession entails. Most managers work closely with owners on developing marketing strategies based around theme nights, entertainment, advertising, and special events. Financial analysis skills—basic cost benefit analysis, for the most part—are important for club and bar managers to propose interesting, yet fiscally sound marketing schemes. Such events as open mic nights, happy hours, and couples nights are examples of themes that many clubs and bars find successful in attracting new patrons. The bar and club manager must be creative without sacrificing the attention to detail that the day-to-day aspects of the profession require.

{ creativity }

Bar or club managers must be comfortable with people: from the professionals with whom they work—accountants, wait staff, suppliers, and government regulators (including representatives from the liquor, fire, sanitation, and health departments)—to the patrons they entertain. Managers must understand local regulations and accounting procedures to ensure the establishment functions legally and smoothly. According to our survey, most people thought the job would be fun (which many say it is), but they didn't understand the degree of responsibility it required. "You have so much to keep track of. Everything is important," noted one club manager. Managers must be comfortable claiming responsibility and enforcing authority as the liaison between the owners of the establishment and the employees.

PAYING YOUR DUES

There is no specific educational requirement to become a bar or a club manager, but most managers have a high school education, and many of them have also completed college accounting, finance, or management coursework. Work experience is more important than educational requirements. Employers seek those people who have experience managing others and keeping track of large budgets and inventories and who have generally demonstrated a strong sense of responsibility. The workday usually extends from late afternoon to late into the night, and weekends are regularly part of established shift schedules. Those who leave the profession often cite the schedule as a significant reason for their departure.

ASSOCIATED CAREERS

The organizational aspects of bar and club managing equips former managers with the necessary skills for inventory control, staff management, human resources, and employment company positions. Others use their patron relations skills as party planners, caterers, public relations professionals, and salesmen. Note that many of these related occupations require a different level of educational achievement than bar and club manager. Only a limited percentage of those employed as bar and club managers see it as a career profession, mainly because only certain establishments offer positions with any benefits whatsoever.

PAST AND FUTURE

Bars and clubs used to be managed by their owners, but as owners opened second and third clubs, they had to find people whom they could trust to run them. The position of manager evolved as one close to ownership and has become, frequently due to corporate ownership, that of intermediary between owners and staff.

Bars and clubs will consistently need creative managers who can ensure that the public has a fresh and exciting perception of the establishment and that the establishment runs as smoothly as possible. Management software is becoming more important for those who are looking to enter this profession, and many three-week courses provide instruction in these systems.

QUALITY OF LIFE

2 YEARS Bar and club managers usually rise from staff positions such as bartenders, waiters, and (less often) bar backs. They usually manage their establishment under strict supervision for two to three nights unpaid, to learn the ropes. There are three months of a probationary period when loose supervision and limited responsibilities are offered. Two-year managers are responsible for assembling, managing, and paying staff, as well as opening and closing the club or restaurant. Duties include ordering supplies and managing inventory. The hours are long (4:00 P.M. to 2:00 A.M., for example) as the new managers learn their job; the pay is reasonable, and many managers are satisfied.

5 YEARS Five-year managers have significant input into promotional efforts that make the public aware of the club or bar. Many managers are given complete latitude to determine and advertise events, with responsibility for the bottom line. Duties remain the same, but managers usually have developed good relationships with vendors and established systems of employee scheduling. At the five-year mark, managers have honed employee evaluation skills and are given reasonable latitude to offer holiday bonuses to exceptional employees. The position becomes one of culture and policy; the five-year manager determines the tone and attitude of the establishment and the way it functions on a day-to-day basis.

10 YEARS A mere 20 percent of managers remain with their initial clubs or bars for 10 years, and the majority of managers leave between years five and nine. Some managers claim that it is difficult to remain fresh and innovative at the same location. Others claim that bar and club popularity levels are cyclical, and when owners see any dip in profits, the first person who carries the blame is the manager. A third group claims that there is little challenge to the job once managers have smoothed operations and reinvented locations. Many of those who choose to remain at their original locations attempt to buy some sort of stake in the bar or club; this new role of ownership seems to provide the spark many need to reinvent themselves.

MAJOR EMPLOYERS

AVALON
47 West 20th Street
New York, NY 10036
Tel: 212-807-7780

BIMBO'S 365 CLUB
1025 Columbus Avenue
San Francisco, CA 94133
Tel: 415-474-0365

CLUB NEW YORK
252 West 43rd Street
New York, NY 10036
Tel: 212-997-9570

MAJOR ASSOCIATIONS

NATIONAL BAR AND RESTAURANT ASSOCIATION
307 West Jackson Avenue
Oxford, MS 38655
Tel: 662-236-5510
Fax: 662-513-3989
E-mail: join@bar-restaurant.com
www.bar-restaurant.com/contact.html

BENEFITS ADMINISTRATOR

A DAY IN THE LIFE

"I like to think of myself as a teacher," remarked one benefits administrator, and her job description seemed to match up with her perspective. Benefit administrators explain, summarize, and publish material that describes to employees their rights and obligations under their benefits plans. Benefit administrators handle grievances, take suggestions, and act as intermediaries between benefits providers and employees. Administrators with strong communication skills, sharp minds, and the instinct to explain and teach find their choice of occupation gives them a high degree of satisfaction. More than 40 percent of the benefits administrator's day is spent on the telephone, either with providers or clients, explaining procedures and getting information. Another 40 percent of the day is spent writing, reading, and researching reports.

{ safety net }

Benefits administration is one outcropping of the corporate culture it supports; many people who enter the industry with the belief that employee benefits should help the employee at any cost are rudely awakened. Decisions on benefits are made in the context of this corporate culture, particularly with an eye on the bottom line. Benefits administration is a way of providing employees with support, a safety net, and advice on investments, but any decisions that help the employees should help the company as well.

Administrators must have a strong sense of self and an ability to explain benefit plans clearly. "Expect to be blamed for everything from the client not filling out their forms properly to a rude pharmacist," said one seven-year veteran. Balanced delicately between the clients and the providers, benefits administrators prove good targets for dissatisfied members of either side. This was cited as the largest downside of the profession and may contribute to the number of administrators who leave the field between years three and six (nearly 35 percent). But this frustration is frequently offset by the general sense of helpfulness that benefits administrators feel in offering people options, educating them about their plans, and helping them through a confusing and intimidating healthcare system.

PAYING YOUR DUES

Candidates should have at least a bachelor's degree. Favorably viewed majors include English, communications, psychology, history, business, and economics. While benefits administrators work for large and small firms alike, most entry-level opportunities exist in larger firms with entire benefits administration departments. Smaller companies usually combine benefits administration duties with other responsibilities. No professional accreditation programs are required in this profession, but a familiarity with issues in the field, an understanding of the areas of responsibility for benefits administrators, and a willingness to work hard and learn are all critical.

ASSOCIATED CAREERS

Benefits administrators make business decisions and help others, and the two fields that people enter from benefits administration most often satisfy these two needs. Business-oriented benefits administrators go into a variety of banking and financial positions, such as management consulting and securities analysis, while people-oriented administrators go into human resources, career counseling, and job-training programs. A few administrators enter the insurance industry.

PAST AND FUTURE

As corporations grew in size and personnel issues and benefits programs became a significant portion of employee compensation beginning in the 1960s, benefits administrators came into being. Initially employed only by the largest companies to handle questions and respond to unusual situations, benefits administrators, or at least their responsibilities, have become part of the human resources department in most companies.

Health care, once an afterthought for most companies, has taken center stage in discussions of employee benefits. As benefit plans and insurance procedures become more complex, the number of administrators is expected to grow. Benefits administrator training programs and professional societies are likely to become more significant, but they are not likely to affect the daily job or to create licensing pressure for people entering the field. Today, benefits administrators are the fastest-growing level of vice president at companies in the United States that employ 30 or more people.

QUALITY OF LIFE

2 YEARS Two years into the profession, the benefits administrator has been exposed to the major areas of responsibility—insurance, compensation, and bonus structure—and has significant responsibility in each. Duties include coauthoring (with more senior personnel) summary description plans of benefits services, managing the distribution of materials to clients of the system, and meeting with members of the insurance industry who explain their products and services. Most administrators attain the title "analyst" and begin to specialize in one specific area.

5 YEARS Five-year veterans separate into two categories: those administrators who have one area of specialization and those who have chosen to cover a number of areas. The latter role isn't necessarily chosen—many people are plucked out of the mix and asked to make themselves experts in a variety of fields. This "star-selecting" is based primarily on performance and capabilities; many administrators mentioned that the political process of networking, while existent, was not the primary means of advancement. Those people who have chosen to specialize have attained the title "senior analyst" in their area of expertise and are managing less experienced employees. Input is accepted on a variety of high-level issues, such as performance of plans and potential modifications to these arrangements. The hours are average; the salaries increase significantly.

10 YEARS Ten-year veterans' lifestyles differ based on the size of the company with which they are associated. Those administrators in smaller firms head up departments, negotiate directly with vendors, work with top executives on benefits packages, and set corporate policy. Those administrators in larger firms have areas of responsibility such as "dental plans for North America." While this requires a degree of specialization, the department head or vice president assumes all the responsibility for planning, implementation, and education. Decisions are still overseen by generalists who have risen faster or who have greater experience, but are rarely countermanded. For those in small firms, salary increases are limited beyond this point; for those in larger firms, salary increases can still be significant.

MAJOR EMPLOYERS
Any medium- to large-size Fortune 500 company will have a need for a benefits administrator.

TARGET CORPORATION
1000 Nicollet Mall
Minneapolis, MN 55403
Tel: 612-304-6073
Jobline: 612-304-4960
www.targetcorp.com

MERCK & CO., INC.
One Merck Drive
PO Box 100
Whitehouse Station, NJ 08889-0100
Tel: 908-423-1000
www.merck.com

MAJOR ASSOCIATIONS
WORLD AT WORK
14040 Northsight Boulevard
Scottsdale, AZ 85260
Tel: 480-951-9191
Fax: 480-483-8352
www.worldatwork.org

BUYER

A DAY IN THE LIFE

Being a professional buyer is a glamorous, powerful job in many respects. But the glitter and glitz should not cloud the hard work and keen intellect required to make it in this competitive field. Professional buyers examine goods and work within reasonable budgets to make competitive bids for products to resell. Don't underestimate the amount and the scale of negotiations necessary. "People eat you alive if they think they can get away with it," wrote one buyer. People who are comfortable with negotiating reported a higher-than-average satisfaction with their job. The decisions a buyer makes—color, size, quantity, and price—are some of the most important in determining whether a company makes a profit in a given year. The power to influence sales, beat competition, and earn high profits through their own { It's addictive. } actions gives many buyers satisfaction in a high-pressure position. The bottom line in this job is "how am I selling and what is my margin." "It's the closest thing to gambling, including picking stocks. You don't really have a lot of research—you have to go with your taste and your gut feeling." "It's addictive," mentioned one long-term buyer. Some buyers said that it is important to stick with what you know and not think about commercial profitability because "you're just as likely to pick a winner or a dog either way. Consumer taste is fickle." Buyers must have confidence in their choices, be able to assert their preferences, and defend their selections.

Buyers work long and sometimes unusual hours and travel to fashion shows, industry conferences, seminars, and trade shows. They investigate producers' lines, then place orders, usually with a limited amount of discussion. Professional buyers work with retail sales people to get feedback on how choices they have made responded to the market. This back-and-forth dialogue is important to a buyer's understanding of any problems the sales force has moving the product. A significant number of respondents mentioned the support the other members of the field provided. While buyers will sometimes come into conflict over purchases and sales, the profession is so grueling that many find themselves sympathetic to one another in spite of that conflict.

PAYING YOUR DUES

Almost any college major can prepare you to become a buyer; it depends on what you want to buy. A book buyer might have been an English major; someone who buys hospital supplies might have majored in biology. Any college major with a business or managerial skills background will prepare you for the career. All employers require new employees to learn the specifics of their own business. Large companies usually have internal buyer training programs lasting from one to five years that expose the new employee to all aspects of the business. Many trainees begin as salespeople and learn about inventory policy, stock maintenance, and shipment checking. Aspiring buyers receive extensive training on proprietary computer and inventory-tracking systems. The ability to plan ahead, predict consumer habits, and make difficult decisions mark those who emerge successfully from training programs. Those buyers who continue in the profession find it helpful to achieve the professional designations recognized in each state, such as Certified Purchasing Manager (CPM) and Certified Purchasing Professional (CPP). To become an official purchasing agent for the government, applicants must pass a two- or three-part exam.

ASSOCIATED CAREERS

Professional buyers are usually in touch with a taste or a sensibility in a given field, and many buyers use their knowledge in other careers. Some buyers become fashion consultants for celebrities; others become internal managers for production firms. A third group of buyers moves into retail and opens their own stores. A significant number of buyers enter advertising, an industry in which their guesses as to consumer preference and experience working with salespeople are invaluable.

PAST AND FUTURE

Professional buyers came about as part of the growth of large retail concerns. Stores would utilize professional buyers to ensure that the same merchandise was stocked in the same region. Professional buyer was a position created to centralize these responsibilities and standardize inventory.

Buyers face a shrinking market for their services. The industry trend among major retail stores has been consolidation. Industry consolidation means shrinkage of redundant positions and further standardization of inventory, so buyers have fewer opportunities to buy. This shrinkage of jobs at large retail stores may be offset by the growth of chains, but there is not yet enough evidence to make a relatively accurate prediction.

QUALITY OF LIFE

2 YEARS — Professional buyers have begun, and in some cases completed, buyer-training programs. Lessons include budgeting, accounting, retail sales, computer systems, inventory control, company protocol, an overview of the industry they are involved in, and some basic financial skills. Many buyers have begun "externship" parts of their program where part of their time is spent in classrooms and the rest is spent working in retail sales departments. Many buyers cite working in retail as invaluable to their development as professional buyers. Salaries and responsibilities are low, but many buyers enjoy these years for the education and free time they offer.

5 YEARS — Buyers involved in long training programs have finished them and become assistant buyers with discrete accounts and responsibilities. Many people pursue additional education through coursework, industry publications, and professional seminars. Those buyers with good reputations for hard work and shrewd bargaining can advance to full buyer status with accountability to the head of the department. Numerous opportunities arise for aggressive buyers to distinguish themselves; the price for this risky behavior can be significant—more than 20 percent of the workforce is let go by year five, primarily for lack of "aptitude" at the profession.

10 YEARS — By year 10, the hours and responsibilities increase, as does the salary. Years 7-11 are when most professional buyers settle into the roles they will assume for most of their careers. Those buyers who have wanted to move into management have done so by this point, and people who wish to remain buyers have carved out a comfortable territory for themselves. Work changes from directly negotiating deals to overseeing other buyers and assistant buyers. Many have established relationships with producers. More than 30 percent of 10-year members of the industry are still with the companies with which they began their careers.

MAJOR EMPLOYERS

BLOOMINGDALE'S
1000 Third Avenue
New York, NY 10022
Tel: 212-705-2383
Fax: 212-705-2399
E-mail: careers@bloomingdales.com
www.bloomingdales.com
Contact: Human Resources

FORD MOTOR COMPANY
5111 Auto Club Drive
Dearborn, MI 48126
Tel: 313-322-0155
www.ford.com

IBM CORPORATION
1 DPA/051
3808 Six Forks Road
Raleigh, NC 27609
Tel: 714-438-5000
Fax: 800-262-2494
www.ibm.com
Contact: Staffing Services Center

MAJOR ASSOCIATIONS

NATIONAL CONTRACT MANAGEMENT ASSOCIATION
8260 Greensboro Drive, Suite 200
McLean, VA 22102
Tel: 800-344-8096 or 571-382-0082
Fax: 703-448-0939
www.ncmahq.org

CLOTHING/JEWELRY/COSMETICS GENERALIST

A DAY IN THE LIFE

People in jewelry, clothing, and cosmetics production and sales need a similar set of day-to-day skills. Each industry employs designers, buyers, production personnel, retail salespeople, and inventory control personnel. With the exception of designers, most initial entrants are hired as generalists who rotate from department to department until a match is found between their skills and a department's needs. A generalist must be flexible and able to switch from task to task at a moment's notice. The skills this occupation requires are best cultivated in someone who has the desire to learn, the ability to take direction, and strong decision-making abilities. Professionals spend their days attending meetings, planning production and shipping, and working with different departments. About 25 percent of their time is spent on paperwork, and more than 20 percent is spent on the phone. Working with others is a large part of this profession: One cosmetics executive wrote, "If you don't listen to people in your division, expect to lose their respect." More than 80 percent of our respondents rated communication skills as either the first or second most important qualification to have. Strong decision-making abilities and aesthetic skills are valued in generalists.

{ rapid and broad exposure }

Since specialization occurs later in this career than most—after 10 years or more—in manufacturing, inventory management, distribution networks, retail sales or advertising, one has a chance to explore the field thoroughly. It is not unusual to be transferred to five, six, even seven different areas during the first three years before spending any significant time at one. This rapid and broad exposure to the full range of career options within the industry is both praised and denounced. "Knowing the whole production process helps me in sales," mentioned one high-end jewelry salesman, referring to an earlier five-month stint abroad at his company's South African manufacturing facilities. Another advertising buyer in the clothing industry countered, "working on the manufacturing floor in Columbus was the biggest waste of two months ever." Satisfaction recorded is below average in this profession, and this discontent is linked to the short-term reliability and the lack of continuity of jobs. Forty percent of the people in the industry change jobs either between companies or within the same company every single year. Also, because the work environment is so fluid and fast-paced, the camaraderie between workers seems to suffer: "For the first two years, I'd look over my shoulder and see a new face every month," said one manager. The competitiveness within these industries and the challenge of achieving success are high, so for those who like a difficult test of their abilities, a career in clothing, jewelry, or cosmetics seems a perfect fit.

PAYING YOUR DUES

No specific bachelor's degree is required for someone to enter the clothing, jewelry, or cosmetics fields, but applicants with finance or inventory backgrounds, communications skills, or computer skills have an advantage. Candidates go through extensive cutthroat training programs, which involve all aspects of clothing, jewelry, and cosmetics manufacturing and sales. Trainees are educated in the entire process, from product conception and development through raw material purchasing, product manufacturing, marketing, sales, and customer service. The bulk of the cost of becoming a professional in these fields is front-loaded into the early years, which involve retail-sales-like rotational structures, low pay, fierce competition, and long hours. Some members of the industry spend hours outside work socializing with colleagues, attending seminars, and taking additional courses to enhance their profiles.

ASSOCIATED CAREERS

People in the cosmetics, jewelry, and clothing industries may go into a number of managerial and sales fields. Many professionals go into industrial management and commercial goods production, corporate strategy, and professional buying. Others use their retail skills to enter other retail or direct-marketing industries. A few gravitate to publishing, advertising, or professional event planning. The ability to rapidly adjust to changing circumstances and different projects makes the transition from these professions to others less jarring.

PAST AND FUTURE

Clothing, cosmetics, and jewelry have been around for centuries. Significant inventions in the clothing industry were the spinning jenny (spinning wheel) in 1764 by James Hargreaves and the invention of the cotton gin, which allowed the mass milling of cotton from plant to usable fiber, by Eli Whitney in 1793. All of these industries are extremely sensitive to imports, and with the dropping of North American tariffs as per the NAFTA agreement, they may face additional competition. Moreover, since over 70 percent of the companies in these industries employ fewer than 50 workers, sensitivity to one bad season or one bad market cycle may prove disastrous to smaller, less well-capitalized companies. Despite these vulnerabilities, the market for these products is strong and should remain unchanging throughout the end of the decade.

QUALITY OF LIFE

2 YEARS Two-year generalists rotate among a variety of departments. Duties may include warehouse inventory control, production assisting, buyers assisting, retail sales agenting, and client complaint department work. These early years provide the generalist with a broad range of experience and determine a solid match between the generalist's temperament and skills and available positions. Satisfaction and wages are low during the first two years, when more than 25 percent of new hires leave the occupation.

5 YEARS Generalists with specific skills who have found a good match begin the process of specialization. Most generalists, however, rotate on an annual basis between different positions. Many are promoted and earn different titles, such as "inventory manager" or "quality control supervisor." Salaries and responsibilities increase, and the hours can become very long. Many generalists switch firms to gain higher salaries and greater responsibility.

10 YEARS Ten-year veterans have found their specialties and earn such titles as "executive materials buyer" or "senior management generalist." They set large-scale policies, manage professionals in charge of day-to-day functioning of each department, and do long-term strategic planning. Salaries rise (beyond cost-of-living increases) only for those who move onto senior executive management. The hours decrease, and quality of life improves.

MAJOR EMPLOYERS

REVLON
625 Madison Avenue
New York, NY 10022
Fax: 212-527-5588
www.revlon.com/corporate/
Email: jobs.mail@revlon.com

POLO RALPH LAUREN CORPORATION
Human Resources Department
650 Madison Avenue
New York, NY 10022
Fax: 212-318-7200
E-mail: jobs@poloralphlauren.com

TIFFANY & CO.
Fifth Avenue at 57th Street
New York, NY 10022
Tel: 212-755-8000
E-mail: jobs@tiffany.com
www.tiffany.com

MAJOR ASSOCIATIONS

AMERICAN APPAREL MANUFACTURERS ASSOCIATION
1601 North Kent Street, Suite 1200
Arlington, VA 22209
Tel: 800-520-2262 or 703-524-1864
Fax: 703-524-6741
www.americanapparel.org

INTERNATIONAL ASSOCIATION OF CLOTHING DESIGNERS AND EXECUTIVES
34 Thorton Ferry Road
Amherst, MA 03031
Tel: 603-672-4065
Fax: 603-672-4064
www.iacde.com

COACH

A DAY IN THE LIFE

Coaches teach athletic skills, provide generalized fitness training, and train athletes to perform in competitive environments. "I'm a teacher, a leader, a friend, and I hate it when we lose," wrote one high school varsity football coach, "but not as much as the kids or their parents do." Being a coach requires successfully juggling these various aspects of the position. The athletes and the coach motivate one another to perform at a higher level; this relationship demands commitment, awareness, and dedication. People who find themselves satisfied in this profession have strong teaching skills, an abundance of motivation to work additional hours, and excellent communication skills. "Leadership skills are essential," wrote one college volleyball coach, "otherwise your good athletes won't respect you enough to listen to you."

> { Leadership skills are essential. }

What sport and age level you wish to coach will have a substantial impact on what preparation is needed beyond knowing your chosen sport very well. The skills required to coach high school tennis, for example, are quite different from the skills required to coach professional baseball. Competition is significant for entry-level positions; on more advanced levels, special skills such as weight-training expertise, stretching, and psychological training become more highly valued. Progression is difficult within and between coaching levels. One person articulated the dilemma clearly: "You want to work for the best coaches to learn your job, but the best coaches never get fired or leave, so you've got to jump into another system somewhere else and start all over again." Many coaches enjoy going to conferences to meet other professionals and learn new methods of fitness training and injury prevention.

PAYING YOUR DUES

Coaching various age levels requires different sets of skills. If you want to coach high school sports, you should have comprehensive knowledge of your sport, knowledge of physical fitness training, and some basic training in injury prevention, first aid, and childhood development. Many employers look for a history of athletics in the sport—being on a high school, college, or professional team will stand you in good stead. It works to your advantage to have worked for a youth league or summer camp as a coach.

On the college level, you should have an understanding of a specialty within a sport—for example, in football, you may be a defensive line coach or a quarterback coach—and the ability to translate that knowledge into terms college athletes can understand and envision. Applicants should have at least three semesters worth of physical training and a history of success coaching at the high school level or above. Many college coaches are hired in part because of personal relationships with the coaching staff, so cultivate contacts. Professional seminars, successful interviewing skills, and recommendations from former coached pupils can help. Many coaches work with "high talent" stars, thereby associating the athlete's fame and prowess with their own skills.

All of the aforementioned criteria are required for coaching professional teams. Strong candidates have had success at the college level, attained national exposure, and most likely, have refined a specialty, such as "special teams coach" (a football term for kicking teams or kick-returning teams) or "shooting coach."

ASSOCIATED CAREERS

Many coaches return to teaching if they leave coaching. More than 25 percent return to school to get graduate degrees in physical therapy, nutrition, exercise physiology, or medical training. A number of them use their leadership skills to run team-oriented projects in business settings. Around 10 percent migrate to occupations that allow them to be outdoors and active, such as policemen, firefighters, park rangers, personal trainers, and semiprofessional athletes.

PAST AND FUTURE

With the advent of professional sports, coaches gained power, money, and additional responsibilities, such as media communication commitments and negotiation involvement. A professional football coach today is as much a recruiter, public relations specialist, and budget director as he is a teacher.

While the number of amateur and professional coaching positions is expected to increase on all levels, competition for these positions is expected to increase as well. But coaches who find the right opportunity and situation should continue to achieve high levels of satisfaction.

QUALITY OF LIFE

2 YEARS Coaches are "jacks of all trades" who work with athletes in a particular sport on issues of general fitness, flexibility (stretching), strength (weight training), skills, teamwork, and attitude. Many coaches are assistant coaches under more experienced professionals. Many of them hone their abilities by expanding their knowledge of strategy, coaching, and training during their free time. The hours are long; the pay is low. Around 35 percent of all coaches leave due to frustration with advancement, wage dissatisfaction, or emotional burnout. This is the largest exodus from the profession; over the course of a career, only half the entrants quit by the 10-year mark.

5 YEARS Five-year veterans are usually assistant coaches at large schools or head coaches at smaller ones. People who have designed their own programs begin to see results around the second or third year of implementation. Few coaches leave the profession between years two and five, as many of them have found positions that suit their level of abilities. Coaches begin to cement professional and personal relationships that are invaluable later in their careers. Satisfaction is high; the pay has become respectable.

10 YEARS Ten-year veterans can go into head coaching, higher level coaching, or specialization. Head coaches are involved with every aspect of the day-to-day job, from overseeing training to making decisions that affect the play of the team. Those coaches who wish to rise to a higher level of coaching (such as national team or professional coaching) concentrate on building winning programs and recruiting high-profile athletes. Self-promotion becomes an important part of the career for those who wish to enter the professional coaching ranks. Specializing in one area of coaching and excelling at it makes it easier for professional teams to envision the role the coach will play with them. Satisfaction is high; few people leave the profession beyond this point.

MAJOR EMPLOYERS

DALLAS COWBOYS FOOTBALL CLUB
1 Cowboys Parkway
Irving, TX 75063
Tel: 972-556-9900
Fax: 972-556-9970
www.dallascowboys.com
Contact: Coaching Department

INDIANA UNIVERSITY ATHLETICS DEPARTMENT
Assembly Hall
1001 East 17th Street
Bloomington, IN 47408
Tel: 812-855-2794
Fax: 812-855-3409
E-mail: athletic@indiana.edu
www.indiana.edu
Contact: Coaching Department

UNITED STATES OLYMPIC COMMITTEE
1 Olympic Plaza
Colorado Springs, CO 80909-5760
Tel: 719-632-5551
Fax: 719-578-4654
www.usoc.org

MAJOR ASSOCIATIONS

NATIONAL HIGH SCHOOL ATHLETIC COACHES ASSOCIATION
PO Box 4342
Hamden, CT 6574
Tel: 203-288-7473
Fax: 203-288-8224
E-mail: dgaliette@hscoaches.com
www.hscoaches.org

CUSTOMER SERVICE REPRESENTATIVE

A DAY IN THE LIFE

Across the many business areas in which they are employed, customer service representatives lend a human face and voice to the sometimes impersonal realties of business transactions. Customer service representatives are in the business of listening to customers' concerns and taking action to address them. Those who have good listening, writing, and speaking skills will do well as customer service representatives; they may find even more opportunities if they are bi- or multilingual. Customer service representatives are employed across a range of businesses. Many find work in the finance and insurance industries and in computer services, typically in large regional call centers. Managers often observe calls to ensure that precise requirements of time spent { **fast-growing occupation** } and material covered are met. Those who work directly in an individual business location may deal with customers face-to-face as well on the telephone and via the Web. Some may find their work in environments as varied as specialty retail boutiques, auto parts dealerships, and technical service firms. In all of these cases, customer service representatives must deal with people who have a question, a concern, or a complaint about a business transaction. Often, such queries come to the representative in close succession, with little time in between calls, especially in call center situations. Customer service representatives need to be effective communicators. They often need to be patient. Dealing with irate customers can be stressful—but searching for solutions and resolving problems can also be highly rewarding.

This is a fast-growing occupation, the expansion of which is driven in part by the current technological boom. Customer service representatives are needed to handle the volume of inquiries generated online as well as to deal in person or on the phone with issues that cannot be resolved electronically. Customer service is becoming a 24-hour occupation; as a result, many customer service representatives may also hold part-time positions or work outside of the conventional business day schedule.

PAYING YOUR DUES

Customer service representatives may enter the profession with a high school diploma. For advancement, especially in technical fields, further education in the specific subject matter of the industry may be useful or necessary. Skills in interacting with others, juggling multiple tasks, communicating clearly, solving problems, maintaining organized records, and communicating effectively via phone and e-mail are essential in the profession—as is, increasingly, the ability to communicate in more than one language. For many, a customer service representative job is an entry-level position in the work force. Customer service representatives may parlay their knowledge of company infrastructure into a position in another department. Those who stick with it and improve their skills in dealing with customers and their knowledge of company products and services may see advancement to supervisory work or more complex problem-solving responsibilities within their first three years in the job.

ASSOCIATED CAREERS

Customer service representatives may enjoy using their communication skills to sell products or services or to work in the hospitality industry. The more technically inclined may choose technical service careers. Those who prefer the record-keeping side may go into accounting services. Those who enjoy interacting with others and seeking solutions may investigate careers in management or human resources.

PAST AND FUTURE

The customer service industry used to be entirely human-driven, and customer service representatives typically had a broad knowledge base that allowed them to respond to general inquiries. The customer service industry has grown substantially in recent years and now often requires individual representatives to cultivate a specific knowledge base about their particular industry and company. Software that can filter customer requests and websites and automated phone systems that allow customers to find information for themselves have resulted in increasingly specialized (and far less routine) training for customer service representatives. The growth potential is excellent due to the twin circumstances of business growth and business downsizing. This latter trend has produced a shift in job responsibilities: Tasks formerly executed by sales or technical employees have shifted to the customer service arena. Representatives who have educations beyond high school may find themselves in particularly high demand for their additional expertise. The industry is becoming increasingly specialized, and customer service representatives will need to cultivate higher-level technical skills as a result.

QUALITY OF LIFE

2 YEARS Whether working in a closely-supervised call center or in a less structured business environment, entry-level customer service representatives interact directly with customers to resolve problems. For this reason, entry-level customer service representatives usually spend the first couple of years learning company policies and how to apply these to customer requests. They also learn how to work effectively in the midst of the constant influx of customer demands. Income potential increases with the ability to handle more complex tasks.

5 YEARS At the five-year point, customer service representatives who work in call centers will be supervising and scheduling other workers and perhaps dealing with more complex or difficult challenges themselves. The same is true of those working in individual businesses, although they are likely spend more time solving complex problems and having face-to-face customer interaction and less time supervising other employees. They may also begin to move into other business areas, such as human resources, sales, or technical support. There is career and income growth potential with increasing subject matter training and management experience.

10 YEARS After 10 years, a call center customer service representative will be supervising other supervisors, often executing primarily management-level and administrative tasks. In an individual business, a customer service representative may combine administrative skills with work in other areas of the business; or he or she may seek highly specialized customer service support opportunities in business-to-business or technical fields. Customer service representatives at this stage may also opt to venture into sales or other aspects of business in which their problem-solving skills will be in demand; possibilities for increased income may be greater in these sectors, as well.

MAJOR EMPLOYERS

Customer service representatives are employed by a wide range of companies across many industries. The broad scope of companies that hire customer service representatives includes such disparate entities as large international businesses, local auto repair shops, and regional grocery stores. Most large companies post qualification information on their websites and accept applications online. The hiring process typically takes place at the regional or local level. The same is true for call centers that handle customer service functions. For smaller local and regional concerns, making contact with the hiring manager or human resources department should help you break into the industry.

MAJOR ASSOCIATIONS

NATIONAL COMMUNICATION ASSOCIATION

1765 N Street, NW
Washington, DC 20036
Tel: 202-464-4622
Fax: 202-464-4600
www.natcom.org

Customer service representatives typically become involved with organizations specific to the industry they serve.

DIPLOMAT/ATTACHÉ/FOREIGN SERVICE OFFICER

BOOKS, FILMS, AND TV SHOWS
FEATURING THE PROFESSION
- **Clear and Present Danger**
- **Protocol**
- **The Ugly American**
- **The XYZ Affair**

YOU'LL HAVE CONTACT WITH
- **Analysts**
- **Government officials**
- **Tourists**
- **Translators**

PROFESSIONALS READ
- **Foreign Affairs**
- **Foreign Policy**
- **International Reports**

A DAY IN THE LIFE

The Foreign Service represents the United States around the world. Members interact with local governments as emissaries of the United States, staff United States embassies and consulates, and provide resources for Americans traveling abroad. More than 60 percent of a foreign service officers' working hours are spent handling reports—assembling facts, writing, proofreading, and reading. "Reading is fundamental," wrote one member of the diplomatic corps, "and if your writing isn't up to snuff, you'll be selected out—fired, that is." Strong communication skills are absolutely essential for anyone thinking about entering the profession. Diplomats are posted to positions abroad for terms of two, three, or four years with nine-month stateside stints every two to four years, but they can be recalled at the discretion of the State Department at any time. { negotiating }

The Foreign Service handles all problems of Americans abroad, including negotiating with local governments for individual United States companies who wish to manufacture, produce, or do business abroad; providing information about the host country; and issuing replacements for lost documentation. Foreign consulates also issue visitation and residency visas to foreigners wishing to enter the United States. These tasks consume a minimum of 30 hours of the workweek: "My hourly wage in 1992 was $3.45. I calculated it, adding in all the unpaid overtime I put in," wrote one diplomat. Since additional internal duties (including writing reports) and social functions (which are an important part of the job) can take up another 40 hours per week, people who are looking for a sinecure are ill-advised to enter the foreign service. Members who are satisfied with their profession enjoy the responsibility: the ability to look at a host country from the inside, write a considered opinion of the state of that country, and have it seriously regarded by officials making decisions about international relations.

PAYING YOUR DUES

To enter the foreign service, you must be an American citizen between the ages of 20 and 54 and have a bachelor's degree. Helpful college or graduate school courses include English, foreign language, government, geography, international history, economics, public speaking, and commerce. Applicants must pass the competitive foreign service exam, offered once a year in most major urban centers and at consulates abroad. Individuals who pass take a secondary exam, which includes a day-long assessment: a physical, a rigorous background exam, and a final review of all the candidates' strengths and weaknesses. Candidates are expected to be familiar with another language, but fluency can be acquired after posting.

Individuals who pass all the tests are given a ranking and put on a list of eligible candidates for future posting. As positions become available, candidates are offered suitable postings. Note that at most, a few hundred slots open up each year. While many start their tenure with a nine-month stint in Washington, DC to learn the protocols of being a diplomat (termed the "pregnancy period" by one of our respondents), others begin in the field and learn and are trained on the fly. Be aware that if you are listed on the sheet of eligibles, and no position opens up within 18 months, you will have to begin the procedure again. All names are removed from the list at that point.

ASSOCIATED CAREERS

More than half of foreign service officers find lifetime careers in the foreign service, particularly with the understanding that retirement is mandatory at age 60, and that one is eligible to retire at age 50 after serving for 20 years. People who leave the field use their unique perspective and their skills to work for other branches of the government, such as the Defense Department, the CIA, the INS, the Commerce Department, or teach at the university level.

PAST AND FUTURE

The Constitution provided that a foreign service be developed, but one did not exist in practice in any reasonably funded form until the mid-1800s. Until 1924, the foreign service was the plumb of patronage and supportable only by individuals in the upper class. The wages were so scandalously low that no one else could afford to take a position. The Rogers Act in 1924 provided reasonable wages and democratized the process of entering the foreign service. The process has become even more egalitarian with current application methods.

The foreign service is and will continue to be a vital service of the United States. As with any government office, it is subject to budget whims, but as it is currently thinly staffed and highly competitive, future funding cuts should not come in this area. Expect competition for limited positions to remain high—strong preparation for the foreign service exam is your best ally.

QUALITY OF LIFE

2 YEARS Halfway through their probationary period, which lasts roughly four years, new diplomats are expected to have made significant headway in learning a foreign language. Many diplomats are called staff specialists; the majority of candidates for positions do not receive officer status upon hire. Duties include filing reports, assembling data, and providing any research or coordination under the direction of foreign service officers or ambassadors.

5 YEARS Five-year veterans have established themselves as officers, information specialists, or staff specialists. Each year, appointees receive ratings from their supervisors and are advanced in the profession through six grades of classification, with grade six being lowest. Around 30 percent of those people who began in the foreign service have left due to low ratings, lack of progress in language skills, or lack of opportunity in their area of expertise.

10 YEARS Individuals who have survived 10 years in the diplomatic corps have been rotated back to Washington for at least two periods of "reeducation" in the American experience, been consistently rated well by superiors, and at least earned a classification of grade three. Diplomats who aspire to "career minister" (a high-level foreign service office position) continue to accrue additional responsibilities and hours. A few diplomats who have shown great promise are sponsored to go to the Foreign Service Institute for high-level additional education—a true feather in the cap of the career diplomat. Individuals who are not advancing find their abroad status in jeopardy and may be asked to return to back-office work in Washington. A few diplomats may become ambassadors, but this position is usually a political appointment.

MAJOR EMPLOYERS

UNITED STATES DEPARTMENT OF STATE
Recruitment Division
2401 E Street, NW, 5H
Washington, DC 20522-0518
Tel: 202-261-8888
Jobline: 202-261-8841
www.state.gov/m/dghr/hr/
Contact: Human Resources

UNITED NATIONS HEADQUARTERS
One United Nations Plaza
New York, NY 10017
Tel: 212-963-1234
Fax: 212-963-4879
www.un.org
Contact: Office of Human Resources Management

MAJOR ASSOCIATIONS

EXECUTIVE COUNCIL ON FOREIGN DIPLOMACY
818 Connecticut Avenue, NW, 12th Floor
Washington, DC 20006
Tel: 202-466-5199
Fax: 202-872-8696

FLIGHT ATTENDANT

A DAY IN THE LIFE

Flight attendants are charged with making sure that passengers arrive at their destinations safely. They do so by enforcing all flight safety regulations and by making the flight as pleasant as possible for passengers. A typical flying day for flight attendants begins an hour before take-off. At that time the captain briefs them on the emergency evacuation procedures and the details of the flight, including its duration and the expected weather conditions on the way. Then they must prepare the cabin for the passengers. Sometimes there is a lead flight attendant, called a purser, who oversees the others in addition to performing the rest of their flight attendant responsibilities. Before take-off, they must brief passengers on safety procedures and make sure that all people and belongings are secure.

{ passionate travelers and social butterflies }

In the air, flight attendants help passengers in the event of any problems, which may range from explaining turbulence to a nervous traveler to evacuating the plane after an emergency landing. They are the firefighters, paramedics, and law enforcement officials at 35,000 feet. Most of the time, though, their in-flight duties involve bringing food and drinks to passengers. As the flight winds down, they begin to prepare for landing by taking inventory, reporting any medical issues with passengers, and taking note of the condition of the cabin equipment. After the passengers have arrived and exited the plane safely, the flight attendants are free to explore the destination—if they don't have to rush off to their next flight. When away from home and on duty, all accommodations and meals are covered. Flight attendants (and their immediate family members, as well) may also fly free on their own carriers and at reduced fares on other carriers.

Good flight attendants are friendly and engaging people. They are passionate travelers, and they are also extremely flexible. Flight attendants may work holidays, weekends, and nights. Generally, flight attendants have 12–14 hour days and fly between 65–85 hours a month. They also spend up to 50 hours on the ground waiting for flights to arrive, preparing the planes, and writing reports. Overall, they may be away from home one-third of the time. As a result of such an unusual schedule, many flight attendants can develop health issues resulting from irregular sleeping and eating patterns, spending time in a pressurized environment, and breathing recycled air. Yet many stay with the position nonetheless: One flight attendant we spoke with said she had become a flight attendant right after graduating from college so she could "see the world" before she pursued another career. Twenty-five years later, she is still catching her next flight back to New York City.

PAYING YOUR DUES

There are fewer preparatory or educational qualifications necessary to become a flight attendant than there are initial character and physical qualifications. Applicants generally must be at least 18 years old, and some carriers require that they be even older. An applicant must be an American citizen in excellent health with exceptional speaking skills. Usually there are height, weight, and vision requirements. Airlines prefer people with a clean-cut look.

Applicants must have a high school diploma or GED, and sometimes even a college degree. Flight attendants on international flights are usually required to speak one or two foreign languages fluently. Once hired, the formal training begins. Three to eight weeks are spent in school at the airline's training hub. The courses cover emergency procedures such as evacuation, operating systems, and water survival tactics. Students learn how to deal with disruptive passengers and dangerous in-flight situations. International trainees learn customs and passport regulations, as well. As students reach the end of the training period, they begin going on practice flights.

ASSOCIATED CAREERS

One interested in a career as a flight attendant may also wish to consider other public safety and service jobs, such as those of emergency medical technician, firefighter, or law enforcement official. If one is a "people person" with a good deal of patience, then waiting tables or bartending may be appropriate options—but of course, those don't offer free travel opportunities.

PAST AND FUTURE

In the early years of flying, there were "skygirls" or "stewardesses," not "flight attendants." "Flight attendant" is a relatively new term that became the norm as the profession diversified. In the 1930s, skygirls were only temporary employees. They had to be 32 years old or younger and weigh no more than 115 pounds. The weight requirement was changed just 10 years ago. Now you need only be a weight "proportionate" to your height. In the very beginning, the sky-girls were also required to be nurses, and the average career only lasted one to two years.

As the airlines and the economy in general continue to recover from September 11th, the employment opportunities for flight attendants are expected to improve. Commercial flight hinges greatly on the economy: The less demand there is for travel, the fewer flight attendants are needed. Competition is always fierce because there are so many more applicants than there are positions. Numerous job openings over the next several years are expected to be created by those leaving the business for a more stable lifestyle.

QUALITY OF LIFE

2 YEARS The first year after training, flight attendants are assigned to an airline base. They are placed on reserve status (typically for about a year), and they are only called on to staff extra flights or to fill in for senior flight attendants. On days off, those on reserve must be ready to report for flight on a moment's notice. Assignments are based on seniority, so those new to the job get little choice in where they fly. Usually, everyone starts at the same base pay and receives the same pay increases. Flight attendants receive extra pay for working nights, international flights, and increased hours. Some carriers even offer incentive pay for working overtime or on holidays.

5 YEARS As flight attendants rise through the ranks, they can choose flights more freely. They can also have their pick of preferred base assignments. There are considerable pay increases. Flight attendants with even more experience may have the option to become supervisors or instructors. Other airline-related positions, such as reservation ticket agent or public-relations specialist, are also available to flight attendants who have devoted many years to the profession.

10 YEARS The most senior flight attendants, those who have flown for a decade or more, can make up to around $90,000 a year at certain airlines. They also have the most freedom to choose flights, hours, and base assignments.

MAJOR EMPLOYERS
AMERICAN AIRLINES
PO Box 619616
DFW Airport, TX 75261-9616
Tel: 817-963-1234
www.aa.com

CONTINENTAL AIRLINES
PO Box 4607
Houston, TX 77210-4607
Tel: 713-324-5080
www.continental.com

UNITED AIRLINES
UAL Corporation
World Headquarters
PO Box 66100
Chicago, IL 60666
Tel: 847-700-4000
www.united.com

MAJOR ASSOCIATIONS
ASSOCIATION OF FLIGHT ATTENDANTS–CWA
501 3rd Street, NW
Washington, DC 20001
Tel: 202-434-1300
www.afanet.org

TRANSPORTATION TRADES DEPARTMENT, AFL–CIO
888 16th Street, NW, Suite 650
Washington, DC 20006
Tel: 202-628-9262
E-mail: michaelb@ttd.org
www.ttd.org

FUND-RAISER/INSTITUTIONAL SOLICITOR

PROFESSIONAL PROFILE

# of people in profession	300,000
Avg. hours per week	45
Avg. starting salary	$40,000
Avg. salary after 5 years	$50,000
Avg. salary 10 to 15 years	$68,000

SALARY   ● ●
HOURS   ● ●
EDUCATION   ● ●

BOOKS, FILMS, AND TV SHOWS
FEATURING THE PROFESSION
- **Direct Response Fund-Raising**
- **Ethical Decision-Making in Fund-Raising**
- **The Nonprofit Handbook**

YOU'LL HAVE CONTACT WITH
- **Direct-response consultants**
- **Event planners**
- **Market researchers**
- **Proposal writers**

PROFESSIONALS READ
- **Currents**
- **Fund-Raising Management**
- **Philanthropy**

A DAY IN THE LIFE

People who are successful at fund-raising develop large plans and execute the tiniest details in them. They also identify a target audience and tailor a unique appeal to that demographic. A fund-raiser should have excellent writing skills, a clear understanding of how and when to approach people, and an unbelievable sense of organization. Fund-raising on a large scale may entail up to seven different appeals to thousands of potential donors; fund-raisers without organizational skills quickly get dragged under by the tide of material that passes through their hands. Planning and attending meetings takes up the majority of the professional fund-raiser's day. Fund-raisers must remain on top of the concerns of potential donors, be responsive to the changing needs of their institution, and build up { **great social ability** } a successful system of reaching donors. Fund-raisers spend plenty of creative energy recreating campaigns to ensure success year after year.

While broad-based fund-raising (letter campaigns, high-profile events, and programs) are important for visibility, publicity, and support, the real work of high-level fund-raisers consists of presentations, education, and funds solicitation from their target market. Meeting others, teaching skills, and a touch of finesse are critical for a fund-raiser to be successful. Meetings with patrons, employees, and executives can take place after quitting time or late in the work day. "It takes a lot of your free time and great social ability to pull it off too," mentioned one director of fund-raising for a private school. "You have to have the courage to sell what you believe and to not blink when you ask for an enormous sum of money," wrote another respondent. The ability to communicate the value and the need of your employer to others is required in this occupation and makes the difference between those who succeed and those who fail.

PAYING YOUR DUES

No specific bachelor's degree is required, but majors such as communications, English, finance, marketing, business, education, and psychology are considered good preparation for entry-level positions. Aspiring fund-raisers need a gentle yet firm touch to communicate a platform and a position in writing and convince people to donate goods, services, and money. Entry-level applicants should be good with numbers, graphics, and design and have an excellent sense of timing, since fund-raising on an ongoing basis requires knowing when not to ask for donations as much as knowing when to ask. One other requirement for this job is the ability to withstand significant rejection. A fund-raiser should be able to bring together disparate elements within a community to reach their goals. Fund-raisers sometimes earn advanced degrees in nonprofit management, finance, marketing, or public relations.

ASSOCIATED CAREERS

Individuals who leave fund-raising find plenty of work in public relations (20 percent), advertising (10 percent), teaching (5 percent), and administration (10 percent). Many of them return to school for advanced degrees in business, education, administration, and law.

PAST AND FUTURE

Fund-raisers have existed since there have been causes that required funding. English private schools long relied on charitable donations from their alumni to support them in times of low enrollment. Orphanages and food houses in early America solicited donations of food and services from local merchants and wealthy patrons. Those who first became professional fund-raisers were the wealthy in America who were connected with other wealthy patrons and could encourage them to donate to specific causes. These people were called "benefactors." As annual, regular fund-raising became significant, they became known as "fund-raisers."

Job opportunities in fund-raising should increase through the end of the decade and very likely beyond. With dramatic cuts in federal and state funding for many nonprofit organizations, private donation solicitation will become increasingly widespread and important. Specialties will be the wave of the future; people who have unique skills in mail solicitations, phone solicitations, organizing fund-raising events, or campaign tracking will be hired for discrete fund-raising tasks under the umbrella of a generalized fund-raising coordinator.

QUALITY OF LIFE

2 YEARS Long hours, hard work, little free time, and an entire fund-raising system to learn make the first few years in this field difficult. Responsibilities are limited; tasks may include proofreading, tracking mail, entering computer data, making phone calls, and arranging meetings with potential donors. Do not expect to attend these meetings or have any impact on policy. Input can be offered and accepted, but people who expect to make an immediate splash in the fund-raising pool should be aware of the limited role they will play these first few years.

5 YEARS Lifestyles for people with five years of experience are significantly different for those people fund-raising for smaller, more specific organizations than those people fund-raising for large, extremely hierarchical organizations. People in small organizations become associate fund-raisers or chief development officers, depending on their success acquiring donations and available opportunities. Many of them remain with their original organizations if advancement opportunities exist. Five-year fund-raisers meet with large, individual donors, propose new audiences to appeal to, devise and organize seasonal campaigns, and make presentations on goals to executives at their organization. Fund-raisers in larger organizations have less responsibility but more defined areas of control. A typical five-year veteran at a large firm may be in charge of Northeast solicitations for the 22–28-year-old age range and people who graduated from college with liberal arts degrees. Duties may include purchasing mailing lists, coordinating production of solicitation materials, and tracking responses. Salaries and hours increase. Many fund-raisers work as fund-raisers for fewer than three years or more than ten; roughly half of them leave between years three and six.

10 YEARS By this point, fund-raisers have most likely held a number of positions at two or more organizations, led and directed successful fund drives or annual campaigns, and reinvented themselves with the times. Experienced fund-raisers often take on challenges of a different scale, such as moving to a much larger organization or heading a department. If you've stayed in this profession for 10 years, you are statistically likely to stay another 15–25 years in this challenging, exciting, and difficult job.

MAJOR EMPLOYERS

Fund-raisers are employed by a broad range of hospitals, schools, religious and social service organizations, environmental and health-related organizations, arts organizations and museums, youth organizations, and retirement homes. Contact local groups in your area for employment opportunities.

MAJOR ASSOCIATIONS

AMERICAN ASSOCIATION OF FUND-RAISING COUNSEL
4700 West Lake Avenue
Glenview, IL 60025
Tel: 800-462-2372 or 847-375-4709
Fax: 866-607-0913
www.aafrc.org

ASSOCIATION OF FUND-RAISERS AND DIRECT SELLERS
5775-G Peachtree-Dunqoody Road, Building G, Suite 500
Atlanta, GA 30342
Tel: 404-252-3663
Fax: 404-252-0774
www.afrds.org

ASSOCIATION OF FUND-RAISING PROFESSIONALS
1101 King Street, Suite 700
Alexandria, VA 22314
Tel: 703-684-0410
Fax: 703-684-0540
www.afpnet.org

HOTEL MANAGER

A DAY IN THE LIFE

A hotel manager oversees all of the daily operations of a hotel, from staffing to coordinating fresh-cut flowers for the lobby. Many managers, over time, are given long-term responsibility for negotiating contracts with vendors, negotiating leases with on-site shops, and physically upgrading the hotel. Hotel managers usually relish "the ability to put your own distinctive style on the [hotel] experience." While managing a hotel and giving it your unique flair are wonderful, they come with full responsibility for failure. "The better you are at what you do, the more responsibilities you are given, the more chances you have to fail," mentioned one hotel manager. When things fall apart, "no one is a hotel manager's friend." Hotel managers can feel great about their positions, create strong relationships with regular customers,

{ No one is a hotel manager's friend. }

and maintain an amicable working environment. But should the bottom line waver and financial woes occur, the first neck on the chopping block is the hotel manager's.

People in the hotel management industry say that sometimes it seems that you need "to be born on the planet Krypton" to be a good hotel manager because only Superman could juggle the administrative, aesthetic, and financial decisions that constitute daily life on the job. Over 70 percent of the respondents said that "tired" was an understatement about how they felt at the end of the day (or night); "Exhausted is more like it," wrote one. A hotel manager's position as a liaison between the ownership and the staff can be difficult and isolating. But people who can put up with the long hours, high degree of responsibility, and variety of tasks emerge with a solid degree of satisfaction and a desire to continue in the profession. The average tenure of a hotel manager is 6.7 years, though this figure doesn't represent the number of managers who work for two years and those managers who work for decades. Many of them work at a variety of hotels, build up their resumes, and then find positions that allow them the freedom to operate their own establishments.

PAYING YOUR DUES

Aspiring hotel managers used to begin at the reception desk, as part of the wait staff, or as members of the cleaning staff, then work their way up the ladder. Since hotels have become more commercial properties and the duties of hotel managers have expanded, this avenue of advancement has more or less closed. Now hotel manager hopefuls typically go to hotel management school. Those who don't should garner as much practical hotel experience as possible. Each chain or specific hotel puts new employees through its own training programs, so people applying for jobs should learn all they can about the scope and functioning of the specific hotels where they wish to work.

Part of life as a hotel manager can be similar to life as a doctor, as managers can be called to duty at any time of the day or night. Hotel managers must handle any and all emergencies, and individuals who wish to remain in the profession must be quick-thinking and decisive. Candidates should have a good organizational and financial background, excellent communication and interpersonal skills, and strong self-discipline. They should also be extremely detail-oriented; when running a hotel, there is no such thing as an unimportant detail. A good manager drives him or herself to improve and upgrade the hotel at every available opportunity.

ASSOCIATED CAREERS

Hotel managers who leave the profession generally go into larger areas of management, such as property management, administrative or financial roles in large hotel chains, or independent ownership of smaller hotels and bed-and-breakfast establishments. The desire for greater control and less uncertainty were cited as the two most important reasons people in the industry seek work elsewhere.

PAST AND FUTURE

In the past, hotel managers were often the owners and ran the establishment themselves. They decided when to fix crumbling walls and how much to charge; aesthetic decisions were less pertinent. In the mid-1800s came the advent of the water-and-rail traveling age, and not only were the very wealthy able to move about more easily than before, but also the merchant class began to travel. This mobility encouraged the rise of the competitive and attractive yet affordable hotel and, thus, arose the need for the permanent manager who could take care of all duties while the owner was involved in expanding, advertising, and popularizing the location.

Hotels have enjoyed a generally consistent demand for their services over the years, despite fluctuations in the economy. At times when lack of prosperity whittles away at the number of business and vacation travelers looking for a bed—threatening to keep the vacancy sign lit and send profits tumbling— efforts to lure in guests, such as lower rates and perks, stimulate the return to full capacity.

QUALITY OF LIFE

2 YEARS The first two years constitute a type of "apprenticeship" in which theoretical coursework is fleshed out by practical experience. Hotel managers sharpen their interpersonal skills, and individuals who wish to advance sometimes continue their education in business, organizational development, or psychology. Duties may include arranging for regular deliveries of supplies and handling client complaints and payroll. Little input is expected from the aspiring managers on issues of design, decor, or promotion. The hours are long, and pay is low; satisfaction levels, unsurprisingly, are below average.

5 YEARS Satisfaction levels leap as hotel managers jump from job to job. Getting positions with increasing responsibility means two-to-three year stints at different hotels, learning a variety of skills—staffing, negotiation skills, event planning—and then moving on. The hours increase during these years, but few managers cite this as a downside. Their input on larger issues, such as hotel renovations and decor, begins to be taken seriously, depending on the individual manager's relationship with the owner.

10 YEARS While many 10-year veterans have impressive resumes, few of them find cause to need them more than a few more times in their careers. As managers understand more and more about what type of hotel they like to run, they choose their positions more carefully. Tenure can run as long as 20 years at a single hotel. Hotel managers' input is significant at this level; most systems have been adjusted to be efficient and responsive to management and client needs, and satisfaction levels are high. Pay can become extremely competitive for people who have good relationships with regular, high-paying clients. A mere 3 percent of hotel managers who've survived 10 years leave; many of them view this as a job for life.

MAJOR EMPLOYERS

COMFORT INN
1120 South College Avenue
Newark, DE 19713
Tel: 800-441-7564
Fax: 302-368-6454

HILTON HOTELS
9336 Civic Center Drive
Beverly Hills, CA 90210
Tel: 310-278-4321 or 800-445-8667
Fax: 310-205-4613
www.hilton.com
Contact: Human Resources

RAMADA
6 Sylvan Way
Parsippany, NJ 07054-0278
Tel: 973-428-9700 or 800-298-2054
www.ramada.com
Contact: Human Resources

MAJOR ASSOCIATIONS

AMERICAN HOTEL AND LODGING ASSOCIATION
1201 New York Avenue, NW, Suite 600
Washington, DC 20005-3931
Tel: 202-289-3100
Fax: 202-289-3199
www.ahma.com

COUNCIL ON HOTEL, RESTAURANT, AND INSTITUTIONAL EDUCATION
2610 North Parham Road, Suite 230
Richmond, VA 23294
Tel: 804-346-4800
Fax: 804-346-5009
www.chrie.org

HOTEL SALES AND MARKETING ASSOCIATION INTERNATIONAL
8201 Greensboro Drive, Suite 300
McLean, VA 22102
Tel: 703-610-9024
Fax: 703-610-9005
www.hsmai.org

INSURANCE AGENT/BROKER

A DAY IN THE LIFE

The people involved in the insurance industry profess that they provide security for a living, since their product is financial protection in the event of a crisis or emergency. This protection is always in demand; therefore, the insurance industry is thus one of the nation's largest employers, with over two million workers. Seventy percent of them are involved in administrative or sales posts in three main areas: life, health, and property and liability. The life insurance agent collects monthly or yearly payments from a policyholder; if the policyholder dies as a result of conditions which are covered in his or her policy, the designated members of his or her family can receive a substantial sum of money. Sometimes life insurance agents arrange for more creative benefits, such as { **work on commission** } college tuition payments for children. Ensuring proper coverage for hospital and doctor visits is the domain of the health insurer, who most likely works for groups of employers rather than soliciting clients among the general public. Some health insurers are employed by the government to enforce Medicaid policies. Finally, property and liability agents insure instances of damage done to and by their policyholders. They must also be fluent in the world of health insurance, since they cover workers' compensation; an employee injured at work will deal with this agent rather than a health insurance agent.

Agents work for one insurance agency, whereas brokers work independently and sell policies through many agencies. Beyond this distinction, however, agents and brokers perform many of the same functions. Both agents and brokers meet with potential clients and advise them on the most appropriate coverage. When claims are made, they have to settle the claim equitably for both the client and the agency. Agents and brokers can be salaried employees of an agency or, more likely, work partly or fully on commission from the premiums they sell. Because most agents work on commission, they must spend quite a bit of time networking and finding new customers. Some large agencies cover all areas under one of the three divisions, while smaller ones specialize in one area. Besides keeping up with customers and courting new ones, insurance agents and brokers have administrative tasks to do, such as keeping records of sales. Fortunate and successful agents will have a staff to handle these matters.

PAYING YOUR DUES

Life and health insurance agents and brokers must be licensed by their state, which means passing an insurance examination. Agents who sell investment-oriented policies must also be licensed by the National Association of Securities Dealers or the Securities and Exchange Commission. While a college degree is not necessary for these positions, many agencies are seeking college-educated applicants, and a degree is an especially good idea if you want to advance to managerial positions. Some agencies even offer training programs for undergraduates, in the hope that students will work part-time while in school and become full members of the company upon graduation. Some of these programs even provide tuition reimbursement for students employed with their agencies.

ASSOCIATED CAREERS

Occasionally insurance agents have dual professions; for example, some property insurance agents are also real estate agents. Field representatives attempt to generate new business for agents and brokers. They conduct and attend insurance conferences to remain fluent in the latest topics in insurance. At times, field representatives will educate insurers about advancements in the field.

The most prestigious title in the insurance industry is held by the underwriter, who has the stressful task of reading applications submitted by agents to determine whether a company should accept the risk a particular client presents. Underwriters depend on studies done by actuaries that determine levels of risk. Insurance adjusters are also players in this industry. When an accident occurs, an adjuster visits the site to assess the damage and determine the funds the insurer will award the victim.

PAST AND FUTURE

The concept of insurance has been evolving for as long as there have been communities. Thousands of years ago, a form of insurance began in China because people wanted to protect their assets when they shipped them across the sea in hazardous conditions. Boat owners began putting a little bit of each owner's cargo in every boat. If one boat sank, each owner would be sure that most of his product would still reach the shore. When European settlers came to America, each member of the community would help if a person's house burned down. By pitching in to help rebuild someone else's house, a community member was ensuring that he would receive help if he suffered a similar loss. As society enlarged and became more complex, insurance began to take the strictly monetary form we are familiar with today. Now people pay one amount, called a premium, to ensure their financial protection if they fall victim to disaster. Thus, if someone's house needed rebuilding in this day and age, the agency would charge the client a fraction of the rebuilding costs and would be able to pay for any reconstruction by using the premiums of those who do not suffer any losses.

The debate over whose insurance will pay whom for what actions—and whether the insurers will be covered by the reinsurers—is in full swing. Politicians and the public will certainly be paying close attention as everyone continues to pay more for insurance. People working in insurance now have better than average chances for advancement into newly developing positions, regardless of the outcome of world events and domestic legislation.

QUALITY OF LIFE

Insurance agents are often frustrated in the beginning of their careers. The mission of the career is to sell policies by playing on people's fears; this weeds out would-be insurers who find the job too much of a downer. It's a lean time when agents are just learning the ropes and do not have many clients. There is a lot to learn, progress seems slow, hours are long, and paychecks are usually small.

Agents who remain in the industry for five years find that they are working long hours to generate even greater numbers of clients. They are relieved by the familiarity of the position and enjoy receiving large paychecks.

When agents are unhappy with the pace at which their careers are developing, many of them break away from their firms to become independent brokers. Others seek advancement by changing fields and becoming underwriters, actuaries, or adjusters.

MAJOR EMPLOYERS

AON CORPORATION
200 East Randolph
Chicago, IL 60601
Tel: 312-381-1000
www.aon.com

AMERICAN INTERNATIONAL GROUP
72 Wall Street, 11th Floor
New York, NY 10270
Tel: 877-638-4299
www.aig.com

CIGNA
1601 Chestnut Street, 46th Floor
Philadelphia, PA 19192
Tel: 215-761-2244
E-mail: jobs@cigna.com
www.cigna.com

MARSH INC.
1166 Avenue of the Americas
New York, NY 10036
Tel: 212-345-6000
www.marsh.com

MAJOR ASSOCIATIONS

NATIONAL ASSOCIATION OF INSURANCE AND FINANCIAL ADVISORS
2901 Telestar Court
Falls Church, VA 20006-4387
Tel: 703-770-8100
www.naifa.org

THE NATIONAL ALLIANCE FOR INSURANCE EDUCATION AND RESEARCH
PO Box 27027
Austin, TX 78755-2027
Tel: 800-633-2165
Fax: 512-345-2167
www.scic.com

INVESTMENT BANKER

A DAY IN THE LIFE

Investment bankers advise their clients about high-level issues of financial organization. They manage the issuance of bonds, recommend and execute strategies for taking over and merging with other companies, and handle selling a company's stock to the public. The work involves a large amount of financial analysis, and it is necessary to have a strong background in finance and economics. Personal and strategic skills are also vital to investment bankers because they serve as strategists for their clients, helping them both develop and implement their financial plans. At the profession's highest level, investment bankers serve as crucial figures in the shaping of the American and world economies, managing mergers of multibillion dollar corporations and handling the privatization of government assets around the world. **{ long hours }**

All this is time consuming, and investment bankers work long hours. Workweeks of 70-plus hours or more are common, and all-night sessions before deals close are the rule rather than the exception. Still, the work is extremely interesting, and those who stay in the profession report high levels of job satisfaction. Investment bankers spend large amounts of time traveling to pitch ideas to prospective and current clients or to examine the facilities of companies being purchased by their clients. In the office, they spend their time developing strategies to pitch to clients, preparing financial analyses and documents, or working with the sales forces of their banks to sell the bonds and stocks that are created by the investment banking department's activities.

PAYING YOUR DUES

In general, an MBA is required so investment bankers can rise in the field; however, entry-level jobs in analyst programs are available to college graduates who want experience in the profession. Analysts perform much of the grunt work required in preparing financial proposals, although they often travel to sit in on meetings with clients and sessions in which senior bankers pitch ideas to prospective customers. After two years, analysts usually move on, either to business school or to another profession, though a few are offered jobs as associates—the position that investment banks offer to MBA holders. In many banks, this is as far as one can rise without an MBA, though there are exceptions; a few prominent bankers never went to business school.

ASSOCIATED CAREERS

Most commonly, investment bankers who leave the profession go on to financial jobs in-house with a client of their former banking firm and work as financial officers and analysts. It is also not uncommon for bankers to move on to management consulting, a field that demands many similar skills. Some bankers get law degrees and become specialists in financial and corporate law, while some lawyers leave their firms to become investment bankers. Bankers who have clients who trust them and have reputations for expertise in their fields can become entrepreneurs, while others leave their firms to set up their own investment banks.

PAST AND FUTURE

Investment bankers have been around as long as stocks have been issued and bonds sold; however, the current industry owes its present form to the demand for expert counsel created by the increasing complexity of financial markets since the 1930s. Until relatively recently, investment banking was a fairly sedate field. The 1980s saw tremendous growth in the field, as the increasing availability of complex securities and high-yield ("junk") bonds made mergers and acquisitions a weapon in the arsenal of every major corporation.

Though the stock markets have their ups and downs, companies always require expert advisors to help them sell stocks and bonds and to make strategic financial plans; investment bankers fill this need. Employment in the investment banking industry should remain strong for the foreseeable future.

QUALITY OF LIFE

2 YEARS During the first two years after finishing business school and taking a job at a bank, most investment bankers work as junior associates, supervising the financial analysis done by analysts and themselves being closely supervised by more experienced bankers. At this level, associates are learning the business, acquiring the skills they will need when they are called on to develop financial plans rather than execute them. They spend long hours running computer analyses, preparing the financial reports that accompany stock issues, and putting together the documents used by senior bankers to pitch ideas.

5 YEARS At this level, investment bankers have significantly more responsibility and mobility. They have become senior associates or vice presidents, depending on the structure of the firm, and oversee the preparation of documents that leave the firm. They also begin to participate in the more creative side of the business, working with senior bankers and clients to develop financial strategies. They have established specialties, whether regional or by type of transaction, and have begun to develop the professional reputations and skills that will enable them to attract clients. The hours remain intense, and still involve all-night sessions and more than 70-plus hours of work per week, but bankers begin to have more control over their schedules. They have more control over their careers as well, as the options of going to work in-house for a client or moving to another bank with a specific need for their expertise become increasingly available.

10 YEARS By this point, investment bankers are involved in strategic and financial planning, creating the plans executed by junior bankers and spending significant amounts of time developing plans with existing clients and attempting to attract new ones. Those who have not left to start their own firms or to work for clients usually now have ownership interests in their firms, and they begin to participate in firm policy and management. They are responsible, either alone or with other senior bankers, for overseeing a sector of the firm's investment banking business, and professional success is now largely dependent on the banker's ability to develop a client base. The hours remain long, but individuals appreciate having significant control over when work must be done. Pay increases dramatically.

MAJOR EMPLOYERS

GOLDMAN, SACHS & CO.
85 Broad Street
New York, NY 10004
Tel: 212-902-1000
http://gs.com

MERRILL LYNCH
250 Vesey Street
New York, NY 10080
Tel: 212-449-1000
www.plan.ml.com

MORGAN STANLEY
1585 Broadway
New York, NY 10036
Tel: 212-761-4000
Fax: 212-392-7451
www.msdw.com

JUDGE

A DAY IN THE LIFE

Judges are the leaders and officiators of the judicial branch of government. Judges apply rules of law to the disputes and disagreements of daily life, whether those disagreements are between two neighbors over excess noise levels, law enforcement officers and an alleged murderer, or nations with international cooperation issues. It is essential for judges to possess the capacity to take in and evaluate large quantities of information; to suspend judgment until all relevant issues have been heard; to decide the exact nature of those relevant issues; and to be fair. Clarity with both the written and spoken word, a keen memory, an ability to communicate clearly, and the capacity to keep issues in strict confidence are also key traits. Though the most visible work of a judge involves presiding over hearings and then rendering decisions in open court, a { officiator } fair proportion of a judge's time is spent taking care of behind-the-scenes work. The judge may hear presentations or read written material to determine which evidence may be admitted in a particular case. He or she may also settle disputes between lawyers. Judges also spend significant blocks of time reviewing case materials, researching the law, evaluating the evidence, and in some cases, writing an opinion on the matter after all arguments have been heard. Scheduling these actions on a number of continuing cases in collaboration with court staff is another aspect of the position of which the judge should be aware. Administrative law judges work for government agencies and make determinations about such issues as workers' eligibility for certain benefits and compensation. Increased willingness on the part of the public to seek judicial resolution for perceived wrongs has resulted in an increase in the number of cases. At the same time, budget constraints in the public sector, in which most judges find work, have reduced the number of judges to hear those cases as well as the number of court workers to assist judges with scheduling and related matters.

A judge often deals with people under stress; typically, at least one party—and often all of the parties—in a dispute will go away less than satisfied. A judge's decisions are part of the public record; nevertheless, many of the factors that help judges come to their decisions often must remain private by rules of confidentiality. This total accountability for decisions rendered—in some cases, despite the confidentiality of key facts—may also present challenges. The position can be very rewarding, however, as judges have the opportunity to affect the daily lives of the communities in which they live and work—and sometimes even the course of history—for the better.

PAYING YOUR DUES

Although it is possible to become a judge without legal training, this career path is by far the exception rather than the rule. A law degree in addition to a bachelor's degree is necessary in almost all cases to advance. Work experience (typically as an attorney) is also required. Most communities respect that a judge's work is demanding and of a high professional level, but few people understand what a judge does or all that he or she must consider when rendering a decision. A judge may start in a lower court and advance to a higher-level court, either by appointment or election; if he or she already has a distinguished law career, then there may be the option start at a higher level initially.

ASSOCIATED CAREERS

As most judges practice law before serving on the bench, many elect to return to that profession, perhaps serving in specialized areas of law or taking senior counsel roles for which their judicial service has prepared them. Some teach law, write about it, or both; and some find careers in business in which their analytical and verbal skills prove especially valuable. Some seek elective office as legislators. They may also find opportunities in the related fields of mediation, arbitration, and conciliation, which are often handled by nonprofit or private business agencies.

PAST AND FUTURE

The work of administering justice, that is, of applying the rules and laws of a society to the disputes of daily life, probably dates back almost as far as humanity itself. As people began to gather in tribes and towns, disputes arose, and decisions by those not directly involved in the disagreement became necessary for the good of the group. Being a judge has always been a difficult and often controversial occupation; but the courts have handed down decisions that have changed the course of history, often for the better (think of the 1954 case *Brown v. Board of Education*). During the Middle Ages in Europe, juries typically determined law by consensus, and then the judge applied such "law" to the facts of a given case; this practice has long since been abandoned in most systems.

Most judges today work for government agencies, and because of the outlook for budget constraints in public service, it is likely that employment opportunities for judges will grow more slowly than the average rate of growth for all professions. Increasing crime and stricter sentencing laws may also bring heavier case loads for judges. As a result, there is likely to be an increased use of arbitration and mediation, particularly in civil law. Excellent time management skills, clear communication, and the ability to handle high levels of stress are likely to prove especially useful for judges in the coming years.

QUALITY OF LIFE

2 YEARS Whether one is employed as a municipal court judge or serves on a higher-level federal court, the first two years consist of a mix of hands-on work: presiding over cases, researching the law, hearing motions, ruling on evidence, and so forth. This is combined with an orientation program of meetings, discussion, readings, mentoring, and continuing education requirements. The early years on the job are brimming with learning opportunities.

5 YEARS As a judge gains experience hearing and resolving cases, he or she may be appointed to courts that decide on more complex issues. Those judges who hold elective office will also have spent some time learning how to be effective political candidates. Specialized training, or a move from one kind of work to another (e.g., from civil to criminal work or from misdemeanor to felony court) is typical at this stage. Dealing with heavy case loads, time demands, and the political pressures of making unpopular decisions are challenges that have already emerged.

10 YEARS At the 10-year mark, a judge will be well positioned for higher office; rendering decisions for more complex cases. He or she may have become an appellate judge or combined high-level court administrative duties with judicial responsibilities. Some judges may return to the practice of law, where prospects for financial rewards may be greater. Others may go into teaching or business careers, while some may seek to use their skills and experience as arbitrators or mediators.

MAJOR EMPLOYERS

Major sources of employment for judges are local civil and criminal courts, including traffic courts, juvenile courts, and felony and misdemeanor courts. These are usually branches of a county, municipality, or regional-governing body. Judges may also find work on a district level as appellate judges in federal courts, in specialized areas such as admiralty law, and as mediators and arbitrators in agencies that are not court-based.

MAJOR ASSOCIATIONS

AMERICAN BAR ASSOCIATION
321 North Clark Street
Chicago, IL 60610
Tel: 312-988-5000
www.abanet.org

LABOR RELATIONS SPECIALIST

SALARY ● ● ●

HOURS ● ●

EDUCATION ● ●

BOOKS, FILMS, AND TV SHOWS
FEATURING THE PROFESSION
- Hoffa
- Matewan
- Newsies
- Norma Rae
- On the Waterfront

YOU'LL HAVE CONTACT WITH
- Attorneys
- Human resource personnel
- Researchers
- Union representatives

PROFESSIONALS READ
- Industrial and Labor Relations Review
- The Wall Street Journal

A DAY IN THE LIFE

Labor relations specialists negotiate contracts, including compensation rates, benefits, working conditions, and rates of advancement, between workers and managers. "If you're doing your job right, no one likes you, but everyone is happy with the deal," said one 10-year veteran of labor relations. This ability to act as the lodestone for others' discontent is important to the success of agreements. Individuals who are most successful in this occupation are able to see creative alternatives that satisfy the needs of one group without neglecting the needs of another. In some cases, these "win/win" scenarios are difficult or impossible to achieve; the savvy labor relations specialist enlists both sides in the quest for such solutions. Labor relations experts trade on their reputation and integrity to bring disparate groups together and conclude deals. Everything else is secondary.

{ **creative alternatives** }

Most of the work a labor relations specialist does takes place before anyone even sits down at a table. A labor relations specialist is an educator on behalf of either the labor or management side and occasionally both. Education about the needs and abilities of either side is critical to not only the successful completion of single negotiations, but also for the long-term relationship between negotiating parties. Current thoughts on negotiation see most ongoing relationships as long-term "partnerships" that need to be maintained and nurtured. Labor relations specialists review documents and meet daily with members of other parties to assess their needs and abilities. A significant 45 percent of their time at the office is spent on the telephone, discussing details, histories, and possible alternatives for cutting deals. Face-to-face meetings are less common than telephone consultations.

Labor relations experts analyze compensation rates, labor needs, and market research, and examine prior contracts between employers and employees. They must be skilled at seeing both the details of the specific negotiations and the larger context into which these negotiations must be placed. This bifocal vision takes time to develop; over half the professional labor relationship experts we surveyed mentioned that given the opportunity, they would redo most of the negotiations they handled in the first five years of their careers.

PAYING YOUR DUES

In few other careers are the requirements for entry so debated. Some people feel that an undergraduate background in personnel relations, labor economics, industrial psychology, or sociology is critical to success in this field. Others think that an MBA and legal training constitute the best preparation. A third group feels that the industry should model itself more on apprenticeship programs and people should learn by sitting in on negotiations and discussions and reviewing past negotiations and solutions. All three groups agree that an undergraduate degree that demonstrates the ability to communicate clearly and argue persuasively is an advantage. For those entering government labor relations, coursework in government issues would be helpful. Graduate-level coursework in industrial relations, economics, law, or history can be advantageous. While you may feel that all this studying should prepare you for serious responsibilities right away, you must realize that competitive entry-level positions may entail fairly lowly work, including library research, computer analysis, and general assistant duties, from scheduling lunches to "ordering office furniture," as one respondent mentioned.

ASSOCIATED CAREERS

Labor relations specialists have to become experts in a variety of industries to do their jobs properly; once experts, many of them choose to assume more certain and less acrimonious roles as advisors in those professions. A number of specialists go into government service, and a large portion of them who are attorneys return to practice in labor litigation on either the managers' or workers' sides. Some of them become authors, lecturers, and teachers in the field of industrial relations.

PAST AND FUTURE

Unions came into their own in the 1930s, after decades of fighting to address the powerlessness of America's workers. Workers were inclined to distrust management, and management was inclined to respond to their own economic needs without consideration for the workers. This gap in communication created the need for the labor relations specialist, a third party who could identify the needs of the two groups and communicate those needs in positive, forward-looking terms. Among significant figures in labor relations are Samuel Gompers, founder of the AFL-CIO, and Jimmy Hoffa, who turned the Teamsters into the nation's largest union.

Personnel issues will become more important for both large and small companies in the future. Consulting firms that mediate between smaller firms and their employees are growing in importance and reputation. Shifting labor national headquarters and the general migration of labor will move the labor job market more to the West Coast from the East Coast and Northeast region of the United States.

QUALITY OF LIFE

2 YEARS Most beginning labor relations specialists learn under the guidance of a mentor or a group. The first few years are a period of education. Responsibilities are limited, but the hours are long; many professionals do research, review documents, and write summary reports. Pay is low, as is input to the negotiations—most young labor relation specialists prefer to be silent, watch, and listen. Successful labor relations specialists cite lessons learned in the early years, such as how to ask productive questions, how to disarm opponents' negotiating ploys, and how to set initial bid levels, as key to their future achievements.

5 YEARS Five years into the profession, many labor relations specialists choose one side—labor or management—to represent. Some of them act as independent arbiters for private organizations, such as the American Arbitration Association, and hone their listening and judgment skills. Client contact, which in years one through three was minimal, becomes important. Specialists define discrete areas of responsibility for themselves, and many of them take a place at the negotiation table. Those individuals who are successful build up their resumes by working on different deals. Others who are not yet successful stay in the background to learn the profession more carefully. Professionals assume the role of lead negotiator between years 4 and 10 of their careers.

10 YEARS A strange phenomenon comes over a number of labor relations specialists in years 10 through 12—a number switch from their original side of negotiations to the other (i.e., from management's side to labor's side, or vice versa). Salaries increase dramatically, as do client expectations. The hours and responsibilities increase, but more on a supervisory level than on a day-to-day negotiation management level. Strong communication skills and client relations skills are critical to continued success at this point. Individuals who cannot complete sound, sensible deals will find themselves moving on to other professions.

MAJOR EMPLOYERS

Labor relations specialists are employed by most corporations with an established union presence. Contact organizations in your area for employment opportunities.

MAJOR ASSOCIATIONS

WORLD AT WORK
1404 Northsight Boulevard
Scottsdale, AZ 85260
Tel: 480-951-9191
Fax: 480-483-8352
E-mail: rjohnson@worldatwork.org
www.worldatwork.org

AMERICAN ARBITRATION ASSOCIATION
335 Madison Avenue, 10th Floor
New York, NY 10017-4605
Tel: 212-716-5800
Fax: 212-716-5905
E-mail: websitemail@adr.org
www.adr.org

LOBBYIST

A DAY IN THE LIFE

Whether lobbyists work for a large organization, a private individual, or the general public, their goals and strategies tend to be similar. First and foremost, lobbyists must be adept at the art of persuasion, which is the mainstay of their job. They must figure out how to sway politicians to vote on legislation in a way that favors the interest they represent. This means tailoring appeals to specific individuals as well as to group voting blocs, such as southerners or pro-choicers. Lobbyists also occasionally lobby one another. When opposing groups find a common area of interest and can present a united front, they are extremely effective.

Lobbying can be direct or indirect. Direct lobbying means actually meeting with members of Congress and their staffs, providing them { core of relationships } with information pertinent to a bill being voted on. The lobbyist imparts his or her information with the help of graphs, charts, polls, and reports that he or she has hunted up or created. Needless to say, this is usually information that the politician may not otherwise have access to and casts the matter in a light favorable to the interest the lobbyist represents. Sometimes, lobbyists will even sit down and help a politician draft legislation that is advantageous for their interest.

Maintaining good relations with politicians who can be relied on to support the lobbyist's interest is key. While their employers cannot themselves make large campaign donations to politicians, lobbyists can raise money from other sources for reelection campaigns and be affiliated with political action committees. The resulting core of relationships a lobbyist has with the decision-makers of this country is what makes a lobbyist worth hiring. To be successful at all of this, the lobbyist must be well-informed, persuasive, and self-confident.

Indirect lobbying, sometimes referred to as grassroots organizing, is a bit less glamorous. Grassroots lobbyists enlist the help of the community to influence politicians by writing, calling, or demonstrating on an organization's behalf. This means long hours spent on the phone and writing letters, trying to rouse the community to get involved. These lobbyists also report to politicians about the concerns and reactions they have gotten from community members. Indirect lobbying is also done through the media. Grassroots lobbyists write articles for newspapers and magazines and appear on talk shows to generate interest in and awareness of their issues.

Lobbyists tend to work long hours; working between 40 and 80 hours per week is the norm. When a bill is up for vote, lobbyists will usually work through at least one night. But the least attractive part of being a lobbyist may be the less-than-spotless reputation of the profession. While many of them are undoubtedly scrupulous, the staggering amounts some high-profile lobbyists can earn causes some degree of mistrust. The fact remains, however, that honest lobbyists are working to promote causes they believe are important and worthwhile.

PAYING YOUR DUES

Lobbying is a profession brimming with people who have changed careers. Lobbyists are required to register with the state and federal governments. Most of them have college degrees. A major in political science, journalism, law, communications, public relations, or economics should provide future lobbyists with a solid foundation. Working in a government or political office, especially as a congressional aide, takes you into the front lines, but it may also be useful to start out in a law or public relations firm.

Many lobbyists also come from careers as legislators; former politicians often capitalize on their years of government service and their connections to old pals still in office. This is the "revolving door" that recent legislation has begun to regulate. Indeed, networking is the name of the game in lobbying, a profession in which people are hired as much for whom they know as for what they know. Someone who can schmooze at high levels will start his lobbying career from a high perch, while others face a long hard climb upward. Although there is no corporate hierarchy, this also means that there is no ceiling for individuals who do well.

ASSOCIATED CAREERS

Primarily, the lobbyist works with legislators and aides. Both professions are career options for former lobbyists because of their inside knowledge of the political system. Public relations is also a natural choice, since packaging and communicating messages is the lobbyist's primary skill. Advertising, journalism, and teaching are also good outlets for the lobbyist's energy and talents.

PAST AND FUTURE

The term "lobbyist" is derived from the location where early lobbyists worked—the lobbies or anterooms of political buildings. As James Madison warned in his writings, bribery is the constant threat lurking in the activity of lobbying. In fact, bribery was rampant in earlier times, but strict legislation resulting from public outcry has made a huge dent. Recent laws, for example, require companies to disclose their lobbyists' names and report all gifts given to politicians, and the value of these gifts has been restricted to no more than 50 dollars. Laws have also been passed to delay politicians from returning to Washington through the "revolving door" as lobbyists after they leave office. Lobbying cannot be legislated out of existence, though, as it is protected by the Constitution. As long as there is legislation, there will be lobbyists. The profession is affected by the economy just like any other; and like many jobs, the lobbyist's professional challenges are heightened in a tight economy where accountability is a must and choices on spending falls under the microscope.

QUALITY OF LIFE

2 YEARS Unless a lobbyist obtained his or her job through well-established connections, he or she is struggling to learn all those names! Individuals who leave the field at this time usually do so involuntarily—they are fired because they can't integrate themselves well enough into the system.

5 YEARS Most lobbyists have proven their ability to get things done by advancing their agendas regardless of the party in office. Their diplomacy and flexibility have allowed them to climb the ladder, and they now have assistants.

10 YEARS Job security for lobbyists grows proportionally with every year of experience. By networking in Washington, DC, lobbyists have become increasingly valuable to their organization and have a high salary and the trust and respect of their employers and colleagues.

MAJOR EMPLOYERS

AMERICAN ASSOCIATION OF RETIRED PERSONS
601 E Street, NW
Washington, DC 20049
Tel: 888-687-2277
www.aarp.org

GREENPEACE
702 H Street, NW
Washington, DC 20001
Tel: 202-462-1177
Fax: 202-462-4507
www.greenpeace.org

SACRAMENTO ADVOCATES
1201 K Street, Suite 2030
Sacramento, CA 95814
Tel: 916-448-1222
Fax: 916-448-1121
Contact: Barry S. Brokaw

MAJOR ASSOCIATIONS

AMERICAN LEAGUE OF LOBBYISTS
PO Box 30005
Alexandria, VA 22310
Tel: 703-960-3011
Fax: 703-960-4070
E-mail: alldc.org@erols.com
www.alldc.org

WOMEN IN GOVERNMENT RELATIONS
801 North Fairfax Street, Suite 211
Alexandria, VA 22314
Tel: 703-299-8546
Fax: 703-299-9233
E-mail: info@wgr.org
www.wgr.org

MARKETING EXECUTIVE

SALARY   ● ● ●

HOURS   ● ●

EDUCATION   ● ●

BOOKS, FILMS, AND TV SHOWS
FEATURING THE PROFESSION
- Big
- Big Game
- Lover, Come Back
- Scrooged

YOU'LL HAVE CONTACT WITH
- Advertising executives
- Market researchers
- Media specialists
- Product designers

PROFESSIONALS READ
- Advertising Age
- Brandweek
- Demographics
- Journal of Marketing
- Marketing News
- Promo

A DAY IN THE LIFE

A marketing executive directs the marketing of a company's products or services. Marketing executives know the company's product line, historical market, potential market, media costs, media response, and budgeting issues. Marketers often have to utilize a number of advertising media, such as radio, television, phone solicitation, mail campaigns, and promotional events, to sell their client's product or service. Their most difficult task is determining how best to take advantage of any or all of them to promote their product. In addition, "You have to know when to sell your own product and when to mow down the other guy's product," wrote one New York marketing executive. Marketing takes three basic forms: positive marketing (the benefits of your product or service), educational marketing (developing a demand for your product by educating people about their needs, such as mouthwash marketers talking about gingivitis), and negative marketing (revealing the flaws in a competitor's product). Knowing when to do which—and how—constitutes both the science and art that marketing executives practice.

 { common sense }

Most marketing executives spend significant amounts of time analyzing demographics, regional sales figures, and the competition. However, more than one marketer told us that in the end, marketing is all about "common sense." Many of the survey respondents said "a general approach to the industry is useless; each product has one specific trait, detail, or role that is unique and valuable, and all the marketing executive does is apply common sense to the promotion of that trait." Another marketer put it this way: A marketing executive has to be able to recognize "unexplored potentialities" that can turn a low-selling item into a high-selling item, and a high-selling item into a mega-hit. The pressure is high, but it has one advantage: Marketers always know how they're doing, as their progress and success is inevitably tracked by an increase or decrease in sales. External events may drive demand for a product in one direction or another; it's the marketer's job to respond to these shifts and take advantage of them. Excuses for low sales don't go over well. The key to being a successful marketing executive is to be proactive and to anticipate trends.

Marketers often work together with developers, advertisers, and production managers to ensure a product's successful promotion. A number of marketers mentioned that although they are called in to consult on production decisions, such as product design, color, and even box shape, "many of the decisions are made without our consent anyway." Once clients fall short of expectations for campaigns, however, they will invariably include the marketer in those decisions going forward. A marketer has to be creative, confident, and thick-skinned—marketing personnel get fired at an above–average rate. Nevertheless, creative thinkers with the ability to analyze statistics and work out long-term logistical plans find sound homes in marketing divisions, in which all their skills are needed to launch a product successfully or to maintain a product's sales.

PAYING YOUR DUES

Marketing executives have no formal educational requirements, but most employers require at least a college degree. Valued courses include those in marketing, statistics, advertising, psychology, sociology, business, finance, economics, and history. Communication skills are very important, so any writing experience is appreciated. Marketing executives need to know their product line and its unique features, so special requirements may apply for those individuals in science, mechanical, medical, or computer-based industries. Professional education is the norm in this occupation, with many marketers attending at least two seminars or lectures a year. Certification is available from a number of professional societies (such as the American Marketing Association and Sales and Marketing Executives International), but employers typically do not require it.

ASSOCIATED CAREERS

Marketing executives often are promoted to strategic planning positions. Others take their skills to advertising agencies, demographic research firms, or public relations firms. Many of them return to school for Master's of Business Administration degrees. Upon completion of their degrees, many marketers head up marketing departments or move into positions of management. A notable few market executives work for consumer advocacy groups and are vocal participants in the debate over fairness in marketing and advertising.

PAST AND FUTURE

Marketing used to be the prerogative of the owner, who made all the decisions about the product line, packaging, and advertising, and negotiated all contracts. The rapid growth of a consumer society has made that one-person-shop practically impossible to maintain, and most companies now hire marketing specialists to ensure that daily marketing management is handled by qualified professionals.

Many marketing positions will become available over the next several years, as many current marketers retire, resign, or move into management positions, but the competition for these positions is expected to intensify. Candidates with more academic credentials will have an advantage, and those individuals who engage in continuing education should be more secure in their positions than those individuals who do not.

QUALITY OF LIFE

2 YEARS At this stage, marketers are assistants, market researchers, and junior marketing personnel as they make the transition from the marketing theory they learned in school to the reality of how the industry functions. Owners make all final decisions regardless of market research or sage advice, and that is one important lesson demonstrated to the new hire. The hours can be long as assistants assemble all data into forms that more senior, strategic marketers can use. Contact with other departments (such as advertising and product design) is limited. Salaries and satisfaction tend to be low.

5 YEARS The work has become more interesting and marketers are better paid, and responsibilities have increased. Many marketers are now marketing executives or strategic marketers with either high-profile positions on marketing teams or lead positions on small products and promotions. Ambitious employees use their few spare hours to get graduate degrees in marketing, finance, or advertising to help them advance beyond their current positions. Within two years, a massive job-swap takes place in the industry—the seven-year-itch strikes hard, as around 25 percent of the workforce changes employers in years seven through nine.

10 YEARS As part of a strategic planning team, 10-year veterans review the reports written by more junior marketers and make recommendations to appropriate departments, with which they now have regular contact. They analyze less and communicate more, translating the work their department does into a form usable by other departments. The hours decrease; salaries and satisfaction increase.

MAJOR EMPLOYERS

MATTEL INC.
333 Continental Boulevard
Mail Stop M1-0908
El Segundo, CA 90245-5012
Tel: 310-252-2000
www.mattel.com

PHILIP MORRIS
120 Park Avenue
New York, NY 10017-5592
Tel: 212-880-5000
Fax: 917-663-5321
www.philipmorrisusa.com

PROCTER AND GAMBLE
1 P&G Plaza
Cincinnati, OH 45202
Tel: 513-983-1100
www.pg.com
Contact: Personnel

MAJOR ASSOCIATIONS

AMERICAN MARKETING ASSOCIATION
311 South Wacker Drive, Suite 5800
Chicago, IL 60606
Tel: 800-262-1150 or 312-542-9000
Fax: 312-542-9001
E-mail: info@ama.org
www.ama.org

DIRECT MARKETING ASSOCIATION
1120 Avenue of the Americas
New York, NY 10036-9700
Tel: 212-768-7277
Fax: 212-302-6714
www.the~dma.org

PROMOTION MARKETING ASSOCIATION
257 Park Avenue South, 11th Floor
New York, NY 10010
Tel: 212-420-1100
Fax: 212-533-7622
www.pmalink.org

SALES AND MARKETING EXECUTIVES INTERNATIONAL
PO Box 1390
Sumas, WA 98295-1390
Tel: 312-893-0751
Fax: 604-855-0165
www.smei.org

MEDIA CONSULTANT

A DAY IN THE LIFE

So, you want to be a media consultant? That's all well and good, but what does it mean? Let's start with the Latin source of the word: *consultare*, which means, "to consider maturely, weigh, ponder." As a general strategy consultant, you may be responsible for analyzing and proposing new ways to improve an organization's structure. But consulting within the media industry comes with much more narrowly-defined sets of tasks and objectives. The position of media consultant typically leads down one of two paths. The first aspect of media consulting deals with assisting a news station, newspaper, or magazine. Consultants in this domain are generally called on to develop new methods to maximize audience size or readership; produce a sharper product; and expand revenue streams. The second kind of media consultant actually coaches clients who deal with the media—on everything from answering questions clearly and succinctly to wearing the right suit. This primarily involves preparing individuals for interviews, press releases, or press conferences and establishing media contacts for future stories.

> { tight timelines and little advance notice }

Consultants travel frequently, sometimes crisscrossing the country to work on projects for multiple clients at the same time. Some projects require a team of consultants; others call for an independent consultant working with the company's managers. All consultants must possess strong analytical skills, the ability to communicate and interact effectively with others, sound judgment, time management skills, and creativity. They are self-motivated and disciplined professionals. The work of a media consultant may be conducted exclusively from a client's office, divided between home and a client's site, or even brought to the site of a live or taped TV or radio program. Due to the somewhat transient nature of the work, those who excel must be able to adapt to changing work environments. Most jobs are based on regular business hours, although media consultants may be required to work long hours as deadlines approach or to come to the set of an early-morning TV show at 4:00 A.M. to offer some last-minute tips to an interviewee and to network with the show's producer. Stress is common among consultants, as they often work on tight timelines with little advance notice—such is the world of media.

PAYING YOUR DUES

Media consulting is a highly competitive field, so experience and education are vital to success. Many media consultants hold bachelor's degrees in journalism, communications, television and radio production, or advertising. Clients seek to hire consultants with tremendous industry knowledge. Undergraduate (and, in some cases, graduate) study should be complemented by work experience at various media outlets. Consultants often come to their profession with several years of experience working on the other side of the desk at news stations, newspapers, and magazines.

ASSOCIATED CAREERS

Working in conjunction with a variety of industries makes it relatively easy for media consultants to segue into different careers. They typically have a solid understanding of many media facets, and they will have cultivated many strong relationships with key players in the field. Professions they may consider include those of publicist or public relations specialist—or, if they hope to venture over to the other side of the business, then the roles of TV, advertising, or publishing executive, journalist, news anchor, or news reporter may also be good fits for them.

PAST AND FUTURE

The emergence of media consultants is a relatively new phenomenon. The field has grown from virtually nothing to the booming industry it is now in roughly half a century.

Consulting, especially within the realm of media, is expected to be one of the most rapidly-growing industries through the year 2012. As all areas of consulting will experience significant growth, a corresponding increase in competition within the field can be expected because of the lucrative and independent nature of the work.

QUALITY OF LIFE

2 YEARS While there is no standard career trajectory for media consultants, most do not begin their professional lives with a media consulting gig. Rather, many spend their first several years out of school working within a particular realm of the media—a role in which they cultivate their expertise, establish key contacts in the industry, and, in all likelihood, develop an area of specialization. Some find entry-level employment at a news desk; others may launch their careers copyediting or designing layout for a magazine. Whatever the position, the first few years should be used to build strong industry connections that will prove indispensable in an eventual consulting career.

5 YEARS Media professionals may begin to think about consulting after five years in the industry. At this point, many have begun to establish themselves and have gained an understanding of how the industry works. Interested candidates will probably begin to have success finding employment with some consulting firms. Those who wish to work independently may start to cultivate a client base. But beware: This latter path, while perhaps more ultimately rewarding, is likely to be slow-going at the outset.

10 YEARS After 10 years, most media consultants have established themselves as industry insiders. They have been working in the field long enough to understand all of its ins and outs. Whether instructing businesspeople on how to approach an interview or helping a magazine increase its circulation, these seasoned professionals know how to get their clients' messages communicated clearly and see their clients' objectives met.

MAJOR EMPLOYERS

CREATIVE CIRCLE MEDIA CONSULTING
169 Weybosset Street, Suite 217
Providence, RI 02903
Tel: 401-277-4817
Fax: 401-277-4818
www.creativecirclemedia.com

MARSHALL MARKETING & COMMUNICATIONS INC.
2600 Boyce Plaza Road, Suite 210
Pittsburgh, PA 15241
Tel: 412-914-0970
Fax: 412-914-0971
www.mm-c.com

SUMMIT MEDIA PARTNERS, LLC.
23454 Waynes Way
Golden, CO 80401
Tel: 303-526-7906
Fax: 303-526-2568
E-mail: info@smpllc.com
www.summitmediapartners.com

MAJOR ASSOCIATIONS

ASSOCIATION OF PROFESSIONAL COMMUNICATION CONSULTANTS
www.consultingsuccess.org

THE INTERNATIONAL GUILD OF PROFESSIONAL CONSULTANTS
5703 Red Bug Lake Road, Suite 403
Winter Springs, FL 32708
Tel: 407-678-7853
Fax: 407-678-8173
E-mail: info@igpc.org
www.igpc.org

MODEL

A DAY IN THE LIFE

You begin the week strutting down the Milanese runway while hordes of paparazzi snap your picture. A few days later you're off to Paris for a fitting and a little celebrity hobnobbing on the side. By week's end on a private jet to New York, you casually thumb through a copy of *Vogue*, an issue in which you happen to grace the cover. Yes, a career in modeling certainly seems glamorous in your fantasies. Unfortunately, the reality doesn't often parallel the dream. Modeling is a very competitive field, difficult to break into, and it's difficult even for seasoned initiates to sustain careers as models in the long term. Few make it to the upper echelons of the profession, and many find second jobs to make ends meet. Aspiring models spend much of their time soliciting agencies and visiting prospective clients, hoping their look strikes a nerve.

{ specific aesthetic criteria }

The hard work doesn't end once you land a plum job on a photo shoot. Days can be long and tiring, and there is often a lot of pressure to finish photo shoots within an allotted time frame. Models are regularly confronted with uncomfortable conditions, such as posing for a swimsuit catalog in the dead of winter. The job can also be physically exhausting, as models frequently have to hold the same position for long periods of time or walk down runways wearing very thin high heels. There's also the emotional challenge of being able to elicit the feeling or mood the photographer stipulates. Additionally, models must cope with the intense demands to keep up their looks and match the standard of beauty the fashion industry dictates—and demands.

Indeed, the industry is known for having very specific aesthetic criteria. Modeling is a youth-oriented profession, and most female models start working between the ages of 15 and 22. A majority of males working in the industry are slightly older, usually in the age range of 18 to 25. Those casting for high-fashion shows typically look for women who are, at minimum, 5'8" and weigh between 108 and 125 pounds. Male models are typically anywhere from 5'11" to 6'2" and weigh between 140 to 165 pounds.

PAYING YOUR DUES

In the modeling industry, an impressive portfolio will open a lot more doors than a degree from a top-name school. Novices aren't expected to arrive armed with an entire album of glamour shots. Aspiring models can attend open calls held by reputable agencies with just a few pictures in hand. They can also send photos into agencies that don't hold calls. There are a multitude of legitimate modeling contests at which new talent is always scouted. A word to the wise: Be sure to do careful research. You should not have to shell out exorbitant sums of money to attend. Modeling is a business rampant with scams and swindlers. When first starting out, be extremely wary of companies and industry "insiders" who attempt to sell you photo shoots and training sessions or charge you registration fees. You should not find yourself faced with huge expenditures when entering this profession.

Models beginning their careers may find that acquiring work initially is difficult and unreliable. As they establish themselves and make key contacts, they will land bigger, better, and yes, more glamorous gigs—not to mention appreciable bumps in pay.

ASSOCIATED CAREERS

While modeling can prove to be an exciting and lucrative career, it's a job with a relatively short shelf life. An increasing number of models move into acting. Many also take advantage of their industry expertise and contacts to find positions with designers, photographers, and fashion magazines. Some even open up their own boutiques or launch their own product lines.

PAST AND FUTURE

Modeling came to the forefront of cultural consciousness with the advent of fashion magazines, and in turn, the birth of the cover girl. Lisa Fonssagrives, with her unprecedented 200 *Vogue* covers, was the world's first real "face of fashion." From the 1930s through the 1950s, she graced almost every magazine, from *Life* to *Town and Country* to *Vanity Fair*. Shortly thereafter, the industry began to grow quickly and substantially. Models like Suzy Parker and Cheryl Tiegs became household names. By 1979 the term "supermodel," which was coined by model Janice Dickinson, had been adopted in everyday vernacular.

The modeling industry continues to thrive today. The potent combination of consumer culture and media saturation keeps the demand for new faces high. Reality shows like *America's Next Top Model* and *Project Runway* abound and provide examples of the potential for this profession.

QUALITY OF LIFE

2 YEARS Life at the two-year mark may be harried and hectic. Modeling is a highly competitive business, and models (even two years into their careers) may find themselves still facing rejection. They must continuously promote themselves and attend numerous cattle calls and "go-sees" at which models meet with prospective clients to see if their look corresponds with the image the client wants to project.

5 YEARS After five years, many working models have landed a contract with an agency. Most likely, they have gained an industry reputation and established a place in a specific niche—on the runway, in a catalog, or on a trade show floor. Importantly, they have attained great working relationships with photographers and an understanding of how to connect with an audience.

10 YEARS Successfully navigating the modeling industry for 10 years is a commendable feat. Definitions of which images are "hot" are in a constant state of flux, so longevity can prove difficult for some. Many models who make it this far are veterans who've achieved supermodel status. They find themselves still leading the walk down the runway at major fashion shows and fielding offers to be the face of designers' campaigns. Alternatively, many models may also extend their careers by transitioning into modeling for adult and older women's/men's fashions.

MAJOR EMPLOYERS

ELITE MODELING AGENCY
111 East 22nd Street
New York, NY 10010
Tel: 212-529-9700
Fax: 212-475-0572
E-mail: info@elitemodel.com
www.elitemodel.com

FORD MODELING AGENCY
142 Greene Street
New York, NY 10012
Tel: 212-219-6500
Fax: 212-966-1531
www.fordmodels.com

IMG MODELS
304 Park Avenue South, 12th Floor
New York, NY 10010
Tel: 212-253-8884
Fax: 212-253-8883
E-mail: modelinfo@imgworld.com
www.imgmodels.com

NEW YORK MODEL MANAGEMENT
596 Broadway, #701
New York, NY 10012
Tel: 212-539-1700
Fax: 212-539-3311
E-mail: info@newyorkmodels.com
www.newyorkmodels.com

WILHELMINA MODELS
300 Park Avenue South
New York, NY 10010
Tel: 212-473-3223
Fax: 212-473-3223
www.wilhelmina.com

MAJOR ASSOCIATIONS

FASHION GROUP INTERNATIONAL, INC.
8 West 40th Street, 7th Floor
New York, NY 10018
Tel: 212-302-5511
Fax: 212-302-5533
E-mail: info@fgi.org
www.fgi.org

MUSIC EXECUTIVE

A DAY IN THE LIFE

Music executives develop and sell music. Some executives seek out new talent; others market new recordings; some expand a particular group's product line. They oversee virtually all aspects of the commercial recording process, including the production of music videos. Their influence is broad, but their tenure may be short-lived if the music they develop or the talent they discover fails to deliver chart-topping hits. It's a tough, competitive business. The music industry rewards the bold, innovative, and aggressive individual who produces large profits for the large recording companies for which they work. Music executives not only keep on top of musical trends and tastes but also try to influence them to keep up with the continuous redesigning of pop culture.

{ deliver chart-topping hits }

There are also music executives who work on their own. The independent producer has become a staple in today's fast-paced, ever-changing music industry, which is tapping into all genres of music and feeding it to a highly impressionable and fickle young audience.

Music executives are in charge of the entire process of producing music: finding new talent; choosing music to be recorded; arranging for studio recording time; hiring studio technicians, background musicians and vocalists, and engineers; and doing marketing and promotional work. Staff producers usually have production support staff, while independent producers often handle these tasks solo. Independent producers can make large sums of money and a name for themselves if they can produce artists who consistently make their way to the top of the charts. Independent producers make their living on what sells, earning 3 to 5 percent of the money brought in by retail sales, so they can literally embrace success overnight or be scanning the classifieds for another career after one disaster.

PAYING YOUR DUES

Music executive jobs cannot be found through the classifieds, nor are there formal courses that prepare you for such positions. If you're interested in the music industry, informational interviews and internships with music industry professionals and companies are key. Any experience in a music-related field, such as the ability to play an instrument or sing, vast and current knowledge of the industry, or technical knowledge or experience in audio and recording technology, sound engineering, and studio setup provide a solid background to this field. Courses in business administration or management are particularly helpful to the independent producer. Because of the highly competitive nature of the business, newcomers must be willing to take just about any entry-level position with a recording company, independent producer, or recording studio and work hard and long hours to get to the top. Stress is a way of life for all music executives, so the aspiring music executive must determine his or her level of tolerance for stress. Even after getting your foot in the door, this industry places considerable emphasis on your record in the field: what you've done, who you've produced, and how much money you've brought in. Thus, an individual's ability to find and sign talent is paramount.

ASSOCIATED CAREERS

Music executives who grow tired of the cutthroat business side may leave for technical positions, such as sound technician, mixer, or audio and recording engineer. Opportunities also exist in talent management and publicity and as agents and road managers. Music executives who are also musicians can use their industry experience and connections to seek out jobs as background musicians, arrangers, composers, and songwriters.

PAST AND FUTURE

The music industry has been around since the invention of the Victrola, which made the recording and selling of music to the masses possible. In the 1920s, flappers bought tons of records. In the 1950s, teenagers bought Elvis Presley and Chubby Checker records, while their 1960s counterparts fell in love with the Beatles.

Now, digital technology has afforded new developments in music recording. The long-playing record (LP) has given way to the digital age and the MP3 format. Splinter and crossover audiences have contributed to the expansion and the redefinition of genres in the music industry. In the future, music executives will have to be creative enough to introduce different styles and various fusions of different genres in an attempt to invent new sounds and determine ways of regulating the file-swapping nature of music on the Internet. Despite the tenuous nature of the business, the music industry will always be in need of innovative, creative, and successful music producers and other executives. It will continue to grow, and ambitious executives in search of the cutting edge will drive this growth.

QUALITY OF LIFE

2 YEARS Music producers with two years experience are finessing the art of recognizing and signing talent. They've had a few hits and misses but are diligently making a name for themselves. They are fine-tuning the subtle art of choosing production people who can work well together. Most importantly, they are learning how to get the most out of their musicians' talent.

5 YEARS Music producers still in the business after five years should consider themselves lucky. Undoubtedly they've sustained considerable successes on the charts and carved out profit-producing niches for themselves. Talent seeks out producers with strong reputations, so music executives do far less scouting.

10 YEARS Ten-year music executives are successful just by virtue of having remained in the field this long. They have very strong reputations, and musicians come crawling to them for contracts. But in this ever-changing industry, staying on the cutting edge is the 10-year veteran's biggest challenge.

MAJOR EMPLOYERS
ARISTA RECORDS
6 West 57th Street
New York, NY 10019
Tel: 212-489-7400
www.arista.com

CLEOPATRA RECORDS
11041 Santa Monica Boulevard, Suite 703
Los Angeles, CA 90025
Tel: 310-477-4000
Fax: 310-312-5653

SONY PICTURES ENTERTAINMENT
10202 West Washington Boulevard
Culver City, CA 90232-3195
Tel: 310-244-4436
www.sony.com
Contact: Human Resources

MAJOR ASSOCIATIONS
RECORDING INDUSTRY ASSOCIATION OF AMERICA
1330 Connecticut Avenue, NW, Suite 300
Washington, DC 20036
Tel: 202-775-0101
Fax: 202-775-7253
www.riaa.com

PERFORMING ARTS ADMINISTRATOR

**BOOKS, FILMS, AND TV SHOWS
FEATURING THE PROFESSION**

- **The Show**
- **Thirty-Two Short Films about Glenn Gould**

YOU'LL HAVE CONTACT WITH

- **Artists**
- **Directors**
- **Fund-raisers**
- **Producers**
- **Venue managers**

PROFESSIONALS READ

- **Culture Front**
- **Performing Arts**
- **Newsletters put out by opera, dance, and fine arts societies**

A DAY IN THE LIFE

Many people see the performing arts as a refuge from the financially motivated corporate world. Performing arts administrators, however, know that the success of a show, a troupe, or a theater is often determined long before the audience shushes and the lights go down. The world of business and the world of art come together in the office of the performing arts administrator. A performing arts administrator controls the finances of a company or a theater with the goal of producing exciting and profitable performances. A performance arts administrator often acts as an artistic director, guiding the focus of a season's shows and hiring directors, and as an internal accountant/promoter/publicist/manager, controlling all the financial decisions that affect a theater, from allocating a budget for props to hiring a janitorial crew to clean up after each show.

{ creative financing }

A performing arts administrator has to make difficult decisions that may be unpopular with directors, performers, and audiences. "You're always the man in the black hat" wrote one performing arts administrator. "Most of the time you're out there trying to get money, publicity, press coverage, and reviews," he said, adding that networking, pitching to supporters of the arts, lining up talent, and negotiating nonessential contracts all contribute to the value of the end product. A number of performing arts administrators come to the profession as former directors, producers, actors, and technical theater personnel, familiar with the day-to-day workings of a performance but unfamiliar with its finances. This education in "creative financing," as one wrote us, seems to satisfy the need for innovation that many people in this profession feel. A performing arts administrator can work long hours, about a quarter of them not in the office but at shows. Many of them firmly believe in their houses' potential profitability; a number invest their own money in struggling or failing shows.

Some performing arts administrators are hired for their contacts and not for their decision-making abilities or their knowledge of the arts. This is one position where a good "rainmaker" can make an enormous difference to a theater or a troupe. Why do people do this? "It's not for the money," wrote one, and others agreed. Performing arts administrators, except at the most prestigious houses and companies, receive unsatisfying wages. They do it because it needs to be done. They love the arts, they want to contribute, and they can. One respondent said, "you work a long day and then, sometimes at night, you open the door to a world that makes people feel alive. That's what everybody should be doing." This level of satisfaction is what keeps many people in the profession, even as they struggle with financial concerns.

PAYING YOUR DUES

Contacts are important, and although there are no specific educational requirements, many performing arts administrators take advantage of the contacts they made in college or graduate school. Some of them attend college and manage theaters there, making sure their studies include finance, economics, drama, and accounting. A great number of performing arts administrators enter the acting, directing, or technical ends of theater production and gravitate to back-office positions as they find the competition fierce and their interests wandering. Most job-related education takes place on the fly, so performing arts administrators should be quick studies with tact and interpersonal skills. Aspiring performing arts administrators often have to relocate to cities where theater has a large market—generally urban environments, such as New York, Chicago, or Los Angeles. Many of them find it helpful to take a course in theater finance sponsored by a local university.

ASSOCIATED CAREERS

Many performing arts administrators become producers. They network among their financial contacts and convince them to invest in ventures as speculative as the ones they have already supported. Other careers that attract the migrant performing arts administrator are those of agent, reviewer, industry analyst, and promoter.

PAST AND FUTURE

Historically, financial decisions at theaters, theatrical companies, and production houses were made on an ad hoc basis, with the company focusing on the needs of the day rather than on its long-term viability. Performing arts administrators became an integral part of the artistic process in the twentieth century with the acknowledgment that a great portion of theater is business and with the recognition of the need for financial management of shoe-string production companies.

Opportunities for performing arts administrators are driven not only by demand for artistic product and available jobs, but also by government and institutional support for the arts. This changes from year to year, and government belt-tightening traditionally makes art a prime target for budget cuts. Then again, this career has always been one in which people pursue longshot events with uncertain payoffs, so the uncertain future for this career may not be a deterrent at all to the aspiring performing arts administrator.

QUALITY OF LIFE

2 YEARS Early in the profession, many performing arts administrators work as producer's assistants or as performing arts administrator's aides, taking notes, fielding phone calls, and handling the administrative work that keeps a theater open. They become familiar with box-office accounting and the basics of promotion; organize fund-raisers, mailings and events; and generally handle the work that the performing arts administrator cannot get to. Relationships in the theater can be intense, and many respondents noted that there is no distinction between a personal social life and a professional social life. Many of them spend hours making industry contacts. The hours are long; salaries are low.

5 YEARS Five-year veteran performing arts administrators have learned how to "schmooze"— how to approach financially well-off patrons of the arts and encourage them to commit funds to their projects. Grant-writing skills are also part of the performing arts administrator's skill-set. Performing arts administrators begin to make a salary that doesn't require them to take another job. Still, knowing the theater company's internal finances can lead to some sleepless nights. The hours are long, and satisfaction is high.

10 YEARS Ten-year veterans describe their experiences as ranging from "blissful" to "execrable" depending on the fate of the ship to which they've tied themselves. Many of them have moved to a larger company with a longer history and more established financial contacts or to a position in which the artistic director and the performing arts administrator have similar views. The hours remain stable. A performing arts administrator's personal and professional lives become even more indistinguishable.

MAJOR EMPLOYERS

LINCOLN CENTER FOR THE PERFORMING ARTS, INC.
140 West 65th Street
New York, NY 10023
Tel: 212-875-5000
Fax: 212-875-5185
www.lincolncenter.org
Contact: Human Resources

MADISON SQUARE GARDEN
2 Penn Plaza, 16th Floor
New York, NY 10121
Tel: 212-465-6330
Fax: 212-465-6026
www.thegarden.com
Contact: Human Resources

THE JOHN F. KENNEDY CENTER FOR THE PERFORMING ARTS
2700 F Street, NW
Washington, DC 20566
Tel: 202-416-8000
Fax: 202-416-8630
www.kennedy-center.org
Contact: Human Resources

ROBERT W. WOODRUFF ARTS CENTER
1280 Peachtree Street NE
Atlanta, GA 30309
Tel: 404-733-4323
www.woodruff-arts.org
Contact: Human resources

MAJOR ASSOCIATIONS

INTERNATIONAL SOCIETY FOR THE PERFORMING ARTS FOUNDATION
17 Purdy Avenue
PO Box 909
Rye, NY 10580
Tel: 914-921-1550
Fax: 914-921-1593
www.ispa.org

PHARMACEUTICAL SALES REPRESENTATIVE

A DAY IN THE LIFE

Pharmaceutical sales is a fast-paced, high-turnover business that rewards assertiveness, persistence, and knowledge. Pharmaceutical sales representatives spend most of their business time on the road; talking with pharmacists, hospital personnel, physicians, patient advocacy groups; and even visiting retirement homes, increasing the visibility of their company's products and the volume of their sales. "Sell sell sell, learn learn learn , sell sell sell," wrote one sales rep, who included his business card with his survey, in case we wanted to purchase any pharmaceutical supplies. Many other sales representatives agreed that the best sellers follow any lead, making every possible effort to sell their product. A number of them attend meetings where contact with purchasing professionals is rich, such as an association of pharmacists or a convention of hospital administrators. { balancing act }

This territory-oriented business can be a hard life, particularly for those individuals trying to maintain their family life as well. The need to sell extends to social functions and free time, and the already precious family moments can erode further to the point where many representatives are forced to reevaluate their commitment to their profession. This difficult balancing act is complicated by the additional pressure of being in a commission-based occupation. For many representatives, a significant portion of their income is riding on their ability to get the product into the hands of the consumer. So why is this job so addictive? Perhaps because the excessive profit margins of many brand-name pharmaceutical products can mean enormous commissions. In addition, products are generally consumed fairly quickly and not stored, so old markets rarely disappear; they need regular servicing.

The second most attractive job feature that the sales reps mentioned was the intellectual challenge the job imposes. Education is the norm in this field; learning about a company's product line is like taking an advanced course in pharmacology (which many of them do take during their initial years in the industry). They have to be familiar with data, statistics, and issues in the health community to be able to communicate successfully with businesspeople and doctors. Although this job has some aspects that are unquestionably grueling—one sales rep said he put in 184 days on the road in a single year—many love it, and love is the only term that accurately describes their zeal, dedication, and willingness to make sacrifices for their job.

PAYING YOUR DUES

Pharmaceutical sales representatives with a science background have an advantage in this profession, in terms of both their credibility and their ability to educate themselves about product lines. A college degree is standard for this job, with many employers looking favorably on graduate work. Useful courses include biology, chemistry, biochemistry, biophysics, organic chemistry, English, public speaking, finance, and negotiation techniques. Professional education is the norm for all sales representatives, both on their own products and on other companies' product lines. The ability to read a scientific study and examine its assumptions is critical to a pharmaceutical sales representative's success. Licensing is available through professional organizations, but it is not required to advance to managerial positions.

ASSOCIATED CAREERS

Pharmaceutical sales representatives go into sales positions in other professions—as systems marketers or service sales representatives, for example—in which their selling skills are valued, but where scientific knowledge is less important. Some pharmaceutical sales representatives are willing to give up the scientific element of their job to go into a profession where it is easier to advance and easier to maintain a satisfying family life.

PAST AND FUTURE

The discovery of penicillin was the beginning of the development of a host of anti-infection and antibacterial drugs. This sparked a nationwide frenzy of biotechnological invention. In 50 years, the United States outpaced the world's production of synthetic biological agents from the dawn of time to the turn of the twentieth century. With this growth of options came the growth of competition—many products had similar effects, and companies found it useful to go directly to physicians and hospitals to show them the benefits of their products. The pharmaceutical industry is a multibillion dollar industry, and sales representatives who keep doctors interested in their supplies are valuable to their employers.

The future of pharmaceutical sales representatives is uncertain, primarily because of the uncertainty surrounding all health care issues. Pharmaceutical products will certainly continue to be important, but it is not clear how much latitude doctors in managed care plans will have to prescribe various medications. Many managed care plans impose generic drug substitution standards on physicians. These standards state that when a generic substitute for a brand-name product exists, the plan will pay only for the cheaper, generic substitute. Other scenarios such as disallowances for research costs may further erode the position of pharmaceutical sales representatives.

QUALITY OF LIFE

2 YEARS At the beginning of the profession, sales representatives have few contacts and little experience selling their products. Their potential clients are usually doctors with a number of years of experience driving bargains and negotiating with other sales representatives, so many new reps view this period as an education rather than a profit opportunity. Many representatives say that doctors will often talk them into handing out free samples. Sales representatives often spend significant time in training programs and at professional conferences learning about industry issues. The hours are numerous.

5 YEARS Five-year veterans have a much rosier day-to-day existence, though it is a very busy one. Many of them spend more than 110 days on the road, visiting hospitals, physicians, and other health care professionals, trying to sell them their products. They have established regular routes, and those individuals who are successful have expanded their client base. Some of them experience financial windfalls; others use those people as models and struggle harder to succeed. Dedication is evident. Satisfaction is high.

10 YEARS Some pharmaceutical sales representatives say 10 years in this profession is a lifetime, but very few people leave it. Many of them have moved into managerial positions or have been given control over a large territory. These individuals start the process again on a grander scale with greater potential income. Only a handful of them make the extremely large amounts of money that mark the superstars in this profession, but the culture makes all representatives aware that the best sales representatives make the most money. Satisfaction is high. The hours are long. Family life may suffer.

MAJOR EMPLOYERS

BIOGEN IDEC
14 Cambridge Center
Cambridge, MA 02142
Tel: 617-679-2000
Fax: 617-679-2456
www.biogen.com
Contact: Human Resources

BRISTOL-MYERS SQUIBB COMPANY
345 Park Avenue
New York, NY 10154-0037
Tel: 212-546-4000
www.bms.com

PFIZER INC.
235 East 42nd Street
New York, NY 10017
Tel: 212-753-2323
www.pfizer.com

MAJOR ASSOCIATIONS

NATIONAL PHARMACEUTICAL COUNCIL
1894 Preston White Drive
Reston, VA 20191
Tel: 703-620-6390
Fax: 703-476-0904
www.npcnow.org

POLITICAL AIDE

BOOKS, FILMS, AND TV SHOWS
FEATURING THE PROFESSION
- The Pelican Brief
- Primary Colors
- Spin City
- The War Room

YOU'LL HAVE CONTACT WITH
- Campaign managers
- Lobbyists
- Politicians
- Researchers

PROFESSIONALS READ
- Local newspapers
- The New York Times
- The Wall Street Journal
- The Washington Post

A DAY IN THE LIFE

"Politics is all-in-the-staff work," said one Senate aide. Politicians are the visible faces of political life, the personalities who spark public debate; but the overwhelming bulk of the processes by which political decisions are made are handled by political staffers. Staffers prepare the reports, conduct the research, draft the legislation, and prepare the negotiation briefs that allow political life to happen. The pay is average, and the hours are long, but many staffers report great satisfaction with work that enables them to have a central role in important public decision-making.

Aides must be aware both of the political developments in their field and of the needs of the home district, and they must be aware of likely public reaction

{ high turnover rate }

to the various positions in a political debate. An effective aide is a valued advisor and resource, and elected officials frequently develop a core senior staffer whom they take with them from office to office throughout their careers. There is a high turnover rate among more junior staffers, however, as they maneuver to work for candidates or officeholders whose careers are on the rise.

Attachment to a particular politician, who often serves as a mentor, is perhaps the most striking aspect of a career as a political aide. The development of long-term commitment and loyalty to a single party or candidate can be extremely rewarding, but an aide's ambitions must be aligned with those of the boss. Moreover, political egos are such that staffers who seek the limelight frequently find themselves seeking alternative employment. In addition, the success of a staffer's career is tied to that of the politician; if the politician changes jobs, so must the staffer, and if the politician loses a reelection bid, the staffers are out of jobs. Despite these uncertainties, however, the life of a political aide can be extremely satisfying, and the dangers of getting turned out of office are offset by the wide range of experiences afforded a political aide.

PAYING YOUR DUES

A college degree is a necessity for staff work at any level—local, state, or federal—and many staffers have graduate and/or professional experience in their fields of specialization. Young labor attorneys will move into labor relations positions, while agricultural consultants may find jobs covering agricultural affairs. Journalism is a useful background for press aide positions. Competition for entry-level jobs can be intense; aspiring aides who have worked on major campaigns or interned in government offices have a good chance of being hired. Frequently, though not always, legislators hire aides from their home districts or states, as a means of maintaining contact between their constituents and Washington or the state capitol.

ASSOCIATED CAREERS

Often, political aides enter their areas of specialization when they leave the profession; others become lobbyists when they depart. A staffer who handled business issues for a state senator would be well-placed lobbying for a state business development organization or working for a consulting firm with local clients. A former military affairs aide to a United States senator would have contacts and knowledge that would be valuable to a military contractor. A significant percentage of aides go on to corporate law, a field in which legislative experience is rewarded.

PAST AND FUTURE

Politicians have always required aides and advisors, though the highly developed staffs of modern American politics are a relatively recent phenomenon. In 1945, Congress employed 4,000 staffers; today it employs 20,000 full-time staff members. Staffs of state governments, though smaller, have similarly expanded. Numerous factors have contributed to this dramatic increase, but the most important has been the increasing role of federal and local government in American life over the last 60-plus years. As governments administer more laws, the complexity of the issues facing legislators increases, and they require increasingly large staffs to be able to make informed decisions. Despite current efforts to trim back the size of American government, the job of legislators in modern society will likely remain extremely complex, and their need for able aides isn't going to disappear.

QUALITY OF LIFE

2 YEARS
The process for a political aide begins with the accumulation of legal and technical knowledge, learning the legislative lay of the land in his or her assigned fields.
Equally important for an aspiring aide is the development of contacts with his or her counterparts in other legislative and committee offices, with journalists who cover his or her field, and with constituents affected by the issues he or she covers.

5 YEARS
The average congressional staffer leaves after four years. Individuals who remain in the profession have become valued advisors, with considerable expertise and networks of contacts in their areas of responsibility. Some of them have become legislative directors, supervising legislative assistants and working with their politicians to set priorities for the legislative resources of the office.

10 YEARS
By now, the political aide is likely one of the most experienced employees in the office. As a legislative director's chief of staff, he or she may have considerable influence over the priorities and time commitments of the politician he or she works for, and throughout the government and legislative offices, he or she has a wide range of contacts with whom her own office participates in decisions and negotiations. Many aides at this level have considerable policy influence and authority to negotiate directly on behalf of the officeholder.

MAJOR EMPLOYERS

DEMOCRATIC NATIONAL COMMITTEE
430 South Capital Street, SE
Washington, DC 20003
Tel: 202-863-8000
Fax: 202-488-5043
www.democrats.org

REPUBLICAN NATIONAL COMMITTEE
310 First Street, SE
Washington, DC 20003
Tel: 202-863-8500
Fax: 202-863-8820
www.rnc.org

Political aides generally work for individual candidates or officeholders, who may change from election to election.

MAJOR ASSOCIATIONS

DEMOCRATIC NATIONAL COMMITTEE
430 South Capitol Street, SE
Washington, DC 20003
Tel: 202-863-8000
Fax: 202-488-5043
www.democrats.org

REPUBLICAN NATIONAL COMMITTEE
310 First Street, SE
Washington, DC 20003
Tel: 202-863-8500
Fax: 202-863-8820
www.RNC.org

POLITICIAN

PROFESSIONAL PROFILE

# of people in profession	910,000
Avg. hours per week	45
Avg. starting salary	$12,400
Avg. salary after 5 years	$15,100
Avg. salary 10 to 15 years	$67,300

SALARY ● ○ ○
HOURS ● ● ○
EDUCATION ● ● ○

BOOKS, FILMS, AND TV SHOWS
FEATURING THE PROFESSION
- **All the King's Men**
- **An American President**
- **The Candidate**
- **Primary Colors**

YOU'LL HAVE CONTACT WITH
- **Campaign managers**
- **Image consultants**
- **Lobbyists**
- **Political aides**

PROFESSIONALS READ
- **Local newspapers**
- **The New York Times**
- **The Wall Street Journal**
- **The Washington Post**

A DAY IN THE LIFE

Politics has been with us for as long as people have had to cooperate to achieve their goals. More than half a million people currently hold full- or part-time elected offices in the United States. They make decisions that affect communities on the local, state, and national levels. For individuals who wish to participate in such decisions, a career in politics should absolutely be considered. Politicians have a hand in thousands of decisions that are important to their communities, from questions of dividing tax revenue for local schools and police funding to issues of federal tax policy. The profession offers great rewards to individuals with a combination of negotiation and public presentation skills. In addition to full-time political jobs, many individuals find that part-time community boards, town councils, or even state assembly jobs make valuable and rewarding adjuncts to their full-time careers.

{ not for shy people }

A career in politics is not for shy people. At all levels, it is characterized by publicity. Most successful politicians enjoy life in the public eye, while individuals who leave the profession often cite loss of privacy as its greatest drawback. Whether in a small town or in the White House, politicians are subject to intense scrutiny. Elected officials have to campaign for reelection every time their term is up, but, for the most part, the first time is the real challenge; incumbency is a strong advantage in many elections. More than 90 percent of the United States House of Representatives is reelected every two years, and the reelection rates at the lower levels of politics are similar.

PAYING YOUR DUES

There is no one career path that reliably leads to office. Working as an aide for an established politician is one common way to meet contacts in the local political party. Law school is another common first step to a political career, since many lawyers achieve public notice or do work for state political parties. In general, political careers begin with an office in state government; most politicians in Washington start as state legislators and work their way up the party hierarchy. In politics, however, the exception is virtually the rule, and people of all academic backgrounds, from peanut farmers to actors, pursue successful political careers. Charisma is important, and being independently wealthy to finance campaigns may prove helpful.

ASSOCIATED CAREERS

A significant majority of full-time, career politicians are lawyers, and many of them return to private practice after leaving office. Many of them represent clients doing business with the government offices they vacated, putting their knowledge of politics in this specific area to work for financial gain; others just go on to ordinary practice. Some former politicians become lobbyists or run professional organizations or foundations that can benefit from their stature and experience. Finally, jobs in academia or appointed positions in government are also quite common career options for former politicians.

PAST AND FUTURE

Modern democracy traces itself to the assembly of ancient Athens, but United States representative government bears little resemblance to the Athenian system. United States politics is a much more sedate affair, even though the public perception of politicians remains rather volatile. In any event, the profession will endure. The public's questions will always need to be answered, and politicians will always be needed to answer them.

QUALITY OF LIFE

2 YEARS At this point, a politician is in the early stages of his or her career, holding a relatively low-level or local office. This may be a school or community board position, a seat in the lower house of the state government, or a position as a small town mayor or town council member. In general, staffs, budgets, and campaign funds are small, and the areas of responsibility of the office are quite limited. Politicians begin to build relationships within their political party that they will depend on throughout their career, attempting to gain the public notice that will provide the foundation for a successful run for higher office. Reelection is a significant concern in these first years, though each successful reelection in a given position reduces the risk of later challenge.

5 YEARS By now the politician has survived at least one, and probably more than one, reelection campaign. The politician has likely established a solid base of support in their local community and is beginning to gain more public attention. Their proposals and initiatives are starting to have a greater chance of success in the local government. The politician is establishing a reputation as a viable candidate for higher office, whether in the city government, the state senate, or Congress.

10 YEARS Successful politicians have by now risen in the party ranks, and they likely have a secure hold on their office and can consider the extent of their ambitions. They are likely among individuals who have the connections and experience to run for senatorial or congressional office, or they could be one of many politicians who build satisfying careers at the state and city level. In any event, politicians who survive the first 10 years can be reasonably confident of lifelong political careers, should they choose to pursue them.

MAJOR EMPLOYERS
Successful politicians end up on the payroll of the U.S. government.

MAJOR ASSOCIATIONS

DEMOCRATIC NATIONAL COMMITTEE
430 South Capital Street, SE
Washington, DC 20003
Tel: 202-863-8000
Fax: 202-488-5043
www.democrats.org

LIBERTARIAN PARTY
2600 Virginia Avenue, NW, Suite 100
Washington, DC 20037
Tel: 202-333-0008
www.lp.org

REPUBLICAN NATIONAL COMMITTEE
310 First Street, SE
Washington, DC 20003
Tel: 202-863-8500
Fax: 202-863-8820
www.rnc.org

PROMOTER

A DAY IN THE LIFE

Promoters develop marketing strategies for events that range from rock concerts to international chess tournaments. Event promoters work with television, radio, special-events coordinators, ticket sellers, reviewers, bulk mailers, and local merchants to market a product. The profession is project-based, so individuals who want predictable hours and a steady workload should look elsewhere. Promoters view working long hours as a benefit: "When you're working, you're working all the time. When you're not, you pretty much make up your own schedule," is how one respondent described the rollercoaster. Promoters work on a team on which people with different skills—artistic, financial, copywriting, and statistical—come together to produce a seamlessly integrated strategy. This helter-skelter mix can turn into a clash of egos, ideas, and concepts. As one respondent said, "If you have to step on someone, do it." You'll also be recognized for your good ideas as well as your bad ones.

{ **tenacity** }

Few other professions place such a premium on creative thinking. Traditional advertising and marketing strategies can often prove too expensive or utilize to diffuse a medium for the standard entertainment event. "You have to be able to think inexpensively. Try pretending your budget was just cut in half, and you have to reach the same number of people," wrote one veteran promoter. A successful promoter has an unlimited imagination that outmatches the most limited budget. "Tenacity," wrote one person surveyed, "is what separated the sharks from the chum (chopped-up fish guts)." Attention to detail is also important. A great promoter will bend over backward for both the paying guests and the talent. Going the extra mile in hospitality for your act is a crucial part of keeping guests and talent coming back in the future.

Promoting is like gambling—a high-risk, high-return industry in which it is amazingly easy to lose your shirt because of one poor decision. People bond while scrambling to find inexpensive media outlets, dashing to events that only moments before were mere ideas, and running to coordinate all the details, but the relationship means nothing if the project is unsuccessful. A promoter cannot afford to be associated with a failed marketing strategy. The fall from grace can be swift and merciless, and many people who have endorsed failures or passed on enormously lucrative projects have quickly found themselves seeking work in other professions.

PAYING YOUR DUES

It takes a particular type of person to become a promoter; confidence and flamboyance help immeasurably. No undergraduate degree is required to enter this occupation, and rightly so—no undergraduate degree would properly prepare you for it. Understanding demographics, business, and publicity is important, but the two most valuable traits mentioned by our respondents are creativity and an ability to be in touch with your audience. Promoters need listening and organizational skills, charm, and style. In many cases, the difference between a financial bloodbath and a smash hit is solely the ability of the promoter, so the pressure is high and rapid career swings are not unusual.

Most concert promoters start out in college, where they can establish contacts with talent buyers and bands who come to play at the school. Booking agents are the most important contacts for promoters. An act can always find another promoter, so establishing and maintaining solid relationships with talent and agents is of utmost importance. Advertising or promotional personnel may go on to start their own businesses with as few as one or two steady clients. Shops tend to be small (65 percent of offices employ fewer than 25 people), and advancement occurs in short, intense flurries. The hours can be long and the future uncertain, but the field can be financially rewarding for those few individuals who achieve star status.

ASSOCIATED CAREERS

Only about 25 percent of promoters stay in the profession for life. More often it is a job for the risk-friendly, aggressive, and creative individual who started out in the field of public relations or advertising. Most people who leave the profession return to public relations, sales, advertising, political consulting, media buying, the film industry, or law.

PAST AND FUTURE

P. T. Barnum and Babe Ruth were two larger-than-life figures who promoted themselves to legendary status. To get people to pay attention to them, they had to build an image, make outrageous claims, or provide something unique, exciting, and exotic. The legacy of these fabulous marketers can be seen in companies like Coca-Cola and celebrity promoters like Don King, who use the media to promote their products and events.

The entertainment industry is expected to continue growing in the next several years. As the number of events that require promotional skills increases, the job market for promoters will expand. The scale of events, however, is likely to be smaller. Individuals with extensive knowledge of statistics, the Internet, and demographics have a bright future.

QUALITY OF LIFE

2 YEARS Two years is a significant period of time in the life of a promoter. A number of projects have gone from idea to completion; a number of them have stalled or failed somewhere during the process; and some of them never developed into anything beyond a mere idea. Promoters have experience researching, modeling, and examining demographics; conducting focus groups; doing interviews; making phone contacts; traveling; and pitching ideas. The ability to successfully pitch ideas is very important to individuals considering a future in this profession.

5 YEARS Sixty percent of individuals who began in the field have departed for other professions or returned to school. The hours get longer, the pay increases, the perquisites increase even more, and the opportunity for significant responsibility emerges for individuals with solid credentials. The farther up the ladder in this industry one wants to go, the more cutthroat it gets. Many promoters, even the best, suffer burnout.

10 YEARS Ten years in the entertainment marketing industry can be a lifetime. Individuals who have worked at a variety of agencies either start their own firms or consolidate their strength at the top of their current one. Another 10 percent leave for high-paying jobs in other fields. Client satisfaction is the telling point for whether the promoter, at this point, will continue to be successful or will decline. Some individuals who specialize in certain types of entertainment marketing—sports events, concerts, or movies—can fall victim to the cyclical nature of public opinion. Individuals who have ridden the elevator up during the boom period of one specialty area may find themselves in a helpless freefall if that field flops.

Every state has at least one large promoter and several smaller, specialized promoters with long histories and talent that is in demand, so this field can be very difficult to break into. Individuals who rise to the top are not always the most pleasant or the easiest to work with, and they rarely take kindly to ambitious young competitors.

MAJOR EMPLOYERS

DELSNER/SLATER ENTERPRISES
650 Madison Avenue
New York, NY 10022
Tel: 212-813-9400
www.livetonight.com

DON LAW COMPANY
36 Bay State Road
Cambridge, MA 01238
Tel: 617-547-0620
Fax: 617-864-9139

FORD MODELING AGENCY
142 Greene Street
New York, NY 10012
Tel: 212-753-6500
Fax: 212-966-1531
www.fordmodels.com

SONY PICTURES ENTERTAINMENT
10202 West Washington Boulevard
Culver City, CA 90232-3195
Tel: 310-244-4436
www.sony.com
Contact: Human Resources

PROPERTY MANAGER

PROFESSIONAL PROFILE

# of people in profession	293,000
Avg. hours per week	40
Avg. starting salary	$25,470
Avg. salary after 5 years	$36,880
Avg. salary 10 to 15 years	$56,000

SALARY ●
HOURS ●
EDUCATION ● ●

BOOKS, FILMS, AND TV SHOWS
FEATURING THE PROFESSION

- One Day at a Time
- The Super
- Three's Company

YOU'LL HAVE CONTACT WITH

- Electricians
- Plumbers
- Property owners
- Tenants

PROFESSIONALS READ

- Journal of Property Management

A DAY IN THE LIFE

Any residential or commercial property must be taken care of from both a physical and a tenant-relations standpoint, and that is what a property manager does. He or she maintains and upgrades facilities while acting as liaison between the owner of the property and tenants. In many cases, the property manager has the responsibility for attracting tenants to the property as well. Since most property managers are in charge of a number of properties at any time, the job can involve frantic work, unusual hours, and extremely difficult schedule coordination. "My desk looks like a hurricane hit it all the time," wrote one manager, adding that his paperwork burden isn't just large; "it scares me." It takes strong communications skills, strong organizational skills, and a flair for numbers to handle this demanding position.

> { My desk looks like a hurricane hit it all the time. }

"Everything that goes wrong is your problem," mentioned one property manager, pointing out that a property manager has the most client contact when disasters occur, such as a flooded basement, a heating system gone awry, or a burglary. This can be daunting for individuals who don't perform well in crisis situations. One respondent told us that the best property managers are "proactive rather than reactive." The more they can anticipate potential problems and prevent them, the fewer problems they have to deal with. When things do fall apart, often due to short-sighted owners who won't lay out sufficient money for upkeep, managers must respond quickly and decisively. More mundane tasks, such as collecting rent and coordinating garbage removal, cannot suffer because of unanticipated events.

Many property managers feel that the best feature of the profession is the chance to work with a variety of people on a number of different tasks: "I never know what my day's going to be like," as one put it. "I think I know. I've made lists of stuff to do. But as soon as you cross one thing out, two new things come up. It's a race to keep on top of everything. I love it." While property managers spend a lot of their day dealing with paperwork and talking on the telephone, the problems they deal with vary greatly from week to week and month to month, giving most property managers a sense of creative challenge that keeps the job fresh. On-site managers also have to show prospective tenants around the site and meet with resident boards and committees, which can mean evenings or weekends spent in meetings.

PAYING YOUR DUES

Most major employers ask that property managers have a bachelor's degree, although no formal requirements are inherent to the field. Course work that proves helpful to candidates includes real estate, organizational behavior, mathematics, accounting, finance, logic, psychology, and public relations. A few property managers who were responsible for recruiting new tenants stated that marketing courses were helpful as well. After being hired, many people attend brief weekend or three-day training programs, sponsored by the hiring company, that acquaint them with the concerns and obligations of the property manager. Individuals who wish to become property managers in the public sector—in subsidized federal housing, for example—must be certified, although certification carries weight in the private sector as well. Professional organizations such as the Institute of Real Estate Management or the National Organization of Home Builders administer these exams.

ASSOCIATED CAREERS

Since they are well-versed in the ins and outs of real estate, many property managers become commercial real estate agents. Only a few property managers with finance experience move into property development, particularly on a local level. Some of them become specialists in building maintenance and repair, using their industry connections to get regular work.

PAST AND FUTURE

While property managers can probably trace their roots back to the rent collectors in the service of extortionate landlords in pre-industrial times, in recent times, the position is more of a liaison between owner and tenant. Property managers can look forward to a strong future. Commercial, residential, and industrial property development is expected to result from growth in all sectors in the upcoming decade, and these newly developed properties will need managers to keep them running smoothly. Property managers will still be at the mercy of local economies, but if relocation is not a problem, the field should be open for at least the next several years.

QUALITY OF LIFE

2 YEARS Property managers are in charge of one or two properties as they learn the business in general and their company's specific protocols. Client contact is immediate in this business, and responsibilities run high right away. The only responsibility that may be withheld from the two-year professional is the ability to negotiate long-term contracts with maintenance companies or custodial services. Large offices will centralize this function; small ones will give that responsibility to experienced managers.

5 YEARS Five years into the profession, property managers may manage one large complex of buildings or a number of small properties. The hours and salaries increase, but responsibility for tenant satisfaction and the smooth maintenance of the property still rest with the manager. Many people switch employers in years three through seven, looking for the right balance between challenge and salary. Satisfaction is above average.

10 YEARS Individuals who have survived 10 years as property managers have developed a system to keep track of maintenance issues, financial obligations, and tenant happiness. A number begin to manage groups of less experienced property managers. Contacts made during the first five years (along with invaluable practical experience) come in handy as emergencies are dealt with swiftly and efficiently.

MAJOR EMPLOYERS

CENTURY 21
6 Sylvan Way
Parsippany, NJ 07054
Tel: 973-428-9700
Fax: 973-496-5955
www.century21.com
Contact: Human Resources

Most property managers operate locally. Look at real estate listings in your area for more employment opportunities.

MAJOR ASSOCIATIONS

INSTITUTE OF REAL ESTATE MANAGEMENT
430 North Michigan Avenue
Chicago, IL 60611-4090
Tel: 800-837-0706
Fax: 800-338-4736
www.irem.org

PUBLICIST

A DAY IN THE LIFE

A publicist gets press coverage for his or her client. The publicist is often the intermediary between the high-profile personality and members of the media. He or she usually wants his or her client to receive positive acclaim, but many publicists surveyed noted the old adage that "the only bad publicity is no publicity." Politicians and captains of industry require a little more specific spin on their press—they want to be seen as forward-looking and confident—but other professions are less picky, as in the case of the rock star who reveals the sordid details of his or her nightlife to cultivate a rough image. Publicists also perform damage control, and attempt to counteract any undesirable press coverage the client receives. This position as "last line of defense" is what distinguishes the adequate publicist from the extraordinary one. Good publicists can transform scandal into opportunity and create valuable name recognition for their clients.

{ go to the hottest parties in town }

Publicists don't work only for the famous. Sometimes they work for a little-known person or industry and generate press coverage. If a company desiring publicity is hampered by its esoteric nature or technical jargon, the publicist must translate its positions into easily understandable language. A major part of the publicist's day is spent writing press releases and creating press packets, which have photos and information about the publicized person or company. Publicists spend a lot of time on the phone. They put in long hours, and most of them receive little financial rewards in return. They operate under hectic conditions and must adhere to strict deadlines that coincide with publicity events, such as the release of a movie or the publishing of a book. They have to ensure that they get the appropriate information to the media in time for the event they are generating publicity for, such as a record release or automotive sale. They must always be available for comment (even when that comment is "no comment") and remain friends with members of the media, no matter how demanding the desires both of clients and of the reporters on whom they depend. But at the end of the day, they go to the hottest parties in town, the ones for their clients.

PAYING YOUR DUES

The most appropriate bachelor's degree for a publicist to hold is in communications, but business degrees are also looked on favorably by employers. In college, aspiring publicists should study public relations, public speaking, and writing. Candidates should also have some experience with copyediting. Depending on the publicist's desired area, other elective courses may include labor relations, economics, and politics. Most publicists recommend interning at a firm before plunging into this job—a low-responsibility position allows them to see the pace of the profession firsthand. Besides, it helps to make as many contacts as possible in this "it's-who-you-know" field. Some publicists have graduate degrees, although they are not required by any employer. All publicists start at the same entry-level positions and work their way up. Experience is the key to obtaining a good job, especially in the entertainment industry, which is the hardest to break into. The music industry is most likely to acknowledge and reward fresh insight given by new employees.

ASSOCIATED CAREERS

Public relations, marketing, and event planning are closely linked to the publicist's field. The event planner creates events to generate interest in whatever the publicist is promoting. Marketers study the community to determine how the client is perceived and how its members feel his or her image could be improved. Advertisers and writers often create the materials used by publicists. Programmers determine where and how frequently the company should advertise. Booking agents are responsible for procuring venues for publicity and anticipating the effect the events will have on the client's image. For instance, he or she may have to weigh the exposure that comes from being a guest on a major talk show against the potential friendliness or hostility of the host. Information officers perform many of the same duties as publicists, only they respond passively to inquiries and publicity, while the publicist actively seeks an interested audience.

PAST AND FUTURE

In the 1800s, to obtain more business, newspapers started the dubious practice of writing positive articles about their advertisers. This practice was halted by legislation soon after it began, but it paved the way for the public relations field. The publicist's field is an offshoot of the public relations arena. Ivy Ledbetter Lee was the first American to work in this capacity. He saw negative press surrounding different blue collar fields and trained the workers to respond to the media so that they would be seen in a more favorable light. Then, the government began hiring people to perform these activities on its behalf, and the label publicist was conceived.

Today, publicists work for anyone desiring coverage in the press, from politicians and companies to actors and lawyers. The future shows average growth for this profession, thanks to the ubiquity and influence of the media.

QUALITY OF LIFE

2 YEARS Most publicists are initially attracted to this field because of its perceived glamour. They soon find out that they have to roll up their sleeves and work hard. They usually stick it out, relying on the well-networked publicists around them for contacts and advice.

5 YEARS By this time, many publicists can relax a bit. They have made enough contacts that they don't have to struggle to be heard. Although they are still working long hours, they can begin to enjoy the glamour factor.

10 YEARS Many publicists are enjoying the influence they have over the media. Some of the best ones are looking to start their own firms or to become television gossip hosts on the small cable channels.

MAJOR EMPLOYERS

Many companies and celebrities have private publicists. Check your area and national trade magazines for more information about employment opportunities.

MAJOR ASSOCIATIONS

NATIONAL COUNCIL FOR MARKETING AND PUBLIC RELATIONS
PO Box 336039
Greesley, CO 80633
Tel: 970-330-0771
Fax: 970-330-0769
www.ncmpr.org

PUBLIC RELATIONS SOCIETY OF AMERICA
33 Maiden Lane, 11th Floor
New York, NY 10038
Tel: 212-460-1495
Fax: 212-995-0757
www.prsa.org
pr@prsa.org

REAL ESTATE AGENT/BROKER

A DAY IN THE LIFE

Buying or selling a house or apartment is one of the biggest decisions of a person's life, and real estate agents and brokers help people negotiate their way through what can be a confusing process. Though both are often called real estate agents, agents and brokers perform different tasks. The broker has more administrative responsibilities. There is usually one broker per estate, but often many agents are working with clients who are interested in the property.

When someone wants to sell or rent property, he or she usually calls a real estate agent. A large chunk of the agent's day may be spent on the phone obtaining listings for his or her agency. The agent also arranges to advertise the properties he or she is showing and may visit each property before it is shown to clients. One needs to know about everything from floor plans to heating systems to cesspools—he or she is a matchmaker and must know both sides of the equation. It's also important for an agent to be familiar with the neighborhoods he or she works in to counsel his or her clients about a property's fair market value. A good real estate agent is informed about things like schools, tax rates, and public transportation systems and should be aware of going mortgage rates.

$\left\{$ evenings and weekends $\right\}$

A real estate agent must manage delicate price negotiations when an interested buyer and seller hook up. "Negotiating skills are not just important but critical for real estate agents," as one respondent put it. The agent also coordinates the "closing" when a property is sold, which means the actual signing of papers and transfer of a property's title. Networking is a big part of the job—most real estate agents develop a group of attorneys, mortgage lenders, and contractors to whom they refer their clients. Finally, a real estate agent should be able to discern and be sensitive to a client's needs during what may be an uncertain time.

To be available when their clients have free time, real estate agents work many evenings and weekends. An experienced agent will sometimes avoid some of the weekend hours by having an "open house" and drafting a new agent to go and answer potential buyers' questions. Commercial real estate agents' jobs involve more research on market trends and an even more detailed attention to the needs of buyers. Since they work longer on each deal, commercial agents and brokers make fewer sales than residential agents but receive higher commissions.

PAYING YOUR DUES

About the only things real estate agents necassarily have in common are high school diplomas and communication skills. More and more people are entering the field with college degrees, and some colleges even offer courses in real estate. These may be helpful, as would other business courses, but most of the learning takes place after you've entered the field. In fact, many real estate agents come to the field from other, unrelated careers because of the flexible hours or the potential for part-time work.

Before you can use the title "realtor" or become a member of the National Association of Realtors, you must have a real estate license. Every state requires that a broker or agent undergo a series of examinations and accumulate some experience before he or she is granted this license. Many real estate boards offer preparatory classes. Once an individual has the license, it's usually renewed yearly without having to repeat the tests. But each state has its own test, so if you want to work in a different state, you need to pass the state-specific exam.

ASSOCIATED CAREERS

Careers associated with real estate often involve working with realtors. On the mortgage end, loan officers arrange the conditions for financing home purchases and act as liaisons between buyers and banks. Another possibility is the field of real estate law, which requires going to law school. Agents seeking further opportunities within the field have a few options, most of which involve setting up shop independently of brokers. Appraisers, for example, assess the fair market values of properties. Real estate counselors, likewise, are independent advisors who offer advice to buyers about the suitability of properties they are interested in.

PAST AND FUTURE

In 1908, the agency known as the National Association of Realtors was started and has continued to strive for high ethical standards in business and tax advantages for home buyers and sellers. The nomadic trend in American life and our ever-expanding population make real estate a business that grows at higher-than-average rates. The downside is that the market is always under the influence of economic fluctuations, and the biggest complaint realtors have is the resulting lack of stability in their incomes. Real estate agents cannot expect to earn steady incomes, since their pay is based on commissions, which may differ greatly.

QUALITY OF LIFE

2 YEARS — The beginning of the agent's career is spent on the phone as well as looking at and showing properties with hopes of finding buyers and sellers. This is a difficult time for agents, as they have not yet established reputations. They rely on the name of their firms to attract clients. There is lots of variety in the daily routine, but these beginners must be prepared for a period of long hours and no commissions as they learn the ropes. As one first-year agent told us, "I made literally zero dollars for seven months, but then suddenly had four sales in a row and made enough for the rest of the year."

5 YEARS — Many agents have developed a reputation by this time and are rewarded with referrals and repeat clients. Some agents will still experience frustration with low sales and meager paychecks, however, which accounts for the high turnover rate in the field.

10 YEARS — By this time most agents have advanced to the highest levels of their firms, often working with blue-chip properties. Many of them now have assistants to help with legwork. But the plateau reached at this point often prompts agents to strike out independently and start their own firms, though the task of getting established can be arduous.

MAJOR EMPLOYERS

CENTURY 21
World Headquarters
One Campus Drive
Parsippany, NJ 07054
Tel: 877-221-2765
www.century21.com

DOUGLAS ELLIMAN
575 Madison Avenue
New York, NY 10022
Tel: 800-355-4626
www.elliman.com

SOTHEBY'S INTERNATIONAL REALTY
450 Columbus Avenue
New York, NY 10024
Tel: 212-400-8700
Fax: 212-400-8799
www.sothebysrealty.com

MAJOR ASSOCIATIONS

NATIONAL ASSOCIATION OF REAL ESTATE BROKERS INC.
9831 Greenbelt Road
Lanham, MD 20706
Tel: 301-552-9340
Fax: 301-552-9216
www.nareb.com

NATIONAL ASSOCIATION OF REALTORS
Corporate Headquarters
3070 Russell Ranch Road
Westlake Village, CA 91362
Tel: 805-557-2300
Fax: 805-557-2680
www.realtor.com

SOCIETY OF INDUSTRIAL AND OFFICE REALTORS
1201 New York Avenue, NW, Suite 350
Washington, DC 20005
Tel: 202-449-8200
Fax: 202-216-9325
E-mail: admin@sior.com
www.sior.com

RESTAURATEUR

A DAY IN THE LIFE

Owning a restaurant is a labor of love, and most restaurateurs work long hours. When his or her establishment is open only for dinner, the restaurateur usually starts his or her day in the late morning. Restaurateurs have a number of daily tasks to complete before the staff arrives. First, he or she checks "the book," which contains reports from managers about whatever happens in the restaurant each night. The owner keeps tabs on items to be ordered, customer complaints, and staff-scheduling conflicts, some of which are recorded in the book. He or she studies the accounting records daily and stays on top of the restaurant's financial situation. He or she may also take on duties like confirming reservations. Usually, restaurateurs also find time to glance through { ready to socialize } wine and food industry papers and read the restaurant review section in the newspaper.

When the doors open, the restaurant owner must be dressed and ready to socialize until the last customer leaves. It is extremely important that a restaurant owner have exceptional name and face recollection. The most successful owners report that the majority of their clientele are regular customers. The easiest way to gain repeat business is by offering seemingly special treatment; remembering a customer's name or favorite table is always impressive. The restaurateur acts as a host, chatting with customers and making sure they are satisfied. Approaching customers while they are dining also helps the owner check on staff members. While this may seem intrusive when done by waiters, restaurant patrons usually love to have the owner inquire about the food and service.

PAYING YOUR DUES

Restaurateurs come from many walks of life, but mostly they have experience within the industry. A restaurant owner can be either a "backer" or an active owner. Backers provide funding to the active owners and entrust them to run the place. Very few people back restaurants as their primary occupation, since the sole job requirement is having access to large amounts of cash. The financial rewards of backing a restaurant can be great, as backers are the first to receive profits. For hands-on owners a good place to start is a college or school that offers a restaurant and hotel management program, but in fact most owners don't follow this formal educational route. Instead, most have paid their dues as waiters, bartenders, and managers, and it's always a plus if they have experience with bookkeeping and accounting, too.

Before opening, the restaurant owner spends some time scouting a location. If he or she is interested in a space that didn't previously hold a restaurant, the owner has to determine whether the building can be affordably converted for restaurant use. Other market studies are usually done to determine what type of restaurant would work best in that particular community and location. When all of this has been figured out, the restaurateur must obtain financing, either through a backer or a bank. The owner then usually hires all the founding staff, seeks out wholesalers and establishes relations with them, and oversees the design of the restaurant, from decor to menu. Then comes the stressful task of procuring a liquor license. Most towns and cities allot only a specified number of licenses, and often the potential owner must negotiate a price from a business that is closing. When the doors open the owner's work is far from finished. Failure rates for new restaurants are high, and an owner must make sure that his or her establishment keeps pace with the times and consistently operates at a high level.

ASSOCIATED CAREERS

Many careers can satisfy food lovers who don't want to commit their time and bank accounts to owning a restaurant. Waiters, bartenders, bus staff, and hosts ensure that the front of the house is running smoothly. The majority of these jobs rely on tips instead of salaries, and so earnings are influenced by the season and night of the week. A restaurant manager runs the front of the house and acts on behalf of the owner in his or her absence. Chefs, sous-chefs, and bakers need formal training at a culinary institute to be taken seriously in the food community. The chef is usually the heart of the restaurant. A chef not only prepares food, but he or she also schedules the kitchen staff, creates and continually updates the menu, and often shops for fine ingredients. The wine steward is another important position in upscale restaurants, where he or she uses an extensive knowledge of wine to select the restaurant's wine list. Wine stewards will also sometimes host wine-tasting dinners to introduce their clientele to new labels. Catering is another venue for food experts who want more variety and a less complicated operation. Franchise owners can open a restaurant without having to worry about any decision-making, such as designing the menu or decorating the establishment. Other aspiring owners open bars or nightclubs.

PAST AND FUTURE

The restaurant as we think of it today did not exist until 1765, when A. Boulanger opened a restaurant in Paris. For about a century after that, restaurants tended to be expensive and mainly catered to the social elite. With the growth of the travel industry at the end of the nineteenth century, restaurants became accessible to almost everyone. Today, 40 percent of our allotted food budget is spent in eating and drinking establishments. The restaurant industry will continue to grow, although it will still be an extremely risky business. Recently, the number both of successful and failed restaurants has climbed each year.

QUALITY OF LIFE

2 YEARS More than three-quarters of new restaurants fail within the first seven months, primarily due to poor cash flow management. Those owners who survive report feeling very stressed—every review brings tears of either joy or pain. At this time, restaurants are usually not showing big profits but are just remaining afloat. In these first years, owners are working long into the night and still anxiously awaiting the possibility of taking some time off.

5 YEARS Most restaurateurs who've made it through the first two years are still working away. They begin to show profits at this time and have usually completely paid off their loans. A few look forward to buying out backers. Mostly, they are happy to be down to working only six 10-hour-days per week.

10 YEARS A decade into the business, restaurateurs spend much less time in the house. They have learned to entrust the late hours to general managers. The most successful ones pay surprise visits to the restaurant to safeguard the high standards of the kitchen. As always, they keep an eye on the books. The owners who flourish tend to hire the most inventive chefs and pay close attention to trends happening in the big cities.

MAJOR EMPLOYERS
BRINKER INTERNATIONAL
6820 LBJ Freeway
Dallas, TX 75240
Tel: 972-980-9917
www.brinker.com

MCDONALD'S CORPORATION
2111 McDonald's Drive
Oak Brook, IL 60523
Tel: 800-244-6227
www.mcdonalds.com

PARK HYATT LOS ANGELES
2151 Avenue of the Stars
Los Angeles, CA 90067
Tel: 310-277-1234
Fax: 310-785-9240

MAJOR ASSOCIATIONS
EDUCATIONAL FOUNDATION OF THE NATIONAL RESTAURANT ASSOCIATION
175 West Jackson Boulevard, Suite 1500
Chicago, IL 60604-2702
Tel: 800-765-2122 or 312-715-1010
E-mail: info@nraef.org
www.nraef.org

RETAIL SALESPERSON

A DAY IN THE LIFE

Retail salespeople can do their jobs from behind a counter, over the phone, or even by visiting their clients personally, whether they're right down the hall or on the other side of the world. Most salespeople pitch their products dozens of times a day, five days a week. Whatever the product, they must convey confidence and goodwill, for making a sale requires a trusting consumer. People in sales must be ready to deal with rejection and with disgruntled customers. As products and market conditions change constantly, salespeople must adapt if they want to survive. In fields such as consumer electronics in general and computers in particular, the rapid pace of change can be as overwhelming as it is exciting.

{ dynamic capitalist economy }

A skilled salesperson knows the product he or she is selling and understands the needs of his or her customers. Salespeople often say they want to help people find what they need and bristle at accusations that they are selling "just for the money." After all, salespeople are a necessary part of a dynamic capitalist economy. Moreover, many salespeople truly enjoy the human interactions as much as the more palpable thrill of closing a sale. For some sales people, the demands of travel detract from the time they can spend with their families; others enjoy the travel or find they can work from home.

A good sales record leads to a better job with a better salary and often extra incentives such as higher commissions. Most of the salespeople we talked to devote their sales-related reading to specialized journals dedicated to the professional salesperson or to the individual markets they serve. The amount of time salespeople devote to their job depends on what they sell and on their own personal needs. Nevertheless, even the best salespeople often work constantly because "you're only as good as your last month's sales."

PAYING YOUR DUES

The sales profession values experience over education. A specialized degree is not necessary to pursue a career in sales. An understanding of the product is important no matter what you sell, but the salesperson must learn to communicate well with clients, whether it's face-to-face, over the phone, or by letter or e-mail. Ambitious salespeople may study marketing and sales techniques at college or business school either before or during their sales careers.

ASSOCIATED CAREERS

The skills involved in sales transfer well to other careers. Practicality, persuasiveness, and tenacity are qualities esteemed in managers, and many salespeople use their job as a stepping stone to consulting or management positions. In addition, some salespeople may be recruited into positions as manufacturer's field sales representatives for products they were formerly selling at the retail level.

PAST AND FUTURE

Complex economies like ours are based on competition from various companies selling similar products. Successful competitors outsell their rivals, and companies know that to succeed they must hire people with expertise in selling.

In these complex and fluctuating economic times, both the local mom-and-pop shops and behemoth superstores have multitiered levels of staff to supervise their operations, and often the training and hiring is done from within. The salesperson on the floor of the ladies lingerie department, for example, may very well be destined to move into commissioned sales, management, finance and auditing, operations, e-commerce and IT, merchandising, buying, or entrepreneurship.

QUALITY OF LIFE

2 YEARS — Entry-level sales jobs may pay minimum wage, often without a commission. Pay scales vary according to the industry. The grind of frequent rejection and the constant interaction with others can be tiring, but for some, the triumph of making a sale can be its own reward. Take this time to learn personal strategies for being a convincing salesperson, no matter what it is you happen to be selling.

5 YEARS — Salaries are considerably higher at this stage, and proven salespeople can negotiate for higher commissions or more lucrative accounts. A change in product lines or entry into a new area can spell a need for rapid reeducation about the product and the best way to sell it.

10 YEARS — After 10 years, many salespeople have settled into management positions and may be responsible for a sales force or important accounts. Veteran salespeople may be able to cut back on their hours while still bringing in significant business to the company. Others may be drawn to the travel and business opportunities of international sales.

MAJOR EMPLOYERS
BLOOMINGDALE'S
1000 Third Avenue
New York, NY 10022
Tel: 212-705-2000
E-mail: careers@bloomingdales.com
www.bloomingdales.com
Contact: Human Resources

GAP, INC.
Resume Center
PO Box 931
Nutting Lake, MA 01865-0931
Attn: GDC
E-mail: careers@gap.com
www.gapinc.com
Contact: Executive Recruiting

MAJOR ASSOCIATIONS
NATIONAL RETAIL FEDERATION
325 7th Street, NW, Suite 1100
Washington, DC 20004
Tel: 800-673-4692 or 202-783-7971
Fax: 202-737-2849
www.nrf.com

SERVICE SALES REPRESENTATIVE

A DAY IN THE LIFE

A service sales representative sells the services his or her company offers, reaching his or her customers over the telephone, in person, and through letter campaigns. A service sales rep can work for nearly anyone who has a service (as opposed to a good) to sell. Service sales representatives have to be good communicators, persuasive talkers, and excellent listeners. The most important quality of a service sales representative, however, is the ability to sell. Indeed, his or her paycheck depends on it—many service sales representatives work for a low base salary plus either commissions on sales or a potentially large bonus. This lays the groundwork for a high-pressure environment; but pressure, as one rep told us, "is what turns coal into diamonds." Sales representatives must first and foremost be { time on the road } confident with their knowledge of the services their company offers. "Most of your job as a sales [representative] is answering questions," wrote one respondent, "and if you don't have answers for your clients, how can you expect them to trust you?" The issue of trust is central to any purchaser/vendor relationship. For the sales representative, having information at his or her disposal is the only way to demonstrate to the potential client that he or she understands the product's uses and limitations. To maintain these high levels of credibility, many companies require that sales representatives engage in internal education programs that keep them up-to-date on changing service lines and improved service features. Sales representatives not only have to adjust themselves to the services their company offers, but also to the needs and sensibilities of their clients. "You don't sell to a mom-and-pop store the way you'd try to sell to IBM," said one telephone service sales rep. Experience is the best way to learn this skill. "Experience is incredibly valuable in sales," wrote a 10-year veteran.

Two aspects of the job were recorded as most frustrating on our surveys. First, simply by virtue of what he or she does, a service sales representative often encounters rejection and puts effort into many deals that do not close. It's important to be able to see that a failed deal is not necessarily a personal failure. Second, the job breeds a certain amount of isolation. "No one is a salesman's friend," wrote one manager of service sales representatives, adding "it can be a very lonely job." Many representatives spend a lot of time on the road, in meetings, and at client dinners, and many of these hours are clocked on the weekends. The price they pay is returned in the form of bonuses, commission, and control over their schedule if not the number of hours they work.

PAYING YOUR DUES

No professional certification is required for service sales representative, and there are no formal educational requirements. A certificate in professional sales is available through continuing education programs such as Sales and Marketing Executives International, and more and more people are entering the profession with a college education. Course work that sales representatives find helpful to them in their profession includes marketing, business, economics, finance, public speaking, sociology, and psychology. Most large employers run established training programs for newly hired service sales reps that last between three weeks and three months. These training programs educate newcomers about services the company offers, the techniques of successful sales representatives, and accounting procedures and generally include interactive exercises to give future representatives some sales experience. Smaller places may not have training programs but will instead pair a newcomer with an experienced sales representative. Employers look for prior experience that demonstrates a self-motivating personality and strong interpersonal along with organizational skills.

ASSOCIATED CAREERS

Service sales representatives often go into other sales-related areas. One consequence, however, of learning all about a company's products is that service sales representatives make excellent internal managers and executives; as a result, sales representatives often take on other, more supervisory positions in their companies.

PAST AND FUTURE

Service sales representatives are a product of urbanization. As greater numbers of people needed more services, competition began to increase between shops and expanding the sales base became critical. Service sales representatives should fare well in the beginning of this century. Service industries are expected to grow faster than all other industries in the United States, and each company is expected to spend significant capital attempting to expand its customer base. Creative and motivated people should find opportunities available that reward their hard work and selling skills.

QUALITY OF LIFE

2 YEARS Those representatives who have been through training programs are having more success than those individuals who have not, due to both superior education in company strategies and generally superior sales representative support. The hours are long, and success is limited, but many people point to one or two difficult sales that went through as turning points. It's hard work to maintain relationships with existing clients and recruit new ones as well. Satisfaction is average, and salaries are low to average.

5 YEARS This is the period in which a sales representative distinguishes him- or herself in the field. Many representatives spend long hours searching for potential clients, but with high levels of success. Skills acquired in the field prove invaluable in years three through seven, and salaries can rise significantly. Some individuals attain the title of senior service sales representative and are put in charge of individuals with less experience. Satisfaction is high; the five-year survivor is, generally, at the top of his or her game.

10 YEARS Individuals who have managed to last 10 years in this field must love the challenge of selling, as many of them tell us that by years eight and nine the profession becomes a bit more difficult. The nature of the work does not change, but the long hours that seemed effortless before are less exciting, and the frustration at deals not closing gets less bearable. Many successful sales representatives consider managerial or executive shifts at this point, giving up life in the field for the stability of the office. Salaries can decrease overall for those individuals making this shift, but the salaries become more stable. The hours decrease; satisfaction drops, but then ultimately improves.

MAJOR EMPLOYERS
THE DUN AND BRADSTREET CORPORATION
103 JFK Parkway
Short Hills, NJ 07078
Tel: 800-234-3867
E-mail: HRSourcing@dnb.com
www.dnb.com

INTEL CORPORATION
2200 Mission College Boulevard
Santa Clara, CA 95052
Tel: 800-628-8686 or 408-765-8080
www.intel.com

MAJOR ASSOCIATIONS
AMERICAN MANAGEMENT ASSOCIATION
1601 Broadway
New York, NY 10019
Tel: 800-262-9699 or 212-586-8100
Fax: 212-903-8168
www.amanet.org

SALES AND MARKETING EXECUTIVES INTERNATIONAL
PO Box 1390
Sumas, WA 98295-1390
Tel: 312-893-0751
Fax: 604-855-0165
www.smei.org

SMALL BUSINESS OWNER

BOOKS, FILMS, AND TV SHOWS
FEATURING THE PROFESSION

- **Bringing Home the Business: The 30 Truths Every Home Business Owner Must Know**
- **Chocolat**
- **Diary of a Small Business Owner: A Personal Account of How I Built a Profitable Business**
- **You've Got Mail**

YOU'LL HAVE CONTACT WITH

- **Consumers**
- **Employees**
- **Suppliers**

PROFESSIONALS READ

- **Business Week Frontier**
- **Entrepreneur Magazine**
- **The Small Business Advocate**

A DAY IN THE LIFE

The small business owner is the backbone of the American economy. Ninety-nine percent of all employers are small business owners. They provide 75 percent of the new jobs created every year, and they are responsible for 96 percent of all exported goods. Small business owners work out of garages, small stores on main streets, and huge corporate campuses. Before you begin selling T-shirts in Times Square or offering oranges in Orlando, you need a business plan. A business plan is your roadmap to success. It includes a description of your product or services, how you are going to finance your business (loans, investors, etc.), deadlines for your business and the ultimate goal. As a small business owner, you need to be aware of the six M's:

{ the most risky legal career you can choose }

1. Mission: You have to know exactly what your services will do for your clients.

2. Market: You have to know who your clients are and how you can find them.

3. Message: Your mission has to be clear enough for your market to understand who you are and what you have to offer.

4. Media: This is the best way to get your message out into the world (via radio, print, television, skywriters).

5. Method: You know what to do, with whom, with what, when, and how to do it. You're in control of your business.

6. Management: This is your way of operating your business so that your clients are completely satisfied.

An ideal small business owner knows how to make plans, solve problems, hire, train, motivate, and lead employees. Being a small business owner is risky; it is probably the most risky legal career you can choose. But, with a lot of hard work—and we mean a lot—a dash of determination, and plenty of luck, the rewards of starting your own business can be excellent (think Bill Gates).

PAYING YOUR DUES

Starting your own business is not easy. Some statistics show that small businesses will not see a significant profit for two years (although you do need to show a profit after the third year, or the IRS may think you are trying to hide something). Owning your own business is not a nine-to-five job. Self-employed contract workers (writers, consultants) may work long hours under tight deadlines, while store owners may spend anywhere from 80–120 hours or more a week maintaining their businesses. And then there are the regulations. Federal, state, and city laws must be followed to remain in business. Small business owners also have to adapt to the ever-fickle customer.

ASSOCIATED CAREERS

Once they've been their own bosses—even if it's for a few years—some small business owners find they can't do anything else. For those individuals who may crave the comfort of large corporations, they can easily find jobs as sales associates, financial analysts, and in other positions that match their skill sets.

PAST AND FUTURE

The small business owner has been around since the days of bartering services. Throughout the years, small business owners have provided goods and services, employment, and government taxes. In a society based on capitalism, small business owners can thrive, as long as they provide a product or a service that people need or want. More than 66 percent of new businesses remained open two years, 49 percent at least four years, and 30 percent at least six years. Three percent of the self-employed own franchises, and more than half of the self-employed work at home.

QUALITY OF LIFE

2 YEARS — Long hours, little rest, and meager amounts of money fill the first two years of being your own boss. This is the make-or-break time, when almost 40 percent of new businesses fold. But if you've got the will, determination, and the means, making it over the two-year hump can give you the confidence and cash to continue.

5 YEARS — By now, the small business owner has been working long enough to get the kinks out. Problems like delinquent suppliers, lack of customers, and possible employee dissatisfaction have been met and hopefully resolved in a way that prepares the small business owner to meet the challenges of some of the bigger bumps in the road (like, say, a global economic slowdown).

10 YEARS — Most small business owners who are still around after 10 years find they have more time on their hands. If business is strong, employees are happy and productive, and customers are satisfied, the small business owner can take more time to ponder the possibilities of expansion—in a word: franchise.

MAJOR ASSOCIATIONS

SBA HEADQUARTERS
409 3rd Street, SW
Washington, DC 20416
Tel: 800-827-5722
www.sba.gov

SMALL BUSINESS HELP CENTER, INC.
PO Box 98
Pleasant Garden, NC 27313
www.helpbizowners.com

STOCKBROKER

A DAY IN THE LIFE

A stockbroker invests in the stock market for individuals or corporations. Only members of the stock exchange can conduct transactions, so whenever individuals or corporations want to buy or sell stocks, they must go through a brokerage house. Stockbrokers often advise and counsel their clients on appropriate investments. Brokers explain the workings of the stock exchange to their clients, gather information from them about their needs and financial abilities, and then determine the best investments for them. The broker then sends the order out to the floor of the securities exchange by computer or by phone. When the transaction has been made, the broker supplies the client with the price. The buyer pays for the stock, and the broker transfers the title of the stock to the client and performs clearing and settlement procedures.

{ fast-paced office }

The beginning stockbroker's first priority is learning the market. One broker said, "First you have to decide whether you have an interest in the stock market. This will determine how well you'll do. If you're just interested in making money, you won't get very far." Stockbrokers spend their time in a fast-paced office, usually working from nine to five, unless they are just starting out or have to meet with clients. The new broker spends many hours on the phone building up a client base. Sometimes brokers teach financial education classes to expose themselves to potential investors who may then become their clients.

PAYING YOUR DUES

A college degree is not required, but most brokers have one. Brokers have to be licensed. A license is obtained by passing the General Securities Registered Representative Examination and, in many cases, posting a bond. Individuals may take this test after they have been employed by a brokerage firm for four months. Firms use these four months as an on-the-job training period to prepare their workers for the test. Many states also require the candidate to take the Uniform Securities Agents State Law Examination. These tests are designed to ensure the candidate's knowledge of all aspects of the stock market. After passing these tests, an individual is considered a trainee. While working full-time, he or she takes classes and trains for up to two years. Employees are expected to take training courses throughout their careers to be aware of developments in the field.

Individuals with prior work experience have the greatest opportunities for becoming a stockbroker. Few people become brokers straight out of college. Most employers seek applicants who have already succeeded in other fields, such as insurance sales. If you know your interests lie in the market, study economics, finance, computers, and business management in college. Many employers view ambition as the most important quality a candidate can possess.

ASSOCIATED CAREERS

The sales aspects and the need to build up a client base are similar for stockbrokers and insurance and real estate agents. Financial planners create and execute financial plans for people or businesses. They ascertain their clients' needs, resources, and goals and use this information to draw up a financial plan that suits the individual or the company. Traders are the people you see in the movies yelling on the chaotic floor of the stock exchange. They perform the actual exchanges.

PAST AND FUTURE

The stock market is strongly affected by economic booms and busts. The most famous bust occurred in October 1929 (also known as the Great Crash, or Black Tuesday), which caused many investors to leap out of the windows of their offices on Wall Street. The industry has matured a great deal since then—now the markets have automatic limits on how far average stock prices can rise or fall in a given session—but historically, only those brokers with iron stomachs have survived in this high-risk, high-stakes industry. The outlook for stockbrokers is positive, as economic growth is anticipated. Deregulation of the industry is allowing many stockbrokers to expand their responsibilities, bringing about a corresponding increase in their client base. Increased concern about financing pension plans is also causing many people to turn to stockbrokers for advice, and the stock market continues to attract increasing numbers of individual investors. This is a boom or bust business, however, so neither upswings nor downturns last forever.

QUALITY OF LIFE

2 YEARS Stockbroking is an extremely competitive business—one of the most competitive of all. There is heavy burnout in the early years due to outrageous hours—all-nighters are routine occurrences for eager and ambitious upstarts—and many novice brokers fail to establish an adequate client base early on. Individuals that stay find the work exciting but anxiety provoking. There is greater security in larger companies but generally a longer wait for advancement and "the big bucks."

5 YEARS Individuals who get through the first few rocky years tend to stay in the field for an extended period of time. Many of them find the high salaries a delicious payback for those first years spent toiling "in the trenches." Leaving for a master's degree in business administration is common at this point for individuals who want to return for top management positions in the industry.

10 YEARS At this point, brokers are enjoying the fruits of their extensive and intensive education and training. Advancement in this field comes in the form of more and bigger accounts or management positions. Occasionally, it culminates in partnership in the firm. Some individuals even retire at this point, but most people like the industry and stick around for years after they've earned pots of money.

MAJOR ASSOCIATIONS
NATIONAL ASSOCIATION OF INVESTMENT PROFESSIONALS
12664 Emmer Place, Suite 201
St. Paul, MN 55124
Tel: 952-322-4322
E-mail: tokeefe@naip.com
www.naip.com

MAJOR EMPLOYERS
BARCLAYS CAPITAL
200 Park Avenue
New York, NY 10038
Tel: 212-412-4000
www.barcap.com
Contact: Human Resources

J.P. MORGAN
345 Park Avenue
New York, NY 10154-1002
Tel: 800-576-6209
www.jpmorgan.com

STUNT DOUBLE

BOOKS, FILMS, AND TV SHOWS
FEATURING THE PROFESSION

- **Crouching Tiger, Hidden Dragon**
- **Die Hard**
- **Double Dare**
- **The Fall Guy**
- **I Am Jackie Chan: My Life in Action**

YOU'LL HAVE CONTACT WITH

- **Actors**
- **Agents**
- **Directors**
- **Producers**
- **Special effects technicians**
- **Stunt coordinators**

PROFESSIONALS READ

- **Burns, Falls, and Crashes: Interviews with Movie Stunt Performers**
- **Fight Direction for Stage and Screen**
- **Sword Fighting: A Manual for Actors and Directors**

A DAY IN THE LIFE

If your heroes include Jackie Chan, Evel Kneivel, or Enzo, the stunt dog for Eddy on the sitcom *Frasier,* or if your hobbies include jumping from 50-story buildings or sword-fighting on top of speeding trains, then you may have a fulfilling career ahead of you as a stunt double. Hired as actors, stunt doubles work on any scene that has the potential for causing injury. Like actors, most stunt doubles work as freelancers. There's no cubicle or suit and tie required in this industry. A stunt double's version of a board meeting may entail working out the kinks of diving into a burning car or colliding head-on with a tractor trailer. It takes a lot of timing, experience, and an occasional prop to work out a logical—and more importantly, safe—sequence. Stunts are often uncomfortable to perform. Some may involve spending long { high-pressure, high-stakes situations } periods of time in an awkward place or position—underwater or on a stunt plane, for example. Most stunt doubles specialize in a certain kind of action, such as driving, piloting, combat fighting, or falling.

Most of the work takes place on location. Locations may range from a studio in Burbank or a rooftop in Manhattan to the Costa Rican rainforest or the Sahara Desert. A 15-second fight scene can take up to two days to perfect, and directors and stunt coordinators spend countless hours planning every moment of every sequence. The hours are long, and if filming starts at 7:30 A.M., then hair, makeup, and wardrobe requirements typically entail a 4:30 A.M. arrival and a subsequent 18-hour day. Time on the set is spent studying the sequence of action, especially if other stunt people are involved; warming up and stretching before performing; and making sure all safety equipment meets the necessary standards. Stunt doubles are not just hired for their skills, though; they must also resemble the actors whose "doubles" they are meant to be. This may involve picking up certain mannerisms or movements characteristic of a particular actor. Though some actors eagerly undertake their own stunts, there are generally a few contractual limitations on what they can and cannot do. As a result, there's always a double on the set who is ready to crash through a window if called on to do so. In many cases, there is time to practice the stunt ahead of time—unless the scene involves something that crashes or burns. In that case, there is often only one chance to get a perfect shot. Once a car is demolished or a set burned, there's no bringing it back to film a second take. In that respect, the job can be particularly stressful and is ideal for those who work well in high-pressure, high-stakes situations.

PAYING YOUR DUES

There are no specific educational requirements for stunt doubles. One of the best ways to break into the world of Hollywood stunts is to cultivate a strong set of the skills that production coordinators seek out, namely those involving gymnastics, tumbling and trampolines, martial arts, advanced driving of motorbikes and cars, stage combat, mountain climbing, horseback riding, and, of course, first aid. There are stunt schools that offer programs for serious professionals interested in pursuing a stunt career. Any of a variety of sports, including waterskiing, scuba diving, high diving, hang gliding, parachuting, and boxing, would also prove invaluable. Stunt people are advised to specialize in one or several types of sporting or physical activities and also to acquire some experience in a range of others.

ASSOCIATED CAREERS

After one too many bumps or bruises, a stunt double may opt to take on the less dangerous role of stunt coordinator, in which he or she would rarely perform stunts, but would still be intimately involved in arranging and planning them. Stunt doubles may alternatively venture into the realm of special effects. Special effects technicians design and manage the effects that bring the action to life, such as fires, explosions, and crashes. As a stunt double, you can always do what others may have predicted: run off with the circus.

PAST AND FUTURE

As trick pilots were performing across the United States during the 1910s and 1920s, Hollywood filmmakers began to capitalize on the public's burgeoning interest in aviation. They did this by incorporating flight scenes in movies. While air shows certainly helped draw attention to aviation, movies arguably helped fuel even greater interest in pilots and in flight. The primary sources of the success of these aviation-oriented films were the stunt pilots who began to emerge in Hollywood during this era. Although many stunt pilots viewed their jobs as "precision work," which implied some degree of safety, in fact the work was extremely dangerous; and Hollywood aerial daredevils, who performed seemingly impossible tasks, took great risks executing a wide range of feats. Their bravery and determination undoubtedly contributed to the growing popularity of aviation in the first half of the twentieth century.

The 1930s marked the beginning of Hollywood's glory days. It was during this action-filled period that the modern profession of stunts truly began. Westerns were the favored genre of the day. Moviegoers fell in love with the romantic vision of cowboy heroes and their adventuresome heritage. Producers quickly hired up all the rough range riders and rodeo stars they could find and set them to work in creating and carrying out stunts. The best of them all was rodeo rider Yakima Canutt, the first true legend of the stunt community.

With the advent of new technology, stunt doubles are placed in dangerous situations less frequently, as filmmakers turn to relatively inexpensive (and much safer) computer graphics effects that employ harnesses, fans, blue screens, and a broad array of other devices and digital effects.

QUALITY OF LIFE

2 YEARS Many stunt performers start out as extras, positions in which they obtain experience on the set and begin to network with the actors, directors, producers, and agents who will help them advance in their careers. After making themselves known to stunt coordinators around town, they may land a job as an assistant, for which they may execute such mundane tasks as carrying knee pads back and forth, all the while trying to absorb as much on-the-set stunt knowledge as possible. Sooner or later, they'll find themselves jumping off buildings and bridges in more low-budget films and garnering experience to add to their head shots.

5 YEARS Many performers spend their first few years doing nonunionized work. They tend to spend more time with mentors on the set than they do in front of the camera. After the first grueling years of extra work and entry-level stunts, a well-rounded stunt performer's best bet is to start focusing on one area of expertise. An experienced stunt double with the right networking skills can become part of a specific actor's support crew and travel from one set to another along with the cooks, trainers, and assistants whom the actor employs.

10 YEARS Age plays heavily in the career path of a stunt performer; and after 10 years in the business, most performers move to coordinating stunts instead of enacting them. Stunt coordinators are usually at the top of the stunt field and may move around the technical sides of the film and theater industry or decide to go into directing or producing. Outside of the entertainment industries, they may become coaches or personal trainers or give workshops and seminars on performing stunts.

MAJOR EMPLOYERS
Stunt performers are freelance employees who typically find work across the entertainment industry with the help of agents.

MAJOR ASSOCIATIONS
AMERICAN FEDERATION OF TELEVISION AND RADIO ARTISTS
4340 East-West Highway, Suite 204
Bethesda, MD 20814
www.aftra.org

SCREEN ACTORS GUILD
5757 Wilshire Boulevard
Los Angeles, CA 90036
Tel: 323-954-1600
www.sag.org

STUNTWOMEN'S ASSOCIATION OF MOTION PICTURES
Tel: 818-762-0907
E-mail: stuntwomen@stuntwomen.com
www.stuntwomen.com

UNITED STUNTMEN'S ASSOCIATION
www.stuntschool.com

TELECOMMUNICATIONS SPECIALIST

BOOKS, FILMS, AND TV SHOWS
FEATURING THE PROFESSION
- The 21st Century
- The History of California
- Videowave

YOU'LL HAVE CONTACT WITH
- Computer engineers
- Construction managers
- Electricians
- Information managers

PROFESSIONALS READ
- Data Communications
- Datamation
- Information Week

A DAY IN THE LIFE

Telecommunications specialists design voice and data communication systems, supervise the installation of these systems, and provide maintenance and service to clients after the installation is completed. Systems can range from a connection between two offices on different floors of the same building to networking databases, voicemail, and electronic mail systems throughout globally distributed offices of multinational organizations. Specializations include voice transmission, cellular capabilities, data communication, cable-to-modem communication, and satellite communication capabilities. Specialists act as information distributors, client representatives, construction supervisors, and maintenance liaisons. Handling this variety of responsibilities requires good communication skills, a firm understanding of technical requirements, and an ability to work closely with other professionals.

{ First, listen. }

According to our respondents, although telecommunications is a technology driven field, the basic rule is, "First, listen." Everything a client wants to be able to do today, tomorrow, and in ten years has to be considered during the planning sessions, and often clients can't identify their needs today and have no idea about tomorrow. Telecommunications specialists work closely with their clients during the planning stages, trying to elicit information from the clients who will help the specialist determine and satisfy their needs. For example, if a company has plans to open a branch office overseas, the telecommunications specialist should be aware of this when planning the system. "It's all systems architecture," one former computer science major said, "except it's in relation to data and voice technology." Many telecommunications specialists work on-site for significant periods of time, supervising system installation and explaining system operation and maintenance to the client. They often step back from the day-to-day management of the project during the installation and let their cabling and wiring experts do their job, as micromanaging a project can be fatal in this profession. Most telecommunications specialists remain their client's contact for any service or maintenance requirements. Although telecommunications specialists are the first to hear complaints from clients, they also get to be heroes when they solve the problems.

Unusual requests to telecommunications specialists are the norm. People don't understand the technology involved, so they usually don't understand their options in terms of features and equipment. Telecommunications specialists help companies determine their own capabilities and discover what good communications support can do for their businesses. Successful telecommunications specialists can juggle multiple tasks, being involved in up to 20 projects and handling 100 maintenance contacts.

PAYING YOUR DUES

No particular degree is required to become a telecommunications specialist. Instead, extensive job-training programs are the norm. Individuals with strong math or engineering backgrounds have an advantage over the candidate pool in general; communication skills are an advantage, too. Training programs usually last two or three months in large companies; on-the-job training in mentor programs isn't unusual for smaller companies. Professional education is also standard in this field, as the technology changes almost as rapidly as the daily newspaper. Professional organizations are gaining respectability in this field, but membership in them isn't required.

ASSOCIATED CAREERS

A telecommunications specialist's skills are valuable in a number of other technology-oriented jobs. Many of them become service sales representatives for high-tech products companies. Others who dislike negotiating deals contract themselves out as wiring specialists and perform installation and maintenance functions for a fee. Still other specialists become computer network administrators, capitalizing on their understanding of the interplay between local wiring (connections) and performance (results).

PAST AND FUTURE

Telecommunications specialists owe the growth of their industry to the growth of the telecommunications technology sector. Decisions about communications used to be based on a simple choice—telephone, mail, or messenger. The development of fiber-optic cable, coaxial cable, and computer routing and data systems all spurred the need for trained professionals who could coordinate the needs of the end-user (the client) with the capabilities of the data/voice server (the provider). Telecommunications specialists fill that role.

The future looks very bright for telecommunications specialists, particularly for individuals willing to continue their education. Positions are growing at roughly double the rate of jobs in the economy as a whole. Technological developments should contribute to this bright future, as the development of cable modems promises to speed transmission rates a thousand-fold, the Internet develops as a telecommunications resource, and companies continue to invest heavily in their communications systems.

QUALITY OF LIFE

2 YEARS Trainees either go through a formal training program or are assigned a "mentor" who takes them along on client meetings. Many of them spend a significant amount of time off-site in these initial years, learning how to help clients examine their current and future needs and how to assess installation possibilities and problems. Many newcomers to the field encounter unusual situations or strange requests that will arm them with horror stories for dissuading future clients from making the same mistakes. The hours are long; satisfaction is reasonable.

5 YEARS Telecommunications specialists initiate client contact and handle their own accounts, from first handshake to negotiations to overseeing final billing. Many of them have considerable leverage to negotiate contracts, and many of them are promoted on the basis of their success at getting good deals. However, positive client feedback is equally important, and complaints from a couple of vociferous clients can sabotage even the most promising of telecommunications specialists' careers. The hours level off; satisfaction and salaries increase.

10 YEARS Many telecommunication specialists hold managerial or supervisory positions. At a minimum, individuals in small companies are now in the "mentor" role. Many telecommunication specialists consider entrepreneurial ventures and begin exploring these opportunities. The majority remain telecommunications specialists, though. Continuing professional education is important in order to keep up with the technological "revolutions" that keep taking place.

· MAJOR EMPLOYERS

AMERICAN TELEPHONE AND TELEGRAPH CORPORATION
32 Avenue of the Americas
New York, NY 10013
Tel: 212-387-5400
Fax: 212-387-5965
www.att.com
Contact: Human Resources

BELL ATLANTIC CORPORATION
1095 Avenue of the Americas
New York, NY 10036
Tel: 212-395-2121 or 800-321-9900
www.22.verizon.com
Jobline: 800-WORK-4-BA

COX COMMUNICATIONS SAN DIEGO
5159 Federal Boulevard
San Diego, CA 92105
Tel: 619-263-9251
Fax: 619-266-5540
www.cox.com
Contact: Personnel

UNITED TECHNOLOGIES CORPORATION
United Technologies Building
Hartford, CT 06101
Tel: 860-728-7000
Fax: 860-728-7028
www.utc.com
Contact: Human Resources

MAJOR ASSOCIATIONS

CABLE TELECOMMUNICATIONS INDUSTRY ASSOCIATION
1400 16th Street, NW Suite 600
Washington, DC 20036
Tel: 202-785-0081
Fax: 202-785-0721
www.wow-com.com

NATIONAL CABLE & TELECOMMUNICATIONS ASSOCIATION
1724 Massachusetts Avenue, NW
Washington, DC 20036
Tel: 202-775-3550
E-mail: webmaster@ncta.co
www.catanet.org

TELEVISION REPORTER

SALARY   ● ● ●
HOURS   ●
EDUCATION   ● ●

BOOKS, FILMS, AND TV SHOWS
FEATURING THE PROFESSION
- Broadcast News
- Good Night, and Good Luck
- He Said, She Said
- Murrow
- To Die For

YOU'LL HAVE CONTACT WITH
- Camera operators
- Researchers
- Television producers
- Writers

PROFESSIONALS READ
- The New York Times
- The Wall Street Journal
- The Washington Post
- Time

A DAY IN THE LIFE

A reporter's job is not for the faint of heart. It requires a great deal of stamina, physical fitness, and unflagging self-motivation. Aspiring television reporters must be strong on perseverance, be able to look danger squarely in the face, be willing to work long hours, forego weekends, holidays, and special occasions, and be ready to be on the road at a moment's notice. Television reporters gather information, investigate leads, and write and report stories live or on the scene. Occasionally they tape their news reports, sometimes called "packages," for a later broadcast. Reporters must be able to accurately compile notes, conduct interviews, determine the focus of a story, and quickly organize and complete a story. Because of the increased pace and efficiency of electronic news-gathering techniques, reporters are sometimes hard-pressed to properly complete their stories before they are called upon to go "live." Reporters with good memory and poise and who are able to speak fluently and extemporaneously will fare well. Reporters must also be both emotionally and psychologically stable so they can report from gruesome crime scenes. They are usually assigned leads to pursue by station assignment editors. Some reporters are given a specific "beat" to cover, such as police stations, city hall, or the courts. Others specialize in areas such as medicine, consumer news, sports, science, and weather.

{ forego weekends }

While most reporters do on-the-spot news coverage, investigative reporters usually cover "long lead-in" stories that often take days or weeks of information gathering and, depending on the subject matter, may involve danger. News correspondents stationed in foreign nations at war or facing civil unrest place their lives on the line with every live report. These correspondents must not only learn how to maneuver through difficult situations to locate sources of valuable information but must also overcome language barriers, cultural barriers, and fear to get to that information.

PAYING YOUR DUES

A bachelor's degree in journalism is the minimum requirement to get your foot in the door of most broadcasting stations, but significant emphasis is placed on collateral experience and internships. Applicants must show college newswriting and demonstrate that they've had reporting experience on school newspapers or at college television stations. Additionally, extensive internship experience and a specialized degree in political science, economics, or business, plus a minimum of three to five years reporting experience, will substantially enhance one's chance of being hired by a major market network.

Most on-air television reporters and anchors in major cities such as New York, Philadelphia, Los Angeles, and San Francisco started out in small-town stations at which they learned everything from the ground up. Although lacking the glamour and pay scale of big-city stations, these small markets are necessary learning grounds and provide invaluable experience for any aspiring reporter.

ASSOCIATED CAREERS

Most television reporters advance by "network hopping," that is, moving from one large station to the next seeking more responsibilities, more exposure, and more money. For the disaffected reporter, there is always the talk show forum, a route that propels many reporters to either fame or infamy and, of course, overnight riches. With demonstrated oral and written communication skills in their favor, die-hard reporters often opt for positions as syndicated columnists with major newspapers, become authors, public relations specialists, editors, or college professors. "I went from newspaper to television reporting, winding up as a network news anchor in New York City," says one 20-year news veteran. "Now I host a daily wellness program on cable television."

PAST AND FUTURE

Today's reporting profession is significantly more stressful than that of yesteryear. The competition among television stations for higher ratings and more advertising revenue has meant that reporters are often required to enter increasingly dangerous situations in order to present the news first and live.

Technology will continue to play an integral role in the television-reporting business. Reporters will therefore have to be on the very cutting-edge of the latest computer software programs, online services, the Internet, and digitized news libraries. Along with the routine of reading most major news publications and generally keeping on top of current affairs, the reporter will have to be alert and savvy enough to filter out useful information from a plethora of sources.

QUALITY OF LIFE

2 YEARS

At this stage the reporter is probably working at a small-town broadcasting station as a General Assignment reporter. The work, though tedious, may sometimes entail behind-the-scenes work such as editing, camera operating, or photography. This is the time when the avid reporter develops contacts, learns every facet of news gathering and dissemination, and fine tunes his or her newswriting skills.

5 YEARS

A seasoned reporter at the five-year mark has the poise and the presence to report from most situations. The reporter may be assigned to a beat, waiting around courts and police precincts for that "big story" to break. The television reporter is now ready and anxious to assume more and varied responsibilities.

10 YEARS

The 10-year veteran is a confident and able reporter. If he or she is still employed by a small station, then this reporter should have an impressive working knowledge of every aspect of the news business and is probably able to operate most if not all related equipment. The ambitious reporter would have specialized in one or more fields, amassing a wealth of knowledge and thereby enhancing his or her value in the broadcast marketplace. The reporter is now ready to be signed by a network in a major news market.

MAJOR EMPLOYERS
ABC INC.
77 West 66th Street
New York, NY 10023
Tel: 212-456-1000
Fax: 212-456-7112
www.abc.com
Contact: Human Resources Department

CBS
524 West 57th Street
New York, NY 10019
www.cbs.com
Contact: Human Resources

NATIONAL BROADCASTING COMPANY
30 Rockefeller Plaza
New York, NY 10112
Tel: 212-664-4444
www.nbc.com

TURNER BROADCASTING SYSTEMS, INC.
1 CNN Center
Atlanta, GA 30303
Tel: 404-827-1700
www.turner.com
Contact: Personnel Department

MAJOR ASSOCIATIONS
AMERICAN FEDERATION OF TELEVISION AND RADIO ARTISTS
260 Madison Avenue, 7th Floor
New York, NY 10016-2401
Tel: 212-532-0800
Fax: 212-545-1238
www.aftra.org/aftra/aftra.htm

BROADCAST EDUCATION ASSOCIATION
1771 N Street, NW, 5th Floor
Washington, DC 20036-2891
Tel: 888-380-7222, or 202-429-3935
www.beaweb.org

TRADER

SALARY ● ● ●
HOURS ● ●
EDUCATION ● ● ●

BOOKS, FILMS, AND TV SHOWS
FEATURING THE PROFESSION
- Boiler Room
- Bonfire of the Vanities
- Liar's Poker
- Wall Street

YOU'LL HAVE CONTACT WITH
- Brokers
- Clients
- Other traders
- Sales and marketing departments

PROFESSIONALS READ
- The Economist
- Futures Magazine
- Reuters
- Stock Market Magazine
- Traders Magazine
- The Wall Street Journal

A DAY IN THE LIFE

A trader buys and sells securities, which include currencies, stocks, bonds, and options, to make a profit. The worth of these securities is derived from the value of an underlying asset—and commodities (oil, gold, cocoa, coffee, sugar, etc.).

Traders are employed by hedge funds (partnerships that invest in stocks, futures, options, and currencies), the 15 or 20 largest banks in the United States and Europe, and large companies. Primary markets are located in New York, London, Singapore, and Tokyo. A company trades to "hedge" its exposure, much like a gambler "hedges" bets. For example, Microsoft sells products in Europe, where the Euro is the common currency. The company, therefore, has to offset its foreign exchange exposure given the current exchange rates.

{ culture and attitude }

While all markets are cyclical, trading currency is generally the most fast-paced, and the currency trader's days are almost always frantic. "I'm a market-maker; I make prices. I'm constantly looking at screens on which the numbers are always changing," says one trader. "At the same time, I have to listen to six brokers shouting different prices all at the same time. I have to listen to what my colleagues are doing and what the spot desk is doing in the back. I have to listen to marketers calling me for prices for their clients. Over time, you learn how to deal with mayhem."

A trader's day starts at 7:30 A.M. and ends at 5:30 P.M., and the work is creative as well as routine. "You go through the same motions and your mind is set to work in the same way, but you have to be creative with ideas in order to make money. You need discipline, which is related to routine, and you must be able to make quick decisions, think fast on your feet, and be a risk-taker. Traders are disciplined and creative gamblers at heart. There's no way you can be calm in this job. Once in a while, I break a phone or a computer. I don't know anybody who is polite and calm during the day."

Trading demands an aggressive, type-A personality. Though culturally diverse, the industry is still very much a virtual old boys' club comprised of nearly 90 percent men. "There's a definite culture and attitude among traders of spending and splurging and carousing with women, and you are expected to take part."

PAYING YOUR DUES

An assistant or junior trader helps traders with routine work such as recording trades or managing the process of "getting the trade to the books" by following the Securities and Exchange Commission's compliance rules. However, an assistant won't advance very quickly; therefore, attending business school while armed with a background in finance and math is essential. A master's in business administration can earn a trader more responsibility. There is tremendous competition for jobs, and getting into a top investment bank is difficult. While a particular pedigree isn't important, attending an Ivy League school is advantageous.

ASSOCIATED CAREERS

Sales and marketing is the flip-side of trading—a company needs a contact in a bank to call to make a price for the company in order to trade. This role is fulfilled by marketers or salespeople, who are called constantly by clients for their ideas about trading.

PAST AND FUTURE

The United States investment market was born in 1790 when the federal government refinanced all Revolutionary War debt and issued $80 million in bonds, the first publicly traded securities. Five securities were traded in 1792—three government bonds and two bank stocks. By the end of the War of 1812, the market for securities in New York began to expand as stocks were traded along with government bonds and bank and insurance stocks. In 1817, New York brokers established the New York Stock Exchange, renting rooms at 40 Wall Street and adopting a constitution with rules governing business conduct. During the 1830s, railroads dominated trading, and the turn of the century saw the first published Dow Jones Industrial Average, with 12 stocks and an initial value of 40.74. World War I was a turning point, as America emerged from the war as a creditor rather than a debtor nation, and New York replaced London as the world's investment capital. Over the next decade, more than 1,700 foreign issues were offered publicly in the United States.

Trading will continue to be profitable, and online trading is quickly revolutionizing the industry as more people on Main Street take to Wall Street. The object of trading will always be the same, but the methods in which business is transacted are quickly changing as decimalization takes hold (allowing trading to the penny), along with round-the-clock markets.

QUALITY OF LIFE

2 YEARS In the first couple of years, a trader will be responsible for a smaller account and allowed to take fewer risks than other players with more seasoned market experience. "Experience is the most important factor. Over time, once your employer trusts you, you'll be allowed to take more risks," says one trader.

A new trader will earn a fairly small salary (by banking standards) of $80–$100, 000, plus a year-end bonus, ranging from nothing to $100, 000, though this varies greatly by field. Equity derivatives, for example, did very well in the last two years with the growth of Nasdaq, while some other fields didn't fare as well.

5 YEARS Bonuses are revenues shared by the team based on the group's and bank's performance, and the senior traders get a larger piece of the pie. After five years, traders' bonuses can reach $500,000, as they are responsible for larger accounts and allowed to take greater risks. "I've heard stories of people who made a lot of money year after year, and then one year just blew everything they've made. There are also people who haven't done well but made a fortune from one great idea." Traders with a good reputation will be lured by headhunters and often jump from one employer to another.

10 YEARS Most traders are in their 20s and 30s, work for two to five years, and then take the high road. The basic exit strategy is simply to retire. "If they've survived 10 years without a heart attack, most traders take their $10 million or $15 million and move on. Some traders who want a less stressful job start a small hedge fund and work out of the suburbs, attracting money from other investors. Others open a bed and breakfast in Vermont."

MAJOR EMPLOYERS

GOLDMAN, SACHS & CO.
85 Broad Street
New York, NY 10004
Tel: 212-902-1000
http://gs.com

MORGAN STANLEY
Firmwide Recruiting
1585 Broadway
New York, NY 10036
Tel: 212-761-4000
www.morganstanley.com

Aspiring traders may seek out work for hedge funds, major banks, and Fortune 500 companies.

MAJOR ASSOCIATIONS

SECURITY TRADERS ASSOCIATION, INC.
420 Lexington Avenue, Suite 2334
New York, NY 10170
Tel: 212-867-7002
Fax: 212-867-7030
www.securitytraders.org

TRANSLATOR/INTERPRETER

A DAY IN THE LIFE

Translators work with written documents, and interpreters listen and translate a message as it is being spoken. The former may work on a variety of documents, including legal, business-related, journalistic, or "literary" texts, and is generally paid by the word. The latter are normally paid either by the hour or as full-time staff in such settings as the United Nations, international businesses, or perhaps within the legal system as a court interpreter.

Translation and interpreting both require extreme professionalism, dedication, knowledge, and attention to detail. Interpreters must be flexible, as they may be called to work at any hour of the day or night, and they must be willing to withstand the significant pressure of attending a diplomatic or business meeting. Translators, however, usually have time to refer to dictionaries and other reference tools and to polish the final product. In recent years, expectations for speedy delivery of work have made translation a high-pressure job.

{ attention to detail }

A variety of working environments exists for translators and interpreters. A broad general education and professional background may be extremely useful; the more knowledge translators or interpreters possess, the better. Technical translators must possess excellent technical writing skills; special certification is not required. Federal court translators must be completely fluent, even in the slang of their second language and must pass the federal certification examination if they work in Haitian Creole, Navajo, or Spanish. Other work is found in academic fields, either studying or interpreting foreign texts. Though literary translation has the most room for creative expression, literary translators must be just as careful as technical translators.

PAYING YOUR DUES

The route into translation is very structured and predictable for employment in the United Nations or other government agency. Individuals seeking the greatest opportunities for employment should be fluent in English and in three of the official languages of the United Nations: French, Spanish, Arabic, Russian, or Chinese. Most translators and interpreters in the United States, however, enter this profession by a circuitous route. There are numerous job opportunities for individuals who are fluent in other languages. Applicants may have a language degree, preferably a bachelor's or master's degree, but an academic degree does not make translators or interpreters: Applicants need to live abroad, immersing themselves in the language, and need specialized training. Employers prefer candidates who have exceptional fluency in at least two foreign languages. Cultural study is an area that potential translators cannot overlook as it is invaluable to understanding the nuances of any work to be translated. Therefore, courses in history, anthropology, and politics are necessary as are courses in grammar and conversation. Time spent studying abroad while in college is also an essential part of an applicant's resume.

Before interviewing for a position, candidates are normally required to undergo a series of tests to ensure language proficiency. First, the candidate has to translate a general text from the host language into the second, or third, language. Then the applicant must choose a more technical text for translation to exhibit fluency in the area he or she has chosen for specialization. These tests can take up to seven hours. After the candidate demonstrates fluency, the employer will invite the applicant to an interview. For this, the applicant is given some time to prepare a topic for translation, and the interview usually begins with the oral presentation of this translation. The interview culminates in an inquiry into the applicant's knowledge of the applicable region's cultural and historical background. Employers will often expect translators, after hiring and training, to work on word processing and other data entry equipment. Computer skills, including familiarity with computer-assisted translation (CAT) software, are essential for translators.

ASSOCIATED CAREERS

During the first year of employment, only a small percentage of translators leave the field. Applicants are well prepared for this position from experience in school, tests and interviews, and training programs.

PAST AND FUTURE

The need for translation has existed ever since divergent cultures came into contact with one another. The great Roman senator Cicero insisted that the interpreter be as loyal to the original text as possible, and this idea persisted in the works of Renaissance theorists, who expected a translator to capture the stylistic possibilities of the host language. In the 19th century, a near reversal of these theories arose. A German theorist, Schleiermacher, claimed that rather than the translator's bringing the work to the reader, the translator should bring the reader to the work. This idea of conveying the culture to the reader continues today.

Computer software is already a huge part of the translation industry. Though the future of translation shows immense growth, the field has become extremely volatile. Pressure from foreign translators and interpreters and the general economic downturn have made translation a somewhat uncertain career. Interpreters in courts especially are suffering from statewide budgetary restrictions that have pulled funding for their services.

QUALITY OF LIFE

2 YEARS Due to the extensive training, interpreters are well aware of what to expect from their profession. Again, the field has become uncertain as of late; applicants who weather the storm can look forward to higher salaries and satisfaction.

5 YEARS Thirty-five percent of all translators leave the profession within the first five years, often because of the ceiling on advancement. This is a position for individuals with a love for language. Continual recognition and perpetual advancement are not likely to occur in this field.

10 YEARS After obtaining some tenure, interpreters report continued satisfaction in the field. This is illustrated by the departure of only another 5 percent of translators beyond the first five years of employment. Interpreters deciding to remain in the field do so because of liberal benefits, increasing flexibility, and comforting security. For some translators, such as individuals employed by the United Nations, there is a slow but positive advancement in salary, benefits, and title—a system that rewards continued employment.

MAJOR EMPLOYERS

U.S. DEPARTMENT OF STATE
HR/REE/REC
2401 E Street, NW, Suite 518H
Washington, DC 20522
Tel: 202-261-8888
Fax: 202-261-8841
www.state.gov/employment

THE WORLD BANK
1818 H Street, NW
Washington, DC 20433
Tel: 202-473-1000
Fax: 202-477-6391
www.worldbank.org

MAJOR ASSOCIATIONS

AMERICAN TRANSLATORS ASSOCIATION
225 Reinekers Lane, Suite 590
Alexandria, VA 22314
Tel: 703-683-6100
Fax: 703-683-6122
E-mail: ata@atanet.org
www.atanet.org

CERTIFIED TRANSLATORS AND INTERPRETERS, INC.
4431 Hidden Shadow Drive
Tampa, FL 33614
Tel: 813-243-8764
www.transinterpreters.com

NATIONAL ASSOCIATION OF JUDICIARY INTERPRETERS AND TRANSLATORS
603 Stewart Street, Suite 610
Seattle, WA 98101
Tel: 206-267-2300
Fax: 206-626-0392
E-mail: headquarters@najit.org
www.najit.org

VENTURE CAPITALIST

PROFESSIONAL PROFILE

# of people in profession	8,474
Avg. hours per week	60
Avg. starting salary	$136,900
Avg. salary 5 years	$201,500
Avg. salary 10 to 15 years	$230,800

SALARY   ● ● ●
HOURS   ● ● ●
EDUCATION   ● ● ●

BOOKS, FILMS, AND TV SHOWS
FEATURING THE PROFESSION

- Confessions of a Venture Capitalist: Inside the High Stakes World of Start-Up
- Financing
- News Radio

·PROFESSIONALS READ
- Business Week
- The Daily Deal
- Institutional Investor
- The Wall Street Journal

A DAY IN THE LIFE

Venture capitalists invest the money of large institutional investors. Here's how it works: Company A has an idea for a product that will revolutionize the way we live, but they don't have the money to get it off the ground. Investor B has the money and is looking for an idea that will make him or her even more cash. The venture capitalist acts as agent for Investor B, seeking out Company A and becoming active in and offering advice to the company's management. The product goes to market, everyone buys it, Investor B gets their money back plus a healthy return, and the venture capitalist takes a percentage of the investment (a "management fee"). A good investment can turn a few million dollars into a few hundred-million dollars. But not all investment { good business sense } opportunities are pots of gold. Venture capitalists and investors need strong business backgrounds to be able to separate the golden investment opportunities from the chaff, but it only takes a few successful companies to make a venture fund successful. Venture capitalists and investors are constantly being approached with ideas that need money. The venture capitalist has to know how to read business plans, understand a company's financial statements, spot trends, and ask the right questions to determine a company's chances for success. Say someone comes to you with this great idea about a website that sells butterfly nets. You know butterfly nets are hot, every kid wants one, but the guy with the website idea has no idea about HTML, for example, much less insights about how to set up a store in cyberspace. You, being the savvy investor you are, wouldn't sink a dime into that project. One survey found that in the recent business climate, venture capitalists typically reviewed 100 business plans before finding a potential investment opportunity with merit. Venture capitalists can finance such broad-ranging plans as bull-sperm farms, Hollywood movies, and Internet providers. Success in this profession requires a little ESP, a good business sense, and a heaping dose of moxy. Some venture capitalists are in the game because of the risks. In a sense, it's legalized gambling. The rush can be intoxicating, and the payoff can be huge.

PAYING YOUR DUES

Most venture capitalists have a Master's Degree in Business, Engineering, or Science; many of them have their Master's in Business Administration. Investing money in a business or project with the hope of making a huge return is, for the most part, an educated crapshoot. Some venture capitalists are going to come up sevens, but most individuals are going to roll snake eyes. You may lose a lot of money before you make a dime. Or you may hit it big with the first company you invest in. Research, patience, knowledge, and a good team can make all the difference.

ASSOCIATED CAREERS

Venture capitalists sometimes find themselves partners in the new businesses that they are funding. Most take an active role in operations: It's not uncommon for a venture capitalist to become chief executive officer, temporarily or permanently, for one of his or her investments, and almost all of them sit on the boards of the companies in which they invest. Few individuals simply provide the funds and step aside.

PAST AND FUTURE

In the 1950s and 1960s—the early days of venture capital investment—individual investors were the norm. While this type of individual investment has not totally disappeared, the past few decades have seen the emergence of the venture firm, partnerships of venture capitalists managing large pools of institutional money. As one financial analyst states, "In the last few years, individuals have again become a potent and increasingly larger part of the early stage start-up venture life cycle. These 'angel investors' will mentor a company and provide needed capital and expertise to help develop companies." The dollar amount of all venture capital investments has declined in recent years. Some individuals maintain that though the stock market is depressed, this is the best of times for venture capitalists. "Not only are valuations low because the stock market is low, but many talented people are looking for work—and it's easier to motivate employees who are happy to have a job to build a new company."

QUALITY OF LIFE

2 YEARS — During the early years of their careers, venture capitalists act as associates, supporting senior members of their investing team, getting exposure to different industries and transactions, working hard, and making few decisions on their own. Learning takes place on the job; for most venture capitalists, the first few years are a chance to see if they like the pace and type of investing they'll eventually do.

5 YEARS — This is the time venture capitalists begin to bring their own investments to the firm for approval and may begin to sit on the boards of portfolio companies, either as a backup to a senior firm member or on their own. The amount of returns on investments made in the early years may encourage or discourage a venture capitalist from continuing to invest in new and established businesses.

10 YEARS — Venture capitalists in business for more than 10 years are able to pick and choose their deals. Many of them sit on company boards and spend time working on business plans and sales processes and working with investors. Senior members—now likely partners at their investment firm—work with associate members, helping them learn the ropes, and have developed expertise in specific industries. At this level, if their firm is successful, venture capitalists are doing very well financially.

MAJOR EMPLOYERS

Most venture capitalists may find work partnered in small, medium, or large firms across the country.

MAJOR ASSOCIATIONS

AMERICAN ENTERPRISE FOR ECONOMIC GROWTH
1655 North Fort Myer Drive, Suite 850
Arlington, VA 22209
Tel: 703-524-3743
Fax: 703-524-3940
www.aeeg.org

NATIONAL VENTURE CAPITAL ASSOCIATION
1655 North Fort Myer Drive, Suite 850
Arlington, VA 22209
Tel: 703-524-2549
Fax: 703-524-3940
www.nvca.org

WEDDING CONSULTANT

PROFESSIONAL PROFILE

# of people in profession	7,000
Avg. hours per week	N/A
Avg. starting salary	$27,680
Avg. salary 5 years	$33,200
Avg. salary 10 to 15 years	$44,300

SALARY ●
EDUCATION ●

BOOKS, FILMS, AND TV SHOWS
FEATURING THE PROFESSION
- **Father of the Bride**
- **The Wedding Planner**
- **A Wedding Story**

YOU'LL HAVE CONTACT WITH
- **Caterers**
- **Hotel and restaurant managers**
- **Photographers**
- **Wedding couples**

PROFESSIONALS READ
- **Bride**
- **Modern Bride**
- **Town and Country**

A DAY IN THE LIFE

Have you ever thrown a party? Do you remember all the little things that went into making your house presentable, the food acceptable, and the amount of liquor adequate? Well, multiply all of these things by 1,000, and you have an idea of what wedding consultants deal with. Wedding consultants are often specialized off-shoots of professional party planners—the folks who organize high-profile charity benefits, entertainment industry parties, debutante balls, and lower key but just as logistically complicated events like charity dance-a-thons. Organization is a wedding consultant's primary skill, but he or she must also have exceptional people skills, since the wedding consultant deals with two families who are acting crazier than usual. In addition to his { **professional relationships** } or her interpersonal skills, the wedding consultant must possess impressive negotiating and business skills to haggle with the numerous vendors needed to supply flowers, music, food, and so forth. Wedding consultants must also have professional relationships with photographers, hotel and restaurant managers, calligraphers, musicians, and videographers. A wedding consultant deals with vendors on a continuing basis, and, because of this, he or she often receives discounts or upgrades from suppliers that he or she can pass on to his or her clients. Part of the reason clients hire consultants is to save money, and most consultants are quick to point out that they should be viewed as part of the wedding budget, not an extra expense, since their connections will hopefully cut wedding costs rather than increase them. Wedding consultants are also troubleshooters, helping their clients avoid cost overruns and planning mistakes, and providing emergency assistance in the event that there are last-minute guests or cancellations of services.

Wedding planners are only as involved as their clients want them to be. Some get hired specifically to deal with the reception, and that includes hours of work booking a space, selecting the caterer, finding the appropriate musical talent or DJs, and negotiating the bill with all parties involved. At other times, wedding consultants work with their clients for nearly a year, getting involved in all aspects of planning the big day, from assisting in the choice of the bride's gown and the design of the pew cards to selecting just who will be supplying the puffed pastries for the reception. This means that wedding consultants must offer a myriad of options to their clients concerning gift suggestions, floral arrangements, transportation sources, and reception locations. Wedding consultants generally charge about 15 percent of the cost of the wedding. Most of them charge an hourly rate, fixed fee, or some combination of these. Depending on the size of the wedding, income can be quite high. The average wedding today costs $20,000; at 15 percent, that's a $3,000 commission. Wedding consultants who organize just two $20,000 weddings a month earn more than $75,000 a year. The variety of work within this career makes for a profession that is difficult to track statistically. Most wedding consultants are self-employed and work as many or as few hours as they choose, depending on how much income they want to earn.

PAYING YOUR DUES

There are no set educational requirements in this profession. Business professionals and individuals with business degrees are at an advantage, however, because organizational and financial skills are essential. Experience pays off more than anything in this profession, though. A solid reputation and connections to vendors and suppliers are crucial. Wedding consultants couldn't perform their jobs without these key elements. Many wedding planners have gravitated to the profession by finding that other work experience has given them a decided advantage. "I worked as a travel agent and in the Orlando/Orange County Convention and Visitors Bureau," says Susan Southerland, owner and president of Just Marry!, Inc. "I turned my travel and event-planning know-how into a full-time profession by starting Just Marry! in 1992." Southerland put a special spin on her wedding consulting by using her travel background to plan destination weddings for clients. Her company has planned weddings ranging in budgets from $600 to $80,000 and served clients from as far away as Japan.

ASSOCIATED CAREERS

As mentioned above, many wedding consultants enter the profession from other related professions, and experienced wedding consultants can cross over into other careers in the same manner. Special-event coordinators, who are found in industries ranging from entertainment to publishing, and even in government (who do you think organizes presidential balls?), are closely related to wedding consultants and deal with many of the same logistical and budgetary issues. Special-event coordinators arrange everything from book signings for authors to fund-raisers for organizations like the Gay Men's Health Crisis.

PAST AND FUTURE

Since both members of most couples work nowadays, wedding consultants are becoming not only more popular but also more necessary; neither the man nor the woman has time to plan their nuptials. Wedding planners have probably been around as long as the institution itself in some form or another, but it was in 1955 that the American Association of Bridal Consultants was founded to represent wedding professionals. It was replaced in 1981 by the Association of Bridal Consultants (ABC), which serves as a professional association and even awards educational designations (there are no licenses in this field) to wedding consultants, ensuring that their members uphold a code of ethics and standards set by the membership. The ABC also provides referrals to prospective clients. As long as people continue to get married, there will be jobs for wedding planners.

QUALITY OF LIFE

2 YEARS — While a wedding planner can be involved with a client for months, the Association of Bridal consultants say that it takes between 60 and 80 hours to plan a wedding. Depending on how many clients a consultant is working with, his or her weekly total can average 40 or many more. It is a competitive industry, and individuals who are new to the career will spend the first few years focusing on developing a solid reputation and strong connections with suppliers to enhance the services and savings they offer.

5 YEARS — Because a planner's client base is always changing (unless they plan weddings for Elizabeth Taylor), the most important road to success for a wedding planner is establishing a reputation for reliability and quality of service. After five years, successful wedding planners have secured a good reputation, worked with clients from all around the country, and developed a stable of vendors who they can depend on to supply the appointments of weddings both small and extravagant.

10 YEARS — After 10 years in the business, wedding consultants are trusted with weddings with budgets exceeding $100,000 and will have the resources to work on a national and sometimes international basis. With these qualifications, a consultant can afford to pick and choose clients and may pull in a large income.

MAJOR EMPLOYERS
Wedding consultants work for people madly in love all across the country.

MAJOR ASSOCIATIONS
ASSOCIATION OF BRIDAL CONSULTANTS
56 Danbury Road, Suite 11
New Milford, CT 06776
Tel: 860-355-0464
Fax: 860-354-1404
www.bridalassn.com

THE YELLOW CAREERS

ACCOUNTANT/AUDITOR

BOOKS, FILMS, AND TV SHOWS
FEATURING THE PROFESSION
- **Midnight Run**
- **Our People: How Arthur Andersen Won Big Business—and Lost Its Way**
- **Paid in Full**
- **The Producers**
- **The Untouchables**
- **Weekend at Bernie's**

YOU'LL HAVE CONTACT WITH
- **Attorneys**
- **Bankers**
- **Bookkeepers**
- **Clients**
- **Record keepers**

PROFESSIONALS READ
- **CPA Journal**
- **Financial Accounting Standards Board publications**
- **Journal of Accounting**
- **Tax Law Digest**

A DAY IN THE LIFE

Accountants keep track of payments, financial positions, and transfers of capital or income for individual or institutional clients. Some accountants are responsible for examining the tax implications of their clients' financial activities. Accountants must be comfortable with numbers, but must also spend a considerable amount of time reviewing other people's work and, in particular, delivering bad news. As a "financial physician" (a term that cropped up more than once in our surveys), you'll be the bearer of unpleasantness more often than blessings and can expect to be greeted, at times, in a less-than-friendly manner. People who enter accounting mention this stigma as the most unanticipated downside of the profession. "I didn't know how many people just don't pay attention to their own numbers and how defensive people are when they're wrong," wrote one frustrated internal auditor.

{ financial physician }

The demand from clients to see their financial pictures improve in the hands of skilled accountants and auditors has led to some spectacular scandals. Accountants who are hired not only to advise but also to participate actively in keeping an individual's, company's, or corporation's assets and losses positioned for optimum return and minimal expense may face a legal and ethical conundrum. The saga of Enron and its role in the collapse of Anderson, formerly one of the biggest accounting firms in the world, is a major case in point. Public scrutiny and internal restructuring has led many of the surviving firms to distance their accounting units from their consulting units, largely to insure that accounting practices do not suffer any ethical breaches by way of pressure from any role the company may also be playing as a consultant.

Tax accountants face a somewhat different lifestyle from auditors and general accountants. Personal income tax accountants are mostly employed at small firms (80 percent of all income tax firms employ five or fewer people) or are self-employed. They are responsible for tracking clients' income, making any quarterly payments due to federal or state agencies, and managing the crush of activity preparing and submitting all required paperwork to the federal and state governments on April 15. Corporate tax accountants, however, are involved throughout the year in corporate decision-making, analyzing the tax effects of corporate investment policy, and advising other company managers on tax-planning issues. Corporate tax accountants face a seasonal surge in April similar to the one personal tax accountants face although to a significantly lesser degree.

PAYING YOUR DUES

Most people in the accounting field enjoy a straightforward path to becoming an accountant. Nearly all firms require at least a bachelor's degree in accounting, finance, or a related discipline. Many employers look favorably on students with significant computer proficiency or work experience in number-intensive jobs, and some job candidates enhance their profiles by earning a master's degree in business, accounting, or finance. The most common certification accountants are asked to complete soon after hire is the state-licensed Certified Public Accountant (CPA) exam. This rigorous four-part exam is rapidly replacing the Public Accountant (PA), Registered Public Accountant (RPA), and the Accounting Practitioner's (AP) exams as the working degree of choice. Different states have different licensing requirements, so write to the National Association of State Boards of Accountancy to find out the requirements for your state. Many boards are currently considering requiring an additional 30 hours of postgraduate accounting.

ASSOCIATED CAREERS

Accounting degrees are often paired with law, marketing, or advertising degrees as a means of specialization, but by no means are these the only careers associated with auditing and accounting. Accountants hold positions in bank operations, budgeting offices, financial analysis, management consulting, the FBI (where accountants track, analyze, and report on illegal interstate money transfers and hidden asset recovery; FBI accountants even brought down Al Capone), and full-service brokerage firms.

PAST AND FUTURE

Financial records certifying transactions and recording inventory levels have been found at the sites of ancient Greek and Roman towns, but accounting didn't become a "science" until 1494 with the publication of a book by mathematician Luca Pacioli that described the principles of accounting, including the double-entry bookkeeping system still in use today. In the United States, accounting grew significantly as a profession with the passage of federal legislation mandating income tax in 1913 and the passage of the Excess Profits Tax in 1917.

The future of accounting looks great for some types of accountants, while potentially bleak for others. Corporate tax advising, tax planning, internal auditing, and small business consulting are expected to grow at a steady pace. Internal auditing, in particular, should grow in popularity as small businesses learn the value of managing their capital soundly. When tax laws change, accounting professionals must reeducate themselves.

QUALITY OF LIFE

2 YEARS Most entry-level accountants and auditors are highly supervised, virtual apprentices to more experienced professionals in the field as cost accountants or junior internal auditors. During the first two years, many people study for their CPA exam, which only 25 percent of test-takers pass at any given administration.

5 YEARS After five years, professionals begin to specialize in private or public accounting and reach levels of greater responsibility, such as budget director or accounting manager. Some start their own firms; others become internal auditors in client firms. Accountants also enter related fields such as banking, financial analysis, and asset management. The 10 to 20 percent who leave the field are dissatisfied by the unpredictability of hours and the unflattering public perception of the industry. For those who remain, both hours and salary increase.

10 YEARS After ten years in the field, private practitioners have established their own firms or, if unsuccessful, reentered the corporate environment. Salary increases significantly at this point for the independent practitioner who has built a considerable client base. A variety of management positions unrelated to accounting, open up, such as strategic planning, operations development, and budget oversight. Some accountants become independent consultants and begin to work shorter hours, deciding to place more emphasis on family life and free time. A significant few enter government service and/or academia.

MAJOR EMPLOYERS

ALTSCHULER, MELVOIN AND GLASSER LLP
One South Wacker Drive, Suite 800
Chicago, IL 60606-7494
Tel: 312-384-6000
Fax: 312-634-3410
www.amgnet.com

DELOITTE TOUCHE TOHMATSU
1633 Broadway
New York, NY 10019-6754
Tel: 212-489-1600
Fax: 212-489-1687
www.deloitte.com

H&R BLOCK INC.
4400 Main Street
Kansas City, MO 64111
Tel: 800-HRBLOCK
www.hrblock.com

KPMG
345 Park Avenue
New York, NY 10154
www.us.kpmg.com

MAJOR ASSOCIATIONS

AMERICAN INSTITUTE OF CERTIFIED PUBLIC ACCOUNTANTS
1211 Avenue of the Americas
New York, NY 10036-8775
Tel: 212-596-6200
Fax: 212-596-6213
www.aicpa.org

NEW YORK STATE SOCIETY OF CPAS
3 Park Avenue, 18th Floor
New York, NY 10036
Tel: 800-633-6320 or 212-719-8300
Fax: 212-719-3364
www.nysscpa.org

ACTUARY

BOOKS, FILMS, AND TV SHOWS
FEATURING THE PROFESSION
- About Schmidt
- Are You with It?
- Mapping the Animal
- Table Talk

YOU'LL HAVE CONTACT WITH
- Accountants
- Auditors
- Computer programmers
- Financial analysts
- Risk managers
- Senior management
- Statisticians
- Underwriters

PROFESSIONALS READ
- Business Insurance
- National Underwriter

A DAY IN THE LIFE

An actuary assembles and analyzes facts and estimates risks and returns to make financial planning decisions in a specific area of expertise. As an actuary, you'll spend a lot of time working with numbers. You'll also spend up to 65 percent of your time working with people, establishing goals, reviewing work, and researching figures. "It's a real learning experience at first—not at all like school," one actuary writes, referring to the interpersonal and communication skills that are required in her job.

A significant portion of the aspiring actuary's time is spent studying for the multifaceted, information-specific exams that every actuary must pass. Employers provide study time during the work week to allow for test preparation and regularly award bonuses each time a fledgling employee passes another exam. Surprisingly, we found little mention of the long hours spent outside of work studying for the exams and the lack of a social life this hard study encourages. Actuaries seem to enjoy the constant education the profession requires, regardless of the personal cost. These exams provide good indicators of progress as an actuary; complete passing of the exams takes between five and ten years.

{ constant education }

PAYING YOUR DUES

Becoming an actuary requires some of the skills of a gambler and some of the skills of a marathoner. You need a gambler's understanding of statistics, probability, and risk analysis. Most actuaries graduate college with a degree in mathematics or a business-related field, although the industry trend of late is to hire more liberal arts students who can demonstrate a high mathematical aptitude. The endurance of a marathoner is required not for the hours, which are fairly acceptable, but to make it through the actuarial examinations, which can take as many as ten years to pass. These tests are administered biannually by three associations: the Society of Actuaries, the Casualty Actuarial Society (for casualty actuaries), and the American Society of Pension Actuaries. While each society provides certification for a certain specialization, the first few tests, at least for pension actuaries, are general enough that they may be taken without regard to any specific career path.

ASSOCIATED CAREERS

As you advance as an actuary, your career path will depend mainly on the complementary skills you bring to the profession. While some move to administrative and executive positions in underwriting, accounting, or information departments, others with more of a business background may move into supervisory positions in such diverse fields as marketing, planning, or corporate strategy.

PAST AND FUTURE

With the rise of the science of probability, described mathematically by Blase Pascal and Pierre de Fermat, came the ability to create probability tables for any given event—death, accidents, even loan defaults. In 1792, the Equitable Society of London (an insurer) decided to use these tables to determine their premiums and, thus, was born the role of the actuary. Edmund Halley—after whom Halley's Comet is named—developed the first table of mortality, thereby giving birth to the life insurance industry.

The need for actuaries should rise over the course of the next decade as insurance companies, pension plans, and large corporations recognize the need for accurate statistical analysis and cash flow management. Computer skills are crucial at the cutting edge of actuarial development, particularly in the field of liability analysis. Another emerging field is actuarial health care science. With unpredictable changes in medical technology and the emergence of epidemic viral strains, life expectancy is becoming more difficult to predict and more variable-dependent. Some actuaries believe these probabilities are describable and are working with complicated mathematics to find a way to explain them. Other emerging fields include terrorism risk-assessment and predictive modeling of catastrophes.

QUALITY OF LIFE

2 YEARS In the beginning, actuaries, referred to by professional societies as "associates," are rotated among different jobs within the company to learn the variety of processes that an insurance or pension company follows. Entry-level actuaries spend much of their time researching and preparing data. Many people enjoy the lack of professional responsibility these early years offer, mainly because it allows plenty of free time to study for the exams that mark the first few years. Attrition is low; satisfaction is average.

5 YEARS "Fast-trackers" diverge from others at this point, and those who have trouble with the exams or find producing analyses on other people's demands unsatisfying leave (18 to 22 percent). Salaries rise, and some attain the professional title of "fellow." Hours increase and specialization becomes critical. Those who leave the profession beyond this point do so primarily because they are dissatisfied with their area of specialization. Job performance is the distinguishing characteristic during these years; actuaries tend to view their jobs and colleagues as "very competitive."

10 YEARS Actuaries who have had success start their own actuarial consulting firms. Many people leave the pure actuarial side and enter management and corporate strategy development. Some continue up the actuarial ladder, moving to "chief" or "head" of actuarial science. Others are recruited by the government or independent research panels for their statistical skill and their experience in a specific area of expertise.

MAJOR EMPLOYERS

MERCER HUMAN RESOURCE CONSULTING
1166 Avenue of the Americas
New York, NY 10036
Tel: 212-345-7000
Fax: 212-345-7414
www.mercerhr.com

TILLINGHAST TOWERS PERRIN
335 Madison Avenue
New York, NY 10017-4605
Tel: 212-309-3400
Fax: 212-309-3957
www.towersperrin.com/tillinghast

WESTON WYATT WORLDWIDE
875 Third Avenue
New York, NY 10022
Tel: 212-725-7550
Fax: 212-644-7432
www.watsonwyatt.com

MAJOR ASSOCIATIONS

AMERICAN ACADEMY OF ACTUARIES
1100 17th Street, NW, 7th Floor
Washington, DC 20036
Tel: 202-223-8196
Fax: 202-872-1948
www.actuary.org

CASUALTY ACTUARIAL SOCIETY
1100 North Glebe Road, Suite 600
Arlington, VA 22201
Tel: 703-276-3100
Fax: 703-276-3108
E-mail: office@casact.org
www.casact.org

SOCIETY OF ACTUARIES
475 North Martingale Road, Suite 600
Schaumburg, IL 60173
Tel: 847-706-3500
Fax: 847-706-3599
www.soa.org/ccm/content

ASTRONOMER

A DAY IN THE LIFE

One would think that staring at the stars and pondering the interactions of large bodies of matter would involve a life of quiet contemplation, removed from the petty day-to-day distractions of the working world. But in fact, astronomers add to the latest in science and technology with their intellect and intuition, working with teams of like-minded specialists to study the universe and its constellations. Using both ground-based and space-borne instruments and equipped with the latest electronic light-gathering instruments, astronomers observe and study stars, galaxies, and quasars while also searching for new planets and previously undocumented celestial bodies. Computers play a key role in astronomical work, as they model, for example, cosmic jets and the environment surrounding pulsars and black holes. Digital models are also vital for simulating phenomena such as the collision of galaxies and enable astronomers to devise better theories about the early stages of the universe. Working with data gathered by physicists, astronomers can address key questions about the nature of the universe through the study of the behavior and force of elementary particles.

{ collision of galaxies }

This profession requires a person who is attentive to details, who is adept at working with others, and who possesses computer skills. One professor described the astronomer's life this way: "We search for all the wonder the universe has to offer by examining every corner and every edge the universe presents us, and yet we are surprised, because in truth, some of the universe we do not understand." Most astronomy jobs are with observatories, research centers, and universities. Observatory jobs usually involve some communication and/or operation with the academic community. It is common for an astronomer to do research at an observatory while employed as an instructor in an astronomy department. Those who are not associated with universities are employed by government labs, research institutions, or planetariums or as consultants for other areas of scientific inquiry, such as electronic communication technology.

PAYING YOUR DUES

Only about 70 American universities offer astronomy as a degree on the undergraduate level, and about 30 offer graduate degrees. A PhD is generally required to work in the field. Only those students with strong undergraduate backgrounds in physics, math, and computer science find the graduate–level work manageable. Close associations with professors during undergraduate and graduate work account for many of the initial positions people attain in the field. Working under close supervision, aspiring astronomers can anticipate long hours, extensive number crunching, and some work as teaching assistants—the latter may entail grading undergraduate papers and tests. Once they receive their doctorates, competition among PhDs for positions is intense. For those astronomers who wish to rise within the profession, publishing academic articles is important. Satisfaction among those employed in this field is, on the average, high.

ASSOCIATED CAREERS

Astronomers who leave the field go into a variety of professions where their science training can be put to use. They may enter the computer science, finance, and private industries.

PAST AND FUTURE

The Mayans, the Babylonians, and the Egyptians all used calendar systems based on the stars. The heliocentric theory of the universe, proposed by Nicolaus Copernicus in 1543, gave birth to modern astronomy, enabling experimental data to match with expected results. Twentieth-century technology, such as radio telescopes, spectroscopy measurements of background radiation shifts, and neutrino detection devices, has added to the basic work of Isaac Newton, Johannes Kepler, Galileo Galilei, and Edwin Hubble. Most agree that the future of astronomy lies in the marriage of technology and breakthroughs in theoretical modeling. Astronomers have untold numbers of questions about the universe, and only with more refined and farther-reaching experimental data will they be able to begin to address them; however, funding will define the future direction of astronomy.

QUALITY OF LIFE

2 YEARS Two years after college, most astronomers are in graduate school and working as research assistants or teaching assistants. The hours are long, and the pay is limited or in the form of academic credits. Others find work at government labs, planetariums, observatories, and university research labs as assistants. Some go into K–12 teaching.

5 YEARS Though still in graduate school, the astronomer who is still in the game at the five-year mark becomes involved in the planning and development stages of research projects (although professors and more experienced astronomers still have final say). Among those employed in the workforce, many who succeed move into more project-manager type jobs and away from the research and number crunching they were doing in the first two years. Teaching assistant positions can evolve into teaching positions. Within the segment of post-PhD employment, the two most accurate bellwethers of success in this field at the five-year stage are the number of articles published in quality astronomy journals and the number of research projects that are approved for funding. Between years two and seven, the greatest migration from this profession takes place—around 30 percent. Hours increase, as does pay, but the most significant aspect of these years is that hands-on responsibility increases.

10 YEARS Ten-year veterans of the astronomy field typically fall into two categories. There are the shooting stars who become tenured professors, research institution heads, and observatory managers because of their professional reputations and their record of performance. There are also the workhorses who have strong records of being team players at research institutions and observatories. The workhorses usually specialize in certain areas, such as exotic phenomena or spectroscopy analysis. Many shooting stars publish books, lecture, and lead conferences on their area of expertise. Duties include setting research agendas, approving grant proposals, acting as consultants to NASA, participating in international astronomy organizations, and serving on government panels in the sciences. Ten-year veterans may find themselves in the unusual position of dealing less with the science of astronomy and more with the politics of academic and governmental funding.

MAJOR EMPLOYERS

NATIONAL OPTICAL ASTRONOMY OBSERVATORY
950 North Cherry Avenue
Tucson, AZ 85719
Tel: 520-318-8000
www.noao.edu

NATIONAL AERONAUTICS AND SPACE ADMINISTRATION
www.nasajobs.nasa.gov

W.M. KECK OBSERVATORY
65-1120 Mamalahoa Highway
Kamuela, HI 96743
Tel: 808-885-7887
E-mail: employment@keck.hawaii.edu
www2.keck.hawaii.edu

MAJOR ASSOCIATIONS

AMERICAN ASTRONOMICAL SOCIETY
2000 Florida Avenue, NW, Suite 400
Washington, DC 20009–1231
Tel: 202-328-2010
Fax: 202-234-2560
E-mail: aas@aas.org
www.aas.org

AMERICAN PHYSICAL SOCIETY
1 Physics Ellipse
College Park, MD 20740-3843
Tel: 301-209-3200
Fax: 301-209-0865
E-mail: personnel@aps.org
www.aps.org

BOOKKEEPER

A DAY IN THE LIFE

Bookkeepers track all cash flow, billing, and lines of credit that affect their companies. They must be detail-oriented and tenacious; they have to track down and rectify any discrepancies, however small, in the company accounts. Most bookkeepers work as internal accountants for small firms that do not have an accountant on staff. They have a large amount of responsibility to the company and sometimes (particularly at the end of the year and around tax-preparation time) have to work long hours to do their job properly. The majority of bookkeepers work for smaller firms. Many become involved in financial tangles mid-stream—they find themselves deciphering records from up to a year before they were hired. Bookkeepers must be flexible and able to adjust to unusual circumstances.

{ double-entry system }

Many bookkeepers we talked with mentioned that the most difficult part of their jobs was not maintenance of financial records—this accounted for a good 50 percent of their time—but rather communication with the other members of the same company. "You have to keep track of everyone's activities, and nobody thinks it is important to keep the bookkeeper apprised every day of what they're doing." This lack of a smooth transfer of information has led many companies to buy bookkeeping software so that each employee can keep track of his or her daily activities, and a bookkeeper can then assemble all the information and verify its accuracy. Computer skills are important in the industry, and even those who are already familiar with the double-entry system of bookkeeping mentioned that being proficient in this software is considered a strong point by employers. Many small firms aren't used to being run as businesses, and many bookkeepers find keeping track of all interaction difficult at first. Bookkeepers must communicate their needs clearly and follow up with consistent requests for similar information. Those who enter the field with an open mind find that being a good bookkeeper "makes all the difference in the world when the boss looks at what direction he wants to take the company." The statistics and data bookkeepers compile provide "snapshots" of the daily activities of the company that make up its history.

PAYING YOUR DUES

Bookkeepers are financial recordkeepers, much like accountants; but they are not required to be accredited by any organization or institution. They have less of an obligation than an accountant and therefore less liability; however, they are paid commensurably less. They usually maintain the records of a single company rather than having many companies as clients. No specific educational requirement is required to become a bookkeeper, but prospective employers favor applicants with finance, record-keeping, or business majors. Basic course work in accounting is very helpful for those who enter the field, but on-the-job training is neither unusual nor discouraged. With the increasing simplicity of accounting software in the workplace, less formal accounting training is required for these positions. The work requires attention to detail and a good method of keeping track of constantly fluctuating items, which leads most bookkeepers to adopt the double-entry method of accounting. Much of a bookkeeper's work involves not only entering information, but also reviewing information and reconciling accounts. While some remain career bookkeepers at a single company, most professionals rotate between or among companies or leave the field altogether for supervisory or managerial positions.

ASSOCIATED CAREERS

Bookkeepers become accountants and inventory control experts at a higher rate than do individuals in any other profession. Those who leave the record-keeping industry altogether use their bookkeeping skills to understand various tasks within an industry, then move to positions of managerial control. The people who take this route, however, usually supplement their bookkeeping skills with courses, seminars, or second positions where they can demonstrate their management ability.

PAST AND FUTURE

At about 3,000 B.C., the Egyptians employed an inventory system to keep track of grain shipments and warehouse storage; this system formed the basis of modern-day bookkeeping. From one of the most active trading centers in the modern world, Venice, came the Italian Luca Pacioli, who developed double-entry bookkeeping. Over the years, this became the worldwide standard method of keeping track of income and outlay, profits and losses. As technology has developed, many bookkeeping systems have become computerized.

Bookkeepers face a strong demand for their services over the next decade, but the trend of computerization in the industry is likely to grow faster than job opportunities. Those who study accounting and current accounting software packages should be in a good position for entry-level opportunities. More positions are expected to become available in the Southeast and Southwest and in urban centers than in rural sectors.

QUALITY OF LIFE

2 YEARS A two-year bookkeeper designs or implements systems of inventory and accounting control and works with each department of a company and with accountants on year-end financial statements. Daily responsibilities include entering account activity and reviewing revenue and expenditure streams. Bookkeepers also cut all checks the company issues. Salaries are reasonable, and the hours are long because new bookkeepers are still learning. Satisfaction is average, but those people who have more input into the bookkeeping systems used seem happier than others.

5 YEARS Five-year veterans offer significant input to bookkeeping systems and methodologies adopted by companies. Bookkeepers work closely with accountants and management to plan expenditures and revenue streams over the course of a year. Many people move from job to job during these middle years, looking for a position that fits their ideal match in terms of size, challenge, and manageability. The hours become more regular; satisfaction is average.

10 YEARS Ten-year veterans head up bookkeeping departments. Many have significant influence on accounting procedures and internal financial controls. The salaries rise, the hours remain average, and satisfaction increases.

MAJOR EMPLOYERS

Bookkeeping positions are available at local companies. Contact companies in your area for more information.

MAJOR ASSOCIATIONS

NATIONAL SOCIETY OF PUBLIC ACCOUNTANTS
1010 North Fairfax Street
Alexandria, VA 22314
Tel: 703-549-6400 or 800-966-6679
Fax: 703-549-2984
www.nsacct.org

NEW YORK STATE SOCIETY OF CPAS
3 Park Avenue, 18th Floor
New York, NY 10016-5991
Tel: 800-633-6320
Fax: 212-719-3364
www.nysscpa.org

BUSINESS VALUATOR

A DAY IN THE LIFE

A business valuator is a certified public accountant (CPA) who has chosen to specialize as an appraiser of businesses, both large and small. Certified public accountants sell their financial services to the public and to private businesses for a fee. A CPA may provide accounting and tax services or aid in appraising the value of a private estate, a small business, or even a large corporation. Business valuators, like their general financial practitioner cousins, will crunch data about the assets, liabilities, and capital of a company to prepare profit and loss statements and show the financial position of a company. However, business valuators aren't necessarily doing this so that a company can determine how much money it has to invest, as CPAs do. A business valuator is often assessing the worth of a company { assessing worth } so that another company can decide whether or not to acquire it, or conversely, what kind of offer they will accept if another company is trying to acquire them.

As the world hurtles toward becoming one very large corporation, business valuators are finding their services in greater demand than ever, and more CPAs are deciding to specialize their skills to capitalize on these opportunities. Although there are more than 500,000 CPAs in the workforce, only some of them specialize in business valuation. Business valuators determine what a company is worth by considering its assets, competitiveness in the market place, and even how much high-profile executives contribute to the company's profits. Valuators must also determine what a company's tax burden will be, since that directly affects profit. There is a lot of work that goes into accurately figuring out all of these numbers. Work hours can be long and the stress level high. Business valuators who have their own businesses tend to work longer hours than those employed by public accounting firms (who average a 40-hour work week). While much of the number crunching is done at their desks, valuators tend to travel often to meet directly with their clients.

Business valuators are also beginning to enter the public world on a larger basis, finding work evaluating assets such as stock options or estates in divorces and bequests. In this day and age, a high-profile divorce can earn a business valuator a fee as attractive as a corporate commission.

PAYING YOUR DUES

A bachelor's degree in accounting, business, or a related field is a requirement, and an MBA in finance or accounting will increase your earning power in the field. But education alone does not make one able to become a business valuator. The best opportunities for employment come to those who are first CPAs, for in most states, CPAs are the only accountants who are licensed and regulated. CPAs must obtain a certificate and license issued by a state board of accountancy.

Because business valuators are not regulated by the federal government, there is a growing sentiment that a regulatory board be created to set up blanket professional standards and ethics. The American Institute of Certified Public Accountants (AICPA), which certifies public accountants, has developed the ABV (Accredited in Business Valuation) designation that offered its first certification exam in November 1997. The AICPA is an independent professional regulatory organization that extends accreditation to those business valuators who pass the ABV examination. As business valuation becomes even more prolific, most clients will look for business valuators, just as they look for CPAs, who are accredited both as CPAs and ABVs and uphold the professional standards of the AICPA.

ASSOCIATED CAREERS

Valuation is a corporate career track, and business valuators must fit the corporate culture, even those who run their own financial planning businesses and are not associated with a bank or accounting firm. Because training in accounting is necessary, business valuators tend to choose other career options that exploit these skills. Some choose to focus on other disciplines under the umbrella of certified public accountancy, while others gravitate to professions as financial analysts and managers, actuaries, and loan officers. Experienced business valuators can find satisfying careers as investment bankers, bank officers, directors or managers of accounting, or full-time teachers at colleges and universities. Most often, business valuators/public accountants shift into management accounting and internal auditing.

PAST AND FUTURE

Business valuators have never been in higher demand than they are now. Business valuators/CPAs enjoy the widest range of job opportunities among qualified accountants, and as state licensing continues to become harder to attain, options will continue to flourish for those people who make the grade. Business valuators with higher levels of education will have the edge over less educated competitors, and computer skills are beginning to play important roles. A broad base of computer knowledge and experience is going to be necessary as accounting software becomes better.

QUALITY OF LIFE

2 YEARS In such a competitive market, it is hard to start out as a self-employed business valuator, and most professionals will have to work for an accounting firm to gain experience and a client base. Capable public accountants can advance rapidly, although those people with inadequate academic preparation will spend their first couple of years playing catch-up with those people who have bachelor's and master's degrees. Professionals on the road to specializing in business valuation will still have to pay their dues, serving in junior accounting positions to advance to more responsible positions. Demonstrating outstanding accounting and appraisal skills on the job is necessary to moving up the ladder.

5 YEARS Business valuators working for accounting firms can expect their own offices and salaries that start above the $40,000 level. At this point, many business valuators choose to become self-employed, having spent their early professional years building a client base to achieve this goal.

10 YEARS Business valuators who have been in the profession for a decade have either advanced to managerial positions or now run their own company. Those business valuators who have moved on to managerial positions or have become directors of accounting at an accounting firm can expect salaries pushing $80,000. Those business valuators who are self-employed may earn upward of $50,000.

MAJOR EMPLOYERS

ARTHUR ANDERSEN, LLP
33 West Monroe
Chicago, IL 60603
Tel: 312-580-0033
Fax: 312-507-6748
www.arthurandersen.com

KPMG INTERNATIONAL
345 Park Avenue
New York, NY 10154
www.kpmg.com

MAJOR ASSOCIATIONS

NATIONAL ASSOCIATION OF CERTIFIED VALUATION ANALYSTS
1111 Brickyard Road, Suite 200
Salt Lake City, UT 84106-5401
Tel: 801-486-0600
Fax: 801-486-7500
E-mail: nacval@nacva.com
www.nacva.com

COMPOSITOR/TYPESETTER

BOOKS, FILMS, AND TV SHOWS
FEATURING THE PROFESSION
- **The Chicago Manual of Style**
- **The Paper**
- **Shattered Glass**

YOU'LL HAVE CONTACT WITH
- **Copyeditors**
- **Editors**
- **Layout artists**
- **Printers**
- **Production editors**
- **Proofreaders**
- **Writers**

PROFESSIONALS READ
- **Editor & Publisher**
- **Electronic Publishing Magazine**
- **Publishers Weekly**

A DAY IN THE LIFE

Compositors, also known as typesetters, are responsible for setting written material into type for public consumption. Compositors have the power to change history, or at least to change the way we read about it. In a famous *Boston Globe* snafu, the typesetter during the Carter administration decided to head an article about the president, "More Mush from the Wimp"—which was certainly not what the editors had submitted. Typesetting entails deciding which parts of a work-in-progress on paper should be marked. It takes into account the dynamics of ink on paper, but leaves the actual rendering of the marks to the printers.

A certain degree of creativity and latitude comes into play, as type size, style, and compositional pattern have to be determined.

{ Compositors must always mind their P's and Q's. }

Using computer software, compositors format text, numerical data, photographs, charts, and other graphics to generate material that is ready to go to press. Depending on the project, typesetters may need to code, write, or edit text; create graphics; design page layouts; and translate electronic information onto paper or other more traditional formats. An entire newspaper or page—text and graphics—can be generated on a computer screen to appear exactly as it will in print. Instead of receiving simple typed text marked with layers of editorial markups, compositors generally retrieve material electronically or from a disk, after it has been edited and copyedited. Since most material published today is also available on the Internet, typesetters may need to know electronic publishing systems for converting text into HTML. After scanning photographs or other images, the graphics are either incorporated directly into page layouts or further manipulated. Compositors also deal with unwanted orphans (a single word or partial last line of a paragraph that appears on the next page), dingbats (a spacer or ornamental font), bangs (exclamation points), and bullets; and they must always mind their P's and Q's.

PAYING YOUR DUES

Students interested in a career as a compositor should study graphic arts or design to gain proficiency in the desktop publishing software that is now widely used to format pages, assign type characteristics, and import text and graphics into electronic page layouts. Courses in other aspects of printing are offered at many vocational or technical institutes, which provide students with an extensive background in imaging, prepress operations, print reproduction, and emerging media. Many employers prefer graduates of these programs because the specific training they receive gives them background in the page-layout process and helps them adapt to new software and techniques. Workers with limited training and experience may start as apprentices and, over time, advance to positions with greater responsibility.

ASSOCIATED CAREERS

While it may be difficult to get your foot in the door of the publishing arena, once you're there, the possibilities for advancement are manifold. Starting out as a compositor, your experience may lead you to other publishing industry jobs: copyeditor, editor, production editor, graphic artist, or layout artist, for example. With any one of these jobs, you may work in-house or on a job-by-job basis as a freelancer.

PAST AND FUTURE

The earliest-known dated printed book known is the "Diamond Sutra," printed in China in A.D. 868. In 1448, the German printer Johann Gutenberg first demonstrated movable type, also called foundry type or hot type. In foundry type, each piece of type was cast into a precise size from metal that was an alloy of lead, tin, and antimony. The setting of individual letters was rendered obsolete by hot-metal setting machines such as the Linotype machine, which permitted one machine operator to do the work of ten hand-type operators. In the late 1980s, desktop publishing on computers became available, starting with the Apple Macintosh. Programs like Adobe PageMaker have not only popularized desktop publishing, but have also given more control to professional compositors. Before the 1980s, most typesetting for publishers and advertisers was performed by typesetting companies, often called typographers. By the year 2000, this industry segment had all but vanished.

The availability of cheap, or free, type fonts made the conversion to in-house typesetting complete, and the advent of the PDF file format has provided a universally readable method of proofing designs and layouts. Compositors in the future may find that they will have more autonomy and flexibility with design features; but they will also need to be increasingly proficient with the newest computer software.

QUALITY OF LIFE

2 YEARS Even though there are innumerable courses and certificate programs out there that teach the basics of the computer programs and techniques used in the field, the best way to master the methods and learn to churn out polished, printable material is to find an office support position. In addition to nondesign duties, administrative employees often use word processors or desktop publishing software to design and produce documents for their employers.

5 YEARS With five years of experience, jobs in major publishing houses (or their third-party vendors) become an option. You may also take on freelance work, provided that you have the necessary software available at home. Advancement depends on experience, whether that's gained in the office or at home after hours.

10 YEARS The 10-year compositor has probably moved into a supervisory or managerial role or taken over editorial or production editorial duties.

MAJOR EMPLOYERS

THE ASSOCIATED PRESS
450 West 33rd Street
New York, NY 10001
www.ap.org

CONDÉ NAST PUBLICATIONS
4 Times Square
New York, NY 10036
Tel: 212-286-2860
www.condenast.com

THE NEW YORK TIMES
229 West 43rd Street
New York, NY 10036
Tel: 212-556-1234
E-mail: digitalresume@nytimes.com
www.nytimes.com

RANDOM HOUSE
1745 Broadway
New York, NY 10019
Tel: 212-782-9000
E-mail: humanresources@randomhouse.com
www.randomhouse.com

MAJOR ASSOCIATIONS

ASSOCIATION OF GRAPHIC COMMUNICATIONS
330 7th Avenue, 9th Floor
New York, NY 10001
Tel: 212-279-2100
www.agcomm.org

ASSOCIATION TYPOGRAPHIQUE INTERNATIONALE
www.atypi.org

GRAPHIC ARTS TECHNICAL FOUNDATION/PRINTING INDUSTRIES OF AMERICA, INC.
200 Deer Run Road
Sewickley, PA 15143
www.gain.net

COPYEDITOR

A DAY IN THE LIFE

Copyeditors are not proofreaders: There's more to their job than replacing commas with semicolons (though copyeditors are certainly expected to know the difference!). Copyeditors are responsible for tidying up prose, correcting inaccuracies, and ensuring that proper grammar and usage are employed. It's also their job to make sure that the red-headed girl who appears on page 67 still has red hair on page 150. They are responsible for ensuring that all cross-references direct readers to the proper places. Depending on the publication, some copyeditors are relied on to catch potentially libelous stories and to alert editors to pieces that require additional consultation with the author. There is often some rewriting involved; for example, copyeditors who find an inappropriate or awkwardly-worded phrase often make the necessary improvement themselves. In smaller publishing houses, copyeditors may find themselves wearing many hats—that of fact checker, layout artist, headline and caption writer, and monitor of wire services. A good copyeditor needs excellent reading and comprehension skills and must be a first-rate writer. You'll find that most people in this field have their noses in books both on and off the job. Copyeditors must also be very detail-oriented. Copyediting is not a job for the disorganized; with so many people to please, egos to manage, and bosses to impress, copyeditors must be highly organized.

{ dedication and determination }

The pay starts off low; the hours can be long; and the competition among those trying break into the publishing industry is fierce. Why stick it out? Most entry-level employees in the field know the pitfalls, but have their eye on the prize—senior or executive editor, positions that come with the task of deciding which material will appeal to readers and how that material should appear in print. At the highest levels, editors can earn six-figure salaries and receive credit for discovering new talent. Assuming that copyeditors don't burn out in the first two years, a promotion to assistant editor, associate managing editor, or production manager is generally right around the corner. In addition to an impeccable skill set, copyeditors must display dedication and strong determination: The more hours you put in and the more work you take home, the more you set yourself apart from your coworkers.

PAYING YOUR DUES

A college degree is required just to get your foot in the door. Most employers prefer to hire candidates with degrees in English, journalism, or communications. For those who want to specialize in particular areas, such as technical or medical copyediting, experience in the given field proves helpful. Familiarity with electronic publishing software is also a definite plus. A good (and sometimes, the only) way to gain some of the experience that larger employers want to see on your resume is to take an internship. Community newspapers, literary magazines, and college publications often supply valuable—yet often unpaid—opportunities to perfect your writing skills; and magazines and newspapers offer internships for students. Interns usually write short pieces, conduct research, and perform various clerical duties. Though post-graduation jobs aren't guaranteed for interns, offers for competent candidates are likely, and the industry experience and contacts are invaluable assets for a position in any sector of the publishing world.

ASSOCIATED CAREERS

If the track to editor, production manager, or managing editor loses some of its appeal, successful copyeditors still have many options. With valuable experience in the publishing industry, copyeditors can move on to become reporters, graphic and layout artists, or free-lance editors for hire. Advertising and public relations agencies are also sources of employment for copyeditors who are seeking work outside the realm of publishing.

PAST AND FUTURE

The Chicago Manual of Style, a handbook for editorial professionals around the world, is perhaps the most essential reference for anyone who works with words. When the University of Chicago Press first opened in 1891, professors who were planning to publish manuscripts brought their work directly to the compositors at the press; the compositors would then attempt to decipher and consistently typeset the manuscripts before passing on these newer versions to proofreaders. To remedy the problems that this process had the potential to create, the compositors teamed up with a proofreader to make a single list of the most common errors they were coming across. This meeting marked the birth of the manual. The list turned into a pamphlet, which grew into a book; and more than a hundred years later, it's still the reference source that sits on the desks of those whose business involves the written word. Equally influential in the history of editing in America, Maxwell Perkins used connections to get his foot in the door of *The New York Times* in 1907. After covering his share of entry-level emergencies (police reports, fires, and disasters), Perkins applied for a job with Charles Scribner's Sons in 1909 and was granted an interview a year later. Working his way out of advertising, Perkins moved up to the editorial floor and made his first discovery in 1919: a Princeton dropout named F. Scott Fitzgerald. Other breakthrough writers soon followed: Ezra Pound, Ernest Hemingway, Thomas Wolfe, and Marjorie Kinnan Rawlings.

Technology now influences every step of the publishing process. Writers, copyeditors, and senior staff members have seen their processes changed and updated on a regular basis with the advent of new methodology. Those who stay on top of new software developments will have an easier time finding work.

QUALITY OF LIFE

2 YEARS Beginning copyeditors spend their first few years of employment perfecting their research and fact-checking skills as well as soaking up the mechanics of the job. As they grow comfortable with the expectations of their supervisors, committed copyeditors can expect to be assigned to more challenging projects.

5 YEARS After the first few years of employment, promotions are fairly predictable. Copyeditors can expect promotion to assistant- or associate-level positions, in addition to more full-scale writing and editing assignments. Assistant editors generally have responsibility for particular subjects, such as local news, human interest stories, or, in book publishing, cookbooks or travel.

10 YEARS Editors with 10 or more years of experience have often earned the title of senior or managing editor. This often involves interaction with industry talent. Top editors with 10 or more years of experience take on additional responsibility for content, ethical conduct, creative vision, and employee management.

MAJOR EMPLOYERS

THE ASSOCIATED PRESS
450 West 33rd Street
New York, NY 10001
www.ap.org

CONDÉ NAST PUBLICATIONS
4 Times Square
New York, NY 10036
Tel: 212-286-2860
www.condenast.com

THE NEW YORK TIMES
229 West 43rd Street
New York, NY 10036
Tel: 212-556-1234
E-mail: *digitalresume@nytimes.com*
www.nytimes.com

RANDOM HOUSE
1745 Broadway
New York, NY 10019
Tel: 212-782-9000
E-mail: *humanresources@randomhouse.com*
www.randomhouse.com

MAJOR ASSOCIATIONS
AMERICAN COPY EDITORS SOCIETY
www.copydesk.org

AMERICAN SOCIETY OF MAGAZINE EDITORS
8107 7th Avenue, 24th Floor
New York, NY 10019
www.magazine.org

EDITORIAL FREELANCERS ASSOCIATION
71 West 23rd Street, Suite 1910
New York, NY 10010
Tel: 212-929-5400
www.the-efa.org

CORPORATE LAWYER

PROFESSIONAL PROFILE

# of people in profession	67,000
Avg. hours per week	50
Avg. starting salary	$64,000
Avg. salary after 5 years	$93,700
Avg. salary 10 to 15 years	$139,000

SALARY ●●●
HOURS ●●◐
EDUCATION ●●●

BOOKS, FILMS, AND TV SHOWS
FEATURING THE PROFESSION
- **The Firm**
- **L.A. Law**
- **The Paper Chase**

YOU'LL HAVE CONTACT WITH
- **Accountants**
- **Bankers**
- **Business executives**
- **Paralegals**

PROFESSIONALS READ
- **Global Legal Studies**
- **Lawyers Weekly**
- **National Law Journal**

A DAY IN THE LIFE

Corporate lawyers ensure the legality of commercial transactions. They must have a knowledge of statutory law and regulations passed by government agencies to help clients achieve their goals within the bounds of the law. To structure a business transaction legally, a corporate lawyer may need to research aspects of contract law, tax law, accounting, securities law, bankruptcy, intellectual property rights, licensing, zoning laws, and other regulations relating to a specific area of business. The lawyer must ensure that a transaction does not conflict with local, state, or federal laws.

In contrast to the adversarial nature of trial law, corporate law is team oriented. The corporate counsels for both sides of a transaction are not strict competitors; together they seek a common ground for their clients. They are, in the words of one lawyer, "the handmaidens of the deal." Facilitating the business process requires insight into the clients needs, selective expertise, flexibility, and, most of all, a service mentality.

{ handmaidens of the deal }

Corporate law requires an incisive mind and excellent written and oral communication skills. Through the negotiation process, lawyers constantly write and revise the legal documents that will bind the parties to certain terms for the transaction. This process is lengthy and typically corporate lawyers work extremely long hours. As a deal moves toward its closing, it becomes an exercise in stamina as much as skillful negotiation. As one person observed, "You've got to be able to put your butt in a chair and do the work."

The upside to this profession is that the compensation is good, and you usually work with smart people. One corporate lawyer remarked that she liked this side of the law precisely because the transactions take place among peers: There is no wronged party, no underdog, and usually no inequity in the financial means of the participants.

PAYING YOUR DUES

In law, the pressure starts early. Law school admissions are extremely competitive—the top 25 schools have an admission rate of about 10 percent. You can get tracked early: The kind of school you attend affects what kind of summer job opportunities you may have; this in turn affects the kind of permanent job you secure. The starting salary and kind of experience you have as a corporate lawyer can vary greatly depending on the size of the firm and geographic location. In a smaller firm, you will have more responsibility and more client contact early on, but the salaries can be tens of thousands of dollars lower than in a large firm. The content of your practice will be different, too: a small-town lawyer may take care of a house closing, drafting a will, and a divorce settlement in a day; big-city lawyers can spend months negotiating a single commercial transaction.

ASSOCIATED CAREERS

If they decide not to pursue partnership in their firms, corporate lawyers often make use of their expertise as an in-house counsel for a corporation. Others go into a related business, such as investment banking, and a few teach.

PAST AND FUTURE

Thomas Jefferson introduced the first academic law program to the United States when he created a professorship in law at William and Mary in 1779. George Wythe, a Virginia judge at the time and, later, a signer of the Declaration of Independence, was the first to fill the post. Harvard was not far behind and was already producing lawyers of repute in the mid-1700s.

The number of corporate lawyers grew in the 1980s when commercial activity was at its peak. When the economy slowed down, so did the need for attorneys. The practice of corporate law is less cushy now; the days of the endless expense account are gone. The state of the economy always shapes the nature of corporate law; changes in the interest rates, the tax code, and other regulations affect the kind of transactions being done and how they are structured.

QUALITY OF LIFE

2 YEARS New associates spend their days reviewing documents and doing legal research. They gather information on statutes that affect their clients' transactions to ensure that it can be done legally and keep track of the paperwork needed for the closing. The work is hard. Expect to put in long hours and work weekends.

5 YEARS By five years, lawyers are negotiating and drafting the major operative documents for their deals. Senior associates are the primary client contact and run deals and closings by themselves. They have increased responsibility and are trying to develop a reputation in their specialty. Often they supervise the training of new associates. At the five-year mark, associates decide if they want to be on a partner track. People who do want to become partners put in very long hours before their review (which usually takes place around seven years). Others leave for a related position in business or become an in-house counsel at a corporation.

10 YEARS At 10 years, corporate lawyers are structuring their own transactions. They have developed keen judgment and create "big picture" strategies. They know what issues will likely arise for a particular case and which experts to call to resolve them. As one lawyer said, "I'm a highly experienced generalist who knows all the right specialists." Usually, associates have made partner by this time. With partnership comes management responsibilities. Partners must recruit and train new associates of the firm, manage the work flow on client transactions, and oversee the internal affairs of the firm. All this work is on top of their normal billable hours. In addition, partners must put in time cultivating clients and selling the business. Firm partners usually get involved in bar association activities, write for professional journals, and speak at national conferences. The compensation at this level is quite good.

MAJOR EMPLOYERS

BAKER & MCKENZIE
One Prudential Plaza
130 East Randolph Drive
Chicago, IL 60601
Tel: 312-861-8000
www.bakerinfo.com

CRAVATH, SWAINE & MOORE
Worldwide Plasa
825 Eighth Avenue
New York, NY 10019-7475
Tel: 212-474-1000
Fax: 212-474-3700
www.cravath.com
Contact: Human Resources

SKADDEN, ARPS, SLATE, MEAGHER, AND FLOM LLP
4 Times Square
New York, NY 10036
Tel: 212-735-3000
Fax: 212-735-2000
www.skadden.com
Contact: Human Resources

MAJOR ASSOCIATIONS

AMERICAN BAR ASSOCIATION
740 15th Street, NW, 9th Floor
Washington, DC 20005-1019
Tel: 202-662-1000
www.abanet.org

ASSOCIATION OF CORPORATE COUNSEL
1025 Connecticut Avenue, NW, Suite 200
Washington, DC 20036-5425
Tel: 202-293-4103
Fax: 202-293-4701
www.acca.com

NATIONAL LAWYERS GUILD
132 Nassau Street, Suite 922
New York, NY 10038
Tel: 212-679-5100
Fax: 212-679-2811
www.nlg.org

COURT REPORTER

A DAY IN THE LIFE

A court reporter's responsibility is to record accurately who says what and when at trials, during depositions, and any time someone feels words being spoken are important enough to hire an accurate transcriber. In a career that requires little emotional commitment for good pay, court reporters find their lives divided into two noninterlocking segments: work and other. "It is a good career to be able to do other things," mentioned one court reporter/actor. Most professionals work through agencies that act as clearinghouses for able, certified court reporters.

Court reporting is a learnable skill requiring strong skills in English language, concentration, and study. Court reporters need strong grammatical skills and lots of patience. "Awareness is the most important thing about this career," a 15-year court-reporting veteran told us. Frequently, the exact words you type in are crucial to the decision rendered in a given case. A court reporter is responsible for certifying that what has been entered is, to the best of his or her abilities, an accurate representation of what took place. Unqualified court reporters usually lose all referrals with the first or second incident that arises from carelessness. Because of this high standard of performance and the natural isolation (only one court reporter is in the court room at any given time), significant pressures are placed on court reporters. Of the 25 percent who leave the profession between the first and second years, most cite "stress" as a major factor in their decision.

{ "I'm scared I'll break a finger." }

At its best, a reporter told us, "You go into a zone where you're not concentrating anymore, and the words are going straight from your ears through your fingers and onto your disk." This near Zen-like experience was mentioned by several of our respondents as the most pleasant and rewarding job features. At its worst, the career places not only mental demands but also physical ones on people in the field. The incidence of repetitive motion disorders (such as carpal tunnel syndrome) in this career is second only to those found in word-processing departments. Since most court reporters work as agents of a larger service, they are responsible for their own health care costs and bear the full burden of any work-precluding injuries. "I can't even play touch football," lamented one reporter new to the field; "I'm scared I'll break a finger." Since there is no true hierarchy in this profession, and therefore advancement is not an issue, little—if any—politics enter the daily routine.

PAYING YOUR DUES

About 80 schools and colleges that offer court reporting programs (either two or four years) are approved by the National Court Reporters Association. The Association requires that schools teach computer-aided transcription, so be careful when choosing a school. If you can study on your own and pass the rigorous Court Reporting Exams, then a degree from one of these institutions is helpful, but not required. Some states demand that court reporters be notary publics, and others demand that they pass additional state-specific certification tests, such as the Certified Court Reporter (CCR) test or the Registered Professional Reporter (RPR) two-part exam. Specialization for such designations as medical transcriber and court transcriber may require additional training and sphere-specific certification. The requirements for employment by the federal government stipulate that court reporters transcribe at least 175 words per minute; private firms often require a minimum of 225 words per minute.

ASSOCIATED CAREERS

Now that all television programming carries closed-captioning, broadcast captioning is fast becoming a burgeoning subset of the court-reporting profession. Another version of captioning, CART (Communication Access Realtime Translation), draws many court reporters. Many can also earn money for their services as "scopists," in which they process and edit the rough drafts of their colleagues' transcripts. The court reporter's unsurpassed skills at data entry are also in demand at hospitals and insurance companies, who employ them to process data into their computers.

PAST AND FUTURE

Accurate transcription of historical events has taken place since the first formalized "trials" of Ancient Greece. These historiographies were originally written after the completion of the trial at the request of the ruler who wanted history to record the verdict (just or unjust), as proof of his enlightened wisdom. With the modern advocacy system in the United States which required trials be open to the public, a more formal means of record keeping was established with the use of court reporters.

Court reporters have become part of the technical revolution that is sweeping America's courtrooms. Once punched into tape, then typed into common 8-1/2 by 11 inch form in a back room (delaying the receipt of transcripts by up to two days), court transcripts are now recorded on computer disks used to store text, thus allowing them to be available within hours. Real-time transcripts are expected to become more common as better technology allows for simultaneous data transfer. The occupation will remain stable and constant (with significant opportunities available for those in entry-level positions) until voice-recognition software has become more refined—most likely not for another few decades, by current estimates.

QUALITY OF LIFE

2 YEARS The court reporter is just getting up to speed for the first few years, continuing with on-the-job training and learning the trade, the different agencies, avenues into working in broadcasting or, if in the legal system, the style of each judge or court.

5 YEARS While the career doesn't change much from one year to the next, the reporter's increasing knowledge of the different courtroom styles gets him or her more frequent assignments.

10 YEARS Employment is fairly secure at this stage, and wages are high due to demand for experienced personnel. Aside from frequent complaints of repetitive strain disorders—"Do you know that the incidence is higher than, say, meat cutters or pianists?" asks a communications executive—job satisfaction is generally high.

MAJOR EMPLOYERS

"The term 'court reporter' is a misnomer because only 25 percent of the court reporters in the United States work in a courtroom," says a communications executive for a major association of the profession. The rest work for attorneys, hired directly or through agencies to cover depositions, with a small percentage employed to create captions for live television or as real time translations for clients who are hearing impaired.

MAJOR ASSOCIATIONS

NATIONAL COURT REPORTERS ASSOCIATION
8224 Old Courthouse Road
Vienna, VA 22182-3808
Tel: 800-272-6272 or 703-556-6272
Fax: 703-556-6291
www.ncraonline.org

DENTAL LAB TECHNICIAN

BOOKS, FILMS, AND TV SHOWS
FEATURING THE PROFESSION

- **First Impressions**
- **Little Shop of Horrors**
- **Practicing Dentistry**

YOU'LL HAVE CONTACT WITH

- **Dentists**
- **Oral surgeons**
- **Orthodontists**
- **X-ray technicians**

PROFESSIONALS READ

- **Dental Lab Entrepreneur**

A DAY IN THE LIFE

Dental technicians (DTs) provide back-office support to dentists. After the dentist has taken a mold of the patient's teeth, the dental technician uses the mold to produce a wax replica of the teeth, from which he or she constructs any needed crowns, bridges, or false teeth, and later makes any adjustments to these appliances as directed by the dentist. Dental technicians work closely with dentists and orthodontists.

Our survey respondents pointed out that DTs are often confused with dental hygienists, who work with the dentist and mostly "clean" teeth and treat periodontal (gum) disease. Dental lab technicians insist that they "don't scrape plaque or put our fingers in anybody's mouth!" In fact they 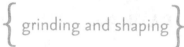 have patient contact only in unusual situations that require a visual inspection of the patient's teeth. Though many labs are large, some technicians are sole practitioners in their studios and can work under contract with a dentist. The painstaking detail work is largely solitary. "If you're afraid of being alone, don't sign up," cautions one DT.

Successful DTs say it's important to be able to make adjustments on the fly. They create facsimiles of people's teeth, and, while impressions can be perfect, they often need minor adjustments, and the DT must work from information provided by the dentist to adjust molds to imitate and accommodate the patient's mouth. "You can get through grinding and shaping three or four times, and the dentist still isn't satisfied," wrote one DT. Another DT added that "it's not personal, but it can be very frustrating." They share certain skills with sculptors and don't mind working hard on making their molds accurate and useful; after all, without a precise fit, these casts are useless. A good eye and a good ear serve candidates well in this exacting profession.

PAYING YOUR DUES

No formal college major is required to become a dental technician. Most candidates learn how to shape, mold, and grind their materials on the job. Many DTs train on the job for two to three years before becoming sole practitioners. About 45 dental colleges in the country offer dental technician programs accredited by the American Dental Association. In their final years at those colleges, students choose one area of specialization, such as orthodontics or crowns and bridges, then take licensing exams (such as the one offered by the National Board of Certification), although these licensing exams are not always required.

ASSOCIATED CAREERS

Construction of medical devices requires attention to detail and knowledge of anatomy; people with these skills become prosthetics manufacturers, lens grinders for optometrists, and oral hygienists.

PAST AND FUTURE

There used to be only a handful of dental technicians who provided highly technical assistance for patients in oral crisis (e.g., massive tooth decay, full bridge replacements, or jaw deformity). With the rapid growth of orthodontics in the 1970s, work for dental technicians expanded, and people began to enter the profession in significant numbers. Over the years, many people have had to return to school to keep up with new technology and new methods of construction, but the most pressing force behind change in the industry has been the use of new materials in making impressions and molds.

Demographic trends suggest there will be a continuing demand for specialists as America's population ages. For people who work in gerontological dentistry in particular, the future looks more promising. Because the bulk of DT work consists of standard procedures (such as brace making and tooth spacing), economies of scale have come into play, favoring larger firms that can process these requests quickly and efficiently. But every set of teeth is slightly different, and specialists must create solutions in unpredictable situations.

QUALITY OF LIFE

2 YEARS
Most dental technicians who work in supervised environments have just completed their on-the-job training programs and are working as assistant dental technicians, grinding molds to specifications, creating wax castings of teeth for crown construction, and shaping jawline impressions. Other relatively new professionals are now full dental technicians and continue to work with their initial employers. Most of them work in offices of five people or fewer, so these early years are marked by close relationships and tight working conditions. The hours are long; satisfaction is average.

5 YEARS
Job mobility becomes significant; over one-third of dental technicians go into private practice at this point, either buying an existing shop or working as an independent contractor affiliated with a number of dentists or HMOs. The remainder move between dental offices, finding temporary matches between themselves and their employers. Satisfaction increases and so do the hours.

10 YEARS
Ten-year professionals have chosen areas of specialization, such as ceramics, partial and complete dentures, orthodontic appliances, or crown and bridge replacements. Salaries increase, and many solo practitioners hire less experienced technicians to help them in their work. Satisfaction is at its highest as 10-year veterans are experienced technicians with a reliable client base and good business-recruiting skills. People who lack any of these elements of a successful technician seek an associated career that satisfies them in a similar way.

MAJOR EMPLOYERS

TOWN & COUNTRY DENTAL STUDIOS
275 South Main Street
Freeport, NY 11520
Tel: 800-925-8696 or 516-868-8641
Fax: 516-868-1309

Employers include local dentists, orthodontists, and oral surgeons. Contact dental specialists in your region to learn about employment opportunities.

MAJOR ASSOCIATIONS

INTERNATIONAL ASSOCIATION FOR DENTAL RESEARCH
1619 Duke Street
Alexandria, VA 22134-3406
Tel: 703-548-0066
Fax: 703-548-1883
E-mail: research@iadr.org
www.iadr.org

NATIONAL ASSOCIATION OF DENTAL LABORATORIES
325 John Knox Road L103
Tallahassee, FL 32303
Tel: 800-950-1150 or 850-222-0053
E-mail: nadl@nadl.org
www.nadl.org

ECONOMIST

A DAY IN THE LIFE

The field of economics rewards creative and curious thinkers. Economists study data and statistics and look for trends in economic activity, economic confidence levels, and consumer attitudes. They assess this information using advanced methods in statistical analysis, mathematics, and computer programming; finally they make recommendations about ways to improve the efficiency of a system or take advantage of trends as they begin. While the majority of economists were previously relegated to the academic community, with about half as many in government, they are striving to maintain consistent employment throughout the private sector in the post-Enron landscape. As many firms split up their accounting and consulting divisions, economists have { strong sense of community } fallen under similar scrutiny to remain ethical as they pursue lucrative client bases. These firms offer advice to and predict economic scenarios for individuals and large corporations and occasionally act as consultants to branches of the government. However, universities and government groups remain the largest employers of economists, followed by industry and research organizations.

"I love being an economist. I get a glimpse of the future or what we think it's going to be," raved one economist we surveyed. High levels of satisfaction are found throughout this field, which encourages discussion, detailed examination, and lively disagreement. Economists work closely with one another and share ideas fairly easily, which leads to a strong sense of community within the profession.

The daily routine of each economist is determined by the specialty chosen. Financial economists meet with members of Wall Street firms and government officials to predict the movement and pace of global financial markets. International economists may spend as much as 30 percent of their time traveling and 40 percent of the time on the phone researching current trends in foreign economic systems (for this subgroup, language skills are important). Other fields include agricultural economics, labor economics, monetary economics, industrial economics, public finance, and law and economics.

PAYING YOUR DUES

Graduates with master's degrees in economics find entry-level positions in which their primary responsibilities are the collection, assimilation, and preparation of data. For positions with greater responsibility, such as those in teaching or government, a PhD is required. The more quantitative course requirements of the economics major include statistics, econometrics, linear algebra, and differential equations. These courses form the core of the discipline, but at the same time, people who are comfortable with the written or spoken word have a significantly higher rate of advancement and overall job satisfaction than those who are not. Applicants should be comfortable with computers, numbers, and long academic papers. Women tend to begin their careers in government and research organizations, and many women who start in academia find they are more successful in the private sector.

The ability to distinguish yourself from other economists is key, but can be difficult, especially within a particular company's or industry's accepted economic assumptions. Creative thinkers with quantitative backgrounds and who have taken cross-discipline course loads, such as philosophy or marketing, seem to find it easier to break from the pack and propose new, interesting additions to the economic canon.

"I get a glimpse of the future or what we think it's going to be."

ASSOCIATED CAREERS

Economists who leave the profession find a wide range of careers open to them. Their statistical and mathematical skills make them well suited for careers as statisticians, bankers, stockbrokers, options traders, equity research analysts, university presidents, and any other profession that requires systems modeling and a thorough understanding of incentives and human behavior. Their research and writing skills allow them to become financial journalists, research analysts, academics in other fields, and administrative managers.

PAST AND FUTURE

Adam Smith, the father of capitalism, extolled the benefits of a laissez-faire (or "hands off") approach to the economy and was a believer in the so-called law of supply and demand. John Maynard Keynes, with his theories on unemployment and the system of economic sponsorship, was one of the first modern economists to garner international fame.

In the future, computer modeling will help economists formulate their economic visions for a broad scope of clients, including third world countries and multinational corporations. In anticipation of an economic boom after a period of turbulence, private industries may hire approximately 30 percent more economists over the next few years, mostly in urban centers, particularly Washington, DC; New York; and Los Angeles (for economists specializing in the analysis of Pacific Rim economies).

QUALITY OF LIFE

2 YEARS Economists who pursue graduate degrees often work while still in school, so these first few years pass at a frenzied pace. For the first few months in the working world, economists learn the assumptions and models used by the hiring company, and more than half of them veer their careers into academia. Tasks focus on computer modeling, report writing, and working as part of larger, highly supervised research teams. Salaries for individuals with PhDs are more than double those of individuals with master's degrees. Projects usually have strict deadlines, so expect some weekend work. Economists in academia start out as assistant professors, lecturing, grading papers, and teaching sections.

5 YEARS Nearly 30 percent of people who began five years ago have either returned to school to pursue higher degrees in economics or get out of the field altogether (in many cases, to become bankers). Since most private consulting firms employ fewer than 50 people, individuals who stay can rise rapidly. Successful economists are team leaders, managing large research projects, working with clients, and reviewing materials prepared by junior associates. Academics, now teaching their own seminars, are likely to have shifted among universities to those schools with strong opportunities for advancement and are publishing papers and articles other than thesis material.

10 YEARS By this point, economists have significant client experience, strong managerial skills, and an ability to deliver promised services. More than 25 percent of 10-year veterans start their own consulting firms. Others become in-house employees at banks, brokerage houses, or other types of financial consulting firms (usually at the vice-presidential level or higher). Academics are now professors, publishing articles, working with graduate students, and angling for the extra university awards and consulting agreements that can provide a significant boost to income and prestige within the profession.

MAJOR EMPLOYERS

FEDERAL RESERVE BOARD
20th & C Street, NW
Washington, DC 20051
Tel: 202-452-3000
Fax: 202-452-3819
Jobline: 800-448-4894
www.bog.frb.fed.us

INTERNATIONAL MONETARY FUND
700 19th Street, NW
Washington, DC 20431
Tel: 202-623-7000
Fax: 202-623-4661
www.imf.org
Contact: Recruitment

UNITED STATES DEPARTMENT OF COMMERCE
1401 Constitution Avenue, NW
Washington, DC 20230
www.doc.gov

WORLD BANK GROUP
1818 H Street, NW
Washington, DC 20433
Tel: 202-473-1000
Fax: 202-477-6391
www.worldbank.org
Contact: Human Resources

MAJOR ASSOCIATIONS

AMERICAN ECONOMIC ASSOCIATION
2014 Broadway, Suite 305
Nashville, TN 37203
Tel: 615-322-2595
Fax: 615-343-7590
www.vanderbilt.edu/AEA

NATIONAL ASSOCIATION FOR BUSINESS ECONOMICS
1233 20th Street, NW, Suite 505
Washington, DC 20036
Tel: 202-463-6223
Fax: 202-463-6239
www.nabe.com

FINANCIAL AID OFFICER

PROFESSIONAL PROFILE

# of people in profession	11,200
Avg. hours per week	40
Avg. starting salary	$24,900
Avg. salary after 5 years	$30,200
Avg. salary 10 to 15 years	$36,300

SALARY ●

HOURS ●

EDUCATION ● ●

BOOKS, FILMS, AND TV SHOWS
FEATURING THE PROFESSION
- **Climbing the Red Tape Mountain**

YOU'LL HAVE CONTACT WITH
- **Bankers**
- **Government officials**
- **School administrators**
- **Students**

PROFESSIONALS READ
- **Adventures in Education**
- **Student Guide (United States Department of Education)**

A DAY IN THE LIFE

Anyone who has requested financial aid knows that the process may transport you into the land of bureaucratic paperwork nightmares. Applying for aid can be confusing and complex. It is the job of an educational institution's financial aid officers to ferry applicants across this river of confusion safely and comfortably. Financial aid officers assess students' needs, determine eligibility, help complete paperwork, and work with students who take out loans to make sure they can make their payments. Our respondents cited interpersonal skills and organizational abilities as the first and second most important qualities an individual needs to succeed as a financial aid officer. People in the field express a strong degree of satisfaction in their choice of occupation. Many financial aid officers are former (or current) clients of the national financial aid system and view their roles as student financial aid advocates. "It's great to be the one helping people get money [to afford a college education]; it's tougher when things don't work out, and there's nothing you can do."

{ fair assessment }

Entry-level positions in this field usually involve managing large paperwork caseloads, following current students through their changes in enrollment status, and informing people of their obligations and options. Individuals interested in this field should be comfortable with numbers and able to learn quickly a structure based on complicated paperwork. People who enter the career should expect occasional brusqueness from clients of the system who are frustrated with the bureaucratic channels and invasive questioning that applying for a loan entails. People who responded to our survey mentioned that the attitude of students who don't receive all the financial aid they want is demoralizing; in many cases, they blame the messenger and lash out at the aid counselor. This can be frustrating, especially when one financial aid officer can be expected to handle up to 2,000 cases per year. The public's often negative impressions of financial aid officers are another drawback.

A good financial aid counselor has to be familiar with the changing restrictions and obligations that face borrowers. The ability to elicit a fair assessment of the student's current loan obligations, work situation, and prospective income is critical to the financial aid officer, who must suggest the amount of money the student should request and determine what programs are available to help the student. Continuing education is very important in this field, and many financial aid officers go to conferences, seminars, and lectures to keep on top of current trends in financial aid.

PAYING YOUR DUES

No specific bachelor's degree is required to become a financial aid officer, but college coursework should include mathematics, statistics, or some finance; coursework covering psychology and English is also helpful. A financial aid officer writes reports, recommendations, and memos, so strong writing skills are necessary. Most importantly, however, a financial aid officer should be a good communicator, able to explain confusing and difficult concepts to people who may be at the end of their financial ropes. Listening skills have been cited as the largest difference between a good and a bad financial aid officer. No official certification is required to be a financial aid officer, but familiarity with Pell Grants, Stafford Loans, Plus Loans, Newman Grants, Federal Nursing Scholarships, and Perkins Loans is key.

ASSOCIATED CAREERS

Financial aid officers, while having a reasonable understanding of complex financial constructs, are statistically more likely ultimately to end up in human resources, career guidance, or individual counseling jobs than in financial ones. The instinct that leads someone to become a financial aid officer lies somewhere between the desire to help others and the ability to manage a large bureaucracy. This mix is best suited for careers that involve a lot of contact with people, such as working in the loan departments at banks or the vocational counseling departments of private companies.

PAST AND FUTURE

Financial aid for education began with the influx of post-World War II GIs returning to school on the GI bill. The federal government decided to encourage soldiers to return to college after the war and provided guarantees on low-interest loans for those who wished to return to college. In the initial years of this program, students had a high rate of repayment of their loans—so much so that the private sector clamored to become involved. Yet with the astronomical rise of education costs in the 1980s, many banks began to move away from this position, fearing that the burden of educational debt might be too great for many students to bear.

Financial aid officers' roles are growing in number and importance; even moderately well-off families need to borrow some money to send a child to college. The big question surrounding this profession is, what role will the government play during times of budget cuts? One thing is certain: Financial aid officers may need to be even more creative about finding ways to help students pay for college.

QUALITY OF LIFE

2 YEARS Junior financial aid officers are thrown into the mix headfirst and assigned cases on their first day. A "sink-or-swim" attitude is part of the entry-level trial facing the beginning financial aid officer; however, coworkers are cited as being extremely helpful in making sure that new employees don't flounder too much. At times, difficult cases are routed away from or reassigned to new personnel. By the end of the first two years, financial aid officers have received two educations: one on how to network through financial aid systems and another on how to work as part of a supportive team.

5 YEARS Pay rises, though not enough, according to many financial aid officers. Their responsibilities and the number of hours they work increase, and the level of difficulty of the cases assigned to them rises. Financial aid officers who have achieved senior status in the office have some supervisory responsibility and may work with the budget and financial offices of the university to reconcile accounts and ensure the smooth progression of money being repaid on loans. Exit interviews, in which a borrower's obligations are explained to them in stark terms, are part of the daily routine at this stage of a financial aid officer's career. Individuals interested in progressing within university administrations take courses in other areas such as management and policy to supplement their skills.

10 YEARS Many 10-year veterans are running financial aid offices by this point, and a significant number of them have switched universities to pursue better opportunities. People who remain "caseworkers" have decided that the managerial life is not for them and that they prefer client contact and student interaction. Individuals who leave after 10 years only do so because of unique opportunities, burnout from exhaustion, or retirement.

MAJOR EMPLOYERS

Financial aid officers are employed by universities and colleges across the country. Contact universities and colleges at which you wish to work for employment opportunities. Many also work for banks.

MAJOR ASSOCIATIONS

NATIONAL ASSOCIATION OF STUDENT FINANCIAL AID ADMINISTRATORS
1129 20th Street, NW, Suite 400
Washington, DC 20036-3489
Tel: 202-785-0453
Fax: 202-785-1487
E-mail: ask@nasfaa.org
www.nasfaa.org

FINANCIAL ANALYST

PROFESSIONAL PROFILE

# of people in profession	298,000
Avg. hours per week	55
Avg. starting salary	$43,660
Avg. salary after 5 years	$76,620
Avg. salary 10 to 15 years	$108,060

SALARY   ● ● ●

HOURS   ● ● ●

EDUCATION   ● ●

BOOKS, FILMS, AND TV SHOWS
FEATURING THE PROFESSION

- **The Assessment**
- **Dealmaking**
- **Wall Street**

YOU'LL HAVE CONTACT WITH

- **Accountants**
- **Bankers**
- **Investment bankers**
- **Researchers**

PROFESSIONALS READ

- **Money**
- **The Economist**
- **The Wall Street Journal**

A DAY IN THE LIFE

Financial analysts gather information, assemble spreadsheets, write reports, and review all pertinent nonlegal information about prospective deals. They examine the feasibility of a deal and prepare plans of action based on financial analysis. Being an analyst requires an awareness of financial trends. Analysts have a heavy reading load, keeping abreast of news stories, market movements, and industry profiles in financial newspapers, magazines, and books. Most analyst jobs are in banking houses or for financial consulting firms, which means following corporate culture and wearing corporate attire. If necessary to close a deal, they must be prepared to travel anywhere. Those who wish to rise in the industry should note the necessity of significant "face time," attending social events and conferences and spending downtime with people in the profession, which can be expensive; this social circle tends to gravitate to expensive clothing, hobbies, habits, and diversions.

{ "face time" }

Analysts sacrifice a lot of control over their personal lives during their first few years, but only a few other entry-level positions provide the possibility of such a large payoff come year's end. Many employers use bonuses—equal to or double the beginning analyst's salary—to attract and retain intelligent personnel. Successful financial analysts become senior financial analysts or associates after three to four years of hard work at some firm. Analysts with strong client contacts and immaculate reputations start their own financial consulting firms. Many of them work as analysts for about three years and then return to school or move on to other positions in banking.

Financial analysts work long hours, and deadlines are strict. "When you have to get the job done, you get the job done. Period," emphasized one. The occasional 15-hour day and night spent sleeping in the office is mitigated by the high degree of responsibility these analysts are given. Beyond this, the long hours breed a close kinship. More than 65 percent called their coanalysts extremely supportive, and many analysts labeled them a "major reason" they were able to put up with the demanding work schedule. Most people become financial analysts because they feel it is the best way to immerse themselves in the world of finance and a great way to earn a lot of money. They're right on both counts, but be aware that the immersion is complete and somewhat exclusive, and although people earn a lot of money, few analysts have the free time to spend it.

PAYING YOUR DUES

Entry-level positions are highly competitive. A bachelor's degree in any discipline is acceptable, so long as the potential analyst's course of study demonstrates his or her ability to understand and work comfortably and proficiently with numbers. Analysts with computer science, physical science, or biological science backgrounds may find the field more welcoming than do liberal arts majors. Business majors don't necessarily have an advantage; each company trains the incoming class of financial analysts before they begin the job. To become a financial analyst you need to have a strong sense of purpose; it is not a job for those who are uncertain that their future lies in the financial world. Candidates must be able to meet and interact with clients, handle a heavy work load, prioritize and complete work under strict deadlines, work as part of a team, and use computer spreadsheet and valuation programs. Many analysts find the business traveling stimulating initially, but "after your third week in Jopbsug, Tennessee, at the ball-bearing plant, it gets old."

ASSOCIATED CAREERS

Individuals who progress along the corporate financial analyst track can expect to find different jobs in the financial community, perhaps as investment bankers, investment advisors, or financial consultants. Analysts who enjoy the more interpersonal side of finance move into management consultant positions, where they can use their people skills as well as their financial skills. More than 45 percent of all analysts head to business school within five years, and another 10 percent go to law school. A few become in-house financial advisors or officers in the industries they covered as financial analysts.

PAST AND FUTURE

The obligations of today's financial analyst were covered by more experienced individuals as late as the 1970s, but with the rapid deregulation of ownership in industries in the early 1980s and the rapid growth of the financial sector during those same years, the need arose for a structured and continuing stream of extensively trained professionals familiar with the financial industry. Larger firms, which downsized their training programs in the early 1990s, are cautiously beginning to expand them again, finding opportunities in such new and developing industries as software development, biotechnology, and aerospace technologies.

QUALITY OF LIFE

2 YEARS

Long hours, low base pay, and a fair amount of responsibility characterize the early years. Analysts travel, pore through documents, meet with clients (on a highly supervised basis), and prepare valuation analyses. Lack of control over hours and personal life are common in the first two years. The burnout rate is surprisingly low in the beginning—around 8 percent—because most individuals who enter the industry have few illusions about the demands of the job.

5 YEARS

At the five-year mark, analysts who remain have achieved the rank of associate or senior financial analyst. Responsibilities shift from producing to pitching, and client contact increases. Many analysts study for professional degrees during these years. More than 70 percent of people who began in the field have either changed firms, returned to school, or changed jobs within the industry. While loyalty is tangible between analysts, the same sense of fidelity doesn't seem to apply to the companies that employ them. Salaries remain relatively stable but bonuses, which once were merely large, can become astronomical; hours, for those who are successful, can actually increase.

10 YEARS

Successful financial analysts have moved on to vice presidential positions in the investment banking, financial analysis, or valuation departments of the company. While bonuses still account for the bulk of income, salaries are significant as well. The hours can decrease, but the amount of responsibility increases and pressure develops to solicit new business. Responsibilities also include personnel decisions and hiring.

MAJOR EMPLOYERS

AMERICAN STOCK EXCHANGE
86 Trinity Place
New York, NY 10036
Tel: 212-306-1000
www.amex.com

CHICAGO STOCK EXCHANGE, INC.
One Financial Place
440 South LaSalle Street
Chicago, IL 60605
Tel: 312-663-2222
E-mail: info@chx.com
www.chx.com
Contact: Employment Specialist

MAJOR ASSOCIATIONS

**FINANCIAL EXECUTIVES
INTERNATIONAL**
200 Campus Drive
Florham Park, NJ 07932-0674
Tel: 973-765-1000
Fax: 973-765-1018
www.fei.org

FINANCIAL PLANNER

BOOKS, FILMS, AND TV SHOWS FEATURING THE PROFESSION
- **Hannah and Her Sisters**
- **The OC**

YOU'LL HAVE CONTACT WITH
- **Accountants**
- **Attorneys**
- **Investment bankers**
- **Trust officers**

PROFESSIONALS READ
- **The Economist**
- **Journal of Financial Planning**
- **The Wall Street Journal**

A DAY IN THE LIFE

Financial planners determine how their clients can achieve their lifelong financial goals through the management of their financial resources. They examine the financial history—and current financial situation—of their client's assets and suggest exactly what steps the client needs to take in the future to meet his or her goals. Although other professional financial advisors usually focus on one area of a client's financial life, the broad-based approach to financial advice that financial planners offer distinguishes them from the rest of the profession. In this sense, financial planners are jacks of all trades, but they do not work alone. Financial planners will inevitably meet with clients' other advisors— attorneys, accountants, trust officers, investment bankers—to fully understand their clients' finan- { **broad-based approach** } cial goals. (The last thing a financial planner wants to do is map out a plan that conflicts with investments that client has already made with their bankers.) It is a research-heavy profession, as well as a stressful one: You are suggesting how to use other people's money. It is a very corporate profession as well, and you will be expected to look and play the part. Although many financial planners are asked to devise comprehensive plans for their clients, some people hire planners to handle a specific interest and financial goal, such as planning for retirement, buying a home, or investing an inheritance. A financial planner will conduct questionnaires and personal interviews, detailing their clients' financial objectives, current incomes, investments, risk tolerance, expenses, tax returns, insurance coverage, retirement programs, estate plans, and other pertinent information to put together a plan that meets the clients' overall or specific financial agenda. The plan itself is a set of recommendations and strategies for the client to use, or to ignore, and financial planners should be ready to answer challenging questions about the integrity of the plan they map out. Because of this, financial planners must constantly update their plans and watch the market for trends that will affect their recommendations. According to the Institute of Certified Financial Planners, planners spend the majority of their time advising clients on investment planning, retirement planning, tax planning, estate planning, and risk management. All of these areas require different types of financial understanding, and planners are generally expected to be knowledgeable about asset management, employee benefits, estate planning, insurance, investments, and retirement funds. On top of all of this required knowledge, a financial planner must also have good interpersonal skills since establishing a client-planner relationship is essential to a planner's professional success. It also helps the planner to be a great presenter since even the best financial plan, if presented poorly to a client, can destroy the client's trust.

PAYING YOUR DUES

Earning a bachelor's degree in any discipline can put hopefuls on the track to becoming financial planners, but it will help if your degree indicates quantitative aptitude, be it in science or business. Education alone is not going to give potential clients the peace of mind they need to turn over their finances. On the issue of trust, it is prudent to note that no federal agency regulates financial planners. There is some regulation on the state level, but only in some states. Because of this, most financial planners choose to become certified by the Certified Financial Planners (CFP) Board. The CFP Board is an independent professional regulatory organization that extends licenses to those planners who pass the CFP certification examination. Most clients will look for financial planners who are certified and are bound to the CFP Board's ethical and educational standards (which include a bachelor's degree, three years of financial planning-related experience, and completion of college-level courses in financial planning).

ASSOCIATED CAREERS

Financial planning is a corporate career track, even for those who run their own financial planning business and are not associated with a bank or investment firm. Because financial planners have so much contact with other professionals in different aspects of the financial profession, career changes can be common. Experienced financial planners can find satisfying careers in investment banking, financial consulting, and financial analysis. Because people skills are also an integral part of being a financial planner, financial consulting—on both personal and corporate levels—are also options. Many financial planners, like many in financial professions, will find themselves attending business school, either to achieve a higher income or to switch to one of the aforementioned professions.

PAST AND FUTURE

The seemingly unstoppable bull market of the last several years has seen a boom in the financial planning profession. Increased activity by banks, brokerage houses, and mutual funds has seen these financial giants scramble to expand their financial planning services for both individuals and small businesses. In fact, financial planning is the fastest growing segment of the industry—good news for people interested in entering an industry in which top salaries push the $200,000 level.

QUALITY OF LIFE

2 YEARS Early in their careers, financial planners will be working for banks, mutual fund companies, or investment firms and will receive extensive on-the-job training. The job responsibilities themselves, however, will consist mostly of client-based and research activities. In many cases, financial planners are beginning their own business, and, as they learn their skills, they build up their personal client base. During these early years, financial planners spend many long hours analyzing documents, meeting with other advisors, and networking to find new clients. The pressure is high, and the pay is low for newly-anointed planners, with incomes starting around $27,000. Financial planners are paid on a fee-only, commission, or fee-and-commission basis. Early on, fees and commissions are apt to be low.

5 YEARS Planners who have not changed their career track can expect to have established some good client-planner long-term relationships, will experience less over-the-shoulder supervision from their employers, and may even have clients who are "feathers in the cap" to their house or firm. Measured success at this point in the career is based on a planner's service fees being considerably marked up from when they started, and, depending on the client, commissions that add up to a nice annual income on their own.

10 YEARS Planners who have survived this long have a myriad of satisfied clients, a good track record, and a six-figure income. Many individuals will have moved onto management positions, overseeing the financial planning services of major investment firms.

MAJOR EMPLOYERS
MORGAN STANLEY
1585 Broadway
New York, NY 10036
Tel: 212-761-4000
www.morganstanley.com

UBS FINANCIAL SERVICES INC.
299 Park Avenue
New York, NY 10171
Tel: 212-821-3000
www.ubs.com

MERRILL LYNCH & CO., INC.
4 World Financial Center
250 Vessey Street
New York, NY 10080
Tel: 212-449-1000
www.ml.com

MAJOR ASSOCIATIONS
FINANCIAL PLANNING ASSOCIATION
4100 E Mississippi Avenue, Suite 400
Denver, CO 80246-3053
Tel: 800-322-4237
Fax: 303-759-0749
www.fpanet.org

FOOD SERVICE MANAGER

A DAY IN THE LIFE

On a daily basis, managers estimate food consumption; place orders with suppliers; schedule the delivery of food and beverages; receive and check the content of deliveries; evaluate the quality of food—before and after it is cooked—meet with sales representatives from restaurant suppliers to place orders for pots, pans, plates and other supplies; monitor the health and safety codes; and adhere to local liquor regulations. They also call in the fix-it guys when repairs on the equipment are needed and the bug guys when pest control is needed. Managers also have to interview, hire, and, when necessary, fire employees. One of the most important tasks of restaurant and food service managers is selecting successful menu items, taking into account the likely number of customers and the past popularity of dishes. Managers analyze the recipes of the dishes to determine food, labor, and overhead costs and to assign prices to various dishes. Menus must be developed far enough in advance that supplies can be ordered and received in time. Food service managers must have initiative, be self-disciplined, and be strong leaders. They need to have communications skills so they can solve problems with suppliers, employees, and customers. Restaurant and food service management can be demanding, so good health is important. Managers are responsible for locking up; checking that ovens, grills, and lights are off; and switching on alarm systems. Food service managers are the workhorses of restaurants. The chef may get all the credit, but without a good manager, the chef would just be cooking at home.

{ good health }

PAYING YOUR DUES

Most restaurants or food service management companies hire management trainees from two- and four-year college hospitality management programs; however, some food managers may be promoted to the position after years of working in the kitchen. More than 150 colleges and universities offer four-year programs in restaurant and hotel management or institutional food service management. For those not interested in pursuing a four-year degree, more than 800 community and junior colleges, technical institutes, and other institutions offer programs in these fields leading to an associate degree or other formal certification. Some programs combine classroom study with on-the-job experience. Internships can help lead to better paying jobs. Some food managers strive for the designation of certified Foodservice Management Professional (FMP). Although the designation is not required for employment or advancement, voluntary certification provides recognition of professional competence, particularly for managers who acquired their skills largely on the job. Because evenings and weekends are when most people go out to eat, working long hours into the night and on being booked Saturdays and Sundays are common among managers. Some managers of institutional food service facilities (schools, and office cafeterias) work conventional, daytime and weekday hours. Most managers, however, work unpredictable hours, filling in for sick workers on short notice. Restaurant and food service managers normally work 50–60 hours per week, depending on the restaurant. It is a highly intense occupation, with the stress of coordinating a wide range of activities extreme at times. The manager is responsible for resolving problems and minimizing disruption to customers. The job can be hectic during peak dining hours, and dealing with irate customers or uncooperative employees can be stressful. However, a calm mind and steady voice can disarm most situations. As a food manager's experience grows, they can be called on to work in more upscale restaurants and hotels.

> "The chef may get all the credit, but without a good manager, the chef would just be cooking at home."

ASSOCIATED CAREERS

Restaurant and food service managers run businesses. Other managers in service-oriented businesses include hotel managers and assistants, health services administrators, retail store managers, and bank managers. Also, many colleges that offer food management training require courses in food preparation. This training can lead to a career as a cook, a chef, an executive chef position, or a restaurateur.

PAST AND FUTURE

There seems to be a McDonalds, Red Lobster, and Romano's Macaroni Grill on every corner. As the number of chain restaurants is expected to grow, so too will the need for food managers, as few restaurant owners will manage the stores themselves. Also, food manager positions will rise in cafeterias of schools, hospitals, and, as the population continues to age, nursing homes and residential-care and assisted-living facilities. As large corporations work to reduce costs, many will turn to outside institutional food service companies within the eating and drinking industry to run their cafeterias. Job opportunities should be better for salaried managers than for self-employed managers. Employment in eating and drinking establishments is not very sensitive to changes in economic conditions, so restaurant and food service managers are rarely laid off during hard times. Competition among restaurants is always intense; this sometimes forces restaurants to close their kitchens.

QUALITY OF LIFE

2 YEARS Most restaurants provide their employees rigorous training programs for management positions. Usually after six months or a year, trainees receive their first permanent assignment as an assistant manager. Some food service managers start out in small schools cafeterias, or as cooks in food service contractors, working their way into higher paying positions within the school or business system.

5 YEARS After five years, an employee has the experience they need to run the daily activities of their own kitchens. Some managers advance to larger establishments or regional management positions within restaurant chains.

10 YEARS Food service managers with 10 or more years of experience may open their own eating and drinking establishments. They may also move to more prestigious restaurants or hotels. Willingness to relocate is essential for advancement to positions with greater responsibility.

MAJOR EMPLOYERS

ARAMARK
Tel: 800-ARAMARK
E-mail: webmaster@aramark.com
www.aramark.com

MRI NETWORK
1801 Market Street, Suite 1350
Philadelphia, PA 19103
Tel: 800-875-4000
Fax: 216-696-3221

MAJOR ASSOCIATIONS

ARG ASSOCIATES, L.L.C.
11 Heard Drive
Ipswich, MA 01938
Tel: 978-356-4942
Fax: 978-356-9606
E-mail: arg2000@msn.com
www.argassociates.com

INTERNATIONAL COUNCIL ON HOTEL, RESTAURANT, AND INSTITUTIONAL EDUCATION
2810 North Parham Road, Suite 230
Richmond, VA 23294
Tel: 804-346-4800
Fax: 804-346-5009
www.chrie.org

NATIONAL RESTAURANT ASSOCIATION EDUCATIONAL FOUNDATION
175 West Jackson Boulevard, Suite 1500
Chicago, IL 60604-2814
Tel: 800-765-2122 or 312-715-5397
www.nraef.org

FOREIGN EXCHANGE TRADER

BOOKS, FILMS, AND TV SHOWS FEATURING THE PROFESSION
- **Bonfire of the Vanities**
- **Danish Kroner**
- **Goldsong**

YOU'LL HAVE CONTACT WITH
- **Bankers**
- **Economists**
- **Interpreters**
- **Statisticians**
- **Translators**

PROFESSIONALS READ
- **FX Week**
- **International Reports**
- **The Wall Street Journal**

A DAY IN THE LIFE

A foreign exchange trader looks at the various factors that influence local economies and rates of exchange, then takes advantage of any misvaluations of currencies by buying and selling in different foreign exchange markets. Those people with the most information, best contacts, and strongest decision-making skills come out ahead. "It's the wild west of trading," wrote one foreign exchange (FX) trader, "and remember: A lot of people died in the wild west." Those individuals who are comfortable with a high degree of risk and uncertainty should look into this exciting career.

A foreign exchange trader manages an account, looks at reports, reads the press from various countries, and most importantly, spends time on the phone. He or she may spend up to 80 percent of the day on the telephone and working at his or her computer. Traders must act fast to exploit valuation differences: "You've got seconds to decide how millions of dollars should be spent," one trader said, "so you have to have confidence." Confidence ranked second only to "guts" as important qualities for new traders to possess. A sharp analytic mind is also crucial; while a variety of degrees are helpful, people with technical or scientific analysis backgrounds tend to find the job more manageable. Accounting strengths are helpful in keeping track of positions and profit and losses throughout hectic days.

> { "It's the wild west of trading." }

FX traders find a specialty early in their careers, following one currency and the underlying economy of its country. Many traders specialize in groups of geographically related countries, such as those who trade Central American currencies or Pacific Rim currencies. Since a trader's work depends on the country or region in which he or she specializes, it can take place at any time of day. Many managers run 24-hour shops and do business around the clock; most employees do have regular shifts, but world events may demand being summoned from bed late at night. Eighty percent of the traders we surveyed were satisfied with their choice of profession, but over 40 percent responded that they were exhausted at every day's end.

PAYING YOUR DUES

Economics, mathematics, and statistics majors have a distinct advantage in applying for positions in this field, as do history majors whose coursework included economics. A bachelor's degree is required. Any experience in a trading environment is valued, as is any work that demonstrates a person's ability to work hard, make fast and accurate decisions, and manipulate numbers. Many employers appreciate study abroad, international work experience, or fluency in a foreign language. As a number of entry-level positions are account representatives as opposed to trading positions, candidates who have good interpersonal skills and access to capital may have an advantage. While on the job, keeping abreast of changes in the industry is important; continuing education is the norm. Few people leave to get advanced degrees in this field—there is a reverse snobbery associated with most trading floors that holds that traders are born, not made, and that no advanced degree will ever make anyone a more competent trader.

ASSOCIATED CAREERS

FX traders are good at strong and immediate decision-making, and many of them apply this skill to other trading environments, such as stock trading, sales, or institutional buying. Their mathematical and financial skills prepare them for positions at Wall Street firms in a number of areas, from back-office account settlement to options valuation analysis. In general, however, FX traders seek the adrenaline rush of trading and enjoy the open unregulated market—the number of them who leave (a meager 20 percent over the course of a career) actually provide the largest single industry donation of manpower to the world of professional gambling.

PAST AND FUTURE

Foreign exchange was originally the province of multinational corporations that would collect revenue in one country and need to return the funds to the parent corporation in another. This process left the companies extremely vulnerable to interest rate shifts over short periods of time and made valuation of foreign assets difficult if not impossible. The in-house foreign exchange manager determined areas of exposure and maintained financial equilibrium among corporations and their foreign outposts. As these divisions proved profitable on their own, a market developed for speculating risk in the 1940s and 1950s in countries with exchangeable currency. To date, these companies control the flow of many billions of dollars across the globe each year.

The market for foreign exchange is growing steadily, and opportunities for individuals interested in the business should grow. Legislative changes will shape the way foreign exchange markets do business, however.

QUALITY OF LIFE

2 | After a general training program in which trading skills, valuation methods, and company protocols are taught, many young professionals become account executives who work with clients, offer advice, and act as liaisons between the trader and the client, before becoming traders themselves. People who enter in the trading arena can expect people to work long hours for little pay in a frantic work environment, all the while learning the process of foreign exchange trading.

5 | Individuals who have not become actual traders by year five often leave. Client contact increases across the board and salary, bonus, and account reviews happen every 6–12 months. The level of satisfaction is highest at this point in traders' careers and actually declines later on; perhaps that is because people who are good at trading tend to move between firms (much of years 5–10 are spent looking for the perfect position), and people who are bad tend to see their responsibilities decline and their pay stagnate. The hours increase, but personal styles and the wealth of experience each person has accrued makes the job more enjoyable and less frantic.

10 | Ten-year veterans either head up trading floors and manage other traders or are major producers with significant responsibilities in their firms. Some traders are in-house consultants for major international firms, while others have become independent traders, capitalizing on past success. Many individuals who are not independent only spend another five years in the profession before retiring or finding another position; the pace and pressure of the business eventually exhaust even the most passionate of traders.

MAJOR EMPLOYERS

AMERICAN STOCK EXCHANGE
86 Trinity Place
New York, NY 10006
Tel: 212-306-1000
www.amex.com

CHICAGO STOCK EXCHANGE, INC
One Financial Place
440 South LaSalle Street
Chicago, IL 60605
Tel: 312-663-2222
E-mail: info@chx.com
www.chx.com
Contact: Employment Specialist

NATIONAL ASSOCIATION OF SECURITIES DEALERS
One Liberty Plaza
New York, NY 10006
Tel: 212-858-4000
Fax: 212-858-4189
www.nasd.com
Contact: Human Resources

OVERSEAS PRIVATE INVESTMENT CORPORATION
1100 New York Avenue, NW
Washington, DC 20527
Tel: 202-336-8400
www.opic.gov
Contact: Office of Human Resources Management

FORENSIC SCIENTIST

PROFESSIONAL PROFILE

# of people in profession	8,400
Avg. hours per week	40
Avg. starting salary	$30,000
Avg. salary after 5 years	$55,000
Avg. salary after 10 to 15 years	$65,000

SALARY ● ●
HOURS ● ● ●
EDUCATION ● ●

BOOKS, FILMS, AND TV SHOWS FEATURING THE PROFESSION
- **The Bone Collector**
- **Crossing Jordan**
- **CSI**
- **Forensic Files**
- **Law and Order**

YOU'LL HAVE CONTACT WITH
- **Attorneys**
- **Crime scene investigators**
- **Drug Enforcement Administration (DEA) officials**
- **FBI agents**
- **Law enforcement officials**
- **Medical examiners**

PROFESSIONALS READ
- **Forensic Science Communications**
- **Forensic Scientist International**
- **Handbook of Forensic Services**
- **Journal of Forensic Scientists**

A DAY IN THE LIFE

Forensic scientists are involved in the search for and examination of physical evidence—gunshot residue, fingerprints, blood and tissue remnants, forged signatures, and any other crime scene clues that can be pieced together by a keen eye and intellect. It's not a career for the fainthearted, but there is certainly not a lot of monotony in the day-to-day activities of a forensic scientist. A day at the "office" could be spent in a morgue, at a crime scene, in a laboratory, or in the courtroom, where you may testify as an expert witness and explain your evaluation of the evidence and the techniques you used to reach your conclusions.

There are several concentrations within the field of forensic science. Criminalists identify evidence; this may include isolating blood at a crime scene that doesn't match the victim, for example. With chemicals, special instruments, and reenactments, the criminalist will analyze and sort the crime scene samples, preparing evidence that can link the victim and crime scene to the suspect. One of the newest areas of criminalistics is wildlife forensics, which seeks to enforce poaching regulations, the Endangered Species Act, and international trade agreements by identifying evidence relating to species illegally killed or sold. Forensic dentistry (odontology) also plays a vital role in the identification of unknown victims and also occasionally in homicide or assault cases. Forensic odontologists are generally called to crime scenes at the request of law enforcement officials or medical examiners. After a postmortem examination, X rays and observations are documented and provided to assist law enforcement with their investigation. Forensic dentists are also called on to give expert testimony in both criminal and civil cases (which may encompass personal injury law, professional malpractice, and the identification of bite marks). One of the most popularized fields of forensic science is forensic pathology—think *Crossing Jordan* and those autopsy room scenes in *Law and Order*. Forensic pathologists investigate the circumstances of death and are relied on to determine the cause of death—natural, accidental, homicide, etc. In addition to investigating violent death, pathologists also look for clues in sudden, unexpected deaths of healthy individuals and deaths that could have been the result of malpractice or negligence. All three areas require a strong problem-solving capacity, good speaking skills, natural curiosity, and excellent note-taking skills.

{ keen eye and intellect }

PAYING YOUR DUES

All members of the field must hold at least a bachelor's degree, and most disciplines require a master's or doctoral degree. Many concentrations call for the scientist to hold a medical degree and undergo training in scene and evidence investigation. This may entail an apprenticeship or residency following medical school graduation, proceeded by a one- or two-year fellowship. Ideally, coursework should include microscopy, statistics, chemistry, and biology. Some labs offer trainee positions that do not require previous experience in the field, but most scientists start out as lab technicians in one of the natural sciences and parlay this experience into a position in the field of forensics. It also should be noted that indiscretions and even excessive traffic violations can prevent you from getting through the application process—so you'll need to make sure you maintain a clean record.

ASSOCIATED CAREERS

Beyond the potential to specialize in one of the many fields that fall under the umbrella of forensic science, career opportunities also exist for educators, forensic artists (who reconstruct faces to help identify victims), coroners, and experienced crime scene photographers.

PAST AND FUTURE

In 1248, a Chinese book entitled *The Washing Away of Wrongs* described how to distinguish drowning from strangulation. This is the first known documentation of medical knowledge applied to crime solving. In sixteenth-century Europe, military and university doctors began gathering information about various causes and manners of death and thus laid the foundation for the vast databases that exist today. In the nineteenth century, it was observed that after someone's hands made contact with a surface, barely-visible marks were left that could be easily observed by a dusting of fine powder. The method of fingerprint classification that arose from this discovery is still the most widely-used method of fingerprinting today.

As technology advances, the field of forensic science grows to encompass new methods and techniques. DNA evidence has become the most well-known type of forensic evidence, and many forensic scientists are emerging from the classroom with the training necessary to meet the demands for DNA testing. Crime scenes are now linked to investigators over the Internet, and professionals trained in this field—teleforensics—allow experts from all over the world to probe virtual evidence. Unfortunately, crime evolves along with new technologies, so forensic scientists will continue to be challenged to improve on established techniques and to develop new disciplines.

QUALITY OF LIFE

2 YEARS   Entry-level forensic scientists seldom go to crime scenes. As members of research teams, they perform laboratory analyses and occasionally testify in court. Scientists at the beginning of their careers will have frequent contact with law enforcement officials as they document the transfer of evidence and lab results from technicians to investigators.

5 YEARS   With experience in basic lab techniques and protocols of analysis, forensic scientists with five years of job training and experience under their belts can begin focusing on the aspects of the field that interest them most—ballistics, DNA evidence, crime scene investigation, or any of the dozens of subsections of the field. Well-trained scientists can explore opportunities with private consulting firms or independent specialists.

10 YEARS   Scientists with 10 or more years of experience can work their way up the ladder to laboratory director or supervisor or apply their expertise in the classroom as an educator at one of the 31 schools around the country that offer programs in the forensic sciences. It is expected—and indeed, the constantly developing technologies demand it—that even established professionals continue their education. Sharing results logged over years of handling evidence and cases is vital to scientists across the world, and there are many scientific journals ready to publish the observations of seasoned scientists.

MAJOR EMPLOYERS

DISASTER MORTUARY OPERATIONS RESPONSE TEAM (DMORT)
Department of Homeland Security
National Disaster Medical System Section
500 C Street, SW, Suite 713
Washington, DC 20472
http://oep-ndms.dhhs.gov/dmort.html

FEDERAL BUREAU OF INVESTIGATION
www.fbijobs.gov

UNITED STATES SECRET SERVICE
Personnel Division
245 Murray Drive, Building 410
Washington, DC 20223
Tel: 202-406-5800
www.secretservice.gov

MAJOR ASSOCIATIONS

AMERICAN ACADEMY OF FORENSIC SCIENCES
410 North 21st Street
Colorado Springs, CO 80904
www.aafs.org

AMERICAN BOARD OF FORENSIC ANTHROPOLOGY
www.csuchico.edu/anth/ABFA

AMERICAN COLLEGE OF FORENSIC EXAMINERS
2750 East Sunshine
Springfield, MO 65804
www.acfei.com

GENETICIST

BOOKS, FILMS, AND TV SHOWS
FEATURING THE PROFESSION
- Alien: Resurrection
- Gattaca
- Genome
- Lorenzo's Oil
- Multiplicity

YOU'LL HAVE CONTACT WITH
- Chemical engineers
- College administrators
- Patients
- Physicians
- Research technicians

PROFESSIONALS READ
- American Journal of Human Genetics
- Genetics
- Genetics in Medicine
- Human Molecular Genetics
- Journal of Gene Medicine

A DAY IN THE LIFE

Geneticists are the leaders of the last frontier within the natural sciences. The four distinct fields within genetics revolve around two fronts: research genetics and applied genetics. In research, a research geneticist attains a PhD over the course of up to 10 years of scholarly, funded research. Genetic counselors study aspects of nursing, psychology, public health, and social work to follow patterns of a family's medical history. On the applied side of genetics, laboratory geneticists apply the latest in technology to assisting advancements of the public and private sectors, from agriculture to legal and police work. After special training including four to six years of university education, a geneticist can develop a particular genetic specialty, such as molecular biology, cytogenics, biochemical genetics, and immunogenetics. Clinical geneticists have a health care side to their training, with a medical school education and a residency in medical genetics that may last up to five years, which is then followed by a fellowship of two or three years.

{ secrets }

The spectrum of specialties within the field of genetics provides a range of daily routines within the research and applied arms of the field. But across the board, geneticists are involved in unlocking and utilizing the last few secrets of biological science. Long hours are typical. Geneticists may work at pharmaceutical companies to uncover the origins of disease and birth defects and then in turn develop ways to prevent or treat them. Geneticists that work in this field are involved in their work from beginning to end, although this could sometimes literally mean a lifetime of work. Geneticists also have the opportunity to be laboratory detectives and use DNA sampling to ensure that the right person is convicted of the crime.

Since medicine, agriculture, and crime the three biggest areas in which genetics plays a role, most geneticists then find employment either in universities, government agencies, or major pharmaceutical companies. These three employers are closely related in how they use research, so geneticists expect to make many contacts within the industry. Aside from the employer and the field of study, there are two types of geneticists: laboratory geneticists—the field that most geneticists choose to enter as it involves an application of genetic technologies—and genetic counselors, who function in the role of as nurse or consultants. Counselors work directly with parents who could be at risk for bearing children with birth defects. It is also common for counselors to consult with insurance and health-care companies about new medical technologies and conditions.

PAYING YOUR DUES

Extensive study in the physical sciences is expected. A bachelor's degree either in biology or chemistry is the foundation from which candidates should plan to enter a doctoral or medical program. Advanced degrees allow them the full range of opportunities in the research, counseling, and applied fields. If the prospect of six–ten years of further education and research doesn't appeal to you, note that some genetic laboratories hire bachelor's degree holders for numerous positions. During the first two years of post-graduate work, students of genetics pursue fellowships to support their faculty supervised research. The competition for funding is excellent practice for the work geneticists do later in their careers, where they must compete nationally for their funding. While the typical work week starts at 40 hours, extra hours are often necessary, whether you are a research geneticist with a deadline for a paper or a laboratory geneticist or genetic counselor whose patients are top priority.

ASSOCIATED CAREERS

If a geneticist leaves the field it is likely because he or she is tired of spending every day in a lab or bogged down by research. Because many geneticists depart their careers with a doctoral or medical degree, they will often leave to practice or continue their research in other areas of medicine. There are also several positions within the government where a geneticist can work as a consultant, especially in the areas of agriculture and security.

PAST AND FUTURE

Genetics is the scientific study of heredity. The first geneticist was Gregor Mendel, who in 1856 presented statistical laws that explained a transmission of certain traits from parent to child. Mendel's work was nothing more than a hypothesis, however, until advanced science techniques proved his theories with the discovery of the chromosome and the gene in the twentieth century. From this discovery, biologists and chemists found the basis of inherited characteristics and created the science of genetics. The field has since exploded, with major steps in technology allowing for more scrutiny in the study of DNA and heredity. The future is very bright because the field is expected to expand substantially in coming years. With the completion of the human genome project, many geneticists will be in the vanguard of developing new medical technologies that will forever alter the way we consider the origins of life and harness genetic codes to pioneer further scientific and medical breakthroughs.

QUALITY OF LIFE

2 YEARS The days are long and the tasks redundant, but enjoyment is typically high after geneticists have spent many years earning their wings in school, residencies, and fellowships. Young geneticists are learning the ropes of laboratory research, but they aren't in charge of their own research.

5 YEARS Geneticists live at the lab, but the work becomes more extensive after five years. They are able to take on individual research projects in direct proportion to their and their project team's abilities to produce results from their efforts and compete successfully to earn funding for their research.

10 YEARS Equipped with seniority and most desirably with a PhD, geneticists after 10 years can be directing research projects and laboratories, lecturing at universities, and consulting with pharmaceutical companies. Geneticists who have maintained their careers with a bachelor's degree may discover a ceiling that prevents them from advancing in the field—unless, that is, they discover a genetic breakthrough that makes them celebrities in the world of science and medicine.

MAJOR EMPLOYERS
CELERA GENOMICS
180 Kimball Way
South San Francisco, CA 94080
Tel: 650-829-1000
Fax: 650-866-6650
www.celera.com

OFFICE OF SCIENCE
United States Department of Energy
1000 Independence Avenue, SW
Washington, DC 20585
Tel: 202-586-5430
www.er.doe.gov

MAJOR ASSOCIATIONS
AMERICAN BOARD OF MEDICAL GENETICS
9650 Rockville Pike
Bethesda, MD 20814-3998
Tel: 301-634-7315
Fax: 301-634-7320
www.abmg.org

NATIONAL SOCIETY OF GENETIC COUNSELORS
233 Canterbury Drive
Wallingford, PA 19086–6617
Tel: 610-872-7608
E-mail: FYI@nsgc.org
www.nsgc.org

HEALTH CARE ADMINISTRATOR

A DAY IN THE LIFE

The health care industry employs hundreds of thousands of physicians, nurses, health specialists, and other nonhealth workers and wields considerable clout on Wall Street. Health care administrators run this behemoth and coordinate and organize the financing and delivery of care and assisting in the management of health facilities.

Two types of health care administrators, generalists and specialists, provide the expertise to run large and small facilities. Generalists are responsible for entire operations; while specialists run specific departments, such as the accounting, budgeting, human resources, policy analysis, finance, and marketing departments. Executive-level administrators of both types are highly educated individuals responsible for overall policy directions. They assess the need for services, equipment, and personnel and also make recommendations regarding the expansion or curtailment of services and the establishment of new or auxiliary facilities. They oversee compliance with government agencies and regulations. Their duties tend to vary with the size and operations of the health facility where they are employed; generally, smaller facilities have less staff support, so administrators have larger work loads. In larger facilities, administrators can delegate duties and devote more time to policy directives.

{ considerable clout on Wall Street }

Assistants to administrators at large facilities typically provide support in the execution of top-level decisions. Depending on their expertise and experience, some assistants oversee the activities of clinical departments such as nursing or surgery, or they may direct the operations of nonhealth areas such as personnel, finance, and public relations. At nursing homes, home health agencies, and other smaller facilities, the duties and responsibilities of administrators are vast and varied. Administrators wear multiple hats in departments such as human resources, finance and operations, and admissions.

Clinical managers are health specialists who supervise specific clinical services in the health care industry. They have job-specific training and are involved with implementing policies and procedures for their departments, while coordinating activities with other managers. Policy decisions do not fall within the purview of managers for small group practices, but larger group practices usually retain the services of a full-time administrator who not only coordinates activities on a day-to-day basis, but also develops and implements business strategies.

PAYING YOUR DUES

To land a plum job in the health care industry, it is sensible first to complete graduate studies. A bachelor's degree will only open doors at the entry level, and only a lucky few will be able to work their way up to a top-level position in a small operation or a middle-management position at a larger facility. A master's degree in hospital or nursing administration, public health, public or business administration, and other related fields is usually a requirement for an executive position. Courses in accounting and budgeting, management principles, hospital organization and management, health economics, and health information systems provide aspiring administrators with a solid foundation. Applicants to the field must be willing to work their way up the corporate health ladder, as even new graduates with master's degrees often start out as assistant administrators or managers of nonhealth departments. As in all management positions, strong leadership qualities, effective communication and analytical skills, and the ability to motivate others will greatly enhance employment opportunities. Specialized expertise in one type of health facility—HMOs, mental health hospitals, nursing homes, general hospitals or outpatient care services—can significantly expand the possibility of easy placement in the industry.

ASSOCIATED CAREERS

Health care administrators can apply their training in health and management as underwriters for health insurance companies and HMOs and in the selling, marketing, and distribution of health care equipment and supplies. Some administrators become directors of public health, social welfare administrators, and directors of health agencies. An administrator with a PhD may consult, teach, or do research.

PAST AND FUTURE

The rise of both private indemnity insurance and government-sponsored health entitlements earlier in this century has spawned a complex medical bureaucracy. As health services continue to expand and diversify, so will job opportunities, though the trend toward managed care and economies of scale in large health management organizations (HMOs) will result in restructuring. As HMOs and other health care providers expand operations, competition for executive-level positions within these organizations will be tough, and overlapping administrators will be squeezed out of merging companies.

A rapidly aging population, especially a growing 75-years-and-older segment who will require the continued services of health care professionals, promises continued employment opportunities in nursing homes and related industries in the coming decade.

QUALITY OF LIFE

2 YEARS With two years of experience, a health care administrator is still making his or her way up the corporate ladder to his or her job of choice. Depending on his or her educational level and the size and operations of the facility, the applicant is either in an entry-level position or a middle-management job. Two-year health care administrators have already developed mentorships and prepared themselves for higher office by asking for and taking on more duties and responsibilities; keeping on top of changes, trends, and developments, in the industry; and executing their prescribed duties exceptionally well.

5 YEARS Five years into the business, the professional is ready to be promoted to executive. He or she has studiously learned the ins and outs of the profession, kept on top of industry trends, completed refresher courses, and obtained necessary licenses and certificates. This is the ideal time for the young professional to evaluate his or her career choice, progress, and advancement potential, as well as review employment options. Returning to school to pursue higher studies is a possibility.

10 YEARS The experienced health care administrator is firmly entrenched in an executive position. Pursuing postgraduate studies while still holding on to that middle-management job will significantly enhance the professional's advancement potential. With a PhD the administrator can enter academia to teach and do research or start-up private consulting services.

MAJOR EMPLOYERS

AURELIA OSBORN FOX MEMORIAL HOSPITAL NURSING HOME
Nursing Home
One Norton Avenue
Oneonta, NY 13820
Tel: 607-432-2000
http://24.97.214.75

BAKERSFIELD MEMORIAL HOSPITAL
420 34th Street
Bakersfield, CA 93301
Tel: 661-327-4647
www.bakersfieldmemorial.org

HOME NURSING COMPANY, INC.
PO Box 669
Lebanon, VA 24266
Tel: 540-889-4318
Fax: 540-889-0403

MAJOR ASSOCIATIONS

AMERICAN COLLEGE OF HEALTHCARE EXECUTIVES
One North Franklin, Suite 1700
Chicago, IL 60606-3424
Tel: 312-424-2800
Fax: 312-424-0023
www.ache.org

ASSOCIATION OF UNIVERSITY PROGRAMS IN HEALTH ADMINISTRATION
2000 North 114th Street, Suite 780
Arlington, VA 22201
Tel: 703-894-0940
Fax: 703-894-0941
E-mail: aupha@aupha.org
www.aupha.org

HOSPITAL ADMINISTRATOR

PROFESSIONAL PROFILE

# of people in profession	230,640
Avg. hours per week	60
Avg. starting salary	$57,500
Avg. salary 5 years	$95,600
Avg. salary 10 to 15 years	$144,000

SALARY   ● ● ●

HOURS   ● ● ●

EDUCATION   ● ● ●

BOOKS, FILMS, AND TV SHOWS
FEATURING THE PROFESSION
- Chicago Hope
- ER
- Hospital Administrator
- St. Elsewhere

YOU'LL HAVE CONTACT WITH
- Medical staff
- Other hospital administrators
- Patients
- Physicians

PROFESSIONALS READ
- FRONTIERS of Health Services Management
- Healthcare Executive
- Journal of Healthcare Management

A DAY IN THE LIFE

Doctors lead exciting and fulfilling professional lives. There are many people who hear the call to save lives, but not all of them like being responsible for people's lives. The hospital administrator plays an indirect yet vital role in saving lives. Hospital administrators manage hospitals, outpatient clinics, hospices, and drug-abuse treatment centers. In large hospitals, there may be several administrators—one for each department. In smaller facilities, they oversee the day-to-day operations of all departments. Administrators make sure hospitals operate efficiently and provide adequate medical care to patients. Their responsibilities are numerous and sometimes require the assistance of the medical and support staff. They act as liaisons between governing boards, medical staff, and department heads and integrate the activities of all departments, so they function as a whole. Following policies set by a governing board of trustees, administrators plan, organize, direct, control, and coordinate medical and health services. Administrators recruit, hire, and sometimes train doctors, nurses, interns, and assistant administrators. Administrators plan budgets and set payment rates for health services. In research hospitals, administrators develop and expand programs and services for scientific research and preventive medicine. In teaching hospitals, they aid in the education of new doctors. They plan departmental activities, evaluate doctors and other hospital employees, create and maintain policies, help develop procedures for medical treatments, quality assurance, patient services, and public relations activities such as active participation in fund-raising and community health planning. Hospital administrators work long or irregular hours. Hospitals are open as around the clock, and administrators may be called in at any hour to make decisions and resolve disputes. Administrators also attend staff meetings, participate in health planning councils, go to fundraising events, and travel to professional association conventions. A hospital administrator's job is difficult and demanding. They need to keep up with advances in medicine, computerized diagnostic and treatment equipment, data processing technology, and changes concerning government regulations, health insurance, and financing options. While doctors strive to keep a patient's blood flowing and heart beating, the hospital administrator is doing his or her job in keeping the hospital alive and healthy.

PAYING YOUR DUES

Health services administrators should have a master's degree in health services administration. A master's degree in public administration or business administration may also qualify graduates for entry into health care administration. The health services administration degree usually includes a one-year internship (residency) in a health care center. Graduates with a bachelor's degree in this field may work in a health care center before starting a master's program. Nursing home administrators need to be licensed by the Nursing Home Administrators State Board of Examiners to work for health care facilities that receive Medicare funds. Health services administrators normally start as administrative assistants in large centers or assistant administrators in medium-sized institutions. They advance by taking on more responsibilities and moving up and into such positions as associate administrator and chief executive officer. Moving to a higher position may require relocating to a smaller state. Some administrators of small facilities may choose to accept a lower-level position in a larger center, which often leads to professional growth.

ASSOCIATED CAREERS

Hospital administrators with a background in medicine can resume their practices. A keen business sense can allow some administrators to move into corporate positions, such as chief financial officer or chief executive officer.

PAST AND FUTURE

Employment for health services administrators is expected to grow at a faster rate than average, especially in states where the population is increasing and more health care facilities are needed to meet the demand. Jobs will be in major medical centers and in large public hospitals. As the population grows older, specialized centers that are caregivers for the elderly or people who may need care frequently and for long periods—such as hospice programs that treat terminally ill patients—will provide excellent opportunities for health care administrators. HMOs that treat large patient lists covered by health insurance are increasing in numbers and will have an ongoing need for administrators at various levels.

QUALITY OF LIFE

2 YEARS A year–long internship (residency) and a year as an assistant administrator will give you the experience you need to apply for administrator positions at small health care centers, hospices, or Medicare facilities. The hours are long and hard as you learn the ropes of running a medical facility.

5 YEARS With more experience comes better job opportunities. Although the work hours may decrease as you gain more experience, work hours increase proportionally to the size of the medical facility you run. The hospital administrator has seen a lot in five years on the job and should be able to settle even the toughest disputes between people in the boardroom and the operating room.

10 YEARS Hospital administrators with 10 or more years of experience are in a prime position to move to large medical centers. Like chief executive officers of Fortune 500 corporations, a seasoned hospital administrator enjoys a good deal of power and can set policies and procedures into place that benefit a hospital's employees as well as the people they serve.

MAJOR EMPLOYERS

Hospital administrators are employed by hospitals and other health-treatment centers. Contact area organizations for employment opportunities.

MAJOR ASSOCIATIONS

AMERICAN HOSPITAL ASSOCIATION
1 North Franklin
Chicago, IL 60606–3421
Tel: 312-422-3000
www.aha.org

ASSOCIATION OF AMERICAN MEDICAL COLLEGES
2450 N Street, NW
Washington, DC 20037–1126
Tel: 202-828-0400
Fax: 202-828-1125
www.aamc.org

INTERNET/INTRANET TECHNOLOGIES MANAGER

BOOKS, FILMS, AND TV SHOWS
FEATURING THE PROFESSION
- **The Net**

YOU'LL HAVE CONTACT WITH
- **Computer programmers**
- **Computer technicians**
- **Webmasters**
- **Website designers**

PROFESSIONALS READ
- **Computer World Magazine**
- **Network Computing Magazine**
- **Wired**

A DAY IN THE LIFE

The average IT manager is a 40-year-old male; females are still largely underrepresented in this field. A 34-year-old Intranet administrator for a small bank in Maine ousted a 20-year-old from that job. As the older man put it, the young gun knew the technology but didn't have much discipline or corporate experience. Because of his success, he received a 17 percent raise.

An IT manager will spend his or her time multitasking in several areas, including managing programmers and designers who implement the systems that make Internet/Intranet technologies a working reality. IT managers also prioritize strategies aimed at accomplishing specific corporate goals, distribute tight budgets to accomplish these goals, write proposals concerning the best use of a company's IT resources, and oversee development and implementation of strategic plans. In addition to all of the technical and managerial responsibilities, IT managers also spend much of their time in meetings, catering to the needs of their employees. If they work as independent consultants, they cater to their own clients' needs. Delivering what the brass wants can be quite stressful. "They want it done yesterday," a senior IT architect at Lockheed Martin gripes.

{ keep up with the pace }

Although IT managers earn roughly the same salaries as network/information systems managers, they tend to be more satisfied with their work, even if the hours tend to be long. It is relevant to note, though, that according to a survey conducted by *Network Computing Magazine*, salary was the biggest cause of dissatisfaction (as expressed by 20 percent of respondents) among Web/Intranet managers, with the number of work hours the second biggest gripe (13.5 percent). To be a successful IT manager, you should have good communication skills, strong technical skills, and an eagerness to work with new technologies. For those who can keep up with the pace of this profession, six-figure salaries are in the future.

PAYING YOUR DUES

Experience tends to get people these jobs, whether they have risen through the IT ranks or have had a few years of previous experience as network/IS technicians and managers. It is unlikely that a person can begin a career in IT as an IT manager. Web/Intranet managers are well-educated and generally have at least a bachelor's degree. There is a close correlation between the level of education and the level of income in this field.

ASSOCIATED CAREERS

Because of the strong technical and communication skills needed to be a Web/Intranet manager, many have come into the field from network and IS jobs. It is possible for an IT manager to jump back into the network/IS field with little problem and command a comparable salary. Those who feel the need for more creative input can use their IT knowledge to be Web designers and Webmasters. Although Web designers don't typically have as much earning power as IT managers, Webmasters sometimes can, depending on the industry. IT managers who enjoy the more technical and computer literate side of the job can become computer consultants or IT security consultants.

PAST AND FUTURE

You can be an IT manager in almost any field, from banking to entertainment. In fact, those in the field of entertainment reported the highest average income. IT managers need to be familiar with the latest in database technologies as well as the latest software; the technical applications in this field seem to change weekly.

QUALITY OF LIFE

2 YEARS Even at this early point in their career, IT managers earn nice wages. Hours can be long, and stress can be high due to deadlines, budgets, and high expectations from clients and corporate boards. Simply keeping up with the latest technological advances can be a challenge. Competition is at a high level within the industry, especially early on, when IT managers are trying to separate themselves from the rest of the pack.

5 YEARS In this occupation, five years is a long time. Many IT managers have the opportunity to change companies at this point. Most IT professionals jump ship to snag promotions or get more interesting work, but salary is often the real motivator; nearly 15 percent go to another company to earn a higher salary. Many IT managers start their own consulting businesses. Some companies hire outside freelance help when they set up their Intranet and Internet architectures, so opportunities abound for the independent consultant.

10 YEARS After ten years, most IT managers are commanding high salaries, and those that have started their own consulting businesses appreciate high levels of autonomy.

MAJOR EMPLOYERS

Most large corporations today have Internet/Intranet technolgieis managers on staff.

MAJOR ASSOCIATIONS

INFORMATION & TECHNOLOGY ASSOCIATION OF AMERICA
1401 Wilson Boulevard, Suite 1100
Arlington, VA 22209
Tel: 703-522-5055
Fax: 703-525-2279
www.itaa.org

INSTITUTE FOR THE CERTIFICATION OF COMPUTER PROFESSIONALS
2350 East Devon Avenue, Suite 115
Des Plaines, IL 60018–4610
Tel: 800-843-8227 or 847-299-4227
Fax: 847-299-4280
www.iccp.org

METEOROLOGIST

A DAY IN THE LIFE

"Meteorologist" and "atmospheric scientist" are different names for the same profession. Meteorologists study the science of Earth's atmosphere—things like air pressure, temperature, and humidity—to arrive at an understanding of how the atmosphere interacts with the rest of our physical environment. Most commonly, this understanding is used to forecast the weather, but there are many other applications. Some meteorologists, for example, analyze past weather trends over hundreds and even millions of years to model how climate changes occurred in the past and to predict future climate patterns. This facet of meteorology proves helpful in a number of arenas: It's used by architects and engineers in designing buildings that need to be suited for a particular climate; by { atmospheric scientist } agriculturalists in developing strategies to maximize food production; by the military, which needs to be aware of weather patterns to plan and carry out its operations; and by you, in planning fishing trips or barbeques.

Entry-level meteorologists start out doing routine weather data collection and analysis. (Sometimes this even entails going up in aircrafts to observe weather conditions from above.) As they develop expertise, they may take on more complex forecasting projects or assume supervisory responsibilities within their organizations. Broadcast meteorologists, in addition to doing data collection and analysis for their local areas, devise the graphics they will need for on-air reports. Weather stations operate 24/7, and this means that meteorologists are often called to work during odd times—days, nights, weekends, and holidays—usually in shifts. During a weather emergency, meteorologists work overtime. Weather correspondents may find themselves standing in the midst of a ferocious storm reporting on the event. Successful meteorologists need to be able to interpret written and graphical weather data under deadline. They must also be proficient in the various technological systems (like Doppler radar and satellite images) that are currently used to collect and analyze weather readings. Though all meteorologists need solid communication skills, broadcast meteorologists need to be especially proficient in this area.

PAYING YOUR DUES

A bachelor's degree in atmospheric science or a closely related field is usually the minimum requirement for an entry-level position in meteorology. (Because meteorology is a relatively small field, not many colleges offer a major in it—but you can find a number of colleges that do on www.PrincetonReview.com.) The federal government is by far the largest single employer of meteorologists and has approximately 2,900 of the 7,700 practicing meteorologists on its payroll. Its hiring practices are relatively representative of those in the field at large, so prospective meteorologists should consult the National Weather Service to review its required courses for hiring. Exceptional grades in computer science, physics, and mathematics are well regarded by employers, as are strong communication skills. Those looking to break into the highly competitive field of broadcast meteorology should pile up on journalism and speech classes while in college. But aspiring broadcast meteorologists should note that it can take nearly an entire working life to make it to a network meteorologist position. Just ask Al Roker, who started broadcasting the weather while in college at SUNY—Oswego and worked in Syracuse, Cleveland, and Washington, DC, before returning to his hometown of New York City, where he worked at local stations for 13 years before becoming the full-time weekday weatherman for the *The Today Show*.

ASSOCIATED CAREERS

After gaining several years' experience within a meteorological organization, some meteorologists seek certification by the American Meteorological Society as consulting meteorologists. This allows them to offer their services in the private sector.

Five years of industry experience, character references, and a passing grade on an exam are required.

PAST AND FUTURE

The philosopher Aristotle wrote the first serious study of the atmosphere, *Meteorologic*, in the fourth century B.C. The Greeks were a seafaring and farming society, and so they did their best to understand and predict weather in order to plan the business of their lives around it—much the same way we try to plan our lives around the weather now. Progress was slow after that. Galileo Galilei did not invent the thermometer until right around the turn of the seventeenth century. His pupil, Evangelista Torricelli, invented the mercury barometer in 1643. Then in the twentieth century, the inventions of radar and satellites and the rapid advance of technology in general allowed meteorologists to monitor the weather across virtually the entire United States in real time.

Meteorologists in coming years are likely to venture into the private sector in greater numbers to assist companies in complying with air quality control legislation (such as the Clean Air Act) and regulation. They may also provide detailed forecasts to weather-sensitive industries, such as farming, commodity investing, utilities, transportation, and construction.

QUALITY OF LIFE

2 YEARS The first two years mainly involve becoming acquainted with equipment and procedures. At the National Weather Service, for example, entry-level meteorologists rotate among various departments to learn how the whole machine operates before being permanently assigned to a specific weather station. One should realize that there are weather stations all across the United States, and it's possible to be permanently assigned to a station that is literally at the end of the world. The pay is modest, and the workload is unpredictable—as unpredictable as the weather itself.

5 YEARS After five years, meteorologists should have operational proficiency of all the processes necessary for basic forecasting. Some develop and supervise less experienced meteorologists. Some go back to school for either a master's degree or PhD, which are usually required to go into meteorological research. Earning potential at the five-year mark has increased dramatically from entry-level rates, but mid-level meteorologists are not laughing all the way to the bank yet. Like all on-air news personalities, the local broadcast meteorologists are hoping for a call up to network.

10 YEARS If still with an organization after 10 years, a meteorologist is probably in a position of some authority. If he or she went back to school for an advanced degree, then career options include joining the faculty at a university or moving into the private or governmental sector for significantly more money. Salaries have surely doubled, and in many cases tripled, from entry-level pay rates. If a meteorologist has launched a consulting business, then he or she has most likely established a solid reputation by this point. Hours as a consultant may be long, but the rewards—at least in terms of income and job satisfaction—can make it all worthwhile.

MAJOR EMPLOYERS
NATIONAL WEATHER SERVICE
1325 East West Highway
Silver Spring, MD 20910
www.nws.noaa.gov

THE WEATHER CHANNEL
Atlanta, GA 30339-2404
www.weather.com

MAJOR ASSOCIATIONS
AMERICAN METEOROLOGICAL SOCIETY
Tel: 617-227-2425
Fax: 617-742-8718
www.ametsoc.org

NEWS ANALYST

A DAY IN THE LIFE

News analysts collect news reported by various sources, interpret it, and facilitate its broadcast to the public. Their purpose is to distill the enormous quantity of news that happens every day. News analysts are often newscasters, either full-time behind-the-desk anchors or reporters called on to comment on specific stories. If a reporter delivers a story live from a specific location, the anchor will often carry on a question and answer session with the reporter to establish important facts for the audience. Sometimes the anchors have time to prepare their questions; at other times, they do it on the fly. Some news analysts specialize. Weathercasters and sportscasters, for example, are news analysts. News analysts who specialize in election coverage may be called on in late October to give a report in which they distill polling numbers, campaign speeches, and key issues.

{ creating the first draft of history }

News analysts usually work long and irregular hours. Depending on how important a news item is, they may have to go on air immediately, with little or no preparation, and stay on indefinitely. On a normal news day, analysts will arrive at their offices several hours before the newscast, review wire reports coming in, and write their stories. For television and radio news, this process also entails working with editors to produce the video or audio clips for taped stories. News analysts who work for newspapers typically write features, op-eds, or regular news pieces. Their deadlines vary depending on the sensitivity of a given story.

The newsroom is a loud and chaotic place in which coworkers constantly talk on the phone, type on computers, and print reports. Qualities of the successful news analyst in such an environment include flexibility and focus. The news does not always happen at convenient times; depending on when it does, news analysts may have to work early, late, and on weekends and holidays. Superb oral and written communication skills are essential. Except for those at the very top (think news anchors) who earn millions of dollars each year, news analysts do not make a lot of money given the long hours they work. Many find, however, that any economic sacrifice is well worth the privilege of having a hand in the creation of the first draft of history, which is exactly what the news is.

PAYING YOUR DUES

News organizations typically require a bachelor's degree for editorial staff positions, and they look most favorably on majors in journalism or communications. They will, however, hire people from other majors, especially when it makes sense for the position. For an economic news analyst position, for example, they may hire someone with a degree in economics. An academic background that includes courses in writing, history, political science, economics, sociology, psychology, and business is very useful in this field. Experience working on school publications is looked on very favorably, and some organizations may even require it of their entry-level hires. In lieu of such in-school experience—or perhaps in addition to it—reporting or editing internships add serious luster to the resume of any applicant. Most news analysts start out as reporters on general assignment and are usually delegated the most undesirable tasks, such as writing obituaries or attending and reporting on civic meetings and summarizing the actions taken. As they accumulate experience, they may be assigned a particular beat, like economics or politics. Over time, they become experts in their given beats, and generally, if they become news analysts, those will be the areas of news on which they will focus.

ASSOCIATED CAREERS

The area-specific expertise and communications skills news analysts develop makes them suitable to assume roles as publicists, editors, and columnists. Some may become teachers of the craft at the high school or college level. Others may make money on the lecture circuit.

PAST AND FUTURE

Mass communication began with the fifteenth-century invention of the Gutenberg printing press. The business of selling printed news evolved over the next 250 years in Western Europe. Newspapers sprouted up throughout the colonies, and the first newspaper with original local news and commentary in Boston was *The New England Courant*, started by none other than James Franklin, the brother of Benjamin Franklin. The more famous Franklin would go on to buy his own newspaper, *The Pennsylvania Gazette*, in 1729. Henry Luce launched the first weekly news magazine in the United States, *Time*, on March 3, 1923. To create value, it not only reported the news, but also analyzed it. Readers praised the magazine, and *Time* spawned numerous imitations, both in print and, later, on television.

Employment opportunities for news analysts are expected to grow more slowly than the average rate for all other occupations over the next several years. This is largely due to increased consolidation of media companies, rising costs, and declining advertising revenue. Internet publications offer some growth potential. The best prospects will be for those writers who can tackle and render coherent highly technical or scientific material.

QUALITY OF LIFE

2 YEARS The first couple of years for any aspiring news analyst are tough. Most of the newspapers in major metropolitan areas and the television networks do not hire reporters directly out of college, so those who eventually want to land those positions have to go out into the bush leagues—small town and suburban newspapers and radio and television stations, for which they report on city council meetings and, if they are lucky, high school football games.

5 YEARS At the five-year mark, a budding news analyst has secured an impressive level of expertise in a specific beat. He or she also has enough experience to be considered for a reporter's position at a station in a larger city. (In fact, he or she may have already traded up into such a position.) Although still not earning the money that he or she may like, there is hope for the future.

10 YEARS If a reporter has wanted to become a news analyst, he or she should officially be one after a decade in the business. If not already working in a major metropolitan area, he or she may still be applying for positions in a large city. Movement from one city to another can happen at any time in a news analyst's career; when bigger opportunities become available, news analysts have to be ready to take them. If a news analyst has made it into a network position or into an anchor chair in a major city, he or she will be earning well into six figures. If not, at least he or she should be making enough for nice vacations and the kids' college funds.

MAJOR EMPLOYERS

CBS
530 West 57th Street
New York, NY 10019
Tel: 212-554-0080
www.cbs.com

CNN
One CNN Center
Atlanta, GA 30303
Tel: 404-878-2276
Fax: 404-827-1995
www.cnn.com

NBC
30 Rockefeller Plaza
New York, NY 10112
Tel: 212-664-2552
Fax: 212-245-4622
www.nbc.com

NATIONAL PUBLIC RADIO
635 Massachusetts Avenue, NW
Washington, DC 20001
Tel: 202- 513-2000
Fax: 202-513-3329
www.npr.org

MAJOR ASSOCIATIONS

NATIONAL ASSOCIATION OF BROADCASTERS
1771 N Street, NW
Washington, DC 20036
Tel: 202-429-5300
Fax: 202-429-4199
E-mail: nab@nab.org
www.nab.org

RADIO/TELEVISION NEWS DIRECTORS ASSOCIATION
1600 K Street NW, Suite 700
Washington, DC 20006-2838
Tel: 202-659-6510
Fax: 202-223-4007
E-mail: rtnda@rtnda.org
www.rtnda.org

SOCIETY OF PROFESSIONAL JOURNALISTS
16 South Jackson Street
PO Box 77
Greencastle, IN 46135
Tel: 765-653-3333
E-mail: spj@link2000.net
www.spj.org:80/spjhome.htm

OFFICE MANAGER

A DAY IN THE LIFE

"An office manager is responsible for the smooth operation of the day-to-day business of the company," one manager wrote us, adding the caveat, "No excuses accepted." A good office manager makes it possible for other people to function efficiently. Office managers work closely with the company partners, owners, or presidents to meet staffing, equipment, and organizational needs. Duties may include pricing products from vendors, interviewing job applicants, managing payroll, and reimbursing members of the firm for out-of-pocket business expenses. An office manager must exercise sound judgment day in and day out, and any lapse can result in termination. This may be the reason that office managers generally take their jobs so seriously. The pressure can be significant, { live on your reputation } particularly for those individuals in charge of large offices. Office managers who succeed have confidence, common sense, loyalty, and the ability to motivate others. Survey respondents who were part-time office managers added the importance of being able to work with others on a team or in pairs to coordinate smooth operations.

Although it is common to think that an office manager should be an angel of tact and discretion, people in the profession disagree. Many office managers said their jobs require them to be somewhat more firm than gentle when projects have to be completed, equipment needs to be serviced, or difficulties with staffing spring up. "You've got to stand up for what you know are the right decisions for the company, even if the boss disagrees. You live on your reputation, and when you have to do your job to someone else's commands, you have to voice your opinion," said one 15-year manager. He was supported by a number of others. "Tough," "precise," and "go-getting" were also words that popped up many times on our surveys.

The greatest satisfaction that office managers mentioned concerned their productivity. Office managers can see immediate results from their decisions; they can control their environments (within the boundaries imposed by their employer). This ability to determine one's own fate cuts both ways, however. Office managers have a very high turnover rate; many are fired, switch jobs, or retire. They are often the first one to be let go when conflicts arise between producers and managers, and they are frequently blamed for office problems that are not of their own making. Office management provides a very structured environment with clearly defined duties for individuals with financial, organizational, and interpersonal skills. An office manager needs to have a high tolerance for risk.

PAYING YOUR DUES

Office managers are not required to have any specific degree, but most employers value a college degree as well as organizational, planning, and communication skills. Suggested courses include organizational behavior, psychology, sociology, finance, and English. Employers at smaller firms also recommend accounting studies, as payroll issues and some financial work may be part of the job.

ASSOCIATED CAREERS

Office managers often use their on-the-job accounting skills to become bookkeepers, bank assistants, and clerks. Some of them use their pricing experience to become professional purchasing agents, but these opportunities are limited, particularly for those individuals in rural locations. Only a few office managers return to school for further degrees, although a small number do go back to study library science.

PAST AND FUTURE

The position of office manager developed along with the growth of the modern firm. As companies expand and diversify, workers are required to perform more and more specialized tasks. Office coordination of the needs and the output of the workers is critical to the productive operation of the company. The office manager helps standardize information, facilitates communication, and makes sure that employees are able to do their jobs.

The future of office managers looks bright. Many economists predict that the economy will allow more office-managing job opportunities in the coming years.

QUALITY OF LIFE

2 YEARS Many office managers direct small firms. They gain valuable experience in purchasing, negotiating deals, smoothing staffing difficulties, and predicting their firm's future needs. This last experience, learning to anticipate problems and requirements, is the most difficult and most important for the new manager. Office managers make contacts with staffing agencies and hone their interviewing skills. The hours are long; salaries are average.

5 YEARS Five-year veterans have gained a good sense of what the job entails. A number of them are beginning to bump into wage ceilings in their current firm, and the race to find new jobs begins. Many office managers work at three, four, or even five firms in five years. A number of them move into jobs with larger staffing requirements than they are used to and must have strong organizational skills to meet this challenge. The hours are long, and salaries are competitive; job security drops as the stakes increase.

10 YEARS Contact with partners and managing directors of firms increases, and many office managers jump to very large firms. Some of them are given a specific area of responsibility, such as staffing needs or supplies and equipment. These are valued positions, and many individuals in them suddenly become averse to big risks and spend much of their time protecting their position. The hours and satisfaction remain steady; pay remains about the same from here on in except for cost-of-living adjustments.

MAJOR EMPLOYERS
HGO TECHNOLOGIES INC.
2110 Lumber Avenue
Wheeling, WV 26003
Tel: 800-300-5543 or 304-242-7600
www.hgo.net
Contact: Human Resources

NEW YORK STATE EDUCATION DEPARTMENT
89 Washington Avenue
Albany, NY 12234
www.nysed.gov

KELLOGG COMPANY
PO Box CAMB
Battle Creek, MI 49016
Tel: 800-962-1413
Fax: 616-961-9047
www.kellogg.com
Contact: Human Resources

MAJOR ASSOCIATIONS
OFFICE AND PROFESSIONAL EMPLOYEES INTERNATIONAL LABOR UNION
265 West 14th Street, 6th Floor
New York, NY 10011
Tel: 800-346-7348
www.opeiu.org

PERSONAL ASSISTANT

BOOKS, FILMS, AND TV SHOWS
FEATURING THE PROFESSION
- America's Sweethearts
- The Big Lebowski
- Jerry Maguire

YOU'LL HAVE CONTACT WITH
- You'll have contact with your boss and with those in his or her profession.

PROFESSIONALS READ
- Personal assistants read materials relevant to the fields of their employers.

A DAY IN THE LIFE

Well-known, wealthy individuals embody the American Dream with the respect, power, and wealth that they wield—not to mention their fashionable taste in clothes. But what would it take to make someone want to work for such a person? The same characteristics that make Donald Trump so revered as an American icon are the same that make him so feared of as a boss. (Not convinced? Just watch an episode of *The Apprentice*.) This job is for the person who wants to know everything about his or her boss. One assistant writes, "Often I would have to get in a cab and run after X if he lost his cell phone (which happened nearly every week) or forgot where he was going. In addition, I had to handle all calls from his manager, lawyer, ex-wives, college-age children, etc. Just a managing of his life." While most person-

{ grunt work—
with a purpose }

al assistants will concede that much of what they do is grunt work, it is grunt work with a purpose. One actor's assistant writes, "I felt that in helping him, I was letting the world know of his talent, and the joy that he has brought to the world is immeasurable."

Managing an office, scheduling meetings and appointments, summarizing projects, and providing information over the phone and e-mail are all typical duties of a personal assistant. Depending on the employer, the position may require much more. Your work may range from more "professional" duties, such as preparing reports, conducting research, and training employees, to the more "informal" ones, such as clothes shopping, purchasing birthday cards, and sending invitations and thank-you notes.

The merits of such a position may not seem obvious, but personal assistants can benefit from their unique positions in a number of ways. There is always the potential to network and meet important industry figures. For many, the position provides an opportunity for free travel. For others, it offers the chance to live vicariously through a favorite celebrity. For one former personal assistant to a major fashion designer, the perk was "the clothes, hands down. We had the best wardrobes in town. I hate shopping now. It was definitely the best." However, potential-assistants-to-the-famous be warned. Not all aspects of the job are glamorous. Some people find the stress and the all-consuming nature of the position too much to handle. Take, for example, this cautionary advice from one assistant who writes, "This job is perfect for someone who wants to be on the 'inside' of a celebrity's personal life because you know everything. I saw my boss naked, saw her break down in tears, watched her fight with her husband. . . . It was all too much for me."

PAYING YOUR DUES

Many personal assistants share similar duties with secretaries. Qualities such as good communication skills, familiarity with computers and office equipment, the ability to absorb and organize business-related data, and, in many cases, the patience of a saint, will be useful to anyone considering this position. Be aware, however, that all of the qualifications in the world may not actually help you land the job. Although some agencies do place personal assistants with employers, many obtain their jobs through a personal connection. It's an odd business from beginning to end, so it should come as no surprise that there's no conventional way to get your foot in the door.

ASSOCIATED CAREERS

Secretary is the position that most often comes to mind when one thinks about a personal assistant. Other positions that may not seem so obvious include babysitter, marriage counselor, personal stylist, and even therapist. Personal assistants may also land industry jobs because of recommendations from their former bosses.

PAST AND FUTURE

Well-off and well-regarded (or at the very least, well-positioned) people have had people around to take care of them since the dawn of recorded history. And although you may not be responsible for fanning your boss down with an oversized palm leaf or for feeding him or her grapes out of a magnificently crafted marble dish, make no mistake, celebrities are the modern-day equivalents of a Pharaoh or Caesar (or at least they sometimes think—and act as if—they are). In choosing this profession, you will voluntarily join those countless numbers of people who have come before you and stood in the shadows of greatness.

Personal assistants are likely to enjoy a comfortable place in American society for the years to come. The level of employment will continue to grow at an average rate compared with the job market at large.

QUALITY OF LIFE

2 YEARS What draws someone to work for a celebrity is most often not the glamour of the work, but rather the potential to ingratiate oneself with someone famous. If your boss hasn't driven you mad by the two-year mark, perhaps it is because you like being around him or her. You may also be benefiting from many opportunities to travel, shop, and meet celebrities.

5 YEARS At this point, you have grown accustomed to the idiosyncrasies of your boss, or else you would have moved on. Your hard work and patience should be paying off. As your boss's most important confidant and advisor, you enjoy a fair amount of job security and are probably earning a salary commensurate with the faith your employer has placed in you.

10 YEARS Although you may decide to stick with your boss for the length of your job, one perk about being a personal assistant—especially if you're a good one—is that you can make great contacts in your boss's industry. One assistant we know of moved to a network position. Another parlayed her experience in the fashion industry into a position as a fashion publicist. An assistant to a film actress got her own agent and is currently writing screenplays in Hollywood.

MAJOR EMPLOYERS

Most personal assistants work for individuals and are not hired by large companies.

MAJOR ASSOCIATIONS

THE FREELANCERS UNION
45 Main Street, Suite 710
Brooklyn, NY 11201
Tel: 718-532-1515
Fax: 718-222-4440
E-mail: info@workingtoday.org
www.workingtoday.org

PLUMBING ENGINEER

A DAY IN THE LIFE

Plumbing engineers are responsible for the design, development, and management of plumbing systems for buildings. These include water, processing fluids, and waste systems. Plumbing engineers have many responsibilities: They are in charge of the coordination and management of those working below them, materials and equipment, schedules, contracts, and safety. The work may be challenging, but it's also rewarding; one plumbing engineer writes of his job, "I love that I'm working on different projects all the time and that I'm not always stuck in front of a desk; I could be out in the field surveying or meeting with clients."

It should come as no surprise that communication skills are essential. Plumbing engineers are in constant contact with potential clients and cowork-

{ identify problems and devise solutions }

ers, including supervisors, electricians, architects, pipelayers, pipefitters, steamfitters, and plumbers. Plumbing engineers are problem solvers. As with all engineers, they must be able to work closely with project managers and superintendents to identify potential problems and devise solutions to remedy those problems. Computer knowledge is also essential, especially for projects with particularly sophisticated design and planning processes. Plumbing engineers must also be familiar with building codes and safety regulations so they may ensure that any construction meets requisite standards. Plumbing engineers typically find full-time work with a single company or are hired on the basis of temporary, or contract, positions.

PAYING YOUR DUES

A bachelor's degree, usually in mechanical engineering (BSME), is usually required for this position. Occasionally, extensive on-the-job experience will suffice. Many employers also require that their plumbing engineers have a professional engineer's (PE) license. This license is particularly useful for engineers who must deal with federal or state officials for the implementation of their projects. Knowledge of AutoCAD is considered essential by many employers, as plumbing engineers are instrumental in the design and construction of a building's plumbing systems, often on a large scale.

After college, many potential plumbing engineers get jobs with mechanical contractors in order to build their resumes and get the on-the-job experience needed to advance. Building on one's experience by working with other professionals, amassing knowledge of federal and state building codes and regulations, gaining valuable customer service experience, and possibly earning a PE license, an individual can plan to apply for a plumbing engineer position after as little as two to five years of experience. Senior plumbing engineer positions usually require some 10 to 15 years of experience to be considered.

ASSOCIATED CAREERS

Plumbing engineers are often likened to mechanical and electrical engineers, since the three fields share similar degree requirements. Plumbing engineers may also venture into architecture, which is similar because of the building planning involved and the use of AutoCAD. Perhaps surprisingly, some plumbing engineers become fire department officials, since that career path requires similar knowledge of building codes and fire regulations. Experienced plumbing engineers may also opt to take jobs with software and consulting companies, for which they may draw on their knowledge of plumbing systems to provide clients with service and technical support.

PAST AND FUTURE

Plumbing engineers are essentially engineer-architects. As buildings became more complex, their construction required the help of more specialized professionals, such as plumbing and electrical engineers. As federal and state governments became increasingly involved with the regulation of building construction, for example, with the Americans with Disabilities Act (1990), professionals with knowledge of intricate building codes became indispensable.

Employment of plumbing engineers is expected to grow at an average rate through 2012. Additional opportunities for people with mechanical engineering degrees will arise with the emergence of new technologies. In particular, the fields of biotechnology, materials science, and nanotechnology will create new job opportunities for people with degrees in mechanical engineering.

QUALITY OF LIFE

2 YEARS During these initial years, you will be gaining the hands-on experience necessary to advance in this field. You will likely start off working under a mechanical contractor, who will act as your supervisor. At this point in your career, it is important to become familiar with as many aspects of the business as possible; advancement is largely dependent on job experience in this field.

5 YEARS At this point, you may be able to apply for an associate plumbing engineer or other similar position. You may, however, wish to hold out until you have more experience and/or certifications under your belt. You will also have to choose, based on availability, whether to work full-time for a company or to take temporary/contract jobs with various employers.

10 YEARS After 10 years, you can expect to be earning a good salary and working full-time for a single company—as long as you have taken advantage of your experience in the field and accumulated the skills needed to make you competitive in this business. In addition to working for a construction company, you may consider employment with a software or consulting company, positions that require less project planning and development and more client advising.

MAJOR EMPLOYERS

EINHORN YAFFEE PRESCOTT
440 Park Avenue South
New York, NY 10016
Tel: 917-981-6000
E-mail: mktgmanagernyc@eypae.com
www.eypae.com

HENDERSON ENGINEERS, INC.
8325 Lenexa Drive
Lenexa, KS 66214
Tel: 913-307-5300
Fax: 913-307-5400
www.hendersonengineers.com

TAI ENGINEERS
11459 Cronhill Drive, Suite A
Owings Mills, MD 21117
Tel: 410-356-3108
Fax: 410-356-3109
www.taiengineering.com

TIGHE AND BOND
Westfield Executive Park
53 Southampton Road
Westfield, MA 01085-1371
Tel: 413-562-1600
Fax: 413-562-5317
www.tighebond.com

Plumbing engineers work for engineering and architectural firms, motor vehicle and equipment manufacturers, and government agencies. Some also find employment through temporary worker agencies.

MAJOR ASSOCIATIONS

AMERICAN SOCIETY OF PLUMBING ENGINEERS
8614 Catalpa Avenue, Suite 1007
Chicago, IL 60656-1116
Tel: 773-693-2773

AMERICAN SOCIETY OF SANITARY ENGINEERING
901 Canterbury, Suite A
Westlake, OH 44145
Tel: 440-835-3040
Fax: 440-835-3488
E-mail: info@asse-plumbing.org
www.asse-plumbing.org

NATION SOCIETY OF PROFESSIONAL ENGINEERS
1420 King Street
Alexandria, VA 22314-2794
Tel: 703-684-2800
Fax: 703-836-4875

PROOFREADER

A DAY IN THE LIFE

Proofreaders are much, much more than human spell-checkers. Attention to detail, sound grammar skills, and the ability to plan, organize, and reorganize written data are all talents that good proofreaders possess. Although particular sets of responsibilities may vary by project—depending on whether the manuscript in question is a book, magazine, newspaper, or technical journal, for example—proofreaders are always responsible for identifying and amending typographical errors, spelling mistakes, errors in punctuation and grammar, and inconsistencies in presentation before a manuscript goes to print. In essence, proofreaders serve as the last lines of defense before a work is released to the sometimes mercilessly critical reading public. Successful proofreaders must be attentive, careful

{ attention to detail and sound grammar skills }

readers; they must know the proper proofreaders' marks inside and out; and they often need to be patient in reading material that may not be of interest to them. They also must be able to organize written words into cohesive, well-organized thoughts.

Proofreaders find work with a variety of employers, from established publishing houses to online businesses. A proofreader who works for a newspaper, for example, will have a different schedule from that of a freelance proofreader, who usually works from home. Those with office jobs should not be surprised, however, to find themselves working amidst the din of keyboards and computer printers, office chit-chat, and other potential distractions. While they may have more job security than freelance proofreaders, members of this latter group enjoy the freedom to set their own schedules and determine their preferred work environments. Proofreaders who wish to advance in this field read manuscripts in their spare time and—if employed by a publishing house—stay late doing extra work to get recognized, and ultimately, promoted.

If you're interested in the creative or development aspects of a project, proofreading may not be your ideal job. Editors primarily interact with authors; whereas proofreaders deal most often with production managers. Copy is not sent to the proofreader for a final read until outstanding creative issues have been resolved between the editor and author. Although the job of a proofreader is not a particularly lucrative profession, it can be rewarding for the person who is detail-oriented and likes to read and work with words. It is also an ideal job for freelancers, as it often allows them the freedom to schedule their own hours and determine their work flow.

PAYING YOUR DUES

No degree is required, although most proofreaders have bachelor's degrees, typically in English, communications, or journalism. The potential to impress employers, nevertheless, depends more on your abilities than your on-paper qualifications. Training is also available, and it may prove helpful for someone who has little or no experience. Classes are offered by many colleges, and some proofreading services even offer online classes.

Finding work can be difficult, but publishers are always in need of proofreaders. If you demonstrate yourself to be a good proofreader, then clients will continue to seek out your services. Available proofreading jobs are typically posted online. If you have already taken a proofreading class, you have probably made valuable connections and may be hired right away; otherwise, you may be asked to take a proofreading test before being offered a job. If you are having trouble finding full-time work, you may consider looking for a company in need of freelance proofreaders. Freelancing offers a great way to get your foot in the door and build your resume.

ASSOCIATED CAREERS

Although proofreaders and editors are often likened to one another, the two positions are distinct. Editors often work closely with authors and iron out most of the errors in a manuscript before sending it off to a proofreader. It is also more common for an editor to have a college or even a graduate degree, usually in English, communications, or journalism.

PAST AND FUTURE

Less famous people have been editing, copyediting, and proofreading the work of more famous people since time immemorial. Originally, publishers were in charge of making sure that manuscripts had been typeset correctly. With the increase in the creation and propagation of published materials over time, however, this job eventually became that of the proofreader.

Growth is expected to increase at about the average rate for all occupations. Competition for jobs is—and is expected to remain—intense, since many who hope ultimately to become writers or journalists launch their careers as proofreaders. Major centers of employment for those interested in working for book and magazine publishers, advertising agencies, and public relations firms include New York, Boston, Chicago, Philadelphia, Los Angeles, and San Francisco. Those interested in working for newspapers and journals may find work in a variety of places. Similarly, freelance proofreaders will be able to find work with few geographical limitations.

QUALITY OF LIFE

2 YEARS Although there is a lot of work out there, you may find at the beginning of your career that you have some difficulty landing a full-time job. Although some are fortunate enough to find jobs or projects right away, most need some time to establish themselves. To get a foot in the door, many enroll in a proofreading class, take entry-level jobs as editorial assistants, or work part-time for companies that need freelance proofreaders.

5 YEARS If you are still a proofreader at the five-year mark, you can expect to have a full workload. If you are working full-time for a publishing house, you will find that putting in extra time at the office will get you recognized and may lead to a higher pay scale. If you are a freelancer, you should be able to work as much as you would like, since you will already have made connections with several publishers.

10 YEARS There is less room for advancement in this field than there is in some others. Unlike editors, who may climb the ranks, there is no analogous career path for proofreaders. Although you may enjoy increased freedom to choose projects that interest you, you should not expect a significant change in your quality of life or earning potential. If you have stayed with the career this long, you are likely a proofreader because you like the work and—if you are a freelancer—because enjoy the freedom of setting your own hours.

MAJOR EMPLOYERS

THE ASSOCIATED PRESS
450 West 33rd Street
New York, NY 10001
www.ap.org

CONDÉ NAST PUBLICATIONS
4 Times Square
New York, NY 10036
Tel: 212-286-2860
www.condenast.com

THE NEW YORK TIMES
229 West 43rd Street
New York, NY 10036
Tel: 212-556-1234
E-mail: digitalresume@nytimes.com
www.nytimes.com

RANDOM HOUSE
1745 Broadway
New York, NY 10019
Tel: 212-782-9000
E-mail: humanresources@randomhouse.com
www.randomhouse.com

MAJOR ASSOCIATIONS

EDITORIAL FREELANCERS ASSOCIATION
71 West 23rd Street, Suite 1910
New York, NY 10010-4181
Tel: 212-929-5400
Fax: 212-929-5439
www.the-efa.org

RESEARCH TECHNICIAN

SALARY   ●

HOURS   ● ●

EDUCATION   ● ●

BOOKS, FILMS, AND TV SHOWS
FEATURING THE PROFESSION

- **Species**
- **Young Frankenstein**

YOU'LL HAVE CONTACT WITH

- **Engineers**
- **Scientists**

PROFESSIONALS READ

- **Communication Skills for the Environmental Technician**
- **Nature**
- **Science**
- **Waste Management and Research**

A DAY IN THE LIFE

The research technician, or lab assistant, is an important part of a scientific lab. Lab assistants participate in high-tech, high-profile research that, in some instances, saves lives. Research technicians are the workhorses of the lab. They set up, operate, and maintain the lab equipment. They test, monitor, and keep detailed logs of the experiments. Most of the work is not glamorous and can at times be mundane. More experienced technicians maintain complex computer equipment, interpret data, develop conclusions, and devise solutions to problems under the direction of the scientist in charge.

There are almost as many different types of research technicians as there are industries. Biological technicians assist scientists in medical
{ dangerous chemicals }
research; they help find cures for diseases. Many assistants work in labs that specialize in DNA research. Environmental technicians conduct field tests to monitor the air we breathe and the water we drink. Agricultural technicians conduct animal research and work with farmers to develop better crops and animal-breeding procedures. Nuclear technicians operate nuclear research equipment to monitor radiation and radioactive materials. Technicians can work either in a lab or outdoors. Some duties of a research technician involve collecting plant samples, examining geological data, collecting weather information, assisting oceanographers, or even testing city sewer water. Research technicians are exposed to dangerous chemicals, toxic materials, and even infectious diseases on a daily basis. It takes a clear mind and a steady hand to work in a lab. The research technician may not get all the glory of the scientist; but without them, the scientist is like a conductor without an orchestra.

PAYING YOUR DUES

Many employers prefer applicants who have at least two years of specialized training or an associate degree in applied science or science-related technology. Some technicians have a bachelor's degree in chemistry or biology or have taken several science and math courses at four-year colleges. Some schools offer internship programs, allowing students the opportunity to work at a local company or other workplace, while attending classes in alternate terms. Participation in such programs can significantly enhance a student's employment prospects. Research technicians need a strong background in science and math. Science courses taken beyond high school in an associate's or bachelor's program should be laboratory-oriented, with an emphasis on bench skills. Because computers and computer-interfaced equipment are often used in research and development laboratories, technicians should have strong computer skills. Communication skills are also important; technicians are often required to report their findings both through speaking and writing. Additionally, technicians should be able to work well with others because teamwork is crucial.

ASSOCIATED CAREERS

Research technicians can use their scientific skills in other fields such as engineering, broadcasting (working with the equipment), and drafting. Research technicians can move into the supply side of laboratories, working as chemical and equipment suppliers. And there is no stopping a research technician from continuing his or her education and becoming a scientist.

PAST AND FUTURE

Research technicians have long enjoyed a stable employment market. However, some statistics show that research positions will grow at a slower-than-average rate for the next ten years. Continued growth of scientific and medical research, as well as the development and production of technical products, should stimulate the demand for science technicians in all areas. In particular, the growing number of agricultural and medicinal products developed from using biotechnology techniques will increase the need for biological technicians. Employment growth will also be fueled by the demand for technicians to help regulate waste products; collect air, water, and soil samples for measuring levels of pollutants; monitor compliance with environmental regulations; and clean up contaminated sites. Job opportunities are expected to be very good for qualified graduates of science technician training programs. In addition to opportunities created by growth, many job openings should arise from the need to replace technicians who retire or leave the labor force for other reasons. Research technicians who are tied to universities usually work under the guidance of a professor. Once that professor retires, loses funding, or simply leaves, these technicians face uncertain employment prospects.

QUALITY OF LIFE

2 YEARS Technicians usually begin work as trainees in routine positions, under the direct supervision of a scientist or a more experienced technician. Job candidates whose training or educational background encompasses extensive hands-on experience with a variety of laboratory equipment, including computers and related equipment, usually require a short period of on-the-job training.

5 YEARS More experience leads to more responsibility. As technology advances, the instrumentation and techniques used in industrial research, development, and production become increasingly more complex. Some technicians find they may need to return to school or take supplemental accreditations to keep up with the changing times.

10 YEARS After ten years of experience, most technicians are considered senior researchers. They manage the everyday happenings in the lab, direct some research, and train lower-level technicians.

MAJOR EMPLOYERS

BAYLOR COLLEGE OF MEDICINE
Human Resources
One Baylor Plaza, BCM 170
Houston, TX 77030
Tel: 713-798-4951
www.bcm.edu

CENTERS FOR DISEASE CONTROL AND PREVENTION
1600 Clifton Road
Atlanta, GA 30333
Tel: 404-639-3311 or 800-311-3435
E-mail: cdcinfo@cdc.gov
www.cdc.gov

ENVIRONMENTAL PROTECTION AGENCY
Ariel Rios Building
1200 Pennsylvania Avenue, NW
Washington, DC 20460
Tel: 202-272-0167
www.epa.gov

MAJOR ASSOCIATIONS

AMERICAN ASSOCIATION FOR THE ADVANCEMENT OF SCIENCE
1200 New York Avenue, NW
Washington, DC 20005
Tel: 202-326-6400
www.aaas.org

ASSOCIATION FOR WOMEN IN SCIENCE
1200 New York Avenue, NW, Suite 650
Washington, DC 20005
Tel: 202-326-8940
E-mail: awis@awis.org
www.awis.org

SOMMELIER

A DAY IN THE LIFE

When customers in an upscale restaurant want to order a bottle of wine with dinner, they may be overwhelmed by or unfamiliar with the selections offered on the wine list. When this is the case, they may ask the sommelier for advice. *Sommelier* is the French term for "cellar-master" or "wine steward." Sommeliers are individuals with a love of wine who are eager to share some of their knowledge with the customer. They can describe the regions, grapes, vineyards, and vintages of an assortment of wines. The best sommeliers talk to, not at, their customers and enjoy when customers tell them about a bottle they have recently tasted. The sommelier either helps to create the wine list or compiles it on his or her own. The sommelier recommends wines that suit the customer's tastes and price range. Even those individuals who are knowledgeable about wine may benefit from the sommelier's advice. He or she has tasted the items on the wine list and knows which wines go best with which entrees. Many patrons are easily intimidated by wines and do not understand the terminology used to describe them. The sommelier must be ready to coax from them a description of their preferences and be understanding of their budgetary limits. When they select a wine, the sommelier brings it to the table with the appropriate glasses and pours it for the customer to taste. The sommelier should encourage the patron to smell the wine first and should describe its components. In a sense, the sommelier must bring the wine to life for the patron before it even touches his or her palate. Sommeliers also decant wines, when necessary. Decanting, usually done to red wines aged for more than 10 years, is the process of pouring the wine into a decanter before serving it. This is done to allow the wine to breathe and to separate it from any sediment that may have settled at the bottom of the bottle. Performing this process in front of the table that ordered the wine, the sommelier demonstrates his or her skills, the nuances of the wine, and the importance of treating precious wines properly.

{ "cellar-master" }

Extensive and frequent travel is part of a sommelier's career. Many travel yearly to different regions to choose wines for their restaurant. At times, they will leave a promising wine behind, but return to it repeatedly until they feel it has aged properly.

PAYING YOUR DUES

While no formal training is required to become a sommelier, professionals in the field utilize a host of skills. A good sense of taste and smell, as well as a detailed memory, complement the business, management, and communication skills required of a good sommelier. A sommelier must also know the finer points of wine service (which include proper table etiquette, decanting, and glassware positioning) and the proper protocol for serving brandies, liqueurs, and cigars. Many aspiring sommeliers gain this knowledge as servers or bartenders at fine restaurants. In these positions, they typically read books about wine and attend tastings in their free time until they feel confident enough to cover for the restaurant's sommelier one or two nights a week. Individuals that seek more formal training attend sommelier education programs, generally offered at colleges and culinary schools in metropolitan areas. It doesn't matter how individuals learn the ropes; certification by The Court of Master Sommeliers—the only internationally recognized organization for certifying restaurant wine professionals—helps immensely when looking for a job. They offer annual wine education programs and testing in the United States.

ASSOCIATED CAREERS

The field of wine is vast, but more traditional and family-oriented than one might expect. Vineyard owners are responsible for tending to the grape harvest and pressing the wine. They employ large numbers of people to do this. Wine production is predominantly a closed area as there are a limited number of good grape-growing regions and families tend to pass the vineyard down through bloodlines. Individuals who are knowledgeable about wine may consider hosting tasting dinners or teaching wine-tasting classes. Still others may write about their experiences for industry publications, such as *Food & Wine* Magazine.

PAST AND FUTURE

The practice of cultivating grapes for wine has carried on for thousands of years. Drinking habits have always fluctuated around the fashions, politics, and customs of the times. Often these three factors have had much to do with the profit generated from wine-growing. The early twentieth century saw the beginning of a movement to ensure the authenticity of wines. This movement culminated in laws stating, for example, that only wine from the French region of Champagne could be called champagne. Since World War II, wine consumption in the United States has grown; the American vineyard has matured, and some vineyards in California produce excellent wine. The best European wines are becoming increasingly expensive, causing many people to view them as investment opportunities. This has created a demand for sommeliers: Given the complexities and the cost of wines, many people recognize the need for guidance in choosing one.

QUALITY OF LIFE

2 YEARS Most sommeliers begin by working under another sommelier's guidance; apprenticeship under a master is the best way to learn about worth stocking. People enter this profession because they have a "taste" for it, and nearly all beginners report great satisfaction with their choice of career.

5 YEARS The majority of sommeliers work independently now and enjoy the increased responsibilities of choosing the house wines (a process typically considered of the utmost importance to restaurateurs). The task of creating the wine list for a restaurant requires diligence and creativity and entails finding the best suppliers of both the choice, inexpensive wines and the higher-priced vintages. After five years, a sommelier has developed the experience to recommend selections for the type of restaurant he or she has been working with.

10 YEARS By this time the sommelier has probably acquired a reputation and may be quoted in magazines and journals as an authority on wine. Some sommeliers do consulting work for several restaurants, bringing their own flair to each house, while others choose to focus on a single restaurant where they are employed full-time or perhaps share a financial interest. Experienced sommeliers may host wine-tasting dinners, speak as lecturers or teach wine education courses, write columns for specialty magazines such as *The Wine Spectator*, or act as mentors to aspiring sommeliers.

MAJOR EMPLOYERS

Sommeliers are employed by fine restaurants across the nation.

MAJOR ASSOCIATIONS

SOMMELIER SOCIETY OF AMERICA
PO Box 20080
West Village Station
New York, NY 10014
Tel: 212-679-4190
Fax: 212-255-8959
www.sommeliersocietyofamerica.org

SURVEYOR

SALARY ● ●
HOURS ● ●
EDUCATION ● ●

BOOKS, FILMS, AND TV SHOWS
FEATURING THE PROFESSION
- **The Great Arc**
- **Measuring America**

YOU'LL HAVE CONTACT WITH
- **Attorneys**
- **Cartographers**
- **Geologists**
- **Urban and regional planners**

PROFESSIONALS READ
- **Professional Surveyor Magazine**

A DAY IN THE LIFE

Surveyors calculate the height, depth, relative position, and property lines of pieces of land. They use theodolites, transits, levels, and satellite technology—known as the Global Positioning System (GPS)—to determine locations and boundaries. They work outdoors most of the time and often have assistants. Surveyors work with many other people and often act as team leaders, in charge of projects for civil engineers, architects, or local authorities. It may seem that a surveyor's job is a nonpressured one, but respondents were quick to point out that, "If a surveyor doesn't do his job properly, everything goes wrong. Imagine the problem if a building straddled two people's properties or an airport runway wasn't level." Surveying is a career that requires an eye for detail, a careful touch, an analytical mind, strong organizational and communication skills, and leadership ability.

{ rigorous physical work }

Surveyors work in a variety of areas. Some delineate property boundaries for legal deeds and titles. Others work on civil-engineering projects, such as airports, highways, and waste-treatment plants. Nearly every construction job requires a surveyor (hence, many surveyors are employed by architects). Surveyors also work with oceanographers, geophysicists (to explore for oil), and miners (to ensure the proper positioning of underground shafts). The variety of the tasks that comprise the job is one of its most interesting features. "You use the same tools in different ways to do different things," one quite happy surveyor noted. Surveyors must stay abreast of technological advances. The development of GPS technology, which triangulates signals from satellites to determine precise locations, has changed the way surveyors and cartographers work together. Continuing professional education is the norm in this occupation.

Surveying can involve rigorous physical work. Often, surveying is done in remote, physically challenging locations and requires the carrying of equipment over undeveloped terrain. Respondents said that their work can be stressful because it is so exacting and because architects sometimes claim a survey was faulty instead of taking responsibility for their own mistakes. Surveyors' positive comments, however, significantly outweighed their negative ones.

PAYING YOUR DUES

Surveyors are not required to have a college education, but state-licensing requirements make it preferable for candidates to earn one. Employers look favorably on college or vocational school courses in surveying, civil engineering, mathematics, physics, statistics, geometry, drafting, and computer science. Many of those who don't attend college find work as assistants and eventually become technicians, for the most part getting their education on the job. All states require that surveyors be licensed. Although requirements vary from state to state, college graduates generally must have two to four years of surveying experience, while high school graduates must have six to ten years. All must pass a written licensing exam. Professional certification, while not required, is available through the American Congress on Surveying and Mapping or the American Society for Photogrammetry and Remote Sensing.

ASSOCIATED CAREERS

Surveyors who leave the profession usually do so because they are dissatisfied with the pay, not with the work. They become construction managers, professional property consultants (on issues of boundaries and the accuracy of other surveyors), and lawyers. Many surveyors return to academic studies, most often to pursue a degree in civil engineering.

PAST AND FUTURE

The profession grew out of the need to map and plan the transit routes for personal and commercial transportation. The planning, construction, and maintenance of America's infrastructure required a constant supply of qualified surveyors. Surveying was once considered a branch in civil engineering, but due to the scope and complexity of work, it is now recognized as a distinct profession.

The need for surveyors is expected to grow significantly in the coming years. Large, long overdue infrastructure maintenance projects are expected to be carried out; the brisk pace of housing starts and property concerns is expected to continue; and satellite technology is likely to compel revisions of existing maps. Job opportunities are expected to increase over the next several years.

QUALITY OF LIFE

2 YEARS Two years into the profession, surveyors usually work as crew chiefs, managers, or technicians. At this stage, all surveyors work under the supervision of experienced surveyors. When state laws do not require a college degree for licensure, many novices learn the techniques and practices they need to become successful surveyors. Salaries are low; satisfaction is average.

5 YEARS Those who are licensed and able to become fully accredited surveyors are more satisfied (and better paid) than those who are not. Responsibilities increase; surveyors begin to work closely with engineers, architects, contractors, and attorneys.

10 YEARS Surveyors have gained considerable experience from working on a variety of projects. A few specialize, but most remain general surveyors who manage assistants and technicians on surveying jobs. Most surveyors remain affiliated with government agencies, contractors, or surveying and engineering firms. Hours and responsibilities remain basically the same; satisfaction is above average.

MAJOR EMPLOYERS

NATIONAL GEOSPATIAL INTELLIGENCE AGENCY (NGA)
Office of Corporate Relations
Public Affairs Division, MS D-54
4600 Sangamore Road
Bethesda, MD 20816-5003
Tel: 703-755-5900
E-mail: recruitment@nga.mil
www.nima.mil

PARSONS BRINKERHOFF, INC.
303 2nd Street, Suite 700 North
San Francisco, CA 94107-1317
Tel: 415-243-4600
Fax: 415-243-9501
www.pbworld.com
Contact: Human Resources

U.S. ARMY CORPS OF ENGINEERS
441 G Street, Northwest
Washington, DC 20314
Tel: 202-761-1024
www.usace.army.mil

MAJOR ASSOCIATIONS

AMERICAN CONGRESS ON SURVEYING AND MAPPING
6 Montgomery Village Avenue, Suite #403
Gaithersburg, MD 20879
Tel: 240-632-9716
Fax: 240-632-1321
E-mail: info@acsm.net
www.acsm.net

NYS ASSOCIATION OF PROFESSIONAL LAND SURVEYORS, INC.
146 Washington Avenue
Albany, NY 12210-2203
Tel: 518-432-4046
Fax: 518-432-4055
E-mail: contactnysapls@nysapls.net
www.nysapls.net

X-RAY TECHNICIAN

BOOKS, FILMS, AND TV SHOWS FEATURING THE PROFESSION

- ER
- Grey's Anatomy
- House
- Scrubs

YOU'LL HAVE CONTACT WITH

- Dentists
- Laboratory technologists
- Nurses
- Patients
- Physicians

PROFESSIONALS READ

- ASRT Scanner
- The Internet Journal of Radiology
- Radiation Therapist
- Radiologic Technology
- Topics in Magnetic Resonance Imaging

A DAY IN THE LIFE

One of the most significant discoveries of the past two centuries, X-ray imaging quickly evolved from a scientific art project (studios began selling "bone portraits" for display in the home) to an indispensable diagnostic tool. X-ray technicians create X-ray images and administer nonradioactive matter into patients' veins for the purpose of diagnosing problems. Some technicians specialize in certain areas of imaging, such as magnetic resonance imaging (MRI) or computerized tomography (CT). In generating X-ray images, these technicians do more than direct patients to "say cheese." There's a lot of preparation—removing items that X rays will not penetrate (such as jewelry and anything containing metal), positioning patients so that the parts of the body in question can be radiographed, and protecting the rest of the body from radiation exposure. Images can be created from film; these require the technician to take very precise measurements and to ensure that the machine gets shots at the right density, detail, and contrast. Technicians with more specialized experience may perform more complex procedures, including fluoroscopies (for these, the technician provides a contrast medium for patients to drink that allows radiologists to see soft tissue and organs not picked up by regular X rays) and MRIs (these employ magnets and radio waves to create images).

{ forefront of one of medicine's fastest-growing industries }

Most technicians will spend some of their off-duty hours on call. Although most technicians work 40 hours a week, their shifts are often not your typical Monday–Friday gig and may include nights and/or weekends. The radiation dangers that come with the territory for technicians are minimized with the use of safety equipment, including gloves, aprons, and shields made of lead. Technicians also wear badges that monitor radiation, and these measurements are recorded to chart their exposure. X-ray technology has paved the way for more sophisticated developments, including ultrasound and CT scanning, and makes it possible for doctors to diagnose some illnesses before symptoms even occur. For this reason, X-ray technicians continue to be at the forefront of one of medicine's fastest-growing professions.

PAYING YOUR DUES

Formal training in radiography can range from shorter certificate programs (usually one year in length) to full bachelor's degrees. Associate's degrees are most common, and these generally take two years to complete. Radiography programs are accredited by The Joint Review Committee on Education in Radiologic Technology and usually require a high school diploma or its equivalent for acceptance. Programs provide classroom and hands-on instruction in anatomy and physiology, radiation physics, medical terminology, and radiation protection. Coursework in mathematics, physics, chemistry, and biology is helpful, and medical professionals in other fields often return for training to build on their knowledge. Most employers prefer to hire registered technicians. To become registered, a technician must complete an accredited program and pass a required examination on completion of that program.

ASSOCIATED CAREERS

In addition to the potential to specialize in diagnostic imaging centers, technicians also have opportunities to become supervisors, chief technicians, and department administrators. Other trained technicians leave the doctor's office and become instructors or sales representatives for equipment manufacturers.

PAST AND FUTURE

Although many of the first technicians to operate an X-ray machine in the early part of the twentieth century had no connection to the medical profession, independent businesspeople began to purchase and operate X-ray equipment as the technology advanced. First falling into the hands of physicians' assistants and secretaries, the job was soon turned over to nurses in hospital facilities; they became the first X-ray technicians. In the 1920s, Eddy Jerman set out to bring uniformity to the profession and founded The American Association of Radiological Technicians.

In the latter half of the century, personnel shortages led to campaigns to recruit and retain technologists. General physicians' offices and medical diagnostic centers are expected to grow rapidly through 2012, in part due to technological advances that allow a growing number of procedures to be done outside the walls of hospitals. Technicians experienced in more complex imaging procedures have better employment prospects, as employers try to manage payrolls by hiring multiskilled employees.

QUALITY OF LIFE

2 YEARS After completing the educational requirements and passing certification exams, newly licensed technicians can expect to find work most easily in physicians' offices or in general practices. Here, technique and procedure is perfected in a less stressful atmosphere, and the experience generally required by hospitals and larger establishments is gained.

5 YEARS With additional experience comes the opportunity to concentrate on areas that have interested you the most in the field and to search for jobs that will allow you to hone your area of specialization. Specialized diagnostic clinics generally require three years of experience. Continuing education is required to maintain certification; and after five years of on-the-job experience and constant classroom instruction about new techniques, the technician at this point is ready to meet the demands of new and more efficient radiological technology.

10 YEARS Technicians with 10 or more years of experience are likely to move on to supervisory positions. Depending on the employer, a master's degree in business or health administration may be necessary for advancement to managerial positions. A decade of experience also leaves technicians with the knowledge necessary to train up-and-coming radiology students, and some may choose to leave the hospital for the classroom.

MAJOR EMPLOYERS

CHILDREN'S HOSPITAL LOS ANGELES
4650 Sunset Boulevard
Los Angeles, CA 90027
Tel: 323-660-2450
www.childrenshospitalla.org

NEW YORK-PRESBYTERIAN, THE UNIVERSITY HOSPITAL OF COLUMBIA AND CORNELL
622 West 168th Street
New York, NY 10032
Tel: 212-305-2500
www.nyp.org

ROOSEVELT HOSPITAL
1000 10th Avenue
New York, NY 10019
Tel: 212-523-4000

The nationwide shortage of health care workers also extends to X-ray technicians. Doctors' offices and diagnostic imaging centers have created numerous jobs, but hospitals are still the largest employers. Online job search engines offer listings for open positions across the country, as do local hospital and health care facility websites.

MAJOR ASSOCIATIONS

AMERICAN SOCIETY OF RADIOLOGIC TECHNOLOGISTS
15000 Central Avenue, SE
Albuquerque, NM 87123
Tel: 800-444-2778
www.asrt.org

AMERICAN REGISTRY OF RADIOLOGIC TECHNICIANS
1255 Northland Drive
St. Paul, MN 55120
www.arrt.org

THE BLUE CAREERS

ACTOR

A DAY IN THE LIFE

One actor we interviewed referred to his life as a modified version of the song "Do the Hustle," in which he ran from audition to audition and checked his answering machine messages every two hours for news of a possible callback. Actors' satisfaction with their profession seems to vacillate with whether or not they are currently working. Many working actors would agree with the one who wrote that he found the occupation "challenging, thrilling, exciting, and wonderful." Some nonworking actors may agree with the one who wrote that acting can be "a dead end to nowhere." In various ways, most actors described their choice of career as not a choice at all: "There was nothing else I wanted to do," wrote one woman; "I guess I'm just demented." { cutthroat career } The community of similarly "demented" professionals is the most supportive aspect of this otherwise cutthroat career. Why else would they stay in a profession in which the average Actors' Equity Association (AEA) member earns less than $7,000 from acting annually?

PAYING YOUR DUES

Formal training is not required to become an actor, but the number of "natural talents" who spring fully groomed into a successful professional career is very small. Most actors study acting, appear in low-budget and local productions, learn (and benefit) from those appearances, and then begin the cycle again. Some study acting in college; others find it helpful to study further and receive a Master of Fine Arts in Acting. Working actors are constantly going on casting calls, finding agents, and getting reviewed (favorably, if possible); all of these are arduous and time-consuming tasks, more often resulting in rejection rather than success. Many actors choose to move to major cities (in particular New York for theater and Los Angeles for film and television) because more opportunities exist in those places. Regional theaters can be excellent but provide only limited exposure. Generally, actors who have been hired for a union production can apply to the Screen Actor's Guild (SAG) and/or Actors' Equity for membership—two unions that demand higher wages for their performers.

ASSOCIATED CAREERS

Actors become many things during and after their acting careers—directors, producers, designers, choreographers, composers, writers, and, in one notable case, president of the United States. Others use their experience to teach acting and related disciplines; still others use their acting talents in careers involving personal interaction, such as marketing or sales. While many careers have a direct line of progression to a pinnacle, acting is an end in itself; many professionals are extremely satisfied to have the chance to work as actors their entire lives.

PAST AND FUTURE

Acting might trace its roots to the campfires of prehistoric people, when hunters would reenact the story of the hunt and praise their deeds in a communal ceremony. It is truly a phenomenon of humankind rather than of any specific country. The Greeks defined the art form with their theological and political plays; Japanese Kabuki theater portrayed historical events intended to illuminate the human condition. Acting is a storied and respected profession that rewards its stars with fame, fortune, and adulation.

More than half of all acting revenues in the United States tend to stem from commercials, and this trend is expected to continue. The remainder of revenue is derived primarily from films. While the career is potentially very profitable for a select few, the likelihood of becoming a star remains slim.

QUALITY OF LIFE

2 YEARS As at all levels in the profession, the attrition rate is high—more than 30 percent. Actors go to open casting calls that may attract hundreds of people auditioning for a single part, audition for everything from commercials to dramatic roles, and juggle paying jobs and, usually, nonpaying acting careers. Most people continue to study acting by attending workshops, enlisting private instructors, and reading. New actors practice their craft by acting in productions at smaller theaters and assisting other productions in unpaid (or low-paying) jobs.

5 YEARS Individuals who survive for five years as actors have an improved quality of life. By this point, they are likely to have agents, who send them on auditions for suitable parts; they've received some reviews, have made some connections in the casting community, and have supplemented money-earning jobs with paying acting jobs. Many actors have become members of the SAG or Actors' Equity unions, which command higher wages for their members; they also offer discounted rates on health benefits. While they may audition for parts more selectively, the level of acceptance remains low. Many actors turn to teaching acting to earn income.

10 YEARS In other professions where a person may have survived for 10 years, he or she would have achieved a reputation or some level of financial security; however, in acting it just means an actor has been working for 10 years. Some members of the profession will have achieved this and more, including international fame; for most, though, the struggle continues with improving their skills and getting work. While actors span a variety of ages, nearly 60 percent of all roles are scripted for people in the 20- to 40-year-old range. This is not to say that there are no parts for younger or older actors; the competition just gets fiercer the longer a person manages to survive in the profession. Of course, those who do remain in the profession for significant periods of time have probably established well-respected reputations.

MAJOR EMPLOYERS
ATLANTIC THEATER COMPANY
336 West 20th Street
New York, NY 10011
Tel: 212-645-8015
Fax: 212-645-8755
www.atlantictheater.com

FOX FILMED ENTERTAINMENT
PO Box 900
Beverly Hills, CA 90213–0900
www.fox.com
Contact: Personnel

PARAMOUNT PICTURES
5555 Melrose Avenue
Los Angeles, CA 90038-3197
Tel: 323-956-5000
www.paramount.com
Contact: Human Resources

MAJOR ASSOCIATIONS
ACTORS' EQUITY ASSOCIATION
165 West 46th Street
New York, NY 10036
Tel: 212-869-8530
Fax: 212-719-9815
www.actorsequity.org

SCREEN ACTORS GUILD
5757 Wilshire Boulevard
Los Angeles, CA 90036–3600
Tel: 323-954-1600
www.sag.org

ANIMATOR

A DAY IN THE LIFE

Nearly everyone has seen some animated sequences in their life, whether it was in a science class filmstrip or a Saturday morning cartoon. Animators create sequences of motion-based art that tell a story or communicate a message. Some animators are graphic artists who draw "cells," which are individual pictures that are strung together to create the illusion of motion. The majority of animators are computer or "technical" animators, whose jobs require less graphic design expertise and more familiarity with animation programs such as the Macromedia Director and other, less commercial ones than those of graphic artists.

Nearly all animators work as part of a team and have a specific area of specialization. The low pay can be a difficult obstacle to overcome.

{ **work as part of a team** }

Another more formidable obstacle is the constant pressure to produce work to others' specifications and then rely on their approval. For creative people, this can be constraining. An animator works on certain characters, scenes, or sequences; but others have the job of assembling these pieces into a coherent whole. Scripting and planning are critical to success for the "large picture" animator. Most animation jobs are in commercials (of which more than 20 percent have animated sequences) and cartoons.

Many animators spend their own money (between $5,000 and $125,000) to produce short animated movies that showcase their talents and then enter these in animation competitions with the hope of gaining exposure and financial rewards. These festivals have grown in reputation and importance over the past 10 years, and it is considered a significant feather in one's cap to have received an award at one of them. Some animators begin their own production companies and recruit funds to develop their own animated products, usually for either foreign markets, sample shorts, or animation festivals.

PAYING YOUR DUES

As in most fine arts fields, no formal education or training is required; if you are talented and are able to get your work viewed, you stand a reasonable chance of finding a job. But it is extremely difficult to achieve the level of professionalism expected in this industry without study. A bachelor's or graduate degree in graphic design with an emphasis on computer skills is extremely helpful in getting interviews or portfolio reviews. Certain universities offer specific semester courses in computer animation on Oxberry Animation cameras (the kind that filmed *Fantasia*) or using Silicon Graphics computer workstations with 2- and 3-D software. Most important for an aspiring animator is that your work be of exceptional quality, and to that end, many aspiring animators intern or work for little pay to learn the craft from established animators, game designers, and programmers. As with most creative fine arts fields, the number of people wanting to become animators exceeds the demand; therefore, open positions are competitive. The rate of success in the field is low, but those who do achieve it are extremely satisfied.

ASSOCIATED CAREERS

Producing animated sequences is like producing any complicated art-and-technology product, so many people who leave the profession move into the realm of software development and design. Some continue on to work on mainstream movies, cartoons, commercials, illustrations, or any area that emphasizes their strongest animation skill.

PAST AND FUTURE

It is impossible to mention the history of animation without mentioning Walt Disney. His popularization of the animated form, through such groundbreaking strips as the "Steamboat Willie" character (which later became Mickey Mouse), and the classic features *Snow White* and *Cinderella*, defined the form and intertwined a sense of magic with the American entertainment experience. Disney Studios still produce what are regarded in the industry as the top-quality commercial animation products.

The marketplace success of *Monsters, Inc.* and *Corpse Bride* has spurred the production of more animated features, and the trend in that direction should continue in the next few years. The majority of projects in the industry, however, lies in commercial work and animating small sequences in limited portions of 30-second spots. Animated commercial sequences have been entering the marketplace at a substantial and increasing pace; the future of animation will be determined by how far technology can progress and how receptive audiences are to the influx of better-produced animation.

QUALITY OF LIFE

2 YEARS Many animators learn the necessary skills traveling from job to job. Exposure to the various sides of animation sketches, drawings, computer skills, and voice-dubbing technology leads the young professional to a greater understanding of how the whole film is developed. The skills critical to success in this business—understanding the technology, working with computers, and film production—are learned while assisting with responsibilities such as production coordination, background design, and progress tracking. The pay is low and the hours are long, but this period of dues paying is critical to learning the process.

5 YEARS Full animation, individual client responsibility, and concept design become part of the job. Animators hone their filmmaking skills—story development, directing, cinematography, and editing as they apply to the task of animation. Many are in charge of location scouting for the preproduction work that marks many of the larger-scale projects, such as Disney productions. The numbers of hours their positions require skyrocket; their pay increases and can rise significantly for those with a strong record of achievement.

10 YEARS Those who have survived 10 years in this occupation (around 20 percent of those who began in it) run projects and are fully responsible for final products. Many find their advancement moves them from the nuts-and-bolts of animating to more of a supervisory and administrative position, where responsibilities include budgeting and scheduling. Industry reputations and networking are the lifeblood of smaller, more commercial houses that produce small animated sequences for commercials in about three months; large houses produce feature films, which may take two to three years to complete. Satisfaction in the profession, at this level, is high.

MAJOR EMPLOYERS
THE DISNEY CORPORATION
500 South Buena Vista Street
Burbank, CA 91521-3020
Tel: 818-558-2868
Fax: 818-556-6969
http://disney.go.com
Contact: Artist Recruitment

WARNER BROTHERS
4000 Warner Boulevard
Burbank, CA 91522
Tel: 818-954-6000
Fax: 818-954-3718
www.warnerbros.com
Contact: Human Resources

MAJOR ASSOCIATIONS
WOMEN IN ANIMATION, INC.
PO Box 17706
Encino, CA 91416
Tel: 818-759-9596
e-mail: info@womeninanimation.org
www.womeninanimation.org

ANTHROPOLOGIST

SALARY   • •

HOURS   • •

EDUCATION   • • •

BOOKS, FILMS, AND TV SHOWS
FEATURING THE PROFESSION
- Blackberry Winter
- Coming of Age in Samoa
- Masai Dreaming
- The Serpent and the Rainbow

YOU'LL HAVE CONTACT WITH
- Editors
- Lab technicians
- Linguists
- Professors
- Students

PROFESSIONALS READ
- American Anthropologist
- American Ethnologist
- Current Anthropology
- Ethnomusicology Today

A DAY IN THE LIFE

Anthropologists examine, analyze, report on, and compare different cultures and how they grow, develop, and interact. How people live offers insights into modern life and how significantly (or, more often, how little) we have changed and how similar we are in our basic systems of interaction. Anthropologists can travel to exotic lands and spend time in primitive conditions or work in developed countries, such as the United States, comparing regional concerns. Cultural anthropologists may compare the culture of the medical world to that of the financial world, or the culture of professional athletes to that of legal professionals. Some anthropologists take a cross-disciplinary approach to the field, studying linguistics, chemistry, nutrition, or behavioral science, and apply the methodologies of those disciplines to their study of culture. Qualities that encourage success in this field include a nonjudgmental, inquisitive mind; patience; and the ability to make inferences from incomplete information. Unlike in other sciences in which significant funding and sizable research teams are usually necessary, an individual can make discoveries while working alone.

{ **grant-writing skills** }

Most anthropologists are employed by universities; they teach and review others' work to earn their daily bread. It is rare for an anthropologist to spend more than 15 percent of his or her career outside the university setting. An anthropologist spends a lot of time writing, editing, doing fieldwork, teaching, consulting with other professionals, and producing papers for professional journals.

Anthropological research relies on the funding decisions of the federal government, universities, and foundations, the three major and nearly exclusive employers in the field. "Don't go into this profession unless you've got the stomach to play politics," warned one professor. "It never gets any easier, and it never gets any better." The immediate return on an investment in anthropology is impossible to quantify, and therefore, hard to justify as a spending item. Anthropology is a competitive field, and those who wish to succeed in it must find creative ways of having their skills recognized. Successful anthropologists quickly learn successful grant-writing skills, find areas of unexplored anthropological concern, and publish articles, essays, and books as early and as often as they can.

PAYING YOUR DUES

Many aspiring anthropologists work as assistants who conduct ground-level research and write surveys before they have earned advanced degrees. College coursework should include anthropology, sociolinguistics, sociology, biology, and language (for those considering anthropology in foreign locations). Specialization takes place very early on. Anthropologists typically must have PhDs. Graduate students choose to study linguistics, sociocultural anthropology, biological-physical anthropology, or archaeological anthropology. Many graduate students associate themselves with an undergraduate or graduate professor for their first field job, while others work with museums, research groups, or government programs to launch their careers. Candidates must have an open mind and strong communication skills to succeed in the field.

ASSOCIATED CAREERS

Anthropology is associated with archaeology, writing, sociology, history, and even geology. Many former anthropologists choose to specialize in one of these other scientific fields. Linguistics and ethnology (reviewing methods of communication and cultural histories) are major fields of choice for the anthropologist who finds physical anthropology less exciting. In the end, few anthropologists leave the profession because of the amount of time, resources, and intellectual energy invested in becoming an anthropologist—not to mention their passion for the field. Usually, those dissatisfied with their choice of career leave during graduate school, before their careers have truly started.

PAST AND FUTURE

Anthropology has existed since ancient Greek times, although it only began to flourish with the rise of mercantilism and the age of exploration. Contact with other cultures and histories led to the development of archaeology and social sciences. The growth of anthropology also has been linked to that of sciences such as geology, biology, and sociology, as each tends to overlap the others.

Anthropology, like many fields, is becoming smaller and more specialized. Those with strong ethnic studies and science backgrounds are being asked to develop their language skills; those with a background in language and cultural studies are asked to learn scientific and statistical skills. Subcategories of study, particularly those with applications in current issues of the day like race relations or economic structure, often follow current trends and gain popularity for brief periods of overexposure and then wane. Funding uncertainties make any venture into this field a calculated risk—but one whose reward can be very satisfying.

QUALITY OF LIFE

2 YEARS Many aspiring anthropologists make initial connections with professors in college or graduate school and work as administrative assistants on research projects. Typical duties include reading and digesting publications for the anthropologist's review, handing out surveys, and coordinating the assimilation of data, transcribing tapes, and proofreading papers. More than 20 percent leave the profession in the first two years, frustrated by these severely proscribed duties; however, the anthropological community is said to be "intensely understanding and supportive."

5 YEARS Five-year survivors focus on getting published in academic journals or writing successful grant proposals. Many industry professionals at this stage move to secondary collaboration positions with established, high-profile anthropologists. Duties include interviewing, writing, and reviewing and analyzing data. Many five-year veterans serve as mentors to entry-level assistants, giving them daily direction on duties. The majority of fieldwork is done in these beginning years, where hours are dawn to dusk. Salaries rise. The life gets more trying, but the potential rewards and interest level are sky-high.

10 YEARS A select few anthropologists remain in the field after 10 years; their anthropological achievements have been well documented and well publicized. The majority of the professionals return to university settings, teaching anthropology, working through government research grants, or working as adjunct professors under foundation grants. Some 10-year veterans act as consultants to government outreach programs and offer advice concerning international industrial concerns. Less than 3 percent leave the profession after 10 years.

MAJOR EMPLOYERS
FIELD MUSEUM
1400 South Lakeshore Drive
Chicago, IL 60605-2496
Tel: 312-922-9410
www.fmnh.org
Contact: Human Resources Department

SMITHSONIAN INSTITUTE
Main Office of Human Resources
750 9th Street, NW, Suite 6100
Washington, DC 20560-0902
Tel: 202-275-1102
Jobline: 202-287-3102
www.si.edu

MAJOR ASSOCIATIONS
AMERICAN ANTHROPOLOGICAL ASSOCIATION
2200 Wilson Boulevard, Suite 600
Arlington, VA 22201
Tel: 703-528-1902
Fax: 703-528-3546
www.aaanet.org

ANTIQUES DEALER

A DAY IN THE LIFE

An antiques dealer buys and sells antiques. These may include art, furniture, jewelry, books, rugs, clothing, or any item that has survived the ravages of time. While some dealers earn specific titles and specialize in one type of relic, many are generalists who examine pieces of any type with historic, aesthetic, and financial value. "It is difficult to describe the life of an antiques dealer," wrote one of our respondents, "because it involves so many things. An antiques dealer must know the pieces they sell, the clients they sell to, [and how to] manage their offices [and] their finances." It is difficult to become and remain an antiques dealer. Few professions require participants to exhibit such a diverse range of skills. The profession provides high { value on both ends } levels of satisfaction at all levels for those people who are interested in history, business, psychology, and aesthetic concerns. The joys of being surrounded daily with items of financial and historical value seem to buoy many people through the long hours, the paucity of compensation, and the difficulty of achieving independence from established dealers. Many respondents had nothing but high praise for their coworkers. One referred to them as "a good resource, both intellectually and emotionally."

Antiques dealers invest substantial capital in inventory. The high level of investment means a high degree of risk and great pressure on the dealer to assess carefully the value of items before they are purchased and to sell items purchased aggressively. The pressure for value on both ends can translate into pressure for those working in the industry; those who are unaware of this "results-based" operation of many antiques houses are surprised at the importance of the bottom line in the business. The job of an antiques dealer requires a person to trust her own understanding of a piece's value and put herself on the line every time she makes a decision. It is natural that betting on your own skills would create worry. People mentioned that if you make a mistake in overpaying for a piece, you can often "sell your way out of it." Successful dealers rarely try to take advantage of long-term customers, however. Those relationships are based on trust.

PAYING YOUR DUES

A variety of undergraduate degrees lend themselves to this career path, but no specific major is required. Art history majors enjoy the interaction with beautiful works; business students appreciate the investment and dealing aspects of the profession; history majors love the continuous education the job allows. Becoming an antiques dealer requires spending long hours inspecting pieces, visiting other antiques dealers, reviewing documentation, and researching histories. Most aspiring antiques dealers begin as interns at auction houses or alongside established professionals and learn as assistants, take care of correspondence, make research trips to the library, and schedule appointments. Attention to detail serves the prospective antiques dealer well, as deciding the value of a piece (the most difficult aspect of being a dealer) can depend on a slight detail. Graduate work is less important than practical experience, and specialization can begin either midway through or late in a dealer's career.

ASSOCIATED CAREERS

Antiques dealers work with restorers, financiers, and auctioneers regularly, and when they leave the profession of antique dealing (as many do), they enter these three fields more than any others. Some become professional valuation specialists, working with auction houses and other antiques dealers as appraisers. A small number of former antiques dealers become teachers and lecturers in graduate fine arts programs.

PAST AND FUTURE

Antiques dealers before the seventeenth century were more closely associated with archaeology, as craftsmanship of prior pieces was less interesting compared with the artisanship, patterning, and construction of artifacts from other or ancient civilizations. Beginning in the seventeenth century, though, craftsmanship emerged as the favorite means of wealthy home beautification, and this demand spurred the production of high-quality, aesthetically pleasing pieces of furniture. Within 70 years, these pieces were being sold as antiques or specialty items.

Antique sales tend to be even more active during years of financial lassitude. Those who aspire to become part of this industry should understand that most successful antiques dealers have to have a critical mass of audience (that is, a client base) to make the profession self-supporting. As a result, urban or suburban antiques dealers have traditionally done better than rural ones. However, such online marketplaces as eBay allow dealers to sell remotely and conveniently, a trend that is expected to grow in the upcoming years.

QUALITY OF LIFE

2 YEARS Two years into the profession, antiques dealers are usually working alongside an established professional and learning inventory systems, bookkeeping methodology, and payment schedules. Many assist with client contact and valuation decisions, learning the less-quantifiable aspects of the profession. The hours are long and the pay is low, but the responsibility levels in terms of inventory management and presentations are high. A number of new dealers take art history, history, and appraisal courses.

5 YEARS The majority of five-year antiques dealers have switched positions at least once during these middle years, either to learn different specialties, gain greater responsibilities, or work in a larger client community. Eight percent return to school to receive their MBAs. Most antiques dealers network with other professionals and seek out areas of opportunity during this time. Few open their own shops at this juncture; good connections are difficult to establish.

10 YEARS Ten-year veterans begin to assemble the pieces they will need to open their own shops. In many cases, that means making a bid to their current employer. One respondent mentioned that "over 90 percent of dealers think about opening their own shop, but only about 40 percent do it." This yen for independence is expected at this stage in a career. Contacts have been established, experience is strong, and dealers have matured, learning the tangible and intangible aspects of the industry. Salaries do not rise beyond this point unless people open their own shops; this encourages the mass exodus to consider self-employment. Of the new dealers, only about 25 percent remain after 18 months.

MAJOR EMPLOYERS
CHRISTIE'S
20 Rockefeller Center
New York, NY 10020
Tel: 212-492-5485
Fax: 212-636-4945
E-mail: careers@christies.com
www.christies.com

SOTHEBY'S
1334 York Avenue
New York, NY 10021
Tel: 541-312-5682
Fax: 541-312-5684
www.sothebys.com

MAJOR ASSOCIATIONS
ART DEALERS ASSOCIATION OF AMERICA, INC.
575 Madison Avenue
New York, NY 10022
Tel: 212-940-8590
Fax: 212-940-6484
www.artdealers.org

NATIONAL ANTIQUE AND ART DEALERS ASSOCIATION OF AMERICA
220 East 57th Street
New York, NY 10022
Tel: 212-826-9707
Fax: 212-832-9493
www.naadaa.org

ARCHAEOLOGIST

BOOKS, FILMS, AND TV SHOWS
FEATURING THE PROFESSION

- **Archaeology**
- **Digging Through the Darkness: Chronicles of an Archaeologist**
- **Indiana Jones trilogy**
- **The Professor's House**

YOU'LL HAVE CONTACT WITH

- **Anthropologists**
- **Archivists**
- **Geologists**
- **Librarians**
- **Soil scientists**

PROFESSIONALS READ

- **American Antiquity**
- **American Journal of Archaeology**
- **Historical Archaeology**
- **Latin American Antiquity**

A DAY IN THE LIFE

Archaeologists study artifacts of the near and distant past to develop a picture of how people lived in earlier cultures and societies. Many in the profession are also involved in the preservation of archaeological sites. Though a popular conception of the archeologist involves a khaki-clad individual in an exotic locale, who cleans sand off ancient crockery with a toothbrush, real-life archaeologists spend as little time as possible in the field. Because fieldwork is both expensive and destructive to the site, the majority of archaeological study takes place in the lab. In the lab, archeologists analyze data, write reports, and interpret findings for the public.

An archaeologist's natural curiosity about the past and the secrets it holds make the profession a fascinating one. However, the work can be slow and exacting. It may take $\left\{ \text{natural curiosity} \right\}$ months to examine thousands of tiny, nearly identical chipped stone axes. Some archaeologists work under the aegis of a major research institution, such as a university or a museum. Many more people in the field, however, are employed by private-sector companies that assist the government and private developers in complying with federal laws aimed at protecting archaeological sites.

PAYING YOUR DUES

A master's degree in anthropology and several years of fieldwork—experience as a site or project supervisor doesn't hurt—will qualify you for most jobs in the field. Coursework valuable to a career as an archaeologist includes ancient history, geology, geography, English composition, and human physiology. Sign up to work on your professors' archaeological digs during your vacations.

Only the most distinguished (or fortunate) archaeologists become prominent in the field, and there are fewer positions available than there are qualified archaeologists to fill them. One way to draw attention to your work is by publishing articles in academic journals.

ASSOCIATED CAREERS

Archaeology is often paired with anthropology. While archaeology is the study of cultures and societies through their material remains, anthropology focuses more on the activities of people within societies and is often applied to current cultures. The two fields share much of the same background, however, and the boundary between allows for mutual exchange. Corporate archaeologists may find work writing environmental impact statements.

PAST AND FUTURE

Since the eighteenth century, with the chance rediscovery of Pompei's well-preserved ruins, the systematic study of lost communities has gripped our imaginations. Napoleon's invasion of Egypt was inspired in part by a desire to explore the remnants of the remarkable culture that once thrived there, and it led directly to the discovery of the Rosetta stone. In the nineteenth century, Heinrich Schliemann fixed the location of Troy's ancient ruins as well as the ruins of Mycenae. Although it has come to light that many of Schliemann's "discoveries" had been made by others and that his excavations often destroyed as much as they unearthed, his work reminded historians that the mythology of the distant past had more than a grain of truth to it.

Hoping to avoid Schliemann's errors, Howard Carter approached his work with a careful eye for procedure and detail. Not only did his discovery of King Tut's tomb cause a worldwide sensation, but it also involved one of the first uses of modern archaeological techniques. Later in the twentieth century, discoveries made in Mexico led to a complete reappraisal of ancient Mayan culture, and dispelled many long-standing myths. Today's broad interest in the history of disparate and distant regions has opened up new avenues of opportunity for archaeologists everywhere.

Contemporary archaeologists pursue these avenues eagerly, in an effort to outpace the encroachment of modern industrial society and prevent the secrets of the past from being lost forever.

QUALITY OF LIFE

2 YEARS Halfway through your undergraduate years, be prepared to plunge into the study of archaeology. Because of the profession's numerous requirements, it will take at least two years of specific and related courses to generate a transcript that will get you into the archaeology department of a well-known graduate school. Since entry into the field is very competitive, your graduate school's reputation and its involvement in current archaeological exploration are important. Obtain as much field experience as you can.

5 YEARS Master's and doctoral candidates in archaeology pursue their studies while they try to gain as much work experience as possible. Hours are long because students must complete their studies and work at the same time. Remuneration is slight, and graduate students rely on grants and other financial aid.

10 YEARS Archaeologists add the role of manager to their many duties. Archaeologists staff and operate their excavations, which often involves coping with the business practices of distant countries, where customs may be quite different. Respected archaeologists have greater opportunity to select and develop their own projects and follow their own curiosity. Those in academia are expected to publish regularly.

MAJOR EMPLOYERS

UNITED STATES DEPARTMENT OF THE INTERIOR—BUREAU OF LAND MANAGEMENT
1849 C Street, Room 406-LS
Washington, DC 20240
Tel: 202-452-5125
Fax: 202-452-5124
www.blm.gov/nhp/index.htm
Contact: Human Resources

THE LOUIS BERGER GROUP, INC.
100 Halsted Street
East Orange, NJ 07018
Tel: 973-678-1960
Fax: 973-672-4284
www.louisberger.com

MAJOR ASSOCIATIONS

ARCHAEOLOGICAL INSTITUTE OF AMERICA
656 Beacon Street, 4th Floor
Boston, MA 02215-2006
Tel: 617-353-9361
E-mail: aia@aia.bu.edu
www.archaeological.org

CENTER FOR AMERICAN ARCHAEOLOGY
PO Box 366
Kampsville, IL 62053
Tel: 618-653-4316
Fax: 618-653-4232
www.caa-archaeology.org

SOCIETY FOR AMERICAN ARCHAEOLOGY
900 2nd Street, NE #12
Washington, DC 20002-3560
Tel: 202-789-8200
Fax: 202-789-0284
E-mail: headquarters@saa.org
www.saa.org

ARTIST

A DAY IN THE LIFE

"If you're lucky, you'll spend most of your time alone and working," wrote one 20-year veteran painter. The artist seeks to express a specific and unique vision through painting, sculpture, drawing, or mixed media. While many spend time in workshops, attending other artists' shows and seminars, and doing research, the heart of the profession—the reason why people choose to join the very selective fine arts—is that they love what they do.

Numerous artists use their specific set of marketable tools as freelance commercial artists, producing work on consignment to another's specifications. Some note that this selling of their skills at times affects their ability to produce their own work. "It's hard to paint my own pictures when I'm sketching a box of oats all day," said one.

{ marketable tools }

PAYING YOUR DUES

History is filled with examples of self-schooled artists with no formal educational training. They are both brilliant and innovative; unfortunately, history is also filled with examples of starving artists who died in obscurity. Formal educational training in this field is becoming the norm, with most earning BFAs in graphic design, painting, or art history. Some find it helpful to continue their education and earn graduate degrees (primarily MFAs), particularly if they desire to teach painting at the secondary level or above. Many academic programs provide at least an introduction to computer-assisted art. Artists tend to congregate around major urban centers, such as New York and San Francisco, in which the multiplicity of galleries and artists makes it easier to form connections; this also offers the unproven artist the opportunity to have his or her work shown.

ASSOCIATED CAREERS

Artists have a number of opportunities available to them, both during their careers as artists and after they've decided to hang up their brushes. Many work as commercial artists, computer artists, and electronic layout consultants using their aesthetic and representational skills in higher-paying professions. Some become art directors for magazines, online services, software companies, or publishing houses. Other artists move into advertising, promotion, and product design.

PAST AND FUTURE

Art has been practiced for ages, as evidenced, for instance, by the animal drawings discovered in caves in Lascaux, France, which date back to 30,000 B.C. Portraiture has a long European history as an honored profession, and one of the greatest supporters of the arts through the ages has been the Catholic Church (also, at times, one of the most strident critics). Commercial art, as a separate industry, arose with the advent of the modern advertising industry and produces more than 75 percent of all art available for view in the United States every year.

The methods and media of art may change, but the intention has remained the same: to reinvent and to communicate fundamental aspects of the human experience in a new and fascinating way. In the future, the role that art plays will not change drastically, but painting, photography, sketching, sculpting, metalworking, and many other historically used media will be joined by computer art, mixed-media art, and other emerging forms that will reflect the ages from which they emerge. The real danger to the prospective artist lies in the future of funding for the arts, both individually and societally. The National Endowment for the Arts may face drastic slashing of funds; tax proposals may eliminate the tax advantages of private contributions; universities may reduce art staffs. Patrons, dealers, and collectors may exert an even greater influence over the life of the artist. Some degree of support for the arts will always continue. That level, however, is uncertain.

QUALITY OF LIFE

2 YEARS These early years are marked by little or no income from the artist's creative work. Hours are long, but many artists say that in these early years, the long hours are spent more on examining other people's art, making introductions to dealers and critics, and networking through the art community rather than on producing their own work. Many aspiring artists take classes, join workshops, and use this time to explore their craft.

5 YEARS Five years down the road, artists continue to hone their craft and spend more time producing their own work. Many of them are still experimenting with different ways to pay the rent.

10 YEARS The sense of frustration is significant for those who haven't received much positive encouragement. Others may experience "second life blues," where initial success has been tempered by the difficulty of following up and reinventing. While 10 years is a significant milestone in a number of professions, as an artist, timing is nothing; continuing and evolving is everything.

MAJOR EMPLOYERS

GUGGENHEIM MUSEUM
1071 Fifth Avenue
New York, NY 10128-0173
Tel: 212-423-3500
www.guggenheim.com

LOS ANGELES COUNTY MUSEUM OF ART
5905 Wilshire Boulevard
Los Angeles, CA 90036
Tel: 323-857-6000
www.lacma.org

MUSEUM OF MODERN ART
11 West 53 Street
New York, NY 10019-5497
Tel: 212-708-9400
E-mail: info@MoMA.org
www.MoMA.org

METROPOLITAN MUSEUM OF ART
1000 Fifth Avenue at 82nd Street
New York, NY 10028-0198
Tel: 212-535-7710
www.metmuseum.org

SEATTLE ART MUSEUM
100 University Street
Seattle, WA 98101-2902
Tel: 206-654-3100
www.seattleartmuseum.org

MAJOR ASSOCIATIONS

AMERICAN DESIGN AND DRAFTING ASSOCIATION
105 East Main Street
Newbern, TN 38059
Tel: 731-627-0802
Fax: 731-627-9321
E-mail: corporate@adda.org
www.adda.org

ART NICHE NEW YORK
498 Broome Street
New York, NY 10013
Tel: 212-941-0130
Fax: 212-941-0138
E-mail: reginas@anny.org
www.anny.org

ASTROLOGER

SALARY ●
HOURS ●
EDUCATION ●

BOOKS, FILMS, TV SHOWS
FEATURING THE PROFESSION
- **The Astrologer**
- **Eliza's Horoscope**
- **Ghost**

YOU'LL HAVE CONTACT WITH
- **Clients**
- **Palm Readers**
- **Psychics**
- **Tarot Card Readers**

PROFESSIONALS READ
- **The Astrological Journal**
- **Culture and Cosmos**
- **Transit: The Astrologers' Newsletter**

A DAY IN THE LIFE

The job of an astrologer is to determine the relationship of behavior, interpersonal relations, and events to the celestial alignment of the stars, sun, moon, and planets. As the alignments in the universe are constantly changing, each new orbital relationship may produce a unique set of outcomes. The astrologer makes his or her predictions for individual clients or, in the case of a few astrologers, for the population at large. The most popular form of Western astrology is typically referred to as "sun sign astrology;" this is exemplified in newspaper horoscopes. The term also applies to the description of the zodiac at the time of one's birth. Astrologers believe that the positions and movements of celestial bodies at the time of birth deeply affect the personality and life of an individual. Astrology in the Western world is based on a variety of premises distinct from those in other cultures.

{ celestial bodies }

Despite the longstanding role of astrologers, the industry, unfortunately, has its share of skeptics and disbelievers. Many in the scientific community view astrologers as charlatans and their work mere superstition. Others accuse some astrologers of taking advantage of those who are gullible and credulous. Astrologers assert that there is a strong correlation between their analyses and events on Earth; yet it is inevitable that some will be believers and others not. In spite of the lack of scientific confirmation available for astrological predictions, many have relied on and continue to seek out the insights of astrologers. Some prestigious newspapers, such as *The Times of London*, publish a daily horoscope; this indicates the degree of mass appeal that the field indeed enjoys.

PAYING YOUR DUES

There's no rigid and established route that must be followed to become an astrologer. In fact, there is no legally-recognized certification for astrology, although a number of state legislatures are currently being petitioned to change that. Both the American Federation of Astrologers (AFA) and the National Council for Geocosmic Research periodically hold monitored exams on several levels, however. Those who pass these exams receive a diploma and a title recognized by virtually all astrologers. The AFA also offers a program to help prepare interested candidates. Completing this course can require as few as six months or may take as long as two years. The speed with which a candidate completes it depends on how dedicated he or she is, as well as how quickly he or she grasps the information presented.

ASSOCIATED CAREERS

Astrologers can opt to apply their knowledge and expertise to print journalism, in which they may write horoscope columns for newspapers and magazines. They can also take positions as reader advisors who use tarot cards or conduct palm readings to consult with clients. Astrologers may also become teachers of aspiring future astrologers.

PAST AND FUTURE

The history of Western astrology traces back to 3,000 B.C., when it was practiced by ancient Babylonians. At that time, astrology was used by priests in an attempt to ascertain the intention and the will of the gods. These priests also constructed astrological charts that allowed them to predict a variety of celestial events as well as the recurrence of seasons.

Although historically astrology has been deeply linked with scientific inquiry, it is not today considered an analytical pursuit akin to that of, say, physics. Nevertheless, astrology is still fairly popular, even though many conceive of the field more as a source of leisure or entertainment than as a serious life guide.

QUALITY OF LIFE

2 YEARS Astrologers who have been in the business for two years are still working to establish a client base. Many may find that they are busy with self-promotion, often launching local or regional marketing campaigns. A number of astrologers at this stage of their careers open up shops in small storefronts and are sometimes hired to offer their services (usually for entertainment purposes) at events such as office functions or carnivals.

5 YEARS After five years, the astrologer has probably built a reputation and has established a regular and loyal client base. Some five-year astrologers may attempt to expand their businesses at this point, perhaps by launching a website or writing a column for a local paper.

10 YEARS After 10 years, an astrologer has probably achieved a noteworthy level of success, having established a practice and steady clientele, among whom may even be a celebrity or two. With this much experience, an astrologer is qualified to pursue larger-scale business endeavors or even to write a syndicated column for a national paper or magazine.

MAJOR EMPLOYERS

There is no leading employer in astrology. Most astrologers are self-employed.

MAJOR ASSOCIATIONS

AMERICAN FEDERATION OF ASTROLOGERS (AFA)
6535 South Rural Road
Tempe, AZ 85283-3746
Tel: 480-838-1751 or 888-301-7630
Fax: 480-838-8293
E-mail: AFA@msn.com
www.astrologers.com

NATIONAL COUNCIL FOR GEOCOSMIC RESEARCH, INC. (NCGR)
1359 Sargent Avenue
St. Paul, MN 55105
Tel: 651-698-1691
E-mail: membership@geocosmic.org
www.geocosmic.org

ASSOCIATION FOR ASTROLOGICAL NETWORKING (AFAN)
8306 Wilshire Boulevard, PMB 537
Beverly Hills, CA 90211
Tel: 800-578-2326
E-mail: info@afan.org
www.afan.org

BOOK PUBLISHING PROFESSIONAL

A DAY IN THE LIFE

Book publishing is an extraordinarily large business, and those who (successfully) enter the profession have no illusions that what they do is merely artistic in nature. "You've got to keep things on schedule. You've got to make them pay for themselves, or you're out of business," said one publishing professional, adding that "publishing" is a term that can encompass many positions within a publishing house. The most high-profile job is that of editor (see entry on "Editor" in this book), who works with authors to produce a quality product. Many other positions are available for those interested in the industry, including managing editors, who control production flow; publicity managers; promotions specialists; subsidiary rights managers; production managers; and salespeople. These

{ contacts are crucial }

occupations are critical to the successful functioning of a publishing house. Those who want to pursue a career in this industry should examine their own skills in light of the variety of opportunities available for ambitious and creative individuals who find the prospect of working with books exciting.

Managing editors are the traffic controllers of the publishing industry. They track production schedules and budgets, allocate personnel, and control the flow of material between departments. A large publishing house can have hundreds of projects running simultaneously, and the managing editor needs to be attentive to detail and be able to anticipate problems before they occur. Publicity, promotions, and sales positions reward creative and outgoing personalities. Successful professionals in this industry utilize their interpersonal skills to drum up consumer interest and encourage sales by bookstores. Salespeople spend significant amounts of time on the road meeting with bookstore buyers and managers. Subsidiary rights departments are usually divided into two arms: domestic and international. Subrights people negotiate international publishing deals with foreign houses or contract for copyrighted work to appear in another medium. The most lucrative rights for works of fiction, movie rights, are usually negotiated only by senior personnel experienced in negotiating with production companies. It requires putting in long hours to rise from assistant and administrative positions to positions of responsibility. For all but the highest up, salaries remain relatively low in this profession.

People in the publishing industry were quick to note that contacts are crucial. Those who want to advance pursue new opportunities zealously, and any advantage one can gain over other candidates is key. Few described the profession as cutthroat, however; instead, many praised their associates and coworkers. Publishing is a financially tough life, but it's ideal for those who are dedicated to books and who want to spend their days with like-minded people.

PAYING YOUR DUES

Publishing has no formal educational requirements, but most professionals have college degrees in fields such as English, literature, or journalism. Degrees that indicate specialized knowledge, such as chemistry or biology, can be useful to those who wish to go into textbook publishing or academic publishing positions. Many return to school for master's degrees in English, writing, or literature; but additional credentials are not necessary to rise in the field. Employers have a paucity of positions available for a large number of candidates, so aspiring book-publishing professionals should be persistent and willing to take anything to get a foot in the door. Editorial or publishing experience in college literary magazines, newspapers, or journals is advantageous for applicants. Those people who wish to advance in this profession should understand that work may occasionally take up all of their free time.

ASSOCIATED CAREERS

Book publishers have experience putting together projects in book production, promotion, or sales. Many move into advertising positions, magazine publishing jobs, project management, and writing. Some return to graduate school for law or business and make the transition to financial careers.

PAST AND FUTURE

Publishing as an industry widened its horizons with the invention of movable type by Johannes Gutenberg and his publication of *The Bible* in the mid-1400s. Paper milling and printing technologies advanced, and small publishing houses in many countries were established. The most recent advance in the industry is the development of desktop publishing, which allows publishers with limited capital to produce quality works.

Publishing is stable in some respects and moving downward in others. Sales positions, promotions, and publicity seem to be areas of future growth opportunities for those just entering the industry. The globalization of product should also lead to a greater demand for subsidiary rights personnel. Publishing houses, however, are receiving a record number of applications for limited positions. Also, publishing is an industry very responsive to the bottom line: Houses are not afraid to fire personnel they cannot afford.

QUALITY OF LIFE

2 YEARS These first two years are marked by menial tasks, limited responsibility, long hours, and "slave wages," as one respondent put it. Many change jobs several times during these first few years, jockeying for the positions most likely to lead to advancement. Many publishing professionals have close relationships with colleagues that prove important in later years.

5 YEARS Many professionals have changed publishing houses and made the decision of whether to work for a small or a large house (a difference in both attitude and type of work). The hours have levelled off, and responsibilities have increased. Those involved in sales are on the road for significant periods of time, making contact with book dealers in a variety of regional markets. Promotions and publicity personnel are running projects of reasonable size but find that they must be creative in using their small budgets wisely. Contact with writers is common at this point, particularly for those in editorial and promotions positions.

10 YEARS Ten-year veterans have made significant choices concerning where they want to work, which department, and at what level of responsibility. Those people who wish to become senior managing editors or chiefs of promotion increase their schedules at this point to demonstrate their abilities. Those professionals who are comfortable at the levels they have attained try to improve their production methods and develop a life outside the profession. Satisfaction is high.

MAJOR EMPLOYERS
FARRAR, STRAUS & GIROUX
19 Union Square West
New York, NY 10003
Tel: 212-741-6900
Contact: Human Resources
www.fsgbooks.com

HARPERCOLLINS
10 East 53rd Street
New York, NY 10022
Tel: 212-207-7000
Fax: 212-207-7279
www.harpercollins.com
Contact: Personnel

RANDOM HOUSE
1745 Broadway
New York, NY 10019
Tel: 212-782-9000
E-mail: humanresources@randomhouse.com
www.randomhouse.com

MAJOR ASSOCIATIONS
ASSOCIATION OF AMERICAN PUBLISHERS
71 Fifth Avenue
New York, NY 10003-3004
Tel: 212-255-0200
Fax: 212-255-7007
www.publishers.org

CAREER COUNSELOR

BOOKS, FILMS, AND TV SHOWS
FEATURING THE PROFESSION

- **Do What You Love and the Rest Will Follow**
- **Guide to Your Career**
- **The Simpsons**
- **What Color Is Your Parachute?**

YOU'LL HAVE CONTACT WITH

- Clients
- Human Resources personnel
- Social workers
- Specialists

PROFESSIONALS READ

- **Adventures in Education (Online)**
- **Chronicle of Higher Education**
- **College Spotlight**
- **NCS Career Magazine**
- **National Business Employment Weekly**
- **Occupational Outlook Handbook**

A DAY IN THE LIFE

Career counselors serve as teachers, confidants, and advisors to their clients. They help people examine their interests, styles, and their abilities to find and enter the profession that best suits them. They can be helpful to people who have yet to choose a career and people who are unhappy with their choice.

Career counselors spend most of their day meeting with clients. Early sessions explore the history and behavior of the client to help the clients understand their own motivations and desires more thoroughly. Working with younger people, especially, career counselors must understand and appreciate the role of parents and the student's home environment. An understanding of the client's peer and familial pressures, { coach the client } along with a familiarity with current events and culture, allow the career counselor to make contact and earn the trust of his or her clients. Most career counselors have a degree in counseling or another mental health field.

After conducting a thorough evaluation of the client's personality traits, counselors must use their expertise to help clients assess their skills base and direct them to a career wherein those skills may be most profitably employed, both financially and in terms of job satisfaction. Counselors are responsible for knowing what skills are needed in a broad variety of professions, how much they pay, and what a hiring authority will want to see in a successful applicant. They then coach the client through the process of researching fields that match their interests, setting up informational interviews with people to supplement their research, and finally targeting or creating specific job positions that meet their needs. Counselors try to empower the clients to become as active as possible in their search.

PAYING YOUR DUES

Most career counselors have a master's degree in a field such as mental health counseling, psychological counseling, or community counseling. At the moment, career counseling is an unregulated field, but most members of the profession are licensed in their state of business as a professional counselor. Nevertheless, people come to the profession through a variety of paths. Some counselors come from social work or human resources management. Others come to career counseling from a discipline such as law or medicine and then use their industry expertise to counsel people in their former field. Many professionals embark on continuing education courses in counseling or psychology.

Familiarity with basic personality, interest, and skills tests, such as the Holland Code, the Myers-Briggs Analogy Test, and the Birkman Personality Assessment (a customized version of which appears in this book) are invaluable aids in assessing clients' occupational aptitudes. Usually, a successful career counselor works as an independent counselor but receives references from other services, therapists, or agencies. The profession may entail long hours, intense listening and assessment, and the ability to think objectively without being swayed by emotion.

ASSOCIATED CAREERS

Career counselors have skills that involve helping other people understand themselves better and take proactive steps to improve the quality of their work lives. Many career counselors are able to transfer these skills to the realms of teaching, vocational counseling in school, social work, and coaching; other counselors go on to obtain advanced degrees, become therapists, and start private practices. Those counselors who are more interested in the business applications of their craft go into outplacement, corporate recruitment, and professional headhunting.

PAST AND FUTURE

Many occupations, such as high school vocational counselors, job retrainers, and psychotherapists, used to have career counseling as one part of their overall job description. The Internet has allowed counselors and potential clients to troll for one another with seeming ease; however, the uncertain provenance behind some career-counseling sites and the tools they offer makes the public wary, as it should be, of snake-oil salesmen with no training in the field.

Indeed, career counseling is a rapidly growing field. At their core, legitimate career counselors depend on the funding from government agencies to do the bulk of their work. It's now estimated that the average person will have as many as half a dozen distinct jobs in the course of his or her career, and the need for this service is likely to increase.

QUALITY OF LIFE

2 YEARS Typically, career counselors start out by working with established professionals who have an existing client base. Many counselors are still moving through training programs associated with established testing authorities and spend significant time attending professional seminars and keeping up with professional reading. A number of career counselors come into the profession as psychotherapists, and many professionals make the transition to career counseling gradually.

5 YEARS By now, most counselors have begun to see progress among their clients—many of whom have successfully shifted careers in these first five years. Among the more successful counselors, client bases have broadened through word of mouth. Salaries have gone up, hours are significant, and satisfaction is strong. Those professionals who began with more established counselors break off between years four and seven to establish independent practices. Marketing skills become important. Many career counselors become involved in professional education seminars, conferences, and other professional establishments to train in cutting-edge counseling techniques.

10 YEARS Those who've survived 10 years in the profession have earned solid reputations and have shepherded many clients to new occupations. Many established professionals begin scaling back hours and professional commitments during these later years. Many 10-year veterans of this profession are prolific contributors to professional journals and mainstream publications. Salaries level off as professionals work fewer hours at higher hourly rates.

MAJOR EMPLOYERS
BIRKMAN & ASSOCIATES, INC.
3040 Post Oak Boulevard, Suite 1425
Houston, TX 70056
Tel: 713-623-2760 or 800-215-2760
Fax: 713-963-9142
E-mail: info@birkman.com
www.birkman.com

INTERNATIONAL SURVEY RESEARCH, LLC
303 East Ohio Street
Chicago, IL 60611
Tel: 800-300-0750
Fax: 312-828-9742
E-mail: chicago@isrinsight.com
www.isrglobalsurveys.com
Contact: Human Resources

Many career counselors are hired by local school districts, private schools, rehabilitation agencies, and social welfare organizations.

MAJOR ASSOCIATIONS
AMERICAN COLLEGE AND CAREER COUNSELING CENTER
2401 Pennsylvania Avenue
Philadelphia, PA 19130
Tel: 215-232-5225
Fax: 215-232-5225
E-mail: henryklein@earthlink.net

AMERICAN COUNSELING ASSOCIATION
5999 Stevenson Avenue
Alexandria, VA 22304
Tel: 800-347-6647
Fax: 800-473-2329
www.counseling.org

NATIONAL BOARD FOR CERTIFIED COUNSELORS, INC.
3 Terrace Way, Suite D
Greensboro, NC 27403-3660
Tel: 336-547-0607
Fax: 336-547-0017
E-mail: nbcc@nbcc.org
www.nbcc.org

CHILD CARE WORKER

A DAY IN THE LIFE

Child care workers live with the reality that there is no perfect substitute for a family in raising a child; but while parents are at work, away, or otherwise unavailable, responsibility for the care and supervision of their children is a serious concern, and there are great possibilities for personal fulfillment in any career of service to young people. "Rewarding" is how most child care workers describe their jobs, and the joy of helping children grow—both intellectually and emotionally—is one of its most appealing features.

A number of child care workers are hired by government agencies and large corporations to run in-house day care centers. These centers allow parents to work and still remain close to their children, a valuable benefit for little or 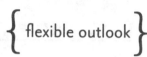 no charge. Firms are increasingly recognizing that having an on-site day care center provides them with significant advantages, notably reduced absenteeism, higher productivity, and better morale among workers, for relatively few dollars.

Other child care workers are employed by individual families; responsibilities in these positions may be more comprehensive, from live-in, 24-hour assistance to cooking duties. Arrangements are made individually between parents and the child care provider. Recent events have brought the widespread lack of Social Security payments for child care workers to national attention. Employers are responsible for these payments by law; many employers do not realize this until it is brought to their attention.

A child care worker manages a child's day, most often attending to the child from early morning through early afternoon, keeping the child engaged with games, exercise, meals, and study. "If you're not organized, you're going to have lots of problems," said one 10-year child care worker. But professionals must be flexible within a framework. With young children, "anything can happen and anything will," wrote another. Children need to trust and feel at home with the people around them, and the successful caregiver deals with situations as they arise, from health care emergencies to calming a very active child. The ability to provide a solid framework of activity, a flexible outlook, and a sense of caring, fun, and energy, are all important facets of being a good child care worker.

PAYING YOUR DUES

Perhaps the most important characteristic of the child care worker is a delicate balance of maturity and wonder. Child care providers work long hours under trying circumstances with children who are grasping to understand the world. A professional must be mature enough to act responsibly with and around the child but be sufficiently filled with wonder to share in the child's excitement about learning. No specific educational requirements exist for the profession, but since child care workers are responsibile for the care of children, courses in basic first aid, childhood development, early childhood education, and nutrition are helpful. The better day care centers require bachelor's or master's degrees in early childhood education. Extensive personal screening is routine in this field, particularly for candidates who work through an agency. Recommendations are more important in this field than in just about any other, and so the worker with excellent references will have a great advantage.

One of the most difficult aspects of being a child care worker is maintaining seemingly infinite patience in handling young and excitable children. Another great challenge is the lack of adult human contact. Most people who are dissatisfied with the profession claim it is due not to lack of enjoyment of teaching and nurturing children, but rather to the desire for peer contact and communication. Wages increase inconsistently for both the day care center worker and the family nanny alike, and without assuming further responsibilities, there is not much of a metaphorical ladder to climb.

ASSOCIATED CAREERS

Child care workers enjoy working with children, and many of them translate this interest into teaching. Many people become teachers, learning specialists, and guidance counselors. Many of them work as child care professionals while young and then go on to a variety of wholly independent careers.

PAST AND FUTURE

During the Middle Ages, branches of the Catholic Church managed orphanages and "public houses" for abandoned children. Royal and wealthy families always employed a staff of specialists who were responsible for raising and educating the children, with each staff member holding a discrete responsibility, such as nurse, tutor, or physical fitness instructor. When both parents work, now, it is common to hire part-time nannies or send children to day care centers.

Child care positions are expected to become increasingly available with rapid job growth over the next few years. Many jobs will become available through religious, private, and community-based organizations that recognize the need for more child care options and the value of economies of scale in this profession (i.e., it doesn't cost that much more to have one person look after three children instead of two). Private companies will also contribute significantly to this job growth, which should take place relatively evenly across the United States.

QUALITY OF LIFE

2 YEARS Two years is a relatively long period for child care workers to be employed at a single location. Many people work part-time to supplement another, less remunerative occupation. Those childcare workers who excel at their jobs are likely to receive raises and supervisional responsibilities within two years. Family child care workers can expect salaries to rise and duties to change, based on the growth and needs of the child. Turnover is significant during these years—around 20 percent of part-time child care workers leave the profession within the first two years.

5 YEARS Five-year veterans generally fall into two categories: people who are running day care centers and child care programs and people who work as individual practitioners for families. At this point, the former have supervisory, staffing, and budget responsibilities. The latter have significant relationships with families—especially those workers with live-in positions; a long-term child care worker has likely bonded with the child and has become a very important person in that child's life. Many caregivers are forced to shift from one family to another when the children begin attending school. Many caregivers find it difficult to sever their ties, as the relationships can become intense.

10 YEARS Child care workers who have lasted 10 years in the profession gain strong satisfaction from their choice of occupation. Nearly all of them have worked a number of jobs and have good reputations and strong opportunities for employment. Many 10-year day care center veterans open their own day care centers, but they may find that while they gain greater control over their work environment, they end up spending more time running the business than actually caring for children.

MAJOR EMPLOYERS

CARONDELET HEALTH CARE NETWORK
1601 West St. Mary's Road
Tucson, AZ 85745
Tel: 520-721-3727
Fax: 520-740-6067
Contact: Human Resources

CHILD SUPPORT ENFORCEMENT
115 Christy Street
New York, NY 10022
Tel: 212-334-7654

NANNIES UNLIMITED
125 East Main Street, Suite 614
American Fork, UT 84003
Tel: 801-756-4119
Fax: 801-847-1558
E-mail: info@nannies-unlimited.com
www.nannies-unlimited.com

NEW YORK NANNY CENTER, INC.
787 Seventh Avenue, 9th Floor
New York, NY 10019
Tel: 212-786-6090
Fax: 212-786-6093
E-mail: info@nynanny.com
www.nynanny.com

MAJOR ASSOCIATIONS

NATIONAL ASSOCIATION FOR THE EDUCATION OF YOUNG CHILDREN
1509 16th Street, NW
Washington, DC 20036
Tel: 800-424-2460 or 202-232-8777
Fax: 202-328-1846
E-mail: naeyc@naeyc.org
www.naeyc.org

NATIONAL ASSOCIATION OF CHILD CARE, RESOURCE AND REFERRAL AGENCIES
3101 Wilson Boulevard, Suite 350
Arlington, VA 22201
Tel: 703-341-4100
Fax: 703-341-4101
E-mail: jobs@naccrra.org
www.naccrra.net

CHIROPRACTOR

SALARY   ● ● ●

HOURS   ● ●

EDUCATION   ● ●

BOOKS, FILMS, AND TV SHOWS
FEATURING THE PROFESSION
- **From Simple Beginnings**
- **Jacob's Ladder**
- **Old Man Chiro**

YOU'LL HAVE CONTACT WITH
- **Nutritionists**
- **Occupational therapists**
- **Physical therapists**
- **X-ray technicians**

PROFESSIONALS READ
- **The Journal of the American Chiropractic Association**
- **The Journal of the NeuroMusculoSkeletal System**

A DAY IN THE LIFE

Chiropractic is a holistic health care discipline that focuses on promoting correct physical alignment to maintain health. Chiropractors believe that structural problems can cause dysfunction in the nervous system, leading to a host of aches, pains, and other conditions. Their objective is to realign the body in a way that restores and preserves health, and to accomplish this without drugs or surgery.

Much of a day in the life of a chiropractor is spent seeing patients and completing the accompanying paperwork. Doctors check the functioning of the neuromusculoskeletal system and analyze the spine using the unique system of chiropractic diagnosis. Chiropractors use "manipulations" to correct spinal alignment, and they treat their patients with massage, heat therapy, and ultrasound to restore balance to the system. They may prescribe changes in diet, exercises, or supports to aid the process. "Compassion is the greatest asset a chiropractor can have," noted one practitioner. Good listening skills help chiropractors detect hidden factors that contribute to their patients' maladies. Strong communication skills also help establish rapport with patients; this in turn helps build the practice. Chiropractors need to continue educating people about the field as the public becomes more interested in holistic health.

{ holistic health }

PAYING YOUR DUES

To be admitted to pursue a Doctor of Chiropractic (DC) degree, applicants must have at least two years of college with courses in organic and inorganic chemistry, biology, and physics as well as a grounding in the social sciences and humanities. There are 21 chiropractic colleges accredited by the Council on Chiropractic Education (CCE). A handful of these grant baccalaureate degrees in conjunction with liberal arts colleges. This reciprocal agreement allows candidates to combine their courses of study and achieve the DC degree a year earlier than usual. The last year of school is spent seeing patients under the supervision of a clinic director. The DC hopeful must see a certain number of patients to graduate.

New graduates must pass the National Board exams. There are also board exams required to practice in some states. In addition, most states require a certain amount of continuing education per year to maintain a chiropractic license.

ASSOCIATED CAREERS

Chiropractors work with nutritionists, exercise physiologists, physical therapists, acupuncturists, neurologists, podiatrists, and other specialists, such as those in ergonomics. A chiropractor may cross over into one of these fields if his or her interests change, but the majority of people with a DC opt to practice or teach.

PAST AND FUTURE

The profession of chiropractic was founded in 1895 by D. D. Palmer, a magnetic healer. The janitor in his employ, Harvey Lillard, was deaf. Palmer was convinced it was due to the strange lump on his shoulder. After one manipulation, Palmer enabled Lillard to hear and began to study the relationship between the musculoskeletal system and other bodily functions. But it was his son, B. J. Palmer, who really developed the discipline. He lectured on the science of chiropractic a great deal and eventually founded the Palmer College of Chiropractic in Davenport, Iowa.

Chiropractic is gaining much greater acceptance as American society becomes interested in alternative medicine. Chiropractic is now covered by almost every HMO and PPO in the country, and in the past five years, hospitals have started admitting chiropractors on their staff. As a result, the field is becoming increasingly competitive. Though officially only two years of college are required to apply to study for a doctor of chiropractic, most candidates nowadays have bachelor degrees. Colleges report that their applicant pool is getting better every year. The Council on Chiropractic Education is in the process of developing the CCAT, a standardized test for admission to chiropractic college. Fortunately, the growing interest in chiropractic means an increased demand for chiropractors and good job prospects.

Technology has also had a dramatic impact on the field of chiropractic. Chiropractors now regularly use CAT scans, MRIs, and thermography as diagnostic tools. Treatment has changed with technological advancements: Ultrasound and electromuscular stimulation are commonplace now. These new practices use expensive machinery, however, which significantly increases the cost of setting up a practice. As a result, there will probably be a trend toward larger practices in the future.

QUALITY OF LIFE

2 YEARS In the beginning of their career, chiropractors generally work for someone else. They could become an associate in a small or midsize practice or assist at a large clinic. Either way, this gives them the mentorship of experienced professionals and helps them begin to build a client base.

5 YEARS At this stage of their career, chiropractors often decide whether they will buy into the practice in which they work and become a partner or open their own practice as a sole proprietor. Many chiropractors also go back to school at this point to train in advanced techniques and develop a specialty. Some of them pursue a PhD in their specialty, which will allow them to teach.

10 YEARS By this time a chiropractor has built his or her practice to the point of it becoming self-generating; some of them may be considering opening a second office. After a decade of practice, many chiropractors teach part-time and have become active in the politics of the profession. They may be involved with groups that want to educate the public about the field of chiropractic, such as their school alumni or other regional or national organizations.

MAJOR EMPLOYERS
Most chiropractors are self-employed or work for small practices.

MAJOR ASSOCIATIONS
INTERNATIONAL CHIROPRACTORS ASSOCIATION
1110 North Glebe Road, Suite 650
Arlington, VA 22201
Tel: 703-528-5000 or 800-423-4690
Fax: 703-528-5023
www.chiropratic.org

WORLD CHIROPRACTIC ALLIANCE
2950 North Dobson Road, Suite #1
Chandler, AZ 85224
Tel: 800-347-1011
Fax: 480-786-9313
www.worldchiropracticalliance.org

CITY PLANNER

PROFESSIONAL PROFILE

# of people in profession	32,000
Avg. hours per week	45
Avg. starting salary	$32,000
Avg. salary after 5 years	$49,800
Avg. salary 10 to 15 years	$62,710

SALARY   • •
HOURS   • •
EDUCATION   • •

BOOKS, FILMS, AND TV SHOWS
FEATURING THE PROFESSION
- **Atlas Shrugged**
- **City Hall**
- **Olmstead**
- **The Power Broker**

YOU'LL HAVE CONTACT WITH
- **Bankers**
- **Civil engineers**
- **Government officials**
- **Sociologists**

PROFESSIONALS READ
- **Journal of the American Planning Association**
- **Planning**
- **Transportation Journal**

A DAY IN THE LIFE

City planners help design cities and make such determinations as the height of buildings, the width of streets, the number of street signs, and the design and location of street "furniture" (everything from bus stops and lampposts to newsstands and wastebaskets). Deciding how a city is set up involves creativity, and a career in city planning demands the knowledge of basic engineering principles, the ability to compromise, political diplomacy, and financial acumen. Strong analytic skills and sheer force of will are required to be a successful urban planner.

Every building or structure must be designed with an understanding of its relationship to other elements of the city, such as coordinating the construction of water and { aesthetic design } power facilities, while still allowing people access to light, heat, and fresh water, or designing housing complexes that will be close to public transportation. Aesthetic design, another feature that the planner must consider, can be the subject of hot debate. The urban planner has to design with an understanding of the policies of the city and create economically viable plans. This last consideration factor can be difficult—urban-planning projects nearly always run over budget and past deadline, and even the most frugal design can be expected to run into opposition from some quarter.

The planner begins by surveying sites and performing demographic, economic, and environmental studies to assess the needs of the community and encourage public participation in the process. If the planner is redeveloping an area (as opposed to groundbreaking or landfilling it), he or she must evaluate existing buildings and neighborhoods before determining what can be done to change the standing structures. During these phases, planners work closely with economic consultants to formulate a plan that makes sense for both the economy of the region and the residents. The next step is to create maps and designs. When the architects draft plans for the construction of bridges, radio and telephone towers, and other large pieces of infrastructure, the urban planner works closely with them. The planner does substantial research regarding zoning and landscaping laws. Occasionally, urban planners must also design or refurbish the town's zoning regulations on building usage, in the manner that is best for the region. He meets with community groups to obtain information on transportation and land usage. Financing is a delicate aspect of the profession, which requires that the planner unite social, budgetary, and developmental concerns to respond to the community's need for progress, while still presenting a fiscally sound proposal to governments and private investors.

PAYING YOUR DUES

Urban developers are employed by many different agencies, and many travel throughout the country to find employment. Recent graduates should look to their state's Department of Transportation or look into civil engineering courses sponsored by the United States Army Corps of Engineers. Experienced engineers often work in private firms or with general contractors, where the planner enjoys far more independence.

Urban planners should have an undergraduate degree in an area such as civil engineering, architecture, or public administration. Most schools do not offer undergraduate degrees in structural engineering, but many employers look favorably on candidates who have studied structural engineering at the master's level. A master's degree in city or regional planning or structural engineering is the highest laurel and respected by all employers. One 30-year structural engineer noticed that many recent graduates handle textbook problems wonderfully, but are less apt at identifying and coping with real-life problems. While studying for a master's degree, students often do internships to acquire as much practical experience as possible to alleviate this problem. Internships can convert to paid positions following graduation.

After four years of working full-time, urban planners are eligible to take a step-one licensing test. There are two of these tests (step one and step two); which one a planner takes depends on his or her interests and area of expertise. After getting this license and working for four additional years, serious candidates take another test to obtain the title of professional engineer. These certifications are not required, but they are respected within the profession. Generally, acquiring these licenses leads to a promotion and increases in salary.

ASSOCIATED CAREERS

Geotechnical engineers explore subsurface areas to determine if the soil and rock will hold up the structure. Architects and draftsmen design the structures. Housing specialists relay the community's needs to the planner. Transport planners design plans for public transportation systems and roads. Any of these professions provides a solid home to the former urban planner.

PAST AND FUTURE

Urban planning began in the United States in the early twentieth century as a response to the rapid development of suburban towns and the renovations of historical cities. Laws placing the control and regulation of building in the government's hands were passed in New York in 1916. Now, every city and many towns have offices for urban planning and development.

QUALITY OF LIFE

2 YEARS
While at any given time two-thirds of urban planners work for the government, neophyte planners find themselves in their employment in even larger percentages. The novice planner is working under the supervision and guidance of other planners. Many planners work as interns for a portion of these initial years. The hours can be long.

5 YEARS
The urban planner's responsibilities increase, and he or she develops a specialty, such as housing, land use, or zoning. Many planners are becoming quite adept at pitching ideas, working within constrained budgets, and political maneuvering. The majority of planners who leave the profession migrate about this time, fed up by lack of professional progress or failure to pass licensing exams.

10 YEARS
Urban planners now lead projects and create policy. Many planners have become directors or senior planners. A number of them have mentor roles where they train and educate newer members of the profession.

MAJOR EMPLOYERS
NEW YORK CITY DEPARTMENT OF CITY PLANNING
22 Reade Street, 6th Floor West
New York, NY 10007-1216
Tel: 212-720-3480
Fax: 212-720-3488
www.nyc.gov/html/dcp/home.html
Contact: Administration Office

UNITED STATES ARMY CORPS OF ENGINEERS
441 G Street, NW
Washington, DC 20314
Tel: 202-272-1024
www.usace.army.mil

MAJOR ASSOCIATIONS
AMERICAN PLANNING ASSOCIATION
1776 Massachusetts Avenue, NW
Washington, DC 20036-1904
Tel: 202-872-0611
Fax: 202-872-0643
E-mail: careerinfo@planning.org
www.planning.org

CLERGY—PRIEST, RABBI, MINISTER, AND IMAM

A DAY IN THE LIFE

Clergy are responsible for the religious education, spiritual guidance, and moral counseling of the members of their faith. Many members of the clergy seem uncomfortable calling their jobs careers or professions; they frequently said in surveys and interviews that they became members of the clergy in response to a calling to the occupation. This sense of divine request supports the clergy member through long hours, low pay, hierarchical politics, and at times, weak congregational support for their own ministries. "You have to be very confident that you are doing the right thing, because when you're preaching to one or two people in the whole church, there's not a lot of positive feedback," wrote one Protestant minister. While many mentioned the demoralizing aspect of sporadic attendance in church or synagogue, all { always on call } respondents agreed with the one who said, "We are not the focus of what we do. Our community is the focus, and how they are doing is how we judge ourselves."

This is not a job for those whose only desire is to help others; clergy often run large organizations and need the willingness and skills to do so. Office and administrative responsibilities, fund-raising, and writing and delivering sermons are important parts of the job. Clergy must be able to get along with all factions of their congregation. Frequently, clergy members will specialize in one aspect of the profession, such as sermonizing or fund-raising, and delegate other aspects of the job to more junior professionals. Being organized and attentive to detail helps in managing administrative tasks while keeping "doctor's hours: We're always on call." In most cases, the rigorous coursework involved in becoming a member of the clergy aids in acquiring these traits. Additionally, strong communication skills, patience, intellect, and dedication are required.

Perhaps the most compelling aspect our surveys noted about the field was the sense of excitement and extreme satisfaction that the clergy felt toward their occupation. The religious community is a growing, vibrant arena in which the free exchange of opinions and ideas and the chance to make real, spiritual insight become possible. "The feeling I get every day," wrote one Presbyterian minister, "is that I'm a witness to everything wonderful about people." Many clergy wrote about their unique opportunity to contribute positively to the human experience.

PAYING YOUR DUES

The education of a clergy member depends on religious and denominational affiliation. Many Protestant churches require their ministers to complete a three-year graduate degree; rabbis complete a course of study lasting four to five years in a Jewish theological seminary; training for the Catholic priesthood usually entails four years of study beyond college at a Catholic seminary. Training tends to include some form of study in homiletics (preaching), history, religious laws, counseling, and the practical aspects of ministering to a congregation.

ASSOCIATED CAREERS

People who leave the clergy do so for a variety of reasons: dissatisfaction with their advancement, a loss of the sense of calling, or the general difficulty of dealing with the downsides of the human condition. When they leave, many continue to apply their ministering skills and become social workers, vocational guidance counselors, psychologists, teachers, and substance abuse counselors. Some people return to school for advanced degrees in fields such as psychology, philosophy, comparative religion, and medicine.

> *"The feeling I get every day is that I'm a witness to everything wonderful about people."*

PAST AND FUTURE

Judaism has been in existence for roughly 4,000 years, and Christianity for about 2,000. While keeping a core set of beliefs intact, these two religions have been in a continuous state of revision and evolution. In general terms, Christians (including Catholics and Protestants) and Jews believe in the sanctity of the Old Testament. Christians believe that Jesus was the Messiah or the son of God and follow the teachings presented in the New Testament. Catholics and Protestants split during the Reformation when Martin Luther put up his 95 theses in protest (hence the *protest*ants) against the abuses of the Catholic Church. Islam can be traced back to the seventh-century Arabia with the emergence of the prophet Muhammad. Muslims believe that during the year 610, Muhammad, while praying in a cave near Mecca, experienced a vision that he later described as a visit from the angel Gabriel. Gabriel informed him that he was the last of the prophets and commanded Muhammad to memorize and recite verses sent by God. These verses were later collected and form the basis of the Quar'an.

The major world religions face the same challenges today that they have always faced: providing each of their believers with moral guidance and educating their adherents. Now, religions must also prove themselves relevant in a chaotic and demanding world. But religion has been around for a very long time, and the demand for new clergy members should remain steady.

QUALITY OF LIFE

2 YEARS Two years into the profession, many members of the clergy continue in their studies and assist an assigned local congregation under the direct-supervision of experienced clergy members. Duties are mainly administrative- and assistant-level, and many new members are merely observers for up to one year on the job. The hours are long in study, but light in pressure.

5 YEARS Five-year clergy members have assumed additional responsibilities, most notably counseling members of the congregation on faith, worship, the teachings of the sect, and issues of family, marriage, and child rearing. A clergy member's success is often based on the depth of his personal involvement. Other duties may involve teaching, sermonizing, inviting speakers, and working with members of other congregations on joint charitable projects. Satisfaction is high, but the hours can be excruciatingly long.

10 YEARS Ten-year clergy members have established strong links to their community and are leaders in both civic and religious matters. Many senior members oversee the more junior members of the clergy and supervise religious education. Moves between congregations, which occur with relative frequency in years one through seven, drop as clergy find their professional matches. Satisfaction is high; the hours continue to be relatively long.

MAJOR EMPLOYERS

MUSLIM CENTER OF NEW YORK
137-58 Geranium Avenue
Flushing, NY 11355
Tel: 718-460-3000 or 718-445-2642
Fax: 718-445-2175
www.muslimcenter.org

PRESBYTERIAN CHURCH U.S.A.
100 Witherspoon Street
Louisville, KY 40202
Tel: 800-872-3283
E-mail: presbytel@pcusa.org
www.pcusa.org

ST. PATRICK'S CATHEDRAL
14 East 51st Street
New York, NY 10022
Tel: 212-753-2261
www.ny-archdiocese.org/
pastoral/cathedral_about.html

THE RABBINICAL ASSEMBLY
3080 Broadway
New York, NY 10027
Tel: 212-280-6000
Fax: 212-749-9166
E-mail: info@rabbinicalassembly.org
www.rabbinicalassembly.org

THE RELIGIOUS SOCIETY OF FRIENDS
E-mail: nelson@quaker.org
www.quaker.org

MAJOR ASSOCIATIONS

NATIONAL CONFERENCE OF DIOCESAN VOCATION DIRECTORS
450 Hewett Street
Neillsville, WI 54456
Tel: 715-254-0830
Fax: 715-254-0831
E-mail: office@ncdvd.org
www.ncdvd.org

RABBINICAL COUNCIL OF AMERICA
305 Seventh Avenue, 12th Floor
New York, NY 10001
Tel: 212-807-7888
Fax: 212-727-8452
E-mail: info@rabbis.org
www.rabbis.org

COLLEGE ADMINISTRATOR

A DAY IN THE LIFE

College administrators make recommendations about admissions; oversee the disbursement of university materials; plan curricula; oversee all budgets from payroll to maintenance of the physical plant; supervise personnel; keep track of university records (everything from student transcripts to library archives); and help students navigate the university bureaucracy for financial aid, housing, job placement, alumni development, and all the other services a college provides. Many administrators eventually specialize in one field, such as financial aid, in which responsibilities include the preparation and maintenance of financial records and student counseling about financial aid. Specialists in information management are responsible for coordinating and producing the majority of university publications. Administrators who specialize in student affairs (sometimes referred to as student services) deal with residence life, student activities, career services, athletic administration, service learning, health education, and counseling.

{ **navigate the university bureaucracy** }

Competition begins with the onset of a specialization. At upper levels, a graduate degree in education, business, student personnel administration, counseling, or information management is required. The hours increase, and administrators spend even more time away from the office at university events or other schools.

PAYING YOUR DUES

There are stringent academic requirements for positions as college administrators. While entry-level positions in financial aid offices, registrar's offices, and admissions and academic offices often require only a bachelor's degree, a PhD or an EdD is standard among those who hold influential positions in college administrations. Candidates for administrative positions should have good managerial instincts, strong interpersonal skills, and the ability to work effectively with faculty and students. People involved in the financial aspects of administration, including administering financial aid, should have significant statistics backgrounds and mathematical skills. Computer proficiency is necessary at all levels.

Universities are just that: miniature universes. Most of their administrations involve all functions of a big corporation, even a small city, within the larger community in which they are located. A person can work for the same university for 20 years and have 20 different jobs during that time!

ASSOCIATED CAREERS

Many college administrators remain college administrators, rather than switch to a different field; 40 percent are career-for-life administrators. People who leave often become professors, teachers, corporate managers, financial aid officers, or human resource coordinators in a variety of settings.

PAST AND FUTURE

In 1865, the average-sized university in the United States employed approximately four administrators for all its students. By 1965, the average administrative staff at a United States university averaged more than 225 people. Today the number is closer to 500 employees.

The number of administrators at a university depends on funding, except for admissions offices, which exist nearly independently of funding decisions. As state education budgets wax and wane, the number of jobs available at publicly funded schools (roughly 25 percent of all institutions of higher education in the United States) varies.

QUALITY OF LIFE

2 YEARS These first two years are the most hectic and difficult years for college administrators. Most administrators train on the job and are assigned responsibilities immediately upon hire. Duties include tracking students' financial aid obligations, counseling students on course of study, and assisting in the resolution of student bureaucratic difficulties. Responsibility levels are high, and the pay is average. The hours can be long as most inherit student caseloads from previous employees, and files must be reviewed.

Entry-level professionals spend a considerable part of their day writing reports, reviewing documentation, and doing research; more time is spent on the road, promoting the school and educating potential students about the benefits of attending. Despite all the time spent embroiled in desk work or on the road, contact with students is highest during the first two years in the profession.

5 YEARS University administrators break into two tracks at the five-year point. People who are happy with their positions frequently begin taking classes at the university that employs them. Administrators who enjoy the profession but dislike their positions aggressively pursue other university administration positions. The majority of position switching among university administrators happens in years three to seven. Geographical mobility is frequently a factor in obtaining the best opportunities.

10 YEARS Ten-year veterans have supervisory authority and administrative responsibility. Many administrators have complete responsibility for the administration of substantial budgets and become more personnel managers than student advocates, a trend that may explain the sag that occurs between years 7 and 11 in terms of satisfaction. Pay increases; the hours remain stable.

MAJOR EMPLOYERS

All colleges and universities in the United States and abroad hire college administrators.

MAJOR ASSOCIATIONS

AMERICAN ASSOCIATION OF COLLEGIATE REGISTRARS AND ADMINISTRATION OFFICERS

1 Dupont Circle, NW, Suite 520
Washington, DC 20036
Tel: 202-293-9161
E-mail: info@aacrao.com
www.aacrao.com

NATIONAL ASSOCIATION OF STUDENT FINANCIAL AID ADMINISTRATORS

1129 20th Street, NW, Suite 400
Washington, DC 20036-3453
Tel: 202-785-0453
Fax: 202-785-1487
www.nasfaa.org

NATIONAL ASSOCIATION OF STUDENT PERSONNEL ADMINISTRATORS

1875 Connecticut Avenue, NW, Suite 418
Washington, DC 20009
Tel: 202-265-7500
Fax: 202-797-1157
www.naspa.org

COMEDIAN

BOOKS, FILMS, AND TV SHOWS
FEATURING THE PROFESSION
- **The Life of Jack Benny**
- **Mr. Saturday Night**
- **Punchline**
- **Seinfeld**

YOU'LL HAVE CONTACT WITH
- **Agents**
- **Club managers**
- **Other comedians**
- **Producers**
- **Publicists**

PROFESSIONALS READ
- **Comedy Magazine**
- **Harvard Lampoon**
- **National Lampoon**
- **The Onion**
- **Spy**

A DAY IN THE LIFE

Comedians get a thrill from making people laugh. A comedian develops a unique style, skill, and body of work as an entertainer. Most noncomedians are only familiar with comic superstars, such as Steve Martin, Jim Carrey, Robin Williams, Whoopi Goldberg, and Jerry Seinfeld, to name a few. Most of the comedians we surveyed mentioned these visible successes as partially responsible for their staying in the profession, however unlikely a similar meteoric rise may be. Most of the surveys received from comedians were distinctly unfunny in their responses to our questions about how they live day to day. "Everybody in the world thinks they're funny. It's just that I'm crazy enough to bet on [my prospects as a comedian]," wrote one professional comedian from Denver who quit his job as a salesman to pursue a full-time career in comedy. A comedian works long hours for little (if any) pay and endures enormous uncertainty, never knowing where the next paycheck will be coming from. The average stand-up comedian earns around $50 for two 20-minute sets at a comedy club. While this translates into a solid hourly wage, a new comedian may do four sets per week, with the rest of the time spent writing material, watching other comedians, and keeping an additional job to pay the rent. A successful comedian must be quick-witted, able to think on his or her feet, dedicated, and lucky. A great deal of self-confidence is required if one is to last over two years in this profession (and over half don't), since failure, disappointment, and rejection are standard.

{ exposure }

Comedy troupes develop, perform, and publicize their own material. Most of the members maintain freelance or day jobs that allow them to pursue this career. They usually schedule a weekly show, bracketed around rehearsals and workshops where they critique one another's sketches and performances. Because attendees will not return to see the same material, it is a highly pressured large-output environment. A troupe comedian must adapt to peers' comments and take criticism well. The ability to work with others is critical to success in comedy groups. The troupes are often formed in major urban centers where actors and comedians congregate due to the larger opportunity for work.

Solo comedians perform on club circuits around the country, usually one after another on a given night, creating a very competitive atmosphere. Being a solo comedian can be an "if-you-win-I-lose" type of career. "There are only so many laughs on any given night, and if possible, you want to get all of them," wrote one regular at a comedy club in New York. Solo stand-up comics face a significant level isolation. At the same time, studying fellow performers' material, style, delivery, and presence are facets of the successful comedian's life.

PAYING YOUR DUES

Being in dingy nightclubs before an audience of one for unpaid stand-up sets are part of the aspiring comedian's dues. No academic requirements exist, but many performers get their start in college acting or comedy troupes, thereby gaining some exposure to large audiences. Stand-up comedians have a more uncertain road than troupe comedians, going from club to club, writing material, practicing and refining it, and hoping for a break. It is not unusual for an aspiring stand-up comic to log more than 200 days per year away from home.

ASSOCIATED CAREERS

More than 30 percent of exiting comedians slide smoothly into acting, where they face much the same odds against success. Others find homes in advertising, teaching, writing, and one mentioned that he ended up in law enforcement. The skills associated with comedy—the ability to make others laugh, defuse tense situations with a well-timed remark, and think on one's feet—are invaluable assets in any other career.

PAST AND FUTURE

Comedy has historically been the mirror of every age, from the Greek playwright Aristophanes to the sarcastic drollery of Dennis Miller. Every known culture has its own form of comedy, and the smile and the laugh seem hardwired as responses in the human brain.

Comedians have been in entertainment ascendancy of late, with Adam Sandler making about $20 million on each of his films. But, in general, comedians should expect to face the same odds in the career tomorrow that they face today.

QUALITY OF LIFE

2 YEARS Progression in this profession is unpredictable, but for the majority of comedians, it follows the scenario outlined here. Two-year comics are just developing their comic personas and getting their feet wet on the comedy circuit. They have just started writing their material and experimenting with different styles. They go to open-mike nights to try out new material, get to know the clubs and vice versa, and make contacts with other comics. The new comic is lucky to get a few bookings. Persistence and confidence are the key to working at all.

5 YEARS Comedians are skilled self-publicists by this point, and some of them even have agents. After five years in the profession, comics know clubs around town and around the country and have, hopefully, performed at many of them. They could even be regulars at one or two clubs. Club managers know them and their style, and they know where their material will be welcomed and where it's not appropriate. Other comedians have seen their work, and they have probably auditioned for a few comedy troupes and maybe even started working with one.

10 YEARS Comedians who have lasted 10 years in the profession have attained a measure of success in their field and probably have a strong regional following. They have had many opportunities to show their work, possibly including TV specials and performing for specific groups, such as political associations or college clubs, depending on their material. They have probably worked for a comedy troupe, at least for a while. Comedians keep seeking out new venues for their performances, writing and developing new material, and hoping for a big break.

MAJOR EMPLOYERS

CAROLINE'S ON BROADWAY
1626 Broadway
New York, NY 10019
Tel: 212-956-4100
www..carolines.com

COMEDY CENTRAL
1775 Broadway, 10th Floor
(212) 767-8600
www.comedycentral.com

SECOND CITY COMEDY
1616 North Wells
Chicago, IL 60614
Tel: 312-664-4032
www.secondcity.com

MAJOR ASSOCIATIONS

AMERICAN FEDERATION OF TELEVISION AND RADIO ARTISTS
260 Madison Avenue, 7th Floor
New York, NY 10016-2401
Tel: 212-532-0800
Fax: 212-545-2242
www.aftra.org

AMERICAN GUILD OF VARIETY ARTISTS
184 Fifth Avenue, 6th Floor
New York, NY 10010
Tel: 212-675-1003
www.home.earthlink.net/~agvala/agva1.html
or
http://americanguildofvarietyartistsagva.visual-net.com

CONDUCTOR

PROFESSIONAL PROFILE

# of people in profession	N/A
Avg. hours per week	30-40
	(plus preparation)
Avg. starting salary	$26,000
Avg. salary after 5 years	$36,000
Avg. salary after 10 to 15 years	$51,000

SALARY

HOURS

EDUCATION

BOOKS, FILMS, AND TV SHOWS FEATURING THE PROFESSION

- Amadeus
- Bolero
- Immortal Beloved
- Interlude
- Money Pit
- Seinfeld

YOU'LL HAVE CONTACT WITH

- Artist managers
- Arts management professionals
- Audio professionals
- Development and fund-raising staff
- Musicians
- Students

PROFESSIONALS READ

- Gramophone
- Symphony

A DAY IN THE LIFE

The most visible work of the conductor involves standing in front of an orchestra or choir during a performance, leading and directing the members of the ensemble with gestures, glances, and even the occasional verbal cue. Of course, the performance is the culmination of hours of rehearsal, during which the conductor will have prepared the orchestra by providing specific musical directions and by working on discrete sections many, many times. If a piece calls for a soloist, the conductor is typically responsible for auditioning candidates and then for guiding the soloist and the ensemble so that they play well together. The conductor is responsible for identifying and then cultivating the kind of musical nuance that renders a piece artistic as well as technically perfect (or near-perfect). The conductor also typically selects the pieces of music on a program, works with media contacts and fund-raisers to secure publicity for the show, and manages administrative aspects associated with directing an ensemble.

{ exceptionally artistic interpretation }

A choral conductor and a band leader of a smaller ensemble will need to have many of the same skills as the conductor of a large orchestra: a great breadth and depth of knowledge about music history, theory, ear training, and composition; a creative imagination; musical insight; the ability to work diplomatically with professionals who may have their own views about how a given piece of music should be presented; the ability to play at least one instrument; and the capacity to convey advanced music concepts. Much of the conductor's work time will be spent in rehearsals. He or she will also need to listen to and select music for the group to perform; make arrangements for performance times and halls; coordinate publicity for upcoming events; and sometimes even manage the finances of the group. These myriad roles require diplomacy and the ability to communicate well, as well as good time management skills. The uncertain nature of arts funding is often the major drawback to this field, as is the unfortunate fact that each ensemble can only have one conductor. Why vie for a coveted conductor position, you ask? There are few career paths as rewarding, so if this is what you love and you land a job doing it, then there can be nothing better. By exhibiting exceptionally artistic interpretation and expression as well as strong leadership skills, the conductor may foster cooperation and collaboration among musicians to communicate unique musical works that may touch the souls of listeners.

PAYING YOUR DUES

Conductors must command respect, both as artists and as professionals. Typically, the path to becoming a conductor begins with learning voice or an instrument; participating in an ensemble (e.g., chorus, orchestra, or chamber group); intensively studying a great breadth of music as well as music theory, ear training, and composition; and earning undergraduate and graduate degrees in music—or, better yet, in music conducting. This training is augmented (pun intended) by course work in the organizational aspects of conducting groups, such as arranging music, communicating musical ideas, managing conflicting personalities, and securing funding. Working (this can sometimes entail volunteering) as a concert master, choir director, or manager/agent for a small group may offer useful practical experience and networking opportunities. Classroom or workshop training in areas of arts management and funding may also prove useful. Many conductors work part-time or work for several groups at once while supplementing their income by teaching, composing, and arranging music.

ASSOCIATED CAREERS

Conductors may also be qualified to work as arrangers, composers, choir directors, instrumentalists, and teachers of music. They may also find work in scoring and arranging for film projects. The capacity to manage the many demands of leading an orchestra or choir may prove useful in the field of arts administration or in the administrative aspects of education, as well.

PAST AND FUTURE

As soon as musicians started coming together to perform in groups, the need for musical leadership arose. Choirs developed song leaders; and with the growth of orchestras as popular entertainment during the Baroque era, many well-known composers also worked as conductors, leading musicians through their own works as well as the works of others. In more recent times, Leonard Bernstein and Aaron Copeland have continued in that tradition.

Both high-profile international touring symphony orchestras and local community groups find themselves in need of musical leadership. Competition for the most prestigious posts is only increasing in intensity. To land your dream job, you'll need large quantities of sheer talent, musical skill, leadership capability, charisma, often an ability to negotiate the politics of fund-raising and promotion, and, of course, luck. Most positions in conducting will remain part-time. Growth of interest in community choirs and orchestras will see some opportunity in these areas, though such positions are likely to be on the lower end of the pay scale.

QUALITY OF LIFE

2 YEARS — Many conductors begin their careers working part-time or on a contractual basis with community orchestras, churches, or theater and dance companies, sometimes as assistant or fill-in conductors. Often, a conductor will combine this with other music-related work (such as teaching or arranging). Adjusting to the uncertainties of income inherent in this profession will prove a challenge in the early years of the career. There is much potential for growth in creative and financial directions, however, although competition for the most high-profile positions is intense.

5 YEARS — As a conductor reaches the five-year mark, he or she will start to enjoy opportunities to conduct larger-scale works (with choir and orchestra, for example) performed by better-funded professional or semi-professional groups. The conductor may become more involved in selecting programs of music for a season, and he or she may even lead a concert tour. Uncertainty of continuing work, the need to balance conducting with other work for the sake of income, and the intense competition for higher-level posts are very real challenges at this point.

10 YEARS — At the 10-year mark, conductors have established themselves and are likely to have ascertained the best way to earn a full-time income. At this point, conductors who don't see lots of potential to direct larger or professional-level ensembles may branch into teaching, composing, or arts administration. Those who combine the field with work in other areas may find this career diversity satisfying; or, they may opt to concentrate on an area with more stable income potential.

MAJOR EMPLOYERS

LOS ANGELES PHILHARMONIC
151 South Grand Avenue
Los Angeles, CA 90012
Tel: 323-850-2000
http://wdch.laphil.com

NEW YORK PHILHARMONIC
Avery Fisher Hall
10 Lincoln Center Plaza
New York, NY 10023-6990
Tel: 212-875-5900
Fax: 212-875-5717
http://newyorkphilharmonic.org

Conductors generally find employment with professional or community orchestras, in religious organizations (for which they work primarily as choral conductors or music directors), in theatrical troupes, and at educational institutions. Many of these positions are part-time and may be contract work.

MAJOR ASSOCIATIONS

AMERICAN FEDERATION OF MUSICIANS
1501 Broadway, Suite 600
New York, NY 10036
Tel: 212-869-1330
Fax: 212-764-6134
www.afm.org

CONDUCTORS GUILD
5300 Glenside Drive, Suite 2207
Richmond, VA 23228
Tel: 804-553-1378
Fax: 804-553-1876
www.conductorsguild.org

COSMETOLOGIST

PROFESSIONAL PROFILE

# of people in profession	754,000
Avg. hours per week	40 (Many in the field work part-time.)
Avg. starting salary	$15,010
Avg. salary after 5 years	$25,600
Avg. salary 10 to 15 years	$35,240

SALARY   •
HOURS   •
EDUCATION   •

BOOKS, FILMS, AND TV SHOWS
FEATURING THE PROFESSION
- Barber Shop
- Legally Blonde
- Steel Magnolias

YOU'LL HAVE CONTACT WITH
- Clients
- Image consultants
- Product manufacturers
- The fashion industry

PROFESSIONALS READ
- Allure
- American Salon
- Glamour
- Modern Salon
- Salon Today
- Vogue

A DAY IN THE LIFE

Cosmetologists are often the initiators of style and change. Cosmetologists help their clients improve on or acquire a certain look with the right hairstyle and hair coloring, manicured nails, and either a properly trimmed beard or carefully chosen makeup, depending on your testosterone and estrogen levels. Cosmetologists also shampoo, cut, color, and style hair and advise clients on proper hair care between appointments. They add permanent waves or straighten hair in addition to giving manicures, facials, and scalp treatments and caring for and styling wigs.

This is a profession that requires considerable tact and diplomacy in dealing with patrons. Cosmetologists are people-oriented and must be able to inspire the confidence of those they service. With an emphasis on personalized care and services, cosmetologists must understand the individual characteristics of their clients to be able to choose the hairstyles and makeup colors and tones that are uniquely suited to them. One New York City stylist remarked, "It's simply important to get to know and understand your clients . . . their likes and dislikes . . . and you work with that, finding styles that enhance aspects of their personality." The move toward more personalized care and services means that cosmetologists with charm, good communication skills, and the ability to inspire trust in their clients will be very successful. For cosmetologists who work in teams where each member has her own specialty—hair, nails, makeup, etc.—interpersonal skills are crucial for success. Constantly updated skills in new hair treatments and techniques give the ambitious cosmetologist the edge. Many cosmetologists regularly attend classes to improve their trade.

{ inspire confidence }

Cosmetologists must keep on top of the latest styles and trends in hair fashion and beauty techniques. If you knew next year's hot hairstyle, you'd be a hit. If you created next year's hot hairstyle, you'd be a star. The hours in the field are flexible, with some professionals working nine to five, others working nights, and some working only weekends. What's not flexible is the considerable amount of time cosmetologists spend on their feet. Professionals are also exposed to hair and nail chemicals that could possibly negatively affect their health.

PAYING YOUR DUES

Cosmetologists face varying licensing requirements in different states, but essentially a high school diploma, formal training at a cosmetology or vocational school, and, in some states, completion of an apprenticeship and passage of a state examination constitute the educational requirements. For most cosmetologists, professional training continues throughout their careers. The recently certified stylist can expect to perform duties that amount to sheer drudgery. Newcomers are left to washing, blow-drying, and setting customers' hair, occasionally being given the task of a simple hairstyle pattern. New workers should perform these tasks with glee, knowing full well that practice makes perfect, and soon enough they'll develop followings of their own, make better wages, and collect bigger tips. New cosmetologists should be especially careful in following the instructions of patrons and seeking help and direction if unsure of a particular procedure. Remember: This is an industry that relies on the proper use and application of chemicals. Hair and nail disasters can make the cosmetologist and the management of the establishment vulnerable to lawsuits.

ASSOCIATED CAREERS

Cosmetologists can virtually step into any area of the beauty business. Hairstylists, hair colorists, nail technicians, makeup artists, estheticians, and massage therapists are in constant demand to help the public look and feel their best. People looking to combine their experience as a cosmetologist with a strong business sense can attempt salon management or ownership or positions in the sales, marketing, and distribution of hair care products. Some cosmetologists become personal consultants to celebrities and VIPs. There are many opportunities for cosmetologists to share their professional knowledge teaching at a cosmetology or vocational school.

PAST AND FUTURE

In the decades prior to the 1960s, women went to the beauty salon once a week for a wash and set, and hair generally wasn't done at home. This changed almost overnight with the advent of the "wash and wear" styles, credited to Vidal Sassoon. These styles allowed a client to care for hair at home in between visits to the salon. The industry was forced to adjust by becoming more diverse. Unisex salons started springing up in the 1970s. The 1980s saw the rise of the full-service salon, which included nail and skin care, as well as makeup services. Today's day spas evolved from these establishments.

Women's tresses have always been their crowning glory, but the extent to which both men and women today rely on their hairstyle as an integral part of their physical identity is significant. Once visited largely by the leisure class, cosmetologists now see clients from every walk of life who are bound together by their sense of fashion and its ever-changing styles and trends.

QUALITY OF LIFE

2 YEARS At this stage licensed cosmetologists have tried a bit of everything, including styling, coloring, nails, skin care, marketing, and consumer service. They are beginning to discover what they excel at and what they enjoy doing. Depending on the salon for which they work, they may already have begun to specialize in specific procedures such as hair coloring or pedicures.

5 YEARS With five years of experience comes a refined technique, an effortless chair-side manner, an unmistakable style, and with it, hopefully, a faithful clientele—people who will move thousands of miles away, but come for a visit because they must get their hair cut by you and only you. At this point a cosmetologist may be mentoring junior cosmetologists and new hires in the salon or may begin training themselves to become a salon manager. People with their creative juices flowing may train to become the salon's artistic director. The cosmetologist at this stage should be on the very cutting edge of the latest techniques in styling and coloring.

10 YEARS The cosmetologist should, after 10 years in the business, be a veritable artist with faithful and ever-flocking patrons. The business-minded will most likely be in a managerial role, while the more artistic will be art directors or specialist image creators at their salon. Depending on their level of responsibility, the cosmetologist may still have the flexible hours that first drew them to the field. Others may try opening a business as a beauty or fashion consultant or becoming a sales representative for a beauty products company. Also, at this point, the enterprising cosmetologist could expand his line of service to include other areas of beauty care.

MAJOR EMPLOYERS
HAIR CUTTERY
2817 Hartland Road
Falls Church, VA 22043
Tel: 703-208-1943
www.haircuttery.com/home.html

THE REGIS CORPORATION
7201 Metro Boulevard
Minneapolis, MN 55439
Tel: 952-947-7777
www.regissalons.com

Many new jobs are listed on the National Accrediting Commission of Cosmetology Arts & Sciences website, www.naccas.org.

MAJOR ASSOCIATIONS
AMERICAN ASSOCIATION OF COSMETOLOGY SCHOOLS
15825 North 71st Street, Suite 100
Scottsdale, AZ 85254-1521
Tel: 800-831-1086 or 480-281-0431
Fax: 480-905-0708
www.beautyschools.org

CURATOR

A DAY IN THE LIFE

Curators (sometimes referred to as archivists in libraries) collect, exhibit, interpret, maintain, and protect objects of historical and aesthetic importance primarily in museums, libraries, and private collections. Curators are responsible for the safety and proper presentation of the works. "It's all so fascinating and beautiful that you can find yourself touching history," wrote one respondent. This sense of connection to the motion and beauty of history as expressed through objects is something nearly all the curators who responded mentioned. Almost none of them entered college with the expectation of becoming curators. The profession seemed to "just appear out of thin air." Satisfaction and responsibility are usually high in this profession at all levels, with the exception of those curators who find that they are { connect to history } unable to spend enough time with the art they love because of their obligations to do publicity, fund-raising, and grant writing.

Curators' duties include creating exhibitions, acquiring works for the collection, meeting with and educating trustees, labeling exhibits, accurately and carefully keeping track of inventory, and, at times, overseeing research on collection pieces to make certain the integrity of the piece is maintained (such as dating tests for fossils or X-ray analysis of paintings to determine origin). "I've got a PhD, and I'm trying to find a good way to deal with termites," said one curator. These varied and wide-ranging duties require someone with a mind attuned to details. Another facet of the curator's job is educating the public about the objects and publicizing their existence. Most literature one receives or audio tracks one listens to at a museum were written by a curator. Grant writing is the third area of responsibility for most curators; much of this is done in consultation with collection managers and curatorial assistants. Curators should have excellent written communication skills. Managing a large staff, including interns and volunteers, is the most unexpected side of the profession. Many curators find the classification and preservation skills they know useless in coordinating the tasks of a full, dedicated staff. "You have to learn to delegate to people's levels of competence," mentioned one veteran curator, and others agreed. "Although you're in charge," said another, "you can't do it alone." Curators who can manage a staff and the details of their job are, for the most part, successful in and excited by their choice of career.

PAYING YOUR DUES

Both graduate education and practical experience are required for people who wish to become curators. Aside from an extensive knowledge of history and art, it is useful to have a basic understanding of chemistry, restoration techniques, museum studies, and even physics and public relations. Curators must have basic skills in aesthetic design, organizational behavior, business, fund-raising, and publicity. Many employers look favorably on foreign language skills as well. To become a collection manager or a curatorial assistant, a master's degree is required. To become a curator at a national museum, a PhD is required, as is about five years of field experience. The market is competitive, and academic standards are very high. Useful graduate degrees include restoration science, curatorship, art history, history, chemistry, and business administration. Nearly all curators find it helpful to engage in continuing education. Research and publication in academic journals are important for advancement in the field.

ASSOCIATED CAREERS

Curators become art historians, critics, college professors, museum educators, and museum directors. A notable few become independent consultants and independent researchers, but significant achievement in the field is required before these opportunities become available.

PAST AND FUTURE

Curatorship arose from the needs of museums, libraries, and societies to maintain and preserve their collections while at the same time publicize them, encourage donations, and expose the public to their artifacts. Curatorship existed as early as 1750 in the United States but without any specific label until the early 1900s. The years 1950–1984 were strong years for museum growth and funding, but beginning in 1985 and continuing into the present, museums have been under severe financial pressure due to lack of government funding and general economic trends.

People who are interested in becoming curators should note that during lean-funding years, the position involves much more grant writing, publicity, and fund-raising than it does collection maintenance and acquisition. Extra time spent at social functions to raise money can be significant. Funding decisions, however, are cyclical; what is true for the industry today may change within a very short period of time.

QUALITY OF LIFE

2 YEARS Most curators at this point are still in graduate school. Many take curatorial assistant positions, as well as collection manager jobs (which are more task-oriented) to gain experience and begin making connections that will prove invaluable later in their careers. Duties of assistant curators include cataloging existing items and research. Some curators with good writing skills may be assigned to grant-writing positions, writing of object labels and other gallery text, as well as printed handouts. A significant number of people get jobs through the recommendations of their professors. The hours are long; the pay is low, if any pay is forthcoming at all.

5 YEARS Five-year veterans have completed at least a master's degree, and many of them continue along the PhD track. A number of curatorial assistants have become curatorial associates with expanded responsibilities and hours. Many people who are not in school may be asked to travel during these periods; others who are in school may be asked to work odd hours, when there is no museum traffic. Duties include assisting with loan agreement forms for the temporary exhibitions; collecting images for publications; overseeing interns, volunteers, and researchers; along with coordinating access to artifacts with scholars and academics who need access for research projects. A few begin to write copy for educational and promotional literature.

10 YEARS A number of professionals have achieved the status of curator or senior curator. These people are involved in planning the museum's exhibition program, curating exhibitions, writing catalog essays, staffing, budgeting, trading items with other museums, and piecing collections together for display. Responsibilities are extraordinarily high; salaries become commensurate with the work. Curators direct any internal museum research on pieces and invite academics to join in the study. The newest responsibility that curators have is working with the president and chairman of the museum to direct all fund-raising efforts. Political skills are crucial for this position. Many curators teach at local schools, publish research, and review academic articles for publication. The hours are long, but satisfaction has never been higher. Ten-year curators face a strong future in this competitive and demanding field.

MAJOR EMPLOYERS

METROPOLITAN MUSEUM OF ART
1000 Fifth Avenue at 82nd Street
New York, NY 10028
Tel: 212-535-7710
www.metmuseum.org

MUSEUM OF MODERN ART
11 West 53rd Street
New York, NY 10019
Tel: 212-705-9400
E-mail: info@moma.org
www.moma.org

SMITHSONIAN INSTITUTE
Main Office of Human Resources
750 9th Street, NW, Suite 6100
Washington, DC 20560-0912
Tel: 202-275-1102
Jobline: 202-287-3102
www.si.edu

MAJOR ASSOCIATIONS

AMERICAN ASSOCIATION OF MUSEUMS
1575 Eye Street, NW, Suite 400
Washington, DC 20005
Tel: 202-289-1818
Fax: 202-289-6578
www.aam-us.org

INDEPENDENT CURATORS INCORPORATED
799 Broadway, Suite 205
New York, NY 10003
Tel: 212-254-8200
Fax: 212-477-4781
E-mail: info@ici-exhibitions.org
www.ici-exhibitions.org

DANCER

A DAY IN THE LIFE

Often prepped from youth for a career in which the average retirement age is in the late 30s, dancers are hard-working, dedicated, patient, and—you guessed it—physically fit. Not only is the profession highly competitive to break into, but it is also very specialized. Dancers appear in such diverse settings as opera, musical theater, television, and commercials. They perform most often in the evenings, with their days spent in long rehearsals. Traveling is also common for anyone pursuing a career as a dancer. Whether working with a dance company, in a musical production, at a school, or on a cruise ship, dancers can expect to spend a lot of time on the road, working very long and late hours. (Often, however, dancers on tour receive additional funds for room and board as well as overtime.) For the person attracted to 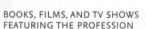 { **long and late hours** } dance by the grace of the art form or the apparent effortlessness with which the professionals move, one may want to reflect on this observation by Martha Graham, one of the twentieth century's greatest choreographers, who says that "Dancing appears glamorous, easy, delightful. But the path to paradise of the achievement is not easier than any other. There is fatigue so great that the body cries, even in its sleep. There are times of complete frustration; there are daily small deaths."

Despite all of its hardships, many are attracted to the profession by the opportunity to participate in something new and creative—and to work on projects that change frequently. Many dancers work with choreographers toward the creation of new dances or the reinterpretation of a preexisting dance. The ability to work with others is essential, as most dancers—contrary to what many believe about the profession—spend their careers performing as part of a large group.

PAYING YOUR DUES

All successful dancers have patience, drive, and above all, a devotion to dance. (Ms. Graham also observes, "Great dancers are not great because of their technique; they are great because of their passion.") Those who pursue dance will, undoubtedly, become accustomed to rather regular rejection when auditioning for work and will almost always face periodic bouts of unemployment. Advancement may be slow and depends largely on the reputation the dancer has built. Dancers must excel as individuals—with respect to their physical and mental health—as well as in their ability to function as members of a group. It is a taxing profession, but dance can also be extremely rewarding for those who have the talent and drive to pursue it.

Most professionals start their training at a young age. While training largely depends on the form of dance in which one specializes, many instructors and dancers agree that a foundation in classical dance is essential. Women typically begin their training in ballet, modern, jazz, or tap around age eight, whereas men often begin between the ages of 10 and 15; ballroom dancers tend to begin in their teens, as well. (Anyone who has seen *Mad Hot Ballroom*, however, knows that some start even earlier.) Training is demanding, requiring around eight physically intense hours every day, and continues to be a necessary part of dancers' lives throughout their careers.

A general education in the arts, including music, literature, and the visual arts, is looked favorably on by industry professionals, who believe that such a background contributes to a dancer's ability to interpret a piece. Moreover, a college degree, while not necessary, can also be helpful. To teach at the high-school or college level, for example, an undergraduate or even a graduate degree in dance and education is necessary. While many dancers pursue a degree to prepare them for a career after dance, many others forgo a formal education to devote more time to practicing and performing.

ASSOCIATED CAREERS

Depending on the kind of performing career a dancer pursues, it may also be helpful to know how to sing. This is particularly true of dancers interested in a career in musical theater. Because many stop performing by their 30s, dancers often find work in a related field such as choreography or teaching. Those with a college degree may seek employment working in a school setting. Others can still teach dance or choreography, but are usually limited to local recreational programs.

PAST AND FUTURE

As an art form, dance has served through the ages as a means of expressing ideas, stories, rhythm, and sound with the body. Since before recorded time, it has been an integral part of human life and is commonly associated with religious rites and social celebrations. In Western culture, one of the earliest references to dance appears in Homer's *Iliad*.

Given the lasting public interest in dance, it is expected that larger dance companies will have continued success in sustaining themselves. Available funding, however, may not meet the needs of many small and midsize companies as they face rising production costs. This may result in fewer performances and a reduction in employment opportunities. Furthermore, industry competition is likely to remain intense, given the relative dearth of available jobs for the sizable and qualified applicant pool.

QUALITY OF LIFE

2 YEARS Particularly at the beginning of one's career, a dancer will usually take on a number of unpaid jobs. The opportunity to gain some experience working with a well-known choreographer or making connections with other dancers can be seen as an investment in one's future. The attrition rate is high, and even many dancers who do stick with their art never see a reward commensurate with their early sacrifices. Those who do find work with a company can initially expect low pay, short-term contracts, and often a lot of traveling.

5 YEARS At this point, dancers tend to have made important connections, learned the industry, and, to some degree, established themselves. If they are in jobs with a dance company, they are probably on their way to attaining principal status.

10 YEARS Because being a dancer is such a physically demanding career choice, professional dancers tend to have peaked by the end of their first decade and may consider pursuing other (often related) career options after about 15 years. Some do continue to dance; others may become dance instructors, choreographers, or even critics; and still others explore alternative career prospects.

MAJOR EMPLOYERS

ALVIN AILEY DANCE FOUNDATION, INC.
The Joan Weill Center for Dance
405 West 55th Street
New York, NY 10019
Tel: 212-405-9000
Fax: 212-405-9001
www.alvinailey.org

MARTHA GRAHAM DANCE COMPANY
316 East 63rd Street
New York, NY 10021
Tel: 212-521-3611
E-mail: info@marthagrahamdance.org
www.marthagrahamdance.org

NEW YORK CITY BALLET
Administrative Offices
20 Lincoln Center Plaza
New York, NY 10023
Tel: 212-870-5656
www.nycballet.com

MAJOR ASSOCIATIONS

AMERICAN DANCE GUILD
PO Box 2006
Lenox Hill Station
New York, NY 10021
Tel: 212-932-2789
E-mail: info@americandanceguild.org
http://americandanceguild.org

DANCE/USA
1156 15th Street, NW, Suite 820
Washington, DC 20005-1726
Tel: 202-833-1717
Fax: 202-833-2686
www.danceusa.org

NATIONAL ASSOCIATION OF SCHOOLS OF DANCE
11250 Roger Bacon Drive, Suite 21
Reston, VA 20190-5248
Tel: 703-437-0700
Fax: 703-437-6312
E-mail: info@arts-accredit.org
http://nasd.arts-accredit.org

NATIONAL DANCE ASSOCIATION
American Alliance for Health, Physical Education, Recreation & Dance
1900 Association Drive
Reston, VA 20191-1598
Tel: 703-476-3400
www.aahperd.org/nda

DENTIST

A DAY IN THE LIFE

A dentist is an accredited medical professional who specializes in the care of teeth, gums, and mouths. As with most medical professions, a keen eye for detail, comprehensive medical understanding, manual dexterity, and strong interpersonal skills are important. Dentists deal with procedures that involve actual manipulation of the teeth or gums. Dentists have also evolved to provide cosmetic care that addresses society's perception of hygiene and health, as with the burgeoning business in whitening teeth. Problems dealing with the jaw or any invasive oral procedure are usually undertaken by an oral surgeon, and dental hygienists and dental assistants do much of the routine dental cleanings, maintenance, and X-rays. A significant part of a dentist's job involves educating patients about ways to preserve a healthy mouth, and the best dentists are skillful communicators. (Gum disease, for example, ultimately attacks more than 87 percent of the population.) Cavities can develop and worsen for a long time undetected by a patient, and sometimes the only remedy is root canal therapy (less painful than in the early days but still expensive) or extraction of the tooth.

{ keen eye for detail }

Dentists are the preventative doctors par excellence, ever alert for early signs of swollen or bleeding gums, tooth decay, etc., but often they simply step in and correct the results of their patients' less-than-stellar personal hygiene. While dentists encourage frequent visits to maintain good health, the reduced likelihood that patients have comprehensive health insurance coverage for dental work as compared to other forms of health care has been known to strain that effort. Dentists work 7–10-hour days, except when emergencies arise, which can occasionally lengthen the workday. The life of a dentist is very similar to that of any other doctor, except that dentists keep regular office hours—one notable attraction of the profession. Many of the dentists we surveyed responded that although the hours are long, one is able to lead a fairly predictable life, take standard vacations around major holidays, and enjoy weekends with family. Reasonable hours were cited on over 90 percent of our surveys as one of the most important features that led people to dentistry as opposed to any other medical specialty.

Dentists pay enormous premiums for liability insurance, large sums for fixed costs such as rent and equipment, and significant overhead for qualified personnel and quality products. Since each patient treated corresponds to additional revenue received, dentists often try to see as many patients as they can on a given day. A dentist usually spends one afternoon a week managing paperwork and insurance claims. The amount of time required to process this paperwork is likely to increase as changes in health care management force doctors to spend more time filing and defending claims of even routine prevention for their insured patients.

PAYING YOUR DUES

Prospective dentists must complete a set of rigorous academic and professional requirements. Academic course work on the undergraduate level should include anatomy, chemistry, physics, and biology. All prospective dentists must complete four years at an American Dental Association-accredited school and pass the individual exams administered by each state. Passage of the National Dental Board Exam (administered twice a year), however, can exempt the candidate from the written portion of the state exams. If you wish to teach, do dental research, or engage in a dental specialty, an additional two to five years of study is required.

After passing the exams and receiving a Doctor of Dental Surgery (DDS) or Doctor of Dental Medicine (DDM) degree, a new dentist may choose to apprentice under an established practitioner for several years, after which time junior associates may either buy a larger share of the partnership or leave to start their own practices. Nearly a quarter of all graduates buy into or purchase outright an existing practice after graduation. Financing is rarely a problem, as most dental practices are considered good investments by banks, as long as the internal cash flow of the practice is properly managed.

ASSOCIATED CAREERS

Including retirement, health problems, death, migration to other fields, and return to school for further education, only 9 percent leave the industry each year. A few professionals decide to specialize in reconstruction, orthodontics, periodontics, oral surgery, or a related medical field. Few people leave the medical field altogether.

PAST AND FUTURE

Records of dental exams have been found among artifacts from ancient Egypt, when dentists doubled as surgeons. Long an independent branch of medicine with its own subspecialties, dentistry will continue to be a growing industry for the coming years. But as with all medical professions, the future of tax and health care reform will significantly affect the financial attractiveness of the career. The field is also changing in other respects. More dentists are entering group practices instead of private practices. This cuts back on insurance and overhead expenses. The focus of dentistry is shifting toward preventive care and cosmetic procedures.

QUALITY OF LIFE

2 YEARS The hours can be long initially, as new dentists must take time to familiarize themselves with their patients' histories, needs, and personalities. It is crucial for new dentists to earn their patients' trust. Job satisfaction increases as dentists begin to hone their "chairside manner" and develop a daily routine that suits them. It should be noted that some dentists find themselves disillusioned with their chosen career. Many dentists are frustrated to find that, although they are similarly educated to physicians, they do not receive the same respect in the public eye. It can also be depressing to repeatedly hear people say, "No offense, but I hate dentists."

5 YEARS Five-year veterans have established reputations and built up a client base. Take-home pay rises as they pay off the initial charge of buying into an existing practice. Many dentists work long hours during years three to eight to build their practice with the expectation of future rewards. The downsides are high-partnership failure and the ongoing crisis in private versus group practice.

10 YEARS Dentists who have practiced for 10 years have reasonable satisfaction from what they do. They have established a consistent and loyal client base, have a range of experience and a degree of expertise, and earn significant income. Many dentists become involved in professional associations and professional philanthropy (where businesses donate services to people in need), and write scholarly articles. The hours are still long, but drop off over the next 10 years. Most dentists are still working full-time even at the 30-year mark, and a significant number continue for as long as four decades before retiring.

MAJOR EMPLOYERS
DENTAL CARE PARTNERS
5900 Landerbrook Drive, Suite 100
Mayfield Heights, OH 44124
Tel: 800-487-4867
Fax: 440-684-6941
www.dcpartners.com

DENT-U-CENTER
3004 28th Street, SW
Grandville, MI 49418
Tel: 800-722-3650
Fax: 616-534-4538

PRESBYTERIAN HOSPITAL OF DALLAS
8200 Walnut Hill Road
Dallas, TX 75231
Tel: 214-345-6789
www.phscare.org

MAJOR ASSOCIATIONS
AMERICAN ASSOCIATION OF WOMEN DENTISTS
330 South Wells Street, Suite 1110
Chicago, IL 60606
Tel: 800-920-2293
Fax: 312-461-0238
E-mail: info@aawd.org
www.womendentists.org

AMERICAN DENTAL ASSOCIATION
211 East Chicago Avenue
Chicago, IL 60611-2678
Tel: 312-440-2500
www.ada.org

INTERNATIONAL ASSOCIATION FOR DENTAL RESEARCH
1619 Duke Street
Alexandria, VA 22314-3406
Tel: 703-548-0066
Fax: 703-548-1883
E-mail: research@iadr.org
www.iadr.org

DIGITAL ARTIST

SALARY   ● ● ●

HOURS   ● ●

EDUCATION   ● ●

BOOKS, FILMS, AND TV SHOWS
FEATURING THE PROFESSION

- **40 Days and 40 Nights**
- **Love Liza**
- **Spiderman (on MTV)**

YOU'LL HAVE CONTACT WITH

- **Animators**
- **HTML coders**
- **Illustrators**
- **Producers**
- **Programmers**
- **Sound designers**

PROFESSIONALS READ

- **Communication Arts**
- **Digital Output**
- **How**
- **MMWire**
- **Print**
- **Shift**
- **Wired**

A DAY IN THE LIFE

A digital artist makes art using the computer as his or her primary tool. This art can be intended for a CD-ROM, video game, or website; but almost as often, it is printed out and hung on a wall.

Individuals who crave stability, please note: Change in this field is constant. Whether you're an illustrator, graphic designer, animator, or game designer, the software you use is constantly evolving. Depending on the company they work for, digital artists may wear many different hats and contribute to five or six projects at one time. Most of their day is spent developing an interface for a project, drawing pictures, assembling the art, and making buttons for users to click on. "The work atmosphere is like a big clubhouse, and we can easily be there until midnight or two in the morning, particularly when working on a deadline. We easily can put in a 12-hour day, and 10-hour days are the average. That's because we're in the hot seat and clients want things yesterday," says one artist at a startup company.

{ change is constant }

PAYING YOUR DUES

A general art education is a good first step, especially for networking, as so much of this industry involves working with creative people in other fields. While a job with a print magazine was once the best way to break into commercial art, the Internet now allows young artists to land jobs as a junior/assistant designer, website designer, art director, illustrator, animator, or game designer. Today there aren't any steadfast rules or traditional channels to paying your dues. You may be relegated to the toilet paper account as a junior art director at an ad agency, but if you're stuck in the same role at an interactive agency, you can make the toilet paper talk, dance, and sing. You're not going to be making complicated video games in the beginning. There is much to learn about how to manipulate the software; it takes time to be able to grasp the intricacies of its usability and understand a language that's not totally developed.

If you can say that you are not only an illustrator and graphic designer, but also know typography, understand color and page layout, and know how to optimize graphics for use on the Web, you will be an extremely valuable commodity. Right now, the demand for creative talent is immense, largely because the Internet is comprised of a world of technicians and engineers, and the people who start companies and develop software generally don't have an understanding of how to create art.

Because every project involves teamwork, communication is as important as artistic skills. In Web companies where technology often breaks inexplicably (particularly around a deadline), being calm, practical, and logical is an asset. While creativity and imagination are the most important attributes, understanding what makes things work and an analytical ability to think like a programmer is often very helpful. In the Internet arena, an artist's unbridled creativity should be balanced with logic and analytical skills.

ASSOCIATED CAREERS

A talented artist is infinitely marketable; he or she can work in virtually any field. An illustrator may work on storyboards for movies or music videos, for example; an animator could move from the Internet into film. While a graphic designer can't jump to industrial design without further training, one could make the transition to packaging design. In school, you generally choose a particular field of design, and unique training is provided for each field. In graphic design, on which Web design is based, you could also make the leap to book or advertising design.

PAST AND FUTURE

Commercial art began with the advent of modern advertising, and graphic design and typography were the world's original interfaces; it is from these interfaces that all modern forms of graphical information are delivered. Internet art has already evolved from having entertainment value to commercial value as an integral part of demonstrating and selling products. "The people in this industry are taking part in creating a language just like filmmakers did in the 1920s. In the future, the Internet will be regarded as an 'age' just like the industrial revolution," believes one digital artist.

How will the role of the artist evolve along with new technologies and forms of communication? Many people are trying to predict its future, but all we know is that change is constant, and it's proceeding so fast that keeping up is no longer even an option. You just have to ride the wave. Managing information, whether it is financial data or cartoons, is always going to be essential. However, the world will always need artists. Whether we watch television through virtual-reality glasses or ditch modern technology and go back to using paper to communicate, someone is still going to have to draw the pictures.

QUALITY OF LIFE

2 YEARS Starting salaries depend on how many programs you know and the extent of your experience. Knowledge of just the baseline illustrator programs will garner the lowest wage. Competition is toughest for animators and illustrators; 3-D artists are the most sought after.

5 YEARS On average, salary jumps about five dollars an hour for every two or three years of experience. The further away you move from making art and the closer you get to making software, the higher the pay—especially if you are adept at doing both. A brilliant artist and programmer could earn as much as $100 an hour.

10 YEARS Digital artists and their software have scarcely been around this long. Check back in a few years to see what the next Internet revolution brings.

MAJOR EMPLOYERS
Any Internet company or CD/CD-ROM manufacturer will probably have need for a digital artist.

MAJOR ASSOCIATIONS
ART SOFTWARE GROUP
E-mail: info@artsoftwaregroup.com
www.artsoftwaregroup.com

DISC JOCKEY

A DAY IN THE LIFE

Whether you're a disc jockey for a radio station or a nightclub, the best aspect of the job is the creativity that it allows (and even requires). Radio disc jockeys play music, chat, deliver news, weather, or sports, or hold conversations with celebrities or call-in listeners. Club DJs mix music, sound effects, and special effects and occasionally provide chatter between songs. Each DJ must be in command of his or her specialty genre of music or demographic of audience—and sensitive to listener responses.

A radio disc jockey must be able to spin off on an item in the news or a hot new song. "I think about how things connect," said one. Being extremely organized and synchronized is critical to the radio station. Songs must fill a certain span of time; commercials have to be aired during specific blocks. Disc jockeys must be able to coordinate what plays when within time and audience constraints while on the air. A radio DJ must build an audience. Most DJs specialize in a specific musical genre, have a consistent approach, and field calls and requests from interested listeners to develop a consistent, loyal listening public. Since only one person is usually on the air at a given time, the DJs get lonely. More than 75 percent of our surveys mentioned "isolation" as one of the biggest drawbacks.

{ **sensitive to listener responses** }

A club disc jockey keeps regular hours, usually working from 8:00 P.M. to 4:00 A.M. Most DJs don't socialize regularly with people who do not keep the same unusual hours. Isolation, again, creeps in. Club DJs must keep the crowd interested in dancing, so they must know a wide variety of styles and songs that appeal to different groups. Record promoters and agents try to flood high-profile DJs with new albums, hoping to provide exposure for their acts. More than 40 percent of all DJs work part-time and find it difficult to land regular, reasonably paying gigs. Many club DJs move to large urban centers to find a market that will support their services, but it's still difficult to get hired initially without a following that you can be expected to draw to the club.

PAYING YOUR DUES

No specific educational requirements exist to become a disc jockey, but most radio disc jockeys have experience at college radio stations or in small markets; others intern while in school to learn the equipment used in the industry and to get a taste of the style of successful radio personalities. Many aspiring disc jockeys create tapes of their shows and save clippings to use as introductions to professional radio stations. Radio jockeys must be familiar with current or specialty (subgenre) musical trends and how specific songs fit together. They must be able to fill empty space with information and have a clear, clean speaking voice and a certain amount of technical skill. A club or nightclub disc jockey must know how to mix beats so music progresses smoothly, how to design a night of music around a specific theme or requested type of music, and how to use lighting and special effects to best advantage. As first introductions, many DJs must work free at established clubs on off nights. Close contact with record promoters is important in getting unreleased demos or other songs that can distinguish you from other DJs. DJs trade on their reputation, so staying current with musical trends and responding to listener feedback is critical to success.

ASSOCIATED CAREERS

More than 60 percent of DJs rotate from one position within the radio industry to another, moving to news anchoring, call-in shows, specialty shows, and sports shows. Another 7 percent write copy for radio broadcasts, television broadcasts, and newspapers. Club disc jockeys move to careers in the record industry, primarily as liaisons between other DJs and the company itself.

PAST AND FUTURE

The first commercial radio station started in 1920 as station KDKA, broadcasting from Pittsburgh, Pennsylvania. During the "golden years" of radio (the 1940s), radio personalities were paid as much as movie stars and treated with the same celebrity. Club disc jockeys reached their apex in the mid-1970s/early-1980s, when disco was the craze and nightclubbing was de rigueur for those in social circuits.

Radio stations are finding it cheaper to buy nationally syndicated shows rather than produce their own, so opportunities for radio DJs could shrink in the coming decade. Successful club DJs will always have followings, but opportunities for success could be limited by an uncertain market for clubs.

QUALITY OF LIFE

2 YEARS Opportunities are difficult to come by. Aspiring DJs pursue auditions, running from club to club or radio station to radio station, actively self-promoting. They bring clippings, taped samples of their work, and recommendations to prospective employers. Many DJs take "test nights" at clubs, where return engagements are determined by the size and activity of the crowd that shows up that night. Radio DJs often take internships or menial jobs at radio stations to get themselves introduced to people who make decisions about on-air talent. The hours are long and often unrewarding.

5 YEARS If disc jockeys are making a living at their profession, they're doing well. The majority have regular stints at a number of clubs or functions or have earned at least secondary on-air responsibilities, and are very busy between promotion, work, and keeping current on musical trends. A number of disc jockeys have made connections in the record industry by this point and spend a significant amount of time scouting emerging bands for signs of talent.

10 YEARS DJs who have survived the club circuit for 10 years are on the back end of their careers because the life is rigorous, and it's rarely forever. The connections 10-year DJs have provide them with ample opportunity to enter the record industry, the promotion industry, or the club-managing scene. Radio disc jockeys who have lasted 10 years in the profession have solid followings, an established taste and attitude, and a regular stint on a local radio station. Individuals who wish for national syndication must make their shows unique, exciting, and creative. The hours increase for those pursuing fame; salaries may become significant between years 7 and 15.

MAJOR EMPLOYERS
HOT 97
395 Hudson Street, 7th Floor
New York, NY 10014
Tel: 212-229-9797
Fax: 212-929-8559
E-mail: hot97@hot97.com

WABC
Human Resources
77 West 66th Street, 13th Floor
New York, NY 10023
http://abc.go.com

WFUV
Fordham University
Bronx, NY 10458
Tel: 718-817-4550
Fax: 718-365-9815
www.wfuv.org

Z100
WHTZ
PO Box 7100
New York, NY 10150
Tel: 212-239-2300
Fax: 800-386-2329
E-mail: z100@clearchannel.com
www.z100.com

MAJOR ASSOCIATIONS
NATIONAL ASSOCIATION OF BROADCASTERS
1771 N Street, NW
Washington, DC 20036
Tel: 202-429-5300
Fax: 202-429-4199
www.nab.org

EDITOR

PROFESSIONAL PROFILE

# of people in profession	130,000
Avg. hours per week	40
Avg. starting salary	$30,770
Avg. salary after 5 years	$41,170
Avg. salary 10 to 15 years	$58,930

SALARY ●●
HOURS ●●
EDUCATION ●●

BOOKS, FILMS, AND TV SHOWS
FEATURING THE PROFESSION

- A Biography of Max Perkins
- Lou Grant
- The Novel
- The Paper

YOU'LL HAVE CONTACT WITH

- Page designers
- Promotion specialists
- Proofreaders
- Writers

PROFESSIONALS READ

- The Copy Editor
- Editor & Publisher
- Kirkus Reviews
- Publishers Weekly

A DAY IN THE LIFE

For people who love the written word and know they have the ability to plan, organize, and see printed material through its several stages of production, editing may be the ideal job. A critical link between authors and the reading public, editors control the quality and nature of printed material, working with authors on rewrites; correcting grammar; and smoothing out inconsistencies. Editors have significant input in the final product. They analyze work for quality of content, grammatical correctness, and stylistic consistency. This requires patience, thoroughness, and an ability to keep in mind both small details and the big picture simultaneously. Editors must be able to work closely with writers, diagnose problems, and offer advice on how to avoid them in the future. This requires a keen, analytical mind and a gentle touch.

{ critical link }

An editor meets frequently with others who are also working on a publication, including artists, typesetters, layout personnel, marketing directors, and production managers. In most areas of publishing, the success or failure of a product relies on continuous and open communication among different departments; a snag in any one may throw off the scheduling of another. As links between departments, editors must be able to handle personality issues diplomatically; be comfortable with the rigorous scheduling and economics of publishing; and coordinate and communicate their requirements clearly and effectively.

Editorial positions are available in many types of companies, from established publishing houses to online service companies. A magazine editor has a different schedule and handles matters distinct from those of an acquisitions editor or a newspaper editor. Interests, opportunities, and luck lead editors to an area of specialization. People who wish to progress in this field nearly always read manuscripts in their spare time or stay late to do extra work. Competence is rewarded, and lateral and upward mobility within large houses is common. More than 40 percent of our respondents registered discontent with their current jobs, but more than 80 percent recorded pleasure with the choice of career and lifestyle. The 15 percent a year who leave the profession do so because their expectations of immediate impact and recognition remain unmet by this competitive and underpaid occupation.

PAYING YOUR DUES

No specific academic degree is required, but most editors were English, communications, or journalism majors in college. A history of editorial positions on college newspapers or literary magazines is important. Most employers require potential editors to take word-processing and proofreading tests before hire, so it's a good idea to be familiar with standard word-processing programs and proofreading symbols. Familiarity with publishing software and graphics systems is extremely helpful. Some find it beneficial to take a six-week publishing seminar to enhance their resumes, but no employers require it. Because of the relative paucity of entry-level editorial positions, many people enter publishing firms, magazines, and newspapers in advertising, marketing, or promotion departments, and parlay these jobs into editorial positions.

ASSOCIATED CAREERS

Individuals who leave editing usually do so because of the lack of mobility and low pay. Editors can apply their skills in business, human resources, and governmental administrative careers. Others go into noneditorial aspects of publishing, such as subsidiary rights or production.

PAST AND FUTURE

With Johannes Gutenberg's invention of the printing press in the fifteenth century, publishing became an industry. Authors would work with printers and sell their work to booksellers, who soon realized that they needed someone in between to assure the quality of the product.

Technology has affected and will continue to affect the field of publishing. More written work is produced each day in the United States than was produced in the world before 1700. Since technological advancement and a lowering of fixed publishing costs now make it easier for smaller houses, magazines, and newsletters to produce quality products, the future of publishing may lie in smaller houses, in which a variety of skills is required by each editor, including those in layout and graphics. The reduction of fixed costs, however, may also mean that larger, well-funded houses that can attract established authors will be in a better position to drive smaller, less organized companies out of existence. Material online will continue to need editing, as well. The position of editor should remain, but the auxiliary skills needed will change.

QUALITY OF LIFE

2 YEARS Expect to work hard and earn little as an editorial assistant or assistant editor. Starting positions include some menial tasks, proofreading, correspondence, assisting senior editors, and photocopying. More than 60 percent of our respondents mentioned that they worked late, worked on weekends, or took work home with them. Many new editors have responsibility for small, easily managed projects to learn the ropes. While new editors sometimes work directly with authors, contact is limited and the responsibility level is low. People are constantly networking to find positions with greater responsibility and better remuneration.

5 YEARS Often a full-blown editor by now, the five-year veteran starts to gravitate to a specialty. Skills have improved both technically and interpersonally, and responsibilities have increased. Earnings have gone up to the point of self-sufficiency (you can go out to dinner occasionally). On average, a five-year editor has held at least two jobs—a significant turnover rate.

10 YEARS At the 10-year mark, an editor has significant editing experience, has been through every major snafu possible, and has a steady stream of responsibilities. Individuals with strong managerial and organizational skills become publishers. A notable few begin their own magazines or imprints. Most editors remain editors for as long as their stomachs and hearts hold out. Most of the lure of editing comes from a love of good writing; that sensibility supports most editors for a long time.

MAJOR EMPLOYERS

CONDÉ NAST PUBLICATIONS
4 Times Square, 17th Floor
New York, NY 10036
Tel: 212-286-3700
Fax: 212-286-5960
www.condenast.com
Contact: Human Resources

RANDOM HOUSE, INC.
1745 Broadway
New York, NY 10019
Tel: 212-782-9000
E-mail: humanresources@randomhouse.com
www.randomhouse.com

MAJOR ASSOCIATIONS

MAGAZINE PUBLISHERS OF AMERICA
810 Seventh Avenue, 24th Floor
New York, NY 10019
Tel: 212-872-3700
E-mail: mpa@magazine.org
www.asme.magazine.org

NATIONAL CONFERENCE OF EDITORIAL WRITERS
3899 North Front Street
Harrisburg, PA 17110
Tel: 717-703-3015
Fax: 717-703-3014
E-mail: ncew@pa-news.org
www.ncew.org

FASHION DESIGNER

SALARY ● ●

HOURS ● ● ●

EDUCATION ● ●

BOOKS, FILMS, AND TV SHOWS
FEATURING THE PROFESSION
- **The Catwalk**
- **Prêt à Porter**
- **Project Runway**
- **Unzipped**

YOU'LL HAVE CONTACT WITH
- **Advertising executives**
- **Models**
- **Production managers**
- **Publicists**
- **Textile manufacturers**

PROFESSIONALS READ
- **Fashion Daily**
- **Vogue**
- **Women's Wear Daily**

A DAY IN THE LIFE

Ever wonder what Giorgio Armani, Betsey Johnson, Donna Karan, and Ralph Lauren do all the time? Work! Few other professions depend so much on keeping on top of fickle popular opinion and watching what competitors produce. The life of a designer is intimately linked to tastes and sensibilities that change at a moment's notice, and he or she must be able to capitalize on or—even better—influence those opinions. Designers reflect society's sensibilities through clothing design. "You have to know just about everything that's been done before so that you can recognize it when it becomes popular again," wrote one respondent. Fashion designers are involved in every phase of designing, showing, and producing all types of clothing, from bathing suits to evening gowns. Those with talent, vision, determination, and ambition can succeed in this difficult, demanding, and highly competitive industry.

{ glamorous }

Fashion design can be more glamorous than a 1940s Hollywood musical or drearier than a bank statement, but it's always taxing. A designer's day includes reading current fashion magazines, newspapers, and other media that reflect current trends and tastes. He or she looks at materials, attends fashion shows, and works with other designers on projects. A designer should be able to communicate his or her philosophy, vision, and capabilities clearly and comprehensively through sketches, discussions, and, occasionally, samples. No matter what his or her personal style is, a designer must produce a creative, exciting, and profitable product line.

As in most professions that produce superstars, it is easy for a competent but otherwise unremarkable designer to wallow in obscurity, designing small pieces of collections, generic lines (the plain white boxer short, for example), or specialties (cuffs, ruffles, etc.). The personality that raises itself above this level must be as large as the vision of the designer; perhaps that's why the word "crazy" showed up in more than 75 percent of our surveys as a plus in fashion design.

PAYING YOUR DUES

People entering the field should have a good eye for color, style, and shape, an ability to sketch, and some formal preparation in design. An excellent portfolio is a must for the job search. A two- or four-year degree in fashion design is helpful, as is knowledge of textiles and a familiarity with the quirks of a variety of fabrics, but no formal certification is required. Candidates should have a working knowledge of business and marketing. The hours are long for a fashion designer, and the initial pay is very limited. This is one of those hit-or-miss occupations where beginners work as someone's assistant until, when they can muster up enough confidence in their abilities and sell that confidence to their superiors, they design a few pieces themselves. The superstar rise is an unlikely event, but it happens. Based on the number of "international star designers" in the last 10 years and the number of people who have entered the profession, the estimated odds of becoming an internationally famous designer are roughly 160,000:1.

ASSOCIATED CAREERS

Fashion designers who become unhappy with the lifestyle (low pay, long hours, hard work, low chance of advancement) leave the field to do a variety of things. Some of them use their color and design skills to become interior designers, graphic designers, or fashion consultants. More than one quarter of the people who leave remain in the clothing industry, either on the production end or on the institutional buying end. Another 10 percent of them enter the advertising or promotions industry.

PAST AND FUTURE

With the invention of the sewing machine by Elias Howe in 1846, cheap reproducible garments became available to the public. Individuals could rapidly design and commission their own wardrobes. Fashion opened up to the public. At its highest levels, called "couture," fashion is available only to the wealthy—couture dresses and gowns can sell for more than $20,000 each. But the concept of fashion, applied to the world at large, has become a democratic principle.

As the fashion market expands, some predictors hold that pockets of smaller, more unique brands of clothing will be marketed over television, the Internet, and the mail. The ability to reach large numbers of people for little cost will determine if this future is real or merely a pipe dream dangled in front of young, aspiring fashion designers.

QUALITY OF LIFE

2 YEARS Surprisingly few people (less than 8 percent) leave the profession in these rough early years, perhaps because they are prepared for the rigorous, unremunerative entry-level jobs. The hours are long, and the duties are ill defined; one day the duties may include tracking down magazine articles on the resurgence of 1970s style, and on another day, duties may include finding the phone numbers of five dance clubs and finding out which night is most popular with the 19–27-year-old crowd. Connections and networking are important during these early years; most designers learn as much about the business as they can. Some of them take part-time jobs in other fields to pay the rent.

5 YEARS Frustration with the slow pace of progression, a leveling of responsibilities for people who have failed to rise, and increased competition for the few available jobs are cited as the main reasons for a massive professional exodus; nearly 50 percent leave the profession at this point. Individuals who remain are actually designing partial lines and simple pieces. Designers gain valuable experience around this time working with production and advertising people.

10 YEARS As competent and proven "senior designers," 10-year veterans have specialized areas of responsibility. One may be in charge of shepherding all designs through the production process. Another may be in charge of scheduling lines based on season and available fabrics. A third may be in charge of overseeing the young designers and their partial lines, scouting for talent. They become both producers and educators, as newer designers look to them for advice and guidance. Wages are solid, the hours are long but manageable, and connections are extensive. The constant challenge 10-year designers face is in reinventing themselves and proving themselves relevant in the fast-changing world of fashion design.

MAJOR EMPLOYERS
DONNA KARAN
240 West 40th Street
New York, NY 10018
Tel: 212-789-1500
Fax: 212-921-3526
Contact: Human Resources

GIORGIO ARMANI
114 Fifth Avenue, 17th Floor
New York, NY 10011
Tel: 212-366-9720
Fax: 212-366-9668
www.giorgioarmani.com

LIZ CLAIBORNE
1441 Broadway
New York, NY 10018
Tel: 212-221-1927
Fax: 212-626-1800

MAJOR ASSOCIATIONS
FASHION GROUP INTERNATIONAL, INC.
8 West 40th Street, 7th Floor
New York, NY 10018
Tel: 212-302-5511
Fax: 212-302-5533
E-mail: info@fgi.org
www.fgi.org

FILM DIRECTOR

SALARY ● ●
HOURS ● ● ●
EDUCATION ● ●

BOOKS, FILMS, AND TV SHOWS
FEATURING THE PROFESSION
- Bowfinger
- Day for Night
- The Final Cut
- Heart of Darkness
- Hollywood Ending
- The Player

YOU'LL HAVE CONTACT WITH
- Actors
- Cinematographers
- Film editors
- Producers

PROFESSIONALS READ
- Hollywood Reporter
- Movieline
- On Location
- Variety

A DAY IN THE LIFE

"What I really want to do is direct." If this applies to you, read on. Directors turn a script into a movie; they are responsible for the quality of the final product and its success. In most cases, directors work on films far longer than any actor, technician, or editor, from the first day of brainstorming to the final release; it is no wonder that directing is physically, mentally, and emotionally draining. Directors work with actors; makeup artists; cinematographers; writers; and film, sound, and lighting technicians. They determine all the particulars of how scenes are to be shot, from visual requirements to the placement of the actors and the appropriateness of the script.

Directors cast actors who can bring their vision to the screen. Sound judgment and an { integrate and cut scenes } open mind are important during these initial phases. A director guides actors to a greater understanding of their characters' motivations and encourages them to perform at a high level—sometimes by gently cajoling and sometimes by yelling—anything to get the job done. A director's unique vision of the final product and ability to communicate that vision effectively and immediately are critical. After the film has been shot, editorial skills are important. Directors must have a good feel for pacing and structure and must know how to integrate and cut scenes so they work effectively.

Issues of finance are important in this industry—making films is expensive. First-time directors find it difficult to get work with any large-budget house, so many of them start with small-budget directing, using existing sites and sets creatively, convincing technical assistants to work for little (or more often, convincing friends to work free), and using editing and cutting rooms during off hours to save money. One director surveyed funded his first film entirely on his credit cards.

PAYING YOUR DUES

Nearly all film directors are film school graduates. Film school students must complete their own short films by graduation; you should be prepared to work under difficult conditions, share space, and convince actors to work for little or no money. Aspiring film directors prove themselves by directing stage productions, doing film lighting design, or establishing a history of assistant or associate directorships. This last route is the most common, as professional experience and networking contacts can be combined in a brief but intense period of time. There is no specific ladder to climb. Many aspiring directors develop clips of their work as a display of their talent when applying for industrial, television, or commercial directing jobs, which pay well and serve as working credentials. Individuals entering this career should be warned that 20-hour days are not unusual.

ASSOCIATED CAREERS

For the most part, directors who leave enter another area of the entertainment industry. A number of them use their financing experience to move into the producing end of film development. Others move into script development or teaching. Some directors become critics, reviewers, or reporters for film-related magazines. Still others become movie or television writers. A few become actors. People who go into business enter a wide variety of fields including costume supply, lighting rentals, casting agencies, site location, and acting schools.

PAST AND FUTURE

Film directors sprang into being with the birth of the industry in the early 1900s. Some important directors who have brought their visions to light include D. W. Griffith (*Birth of a Nation*), Orson Welles (*Citizen Kane*), Alfred Hitchcock (*Rope*), and Martin Scorsese (*Raging Bull*).

Directing will either become larger and more megalithic as a profession, as suggested by the consolidation of major film companies. Alternatively, it may lean toward small and independent projects, as the popularity of such independent film festivals as Sundance heralds. In the first event, directing possibilities will be limited and difficult—extremely difficult—to obtain. In the second event, directing positions will be more available but much less remunerative. In either case, the road to becoming a director is long, and the odds are slim, but the rewards for individuals who succeed are great.

QUALITY OF LIFE

2 YEARS Hopeful directors start out doing production work and learning how to piece a film together. Academic lessons from film school are supplemented with practical experience in the different facets of making a movie, from choosing locations and getting proper permits to budgeting, scheduling, and arranging transportation. These early years are marked by low responsibility, long hours, little pay, and an enormous amount of learning.

5 YEARS Five years into the profession, young directors have had a chance to produce at least a short film to enter in competitions or to use as an audition reel. Areas of strengths and weaknesses have been identified; individuals willing to pay the hard wages of growing as filmmakers will work on their weaknesses. They may become subdirectors with discrete areas of authority. Opportunities exist for directors who have made strong networking connections and have distinguished themselves through good work and aggressive self-promotion. People who are less vocal about their accomplishments either remain in assistant positions or leave the profession altogether. As a matter of fact, even directors who have good reputations begin to leave the profession due to the long hours and competing offers in specialty industries for much more certain pay.

10 YEARS A mere 35 percent who began with the intention of becoming a director are still around, and many of them leave the field over the next five years. Directors who remain have significant opportunities available to them, if they have managed to refine their craft, communicate their vision clearly, match up a script with a production company, and land the job of directing it. If it seems like the success stories at the 10-year mark are qualified by a number of ifs, that's because they are. The success rate in this field is abysmal. But individuals who manage to fight their way to the top reap financial and emotional rewards.

MAJOR EMPLOYERS

THE DISNEY CORPORATION
500 South Buena Vista Street
Burbank, CA 91521-3020
Tel: 818-558-2868
Fax: 818-556-6969
http://disney.go.com
Contact: Artist Recruitment

PARAMOUNT PICTURES
5555 Melrose Avenue
Los Angeles, CA 90038
www.paramountpictures.com

SONY PICTURES ENTERTAINMENT
10202 West Washington Boulevard
Culver City, CA 90232-3195
www.sonypictures.com
Contact: Human Resources

WARNER BROTHERS
4000 Warner Boulevard
Burbank, CA 91522
Tel: 818-954-6000
www.warnerbros.com

MAJOR ASSOCIATIONS

AMERICAN FILM INSTITUTE
2021 North Western Avenue
Los Angeles, CA 90027-1657
Tel: 323-856-7600 X870
Fax: 323-467-4578
www.afionline.org

ASSOCIATION OF INDEPENDENT VIDEO & FILMMAKERS
304 Hudson Street, 6th Floor
New York, NY 10013
Tel: 212-807-1400
Fax: 212-463-8519
www.aivf.org

DIRECTORS GUILD OF AMERICA
Los Angeles Headquarters:
7920 Sunset Boulevard
Los Angeles, CA 90046

New York Headquarters:
110 West 57th Street
New York, NY 10019

MOTION PICTURE ASSOCIATION OF AMERICA
15503 Ventura Boulevard
Encino, CA 91436
Tel: 818-995-6600
www.mpaa.org

TRIBECA FILM INSTITUTE
375 Greenwich Street
New York, NY 10013
Tel: 212-941-2000
www.tribecafilminstitute.org

FILM EDITOR

A DAY IN THE LIFE

Film editors assemble footage of feature films, television shows, documentaries, and industrials into a seamless end product. They manipulate plot, score, sound, and graphics to refine the overall story into a continuous and enjoyable whole. On some films, the film editor is chosen before cast members and script doctors; people in Hollywood recognize that the skills of a good film editor can save a middling film. In the same way directors use certain actors they appreciate over and over again, they also use film editors they know and are comfortable with. Martin Scorcese, Spike Lee, and Robert Wise are a few of the directors who work with the same editors over and over again. Such relationships lend stability to a film editor's life; otherwise, they must be prepared to submit video resume after video resume, in the struggle to get work. Editors can express themselves through their unique styles; Spike Lee's editor, for example, is well-known for his editing style.

{ dawn/dusk }

The hours are long, and the few editors who had the time to write comments to us tended to abbreviate their thoughts. "Dawn/Dusk. Rush jobs. After test audiences, do it again. Lots of frustration. Lots of control, though," wrote one. Just as directors do, film editors spend a long time perfecting and honing their craft. Like most industries, the film industry has embraced new technology. Assistant editors must now have strong computer skills to work in the industry.

While some editors stay removed from the project during the filming process so as not to steer the director away from his or her concept of the film, many of them do visit the director on set while production is under way. Nevertheless, the majority of a film editor's work is done alone. Despite that solitude, interpersonal skills are just as important as endurance is in an editor's career. Film editors work closely with sound editors and musical directors as the film nears completion. Long hours and significant isolation while actually editing can make even the most positive-minded film editor question the career choice. But an interesting, well-edited film can restore faith in the profession.

PAYING YOUR DUES

Film editors need extensive academic and professional experience. Standard coursework should include filmographies, basic editing, and commercial editing. Some aspiring editors may take directorial courses and direct plays or films; this training typically proves helpful in the working world. It costs a lot to borrow film-editing equipment from the university and graduate school film departments that have it. Most aspiring film editors work as interns, production assistants, or animation-editing assistants while in graduate school. Once out of school, editors usually work in the production field or for an established film editor for little money. People who want to pay their dues and become independent, self-supporting film editors take note: 4–10 years of on-the-job training before making enough connections, building up a significant body of work, and being able to start your own editing service is more than common. For the most part, it's the only way to succeed in this profession.

ASSOCIATED CAREERS

Film editors sometimes become directors and sound editors, but more often, the switch occurs the other way around. Individuals who leave film editing often go into video promotion and sales, film-equipment sales, and editing-equipment sales and development. A few editors enter animation companies, in which there is less footage. In this case the film editor's mission is to ensure that every single piece fits together and that everything "flows" as it should.

PAST AND FUTURE

In 1980, the average feature film had one film editor assigned to it, and that person, for all intents and purposes, exerted as much influence over the final product as the director of the film did. Now, with the increasing complexity of film editing, graphic overlays, computer animation sequences, and rising budgets, an average of nine editors are attached to each feature film.

Editors will continue to enjoy strong demand for qualified professionals who produce quality work. Editors who have ability and a willingness to work with others will be rewarded with good jobs. While there are editing jobs to be found among the communications and entertainment industries throughout the country, most career opportunities for editors will continue to be found in Los Angeles and New York.

QUALITY OF LIFE

2 YEARS Beginning film editors are expected to bring some proficiency in computer editing tools to the trade even as they get their first on-site training in the technical skills of editing, cutting, splicing, and seamlessly integrating different scenes. Long hours and low pay are mitigated by a rapid learning curve. Beginners gain valuable experience by working with sound and music editors. This collaboration is a must for editors who wish to continue in the profession. What little responsibility you do get is important; individuals who don't demonstrate maturity and quickness are encouraged to leave the profession.

5 YEARS Five-year veterans have gained more responsibilities, a network of contacts, and enough editing experience to begin a solo career, join an existing editing company as a partner, or go under contract for a large production house. By now, editors specialize in commercial, industrial, or software/Internet work, or in drama, comedy, or thriller genres. For editors to be successful, forming close relationships with directors and producers is significant. Pay, responsibilities, and hours increase.

10 YEARS A film editor now has a solid reputation, a healthy paycheck, and reasonable hours. Most work as independent contractors, editing films and video releases of films. Some editors act as consultants to other editors. Contact with other editors becomes important at this stage, and duties become more expansive in general.

MAJOR EMPLOYERS
THE DISNEY CORPORATION
500 South Buena Vista Street
Burbank, CA 91521-3020
Tel: 818-558-2868
Fax: 818-556-6969
www.disney.go.com
Contact: Artist Recruitment

PARAMOUNT PICTURES
5555 Melrose Avenue
Los Angeles, CA 90038
www,paramountpictures.com

SONY PICTURES ENTERTAINMENT
10202 West Washington Boulevard, Suite 3900
Culver City, CA 90232-3195
www.sonypictures.com
Contact: Human Resources

WARNER BROTHERS
4000 Warner Boulevard
Burbank, CA 91522
Tel: 818-954-6000
www.warnerbros.com
Contact: Human Resources

MAJOR ASSOCIATIONS
AMERICAN CINEMA EDITORS
100 Universal City Plaza
Building 2352, Room 202
Universal City, CA 91608
Tel: 818-777-2900
Fax: 818-733-5023
www.ace-filmeditors.org

ASSOCIATION OF INDEPENDENT VIDEO & FILMMAKERS
304 Hudson Street, 6th Floor
New York, NY 10013
Tel: 212-807-1400
Fax: 212-463-8519
www.aivf.org

FLORIST

PROFESSIONAL PROFILE

# of people in profession	104,000
Avg. hours per week	40
Avg. starting salary	$13,440
Avg. salary 5 years	$19,480
Avg. salary 10 to 15 years	$23,560

SALARY ●

HOURS ●

EDUCATION ●

BOOKS, FILMS, AND TV SHOWS
FEATURING THE PROFESSION
- **Bed of Roses**
- **Three's Company**

YOU'LL HAVE CONTACT WITH
- **General public**
- **Wedding designers**

PROFESSIONALS READ
- **Floral Management**
- **Florist**
- **Florists' Review**

A DAY IN THE LIFE

Roses are red, violets are blue—if that's the extent of your knowledge of nature's green-ery, a job in the floral industry may not be for you. But if you know the difference between a petal and a pistil, if you have an eye for arrangement, and if you don't sneeze at the mere men-tion of magnolias, then FTD wants you. The role of the florist is one of creating a more pleas-ant, beautiful place to live. Think about it. Almost every occasion provides an excuse to fill the room with flowers; these include births, weddings, anniversaries, graduations, holidays, bon voyages, even Thursdays. Parade floats, pageant winners, and Derby horses are draped in flow-ers. Flowers can also brighten sad times and help a person cope with an illness or loss. So who has the potential to bring { **Valentine's Day** } so much pleasure to the world? The florist. Most florists own their own shops or work in the floral department of grocery stores. Florists don't just arrange flowers. Presentation is only half of a florist's job. That said, to cultivate a regular client base, florists must be able to arrange skillfully and beautifully dried, artificial, and live flowers into bouquets or arrangements that suit the tastes and needs of their clients and occasions. They also have to know how to grow, cut, and clean a flower. Florists in smaller operations may also need to grow or purchase flowers, do the bookkeeping for the shop, and make deliveries. Being a florist is not always a bed of roses, though. The week of Valentine's Day is probably the most stressful time in the life of a florist (and potentially the most profitable). It's like the post office during Christmas. Large weddings (the month of June, in particular) can also be stressful for some florists. Florists don't rake in the cash as a rule. Most are in the business because they love their work; they love flowers and plants; and they love knowing that they've added a little color to someone's life.

PAYING YOUR DUES

Some community schools offer classes in floral design, but if you really want to be a florist, you need the heart and hands-on experience. Most florists start off as apprentices in a flower shop. After years of learning the trade, some move on to open their own shops. The American Institute of Floral Designers offers aspiring florists the chance to be "Accredited in Floral Design." Prospective members must send in pictures of their arrangements and then do a live showing in front of AIFD judges. The AIFD also offers grants for student research in the area of floral design. AIFD accreditation gives you a higher standing in the world of floriculture.

ASSOCIATED CAREERS

Florists are typically small-business owners. Jobs that require similar skills include party and wedding designers, gardeners, landscapers, parade consultants, and corporate advisors.

PAST AND FUTURE

Although humans have cultivated flowers throughout history, the modern florist has been around for only a few hundred years. In 1910, a handful of American retail florists founded the Florists' Telegraph Delivery. Today FTD is the largest floral company in the world. It connects more than 20,000 florists in North America and 50,000 florists in 154 other countries. The floral industry is a multibillion-dollar industry that is expected to continue to grow. As long as there are happy occasions or a need to make amends, there will be an industry for florists.

QUALITY OF LIFE

2 YEARS A beginning florist can hold any position, from a floral delivery person to a grower who sells roses by the side of the road. The first few years of a floral arranger's career are filled with learning which flowers go with which other flowers and assorted greenery. Beginning-level florists usually work under the tutelage of a more experienced florist during this time.

5 YEARS At this point, most florists have their own shops or manage the floral departments of grocery stores. Along with delivering flowers around town for birthdays and holidays, these florists have built a reputation as excellent sources of flower arrangements for local weddings and parties.

10 YEARS An established florist may want to expand his or her business by adding stores. Some florists with 10 years experience can be called on to arrange the flowers of large-scale, high-profile weddings, parties, and other special occasions.

MAJOR EMPLOYERS
FTD
3113 Woodcreek Drive
Downers Grove, FL 60515
Tel: 800-SEND-FTD
www.ftd.com

Most florists are either self-employed or work in the floral departments of larger stores. Contact local stores for employment opportunities.

MAJOR ASSOCIATIONS
THE SOCIETY OF AMERICAN FLORISTS
1601 Duke Street
Alexandria, VA 22134
Tel: 800-336-4743 or 703-836-8700
Fax: 703-836-8705
E-mail: memberinfo@safnow.org
www.safnow.org

FREELANCER

PROFESSIONAL PROFILE

# of people in profession	N/A
Avg. hours per week	N/A
Avg. starting salary	N/A
Avg. salary after 5 years	N/A
Avg. salary after 10 to 15 years	N/A

SALARY ● ● ●
HOURS ● ● ●
EDUCATION ● ● ●

YOU'LL HAVE CONTACT WITH

- Agents
- Art directors
- Directors
- Editors

A DAY IN THE LIFE

While it's true that freelancers come in all shapes, sizes, and specialties, there are a number of attributes that, for better or for worse, nearly all independent contractors share in common. First and foremost: freedom and flexibility. They're called independent contractors for a reason, and that independence shows itself in the freelancer's ability to determine which jobs to take and when to work on them. Sure, there are limits to both of these liberties. Depending on your field and whether it requires you to work outside the home, for instance, late nights may be out of the question—but even freelancers with fairly regular nine-to-five gigs have a lot more say in terms of what they work on and when they do their work than the conventional employee. This authority comes not only

$$\left\{ \begin{array}{l} \text{self-employed, independent} \\ \text{contractors} \end{array} \right\}$$

from the fact that for most intents and purposes, independent contractors are self-employed, but also because the services they provide, which are often artistic in nature, often require specific talents and background that most clients and their employees don't have. (That's why they come to you.)

The creative nature of many freelance positions renders good freelance gigs highly sought-after by people looking to devote time to the artistic aspirations that don't always pay for themselves. It's hard to write a novel when you can devote all of your time to it, and doing it when you've got a conventional job is nearly impossible. That's why most would-be novelists would jump at the opportunity to write freelance copy for, say, a travel guide, if it means they would be freeing up the time and energy so often sapped by the typical nine-to-five job. Of course, it's not all chocolate boxes and roses. The independence that looks so attractive carries with it a very real drawback when it comes to the topic of job security: namely, freelancing provides very little of it. If you're working for a single employer, then you probably rely on the basic belief that, as long as you do your job well, it will still be there for you in a week, a month, or a year; if you're salaried, your company may pay some or even all of your health insurance premiums; they'll pay you when you're on vacation and when you're ill. That's all very nice to have. Employers know that good employees are valuable. They pay to keep them happy. They pay to keep them around. Freelancers don't have the luxury of loyal employers. They have clients who, regardless of performance and loyalty, may only call on them for one job. Freelancers must therefore have a number of regular clients who can be relied on for repeat business. Still, even the most successful freelancers will have occasional lulls of little or no work, especially early in their careers.

PAYING YOUR DUES

Depending on the services that you plan to provide, freelancing doesn't necessarily require a specific educational background. This is not to say that pursuing a degree in the area in which you plan to freelance would not make things easier on you. Freelancers have to know their stuff—indeed, the whole point of being an independent contractor is that you possess skills uncommon for most of the population. A background including formal training and a certificate or bachelor's degree, especially for those working in creative or technical fields, is usually par for the course.

ASSOCIATED CAREERS

Since the potential fields in which freelancers work are so varied, pinning down a short list of associated careers is not possible for the career at large. Since most freelance opportunities are in creative fields, many people who find it too daunting a task to make their living as, say, artists or writers, may start out as freelancers until they reach a point of stability, and then ultimately move into their chosen vocation full-time.

PAST AND FUTURE

The term "freelance" finds its origin in medieval Europe and knights who would make their services—and their lance—available to those willing to pay a price. In a word, the original freelancers were mercenaries, but things have changed. An increasingly complex world has brought with it a growing number of on-demand talents and services that, while not necessarily excluding the occasional need for some hired muscle, don't typically require the use of a lance, mace, sword, or any other weapon of war.

Today, freelancers—or independent contractors—offer out their skills to bidders in virtually any field imaginable. Freelance opportunities may grow in number as companies downsize and seek to outsource specialized labor.

QUALITY OF LIFE

2 YEARS At this point in a freelancer's career, he or she may still be establishing a client base. Freelancers at the two-year mark typically still have to take on projects that may not be of particular interest to them so they can pay the bills, and they may experience relatively frequent lulls in workflow.

5 YEARS At the five-year mark, professional, full-time freelancers are likely to have established a steady client base. They probably worry less about money than they did at an earlier stage of their careers; and they probably enjoy their freedom more.

10 YEARS If, at the 10-year mark, you are still working as a freelancer, then you are probably picking and choosing the projects that you take on—and earning an attractive salary doing it. If you're not still working in the world of freelancing, then the skills that you gained during the early part of your career—about client management, money management, and time management—are probably serving you well in your new chosen field.

MAJOR EMPLOYERS

Freelancers are independent contractors who have clients at all levels of the private and public sectors.

MAJOR ASSOCIATIONS

THE EDITORIAL FREELANCERS ASSOCIATION
71 West 23rd Street, Suite 1910
New York, NY 10010-4181
Tel: 212-929-5400
Fax: 212-929-5439
E-mail: info@the-efa.org
www.the-efa.org

WORKING TODAY
45 Main Street, Suite 710
Brooklyn, NY 11201
Tel: 718-532-1515
Fax: 718-222-4440
E-mail: info@workingtoday.org
www.WorkingToday.org

GRAPHIC DESIGNER

A DAY IN THE LIFE

Graphic designers generate the visual presentation and design of goods, including websites, detergent boxes, album covers, and dog food cans. Their work is usually done on a project basis. Designers must be able to work under extreme time constraints and very defined financial and design limits to produce quality material. A graphic designer must be able to synthesize feedback from a number of different sources into a distinctive image; use research prepared by a marketing department and cost specifications determined by a budgeting department; and produce a variety of sketches and models that demonstrate different approaches to the product. This takes a person who can listen to comments and has a good eye for aesthetic design, a flair for color, and a solid understanding of the needs of the corporate world.

{ visual presentation }

"Graphic design isn't one job. It's 20," wrote one overworked designer. "Sales[person] skills are very important if you want to see your designs accepted," wrote another. Nearly all respondents listed communication skills as either second or third in importance for success in this profession. Over time, choosing a specialty is the name of the game, either in website design, product or packaging design, material use, or object arrangement.

When projects are under way, graphic designers can expect to work long hours brainstorming and meeting with executives to discuss ideas. The job is highly visible; successes and failures alike are recognized and are put on display. Individuals who are insecure about their skills or their ideas have a hard time accepting the amount of risk and rejection this career entails. A successful graphic designer has an enviable life, choosing clients and earning significant amounts of money. However, be warned: An artist's style may be very hot one season and turn into a parody the next. People who are unwilling or unable to change could find promising careers declining. Of the nearly 25,000 people who try to enter the field of graphic design each year, only about 60 percent last the first two years, and about 30 percent remain in the field at five years.

PAYING YOUR DUES

The majority of graphic designers have a four-year degree, usually in product design, art, or art history. Graphic designers must have talent and an understanding of the business world, including issues of finance and production, and should be familiar with computer software such as InDesign, Quark XPress, Photoshop, Adobe Illustrator, and other painting and graphic design tools. Graphic designers must be able to work in a variety of media and meet deadlines, sizing limits, and financial restrictions, especially those designers who wish to work as freelance graphic designers rather than in-house salaried designers. Basic pre-professional coursework should include design, drawing, computer artwork, and specific knowledge (for example, anatomy for medical graphics designers) relating to any area of specialization. Professionals must assemble a working portfolio to approach companies for work of any scale. For individuals who wish to pursue further study, more than 100 schools offer accredited graphic design programs, according to the National Association of Schools of Art and Design, and each addresses issues of the working life of the graphic designer along with issues of design.

ASSOCIATED CAREERS

Many artists turn to graphic design to make a living during their lean years and then return to art. A number of them become gallery owners and patrons and use the contacts they made as designers to help out new talent in need of remunerative work. The significant number of graphic artists who leave do so because of the scrambling lifestyle: the need to pursue work constantly and the requirement to act as a salesperson for their ideas. Others take in-house positions as design consultants and as magazine layout editors.

PAST AND FUTURE

Graphic design has been around since shopkeepers started hanging signs to advertise their wares. In the 1700s, artisans were approached by merchants eager to make their goods and services recognizable to a largely illiterate population.

Graphic design will become even more significant as computer technology becomes increasingly available and as more companies realize that a definitive, distinctive logo and product design can make an enormous difference in product sales. Job opportunities should increase during the next few years with even more openings seasonally for such projects as holiday window displays and specialty sales events. Currently, more than a third of all graphic designers are self-employed. This figure is expected to increase in the coming years.

QUALITY OF LIFE

2 YEARS Unproven graphic designers negotiate a difficult road as they try to assemble portfolios, bid competitively for small jobs, and build their reputations. Those designers with good connections have an easier time getting a foot in the door, but unfamiliarity with standard working conditions and standard practices still may make the beginning rocky. The hours can be long and unrewarding; be prepared to withstand significant rejection. Forty percent of all graphic designers leave the profession in the first two years.

5 YEARS The field evens out at the five-year mark; only individuals with proven records, solid connections, and strong references survive. Around a third of those designers who began in this career stay in it to this point, and around 10 percent remain independent freelance graphic designers. The majority of graphic designers become in-house consultants, designers, and producers. For the most part, designers are satisfied with their work, although the hours are long and salaries are average. Those who have shown good judgment sometimes choose other graphic designers to produce out-of-house work or recommend other designers for hire.

10 YEARS Ten-year veterans have established sound (and profitable) reputations; their designs remain fresh, and they should be able to find a number of fairly lucrative in-house graphic design positions. Many of them spend more time supervising design departments or "stables" of newer, less expensive designers. People who've started their own businesses begin to reap significant profits if their ventures are successful.

MAJOR EMPLOYERS
MICROSOFT CORPORATION
One Microsoft Way
Redmond, WA 98052-6399
Tel: 800-642-7676
Fax: 425-936-7329
www.microsoft.com

MTV NETWORKS
1515 Broadway
New York, NY 10036
Tel: 212-258-8000
www.mtvncareers.com
Contact: Human Resources

OGILVY & MATHER
309 West 49th Street
New York, NY 10019
Tel: 212-237-5627
www.ogilvy.com

MAJOR ASSOCIATIONS
SOCIETY OF ILLUSTRATORS
128 East 63rd Street
New York, NY 10021-7303
Tel: 212-838-2560
Fax: 212-838-2561
E-mail: info@societyillustrators.org
www.societyillustrators.org

THE AMERICAN INSTITUTE OF GRAPHIC ARTS
164 Fifth Avenue
New York, NY 10010
Tel: 212-807-1990
Fax: 212-807-1799
E-mail: commentscaiga.org
www.aiga.org

THE SOCIETY OF PUBLICATION DESIGNERS
17 East 47th Street, 6th Floor
New York, NY 10117
Tel: 212-223-3332
Fax: 212-223-5880
E-mail: mail@spd.org
www.spd.org

GUIDANCE COUNSELOR

A DAY IN THE LIFE

Few careers are as potentially rewarding—or as frustrating—as that of a guidance counselor, whose job it is to help guide and structure children's educational and vocational direction as they pass through an unstable and confusing time in their lives. It can be frustrating because you will have limited power to make students follow your advice, and often you will face students "who don't want to think about the day after tomorrow," as one counselor put it. A guidance counselor helps students determine courses of study and possible vocations. Counselors try to understand what motivates each student as well as his or her skills and desires. "When you're doing things right," wrote one, "it's like you're another parent, except they trust you a little more." Individuals who aspire to enter the field should be aware that emotional as well as intellectual demands come with the territory.

{ continuing education }

As most guidance counselors spend over a third of their time in consultations with students and parents, prospective counselors should be comfortable with teenagers and have excellent communication skills. Another 25 percent of a guidance counselor's day is spent administering and evaluating tests. Guidance counselors use the results to provide context for existing records of academic performance, teacher evaluations, and a better overall understanding of students' needs.

Some guidance counselors call the continuing education they receive from the students with whom they work the most interesting feature of the profession. "I learned more from them than from any class in college," wrote one enthusiastic counselor. "I learned more in the first day." Not all counselors are as positive as this, but the level of satisfaction guidance counselors recorded was one of the highest of any career in this book. Of course, people who don't love the profession usually leave quickly; guidance counselors have one of the highest initial attrition rates of any profession in this book—a staggering 60 percent within the first two years. Careers that require this degree of emotional commitment can be rough on those individuals who are not prepared to make one on a regular basis.

PAYING YOUR DUES

A bachelor's degree is required to become a high school guidance counselor, and some states require that the candidate have a master's degree, as well. To work in public schools, guidance counselors also typically need to be licensed. Coursework should include social studies, psychology, and communications work, with an emphasis on public speaking. Courses dealing with education are important, too; many private schools require that guidance counselors teach courses in addition to performing their counseling duties. A background in statistics and mathematics is important for evaluating students' standardized tests. By far the most important skill a potential guidance counselor can bring to this profession is the ability to relate to adolescents. This skill requires a combination of the ability to listen, honesty, an open mind, and a sense of humor. Individuals who succeed in this profession communicate well with students.

ASSOCIATED CAREERS

People become guidance counselors because they want to help students, and individuals who leave find many other ways to satisfy that desire: They return to school and become therapists, they head up substance-abuse programs, they run educational centers and programs, they become teachers without counseling duties, and they even become tutors. Some of them decide that they would like to continue helping people, but in a different age range, and they become professional career advisors, recruiters, and human resources personnel.

PAST AND FUTURE

Guidance counselors were first introduced in the United States in the Northeast in the early 1900s, but this profession didn't experience any significant growth until the end of World War II. Pushed by the Department of Education, school systems across the country soon "strongly encouraged" the position in every public and private school.

Guidance counselors face daunting tasks every day, but their roles at the center of youth education have never been more important. The job market for guidance counselors should be full of opportunity for the next 10 years or so, as enrollment is growing in United States school systems. The problem is that institutional support for guidance counselors is waning. Guidance counselors can be the first to face the consequences of budget cuts, since they are "noninstructional personnel."

QUALITY OF LIFE

2 YEARS These early years are the most trying years for guidance counselors. The full emotional impact of helping guide teenagers through difficult personal decisions and life-changing options presents itself to the new hire. Many counselors opt for different occupations after the first couple of years. Individuals who remain must learn to keep personal and professional decisions separate while maintaining warm relationships with students. This juggling act is difficult to manage, particularly in the first few years when older students are making critical decisions but have no context in which to trust in your ability to help them.

5 YEARS Individuals who've survived five years as guidance counselors face a much more stable work environment, from which less than 5 percent leave each year. Counselors learn to interpret standardized tests and improve their communication skills with students. Many of them become involved in conferences, lectures, and conventions where issues about vocational and academic counseling are discussed. The hours decrease and pay increases, but administrative duties may increase as well. Many schools like to see a continuous development of guidance-counseling programs, so creative thinking is a must.

10 YEARS Ten-year veterans, for the most part, have found positions where they are happy and satisfied. Pay levels off, and, unless they want to assume additional duties, guidance counselors can expect only cost-of-living salary adjustments. Guidance counselors continue in the same roles as before, but many of them exercise their seniority to initiate parent/teacher programs that provide a further safety net for troubled teens.

MAJOR EMPLOYERS
LOS ANGELES UNIFIED SCHOOL DISTRICTS
Board of Education
333 South Beaudry Avenue, 24th Floor
Los Angeles, CA 90017
Tel: 213-241-6389
Fax: 213-248-8953
www.lausd.k12.ca.us
Contact: Personnel Selection

NYC BOARD OF EDUCATION
Division of Human Resources
65 Court Street
Brooklyn, NY 11201
Tel: 718-935-2000
www.nycenet.edu

TEACH FOR AMERICA
315 West 36th Street, 6th Floor
New York, NY 10018
Tel: 212-279-2080 or 800-832-1230
Fax: 212-279-2081
www.teachforamerica.com
Contact: Admissions

TEXAS EDUCATION AGENCY
1701 North Congress Avenue
Austin, TX 78701
Tel: 512-463-9734
www.tea.state.tx.us
Contact: Human Resources

MAJOR ASSOCIATIONS
AMERICAN COLLEGE AND CAREER COUNSELING CENTER
2401 Pennsylvania Avenue
Philadelphia, PA 19130
Tel: 215-232-5225

AMERICAN SCHOOL COUNSELOR ASSOCIATION
1101 King Street, Suite 625
Alexandria, VA 22314
Tel: 703-2722 or 800-306-4722
Fax: 703-683-1619
www.schoolcounselor.org

HOSPICE NURSE

A DAY IN THE LIFE

Hospice nurses perform many traditional nursing duties such as observing, assessing, and recording symptoms, and they still work closely with physicians, administer medications, and provide emotional support. Hospice nurses have a particularly tough job because, from the outset, they know that the patient for whom they are caring is terminally ill. The medications that hospice nurses administer and the symptoms they record aren't intended to aid a patient in his or her recovery, but rather to make his or her remaining days as comfortable as possible. Most of the nurse's duties involve minimizing pain. Although being a nurse of any kind is very difficult, dealing every day with a dying person requires an exceptional temperament, one that embodies great caring, patience, and resolve.

> { embodies great caring, patience, and resolve }

Hospice care is what is known as comprehensive palliative medical care, i.e., treatment to reduce pain and other troubling symptoms as opposed to treatment to cure. The hospice doctrine states that terminally ill patients have the right to spend their last days in the comfort of their own homes, with their families, and hospice care provides professional medical care as well as supportive social, emotional, and spiritual services to accomplish this. The hospice nurse's duties fall somewhere in between all of these ideals, with emphasis on medical care. Because they essentially act as home-care nurses and spend several hours a day with their patients in their homes, they become emotional caretakers as well.

The majority of hospice patients have cancer, but others suffer from AIDS, Lou Gehrig's disease, heart or lung disease, and other fatal conditions. Patients can be any age, race, or creed, and it can be especially trying on hospice nurses to attend patients who are as young, or younger, than they are. Hospice nurses coordinate the care of every hospice patient through an advising physician, provide direct patient care, evaluate the patients' conditions, and serve as the liaison between families and physicians. A hospice nurse may also work with a patient's social worker, home-care aide (who may do housework and provide hygienic care to a patient who is incapable of bathing and caring for him- or herself), and physical, occupational, or speech therapist.

PAYING YOUR DUES

All hospice nurses must be registered nurses (RNs) in addition to being certified by a state health department as a hospice worker. The first step is obtaining a bachelor of science degree in nursing (BSN). Although RNs aren't required to have bachelor's degrees, many nursing career paths are only open to those with a bachelor's degree or even a master's degree. Nursing education includes classroom instruction and supervised training in hospitals, as well as courses in anatomy, physiology, microbiology, chemistry, nutrition, psychology, behavioral sciences, and, of course, nursing. On top of the recommended bachelor's degree, all states require prospective nurses to graduate from an accredited nursing school and successfully pass a national licensing examination. Then, to become a certified hospice nurse, you must have a current license as an RN and at least two years of full-time experience as an RN in a hospice-nursing practice, and you must pass the exam administered by the National Board for the Certification of Hospice Nurses.

ASSOCIATED CAREERS

Hospice nursing requires a unique assembly of traits and talents. Careers that are most likely to attract hospice nurses require medical knowledge and involve patient care, but tend not to deal with terminal cases and have higher salaries on average. Hospice nurses come into contact with many of these occupations during their work. Former hospice workers may pursue careers as occupational therapists, paramedics, physical therapists, and physician assistants.

PAST AND FUTURE

The first hospices were founded and operated by volunteers to help the ill with everyday tasks like shopping, babysitting, and carpooling, almost any aspect of a common family routine that may be impeded by illness. Hospice care has evolved into a nationwide network of health care professionals, volunteers, and social service professionals whose goal is to help the terminally ill live out their illnesses with dignity. Today, hospice care is a benefit of Medicare and is also covered by Medicaid. Private insurance companies, HMOs, and managed health care plans also offer hospice care among their benefits. Employment in home health care is expected to grow exponentially over the next several years, and opportunities will be best for nurses with high levels of education and advanced training.

QUALITY OF LIFE

2 YEARS For those registered nurses attaining certification as a hospice nurse, the first two years mean gaining the experience to become certified. As such, earnings won't be great. Many RNs will work additional nursing jobs, and hospice nursing can be a part-time occupation. The hours can be long, and the hazards of the job are plentiful. There are physical threats (nurses can throw their backs out moving patients); nurses can, and often do, become attached to their dying patients. Hospice nurses, however, are often of a superior strength who fervently believe that what they learn from their patients and can give back to them and their families far outweighs any emotional suffering they must endure.

5 YEARS At this point in a hospice nurse's career, he or she is certified and can expect to enjoy higher earnings. Responsibilities change little for a hospice nurse, however, and physicians still oversee patient care and expect nurses to carry out their orders to the letter.

10 YEARS At this point, the hospice nurse's salary has probably leveled off. Having experience, however, can lead to a higher-level administrative job within a hospice. For example, hospice nurses can become the executive directors of an agency, the directors of nursing or clinical services, or quality assurance managers. These positions will take a nurse out of the field, away from actually caring for patients, and place him or her in an office, where the nurse will make ethical, financial, and administrative decisions that focus on the patient in a different realm. Hospice nurses who choose to make such a move can increase their annual incomes to as much as $63,000.

MAJOR EMPLOYERS

ALL METRO HEALTH CARE
50 Broadway
Lynbrook, NY 11563
Tel: 516-887-1200
www.nyshcp.org/lichapter.shtml

UNITED STATES HOMECARE
253 West 35th Street
New York, NY 10001
Tel: 212-563-1979

HOME CARE ASSOCIATION OF NEW YORK STATE, INC.
194 Washington Avenue, Suite 400
Albany, NY 12210
Tel: 518-426-8764
Fax: 518-426-8788
E-mail: info@hcanys.org
www.hcanys.org

MAJOR ASSOCIATIONS

AMERICAN NURSES ASSOCIATION
8515 Georgia Avenue, Suite 400
Silver Springs, MD 20910
Tel: 800-274-4262 or 301-628-5000
Fax: 301-628-5001
www.nursingworld.org

HOSPICE ASSOCIATION OF AMERICA
228 7th Street, SE
Washington, DC 20003
Tel: 202-546-4759
Fax: 202-547-9559
www.hospice-america.org

NATIONAL HOSPICE AND PALLIATIVE CARE ORGANIZATION
1700 Diagonal Rod, Suite 625
Alexandria, VA 22314
Tel: 703-837-1500
Fax: 703-837-1233
www.nhpco.org

HUMAN RESOURCES MANAGER

BOOKS, FILMS, AND TV SHOWS
FEATURING THE PROFESSION

- Dave
- The Drew Carey Show
- Matching Pairs
- The Value Survey

YOU'LL HAVE CONTACT WITH

- Attorneys
- Benefits administrators
- Office managers
- Recruiters

PROFESSIONALS READ

- Crimson and Brown Reports
- HR Magazine
- Human Resource Development Quarterly
- Training and Development Journal

A DAY IN THE LIFE

Human resources managers handle personnel decisions, including hiring, position assignment, training, benefits, and compensation. Their decisions are subject to some oversight, but company executives recognize their experience and skill in assessing personnel and rely heavily on their recommendations. Although physical resources—capital, building, equipment—are important, most companies realize that the quality and quantity of their output is directly related to the quality and commitment of their personnel. Human resources professionals make sure that appropriate matches are made between support staff and producers, between assistants and managers, and between coworkers to enhance productivity, support the company's business strategy and long-term goals, and provide a satisfying work experience for employees.

{ handling the dirty work }

A human resources professional in a smaller firm is a jack-of-all-trades who is involved in hiring, resource allocation, compensation, benefits, and compliance with laws and regulations affecting employees and the workplace and safety and health issues. This multiplicity of tasks requires individuals with strong organizational skills who can quickly shift from project to project and topic to topic without becoming overwhelmed. "You're the last line of defense between your company and confusion," wrote one human resources manager at a small firm, "and sometimes confusion wins." Strong interpersonal skills are crucial for managers at small firms. These managers spend much of their day handling questions, attending budgeting and strategic planning meetings, and interviewing prospective employees. The rest of the time, they take care of paperwork and talk on the telephone with service providers (insurance, health care, bank officers, etc.). At larger firms, human resources managers often specialize in one area, such as compensation, hiring, or resources allocation. Compensation analysts work with department managers to determine pay scales and bonus structures. Hiring specialists (also known as recruiters) place ads in appropriate publications, review resumes, and interview candidates for employment. Allocation managers match assistants, support staff, and other employees with departments that have specific needs. Sensitivity to both personality issues and corporate efficiency are a plus for allocation managers.

The most difficult feature of the human resources professional's job is handling the dirty work involved in the staffing of a company: dealing with understaffing, refereeing disputes between two mismatched personalities, firing employees, informing employees of small (or nonexistent) bonuses, maintaining an ethical culture, and reprimanding irresponsible employees. Performing these tasks can be disheartening for human resources managers who are supposed to support and assist employees, and many human resources managers feel that employees dislike or fear them because of this role.

PAYING YOUR DUES

Academic requirements for a career in human resources vary, but most employers prefer that each candidate have a bachelor's degree. Undergraduates should pursue a balanced curriculum that includes behavioral sciences, English, economics, general business, business and labor law, accounting, and statistics. Master's degrees in human resource management, industrial relations, organizational development, organizational behavior, and business administration are also considered worthwhile. Each company has its own internal protocols, and most new hires are trained in them when they begin. A human resources manager must have strong interpersonal skills, and many employers conduct multiple interviews that test a candidate's ability to relate to a diverse group of people.

ASSOCIATED CAREERS

Many human resources professionals feel that they must focus too much on the financial aspects of their duties to allow them to provide the assistance they want to give. Individuals who leave the profession often go into career counseling, industrial psychology, guidance counseling, and labor relations. Individuals who prefer the financial side of being a human resources manager go into budgeting, inventory control, and quality control management.

PAST AND FUTURE

The transition of the American economy from an agricultural society to an industrial society created the need for talented, creative workers and a need to manage these resources. Growing companies wanted to have more control over hiring, salary structure, and resource allocation.

The future is bright for human resources managers in both small and large firms. Managing a labor force entails an understanding of a number of complicated issues, and many companies have discovered that specialists handle the job more competently than do company managers. In addition, many companies are subdividing their human resources departments into smaller, specialized units, dealing with compensation analysis, benefits administration, or recruiting. Human resources positions are expected to increase more quickly than jobs in the general market.

QUALITY OF LIFE

2 YEARS Responsibilities in the field of human resources are significant in these first two years, as are the hours. New hires are expected to learn the company's protocols and procedures while carrying out their assigned duties. Most human resources managers establish mentor relationships with more senior human resources practitioners and learn effective techniques for managing people. Satisfaction is average; the hours are long.

5 YEARS Five-year veterans of small companies have become important staff members, and many of them have discrete areas of control. Individuals who work for large companies have begun to specialize in health benefits, pension plans, 401(k) plans, corporate recruiting, or another area of human resources. Many of them feel that working long hours will earn them a position as vice president or director of human resources. Salaries increase, but many people who want larger salaries move to bigger corporations. Satisfaction is high for career-track professionals.

10 YEARS Many human resources professionals assume managerial duties, with the goal of heading up a large human resources department or directing a benefits, recruiting, or personnel department. A significant number of human resources professionals return to graduate school to acquire more credentials that will distinguish them from other candidates. The hours can increase for individuals still trying to get ahead.

MAJOR EMPLOYERS

EASTMAN KODAK COMPANY
343 State Street
Rochester, NY 14650
www.kodak.com
Contact: Staffing, Department HEKHP

SMITH BARNEY CITIGROUP
380 Greenwich Street
New York, NY 10013
Tel: 212-464-6000
www.smithbarney.com
Contact: Human Resources

SONY PICTURES ENTERTAINMENT
10202 West Washington Boulevard, Suite 3900
Culver City, CA 90232-3195
www.sony.com
Contact: Human Resources

MAJOR ASSOCIATIONS

SOCIETY FOR HUMAN RESOURCES MANAGEMENT
1800 Duke Street
Alexandria, VA 22314
Tel: 703-548-3440 or 800-283-7476
Fax: 703-535-6490
www.shrm.org

WORLD AT WORK
1404 Northsight Boulevard
Scottsdale, AZ 85260
Tel: 480-922-2020 or 877-951-9191
Fax: 480-483-8352
www.worldatwork.org

INTERIOR DESIGNER

PROFESSIONAL PROFILE

# of people in profession	60,000
Avg. hours per week	45
Avg. starting salary	$21,200
Avg. salary after 5 years	$39,100
Avg. salary 10 to 15 years	$69,640

SALARY   • •
HOURS   • •
EDUCATION   • •

BOOKS, FILMS, AND TV SHOWS FEATURING THE PROFESSION
- Cloth and Paper
- Designing Women
- Using Color
- Will and Grace

YOU'LL HAVE CONTACT WITH
- Architects
- Carpenters
- Suppliers
- Textile manufacturers

PROFESSIONALS READ
- Architectural Digest
- Interior Design

A DAY IN THE LIFE

An interior designer is responsible for the interior design, decoration, and functionality of a client's space, whether the space is commercial, industrial, or residential. Interior designers work closely with architects and clients to determine the structure of a space, the needs of the occupants, and the style that best suits both. The position is a combination of engineer and artist, and it takes a unique type of mind to handle both of those concepts well. Interior designers have to be good with more than color, fabric, and furniture; interior designers must know materials, have budgeting skills, communicate well, and oversee the ordering, installation, and maintenance of all objects that define a space. They also have to know about electrical capacity, safety, and construction. **{ balance the practical with the aesthetic }** This broader range of required knowledge distinguishes them from interior decorators.

Interior designers have to be able to work with contractors and clients alike, planning and implementing all aesthetic and functional decisions, from faucet handles to miles of carpeting—and all this usually must be done within a fixed budget. Interior designers are hired for their expertise in a variety of styles and approaches, not merely their own personal vision. Therefore, they have to be able to balance their own tastes and their clients' tastes—and be willing to put their clients' tastes first. This requirement can be frustrating at first for many who enter the profession.

Interior designers are often asked to begin their planning before construction of a space is finished; this means that they must be good at scheduling and comfortable reading blueprints. This element of the job comes as a surprise to many new interior designers, who expect to have less of an administrative and technical role and more of a role in influencing the overall feel and appearance of a space. Those who thrive in the industry say this ability to balance the practical with the aesthetic is crucial to being a successful interior designer. Interior design is hard work, but those who do it well find the work very satisfying.

PAYING YOUR DUES

The academic and professional requirements for most areas of design are fairly general, with the emphasis on portfolio development and professional experience. Interior design, however, has nationally-standardized requirements. Interior designers must have a bachelor's degree. Employers look favorably on those who have studied engineering, design, and art. Those who want more specific study complete interior design programs. Across the United States and Canada, there are 105 colleges and universities accredited by the Foundation for Interior Design Education Research. Interior designers must also be familiar with federal, state, and local interior design codes (involving such issues as capacity, flammability, and stress levels). To be federally licensed, prospective interior designers must pass the qualification exam given by the National Council for Interior Design. Professional organizations are significant in this field, and many interior designers find it helpful to join one or more of them. To become eligible for membership, one must have completed two to three years of graduate work, worked in the field for two to three years, and passed the federal licensing exam.

ASSOCIATED CAREERS

Interior designers deal with technical engineering issues and aesthetic design issues. Those who leave this field usually choose another area involving aesthetic design. Many become interior decorators, graphic designers, and computer graphics consultants. A notable few become architects. Few leave the arena of aesthetic decision-making altogether.

PAST AND FUTURE

In years past, only the wealthy could afford to hire an interior designer. Most people designed their interiors themselves. With the expansion and popularization of the field, along with significant reductions in the cost of materials, even modest-income families may now hire interior designers. However, many still design their interiors without professional help.

Interior designers should have a bright future and are expected to be in demand. Many owners and occupants of professional and residential complexes are turning to professional interior designers to shape their spaces. There is also significant age-pressure in the industry, and a significant number of interior designers are expected to retire soon. This will open additional positions for younger interior designers. Discussions about making the requirements for the profession more stringent have been broached, but no specific legislative proposals have emerged to date.

QUALITY OF LIFE

2 YEARS Two years into the profession, many aspiring interior designers are working as interns or assistants, as entry into the field is competitive. A number of students make connections through relationships their schools have with major employers.. During these first two years, many act as assistants, learning budgeting, competitive pricing, and client communication skills. Salaries are low or nonexistent in these early years, hours are long, and satisfaction may be low. About 20 percent of potential interior designers leave the profession within the first three years.

5 YEARS After five years, interior designers have significant professional experience and a paying job in the industry. The large majority have passed the federal licensing exam. Many have associate-level responsibility for projects and work relatively unsupervised. Budgeting and cost-estimating are still reserved for more senior members of the profession. Many consider starting their own interior design firm during these middle years. Hours become more stable, and salary increases.

10 YEARS Ten-year interior designers have significant budgeting and cost-estimating responsibility and extensive client contact. The majority of those who wanted to start their own interior design firms have done so by this time, and many can point to a number of homes, offices, or stores where potential clients can see living examples of their work. Hours remain stable, and salaries increase.

MAJOR EMPLOYERS
ETHAN ALLEN
PO Box 1966
Danbury, CT 06813-1966
Fax: 203-743-8298
www.ethanallen.com

IKEA
1100 Broadway Mall
Hicksville, NY 11801
Tel: 516-681-4532
www.ikea.com

MAJOR ASSOCIATIONS
AMERICAN SOCIETY OF INTERIOR DESIGNERS
608 Massachusetts Avenue, NE
Washington, DC 20002-6006
Tel: 202-546-3480
Fax: 202-546-3240
www.asid.org

FOUNDATION FOR INTERIOR DESIGN EDUCATION RESEARCH
146 Monroe Center, NW, Suite 1318
Grand Rapids, MI 49503-2822
Tel: 616-458-0400
Fax: 616-458-0460
E-mail: fider@fider.org
www.fider.org

INVENTOR

A DAY IN THE LIFE

Inventors are some of the icons of American history; they industriously work to create new products for the American public. The image of Alexander Graham Bell inventing the telephone in a relatively primitive lab is firmly printed on our mind's eye. Engineering and development costs have dramatically increased, and invention today more often occurs in corporate labs and research and development departments; still, 20 percent of U.S. patents are issued each year to private inventors. A skilled inventor can still transform good ideas into significant sums of money. There are great rewards in designing a product that is better than any that have come before it.

{ uncertain living }

In addition to being creative, successful inventors must also be effective businesspeople. Developing a useful product is only the first step in the process. The inventor must also be able to negotiate a favorable licensing contract with an established manufacturer or have the wherewithal to become an entrepreneur and go into the business of manufacturing his or her ideas. Designs must be developed that avoid infringing on existing patents, and investors must protect themselves from others who would copy their existing design. Knowing the fields or backgrounds of inventions makes inventors' lives much easier, both when they develop new products and assess the value of inventions as they are developing them.

As a full-time career, inventing provides an uncertain living for all but the most talented. Developing new products is time-consuming and often expensive, and income doesn't start to flow until a marketable prototype is ready. Many inventors work part-time as inventors and spend the rest of their time in jobs as engineers, corporate research scientists, or in academia. Still, a good idea can be worth pursuing.

PAYING YOUR DUES

With rare exceptions, a background in science or engineering is a must. Many private inventors spend years working as designers for private corporations before they develop the ideas that let them set out on their own. Experience in product design and development is crucial, as is knowledge of the new product's potential market. Years working in industry or in academic research are the best methods to acquire the skills of a successful inventor.

ASSOCIATED CAREERS

Many inventors continue to work as research scientists and engineers while they develop their ideas, and these are the fields that most return to if they are unable to make it as inventors. Many return to inventing over and over again, accumulating successes and failures over many years. The first idea an inventor develops is often not the best one, but the experience gained with each try can be invaluable to later efforts.

PAST AND FUTURE

Archimedes is the first legendary engineer. The notebooks of Leonardo da Vinci contain visionary sketches and plans for literally hundreds of devices—although many, such as his designs for submarines and flying machines, ventured beyond his ability to "invent" them, given the limited resources available at the time. In more modern times, invention became central to the American self-image with the onset of the industrial revolution, when improved mass manufacturing techniques made it possible to rapidly make fortunes from a design for a useful new product. In turn, large manufacturing corporations built on the profits of the inventions of private inventors arose. Those corporations built up the large research and development staffs, which have largely displaced the role of the individual inventor. Private inventors and entrepreneurs are likely to continue playing a role in the development of the American economy.

QUALITY OF LIFE

2 YEARS Two-thirds of all inventors never see any profits from their creations. By the two-year mark, the inventor is either making money (either through a licensing agreement or private manufacturer) or should be considering another line of work. These first two years are the most difficult; developing an idea is perhaps the easiest part of invention, and many inventors find that developing business and distribution contacts is the most challenging aspect of the process.

5 YEARS The inventor who is still working as an inventor at this point has probably succeeded in establishing manufacturing and distribution relationships. This makes it much easier to generate profits from additional inventions, and it allows the professional to spend more time focusing on inventing and less on pounding the streets looking for business contacts. Quality of life has likely improved significantly by this point.

10 YEARS By now, the inventor's operation probably resembles a small business. If inventions have been profitable, additional researchers and business assistants may be employed, and the inventor has probably developed a stable market for his or her products. Very few inventors make it to this point, with the exception of those who do reap the rewards of owning and operating a business that allows them to make a living on their creations.

MAJOR EMPLOYERS
UNITED STATES COPYRIGHT OFFICE
Library of Congress
101 Independence Avenue, SE
Washington, DC 20559-6000
Tel: 202-707-3000
www.loc.gov/copyright

UNITED STATES PATENT AND TRADEMARK OFFICE
Mail Stop USPTO Contact Center (UCC)
PO Box 1450
Alexandria, VA 22313-1450
Tel: 571-272-1000 or 800-786-9199
Fax: 571-273-3245
www.uspto.gov

MAJOR ASSOCIATIONS
AMERICAN SOCIETY OF INVENTORS
PO Box 58426
Philadelphia, PA 19102
Tel: 215-456-6601
E-mail: info@casoi.org
www.americaninventor.org/

NATIONAL CONGRESS OF INVENTOR ORGANIZATIONS
PO Box 931881
Los Angeles, CA 90093-1881
Tel: 323-878-6952
E-mail: ncio@inventionconvention.com
www.inventionconvention.com/ncio/

JOURNALIST

PROFESSIONAL PROFILE

# of people in profession	70,000
Avg. hours per week	45
Avg. starting salary	$28,100
Avg. salary after 5 years	$44,600
Avg. salary 10 to 15 years	$69,300

SALARY   ● ●
HOURS   ● ●
EDUCATION   ● ● ●

BOOKS, FILMS, AND TV SHOWS FEATURING THE PROFESSION

- Absence of Malice
- All the President's Men
- His Girl Friday
- The Killing Fields
- The Paper

YOU'LL HAVE CONTACT WITH

- Editors
- Photographers
- Publishers
- Researchers

PROFESSIONALS READ

- American Journalism Review
- Broadcast & Cable
- Columbia Journalism Review
- Editor & Publisher
- The New York Times

A DAY IN THE LIFE

There are many types of journalists, from the local beat newspaper reporter to the foreign correspondent, the magazine feature writer to the freelance book reviewer, and so on. It is difficult to pin down the daily routine of an average journalist. Journalists interview sources and review records to assemble, collect, and report information and explore the implications of the facts. Journalism informs, educates, chastises: Do not underestimate the power a journalist holds. Remember Watergate, when Robert Woodward and Carl Bernstein, two reporters working for *The Washington Post*, discovered and published information that led to the resignation of President Richard Nixon?

Professionals must be able to report quickly and accurately. More than 80 percent of our respondents listed { chaotic schedule } time pressure as one of the most distinguishing features of this job. Journalists must maintain a point of view while remaining objective about their subjects, which can be difficult; around half our respondents said that their colleagues sometimes got too involved in the stories. Interpersonal skills, excellent writing skills, and a reporter's instinct (the ability to accurately assess the significance of obscure and incomplete information) are essential to success.

The uncertainty of the daily routine makes it difficult to incorporate family, hobbies, and any regularly scheduled plans; but those who detest the predictability of nine-to-five jobs are attracted to journalism because "no day is a carbon copy of the day before." Long hours and chronic deadline pressure can be significantly negative factors. When an editor calls you in on a breaking story, you have to be prepared to drop everything; when you're on deadline, you can get crazed trying to write a complicated story in half the time you need. This ball and chain to the offices leads many to resent, and eventually reject, the reporter's life. Some journalists complain about being "under the thumb of Napoleonic editors who control your every word based on their own taste." (Editors are sometimes Napoleonic, but more often, they are simply perfectionists.) Journalists who are protective of their prose rarely last in this profession, since articles are often edited for publication without their consultation. More than 40 million people read newspapers in the United States each day, and more than 50 million people read magazines each week. The opportunity for your writing to reach a large audience is tempting indeed, and many find the initial low pay, uncertain and occasionally dangerous conditions, and chaotic schedule a fair tradeoff to be allowed to do what they do. In fact, many seem drawn by the excitement and challenge of these very conditions.

PAYING YOUR DUES

Most journalists hold a bachelor's degree in journalism, communications, English, or political science. More than a few distinguished careers have begun at the school newspaper or at a neighborhood magazine or newspaper. Many journalists come to the profession later in life after gaining expertise and connections in other professions. Journalism jobs are highly competitive: Credentials and experience must be accompanied by gumption and hard work.

Excellent writing skills are a must, as are computer word-processing skills. Bone up on proofreading skills before applying for any job. Foreign language skills may be necessary for those reporting on the international scene. Persistence, initiative, stamina, and the desire to tell real stories about real events are critical to the survival of the budding journalist. The best journalists have a knack for putting contemporary events into historical perspective.

ASSOCIATED CAREERS

Journalists who leave the profession often become editors, professors, researchers, and analysts. Many teach high school and run school papers; others take jobs in whatever industry they once covered as a reporter. Those who leave the field usually do so because of the uncertain lifestyle and the long hours.

PAST AND FUTURE

The first American newspaper was printed in 1690 and was quashed four days later. Since 1776, the number of daily newspapers printed in the United States has risen from 37 to nearly 1,500, not including weeklies, magazines, and computer-generated newsletters.

Journalism, like most occupations concerned with communication, is becoming more electronic. Online services and electronic publishers deliver expertly written pieces 24 hours a day, seven days a week on the Internet. But somebody still needs to write those pieces. Competition for jobs will remain fierce, but specialized jobs should increase; those with unique skills, such as technological expertise or foreign language skills, should enjoy a distinct advantage.

QUALITY OF LIFE

2 YEARS Many aspiring reporters begin their careers by pitching story ideas to local newspapers and magazines on a piecemeal basis. Writers who can show clippings from school newspapers or other publications—no matter how minor—begin with an advantage if the prose is good. Aspiring writers may have to survive repeated rejections before a story idea is finally accepted for publication, and the income stream from freelance journalism is so unpredictable that many take more regular-paying jobs. Most aspire to a salaried job at a local newspaper during these scrambling years. As at all levels of this profession, satisfaction is high despite low income.

5 YEARS By now most journalists have held at least two full-time salaried positions. The most desirable jobs at this level are daily newspaper reporting jobs, especially those with a specialized "beat." It's hard for a journalist to break past the low $30,000s without daily deadline experience, and this is often what separates "the men from the boys."

10 YEARS Ten-year survivors in journalism still work long hours, but they have established a strong tone and style, enjoy a dedicated readership, and are finally making a wage commensurate with their abilities. The majority (more than 60 percent) of those who began as journalists do not make it to the 10-year mark, dissuaded by lack of opportunity and lack of advancement. Many turn to editorial duties as well as reporting duties. A number switch their specialties after 10 years to keep their jobs interesting and their writing fresh.

MAJOR EMPLOYERS

ASSOCIATED PRESS
450 West 33rd Street
New York, NY 10001
Tel: 212-621-1500
E-mail: apjobs@ap.org
www.ap.org
Contact: Staffing Department

CABLE NEWS NETWORK
1 CNN Center
Atlanta, GA 30303
Tel: 404-827-1700
Fax: 404-681-3578
www.cnn.com
Contact: Personnel

THE NEW YORK TIMES
229 West 43rd Street
New York, NY 10036
Tel: 212-556-1234
www.nytimes.com
Contact: Employment Department

TIME INC.
One Time Warner Center
New York, NY 10019-8016
Tel: 212-484-8000
www.pathfinder.com/time
Contact: Human Resources

MAJOR ASSOCIATIONS

AMERICAN SOCIETY OF JOURNALISTS AND AUTHORS
1501 Broadway, Suite 302
New York, NY 10036
Tel: 212-997-0947
Fax: 212-937-2315
www.asja.org

THE NEWSPAPER GUILD
501 3rd Street, NW, Suite 250
Washington, DC 20001
Tel: 202-434-7177
Fax: 202-434-1472
E-mail: guild@cwa-union.orgwww.newsguild.org

SOCIETY OF PROFESSIONAL JOURNALISTS
Eugene S. Pulliam National
    Journalism Center
3909 North Meridian Street
Indianapolis, IN 46208
Tel: 317-927-8000
Fax: 317-920-4789
www.spj.org

LANDSCAPE ARCHITECT

SALARY   • •

HOURS   • •

EDUCATION   • •

BOOKS, FILMS, AND TV SHOWS
FEATURING THE PROFESSION
- Caddyshack
- Can't Buy Me Love
- Edward Scissorhands

YOU'LL HAVE CONTACT WITH
- Architects
- Clients
- Construction managers
- Engineers
- Scientists

PROFESSIONALS READ
- ASLA.org
- Landscape Architecture Magazine
- Landscape Architecture News Digest

A DAY IN THE LIFE

If you are thinking about becoming a landscape architect, you should have an appreciation for nature, a creative flair, and a passion for working with your hands. You should also have strong writing and researching skills and an affinity for engineering and environmental sciences. All of these skills will be useful for mastering the art and science of the analysis, planning, design, management, preservation, and rehabilitation of land. Landscape architects apply their skills to site planning, garden design, environmental restoration, town and urban planning, park and recreation planning, regional planning, and even historic preservation. The growing popularity of this profession is understandable. Where else could consecutive job assignments find you planning a { urban or suburban areas } site for corporate office buildings, then have you managing a large wilderness area, and next creating public parks that won't interfere with the natural environment?

Even though landscape architects appear to keep average hours, project deadlines can create a lot of overtime. Working through weekends is very likely. A major job, like planning a corporate site, can take more than a year to complete. A landscape architect must work with all the other professionals involved in a project. The list includes architects, engineers, and construction contractors, and a landscape architect must see that their design concepts will work with the overall project. Surveys of the land at the site itself must often be made, taking into consideration complex factors such as drainage, slope of the land, and even how sunlight falls on the site. Once this is done, they spend the majority of the remainder of the project in the office, preparing presentations for clients that include cost estimates, sketches, and models. After a project is approved, landscape architects prepare even more detailed working drawings and outline explicitly the methods of construction and lists of construction materials. Some landscape architects even supervise the installation of their designs, although this is often left to a developer or separate contractor.

Landscape architects can also choose to specialize in areas such as residential development, parks and playgrounds, restoration, or even shopping malls. Only a few, however, are exclusively devoted to individual residential designing because the income is too small compared to the earnings from larger, commercial projects. Most of the profession is centered in urban or suburban areas, and while the majority of landscape architects work for landscape architecture services and firms, a full 20 percent of people in the profession are self-employed.

PAYING YOUR DUES

Entrance into the profession requires a bachelor's or master's degree in landscape architecture (from an accredited school), training, licensure (in all but five states), and specialized skills. It is a long road to becoming a licensed and professional landscape architect. The bachelor's degree in landscape architecture takes between four and five years to complete; a master's can take two to three years. During and after school, prospective landscape architects serve as interns to professionals in the field for a period of at least two years. Finally, they will have to pass the L.A.R.E. (Landscape Architect Registration Examination) to obtain their licenses to practice landscape architecture as certified professionals. However, if they choose to take jobs with the government, the process can be somewhat shorter; the federal government doesn't require its landscape architects to be licensed.

ASSOCIATED CAREERS

Because of the numerous skills involved in landscape architecture, there are many related careers that landscape architects can move into. The most closely related field is, of course, architecture itself, but a career switch to straight architecture will require even more time and education. Many landscape architects find satisfying careers as landscape supervisors, landscape designers or consultants, drafters, environmental planners, or golf course designers. Civil engineering and urban planning are also fields of interest to landscape architects, as is the field of botany.

PAST AND FUTURE

The American Society of Landscape Architects (ASLA) was founded in 1899, and one of its charter members was 77-year-old Frederick Law Olmsted, the landscape architect who designed New York City's Central Park. Today, the ASLA has more than 15,000 members across 48 chapters. An ever-growing number of landscape architects are using computer-aided design (CAD) systems to assist them with presentations. Proficiency with this technology is becoming a requirement in the field. Larger-scale projects are often planned using geographic information systems technologies and computer-mapping systems. The level of computer-assisted design in the profession will continue to increase. Job opportunities will be best for landscape architects who develop strong technical and computer skills.

Knowledge of environmental issues, codes, and regulations will also give landscape architects an edge in the marketplace. The continued and growing concern for the environment should see the demand for landscape architects increase as the need to design environmentally sound development projects becomes even more pressing. Urban planners have cited the greening of roofs and courtyards in cities as effective approaches to cut down on energy costs and reduce pollution, making landscape architects in greater demand as society increasingly understands how the natural world can alleviate some of the strains people place on the environment.

QUALITY OF LIFE

2 YEARS These years are spent interning under the guidance of a licensed landscape architect. Although the tasks will vary depending on the type and size of the firm the intern is working for, standard work includes project research, preparing maps of areas to be landscaped, and, occasionally, participation in the actual design of a project. All the intern's work is closely supervised, though; the hours can be long, and the pay is low.

5 YEARS At this point in their careers, many interning landscape architects are either studying for the L.A.R.E. or have just taken it. For individuals who have passed the L.A.R.E., responsibilities will increase dramatically as they are now legally able to carry a design through from start to finish without supervision. With this privilege comes direct client contact and even the chance to oversee certain aspects of a project. The hours may increase, and income certainly rises.

10 YEARS Landscape architects who have lasted this long without switching career tracks should at this point be enjoying the privileges of their experience. It is not unlikely to be an associate at a firm, and the more ambitious individuals may possibly have achieved the title of partner. In either case, associate or partner, they are seeing an income that is at the top range of the profession. Landscape architects with 10 years under their belts and a talent for small business management often open their own firms.

MAJOR EMPLOYERS

Many landscape architects are self-employed or serve as part of small landscape architectural firms located in urban or suburban areas throughout the United States. A large segment of those in the career are employed by federal, state, and local government agencies.

MAJOR ASSOCIATIONS

AMERICAN SOCIETY OF LANDSCAPE ARCHITECTS
636 Eye Street, NW
Washington, DC 20001-3736
Tel: 202-898-2444 or 888-999-ASLA
Fax: 202-898-1185
www.asla.org

COUNCIL OF LANDSCAPE ARCHITECTURAL BOARDS
144 Church Street, NW, Suite 201
Vienna, VA 22180
E-mail: info@clarb.org
www.clarb.org

LIBRARIAN

BOOKS, FILMS, AND TV SHOWS
FEATURING THE PROFESSION
- **Foul Play**
- **Goodbye, Columbus**
- **The Name of the Rose**
- **Party Girl**

YOU'LL HAVE CONTACT WITH
- **Computer programmers**
- **Information managers**
- **Inventory managers**
- **Publishers**

PROFESSIONALS READ
- **Library Journal**
- **Library Technology Reports**
- **Library Trends**
- **Publishers Weekly**

A DAY IN THE LIFE

Librarians are the custodians of our culture's retrievable media—books and audio and visual materials—and other data or physical objects that can be catalogued and stored. The modern librarian is the manager of an enormous warehouse, and people rely on him or her to help them navigate the increasingly voluminous world of data.

Research and computer skills are important; therefore, people who are generally less comfortable with computers find the transition to online archives much more difficult. Be prepared to work under real deadlines and significant pressure; individuals with corporate library jobs will find that although the salaries are higher, "if you can't do the job when they really need you, they'll show you the door." Librarians who specialize in medicine or law will find their professions more lucrative than general librarians, but the books won't be the kind you take home and read for a little relaxation. Especially for specialists, graduate studies prove invaluable for a successful transition to working life.

{ the custodians of our culture's retrievable media }

A librarian spends more than 60 percent of his or her day working with people, either library patrons or other staffers and back-office workers. Strong interpersonal skills are required for individuals who hope to succeed in this field. "You've got to be polite even when you want to break someone's neck, which happens Monday morning about 10 and lasts through Saturday at four," said one 15-year veteran of the St. Louis public library system. Librarians also work closely with their colleagues; they loan books, advise one another, and discuss daily work issues on a regular basis. More than 50 percent of our respondents called their professional community "supportive."

"I'm surrounded by books all day, and that's all I've ever wanted," reported one happy librarian. A librarian does far more than sit at the desk and check books in and out of the library. A large part of his or her job is research. The most-cited positive feature about being a librarian was the sense of continuous education. Librarians are challenged daily to find creative ways of retrieving a different information; and how well they can satisfy these requests determines their success and satisfaction in the profession.

PAYING YOUR DUES

A bachelor's degree is required, and a master's in library science is a plus; PhDs are becoming more common among professional librarians, as well. Some states require certification. Only 59 schools offering graduate degrees are accredited by the American Library Association, so check before you enroll. Graduate classwork includes classification, cataloging, computer courses, and reference work. Some graduate programs require students to know a foreign language. A strong sense of current events and contemporary themes is helpful. A sense of aesthetics helps, too; it is not unusual for a librarian to design a library exhibit. Individuals wishing to become school librarians must also complete any teaching certifications required.

ASSOCIATED CAREERS

Librarians often move into specializations of information science, in acquisitions, cataloging, reference, and special collections. Others become antiquarians, antiques dealers, or collectors, or transfer their skills to the corporate arena by becoming research specialists. Others become consultants in their areas of specialization or perhaps library directors, who make personnel and staffing decisions, track inventory, set and follow a budget, and oversee the general operations of the library.

PAST AND FUTURE

John Harvard created the first library in the United States when he left his book collection to the Massachusetts Bay Colony's college in 1638; before long, Benjamin Franklin democratized the library concept by proposing that people have the right to borrow and use books. Today there are more than 117,000 libraries in the United States, with the Library of Congress housing 130 million items on approximately 530 miles of bookshelves. And that's just one collection (albeit a large one).

The future of librarians is linked to three things: public funding for the public library system, private donations that support libraries, and the growth of technology within the public and private library system. Technological by-products expected to change the field include the development of Web-based information architecture, the shift of emphasis from privately owned to publicly shared information, and the increased acquisition of nonprint materials. Although the online cataloguing of books may seem to threaten the position of the librarian, aspiring professionals should remember two key facts: frequently, librarians are the people responsible for creating and maintaining online catalogs; and books aren't going anywhere any time soon.

QUALITY OF LIFE

2 YEARS In larger libraries, assistant or junior librarians manage discrete library areas that focus on organization and tracking, such as the periodicals desk or reshelving. Librarians with two years of experience sit in on meetings and are expected to provide input. These first two years are educational years, spent learning the system and the people associated with the specific library you enter. Recognition is limited, the hours are average, and pay is mediocre in the early years. Individuals in the corporate sector are likely to face long hours and potentially much more responsibility, along with higher wages. Many new librarians are overwhelmed by the responsibilities of being a librarian; perhaps that is why the profession has a 30 percent first-year attrition rate. But those individuals who survive the first year seem very capable of surviving in the profession for the long haul.

5 YEARS The attrition rate after the first two years settles off at about 5 percent. Responsibilities increase, as do hours and pay. Daily tasks may include helping to plan fund-raising drives, looking into book-tracking systems, negotiating with vendors for library supplies, handling complaints, and satisfying unusual requests for information. Most librarians who wish to rise in rank have completed their master's by this time; they attend lectures and conferences and subscribe to librarian newsletters. Librarians start managing large staffs of reshelvers, checkout personnel, and administrators.

10 YEARS Ten-year veterans have significant input and responsibilities. They may work closely with directors in deciding budgetary priorities, steering the direction the library takes. Satisfaction is highest during these influential years, and individuals who stay in the profession for 10 years are expected to remain for many more.

MAJOR EMPLOYERS
LIBRARY OF CONGRESS
101 Independence Avenue, SE
Washington, DC 20540
Tel: 202-707-5000
www.loc.gov
Contact: Human Resources

NEW YORK PUBLIC LIBRARY
Human Resources Department
188 Madison Avenue
New York, NY 10016-4314
Tel: 212-930-0800
Fax: 212-592-7327
E-mail: hrd@nypl.org
Contact: Employment and Placement Office

SAN FRANCISCO PUBLIC LIBRARY
100 Larkin Street
San Francisco, CA 94102
Tel: 415-557-4400
www.sfpl.lib.ca.us
Contact: Personnel

MAJOR ASSOCIATIONS
AMERICAN LIBRARIAN ASSOCIATION
50 East Huron Street
Chicago, IL 60611
Tel: 800-545-2433
E-mail: library@ala.org
www.ala.org

AMERICAN SOCIETY FOR INFORMATION SCIENCE
1320 Fenwick Lane, Suite 510
Silver Spring, MD 20910
Tel: 301-495-0900
Fax: 301-495-0810
E-mail: asis@asis.org
www.asis.org

SPECIAL LIBRARIES ASSOCIATION
331 South Patrick Street
Alexandria, VA 22314-3501
Tel: 703-647-4900
Fax: 703-647-4901
E-mail: sla@sla.org
www.sla.org

MANAGEMENT CONSULTANT

BOOKS, FILMS, AND TV SHOWS
FEATURING THE PROFESSION

- **Behavior and Management**
- **Listen to Your Workers**
- **Office Space**
- **The Swami**

YOU'LL HAVE CONTACT WITH

- **Accountants**
- **Organization development consultants**
- **Production managers**
- **Quality control managers**

PROFESSIONALS READ

- **Consultants News**
- **Consulting Magazine**
- **C2M**
- **Institutional Investor**

A DAY IN THE LIFE

Companies, to improve efficiency and profitability, hire management consultants to identify problems and recommend solutions. Consultants' objectives can be limited to analyzing such issues as shipping functions and then streamlining procedures. Alternatively, their goals may be broadly defined and include reorganizing a multinational corporation to take advantage of the synergies that developed when it acquired new businesses. "Sometimes you're asked to solve a particular problem, and you find that the problem is just a symptom of another problem, so you need to spend a lot of time at the beginning identifying where to start and what you need to do," wrote one consultant. The need to spend time at the beginning doing research, identifying areas of concern, and { how to fix things today } mapping out how the different areas of a business affect one another is often a difficult sell to clients who want immediate results. "No one wants to hear that you've got to look at five years of data—they want you to tell them how to fix things today," wrote another. Management consultants have to be accomplished analysts, attentive listeners, and firm but tactful communicators. They are thinkers and problem solvers who know how to convince others that change is needed.

Though even starting management consultants make good money (and income rises considerably with experience), our surveys indicate that candidates must be willing to sacrifice time from their personal lives. Nearly all survey respondents say that 60-hour workweeks are part of the training and education process—some report up to 90-hour workweeks—and that travel and time spent on-site at clients' offices can be considerable. Consultants must get used to leaving home on Sunday for a business trip and not returning until Thursday or Friday. Individuals who do management consulting in government agencies tend to be more serene about their lot, citing more regular hours and interesting work. Satisfaction is generally high in this career, despite its demands.

PAYING YOUR DUES

No specific academic requirements exist for management consultants, but nearly all employers require at least a college degree in a related field. Employers generally prefer candidates who majored in one of the following areas: business, economics, statistics, mathematics, computer science, and logic. An Ivy League education is a distinct plus, and many employers look extremely favorably on MBAs, which are necessary requirements for upward mobility in this profession. Very little guidance is available, so candidates should demonstrate academic, work, or entrepreneurial experience that shows them to be self-starters and interested in excellence in whatever they do. Most major employers run their own programs to train junior consultants in accounting, internal policy, research techniques, and how to work as part of a close-knit, hardworking team. Experience is always valuable, but professional certification—granted by the Institute of Management Consultants USA, Inc. only after rigorous review—is often more important when it comes to getting hired and promoted, especially at smaller firms. The majority of management consultants are self-employed and work in firms of 10 or fewer people, but the highest-paid ones usually do a significant stint at a large company, making professional contacts and building a solid reputation.

ASSOCIATED CAREERS

Management consultants are exposed to a variety of industries to which they frequently migrate. Manufacturing, banking, and production are areas populated by ex-management consultants. Other management consultants see their counterparts on the financial side—investment bankers—making as much or more money than they do and use their financial skills to emigrate to this field.

PAST AND FUTURE

Management consulting is a relatively new occupation and one that took off in the 1960s with the growth of management sciences as a valid academic course of study. Business schools and economics departments across the nation produced a spate of literature on the subject of "management organization" and analysis of worker and company efficiency. To support this purely theoretical science, they began collecting and distributing data on organization, productivity, and capacity, giving companies a greater understanding of the forces affecting their organizations. Small consulting firms with specific areas of expertise developed in the 1970s, and the 1980s saw the birth of the management consultant generalist, who applied general principles of management to individual companies and emerged with recommendations. The work of these management consultants was validated in the 1990s: companies with more than 10,000 employees who followed their consultants' recommendations experienced an average increase of 21 percent in revenue after five years.

Management consulting is a growing profession, and significant opportunities are projected for the future. Competition for these positions will, however, be intense.

QUALITY OF LIFE

2 YEARS Management consultants reported that quality of life is a trade-off at first. Most individuals have gone through initial training programs and are junior members of consulting teams. The hours are very long. Salaries—consisting of an average base wage and significant potential for bonuses—are high for entry-level positions. A number of consultants said that in these initial years, they learned not only how to analyze a company's management but also how to enjoy working hard and getting results with a small group of bright and dedicated people.

5 YEARS Five-year management consultants are team leaders who manage projects instead of working on-site all the time. Satisfaction jumps as people who are successful receive salaries commensurate with their staggering hours. Duties at this stage for management consultants include managing accounts, directing production of reports, and reviewing the analyses of more junior associates.

10 YEARS Ten-year veterans continue to find their work very exciting. Why else would they be willing to work 60 hours a week after 10 years on the job? One answer may be that salaries can be enormous. They are experienced, dedicated professionals who very much enjoy applying their skills to their work. At the most senior levels, management consultants are involved in such sensitive areas as recruiting new business, working closely with clients, and directing company policy.

MAJOR EMPLOYERS

ACCENTURE
1345 Avenue of the Americas
New York, NY 10105
Tel: 917-452-4400
www.accenture.com

BAIN & COMPANY INC.
131 Dartmouth Street
Boston, MA 02116
Tel: 617-572-2000
Fax: 617-572-2427
E-mail: recruiting@bain.com
www.bain.com

DELOITTE CONSULTING
1633 Broadway
New York, NY 10019-6754
Tel: 212-489-1600
Fax: 212-489-1687
www.dc.com

IBM BUSINESS CONSULTING SERVICES
1133 Westchester Avenue
White Plains, NY 10604
Tel: 800-426-4968
www-1.ibm.com/services/us

MAJOR ASSOCIATIONS

AMERICAN MANAGEMENT ASSOCIATION
1601 Broadway
New York, NY 10019
Tel: 800-262-9699 or 212-586-8100
Fax: 212-903-8168
www.amanet.org

INSTITUTE OF MANAGEMENT CONSULTANTS
2025 M Street, NW, Suite 800
Washington, DC 20036-3309
Tel: 800-221-2557 or 202-367-1134
Fax: 202-367-2134
www.imcusa.org

MARKET RESEARCHER

BOOKS, FILMS, AND TV SHOWS
FEATURING THE PROFESSION
- 99 Calls
- Kate and Leopold
- Late Night Stories

YOU'LL HAVE CONTACT WITH
- Advertising executives
- Marketing executives
- Researchers
- Statisticians

PROFESSIONALS READ
- Journal of Advertising Research
- Marketing News
- Research Alert

A DAY IN THE LIFE

"People will tell you market research is a science, and there are scientific parts to it, but when it's done well, it's an art," wrote one market researcher. Market researchers prepare studies and surveys, analyze demographic information and purchasing histories, review the factors that affect product demand, and make recommendations to manufacturing and sales forces about the market for their product. This multifaceted job requires financial, statistical, scientific, and aesthetic skills, as well as common sense.

Market researchers work on projects that proceed in stages. At the beginning of a project, a market researcher may spend three weeks with other market researchers designing a survey and testing it on small samples of their intended population. In later stages, they may define demographics, distribute the survey, and collect and assemble data. In the final stages, they may analyze survey responses to uncover consumer preferences or needs that have not yet been identified. Like all scientific experiments, "the assumptions we make are key. If we don't get those clear at the beginning, it's going to affect our entire study," wrote one respondent. Those people who specialize in public opinion surveys are particularly careful about how they phrase their questions, as a single misplaced modifier can dramatically affect the meaning of a question and, likewise, its responses.

{ perfect survey }

Market researchers work on their own and on teams. Many researchers find it difficult to adjust to working on a team. As one respondent said, "There are a lot of opinions about what constitutes the perfect survey. Four market researchers are going to have four different opinions." This diversity of opinion, while celebrated in the world at large, can make for difficult strategizing sessions and even more difficult interpretations of results. Good market researchers are careful listeners and remain flexible in their assumptions. They have to be good at communicating their results; a miscommunication between the market research department and management can lead to a financial disaster.

PAYING YOUR DUES

An entry-level market research position requires only an undergraduate degree. Employers look favorably on a degree in marketing and courses in statistics, mathematics, survey design, advertising, and psychology. Graduate degrees in marketing, business, or statistics are becoming more common among individuals in management positions. Work experience that demonstrates a creative intellect and the ability to work on teams is also well received. Prospective market researchers should be aware that early jobs in the field entail plenty of menial work—copying, proofreading, inputting data, and the like. Individuals who are willing to carry out these entry-level tasks go on to fill positions of responsibility.

ASSOCIATED CAREERS

Market researchers have statistics and survey skills, and many of them acquire business and production skills while employed by companies or lobbies. Market researchers who change careers usually become executives, advertising managers, demographic analysts (for the Census Bureau), and statisticians. Market researchers do well in any position that combines numerical analysis with interpersonal skills; many of them become economists or bankers.

PAST AND FUTURE

Market research as a distinct profession emerged out of the multiple-product nature of large companies. In the 1950s, many successful organizations began to analyze who their customers were and what other products they might be interested in buying. As advertising and marketing techniques became more sophisticated, so did market research techniques. Companies found customer information so valuable that they established in-house research departments to examine all aspects of a product, from concept to price, and to make recommendations to the company's top executives.

The job market for market research remains strong as the brisk pace of manufacturing consolidation, growth, and development continues. The pendulum has come full swing as today's companies move away from in-house research, finding it more profitable to contract out than to support their own marketing staff. New technology continues to redefine the role of the market researcher, as computers expedite, expand, and sometimes even replace their functions. But thanks in part to an increasingly competitive economy, the outlook of the market research profession looks bright, with the field expected to grow faster than average for all jobs in the next five years.

QUALITY OF LIFE

2 YEARS During these years, market researchers hand out surveys, record information, set up appointments, proofread, etc.—any task that more senior-level market researchers need done. Although these tasks are not very stimulating intellectually, understanding all the steps required to conduct supportable market research is crucial to a market researcher's long-term success. The hours and salaries are average. Responsibilities and satisfaction are low. After two years, market researchers emerge from administrative assistant duties and begin to have limited input in market research decisions.

5 YEARS By the five-year mark, most professionals are members of research teams and have earned the title of market researcher. Many of them have sole responsibility for areas of a given project and meet with team members to coordinate the project into a whole. The hours, salary, responsibilities, and satisfaction increase.

10 YEARS Ten-year veterans of this profession are senior market researchers and often are more involved in policy and the focus of research than in project coordination. A number of them have moved into higher management. Those researchers who remain in the field work more closely with upper management than with other market researchers. The hours decrease, but responsibilities skyrocket. Mobility becomes important, but opportunities depend on the industry and the market for the industry at the time.

MAJOR EMPLOYERS

THE ARBITRON COMPANY
9705 Patuxent Woods Drive
Columbia, MD 21046-1572
Tel: 410-312-8000
www.arbitron.com
Contact: Recruiter

INFORMATION RESOURCES, INC.
150 North Clinton Street
Chicago, IL 60661-1416
Tel: 312-726-1221
www.infores.com
Contact: Human Resources

MAJOR ASSOCIATIONS

AMERICAN ADVERTISING FEDERATION
1101 Vermont Avenue, NW, Suite 500
Washington, DC 20005-6306
Tel: 202-898-0089
Fax: 202-898-0159
E-mail: aaf@aaf.org
www.aaf.org

AMERICAN MARKETING ASSOCIATION
311 South Wacker Drive, Suite 5800
Chicago, IL 60606
Tel: 800-262-1150 or 312-542-9000
Fax: 312-542-9001
E-mail: info@ama.org
www.ama.org

MARKETING RESEARCH ASSOCIATION
110 National Drive
Glastonbury, CT 06033
Tel: 860-682-1000
Fax: 860-682-1010
E-mail: email@mra-net.org
www.mra-net.org

MEDIA SPECIALIST

A DAY IN THE LIFE

If you were about to give a talk to a class or present something at a meeting, to whom would you turn? The best option would be a media specialist. Media specialists get to work with multimedia equipment (such as television and video equipment), cameras, film projectors, slides, and recording equipment, usually on behalf of a school, library, or business. A media specialist is a type of teacher who works with multimedia equipment to make classes, presentations, and lectures more vibrant and exciting. They are sometimes called library media specialists, and, like librarians, they help teachers and lecturers choose and locate audiovisual aids that are used in classrooms, training sessions, conferences, seminars, and workshops. They acquire, catalog, and maintain collateral material such as films, video { *knowledge and enlightenment* } and audiotapes, photographs, and software programs. Media specialists largely work for schools and institutions of learning, but some of them work in libraries, government agencies, private industries, and other businesses.

Media specialists working in school systems help teachers by finding relevant material to be used as teaching aids. They work closely with teachers in ordering course materials, determining what training aids are best suited for particular grade levels, and instructing teachers and students in the operation of audiovisual equipment. They also perform simple maintenance tasks such as cleaning monitors and lenses and changing batteries and lightbulbs. Technicians usually handle repairs and more complex maintenance work.

Government agencies, medical and industrial corporations, international humanitarian organizations, and other nongovernmental organizations that need to train workers and distribute information to the public require the services of media specialists. Some media specialists will find work researching and developing public service announcements run by health, welfare, and social services; community action groups; and radio and television stations. Professionals keep on top of developments in media and learning methods by attending conventions, conferences, and seminars; reading trade journals; and communicating with industry insiders. Much of their time is spent previewing products, ordering supplies, and organizing materials. Even though most media specialists have heavy schedules, their reward comes with the knowledge and enlightenment they help bring to students and other audiences.

PAYING YOUR DUES

A bachelor's degree in educational media or instructional technology is the basic requirement for this profession. A master's degree in these programs or in communications, library science, library media, or education will benefit individuals applying for work in the school system. Many media specialists start out as teachers and, with additional training, move into this profession. Aspirants to the profession can greatly enhance their job prospects by doing volunteer work in media centers at local libraries or finding part-time employment with companies that sell or produce audiovisual programs and equipment. They must be able to operate different kinds of audiovisual equipment and instruct others on how to operate them as well. Applicants must be inventive, creative, and able to adapt to different environments. Since a media specialist's salary depends on experience and geography, the specialist will have to work hard at his or her craft before salary scales rise to an optimum level.

ASSOCIATED CAREERS

Since most media specialists start out as teachers, people who leave the profession often return to teaching. Even professionals without a basis in education can quite easily make the transition to this profession. With a PhD, media specialists may find work teaching at colleges and universities and as directors of media programs.

PAST AND FUTURE

Technology has redefined the principles of education. Teaching tools such as charts and maps have been replaced by computers, CD-ROMs, DVDs, and PowerPoint presentations. As more companies set up in-house libraries and research and training departments, opportunities will continue to increase for media specialists who will be needed to locate, catalog, and maintain reference materials. Whereas teachers and students have more access to information today, the effective delivery of this information is now the job of media specialists.

With rapid expansion of technology and the explosion of information sources, the job of the media specialist, who is versed in the use of media resources, is virtually assured. As technology continues to drive the growth of industries, training will continue to be an integral part of preparing workers for new job situations and improving and updating current skills.

QUALITY OF LIFE

2 YEARS The two-year media specialist has to learn about the business and keep current of all new developments in the industry. Reading trade journals and attending conventions, exposés, seminars, and workshops are crucial for media specialists who wish to succeed in the field.

5 YEARS With considerable experience working with a variety of audiovisual equipment, developing collateral material, and acquiring and maintaining stock, the media specialist should now be able to command a relatively higher salary if he or she is in the right market. Media specialists who are working in the school system start to consider becoming media program coordinators for their school districts, if such a move is possible. At this stage, the professional is still making the rounds at conventions and audiovisual outlets as well as scanning trade publications to keep updated. Returning to school for further education is a possibility for the professional in search of upward mobility.

10 YEARS The media specialist at the 10-year level is a marketable commodity with wide-ranging and current knowledge of the industry. If he or she is working within the school system, a move to the private sector will probably prove considerably more lucrative and challenging. Social, health, and welfare services may prove interesting for the socially and politically conscious. With higher education and a PhD, the ambitious media specialist can find work as a college professor or director of a college media program.

MAJOR EMPLOYERS
Media specialists are employed primarily to conduct local market analysis. Contact media specialists in your area for employment opportunities.

MAJOR ASSOCIATIONS
INTERNATIONAL TECHNOLOGY EDUCATION ASSOCIATION
1914 Association Drive, Suite 201
Reston, VA 20191-1539
Tel: 703-860-2100
Fax: 703-860-0353
E-mail: itea@iteaconnect.org
www.iteaconnect.org

MEDIATOR

A DAY IN THE LIFE

Being a professional mediator is all about conflict resolution, and so the job demands a person with excellent reasoning, problem-solving, and peace-making abilities. When two parties have a dispute and wish to avoid the legal intricacies of litigation, they may call in a mediator to facilitate an equitable solution. While many are suspicious of lawyers and attorneys, mediators are more often attributed with qualities of wisdom, trustworthiness, and neutrality. Unlike lawyers and judges, who evaluate, assess, and decide for others, mediators help participating parties evaluate, assess, and decide for themselves. Parties wishing to avoid the delays, high costs, publicity, and ill will brought on by litigation look to mediators as a more peaceful, inexpensive, and expedient alternative.

{ **conflict resolution** }

The mediator's job is to listen, sort through differences between the two parties involved in a dispute, and find common ground upon which to ascertain a solution. A good mediator is honest, neutral, and encouraging; listens well; and has excellent communication skills. Helping two parties arrive at a mutually agreeable solution also takes a fair amount of creativity. Mediation is considered a form of Alternative Dispute Resolution (ADR). Although ADR sounds like a terrible syndrome, it's in fact a more Zenlike approach to conflict resolution, with mediators as the master practitioners. Corporations, government agencies, community organizations, schools, neighborhoods, and even families will turn to mediators when they seek mutually acceptable answers to their problems. Examples of conflicts they work to resolve include labor/management issues, health care disputes, environmental/public policy issues, and international conflicts.

PAYING YOUR DUES

The educational background of a professional mediator varies widely. A fair number in the field hold law degrees, while others may not even hold a bachelor's degree. Most important is an education in mediation, whether taken as part of an undergraduate degree or as individual training courses. University degrees in public policy, law, and related fields also provide helpful backgrounds. While few states require licenses or certification to practice mediation, most individuals in the profession have completed training and pledged to abide by certain ethical standards.

ASSOCIATED CAREERS

Lawyers, religious leaders, social workers, counselors, and educators are often called on to mediate. Judges and magistrates also play the role of mediator. Strong mediators have many possible professions open to them, including diplomats and politicians.

PAST AND FUTURE

Historically, mediation has been used to settle many different types of disputes. Mediation was a solution sought after by warring Greek city-states. Catholic popes became mediators between European countries during the Renaissance, and recently, Bishop Desmond Tutu and former President Jimmy Carter have served as mediators in unstable parts of the world. In the business realm, mediation has long been used as a source for conflict resolution. Since 1887, the American government has promoted arbitration and mediation for contractual disputes involving commerce.

Today, increasing numbers of colleges and universities offer degrees in dispute resolution and conflict management. The field is expected to grow faster than average for all occupations in the coming years.

QUALITY OF LIFE

2 YEARS — Mediators don't often work irregular hours. A dispute may arise at any time, but unless there is a pending deadline, mediators tend to work eight-hour days. For the first several years, mediators will stick to smaller problems to build their reputations.

5 YEARS — As a mediator's experience increases, they are called on to help resolve larger disputes. Mediators aren't usually called on to travel, although some of the more experienced mediators travel extensively to help resolve disputes anywhere in the world.

10 YEARS — Highly competent mediators who have lasted 10 years or more may be called on to handle high-profile cases ranging from corporate disputes to international peacekeeping missions.

MAJOR EMPLOYERS
Most mediators are self-employed.

MAJOR ASSOCIATIONS
AFCC
6525 Grand Teton Plaza
Madison, WI 53719-1085
Tel: 608-664-3750
Fax: 608-664-3751
E-mail: afcc@afccnet.org
www.afccnet.org

ASSOCIATION FOR CONFLICT RESOLUTION
1015 18th Street, NW, Suite 1150
Washington, DC 20036
Tel: 202-464-9700
Fax: 202-464-9720
www.acrnet.org

SOUTHERN CALIFORNIA MEDIATION ASSOCIATION
10850 Wilshire Boulevard, Suite 400
Los Angeles, CA 90024
Tel: 877-963-3428
E-mail: scma@scmediation.org
www.scmediation.org

MUSICIAN

A DAY IN THE LIFE

Musicians include rock stars, opera singers, folk guitarists, jazz pianists, violinists, drummers—anybody who creates and performs music. Musicians consist of a broad group of artists who play musical instruments, sing, compose, and arrange music in a variety of settings. They perform before live audiences or record in music studios. Instrumental musicians use such items as the saxophone, guitar, drums, piano, or clarinet to create music. Singers use their voice. Composers are the creators of original music. Orchestra conductors lead orchestras and bands, and choral directors direct choirs, singing clubs, and other vocal ensembles. It's a tough field, but individuals in it usually feel an inner compulsion to play and share their music, so much so that they're willing to sacrifice a lot. "Music is in the soul, so I must play on and on; it's a given," says one saxophonist who finally signed a major recording contract. Some lucky musicians—orchestra members, opera singers, and a few pop artists—make a living at their profession. Very few become rich and famous—Frank Sinatra, Ella Fitzgerald, Paul McCartney, and Aimee Mann are rare examples—but most musicians are happy just to be able to play for an audience once in a while.

{ Music is in the soul. }

The serious musician spends a lot of time practicing and rehearsing. "You have to constantly better your best, for you're only as good as your last performance," said one musician. Musicians also spend a substantial amount of time on the road, traveling to and from performances, or just seeking performing opportunities. Since most musicians' gigs are at night and on weekends, those people who don't fully support themselves through their art often take day jobs to cover the bills.

Musicians can play and compose for a variety of sources. The television, motion picture, and advertising industries employ musicians to perform live shows, score music for movies, and compose and arrange theme songs for television programs and advertisements. Theater orchestras provide live music for plays and other productions. Because live audiences and auditions are a fact of life for musicians seeking to establish a reputation or find a niche, they must be able to deal with their anxieties and deliver a quality performance in front of any gathering of people. Musicians face rejection all the time, but the most disciplined individuals maintain confidence in their abilities; they can never allow themselves to become complacent if success is the goal. Most of them work at small-time gigs wherever they can—in clubs and churches and at weddings, birthdays, and bar mitzvahs—while waiting for their big breaks.

PAYING YOUR DUES

The road to becoming an accomplished musician starts at a very early age and involves rigorous study and training. For singers, training begins when their voices mature, and it never ends. Most other musicians start to play their instruments very early in their lives. Some musicians enter into private study with a highly reputed master musician, while others pursue a formal training program at a college or university, gaining a degree in music or music education. Talent, persistence, and having excellent mentors are essential to becoming a good musician.

For the recording artist, entertainment lawyers have become more of a necessity than even a manager, whereas musicians who rely mainly on live performances require only a road manager (if gigs pay enough to salary one) and an independent booking agent. Mastering the convoluted relationships among agents, managers, lawyers, and other industry professionals is a job in itself.

ASSOCIATED CAREERS

Musicians almost never give up music completely. Even when they leave for more stable, lucrative fields, they often seek out nightclub engagements at nights and on weekends. Take, for example, director Woody Allen, still playing his clarinet at Michael's Pub in New York on occasion. Some musicians find music-related jobs as teachers, songwriters, and even music therapists. Musicians with vast technical knowledge may find an opening in the specialized area of instrument repairs and tuning. They may also find jobs as music librarians, critics, and disc jockeys. Those who enjoy the business side may become concert managers, booking agents, music industry executives, and publicists. Some go into the sales and marketing of musical instruments and record store management.

PAST AND FUTURE

Music has been around since the beginning of time. Since there can be no music without musicians, their place is virtually assured—even if lucrative recording deals and a place in the limelight will continue to elude many of even the most gifted artists. As it is often not talent but public relations packaging that guarantees success, talented musicians will have to invent ways of selling themselves and their music to the public. Musicians able to compose, play several instruments, and arrange will find more employment opportunities open to them.

QUALITY OF LIFE

2 YEARS The musician with a bare two years of experience grabs at any and every opportunity to play—school or community concerts, bars, restaurants, birthday parties, bar mitzvahs, weddings, and even funerals. The newcomer to the music world is up against a vast array of talent, experience, and abilities, so practice sessions continue to be as arduous as they were in childhood. There is no corporate ladder or any of the scheduled raises and promotions that go with it; from day one, it's all about getting gigs and exposure.

5 YEARS The musician with five years of experience is still young in the business. Self-discipline is vital to the success of any musician, so practices and rehearsals continue to take up the greater part of the day. A day job supplements income earned from sporadic and low-paying gigs at nightclubs, while the musician continues to search for regular work as a performer. Many musicians give private lessons or opt to take work in an unrelated field.

10 YEARS To the musician with only two years of experience, 10 years seems considerable. But seniority, like talent, does not always translate into success or even modest recognition. The 10-year veteran is still practicing and developing his or her own musical style. Auditions, weekend gigs, and intermittent employment may still be the mainstay of the musician's life. The exceptionally talented have enlisted the services of an agent or manager to help find them engagements and manage their careers.

MAJOR EMPLOYERS

INTERSCOPE RECORDS
2220 Colorado Avenue
Santa Monica, CA 90404
Tel: 310-865-1000
Fax: 310-865-7096
www.interscope.com

NEW YORK METROPOLITAN OPERA GUILD
70 Lincoln Center Plaza
New York, NY 10023
Tel: 212-769-7000
E-mail: info@metguild.org
www.metguild.org

MAJOR ASSOCIATIONS

AMERICAN FEDERATION OF MUSICIANS
1501 Broadway, Suite 600
New York, NY 10036
Tel: 212-869-1330
Fax: 212-764-6134
www.afm.org

AMERICAN GUILD OF MUSICAL ARTISTS
1430 Broadway, 14th Floor
New York, NY 10018
Tel: 212-265-3687
Fax: 212-262-9088
E-mail: AGMA@musicalartists.org
www.musicalartists.org

MUSICIANS FOUNDATION
875 Sixth Avenue
New York, NY 10001
Tel: 212-239-9137
Fax: 212-239-9138
www.musiciansfoundation.org

NEWS ANCHOR

A DAY IN THE LIFE

Bombs dropping on Baghdad; Neil Armstrong walking on the moon; the Challenger shuttle exploding; the fall of the Berlin Wall: Whatever the occasion, journalists are always there, capturing the times that test us and the events that shape us. They keep us apprised of what's going on in our world. And when we hear anchors utter that indelible phrase, "We interrupt this broadcast," we know that news of a defining moment is about to be released.

News anchors must have their pulse on global social, political, and cultural movements. They are always anticipating the next big trend or history-making event. Newscasters spend their days examining, interpreting, and broadcasting news. While on the air, { **stamina, a keen memory, and resourcefulness** } their main function is to introduce stories and videotaped segments or live transmissions from on-the-scene reporters. Although most anchors are assigned either to a day or an evening shift, working hours may vary tremendously, especially if there is a late-breaking news development. Given the demands of the 24-hour news cycle, anchors often need to be ready to go on the air with virtually no time for advance preparation. As a result, a typical day is one that has the potential to change drastically at a moment's notice; and news anchors have to be able to maintain their composure and think on their feet, because life in the newsroom unfolds at a frenzied and furious pace.

With stories continually arising and a definite broadcast time always looming, the pressure to meet deadlines is intense. On top of the stamina required for the job, a keen memory is also a valuable trait, since the volume of news is immense. Resourcefulness is paramount, especially in extemporaneous speaking situations. On top of that, anchors need to be able to adapt quickly and easily to new situations. Perhaps most importantly, anchors must continually seek to provide accurate facts and impartial news, since the public places its trust in journalists. Lastly, having an on-camera job typically requires an eloquent speaking voice and a pleasant appearance, and so a typical day may involve activities related to physical appearance maintenance.

PAYING YOUR DUES

Anchors usually hold a degree either in journalism or in communications. Television news is a competitive field, and a BA alone won't land you a seat behind the nightly news desk. When looking to hire, most newsrooms want an individual who has reporting experience. It is essential that aspiring news anchors seek out internships in broadcasting and/or work at the broadcasting stations of their universities. Entry-level positions are usually of the desk-assistant variety. Although some of the work in such positions may be challenging, these positions involve a lot of grunt work, not to mention a lot of work in general. Desk assistants who get promoted tend to take initiative and be proactive, sometimes even aggressive. The bright side? All of your favorite news anchors have been there. One first jobber at a major news network reports: "Everyone has been a desk assistant at one point." Once you demonstrate your aptitude, the next step is usually to become a correspondent. This position is slightly more glamorous, but it often entails a lot of travel, much of which may be last-minute. You and the firefighters will be the only ones heading in the direction of a burning building, and you may often find yourself heading toward the eye of the storm, both literally and figuratively. Those who prove their abilities at this stage may eventually receive the cushier offer of a news anchor position. One last tip: If you're just starting out, smaller local stations tend to be more apt to hire new talent.

ASSOCIATED CAREERS

Do you fear that sitting behind a desk and getting your face powdered 10 seconds before you go on the air may eventually lose its luster? There are a multitude of other "behind-the-scenes" positions that may also be of interest to you. Many former news anchors have moved on to produce or edit news shows and specials. Others begin writing for television or print. Still others can't seem to resist the lure of the field and return to reporting.

PAST AND FUTURE

Edward R. Murrow is credited with the birth of broadcast journalism. His original show, *See It Now*, first aired on November 18, 1951. It was adapted from his radio program of the same name. By April of 1952, the program had been moved to primetime and was averaging about three million viewers per broadcast. *See It Now* earned four Emmy Awards in the course of its run. Many of the broadcasts, such as Murrow's debate with Senator Joseph McCarthy in March of 1954, were often hailed as breakthroughs for the medium.

Broadcast news, and hence news anchors, continue to gain momentum. Certainly, the advent of cable perpetuated and intensified 24-hour news coverage. Viewers are continually tuning in to networks like CNN to get up-to-the-minute information. And as the world grows more complicated and conflicted, people will come to rely on anchors all the more to provide accurate, timely news reports.

QUALITY OF LIFE

2 YEARS At two years into their careers, aspiring news anchors are still considered to be in the nascent stages of their careers. Most opportunities are with smaller local stations. Individuals in this group generally find themselves taking on multiple roles—not only introducing stories, but also conducting both on-camera and on-location interviews, as well. Typically, they write their own material.

5 YEARS Five years in television broadcasting marks a career crossroads for most anchors. At this point, they've gained a lot of reporting experience, become well-rounded journalists, and built strong industry foundations. They can begin to focus their attention on attaining positions at larger local affiliates, perhaps anchoring the weekday or weekend news. They may also start to acquire correspondent opportunities with major urban stations.

10 YEARS After 10 years on the air, anchors will be regarded as news veterans. While they may not always be broadcasting nationally during primetime, working in bigger markets is a viable option. Many journalists with this much experience obtain positions at larger stations in major metropolitan areas. They tend to stay behind the desk, presenting stories and introducing live transmissions and taped segments, the material for which is often written by others—but their extemporaneous comments and reflections peppered throughout are the fruits of their experience and expertise.

MAJOR EMPLOYERS

ABC TELEVISION
77 West 66th Street
New York, NY 10023
Tel: 212-456-7777
www.abc.com

CBS
530 West 57th Street
New York, NY 10019
Tel: 212-554-0080
www.cbs.com

CNN
One CNN Center
Atlanta, GA 30303
Tel: 404-878-2276
Fax: 404-827-1995
www.cnn.com

NBC
30 Rockefeller Plaza
New York, NY 10112
Tel: 212-664-2552
Fax: 212-245-4622
www.nbc.com

MAJOR ASSOCIATIONS

BROADCAST EDUCATION ASSOCIATION
1771 N Street, NW
Washington, DC 20036-2891
Tel: 202-429-3935 or 888-380-7222
E-mail: beainfo@beaweb.org
www.beaweb.org

NATIONAL ASSOCIATION OF BROADCASTERS
1771 N Street, NW
Washington, DC 20036
Tel: 202-429-5300
Fax: 202-429-4199
E-mail: nab@nab.org
www.nab.org

RADIO–TELEVISION NEWS DIRECTORS ASSOCIATION
1600 K Street NW, Suite 700
Washington, DC 20006-2838
Tel: 202-659-6510
Fax: 202-223-4007
E-mail: rtnda@rtnda.org
www.rtnda.org

NURSE

BOOKS, FILMS, AND TV SHOWS
FEATURING THE PROFESSION
- ER
- Nurse Betty
- Nurses
- One Flew Over the Cuckoo's Nest
- That 70s Show

YOU'LL HAVE CONTACT WITH
- Housekeeping
- Lab technicians
- Nutritionists
- Patients
- Pharmacists
- Physicians
- Social service workers

PROFESSIONALS READ
- American Journal of Nursing
- Journal of Practical Nursing
- Nursing
- Nursing Connections

A DAY IN THE LIFE

Nurses help prevent disease and injury and care for the sick and injured, but within these parameters, there are no limits to what the job can entail. "Nursing offers you the opportunity to do a million different things, in a million different places," as one survey respondent put it. Nurses work in hospitals, long-term care facilities, clinics, schools, corporations, and sometimes even in businesses of their own. While there are many different areas of specialization, some individuals are general nurses, who assist doctors by performing a variety of tasks as needs arise, and will often have secretarial duties as well if they work in HMOs or private offices. More specialized nurses include surgical nurses, who ensure the sterility of instruments and assist doctors during surgery; obstetric-gynecological nurses, who help to deliver babies; neonatal nurses, who care for newborns and teach new mothers how to feed their babies; nurse anesthetists, who work with anesthesiologists to provide proper sedation for patients; or psychiatric nurses, who care for patients with mental or emotional disorders. Occupational health nurses work at factories or other worksites to offer preventive education, and community or public health nurses spend time on the road to instruct various groups in their community on diverse health-related topics. Another variety of nurse is the private duty nurse, who has only one patient in his or her charge and works in the patient's home or in the hospital. Some are also hospice nurses (refer to page 62 of this section).

{ clear directions }

These days, nurses with more advanced degrees handle many things that were once the sole province of physicians, such as treating some ailments and setting fractures. Nurse practitioners can even make diagnoses and write prescriptions. Clinical nurse specialists also have additional patient responsibilities in such areas as geriatrics or pediatrics, depending on the nurse's specialty. Nurses can advance to become department heads or supervisors, overseeing other nurses as well as caring for patients. Each facility also has a director of nursing, who establishes standards of patient care, composes the department's budget, and advises other hospital employees on nursing issues.

Nurses generally work in eight-hour shifts day and night, although some hospitals have recently been experimenting with having nurses work 10 or 12-hour shifts on three or four days a week. Communication skills are critical—nurses must listen well and be able to give clear directions to patients and aides.

PAYING YOUR DUES

People who want to become nurses can choose among four educational programs. The two-year program takes place in a junior or community college combined with some hospital training. The diploma program, run entirely by a hospital or school and based solely on nursing, takes three years to complete. The longest is the BSN program, which awards candidates a bachelor's degree of science after four or five years of study at a college or university. None of these programs qualifies the nurse for practice, though. To practice, every nurse must pass a national licensing exam. After completing any of these programs and passing the exam, the nurse becomes an RN, or registered nurse. The fourth and quickest option is to become an LPN, or licensed practical nurse, which requires only one year of training. While for most beginning jobs the RN license opens the door, a BSN is necessary to be eligible for some supervisory positions. For the highest managerial positions or to teach in a nursing school, a master's degree in nursing is the norm. Some specialties even require a doctorate degree.

A background in science and liberal arts will serve future nurses well. Nursing programs place a large amount of emphasis on science and math for obvious reasons, but liberal arts courses are also helpful, since nurses spend much of their time educating patients and staff.

Registered nurses from all three programs can rise to become supervisors, directors of nursing, and other managerial roles. Codes that define the scope of nurses' practices are defined independently from state to state.

ASSOCIATED CAREERS

Some nurses go on to become instructors of nursing at hospitals and universities. Another burgeoning nursing-related profession is midwifery. After having been forced out of the field by doctors in the nineteenth century, midwives are returning to their centuries-old role of delivering babies. Now, midwives who are certified nurses actually deliver babies in hospitals, birthing centers, or the mother's home. Midwives also offer care to pregnant women and educate new mothers. Many women prefer their care to that of obstetricians.

PAST AND FUTURE

While hospitals have, in some form, been in existence for many centuries, it wasn't until the nineteenth century that Florence Nightingale transformed the nursing profession. During the Crimean War, she began a training program that taught citizens how to administer proper patient care, including sterilization, which was then a radical concept. Today, all nurses are trained, educated, and licensed professionals, and the field continues to grow, with more men entering this previously all-female profession every year.

The outlook for the future is bright, as the demand for qualified nurses far exceeds the supply in the health care industry. One effort that some states have made to make it easier to hire nurses is to waive the licensing exam for nurses coming into a job from out of state, provided that the nurse has already passed the exam in his or her state of residence.

QUALITY OF LIFE

2 YEARS Very few nurses leave the field at this point. Entry-level salaries are relatively high, and most nurses are becoming oriented to their surroundings and finding gratification in their work.

5 YEARS More nurses leave the profession at this time. Our respondents cited frustration with budget cutbacks that have interfered with the quality of nursing care as their main reason for leaving. Individuals who stay still enjoy the challenges and flexibility the profession offers. As many as 32 percent of all nurses work part-time.

10 YEARS Some veteran nurses find themselves making a lateral move from hospital to private care, which can ensure more regular hours and a stable atmosphere. After 10 years in the profession, many nurses have also advanced to higher-paying supervisory positions.

MAJOR EMPLOYERS

AURELIA OSBORN FOX MEMORIAL HOME NURSING COMPANY, INC.
One Norton Avenue
Oneonta, NY 13820
Tel: 607-431-5876

BAKERSFIELD MEMORIAL HOSPITAL
420 34th Street
Bakersfield, CA 93303
Tel: 661-327-1792
Contact: Human Resources Department

MEMORIAL SLOAN-KETTERING CANCER CENTER
1275 York Avenue
New York, NY 10021
Tel: 212-639-2000
www.mskcc.org
Contact: Nurse Recruitment

MAJOR ASSOCIATIONS

NATIONAL LEAGUE FOR NURSING
61 Broadway, 33rd Floor
New York, NY 10006
Tel: 212-363-5000
Fax: 212-812-0391
E-mail: generalinfo@nln.org
www.nln.org

NUTRITIONIST

**BOOKS, FILMS, AND TV SHOWS
FEATURING THE PROFESSION**

- **Eating Right**
- **Facts of Life**
- **In the Kitchen with Rosie**
- **Super Size Me**
- **What Doctors Don't Tell You**

YOU'LL HAVE CONTACT WITH

- **Chefs**
- **Child care workers**
- **Patients**
- **Psychologists**
- **Teachers**

PROFESSIONALS READ

- **Nutrition Forum**
- **Nutrition Research Newsletter**
- **Nutrition Today**

A DAY IN THE LIFE

Nutritionists have a healthy regard for food and its life-sustaining properties. They are primarily concerned with the prevention and treatment of illnesses through proper dietary care. Nutritionists evaluate the diets of patients and clients suffering from medical disorders and suggest ways of fighting various health problems by modifying the patient's intake of certain food items. As one nutritionist puts it, "It's basically all about balance—the older you get, the more you begin to understand the importance of balance in your life, and your diet is no exception." Hypertension, diabetes, and obesity are some of the common health problems that nutritionists work to alleviate. Through education and research, they also promote sensible eating habits in communities, schools, hospitals, prisons, clinics, and nursing homes. Like all other health professionals, nutritionists are motivated by a concern to improve people's quality of life.

{ life-sustaining }

Food manufacturers, advertisers, marketers, and some enlightened restaurateurs employ nutritionists to organize, develop, analyze, test, and prepare meals that are low in fat and cholesterol and virtually devoid of chemical additives. Nutritionists usually specialize in one of three major areas of practice: clinical, community, or administrative management. Clinical nutritionists service the needs of clients who are institutionalized. They develop, implement, and maintain nutritional programs for individuals in hospitals, nursing homes, retirement communities, day care centers, and prisons. Before proposing or implementing any dietary program, nutritionists must consult with doctors or other health professionals to ensure that medical and dietary needs are optimized. Community nutritionists are an integral part of health clinics, clubs, agencies, and HMOs. They advise individuals and groups on the nutritional practices that will promote good health. They also structure and recommend diet plans for whole families, often including guides to the correct preparation of meals and shopping for the right foods. Meal planning and preparation on a large scale, such as for a school district, requires the careful supervision of administrative or management nutritionists. Their responsibilities include preparing food budgets, purchasing food, ensuring that health and safety codes are strictly observed, maintaining records, and writing reports.

Nutritionists often spend the greater part of their workday on their feet. Hot, steamy kitchens also figure prominently in a nutritionist's career, although many of them end up working in well-lit, properly ventilated environments. But nutritionists must be prepared to work in environments that are not always equipped with modern conveniences or sometimes fall short of prescribed standards. In such work situations, the primary concern of the nutritionist will be to bring the work environment up to standard by enforcing health and safety codes and improving overall production capacity.

PAYING YOUR DUES

A bachelor's degree with a major in dietetics, food and nutrition, food service systems management, or a related subject is the basic requirement of this profession. Courses in the sciences, such as biology, microbiology, mathematics, statistics, psychology, and sociology are core course requirements.

ASSOCIATED CAREERS

The principles of nutrition are readily applied to a number of areas of modern life. Home economists, nurses, therapists, home-care attendants, health educators, and even chefs all require a working knowledge of nutrition. Some nutritionists report or prepare publications on food and health-related issues, such as the importance of fiber in the diet and the efficacy of vitamin supplements. The growing popularity and marketing power of the fitness industry coupled with an overall movement toward healthier lifestyles as a consequence of the growing incidence of heart disease and obesity among America's aging population has ensured the place of nutritionists in the scheme of things.

PAST AND FUTURE

The study of nutrition dates back at least as far as the eighteenth century, when the French scientist Antoine Lavoisier linked respiration with metabolic function.

The employment prospects for dieticians and nutritionists are expected to grow at an average rate through 2012.

QUALITY OF LIFE

2 YEARS At this early stage, nutritionists are still learning how thoroughly to evaluate a patient's or client's dietary needs. They should understand the absolute importance of communicating clearly and directly with the attending physician or health care professional before developing or recommending any nutrition program. Nutritionists should also be establishing their professional style in dealing with and relating to patients. Their focus is on creating an environment in which the patient feels at ease.

5 YEARS Nutritionists at this stage are now seasoned professionals who perform their duties with minimal or no supervision, cross-reference their information with doctors, are thorough in their research, are accurate in their recommendations, and have a good rapport with their patients. At this stage, individuals seeking a challenge will begin to examine their options for advancement in their current field, weighing them against employment opportunities in other areas.

10 YEARS At the 10-year mark, highly experienced nutritionists are ripe for setting up their own private consulting firm. They should have developed a considerable amount of contacts to easily facilitate such a move. 10-year veterans have kept abreast of industry developments through trade journals and other publications, revising and updating their own nutrition programs at every step of the way. They may also write their own books and articles for publication. Academia will require the services of many nutrition veterans as the industry continues to expand at its record fast pace and more universities and colleges begin to offer nutrition and dietetics programs.

MAJOR EMPLOYERS
AMERICAN HEART ASSOCIATION
7272 Greenville Avenue
Dallas, TX 75231
Tel: 800-242-8721
www.americanheart.org
Contact: Human Resources

U.S. DEPARTMENT OF HEALTH AND HUMAN SERVICES
200 Independence Avenue, SW
Washington, DC 20201
Tel: 202-619-0257 or 877-696-6775
www.os.dhhs.gov

WEIGHT WATCHERS INTERNATIONAL
175 Crossway Park West
Woodbury, NY 11797
Tel: 516-390-1400
Fax: 516-390-1334
E-mail: hr@weight-watchers.com
www.weight-watchers.com
Contact: Human Resources

MAJOR ASSOCIATIONS
THE AMERICAN SOCIETY FOR CLINICAL NUTRITION
9650 Rockville Pike
Bethesda, MD 20814-3998
Tel: 301-634-7110
Fax: 301-634-7350
www.ascn.org

OCCUPATIONAL THERAPIST

A DAY IN THE LIFE

Occupational therapists care for persons with disabling mental, physical, developmental, and emotional conditions and help them recover or develop and maintain their daily living and work skills. With clients who are overcoming everything from strokes to attention deficit disorder, occupational therapists help their patients have productive and independent lives. They help patients compensate for the loss of functions, as in the case of amputees or recently disabled individuals, as well as improve motor skills and reasoning and perceptual abilities. Some therapists work solely with specific disabilities or with certain age groups. Specialties include alcoholism, drug abuse, eating disorders, mental health, and industry-specific injury and pain management. Occupational therapy requires unequivocal dedication, and often rewards its practitioners with a tremendous sense of accomplishment. The profession calls for the best of those individuals who practice it; occupational therapists must be compassionate, caring, patient, and capable of commanding the respect and trust of people within their care. "The satisfaction you get from helping someone reclaim their life is enormous," one student intern enthused. "Sometimes they come in depressed and angry and gradually their spirits are renewed with each day of therapy, and hope is in their eyes and their future."

{ tremendous sense of accomplishment }

The well-trained professional is familiar with a wide range of activities that will be employed as a matter of course in the patient's recovery. Patients suffering from coordination problems, for example, may be given manual art projects, such as creative handicrafts, to improve hand-eye coordination. Practical activities such as gardening and weaving increase strength and dexterity. Although most occupational therapists work an average 40-hour week, it is often emotionally draining and backbreaking work. Practitioners are challenged to develop and implement exercises that will gain the maximum participation and interest of patients. Occupational therapists face significant challenges when dealing with patients with permanent physical handicaps, such as muscular dystrophy, cerebral palsy, or spinal cord injuries. They develop and teach patients how to operate adaptive equipment such as wheelchairs, splints, and other devices that allow individuals with limitations to exercise a measure of control over their environment. Occupational therapists who work with the physically disabled must have strength, agility, and stamina to help patients in and out of beds and wheelchairs and allow patients to lean on them while they assist them with various exercises, such as walking and lifting weights. Not all therapists need to be physically strong and powerful, but all, including industrial therapists who assist patients in finding and holding jobs, are challenged to inspire trust, motivate progress, and demonstrate concern and compassion.

PAYING YOUR DUES

Starting in 2007, all certified occupational therapists will be required to have an entry-level master's or doctoral degree. Until then, they can get by with a bachelor's degree in occupational therapy. But they too will have to pass the test administered by the National Board for Certification in Occupational Therapy, which enables those who pass to apply to their state regulatory board to practice. Internships or volunteer work in the health care field demonstrate to potential employers the commitment that is a necessary prerequisite to this profession. Applicants should carefully consider their ability to physically and emotionally cope with the demands of the job. By far the most significant qualification applicants to this profession could have is a sincere commitment to the care of others.

ASSOCIATED CAREERS

With a rapidly aging population, the need for assorted health care professionals to provide specialized rehabilitative care will remain constant. Because therapists are required to be versed in a number of activities that are used in the care of the disabled, this facilitates an easy transition to alternative occupations. Horticulture, music, dance, manual arts, and creative handicrafts are exercises for the physically challenged as well as those individuals suffering from stress-related illnesses. Some occupational therapists, with further studies, will move into orthotics, chiropractic treatment, speech pathology, audiology, prosthetics, physical therapy, and rehabilitation counseling areas.

PAST AND FUTURE

Occupational therapy was established as a career in science after World War I, when the nation had to offer services to the thousands of injured soldiers who were returning to the United States. The American Occupational Therapy Association was established in 1923 and began offering accreditation in 1935. It now has approximately 35,000 occupational therapists associated with it.

The field of occupational therapy is forecasted to increase its demand for new professionals at a pace faster than average, as compared to all other industries, for the rest of the decade. As scientific discoveries continue to extend the life expectancy of the average American, patients will need extensive therapy to combat a number of disabling conditions. Therefore, occupational therapists will have to update their knowledge of new adaptive equipment and its uses as they also develop new skill sets.

QUALITY OF LIFE

2 YEARS If he or she is practicing in a state that requires licensing, the occupational therapist should be thinking of and making steps toward becoming a registered professional. The ambitious therapist seeks the guidance and advice of mentors and develops professional contacts. This is an ideal time for the practitioner to decide whether he or she wants to work exclusively with a specific age group or service the needs of individuals with particular disabilities.

5 YEARS With five years of on-the-job experience, the occupational therapist is now board-certified and has updated his or her skills through job-training programs, college courses, and professional workshops. Thus the occupational therapist is ready for and probably actively seeking advancement. At this juncture an evaluation of existing employment opportunities or the possibility of shifting to an alternate career is foremost in the mind of the practitioner. Private or group practice is a distinct possibility for the five-year veteran.

10 YEARS If the occupational therapist is not in a top-level administrative post at a health care facility after 10 years of service, then he or she should definitely be moving in the direction of establishing a private practice. With considerable years of experience, professional and personal contacts, and a growing number of adult day care programs, nursing homes, and health care agencies, private or group practice should be a lucrative and worthwhile endeavor.

MAJOR EMPLOYERS
CARONDELET HEALTH CARE CORPORATION
120 North Tucson Boulevard
Tucson, AZ 85716
Tel: 520-873-5000
Fax: 520-873-5030
www.carondelet.org
Contact: Human Resources

Occupational therapists are primarily employed by hospitals, outpatient clinics, rehabilitation centers, nursing homes, schools, and other social service agencies, at which they work in conjunction with other therapists and counselors. Some of them also go into private practice and work as consultants with companies. Contact local health and mental health care agencies in your area for employment opportunities.

MAJOR ASSOCIATIONS
AMERICAN OCCUPATIONAL THERAPY ASSOCIATION
4720 Montgomery Lane
PO Box 31220
Bethesda, MD 20824-1220
Tel: 301-652-2682
Fax: 301-652-7711
www.aota.org

NATIONAL BOARD FOR CERTIFICATION IN OCCUPATIONAL THERAPY
800 South Frederick Avenue, Suite 200
Gaithersburg, MD 20877-4150
Tel: 301-990-7979
Fax: 301-869-8492
www.nbcot.org

OPTOMETRIST

A DAY IN THE LIFE

"If you are looking for a dynamic and challenging career that allows you to help people and achieve personal growth, community respect, flexibility, and financial success, optometry is for you," says one optometrist with a private practice in New York City. "I've had this business for nearly 40 years, and I don't plan on retiring anytime soon. In my opinion, this field offers unlimited opportunities." Like this doctor, most optometrists are in private practice, either solo or with a group of fellow optometrists. A growing number of optometrists are employed by other optometrists or ophthalmologists, hospitals, HMOs, or retail optical stores. Still others pursue careers in the military or public health service, teaching, and research. They may also specialize in working chiefly with elderly patients, children, contact-lens patients, and the partially blind.

{ **primary eye-care provider** }

Whether they work in a private practice, group practice, or clinic, optometrists all perform a number of duties. They examine the internal and external structure of the eye to assess its neural connections, determine its ability to see color accurately, and measure depth perception. They also assess and, with corrective lenses, improve the patient's ability to see both close up and from a distance. Perhaps most importantly, they can diagnose eye disease. Optometrists will consult with ophthalmologists regarding the care for cataract patients and can often provide much of those patients' pre- and post-operative care. As the primary eye-care provider, they are on the front lines to observe early signs of systemic conditions, and, by acting in due course of their examination, contribute to their patients' overall health. All optometrists need great people skills and the ability to deal with patients tactfully. Those individuals with private practices also need business skills.

PAYING YOUR DUES

Just as an optometrist's professional responsibilities are varied and difficult, so may be the road to becoming an optometrist. Admission into any of the 17 accredited optometric colleges in the United States is very competitive. As an undergraduate, superior grades in math, physics, chemistry, biology, anatomy, physiology, and even English are a must. Applicants must also take and score highly on the OCAT (Optometry College Aptitude Test). Graduate study lasts four years and includes classroom and clinical training in ocular anatomy, disease, myotology, pharmacology, neuroanatomy and neurophysiology of the vision system, vision performance, and vision screening. Unique to optometric education is the study of optics and extensive training in lens design, construction, application, and fitting. And, since optometrists are members of the primary health care team, they also must study human anatomy, general pharmacology, pathology, psychology, biochemistry, statistics, and epidemiology, much like any medical student. After completing this study successfully for an OD (Doctorate Degree of Optometry), optometrists must pass a state board examination to become licensed to practice in their state.

ASSOCIATED CAREERS

Very few optometrists transfer to other occupations, but individuals who do sometimes look at ophthalmology. Ophthalmologists are specialized physicians concentrating in treating eye diseases, repairing injuries, and performing eye surgeries. Optometrists may become ophthalmologists, but only after several more years of schooling. Because optometrists apply scientific knowledge to prevent, diagnose, and treat disorders and injuries, those few individuals who want to change career tracks before committing to the years of education ahead of them also consider careers as chiropractors, podiatrists, and even speech-language pathologists. A scant few of them become enchanted with optics and turn their career track to the practical applications of optics in industry, such as laser technology or lens technology used by NASA and in industrial research.

PAST AND FUTURE

Breakthroughs in technology have made optometry a more accurate science and have made treatments once unthinkable, such as a radial keratotomy, a reality. More and more optometrists are hiring optometric assistants and other support personnel to meet the growing demand for eye care. Because more HMOs and health care plans include vision plans, optometry is a growth industry, and not just for those individuals with private practices. Employment in this field is expected to grow as fast or faster than average when compared to all other occupations.

QUALITY OF LIFE

2 YEARS Starting salaries for optometrists are relatively high, although income varies greatly depending on geographic area and specialization. Optometrists who begin working as salaried employees tend to earn more initially than those individuals who start their own practices. Beginning optometrists enter into associate practices with other optometrists to earn enough money to start their own practice.

5 YEARS Professional reputation and the number of years in practice affect earnings level. Optometrists who have their own practice in the six-figure range will start to develop a client base and a reputation. Those optometrists who are working for group practices or HMOs with four or five years of experience can be pulling in anywhere from $30,000–$85,000. At this point, some professionals may have gone back to school for a master's degree or PhD to acquire the necessary training to teach or to specialize in areas like neuro-optometry or pediatric optometry. Some optometrists decide to pursue research positions.

10 YEARS In the long run, it is those who have private practices who end up with the most lucrative jobs. With years of experience and a solid reputation, an optometrist in a major metropolitan area can make as much as $160,000 per year.

MAJOR EMPLOYERS
LENSCRAFTERS
8650 Governors Hill Drive
Cincinnati, OH 45249
www.lenscrafters.com

A substantial majority of optometrists are self-employed.

MAJOR ASSOCIATIONS
AMERICAN OPTOMETRIC ASSOCIATION
243 North Lindbergh Boulevard, 1st Floor
St. Louis, MO 63141
Tel: 800-365-2219
Fax: 314-991-4101
www.aoanet.org

ASSOCIATION OF SCHOOLS AND COLLEGES OF OPTOMETRY
6110 Executive Boulevard, Suite 510
Rockville, MD 20852
Tel: 301-231-5944
Fax: 301-770-1828
www.opted.org

PARALEGAL

PROFESSIONAL PROFILE

# of people in profession	200,000
Avg. hours per week	40
Avg. starting salary	$30,020
Avg. salary after 5 years	$37,950
Avg. salary 10 to 15 years	$48,760

SALARY • •
HOURS • •
EDUCATION • •

BOOKS, FILMS, AND TV SHOWS
FEATURING THE PROFESSION
- **Case #11072**
- **The Firm**
- **Night Shifts**
- **Paralegals: Enhancing the Practice, Professionalism and Profitability**

YOU'LL HAVE CONTACT WITH
- **Administrative support staff**
- **Attorneys**
- **Clients**
- **Judicial personnel**
- **Librarians**
- **Proofreaders**
- **Public officials**
- **Secretaries**
- **Vendors**

PROFESSIONALS READ
- **Legal Assistant Today**
- **NALA Facts & Findings**
- **Paralegal**

A DAY IN THE LIFE

Through a combination of education, training, and work experience, a paralegal performs "substantive" legal work and is "an integral part of the legal team," according to a vice president of a major association. If you want to learn the nuts and bolts of the legal profession and understand the importance of careful and thorough research, then paralegal studies may be the right occupation for you. The paralegal, or legal assistant, profession is the ground floor to lawyering and often, every bit as important. In many distinct ways, their duties include the same tasks lawyers who assume responsibility for the legal work do, but paralegals do not practice law and are prohibited from dispensing legal advice, trying a case in court, or accepting legal fees. Paralegals work hand in hand with lawyers, helping to prepare cases for trial. In their preparatory work, they uncover all the facts of the case, conduct research to highlight relevant case laws and court decisions, obtain affidavits, and assist with depositions and other materials relevant to cases.

{ an integral part of the legal team }

A significant portion of a paralegal's work involves writing reports and drafting documents for litigation. After the initial fact-gathering stage, the paralegal prepares reports for use by the supervising attorney in deciding how the case should be litigated. Paralegals who work in areas other than litigation, such as patent and copyright law and real estate and corporate law, also assist in the drafting of relevant documents—contracts, mortgages, estate planning, and separation agreements. Paralegals who work for government agencies maintain reference files, analyze material for internal use, and prepare information guides on the law. Those paralegals involved with community legal services help disadvantaged persons in need of legal aid. Much of their time is spent preparing and filing documents and doing research. Employee benefit plans, shareholder agreements, and stock options are the primary concern of the paralegal working for corporations.

PAYING YOUR DUES

Paralegals usually enter the profession after completing American Bar Association (ABA)-approved college or training programs or are trained on the job. Although most paralegal programs are completed in two years, a growing number of colleges and universities offer four-year bachelor's degree programs. Beyond this, some firms hire liberal arts majors as paralegals directly after college and then train them on the job. This is a growth profession that attracts large numbers of applicants, and the competition is strong and healthy. A four-year program at a reputable college and certification by the National Association of Legal Assistants, the Certified Legal Assistant (CLA) designation, will greatly enhance employment opportunities. The paralegal who has demonstrated competence in computer applications will distinguish him- or herself from the pack and be able to move ahead. Practical experience gained from student internships, familiarity with legal terminology, and strong investigative skills are also advantages.

ASSOCIATED CAREERS

A number of occupations call for specialized knowledge of the law but fall short of the need for a lawyer. Should a paralegal become disenchanted with his or her career, there are possibilities in law enforcement or as an insurance claims adjuster, occupational safety and health officer, patent agent, and title examiner. And there is always the option of ultimately becoming a lawyer.

PAST AND FUTURE

The paralegal profession is a relatively new and rapidly expanding area. Previously, much of the groundwork now covered by the paralegal was part and parcel of being a lawyer. Now lawyers can afford to focus more intently on the strategies of trying cases and resolving legal problems, thanks to the invaluable preparatory work of the paralegal. Computer technology will continue to play a significant role in the fact-finding and fact-gathering stages of most legal cases. Instead of poring over volumes of research material in law libraries, much of this information is easily accessible from online digitized law libraries and software programs. Of course the paralegal who specializes in a particular field and who is computer literate will have the added edge on advancement. Because of the continuous enactment of new legislation and revised interpretations of existing laws, the paralegal must keep constantly updated on every change, every proposal, and every nuance of the law.

QUALITY OF LIFE

2 YEARS These are the critical years for the newcomer to the profession to take stock, gain valuable all-around experience, and simply feel his or her way around the profession. At this stage the paralegal is probably given minimal responsibilities but loads of work— and working up to 90 hours a week should be expected at times, for those individuals who want to get anywhere in the profession. The day will be spent doing research in the law library, poring over tedious documents (looking for witness names through word-searches and similarly mind-numbing tasks), and preparing reports for presentations (three-hole punching, formatting labels, etc). The paralegal should expect to be under constant supervision, assist with clerical matters, photocopy articles, and compile files. The work may seem never-ending and tedious, but the paralegal with perseverance will take it in stride and absorb this experience.

5 YEARS If he or she hasn't opted to attend law school, by now the experienced paralegal has decided on and begun to pursue a specialized field. The professional paralegal has more responsibility and significantly reduced supervision. In a corporate environment, advancement opportunities are possible at this juncture. Usually, paralegals move up to supervisory or managerial capacities, but many of them may find it easier to move to another law firm in search of advancement and better salaries.

10 YEARS The 10-year mark is the ideal time for reassessment of one's career as a paralegal. By now the professional has undergone several career-enhancing changes, such as college refresher courses, workshops and seminars on changes in the law, becoming familiar with new computer applications in legal research, and developing an area of specialty. At this stage, if the paralegal still yearns for more responsibilities and challenges, he or she should make the decision of whether to pursue a law degree or undertake an alternate career.

MAJOR EMPLOYERS

CANDICE APPLE & ASSOCIATES
403 West Fisher Avenue
Greensboro, NC 27401
Tel: 336-370-1652 or 800-669-2390
Fax: 336-370-0032
www.candiceapple.com

SKADDEN, ARPS, SLATE, MEAGHER & FLOM LLP
Four Times Square
New York, NY 10022
Tel: 212-735-3000
Fax: 212-735-2000
www.skadden.com
Contact: Human Resources

In addition to law firms, paralegals are also hired by corporations, branches of the government, universities, and nonprofit organizations.

MAJOR ASSOCIATIONS

AMERICAN ASSOCIATION FOR PARALEGAL EDUCATION
19 Martin Road
Mt. Royal, NJ 08061
Tel: 856-423-2829
Fax: 856-423-3420
E-mail: info@aafpe.org
www.aafpe.org

NATIONAL ASSOCIATION OF LEGAL ASSISTANTS
1516 Boston Avenue, Suite 200
Tulsa, OK 74119
Tel: 918-587-6828
www.nala.org

NATIONAL FEDERATION OF PARALEGAL ASSOCIATIONS
2517 Eastlake Avenue East, Suite 200
Seattle, WA 98102
Tel: 206-652-4120
Fax: 206-652-4122
www.paralegals.org

PHARMACIST

A DAY IN THE LIFE

Pharmacists dispense drugs and medicines prescribed by physicians and health practitioners. As such, a pharmacist must possess the medical knowledge necessary to inform his or her customers about the purpose, hazards, and side effects of any drug he or she dispenses. Pharmacists also keep computerized and often detailed records of patient drug use and medical profiles to ensure that patients won't combine drugs that shouldn't be taken with one another and that they are following their doctors' instructions concerning dosage. It is an increasing part of the pharmacist's job to be actively involved with patients, providing information on prescription drugs, referring patients to appropriate over-the-counter drugs, and advising physicians on the proper selection and use of medications.

{ actively involved with patients }

Pharmacists employed in community pharmacies, as nearly 60 percent are, may also take on the responsibilities of running the business, such as buying and selling non-pharmaceutical merchandise (think of what else you can get at Rite Aid), hiring and supervising personnel and pharmacy technicians, and overseeing much of the day-to-day operation of the pharmacy itself. Although pharmacists who run their own business certainly perform these tasks, even salaried employees of big-chain pharmacies can find themselves taking on some managerial responsibilities in addition to their pharmaceutical duties.

Pharmacists who are employed by hospitals (this group makes up 25 percent of the profession), clinics, and HMOs dispense prescriptions and work as consultants to the medical team. They also make sterile solutions for use in the emergency room and in surgical procedures, purchase medical supplies, instruct interns, and perform administrative duties. Some of them in the hospital and medical field continue their education and conduct research into new medicines and areas of drug therapy, specializing in drug therapies for psychiatric disorders, for example, or the use of radiopharmaceuticals.

Most pharmacists spend an average of 44 hours per week at their jobs, but individuals who are self-employed tend to work longer. In any case, the work is not sedentary, and pharmacists report spending a lot of their time on their feet.

PAYING YOUR DUES

The majority of students enter pharmacy school with at least three years of college under their belts. Undergraduate study should consist of mathematics and sciences such as biology, chemistry, and physics, as well as humanities and social sciences. Students on this track need to pay close attention to the curriculum recommended by the college of pharmacy they intend to apply to in order to fulfill admissions requirements. Students must then complete at least two years of special pre-pharmacy coursework followed by four academic years of pharmacy study.

In addition to being knowledgeable, a pharmacist needs to have good people skills. Successful completion of the academic and clinical requirements of a professional degree from an accredited program and passage of a state board examination are required to obtain a license to practice pharmacy.

ASSOCIATED CAREERS

Education and training in the pharmaceutical sciences open up more career choices than just the practice of pharmacy. Drug manufacturers and wholesalers hire pharmacists as sales and medical service representatives. Drug companies see the advantages of having informed salespeople pitching their products to retail pharmacies and hospitals, and pharmacists provide credible information on new drug products to prospective buyers. With additional education and training, a qualified pharmacist can also teach in colleges of pharmacy, supervise the manufacture of pharmaceuticals, or become involved with the research and development of new medicines. With more academic work, pharmacists can move into pharmacology or become pharmaceutical chemists. The academically minded pharmacists combine pharmaceutical and legal education to pursue jobs as patent lawyers or consultants on pharmaceutical and drug laws.

PAST AND FUTURE

The days of a pharmacist's work resembling that of an ancient alchemist are gone. The actual mixing of ingredients to form powders, tablets, capsules, ointments, and so on is the smallest part of a pharmacist's job. Most medicines are now produced by pharmaceutical companies and come pre-packaged. Though technology has taken over one aspect of a pharmacist's job, it has also created a need for more pharmacists. Scientific advances in medicine have made drugs for the treatment and prevention of disease widely available, and with more and more new drugs and drug treatment options available, there is a demand for pharmacists who can consult physicians, health care practitioners, and patients on the proper use of these new drugs. Also important to the projected growth in the profession is the increase in the elderly population—the primary consumers of medicines—as the average life expectancy of Americans rises every year. This puts the career of pharmacist among an elite group of professions that are luring new graduates into the field with perks, incentives, and generous salaries.

QUALITY OF LIFE

2 YEARS Many pharmacists will start out as employees of community pharmacies and retail chains, while others will work in hospitals with limited responsibilities under the watchful eyes of their supervisors. Starting salaries range widely for entry-level pharmacists, depending on region and practice setting.

5 YEARS By this point, pharmacists who can afford to start up their own businesses have the experience to do so. Those individuals working in community pharmacies have the professional experience to move into managerial and supervisory positions, and pharmacists working in hospitals will assume senior supervisory positions and direct the actions of interns and newly licensed pharmacists. Pharmaceutical companies are also searching for pharmacists with this level of experience to act as sales representatives. Others pharmacists choose to pursue a master's or doctorate degree to move into teaching and research positions.

10 YEARS Well established by this point in their careers, those individuals who have stayed within the community pharmacy field are managers, and some of them have achieved executive positions within the company. People who have remained in hospitals assume administrative positions or have achieved the position of director of pharmacy service and are in charge of all of the hospital's pharmaceutical services. But nearly any pharmacist with this much experience can find gainful employment in the manufacturing side of the industry in management positions, sales, research, quality control, advertising, production, and other areas. After 10 years, many pharmacists have enough capital to finally start their own practices, while those individuals who have had their own businesses should enjoy continued success.

MAJOR EMPLOYERS

CVS
One CVS Drive
Woonsocket, RI 02985
Tel: 888-607-4287
www.cvs.com

GENOVESE
80 Marcus Drive
Melville, NY 11747
Contact: Recruiting Department

RITE AID CORPORATION
30 Hunter Lane
Camp Hill, PA 17011
Tel: 717-761-2633
E-mail: recruiter@riteaid.com
www.riteaid.com

MAJOR ASSOCIATIONS

AMERICAN ASSOCIATION OF COLLEGES OF PHARMACY
1426 Prince Street
Alexandria, VA 22314
Tel: 703-739-2330
Fax: 703-836-8982
E-mail: mail@aacp.org
www.aacp.org

AMERICAN COUNCIL ON PHARMACEUTICAL EDUCATION
20 North Clark Street, Suite 2500
Chicago, IL 60602-5109
Tel: 312-664-3575
Fax: 312-664-7008
www.acpe-accredit.org

AMERICAN PHARMACIST'S ASSOCIATION
2215 Constitution Avenue, NW
Washington, DC 20037-2985
Tel: 202-628-4410 or 800-237-2742
Fax: 202-783-2351
www.aphanet.org

PHILOSOPHER

BOOKS, FILMS, AND TV SHOWS
FEATURING THE PROFESSION
- **A Confederacy of Dunces**
- **Kafka**
- **Rope**
- **Sophie's World**
- **Tom & Viv**

PROFESSIONALS READ
- **Computational Intelligence**
- **Critical Inquiry**
- **Psyche**

A DAY IN THE LIFE

What is the nature of truth, the meaning of life, the ideal structure of a society, the basis of morality, or the essential makeup of reality? Philosophers spend their lives attempting to answer questions like these. A taste for intellectual debate is a must in this profession. If you enjoy speculative reasoning, you'll probably enjoy being a philosopher, but be warned: it's a tough way to pay the rent. Most philosophers make their livings as college professors (see the Professor profile), but there aren't many full-time teaching positions in philosophy, and philosophers do not have many outside employment opportunities as do engineers or economists. The French government has occasionally employed its own philosophers, once hiring noted philosopher Michel

{ **a life of pure contemplation** }

Foucault to serve on a committee to rewrite the French penal code, but the United States government is not known for doing the same. For individuals who do find teaching positions in philosophy, the work is quite similar to that of other professors in the humanities. Aside from teaching responsibilities, which usually occupy approximately 12 hours of his or her time per week, a philosopher's time is largely his or her own. Professors stay busy, however; long hours are the norm. Yet the work is a pleasure if you enjoy reading and writing about philosophy, and why else would you enter the field? Particularly in the first few years, philosophy involves much writing, as young philosophy professors' publishing records are important parts of tenure evaluations. Once tenured, however, philosophers can probably live the closest approximation of a life of pure contemplation in our society.

PAYING YOUR DUES

Unless you plan on taking the Thoreau-Walden Pond approach, you'll probably need a PhD in philosophy. This is a prerequisite for teaching in the field. It involves five to seven years of study after completion of a college degree, including two to three years of course work. The rest of the time is spent writing a dissertation, which must be an original manuscript that analyzes some aspect of philosophy. More than in many of the other humanities professions, universities have philosophy departments that are specialized, choosing to hire a majority of analytic philosophers, continental philosophers, comparative philosophers, or some other branch of the field. The young philosopher's choice of a dissertation topic, therefore, has a significant impact on the institutions at which jobs will be available after graduation. Like all the academic disciplines, relationships with senior faculty are extremely important in finding a job, as doors to employment opportunities are often opened through recommendations from colleagues.

ASSOCIATED CAREERS

Individuals with backgrounds in philosophy turn up in a wide variety of fields. The training is flexible enough that philosophers can become writers, policy analysts, editors, or almost any other profession imaginable. Perhaps because the training often includes substantial elements of political philosophy, many people decide to go from philosophy to the legal profession.

PAST AND FUTURE

Contemporary philosophy, as it is taught in United States universities, traces its roots to the ancient Greeks; but other systems of non-Western philosophy find their origins in a vast range of sources, from the political debates of the Iroquois Confederacy to the Confucian writings of early China. Western philosophy is divided into two camps: continental philosophers, who concentrate on traditionally defined philosophical writers like Nietzsche and Hegel, and analytic philosophers, who owe much of their methodology to logic, mathematics, and theoretical physics. While this profession will likely remain limited in size, it should see the same increase that is expected for all the academic professions as the number of college-age Americans continues to grow. In recent years, however, the humanities have lost ground to the more professionally oriented fields of American academia, and this trend will likely continue.

QUALITY OF LIFE

2 YEARS — At this stage, the recent philosophy PhD graduate is either in a tenure-track job as an instructor or assistant professor or is a part-time or adjunct professor looking for a job that will eventually lead to tenure. The young assistant professor works long hours, teaching several undergraduate classes and beginning to establish the research and writing record necessary to advance in his or her field. In addition, the recent PhD recipient is expected to present papers at philosophy conferences to establish professional contacts and submit his or her work to the scrutiny of other philosophers. In smaller and two-year colleges, there is often less pressure to publish, but these are busy years wherever the young philosopher teaches.

5 YEARS — A career in academia has begun to take shape at this point. The philosopher has probably published a handful of articles that have begun to establish clear areas of expertise. At this stage, assistant philosophy professors have more control over their teaching schedules; they are likely to be teaching fewer introductory classes and more classes and seminars in their areas of specialization with enrollments consisting of upper-level undergraduates and graduate students. Since academic marketability is determined by a university's specific needs, professors are able to move from one institution to another as they establish themselves in their respective philosophical fields.

10 YEARS — By now, philosophers have either made tenure at the university in which they started, found another university that will give them tenure, or left the profession. With tenure comes the rewards of the philosophical life: the ability to say, write, and teach what one wishes with almost complete freedom.

MAJOR EMPLOYERS

Philosophers are employed primarily by universities. Occasionally, however, they find work outside of academia as editors at book publishers, for example, or as logic puzzle designers for standardized test companies.

MAJOR ASSOCIATIONS

AMERICAN CATHOLIC PHILOSOPHICAL ASSOCIATION

Administration Building
Fordham University
Bronx, NY 10458
Tel: 718-817-4081
Fax: 718-817-5709
www.acpaweb.org

AMERICAN PHILOSOPHICAL ASSOCIATION

31 Amstel Avenue
University of Delaware
Newark, DE 19716-4797
Tel: 302-831-1112
Fax: 302-830-8690
E-mail: apaonline@udel.edu
www.apa.udel.edu/apa

PHOTOGRAPHER

PROFESSIONAL PROFILE

# of people in profession	130,000
Avg. hours per week	40
Avg. starting salary	$17,740
Avg. salary after 5 years	$24,040
Avg. salary 10 to 15 years	$34,910

SALARY ● ●
HOURS ● ●
EDUCATION ● ●

BOOKS, FILMS, AND TV SHOWS
FEATURING THE PROFESSION
- **Absolute Beginners**
- **Blow-Up**
- **The Bridges of Madison County**
- **The Eyes of Laura Mars**
- **The Girl in the Picture**

YOU'LL HAVE CONTACT WITH
- **Advertising executives**
- **Clients**
- **Event planners**
- **Graphic designers**
- **Journalists**

PROFESSIONALS READ
- **Communication Arts**
- **Photo District News**
- **Professional Photographer**

A DAY IN THE LIFE

A photographer takes pictures of people, places, objects, and events, which he or she tries to capture artistically. Photographers also seek to evoke a mood, feeling, or drama surrounding a particular subject. Photography is both an artistic and a technical job that allows an individual the opportunity to demonstrate his or her creative abilities and technical proficiency. A photographer uses his or her camera much the same way an artist uses his or her brush, as a tool to capture his or her unique perspective of the world. For example, the famous photographer Ansel Adams popularized the genre of landscape photography as art through his pictures of Yosemite; and Alfred Steiglitz recorded the charm of the drama of the modern world around him in great photos such as "The Steerage" and earned fame for his series of portraits of Georgia O'Keeffe. A photographer must practice extensively to master the technical applications of light, camera settings, lenses, film, and filters and use these applications creatively. Photographers use a wide variety of lenses and filters designed for close-up, midrange, or long-distance photography. Some photographers do their own developing and printing, especially art photographers, but many of them hand their film over to their employer or a commercial lab for processing.

{ **unique perspective** }

More than half of all photographers are self-employed, and most specialize in commercial or portrait photography or photojournalism. Commercial photography involves taking pictures of merchandise, buildings, machinery, fashion, and landscapes to be used in advertisements, marketing reports, brochures, catalogs, and websites. Editorial photographers work for magazines, book publishers, and newspapers—the last of these being the single biggest employer of photographers in the country. Industrial photographers' work is usually used in reports and to evaluate machinery or products used. Forensic photographers travel with police to crime scenes to photograph evidence. Portrait photographers work either in their own studios or on location, taking pictures of individuals, families, and small groups.

Photojournalists often face a significant amount of danger in attempting to take pictures of newsworthy events, people, places, and things for newspapers, websites, journals, and magazines. Some photojournalists also work in the field of educational photography, preparing slides and film strips for use in the classroom. Still others become aerial photographers, taking photos from airplanes for industrial, scientific, military, or journalistic purposes. Scientific and biological photographers provide images for science publications, research reports, and textbooks. Archaeological photographers take pictures of finds *in situ*. Finish photographers photograph horse races as the animals cross the finish line. Motion picture photographers film movies, commercials, and television programs.

Photographers work long and irregular hours and sometimes have to be available on short notice. They must be able to work under the pressure of tight deadlines. Self-employed photographers enjoy a more flexible and relaxed schedule but must devote a significant amount of time to marketing themselves and expanding their client list.

PAYING YOUR DUES

Skill, creativity, determination, and business savvy are the keys to success in this profession. No formal education is necessary, but for the photographer who intends to specialize in areas such as scientific or industrial photography, a college degree in the area of specialty is recommended. Photojournalists looking for entry-level positions should have an undergraduate degree in journalism and/or photography.

Photographers must have good vision, in both the literal and figurative sense of the word. An appreciation of light and shadow, an eye for form and line, and a distinctive and creative approach to photographs are very useful. Because success in this field is closely tied to experience and exposure, aspiring photographers are advised to serve as interns or apprentices for experienced photographers to acquire broad technical knowledge of the field and the practical experience that comes with handling many different kinds of cameras and equipment. Apprentices are trained in equipment setup and use, darkroom techniques, lighting and background, and digital editing. Because they are so often self-employed, photographers should take business, marketing, and public relations courses to facilitate the less creative, but essential side of their careers.

ASSOCIATED CAREERS

Photographers who grow tired of the business or wish to get a steadier second job can use their skills as graphic artists or in the art departments of publishers, magazines, newspapers, or advertising agencies. Becoming developers is another option for those photographers seeking to expand their operations. Some individuals teach photography. Also, with additional training, photographers can become camera operators.

PAST AND FUTURE

Photography first "developed" in the mid-nineteenth century. Early photographers captured images on heavy plates and printed them on sepia-toned paper. The first candid or 35mm camera was marketed in 1925, and by the mid-century became a common household item. With recent developments in digital photo technology, photographers find their roles now incorporating many more production duties, including touch-ups, airbrushing, and color edits, all of which are done digitally. As online media expand, so will the need for photographers to provide and manipulate digital images for websites.

QUALITY OF LIFE

2 YEARS The newcomer in this profession is probably still assisting a seasoned photographer. He or she may be a proficient photographer, but has not yet acquired enough experience to compete against the more experienced and versatile photographers in the profession.

5 YEARS At the five-year level, the self-employed photographer is slowly building a reputation and scouting for more clients. If lucky, some of the photographer's work may have been placed in magazines and trade journals—a significant step. Photographers should consider signing with stock photo agencies that grant magazine and other clients the rights to an individual's photographs on a commission basis. Some photographers work in-house at magazines or newspapers, or as part of a stable of professionals at large photography businesses that specialize in weddings and events.

10 YEARS Photographers have usually set up their own studios by this point and may spend more time running their businesses than actually taking pictures. The 10-year veteran has significant professional contacts that will lead to bigger and more high-profile assignments.

MAJOR EMPLOYERS
ASSOCIATED PRESS
450 West 33rd Street
New York, NY 10001
Tel: 212-621-1500
E-mail: apjobs@ap.org
www.ap.org
Contact: Staffing Department

GETTY IMAGES
75 Varick Street
New York, NY 10013
Tel: 646-613-4000
www.gettyimages.com

MAJOR ASSOCIATIONS
AMERICAN SOCIETY OF MEDIA PHOTOGRAPHERS
150 North 2nd Street
Philadelphia, PA 19106
Tel: 215-451-2767
Fax: 215-451-0880
www.asmp.org

PHYSICAL THERAPIST

PROFESSIONAL PROFILE

# of people in profession	137,000
Avg. hours per week	45
Avg. starting salary	$48,480
Avg. salary after 5 years	$57,330
Avg. salary 10 to 15 years	$70,050

SALARY   ● ●

HOURS   ● ●

EDUCATION   ● ●

BOOKS, FILMS, AND TV SHOWS FEATURING THE PROFESSION

- **Born on the Fourth of July**
- **Forrest Gump**
- **Regarding Henry**

YOU'LL HAVE CONTACT WITH

- **Athletes**
- **Nurses**
- **Occupational therapists**
- **Physicians**

PROFESSIONALS READ

- **Advance**
- **PT Bulletin**
- **PT Forum**
- **PT Journal**

A DAY IN THE LIFE

Working with patients who have limited use of their bodies due to injuries or disabilities, a physical therapist builds flexibility, strength, and spirit. His or her goals are to reduce patients' pain, to increase range of motion, and to instill a sense of self-determination. "All day, I help people get back in charge of their lives," wrote one physical therapist from Tucson, Arizona, "and that makes me feel great!" This sense of contributing to people's quality of life is important to individuals entering the field. Physical therapy is emotionally and physically demanding, and a patient's progress is measured in extremely small increments. Still, individuals who find it a rewarding profession are extremely happy with what they do.

{ Patience is key. }

A physical therapist works in either a hospital or a private office setting and sees roughly 10 patients per day. Some physical therapists have specialties that require additional certification, such as gerontology, sports physical therapy, OB/GYN, pediatrics, orthopedics, neurology, or degenerative diseases, such as multiple sclerosis or cerebral palsy. Most physical therapists are generalists and must be able to evaluate a patient's condition and design a reasonable (and effective) rehabilitation program. Often, physical therapists see patients after traumatic injuries sustained in car crashes, sports mishaps, or other types of accidents. In these cases, physical therapists work closely with physicians to determine the pace and expected progress of the patient. A physical therapist has to be sensitive not only to the physical limitations of his or her patients but also to their emotional limitations as well. "You have to be able to motivate people to do exercises that hurt and remind them of their limitations," wrote one physical therapist, "and the last part is the most difficult part for them." "Patience is key," as another put it.

The emotional strain of working with people who are frustrated with their recent limited abilities can take its toll. "When a patient's body isn't responding, they can take it out on you," mentioned one survey respondent. Emotional attachment to patients is nearly inevitable after months or even years of close association, and being the target of people's anger and frustration can be daunting; of the 10 percent who leave physical therapy each year, more than half of them cite "depression" as one factor. The profession is physically demanding, too; most of a physical therapist's time is spent standing, crouching, bending, and using his or her muscles, and long days followed by sore evenings are common. Also, physical therapists spend about 10 percent of their time on tedious paperwork, filing progress reports and filling out insurance claim forms. This aspect of the job is expected to become more demanding in the future, as insurers are now targeting rehabilitation therapy for cuts.

PAYING YOUR DUES

All physical therapists are licensed by the state in which they practice and must have fulfilled standard academic requirements. You can find work with a bachelor's degree in physical therapy from one of the 700 or so accredited undergraduate programs in the United States, but those individuals who did not take this route in college can attend master's programs to study rehabilitation therapy—around 60 graduate schools offer this degree. Aspiring physical therapists should study biology, biomechanics, calculus and statistics, chemistry, nutrition, human growth and development, physics, and psychology. Students may be required to do fieldwork in addition to their academic studies. As a career, physical therapy offers flexibility: More than 20 percent of all physical therapists work in the profession part-time while finishing other degrees, pursuing other careers, or taking care of family.

ASSOCIATED CAREERS

Physical therapists who leave the field often continue as therapists in related or specialized areas, such as speech therapy, occupational therapy, chiropody, flexibility and strength training, and audiology. A notable few train to become physicians.

PAST AND FUTURE

The wide-scale application of physical therapy didn't take place until a substantial number of soldiers returned from World War I with injuries that required extensive physical rehabilitation. Physical therapy soon became a widely practiced and respected profession in the United States.

The expected demand for physical therapists in the United States is expected to grow very significantly within the next few years. America's population is aging, and increasing numbers of physicians are recognizing that physical therapy is critical to the successful recovery from surgery, injury, and illness. The only possible roadblock is potential limitations by insurance carriers; should insurers place overly restrictive caps on physical therapy payments, the industry will see a slower rate of growth, but still an increased number of available positions.

QUALITY OF LIFE

2 YEARS Two years into the profession, physical therapists are, for the most part, working in internships and as assistants while they complete their studies. Many of them use these years to learn client skills—the most difficult part of the profession. Therapists at this stage in their careers are generally still developing the persona that marks the successful physical therapist: a combined friend, therapist, and drill sergeant. The hours are average; the wages are reasonable.

5 YEARS Five-year practitioners have satisfied all licensing requirements and are now considered full members of the profession. This means that the hours rise and responsibilities increase for most of them. A number of therapists switch positions during these middle years, trying on both hospital and private settings for size. Salaries increase, and many therapists begin to see significant results with their patients. This, in turn, increases their job satisfaction. The majority of individuals who leave the profession do so between years two and six.

10 YEARS Ten-year professional physical therapists follow one of two tracks. Many of them go into private practice and open their own offices, often hiring other physical therapists. Others continue their affiliations with hospitals and employers but move into a more supervisory role, overseeing the work of other physical therapists and handling complicated or difficult cases. Many therapists go back to school in years 8–12 to develop specialties in the areas that they find most exciting.

MAJOR EMPLOYERS
CARONDELET HEALTH CARE CORPORATION
1601 West St. Mary's Road
Tucson, AZ 85745
Tel: 520-721-3727
Fax: 520-740-6067
www.carondelet.org

Physical therapists are employed primarily by hospitals, rehabilitation centers, and doctors. Contact these facilities in your area for more information.

MAJOR ASSOCIATIONS
AMERICAN PHYSICAL THERAPY ASSOCIATION
111 North Fairfax Street
Alexandria, VA 22314
Tel: 703-684-2782
Fax: 703-684-7343
E-mail: aptacareer@apta.org
www.apta.org

NATIONAL REHABILITATION ASSOCIATION
633 South Washington Street
Alexandria, VA 22314
Tel: 703-836-0850
Fax: 703-836-0848
www.nationalrehab.org

PHYSICIAN

SALARY   • • •
HOURS   • • •
EDUCATION   • • •

BOOKS, FILMS, AND TV SHOWS
FEATURING THE PROFESSION
- ER
- Fatal
- Grey's Anatomy
- Vital Signs

YOU'LL HAVE CONTACT WITH
- Hospital administrators
- Insurance executives
- Nurses
- Patients

PROFESSIONALS READ
- Clinical journals in areas of specialty
- Journal of AMA
- New England Journal of Medicine

A DAY IN THE LIFE

Physicians can pursue careers in private practice, university-hospital work, or health maintenance organizations. The first option lets you be your own boss. The second option offers you the opportunity to divide your work between treatment, research, and instruction, in varying proportions. The third option means you work for a large corporation, which provides you with patients and handles most of the administrative and business tasks that physicians in private practice have to handle on their own. Physicians can also work in inner-city clinics or in rural areas, where shortages of physicians exist. Physicians can be family physicians, or they can specialize in internal medicine, cardiology, endocrinology, neurology, oncology, sports medicine, or one of many other specialties. { relate to their patients as people }

Medicine is a rewarding profession, but it is hard work. Physicians are often exhilarated when they know they have helped someone get well and devastated when they lose a patient. It is a job that can take a physical and mental toll on you. Since the average patient is not a doctor, physicians must not only be able to communicate difficult, often painful information to those individuals in their care, but also they must learn how to interpret their patients' needs. They must relate to their patients as people and not reduce them to just the illness that needs to be treated. One element of this is collaborating with their patients to determine the best course of treatment for them as individuals. This requires patience, empathy, and compassion. "Compassion," remarked one physician, "is absolutely necessary."

PAYING YOUR DUES

In college, enroll in a pre-med program. Volunteer to work at your local hospital or with emergency medical services. During your last year of college, apply to medical school and take the MCAT. The four-year program at medical school encompasses clinical work and book learning, with two years in the classroom and two in the clinical setting. Some of the usual courses taken in medical school are pathology, pharmacology, neuroanatomy, biochemistry, physiology, histology, and gross anatomy. Clinical study takes place at local hospitals or medical practices. Students are expected to offer diagnoses and suggest courses of treatment in real-life situations, although a medical doctor instructor makes the final decisions. In standard programs, students enter clinical clerkships in their third year, and, in their fourth year, they can choose among various elective subspecialties. Students also spend the fourth year applying for their first year of residency training.

Medical students must take Steps 1 and 2 of the United States Medical Licensing Exam (USMLE) to receive their medical degrees. Residency training is next, and this lasts three to seven additional years, depending on the specialty. Residents will take Step 3 of the USMLE during their residency training. This will then enable them to get a state license to practice medicine. A medical education is never truly complete. New challenges and breakthroughs keep the medical landscape in a constant state of flux. Nevertheless, the initial years of medical school have an enormous impact. One physician with whom we spoke could name instructors who still influence his work more than 30 years after he earned his degree.

ASSOCIATED CAREERS

Nursing is the clearest alternative to medical practice. Although the educational demands are less rigorous, the responsibilities are essential. Nurse practitioners prescribe medicines and play a key role in patient care. There are also many opportunities for lab technicians. You may also be interested in a career in pharmacology, biology, biochemistry, or biophysics.

PAST AND FUTURE

Not even the elimination of disease would eliminate society's need for specialists in the working of the human body. The first physician, Hippocrates, began with this motto: "First do no harm," a credo by which physicians still practice medicine today (physicians are asked to take the "Hippocratic oath," which affirms this belief, among others). With the institution of formalized training and strict professional certification, physicians gained more respect and were more widely used in the modern world.

The medical profession is undergoing a downsizing process similar to that of many other industries. Medical schools are placing a greater emphasis on general knowledge, although there is still a need for specialists. The growth of managed care has increased the demand for obstetricians, pediatricians, and family practitioners who can treat a wide variety of ailments and look after the health of many patients.

QUALITY OF LIFE

2 YEARS Residents work long hours and are expected to put their classroom experience into practice right away. Physicians must quickly learn the difference between books and people. Residents work under the supervision of veteran physicians. Although residents' hours have traditionally been very long, hospitals have recently begun reducing the schedules of their young physicians. After satisfying residency requirements, a physician can strike out on his or her own as a full-fledged medical practitioner. Wherever physicians work, however, they will spend much of their salary (in the early years especially) paying off student debt, which can exceed $100,000.

5 YEARS In private practice, a full partnership usually comes after five years. Physicians have a vested interest in attracting and keeping patients. In addition to clinical responsibilities, physicians in private practice will have the management duties that come with running any business. University-hospital-based physicians may work their way up the faculty ladder, devote more time to clinical work, or spend their days in the lab conducting research. Physicians at HMOs can look forward to some vested interest in their organization.

10 YEARS Experienced physicians, whether general practitioners or specialists, command very high salaries. A thriving private practice is demanding but lucrative. Medical instructors at major universities often earn more than the university's president. With the boom in managed health care, physicians at HMOs can expect similar rewards in exchange for accepting certain restrictions on their professional autonomy.

MAJOR EMPLOYERS
CEDARS-SINAI MEDICAL CENTER
8700 Beverly Boulevard
Los Angeles, CA 90048
Tel: 310-423-3277

MASSACHUSETTS GENERAL HOSPITAL
55 Fruit Street
Boston, MA 02114
Tel: 617-726-2000
Fax: 617-724-2266
www.mgh.harvard.edu

MOUNT SINAI HOSPITAL
One Gustave L. Levy Place
1190 Fifth Avenue
New York, NY 10029
Tel: 212-241-6500
www.mountsinai.org

MAJOR ASSOCIATIONS
AMERICAN ACADEMY OF FAMILY PHYSICIANS
11400 Tomahawk Creek Parkway
Leawood, KS 66211-2672
Tel: 800-274-2237 or 913-906-6000
www.aafp.org
Contact: Human Resources

AMERICAN MEDICAL ASSOCIATION
515 North State Street
Chicago, IL 60610
Tel: 800-621-8335
www.ama-assn.org

POLITICAL SCIENTIST

A DAY IN THE LIFE

Political scientists study the structure and theory of government and seek practical and theoretical solutions to political problems. Most current studies and research concentrate on tangible topics such as welfare reform, political campaigns and elections, foreign relations, and immigration. The vast majority of political scientists are teachers at colleges and universities at which they conduct research and write books and articles on political theory. Political scientists armed with the practical and theoretical knowledge of government may enter political life. They generally do not run for public office, but very often their expertise is enlisted by candidates to ensure a successful run or reelection. A great many of them become political aides, helping elected individuals analyze and interpret legislative { **participant observer** } issues and their constituencies. Some political scientists become political commentators on television and radio or write columns for newspapers; others become public opinion pollsters.

Political scientists approach problems using one or a combination of four distinct methods: objective, analytical, comparative, and historical. The adequacy and integrity of a political scientist's theory rests on his or her ability to set aside his or her own prejudices and remain objective in gathering, analyzing, and presenting his or her findings. Using commonly available research—interviews, newspaper clippings, periodicals, case law, historical papers, polls, and statistics—to test theories and develop new ones, political scientists analyze, compare, and even trace problems back to their sources. In gathering data, political scientists sometimes employ the technique of the participant observer, blending with crowds while carefully observing a particular interaction. The questionnaire is another research tool the political scientist uses. Questions are carefully ordered and worded to be as objective as possible.

PAYING YOUR DUES

The job of a political scientist is an intellectually challenging one and places a premium on higher education. Most jobs require a master's degree. If teaching at the college and university level is your goal, then nothing less than a PhD will do. Students who specialize in a particular field such as public administration, public policy, international relations, or American politics will fare well in seeking jobs. Computer and language skills will also significantly enhance a candidate's job prospects. Entrants start out as trainees in political science research at universities and think tanks or as assistants in independent public opinion research organizations. Education, experience, knowledge, and an area of specialty—especially public administration or public policy—are indices of high salary levels.

ASSOCIATED CAREERS

Some political scientists move on to law school. A few become consultants to political groups, think tanks, nongovernmental organizations, businesses, and industries. The vast majority of political scientists who end up in teaching posts at colleges and universities also establish double careers as writers and researchers. A few of them hold positions as directors or department heads of college programs.

PAST AND FUTURE

Plato, considered by many scholars an early patriarch of political science and a major influence on the discipline, attempted to classify forms of government. Computers now figure in greatly to the organization and analysis of data that forms the core of the political scientist's work. Individuals with strong computer training and language skills will fare far better in the field—particularly those specializing in the areas of public administration and public policy—than will those who do not. Fewer vacancies at colleges and universities will mean that competition for existing jobs will be intense. While future job opportunities are limited, the position itself has been around for a long time and should remain secure.

QUALITY OF LIFE

2 YEARS At the two-year level, political scientists are probably employed as trainees or research assistants. They are concerned about acquiring significant experience and working up through the ranks. It is important for the relative newcomer to establish mentorships. Individuals who have finished their PhDs are either seeking or already have positions as assistant professors.

5 YEARS Five years into the profession, the emphasis is still on experience. Individuals who have specialized in public administration may see greater progress in their career, moving up the ranks and being called on to head research projects. Professors, usually associates by now, are publishing and seeking tenure.

10 YEARS At this level the political scientist teaching at a college or university should be a tenured professor with a body of scholarly research, articles, and books to show for years of work. The political scientist who started out in research may have advanced to research director at his or her organization. With 10 years of experience, the political scientist has a fairly secure position and commands the respect of peers and potential employers.

MAJOR EMPLOYERS

HARVARD UNIVERSITY
JFK School of Government
79 John F. Kennedy Street
Cambridge, MA 02138
Tel: 617-495-1100
www.ksg.harvard.edu

PRINCETON UNIVERSITY
Department of Politics
Corwin Hall
Princeton, NJ 18544
Tel: 609-258-4760
www.princeton.edu/politics
Contact: Human Resources

YALE UNIVERSITY
Department of Political Science
124 Prospect Street
PO Box 208301
New Haven, CT 06520
Tel: 203-432-5230
Fax: 203-432-6196
www.yale.edu/polisci
Contact: Human Resources

MAJOR ASSOCIATIONS

AMERICAN ACADEMY OF POLITICAL AND SOCIAL SCIENCE
3814 Walnut Street
Philadelphia, PA 19104-6197
Tel: 215-746-6500
Fax: 215-898-1202
www.aapss.org

AMERICAN POLITICAL SCIENCE ASSOCIATION
1527 New Hampshire, NW
Washington, DC 20036
Tel: 202-483-2512
Fax: 202-483-2657
www.apsanet.org

PRODUCT DESIGNER

A DAY IN THE LIFE

"If you can spend hours walking down the drugstore aisle critiquing everybody's products, you were born to be a product designer," wrote one respondent. Who would argue with that? Product designers have agonized over the shape, size, and material content of every tube of toothpaste, every bottle of conditioner, and every bar of soap produced in the United States today. A product designer combines a talent for design with an understanding of the production and marketing of consumer goods. Over two-thirds of all product designers work for consumer goods manufacturing concerns, which produce most drugstore and food items. These designers play a critical role in differentiating their products from those of their company's competitors. "So much of what you buy is influenced by how it looks on a shelf," as one advertising executive told us, "that companies cannot afford anymore to not have product designers on staff." These consumer product designers also work to give their companies the edge by keeping production costs low; production costs translate directly into consumer costs for the product, and a designer who can reduce a per-item cost even a tiny bit can give an employer a competitive advantage at the supermarket or drugstore.

{ business savvy }

A product designer spends around 30 percent of his or her day meeting with executives, researchers, production managers, and advertising people, either on the telephone or in person. It's important that the prospective designer be able to work as part of this team, which means understanding that his or her personal preferences may not be chosen. Besides the time spent actually working on designs, the remainder of his or her time is spent working with engineers, graphic designers, and cost estimators to coordinate the production of potential product lines. Because of the collaborative nature of the process, this job requires strong interpersonal skills; over half the surveys we received cited "the ability to listen" as extremely important to success.

While aesthetic skills are obviously critical to product designers, business savvy is just as important. In the industrial sector, designers evaluate options to improve the production process that brings something to the marketplace, finding ways to reduce time to market and save costs in manufacturing. Successful product designers are equally comfortable producing three-dimensional models of their designs and providing cost estimates to production executives. Every design accommodates specific cost limitations, and designers who can't keep to those limitations, as one package designer put it, "find themselves designing packages at home. Unemployed." This forces the product designer to be creative with materials, production methods, and forms. Many of them cite this pressured creativity as one of the most exciting parts of the job. At the same time, this is a profession in which more than 70 percent of what the designer designs will never be produced for either cost, preference, or advertising reasons, so product designers should be thick-skinned enough to be able to watch their work be discarded on a daily basis. Those individuals whose designs prove financially successful can expect to have more influence over the process as time goes on.

PAYING YOUR DUES

Product designers face specific academic requirements that allow them entry to the field but certainly do not guarantee them success. No specific licensing requirements exist for product designers; applicants should concentrate on developing a portfolio of designs, an awareness of cost specifications, and a demonstrated ability to work with a team. Most product designers have a bachelor's degree in industrial design, and their coursework should include manufacturing principles, psychology, sociology, finance, materials' use, and organizational behavior. But beyond academics, the more a prospective product designer can become familiar with the production process, the more likely he or she is to be successful in the field. An aspiring product or industrial designer should also be well-versed in current packaging trends in the industry that he or she intends to enter. For example, if someone wants to design products for the music industry, he or she should be aware that while the plastic two-hinge case is the industry standard now, many companies are choosing to replace it with a cardboard foldout case favored by recycling-minded consumers.

ASSOCIATED CAREERS

Product designers often become graphic designers, commercial artists, cost estimators, and product-manufacturing executives—all careers with which they come into contact as product design specialists.

PAST AND FUTURE

With the demonstrated effectiveness of advertising in the twentieth century, manufacturers looked to gain an advantage over one another by providing more attractive, identifiable product design. Producers who lacked these aesthetic skills hired professional consultants to redesign their products. These redesigns proved so effective that many design people were hired in-house. Product designers are involved at every stage of product development today, and the future of product design looks stable. Jobs should increase at the same rate as jobs in all other manufacturing occupations. The market for consumer products is healthy, and the rate of growth is steady. With the dawn of an increasingly global economy, product designers for overseas companies who want to sell their products in the United States may be in high demand.

QUALITY OF LIFE

2 YEARS — As assistants during the early years, product designers normally undergo a training program in which they are rotated to various positions within the company. Many begin their careers as staff industrial designers for consultancies or manufacturing companies. They gain valuable experience in finance, production, development, marketing, and sales. Responsibilities are limited, and although many of them are itching to begin designing, most designers merely assist the design department in the production of already-designed products. Salaries are average; the hours aren't that long.

5 YEARS — Five-year survivors find their hours have increased tremendously and so have their responsibilities. Many of them are in the midst of actual designing and mock-up production and use their knowledge of materials pricing, cost estimating, and consumer taste. Satisfaction skyrockets during these middle years, and many of them find work obligations can extend into off-hours and weekend time; a few on our surveys noted that other interests "suffered" during this period.

10 YEARS — Veterans of product design are faced with the same challenges as graphic designers and commercial artists at this stage of their careers: to renew their visions and keep themselves relevant to the industry they represent. Mobility is a feature of the 10-year product designer, as many switch jobs searching for the spark to keep their work fresh. Salaries increase, and satisfaction evens out. A number of very successful designers become independent consultants to industries, providing analyses of product lines or cost-structure estimates for startup companies.

MAJOR EMPLOYERS

3M CENTER
Building 224-1W-02
PO Box 33224
St. Paul, MN 55133-3224
Tel: 888-364-3577
www.3m.com
Contact: Staffing and College Relations

FISHER-PRICE
636 Girard Avenue
East Aurora, NY 14052
Tel: 716-687-3000
Fax: 716-687-3636
www.fisher-price.com
Contact: Employment Office

PROCTOR & GAMBLE
1 P&G Plaza
Cincinnati, OH 45202
Tel: 513-983-1100
www.pg.com
Contact: Personnel

MAJOR ASSOCIATIONS

INDUSTRIAL DESIGNERS SOCIETY OF AMERICA
45195 Business Court, Suite 301
Dulles, VA 20166
Tel: 703-707-6000
Fax: 703-787-8501
www.idsa.org

PROFESSOR

A DAY IN THE LIFE

College professors organize and conduct the functions of higher education. They engage in a variety of activities, from running laboratory experiments and supervising graduate student research to giving large undergraduate lectures and writing textbooks. With the exception of scheduled classes—which can consume as few as three hours a week in graduate universities or up to 12–16 hours per week for undergraduates—a professor's time is largely spent on research, preparing class material, meeting with students, or writing. This profession is thus best suited for motivated self-starters, and its highest rewards are given to individuals who can identify and explore original problems in their fields.

Tenured professors have relatively high job security and professional freedom. Once tenured,

{ motivated self-starters }

a professor can largely set his or her own responsibilities and decide to a large extent how to divide his or her time between teaching, writing, researching, and administration. However, tenure no longer means complete immunity; post-tenure review is now mandated at most universities, and individuals who fall behind on teaching and independent scholarship may not be so secure in their positions nowadays.

The most difficult years of being a professor are the early ones, during which there is great pressure to publish a significant body of work to establish the credentials that lead to tenure. However, the work of junior and senior faculty is quite similar, and the profession offers intellectual stimulation and freedom to all its members.

PAYING YOUR DUES

The path to becoming a tenured college professor is arduous. While a master's degree may be sufficient to qualify to teach in a two-year college or in some cases, as an adjunct, a doctoral degree is required to teach in four-year colleges and universities. PhDs generally take four to seven years to complete; after completing two to three years of course work, the graduate student will usually teach classes and write a dissertation (an original piece of research taking about three years to complete that is the most important element of the search for a first job as a professor). In addition, post-doctoral experience is an added advantage. For the coveted tenure-track positions, virtually every successful job candidate now boasts at least one and usually two post-doctorate years, and these years are necessary to remain competitive, which means gathering a sufficient backlog of publications and writings. Personal relationships with faculty are also critical in this hunt for a first job, as teaching positions in many areas (particularly the humanities) can be scarce. While approximately 80 percent of college jobs are in four-year institutions, about a third of all college faculty are employed part-time or in nontenure-track positions, and this percentage has risen in recent years as colleges attempt to control costs.

ASSOCIATED CAREERS

Because of the relatively flexible structure of the profession, many full-time faculty engage in outside professional activities. Economists consult with governments and corporations; engineers and academic labs develop products for private industry; humanities professors write articles that appear in newspapers and magazines. Many find this ability to work professionally on terms they define, while remaining in their institutions, to be among the most satisfying aspects of the profession. In addition, the significant administrative positions in colleges and universities are usually filled by former and current professors, and it is not uncommon for careers in university administration to develop from teaching careers.

PAST AND FUTURE

The mission of the first colleges in the United States was to train ministers for the new colonies. The concept of the modern liberal arts education did not appear in America until 1825, with the founding of the University of Virginia; today, this principle of the secular faculty is the norm rather than the exception. Higher education for women originally developed separately; the first women's college, Wesleyan Female College, was founded in Macon, Georgia, in 1836, and single-sex education was the norm until the 1960s. Since then, coeducation has become the rule.

Demand should grow for professors in fields such as computer science and engineering, while employment for humanities professors will likely remain tight.

QUALITY OF LIFE

2 YEARS At this stage, the recent PhD graduate is either in a tenure-track job as an instructor or assistant professor or is working as a part-time or adjunct professor and looking for a job that could eventually lead to tenure. In the sciences, 50 percent of PhD holders work with academic institutions, and many of them work in the private sector in lucrative jobs they have chosen in lieu of academic careers. For humanities PhDs, the job market is tougher; 20 percent of them find junior positions on a tenure track in their first year after graduation, and another 30 percent of them find nontenure-track work. Half of all doctorate degree holders do not find academic jobs. The young assistant professor works long hours for minimal pay, teaching several undergraduate classes and beginning to establish the research and writing record necessary to advance in his or her field. In smaller schools and at two-year colleges, there is often less pressure to publish, but these are busy years regardless of where the junior professor teaches.

5 YEARS If the professor has been aggressive (and fortunate) enough to get a monograph published and establish a clear area of expertise, he or she is on the verge of being promoted to associate professor and awarded tenure, events that are normally expected after the sixth year. Associate professors have more control over their teaching schedules; they are likely to be teaching fewer low-level classes and more classes and seminars in their areas of specialization with older undergraduates and graduate students. In addition, as academic marketability is determined by a university's specific needs for expertise, professors become more able to move around among institutions when they establish themselves in their fields.

10 YEARS By now, professors have probably made tenure at the university in which they started their careers found another university that will give them tenure, or left the profession altogether. Failing these options, he or she may remain exploited as an adjunct professor, with all the demands of a tenured position but not the freedom, prestige, or security. With tenure come the real rewards of the academic life: the ability to say, write, and teach what one wishes with the greatest possible freedom. Job satisfaction is extremely high, and few tenured professors leave the profession. Individuals who do leave generally take lucrative positions in private enterprises or positions in government agencies.

MAJOR EMPLOYERS
HARVARD UNIVERSITY
Faculty of Arts and Sciences
University Hall
Cambridge, MA 02138
Tel: 617-495-1000
www.harvard.edu

STATE UNIVERSITY OF NEW YORK
State University Plaza
Albany, NY 12246
Tel: 518-443-5555
www.suny.edu

YALE UNIVERSITY
153 College Street
New Haven, CT 06520
Tel: 203-432-4771
E-mail: jobs@yale.edu
www.yale.edu

MAJOR ASSOCIATIONS
AMERICAN ASSOCIATION OF UNIVERSITY PROFESSORS
1012 14th Street, NW, Suite 500
Washington, DC 20005
Tel: 202-737-5900
Fax: 202-737-5526
www.aaup.org

COLLEGE & UNIVERSITY PROFESSIONAL ASSOCIATION FOR HUMAN RESOURCES
2607 Kingston Pike, Suite 250
Knoxville, TN 37919
Tel: 865-637-7673
Fax: 865-637-7674
www.cupahr.org

PSYCHIATRIST

A DAY IN THE LIFE

Psychiatry is uniquely situated within the realm of science. As the branch of medicine that deals with the study of mental illness, psychiatry helps bridge the gap between the ethical and empirical as well as that between the social and the physical beings. Those who practice psychiatry are concerned with the diagnosis and treatment of mental, emotional, and behavioral disorders, such as depression, schizophrenia, and anxiety. These illnesses may impede a person's ability to function effectively and happily. Psychiatrists generally treat mental and behavioral conditions with a combination of therapy, counseling, and medication.

Many psychiatrists report that a typical day is, well, atypical. Of course,

{ **Psychiatry is uniquely situated within the realm of science.** }

there are standard practices, such as taking a patient's history, completing physical exams, and administering diagnostic tests. But patients may present a wide range of ailments, so treatments must always be case-specific. A doctor may begin the day administering electroshock therapy to someone who is severely depressed, move on to consult with the family of someone afflicted with schizo-affective disorder, monitor a manic-depressive's lithium intake, and finally, meet with a patient who has been hampered by obsessive-compulsive tendencies.

While numerous psychiatrists maintain a general practice in which they see a variety of patients, some choose to specialize in a specific psychiatric subfield. For example, neuroscientists spend their days studying the structure and functions of the brain. Geneticists focus on genes and chromosomes and the possibility of genetically-linked mental disorders. Pharmacologists examine the mechanisms of assorted drug actions and develop more effective medications. Clinical researchers test the efficacy of a variety of treatments with medication and psychotherapy trials.

PAYING YOUR DUES

A career in psychiatry requires many years of education and training. While it's not necessary to have a science-related major as an undergrad, you'll nevertheless need to fulfill premed requirements. After taking the MCATs, applying and gaining admission to medical school, and then actually attending medical school, aspiring psychiatrists still need to complete a four-year psychiatric residency. After this training, psychiatrists must take written and oral examinations to gain board certification. Be warned, though: The failure rate for these exams is nearly 50 percent. Once a psychiatrist has completed this process, he or she still needs to build up a practice, patient base, and reputation in the field.

ASSOCIATED CAREERS

Psychiatrists who decide to give up their practice may enjoy myriad other career options. Some may opt to move into research and conduct clinical studies. Others may choose to go into teaching. Still others may apply their expertise by moving into such fields as social work.

PAST AND FUTURE

The etymological basis of the terms psychology and psychiatry is the Greek word *psyche*, which means "spirit." The field of psychiatry in its earliest conception was a niche within general medicine that combined medical practice with that of psychology. At the beginning of the twentieth century, German psychiatrist Emil Kraepelin established the foundation of the field when he sought to group and identify patterns in hundreds of mental disorders and to develop a new diagnostic system. The famous Austrian neurologist Sigmund Freud used medical observations to develop the field of psychoanalysis; Freud continues to be highly influential in psychiatry today.

Psychiatry has waged a hard-fought battle to be recognized as a serious science and respected branch of medicine. Since most mental illnesses lack a simple, biologically-based test that can ascertain their presence, it is still difficult to diagnose some patients. With the advancement of technology (neuroimaging now identifies diseases such as schizophrenia and severe depression, for example), psychiatrists are gaining a greater understanding of the human mind and are thus continually improving treatments. The potential to do cutting-edge research in this field is promising at present and in the future.

QUALITY OF LIFE

2 YEARS At the two-year mark, doctors are only halfway through their residencies. They spend this time plumbing research about mental illness and treatment and training with experienced psychiatrists. Importantly, they complete rotations within various psychiatric subdivisions (e.g., child psychiatry, geriatric psychiatry, etc.). This not only makes them well-rounded physicians, but it also sharpens their decision-making processes and prepares them to specialize, should they opt to do so later in their careers.

5 YEARS At the five-year mark, psychiatrists have completed their residencies and have cultivated a comprehensive understanding of the spectrum of psychiatric disorders. If they wish to specialize, psychiatrists usually do so at this point in their careers. At this level, psychiatrists are typically concerned with establishing their practices and building up a client base.

10 YEARS The practice of psychiatry does not change drastically from 5 years to 10 years. At this point, however, psychiatrists are well established and may be publishing articles on a semi-regular basis.

MAJOR EMPLOYERS
There is no leading employer within the field of psychiatry. Most psychiatrists work either in private practice or for one of the many hospitals across the country.

MAJOR ASSOCIATIONS
AMERICAN BOARD OF PSYCHIATRY AND NEUROLOGY, INC.
500 Lake Cook Road, Suite 335
Deerfield, IL 60015-5249
Tel: 847-945-7900
Fax: 847-945-1146
www.abpn.com

AMERICAN PSYCHIATRIC ASSOCIATION
1000 Wilson Boulevard, Suite 1825
Arlington, VA 22209-3901
Tel: 703-907-7300
E-mail: apa@psych.org
www.psych.org

PSYGHOLOGIST

A DAY IN THE LIFE

By doing research and performing examinations, psychologists study all aspects of the mind. Health facilities employ approximately 30 percent of all working psychologists, while 40 percent of them work in educational environments, in such positions as counselors, educators, and researchers. Most often, these academically connected psychologists maintain a private practice while teaching or conducting research. Psychologists working in academic settings have flexibility in their schedules, but the demands on their time are high.

Working in private practice is the goal of many psychologists. While seeing private patients means a psychologist is his or her own boss, it also means accommodating patients with evening or weekend hours, so demands on time can be high. A

{ helping others }

government or corporate psychologist, by contrast, works in a more structured environment. Their hours are fixed, and they often work alone. There's some relief and enjoyment in the occasional conference that takes them away from writing reports. Despite potentially grueling schedules and emotional demands, psychologists report great satisfaction in their jobs; the gratification they receive from helping others keeps them in the field. One psychologist wrote, "The best thing about this job is that people open up their lives to you—that's a great responsibility but also an honor."

PAYING YOUR DUES

Plan on spending many years in school if you want to embark on a career in psychology. A PhD will enable you to work in the widest range of positions, and doing graduate work toward a doctoral degree takes between five and seven years to obtain. Obtaining this distinguished degree hinges on completing a dissertation based on original research. Before you begin this research, you must complete course work in quantitative research methods, statistics, and computers. If you want to work in a clinical or counseling setting, you will begin to work with patients under supervision before the degree is completed, and at least another year of supervised work experience is required afterward. Most academic programs require counseling psychology students to undergo psychoanalysis as part of their training. The newer Doctor of Psychology (PsyD) will qualify you for clinical positions. The PsyD is awarded based not on a dissertation but on clinical experience and exams. The time and effort it takes to get this degree are comparable to the PhD. The difference is the emphasis on counseling to obtain a PsyD, while the PhD candidate does research. Thus, employment options for individuals who hold a PsyD are less flexible than for individuals who hold a PhD.

Besides the years of study and internships, psychologists offering patient care must be certified and licensed by the state in which they intend to practice. Most of these licensing exams are standardized tests, but some states require applicants to pass essay or oral exams. These tests are designed to ensure that candidates have both knowledge of the field and appropriate personal qualities.

Without a doctoral degree, you can find job options within psychology, but these positions will always require supervision by doctoral-level psychologists. Candidates holding master's degrees can work as assistants and may administer tests, conduct research and psychological evaluations, and counsel certain patients. The master's degree requires a minimum of two years of full-time study and a one-year internship. The candidate has the choice of obtaining practical experience or completing a research-based thesis. Individuals with only a bachelor's degree in psychology find their options more limited. They can work as assistants to psychologists and other mental health professionals. Graduate schools tend to look favorably on undergraduate degrees in psychology. Other good majors for future psychologists are biological, physical, and social sciences; statistics; and mathematics.

ASSOCIATED CAREERS

A PhD in psychology creates numerous opportunities to work in fields other than counseling. Teaching and research are the areas most populated by nonpracticing psychologists. With master's-level qualifications, teaching in high schools or junior colleges is possible, while doctoral-level qualifications allow you to teach at the college and post-graduate levels.

PAST AND FUTURE

In the seventeenth century, the French philosopher Rene Descartes separated human behavior into two classes, involuntary and voluntary; the field of psychology stems from his theory of involuntary behavior. In 1892, Edward Titchener brought this "psychology of introspection" to the United States, at the same time that Sigmund Freud was developing his theory of the unconscious. Since then the study of psychology has grown into many disparate areas. As a profession, psychology has enjoyed formal recognition in this country since World War II. As a relatively new science, psychology enjoys wide and varied prospects for the future. The contributions of psychology to understanding the effect of personal behaviors on health will help encourage its growth over the coming decade. The demand for psychologists is expected to be high in corporate, correctional, educational, and public settings. The old stigma attached to therapy is fading, as more people turn to therapists to help them get through difficult times and as chronic problems like depression are recognized as treatable disorders rather than personal failures.

QUALITY OF LIFE

2 YEARS — Because of the extensive academic and emotional commitment required to obtain their degree, very few psychologists leave the field at any time in their careers. New psychologists are busy starting research programs, teaching students, and establishing practices.

5 YEARS — After a few years, psychologists are earning intellectual rewards through their research, practice, and teaching. Now is the time a psychologist may become more involved in outreach, having become comfortable in his or her work. Psychologists are rarely involved in only one endeavor—they're often working at more than one activity, including research, teaching, and seeing patients.

10 YEARS — Ten years in a career can bring additional administrative responsibilities for individuals in all positions and advances in rank and tenure for individuals in teaching positions.

MAJOR EMPLOYERS

HAZELDEN TREATMENT CENTER
PO Box 11, BC16
Center City, MI 55012
Tel: 651-213-4000 or 800-257-7810
Fax: 651-213-4394
E-mail: jobs@hazelden.org
www.hazelden.org
Contact: Human Resources

PAYNE WHITNEY CLINIC
525 East 68th Street
New York, NY 10021
Tel: 212-434-5500
Fax: 212-434-5547

Besides private practice, psychologists are employed by schools, hospitals, clinics, social service agencies, consulting services, and private companies involved in marketing research and statistical analysis. Contact these facilities in your area for employment information.

MAJOR ASSOCIATIONS

AMERICAN PSYCHOLOGICAL ASSOCIATION
750 1st Street
Washington, DC 20002-4242
Tel: 202-336-5500
Fax: 202-336-5568
www.apa.org

NATIONAL ASSOCIATION OF SCHOOL PSYCHOLOGISTS
4340 East West Highway, Suite 402
Bethesda, MD 20814
Tel: 301-657-0270
Fax: 301-657-0275
www.naspweb.org

PUBLIC HEALTH ADMINISTRATOR

PROFESSIONAL PROFILE

# of people in profession	33,000
Avg. hours per week	40
Avg. starting salary	$25,400
Avg. salary after 5 years	$45,700
Avg. salary 10 to 15 years	$72,500

SALARY   ● ●
HOURS   ● ●
EDUCATION   ● ● ●

BOOKS, FILMS, AND TV SHOWS
FEATURING THE PROFESSION
- **The Black Plague**
- **The Coming Plague**
- **Hot Zone**
- **Outbreak**

YOU'LL HAVE CONTACT WITH
- **Epidemiologists**
- **Physicians**
- **Sociologists**
- **Statisticians**

PROFESSIONALS READ
- **Family Planning Perspectives**
- **Journal of Epidemiology**
- **Public Health Reports**

A DAY IN THE LIFE

Public health administrators focus on community-wide disease prevention and health promotion. As the name of the profession shows, there are two parts to their jobs. Public health administrators try to improve the welfare of the community at large and run the organizations that disseminate information about health. The majority are employed by governmental health agencies, while others work for not-for-profit organizations and educational institutions. They assess community health issues and educate members about the prevention or alleviation of health problems. The public health administrator executes community outreach programs to make people aware of dangers such as lead poisoning and to address chronic problems afflicting the community, like sexually transmitted diseases.

{ designing new ways to handle issues }

The administrator's job calls for the management skills of a chief executive officer. He or she creates budgets, hires staff, organizes the office, and obtains any necessary equipment. Writing grant proposals and fund-raising take up more and more of the administrator's time as budget cuts flourish. Whenever he or she notices a health-related trend or event, he or she must write a report on what he or she believes its effect on the community will be. The public health administrator must be prepared to delicately balance limited budgets with the compassion needed to provide basic care. Since he or she is often faced with contradictory information and demands, he or she must be able to make decisions. He or she also needs self-confidence when called on to defend decisions to public officials or the press. The administrator attends community events frequently. Usually he or she devotes five and a half days a week to his or her career, but some of them are on 24-hour call. In an era of shrinking health care budgets, officials are expected to complete projects faster and with less support staff than ever before. This has forced many administrators to exercise their creative juices in designing new ways to handle the issues they face.

PAYING YOUR DUES

There is no one way to become a public health administrator, but most professionals have worked in related fields and acquired advanced degrees. Employers require at least a bachelor's degree in health care administration or a related field, but the field is so competitive that master's-degree holders have a significant advantage. While health-related courses, business administration and finance are important parts of your academic background (make time for communications and English, too). You will need to write and present many reports professionally and confidently. Many administrators receive their degrees after having worked in other areas in the field. They are often former health inspectors, who insure that consumer products meet federal health and safety standards, or regulatory inspectors, who enforce observation of public welfare laws and regulations. Individuals with keen entrepreneurial skills and backgrounds are encouraged to enter the field, bringing their efficiency to it. Some people gain their initial training in the Peace Corps before returning to school.

Many graduate programs offer specialized joint degrees, such as a combined health care management and law degree. While dozens of schools offer graduate and undergraduate degrees in public health administration, only 26 are accredited. Whether you choose an accredited school or not is largely dependent on your plan of study, career expectations, and financial situation. Public health administrators enjoy a combination of study and work throughout their careers. Most public health administration students enroll in internship programs to gain experience. Once they start working, they are expected to take continuing education courses every year to keep up with the latest in health care services. Beginning in school and continuing throughout their careers, public health administrators should read trade papers about health care and the literature supplied by its providers.

ASSOCIATED CAREERS

The public health administrator works with a host of people in different professions and can apply his or her skills, with some extra training, to these other fields if he or she wishes to change careers. Biostatisticians compile and study vital statistics. They determine the incidence of diseases in different populations and create life expectancy tables. Public health administrators turn to them for advice regarding issues such as which vaccines are better than others. Public health administrators can become health economists, who examine financing and organization of health care facilities, and advise them on running their businesses. The demand for health economists is growing due to the changing organization of the health care industry.

PAST AND FUTURE

A century ago, health care officials were concerned entirely with preventing and controlling infectious diseases. As the variety of factors affecting health gained recognition, the field of health care administration was born. One professional growth consultant recently commented, "What's happening in health care today is that no one knows what's happening in health care today." Recent budget cuts and government debates are making individuals in the field very anxious. Should national health care reform legislation be passed, it will further change terms of delivery and provision and payment for health care services. Future public health administrators will have to display creativity and flexibility in finding solutions to health care problems.

QUALITY OF LIFE

2 YEARS Approximately 80 percent of recent graduates who enter this field feel prepared for the challenges they face as public health administrators. They are often dedicated and well integrated into the system and are only new to their particular positions, not the field as a whole. New administrators learn about the problems faced by the community they work in and get their first tastes of running an office.

5 YEARS Some public health care officials find that they are tired of the long hours and increasing responsibilities. Trying to get people to take basic health precautions can be frustrating when they ignore crucial advice. Administrators sometimes move from working on public health for a public office to working on public health in the private sector, such as in hospitals, where they can continue their satisfying work in a more temperate environment. Others remain with the communities of which they have become a part.

10 YEARS The 10-year veteran is skilled at running his or her office and effectively advising the community about preventative health care. He or she has become a critical member of the community, depended on for practical and trustworthy advice. Administrators enjoy the recognition they receive from the community and public officials.

MAJOR EMPLOYERS

POPULATION COUNCIL
1 Dag Hammarskjold Plaza
New York, NY 10017
Tel: 212-339-0500
Fax: 212-755-6052
E-mail: jobs@popcouncil.org
www.popcouncil.org

ROCKEFELLER FOUNDATION
420 Fifth Avenue
New York, NY 10018
Tel: 212-869-8500
www.rockfound.org
Contact: Health Equity

SEXUALITY INFORMATION AND EDUCATION COUNCIL OF THE UNITED STATES
130 West 42nd Street, Suite 350
New York, NY 10036
Tel: 212-819-9770
Fax: 212-819-9776
www.siecus.org

MAJOR ASSOCIATIONS

ASSOCIATION OF UNIVERSITY PROGRAMS IN HEALTH ADMINISTRATION
2000 North 14th Street, Suite 780
Arlington, VA 22201
Tel: 703-894-0940
Fax: 703-894-0941
www.aupha.org

NATIONAL HEALTH COUNCIL
1730 M Street, NW, Suite 500
Washington, DC 20036
Tel: 202-785-3910
Fax: 202-785-5923
www.nationalhealthcouncil.org

RARE BOOKS DEALER

A DAY IN THE LIFE

While the profession of rare books dealer may itself be rather rare, it is the dream job of some and offers members of this small but passionate group the opportunity to work with historical artifacts on a daily basis. The allure of the field stems partly from the search for particular editions of rare book lore; indeed, rare books dealers must always be on the lookout for new additions to their collections. Rare and significant books can found anywhere from private libraries to garage sales, or even in a neighbor's basement or attic. For rare books dealers, the potential for the next great find to happen at any moment may be tantalizing.

Rare books dealers function as more than salespeople and collectors; they are also experts who possess immense quan-

$$\left\{ \begin{array}{l} \text{work with historical artifacts} \\ \text{on a daily basis} \end{array} \right\}$$

tities of knowledge about printing, book making, literature, history, science. . . the list goes on. It takes a trained eye; proficiency in Secretary; fluency in other languages such as Latin, German, Italian, and French; and knowledge of the history of books to be successful in this career. Because of the breadth and depth of their skill sets, rare books dealers are frequently approached by both collectors and other booksellers to appraise the value of their finds. Many dealers, especially those who have worked in the business for a while, have an impressive understanding of market trends, and have probably already handled the book or books in questions. They are quite aware of the criteria routinely used by industry peers and know how to determine authenticity (of the book and of the author's signature, for example), condition, age, and value. Individuals may also call on rare books dealers for consultations as they establish their own personal libraries. Taking into consideration the dimensions of the library as well as the client's interests and preferences, dealers recommend works that the client may enjoy and find valuable. They also provide advice as to how to keep acquired books is good condition. After all, the book may depreciate if it deteriorates. Most dealers recommend that books be kept in a relatively stable environment with low exposure to humidity. Books should also be kept out of direct sunlight, as pages tend to fade and leather bindings tend to get destroyed. Because rare books are artifacts, some disapprove of large private collections and argue in favor of keeping rare books in libraries, where the general public may access them. Nonetheless, the rare books industry is a thriving (but small) one, and many collectors and dealers make their holdings accessible to historians and others conducting primary-source research.

PAYING YOUR DUES

Apprenticeship offers one of the best means of entry into the world of rare books. Because the business can be a bit quirky, an established dealer may really help a novice learn the ropes. Most come into the field with an interest in (or in many cases, a passion for) rare books, and may already be familiar with various scripts, one or more foreign languages, and book-making techniques. Nevertheless, neophytes need to learn about how to run a rare books business, as well as how to ascertain the origin and authenticity of a given sample. It is also essential for them to learn the history of the books in their mentors' collections, to gain a sense of the contents of other collections across the globe, and to be able to determine with relative certainty the provenance, edition, and authenticity of a book. While there is no definitive educational path a dealer must take, an extensive knowledge of history, the history of science, and the history of the book, as well as of literature will prove extremely useful. And of course, a passion for books is a given.

ASSOCIATED CAREERS

While working as a rare book dealer puts an individual in a very specific niche, there are several other career alternatives that a dealer may opt to explore. Individuals who work with rare books have the qualifications to work for an auction house or to parlay their experience into dealing with other antiques and collectibles. They can also find positions in bookstores, as archivists, or even as curators of rare books library collections.

PAST AND FUTURE

Book collecting in the Western world is a relatively new phenomenon, given that the advent of the printing press only dates back to the mid-fifteenth century. The personal collections of royalty in the late fifteenth century would not have exceeded a hundred books. Yet just one hundred years later, Montaigne claimed having a collection of about a thousand books; and large seventeenth-century collections were known to have more than 2,000 books. The end of the seventeenth century saw interest in book collecting erupt. By 1676, book auctions had been introduced across Europe.

Today, the field of rare book dealing continues to grow, albeit at a conservative pace. There has not been a dramatic fluctuation in the prices of books; but rare books have proven to be sound investments, and there is every indication they will remain so.

QUALITY OF LIFE

2 YEARS At two years into their careers, rare books dealers probably still work as apprentices and are considered novices. They are gaining experience in the realms of acquisitions and sales and are in the process of mastering assessment and appraisal skills.

5 YEARS At this point in a rare books dealer's career, he or she has probably amassed a substantial understanding of the trade. He or she has probably also built a strong professional foundation. Some may seek to open their own shops; take on managerial roles at their current shops; or move to other shops. By this point, rare books dealers have probably established an area of specialty in a particular genre of books.

10 YEARS The routine for rare book dealers does not drastically alter from 5 years to 10 years, although many, by this point, have probably opened their own shops. After this much time in the industry, rare books dealers have most certainly established a solid reputation. Their business may be sought out by active collectors as well as by auction houses. Their expertise may be called on by professors, collectors, librarians, archivists, and perhaps even fellow rare books dealers. Many dealers have become especially well-versed in a specific category of literature, such as Renaissance Bibles or English books printed before 1641.

MAJOR EMPLOYERS

BAUMAN RARE BOOKS
1608 Walnut Street, 19th Floor
Philadelphia, PA 19103
Fax: 215-546-9064
E-mail: booksforsale@baumanrarebooks.com
www.baumanrarebooks.com

CHRISTIE'S
20 Rockefeller Plaza
New York, NY 10020
Tel: 212-492-5485
E-mail: info@christies.com
www.christies.com

JAMES & DEVON GRAY BOOKSELLERS
12 Arrow Street
Cambridge, MA 02138
Tel: 617-868-0752
Fax: 617-868-0753
www.graybooksellers.com

SOTHEBY'S
1334 York Avenue
New York, NY 10021
Tel: 541-312-5682
Fax: 541-312-5684
www.sothebys.com

MAJOR ASSOCIATIONS

ANTIQUARIAN BOOKSELLERS ASSOCIATION OF AMERICA
20 West 44th Street, 4th Floor
New York, NY 10036-6604
Tel: 212-944-8291
Fax: 212-944-8293
www.abaa.org

INTERNATIONAL LEAGUE OF ANTIQUARIAN BOOKSELLERS
E-mail: info@ilab.org
www.ilab-lila.com

RESEARCHER

BOOKS, FILMS, AND TV SHOWS
FEATURING THE PROFESSION
- **Bright Lights, Big City**
- **The Daughter of Time**
- **The Hunt for Red October**
- **Three Days of the Condor**

YOU'LL HAVE CONTACT WITH
- **Advertising executives**
- **Biologists**
- **Chemists**
- **Marketing executives**

PROFESSIONALS READ
- **Research Review**

A DAY IN THE LIFE

How many people prefer premium-brand toilet paper to generic toilet paper? How many 21-year-olds voted in the last election? How many politicians does it take to screw in a lightbulb? If you're curious about what people think and how they make decisions, you may want to become a researcher. Researchers collect, organize, analyze, and interpret data and opinions to explore issues, solve problems, and predict trends. Most researchers measure public opinion. Social science researchers gauge the public's opinion regarding social issues, services, political campaigns, parties, and personalities. Market researchers design and administer surveys to find out what people are most likely to buy. Their results influence policy and decision-makers and help provide business owners, advertising agencies, and politicians with a better idea of what is important to their customers and constituents.

{ **target audience** }

A four-step approach forms the core of the researcher's methodology: objective descriptions, problem analysis and classification, comparative studies, and historical review or development. Objectivity is critical to research work as prejudices and biases may distort the fact-gathering effort and the conclusions drawn. Researchers analyze and classify data in terms of responses and inclinations and compare studies on the same subject. They also investigate previous surveys to compare results. While researchers often conduct interviews and administer questionnaires, they also use information sources including libraries, newspaper clippings, encyclopedias, magazines and periodicals, case laws, legislative records, historical documents, and public opinion polls. Computers now play a pivotal role in the collection and organization of data and in the statistical methods of analysis. Public opinion researchers work a standard 40-hour workweek, sometimes with tight deadlines, but individuals in supervisory or management positions often work longer hours overseeing particular projects.

Carefully worded interviews or questionnaires are the most significant of the methods researchers use to collect data. The target audience and the specific type of information desired affect the choice of data collection methods. Researchers interested in buying trends during the Christmas shopping season may station interviewers at shopping malls. Market researchers often use telephone surveys to reach a particular demographic. Questionnaires may be administered to a carefully selected group or sample of people called a focus group. This group corresponds to the pollster's or marketer's target audience, who may be concerned about a certain issue, may shop at a certain location, or may buy certain brands of food or clothing items.

PAYING YOUR DUES

A bachelor's degree in business administration or economics provides a good foundation for individuals interested in public opinion research. A degree in sociology or psychology is best for individuals interested in exploring consumer demand or opinion research. People with a strong basis in statistics or engineering may find opportunities in industrial or analytical research. But increasingly, employers are looking to hire individuals with strong computer skills and higher degrees, such as a degree in business administration. A master's degree in sociology or political science will greatly improve employment and advancement opportunities. In addition, researchers must have strong people skills, be able to relate to people in a variety of social and cultural contexts, be good listeners, and be able to command the attention of the interviewee. Patience and objectivity are critical.

Whereas entrants with the requisite education, training and experience may start out as interviewers and data analysts, most applicants to the field of public opinion research enter as survey workers, research assistants, or coders and tabulators and move up to become interviewers or data analysts as they gain experience. Since starting salaries are commensurate with the training and experience of the applicant and the professional capacity and size of the company, entrants should try to gain experience and carefully explore salary levels and advancement potential of prospective companies.

ASSOCIATED CAREERS

Researchers with doctoral degrees often become instructors or professors at colleges and universities, while others become writers and pundits, publishing articles and books on survey techniques, studies conducted, and forecasting trends. Individuals with political science degrees sometimes become public opinion pollsters, making a name for themselves by predicting voting trends in presidential campaign years. Still others move on to work for the various political groups, organizations, and government agencies they once surveyed. Consumer pollsters find ready employment with advertising agencies and industries. Urban and regional planners, demographers, and statisticians call for research skills in their various fields.

PAST AND FUTURE

The expanded awareness of the power and importance of polls and surveys in influencing consumers, policy makers, and businesses ensures that public opinion research will continue to be a growing field. As computers continue to play an increasingly important role in this area, applicants will need to demonstrate strong computer skills in addition to pursuing extensive training and higher degrees.

QUALITY OF LIFE

2 YEARS Entry-level workers concentrate on acquiring the widest range of experience possible. The onus is on the worker to show initiative and drive by completing tasks according to schedule and volunteering for added duties and responsibilities.

5 YEARS At the five-year level, the researcher is well on his or her way to establishing him- or herself as a thorough, highly motivated professional. The ambitious worker has probably returned to school for refresher courses, attended various seminars and workshops, and is skilled in the latest computer applications. At this juncture, the professional is likely to consider pursuing doctoral studies.

10 YEARS With a decade of research experience to his or her credit, the professional should now be in a top-level management or advisory position. Researchers in academia are tenured professors or department heads with a body of research material, books, and articles to show for it.

MAJOR EMPLOYERS

IIT RESEARCH INSTITUTE
10 West 35th Street
Chicago, IL 60616
Tel: 312-567-4972
Fax: 312-567-4021
www.iitri.org

PFIZER INC.
235 East 42nd Street
New York, NY 10017
Tel: 212-733-2323
www.pfizer.com
Contact: Personnel

MAJOR ASSOCIATIONS

AMERICAN ASSOCIATION FOR PUBLIC OPINION RESEARCH
PO Box 14263
Lenexa, KS 66285-4263
Tel: 913-310-0118
Fax: 913-599-5340
E-mail: AAPOR-info@goAMP.com
www.aapor.org

AMERICAN STATISTICAL ASSOCIATION
1429 Duke Street
Alexandria, VA 22314-3415
Tel: 888-231-3473 or 703-684-1221
Fax: 703-684-2037
E-mail: asainfo@amstat.org
www.amstat.org

SOCIAL RESEARCH ASSOCIATION
175-185, Gray's Inn Road
London, England
WC1X 8UP
Tel: 020-8880-5684
E-mail: admin@the-sra.org.uk
www.the-sra.org.uk

SCHOOL ADMINISTRATOR

BOOKS, FILMS, AND TV SHOWS FEATURING THE PROFESSION
- Boston Public
- Keeping Pace with Our Children
- Lean on Me
- Stand and Deliver

YOU'LL HAVE CONTACT WITH
- Admissions personnel
- Financial aid officers
- Professors
- Students

PROFESSIONALS READ
- Chronicle of Higher Education
- Journal of Student Development
- Pathways

A DAY IN THE LIFE

Administrators, unlike teachers, work a 12-month year. They are fairly busy for most of that time. Whether running a small, private day care center or an overcrowded public high school, an administrator's tasks are numerous and varied, ranging from curriculum development to student discipline. The most familiar school administrator is the principal. Assisting the principal are vice principals, whose duties tend to be more specialized and who have more responsibility for the day-to-day operation of the school than does the principal. In a central administration office, other specialists work with some or all the schools in a given district, overseeing particular programs, such as the evaluation of student academic achievement. Any one of these administrators may be { understanding children's needs } responsible for infrastructure maintenance, the hiring and training of teachers, and student affairs.

Administrators work at colleges and universities, as well. Among them are the deans of faculty, who handle academic issues, and the deans of students, who see to the well-being and appropriate conduct of the student body. Registrars process student records and many financial matters, while provosts serve as university-wide troubleshooters. As in smaller primary and secondary schools, colleges often require their teachers to perform administrative work. To a college student, the most familiar teacher-administrator is probably the department chair, and anyone who has applied to college knows all about the dean of admissions.

School administration is a combination of intellectual work and grunt work. Organizational skills are key, as is the ability to operate within constantly tightening budgetary constraints. Since duties can range from hiring a basketball coach to providing AIDS education, administrators need to be versatile and flexible. An administrator must have a great deal of patience to deal with the enormous bureaucracy often associated with educational institutions. Finally, and perhaps most importantly, since administrators are responsible for the education of young people, a particular dedication to and an understanding of children's needs are essential.

PAYING YOUR DUES

Most beginning administrators have acquired related work experience—usually in teaching or management posts—and, as might be expected in an academic environment, they also have advanced degrees, including doctorates, in education, administration, or a combination of the two. Recently, some schools have begun to demand that their applicants have a Master of Business Administration degree. At the university level, deans, are, of course, expected to bring a rich academic and professional background to their jobs. As with many educational jobs in the United States, applicants must be certified, which is usually determined by the state government.

ASSOCIATED CAREERS

For those individuals who want summers off, teaching is a viable alternative to administration, and it brings with it many rewards. If you would rather work during the summer, look into camp counseling and administration, although these too can be year-round tasks. More and more religious communities are taking charge of the education of their children, and they consequently require the services of qualified school administrators.

PAST AND FUTURE

Teachers once ran their own schools, and some of them still do, but most schools have become more specialized. The need for specialists to maintain an ever-increasing public and private educational system became apparent early in United States history. In the nineteenth century, it became clear that administrators and teachers could be the reformers of America's educational programs, as was the case with Horace Mann. To this day, educators and school administrators sometimes find themselves in the thick of great controversies and revolutions. The future holds even more complicated challenges for school administrators. Health, political, and cultural issues play significant roles in the life of the contemporary school administrator.

Because so many administrative jobs are tied to state funding and a strict hierarchy, few administrators can expect to get rich quick running schools. Nevertheless, many administrators belong to unions, which see to it that the school system provides such benefits as health insurance and child care. At private schools, salaries tend to be lower and fringe benefits are uncommon.

QUALITY OF LIFE

2 YEARS Many school systems assign new administrators to posts that are low on the ladder and allow them to advance only according to a set timetable. Other systems are quite willing to convert a seasoned teacher into a principal overnight, but this is less common in larger systems. Some beginners may work in school headquarters before moving on to a particular school as a vice principal or principal.

5 YEARS Because school administration involves so many specialized tasks, some administrators at this stage have greater responsibilities in one aspect of education administration, such as curriculum development. Other administrators, such as a school principal or, in the case of college administrators, a student dean, have more generalized duties. A principal's duties vary according to the school system. Some must refer constantly to a central administrative body before instituting changes, while others operate with virtual autonomy. Another option for administrators is to move to a larger school system, where greater opportunities and challenges exist.

10 YEARS Many respected principals hold their jobs for decades, leaving an indelible impression on entire generations of students. Others move on to different challenges and seek the position of school superintendent. At the college level, the trend is somewhat different. Respected college deans often hang up their administrative hats and return to the classroom or the research center. Still others seek the office of university president or chancellor. Dwight D. Eisenhower left his job as president of Columbia University to run for president of the United States.

MAJOR EMPLOYERS
CHICAGO BOARD OF EDUCATION
125 South Clark Street, 2nd Floor, MR#125
Chicago, IL 60603
Tel: 773-535-8000 or 800-593-5700
Fax: 773-535-7625
www.cps.k12.il.us
Contact: Department of Human Relations

COLORADO DEPARTMENT OF EDUCATION
201 East Colfax Avenue
Denver, CO 80203-1799
Tel: 303-866-6600
Fax: 303-830-0793
www.cde.state.co.us

MAJOR ASSOCIATIONS
AMERICAN ASSOCIATION OF SCHOOL ADMINISTRATORS
801 North Quincy Street
Arlington, VA 22203
Tel: 703-528-0700
Fax: 703-841-1543
www.aasa.org

AMERICAN FEDERATION OF SCHOOL ADMINISTRATORS
1101 17th Street, NW, Suite 408
Washington, DC 20036
Tel: 202-986-4209
Fax: 202-986-4211
www.admin.org

NATIONAL ASSOCIATION OF SECONDARY SCHOOL PRINCIPALS
1904 Association Drive
Reston, VA 20191
Tel: 703-860-0200
Fax: 703-476-5432
www.nassp.org

SECRETARY

A DAY IN THE LIFE

A secretary manages information. Responsibilities can include everything from scheduling staff appointments to office management to managing an entire database. Since the computer is central to any modern office, mastery of the latest office technology is essential. Secretaries are often the primary conduit of information from their employers to the rest of the world, so they must be comfortable communicating with others in person and on the telephone. Secretaries who work in specialized fields, such as law and accounting, are familiar with the intricacies of their field. Executive secretaries often initiate and execute independent projects. One secretary with whom we spoke described her view of keeping busy after accomplishing a day's assignments well

{ Be prepared for anything. }

before deadline: "You can bury your nose in a magazine, or you can find something constructive to do. Good secretaries are self-starters." Few professions call for such careful execution of so many specialized tasks. Such professionalism combined with the almost constant changes in business technology has led secretaries to turn to one another for support, training, and solidarity. "You often don't know exactly what's expected of you," remarked one secretary. "It's easier if there are other secretaries there to help you clarify things, especially in a place like a law office." Because so much of the job depends on organization, secretaries' skills are tested when they work for particularly disorganized bosses. "Your main task is making sure everything goes smoothly, anticipating as well as accomplishing particular tasks." And secretaries are still expected to handle their employers' moods and foibles in the course of everyday business. The best advice we heard: "Be prepared for anything."

PAYING YOUR DUES

Some of the clerical skills expected of secretaries can be picked up on the job, but secretarial candidates should have already mastered typing and word processing in high school, college, or vocational school. The journey through the ranks can begin as an administrative assistant with graduation up through the ranks of regular and senior executive assistant and lateral moves from department to department and then to office manager and senior office manager. Medical secretaries earn a separate distinction. Competition in the field allows employers to place greater demands on applicants: A college education is a valuable asset. In a global economy, being bilingual or even trilingual is often a plus. Stenography has become something of a lost art, but it may come in handy with an old-fashioned boss.

ASSOCIATED CAREERS

"Secretary" is an umbrella term for any number of administrative jobs, and the most qualified secretaries have mastered them all. Many secretaries use their experience to enter a particular profession and find that their ability to multitask and work with others can allow them keen insight into the management of their own company. Some secretaries develop editorial skills in their positions and move into editorial jobs. Many secretaries who are responsible for office management, including payrolls, bookkeeping, bill paying, and maintenance of the office's physical plant find more specialized opportunities in these areas. Those individuals interested in doing secretarial work on a temporary basis may seek assignments through an agency that places temporary workers with companies. These agencies provide companies with administrative workers on a daily, weekly, or monthly basis. Temp work has the advantages of flexibility and variety—of bosses, office settings, and tasks. It also has the drawbacks of routines—you will quite possibly be given one boring task to do for a week—and the possibility that the work may dry up at certain times of the year when you could really use a paycheck.

PAST AND FUTURE

Paperwork and other clerical tasks, which were often a woman's first exposure to the world of big business at the beginning of the twentieth century, formed the early composite of the secretary's duties. With the demands placed on the male population by two world wars, the position of secretary came to be held almost exclusively by women by midcentury. The image of the "working girl" making coffee for the boss persisted through the 1980s. Today, however, the occupation has become less closely associated with women. With corporate downsizing, secretaries often find themselves working for as many as three bosses while coping with constant innovations or limitations in technology. As in any profession, a good secretary is a rare and valued employee. Salaries start at around $27,000, but veterans can take home substantially more.

QUALITY OF LIFE

2 YEARS The early part of your secretarial career is the time to lay the groundwork for greater responsibility and reward in the future. As a new secretary, you'll hone your skills in typing, word processing, and data processing and spend much of your time answering the phone and screening calls. You'll begin to identify your niche as an executive, administrative, legal, medical, or other type of secretary. Employers will ask you to do faxing, filing, and photocopying and to handle correspondence. Paralegals can expect to have a demanding schedule. During these years, many secretaries discover how to operate efficiently in the face of unending, unexpected, or loosely defined responsibilities.

5 YEARS Thousands of secretaries move on to other jobs in this period, often getting hired on the basis of their achievements as office professionals. Secretaries who stay on have found a means of coping with a tremendous volume of work and derive satisfaction from helping to make a business run smoothly. At this point, many secretaries train new secretaries, often in a training program of their own devising.

10 YEARS For those individuals who have made the most of a secretarial career, the rewards are palpable. It is hard to last in a profession that demands organizational skill, meticulous attention to detail, efficiency, and patience. Secretaries who possess these qualities know how rare they are and can expect to reap the rewards they deserve, including a pension and benefits.

MAJOR EMPLOYERS
CAREER BLAZERS
590 Fifth Avenue, 6th Floor
New York, NY 10036
Tel: 212-719-3232
Fax: 212-921-0452
www.careerblazers.com

MAJOR ASSOCIATIONS
INTERNATIONAL ASSOCIATION OF ADMINISTRATIVE PROFESSIONALS
10502 NW Ambassador Drive
PO Box 20404
Kansas City, MO 64195-0404
E-mail: service@iaap-he.org
www.iaap-hq.org

SET DESIGNER

A DAY IN THE LIFE

Okay, so it's not the award everyone stays up until midnight to see who won, but the importance of a set designer to a play, musical, or movie is paramount. From minimal productions, like grade school plays, to multimillion-dollar movies, the set is a silent supporting actor. Moods, meaning, and media are all affected by the set design. Any flaw—a misplaced building, an uncomplimentary color scheme—can ruin the authenticity of any production. Set designers are involved in all aspects of "creating the scene," from stage construction to costume creation to the use of props. They research, design, and supervise construction of the visual aids required in stage, film, and television productions. Set designers have above-average artistic ability. They are drawers, painters, sculptors, sewers, and

{ creating the scene }

carpenters of the set. Set designers usually start with freehand sketches of what the scene should be. They then move to scale models, working in tandem with the director of the production, the production manager, and writers. Once their plans are finalized, the set designer supervises construction workers who build the sets. They also work with people in charge of lighting and sound. They have to have a strong understanding of theatrical rigging and safety. Lately, as the trend of movies using computer-generated worlds grows, specially trained set designers are called on to create fantastic worlds using a mouse and a keyboard. The set designer has to take into consideration a production's budget when building sets. The smaller the budget, the more creative the set designer may have to be to build a world that entrances the audience without costing a fortune. Set designers mostly work in large production theaters and movie studios, and they work long hours, particularly up to the night of the first performance.

PAYING YOUR DUES

Set designers usually attend specialized design institutes or artistic academies. However, the ability to build a set can also be gained through on-the-job training. It's not hard to imagine a set designer starting out his or her career with small church productions, working his or her way up to school plays, college productions, and then Broadway. It's a long shot, but with a ton of talent and determination, it's not impossible. Most set designers study specific courses, gaining degrees in theater. Set designers are required to attend interviews or auditions and to bring with them a portfolio of past design or artwork. Some work under the tutelage of more experienced set designers.

ASSOCIATED CAREERS

Good set designers have an artistic ability that can translate into many other professions, including painters, sculptors, carpenters, and florists. The skills needed to build entire worlds in a limited space come in handy if a set designer wishes to pursue similar—but technically more demanding—careers as architects and even city planners. Being in the theater profession, set designers can also make the transition to stage manager or director.

PAST AND FUTURE

Theater has been around for thousands of years. Greek tragedies were admittedly minimalist in set design—masks. But through the ages, plays have found more and more need for set designers. Now, set designers are employed by theater, film, and television production companies, usually under contract for the duration of a particular production. Some set designers work on a freelance basis. But it's not just traditional media that set designers are working in. With movies like the *Matrix*, *Star Wars*, and *Lord of the Rings*, set designers may find themselves in front of a computer screen, developing otherworldly sets that exist only in cyberspace. One study showed that competition for jobs in this field is intense. Getting the high-profile, high-paying jobs requires an outstanding ability and artistic flair. Demand for set designers is linked to the number of films, television programs, and stage shows under production at a given time, the level of funding available, and popular trends in entertainment.

QUALITY OF LIFE

2 YEARS Without much training or education, young set designers may find themselves stuck building Noah's ark or straw houses for the *Three Little Pigs*. With at least two years of college, set designers can take on university productions and community theater. Some set designers may create sets for low-budget movies at this point. During this time, set designers gain knowledge and understanding of building materials and techniques. No matter the level of production, set designers learn how to handle high stress and adapt well to last-minute changes in a performance environment.

5 YEARS The stress of putting on a show never goes away, but after five years, being able to anticipate problems before they occur is a likely and much-appreciated skill. Most set designers with five years of experience in community theater may decide it's time to move on to bigger projects. Others may feel that bringing joy to their hometown audiences is reward unto itself.

10 YEARS The value of a set designer with 10 years or more of experience to a producer and director is extraordinary. At this stage in a set designer's career, he or she should be able to see the world the director wants to create—sometimes before the director sees it. As a set designer's reputation grows, he or she may be called on to do bigger productions, until someday he or she is up on stage him- or herself, thanking his or her parents and the producers and everyone else he or she can remember for the award he or she has just received.

MAJOR EMPLOYERS

Set designers work for productions, both large and small, across the nation and the globe.

MAJOR ASSOCIATIONS

ART DIRECTORS GUILD
11969 Ventura Boulevard, Suite 200
Studio City, CA 91604
Tel: 818-762-9995
Fax: 818-762-9997
www.artdirectors.org

UNITED SCENIC ARTISTS LOCAL 829
29 West 38th Street
New York, NY 10018
Tel: 212-581-0300
Fax: 212-977-2011
www.usa829.org

SOCIAL WORKER

SALARY   • •

HOURS   •

EDUCATION   • •

**BOOKS, FILMS, AND TV SHOWS
FEATURING THE PROFESSION**

- **Boys Town**
- **Losing Isaiah**
- **The Statue of Liberty**
- **The Welfare State**

YOU'LL HAVE CONTACT WITH

- **Attorneys**
- **Government officials**
- **Occupational therapists**
- **Psychologists**

PROFESSIONALS READ

- **The Hand**
- **Journal of NACSW**
- **The Social Worker**

A DAY IN THE LIFE

Social workers spend their days helping people with complicated psychological, health, social, or financial problems. They assist families in need and people who are the victims of abuse. They provide counseling, advice, and direction for people who would otherwise have no way of bettering their situations. While seeing people who are confused, scared, and beset by problems all day long may sound disheartening, social workers told us that they were uplifted by their job and that they truly felt they were doing work of value. "People need your help, and you give it to them," said one respondent, adding, "The only strange thing is that you get paid to do it."

Social workers, around half of whom work for local and federal governments, have to be familiar with all assistance programs and services available for those individuals in need. This requires continuing education to keep abreast of programs, their funding, and their efficacy. "The quickest way to lose your client's trust is to send them to an agency that tells them they're not eligible," said one by way of explaining that the trust of one's client is difficult to earn and easily lost. Social workers have to be prepared for disappointments from their clients as well. More than 30 percent of urban families assigned a social worker miss one of their first three appointments. Still, most professionals invest themselves heavily in the fates of their clients, and a number of our respondents called this involvement emotionally draining. While this contributes to the reasonably high attrition rate for first-year workers (15 percent), respondents noted that it was valuable in that it kept them aware of the significance of what they do.

{ trust }

More and more, social workers are being asked to find an area of focused responsibility, such as criminal justice issues, gerontological services, or medical issues. This can leave the social worker a bit dissatisfied, as often a client will have a number of concurrent problems, and they have a prescribed range of duties they can perform. For people with a natural instinct to help others, this is tantamount to "telling a millionaire he can only give away $20 at a time." Private professionals are under no such restrictions, and they record generally higher levels of satisfaction.

PAYING YOUR DUES

Social workers face significant educational requirements. Most initial positions, which are primarily clerical, require only a bachelor's degree in social work or a related field, such as psychology or sociology. For positions that involve psychological recommendations or assessments or for positions with more responsibility, a master's degree in social work is required. More than 300 colleges offer bachelor's degrees in social work, and more than 100 offer master's degrees in social work and are accredited by the Council on Social Work Education. Individuals who wish to advance to policy or director positions are asked to complete a doctorate program in social work. Nearly all programs in social work require extensive fieldwork and client contact. Traditional course work includes social welfare policies, political science, human behavior, research methodology, and abnormal psychology. All states have strict licensing requirements for social workers, and additional professional certifications are available from the National Association of Social Workers (NASW). Private practitioners are encouraged to earn professional certifications, as these help in collecting reimbursement for services from insurance providers.

ASSOCIATED CAREERS

Social workers have a strong instinct to help people, and this often serves people well in positions such as therapists, guidance counselors, and not-for-profit counseling service providers. Individuals who become burned out by the intense nature of the client/worker relationship find work in slightly more distancing professions, such as teaching, writing promotional literature for programs, and fund-raising.

PAST AND FUTURE

Poorhouses used to be basically jails for people who couldn't support themselves, and destitute parentless children used to live in state-run orphanages much like the one featured in *Oliver Twist*. In the twentieth century, reformers like Samuel Barnett and Jane Addams began to establish public programs and encourage self-sufficiency and education. Now there are a wide variety of programs to help people in need, though of course there could be more, and social workers are needed at each one of them.

Social workers can look forward to a bright future as current demand, particularly in rural regions, exceeds supply. New opportunities for social workers in all regions are expected to develop faster than the national average for the creation of new jobs. Professionals with advanced degrees and specialized experience will have an advantage in the industry. The only uncertainty in the profession is proposed federal cuts to existing social programs, which would not have an immediate impact on jobs, but could dim long-term prospects for both social workers and their clients.

QUALITY OF LIFE

2 YEARS New social workers either love what they do or find that they are too drained by its emotional intensity. Many individuals leave after one or two years, frustrated at their inability to help their clients and exhausted by their anxiety over their clients' prospects. Individuals who make it through these early years tend to remain in the profession. Specialization begins for people at public agencies. The hours are long, but salaries are reasonable. Satisfaction varies widely.

5 YEARS Five years into the profession many social workers have chosen the area of specialization that they will remain in until they assume positions of managerial responsibility. Caseloads can be overwhelming, as the average five-year veteran is in charge of over 200 client cases at any given time. Many individuals are involved in continuing education and spend considerable amounts of their free time reading publications about their area of specialty or attending conferences. Private practitioners begin to earn higher incomes and work to develop strong community reputations. The hours increase.

10 YEARS Many social workers earn managerial or senior case officer status, which unfortunately removes them from the day-to-day counseling that drew them to the profession in the first place. A number of social workers turn down opportunities for advancement for this very reason. Individuals who do accept these higher positions become caseload managers and assign people to cases, exercising large discretionary powers of assessment and approval for clients' unusual needs. Satisfaction is high, and the hours remain stable.

MAJOR EMPLOYERS

CARONDELET HEALTH CARE CORPORATION
1601 West St. Mary's Road
Tucson, AZ 85745
Tel: 520-721-3727
Fax: 520-740-6067
www.carondelet.org

HACKENSACK UNIVERSITY MEDICAL CENTER
30 Prospect Avenue
Hackensack, NJ 07601
Tel: 201-996-2000
Fax: 201-489-1766

MAJOR ASSOCIATIONS

AMERICA ASSOCIATION OF MARRIAGE AND FAMILY THERAPY
112 South Alfred Street, Suite 300
Alexandria, VA 22314
Tel: 703-838-9808
Fax: 703-838-9805
www.aamft.org

NATIONAL ASSOCIATION OF SOCIAL WORKERS
750 First Street, NE, Suite 700
Washington, DC 20002-4241
Tel: 202-408-8600
E-mail: membership@naswdc.org
www.naswdc.org

SOCIOLOGIST

A DAY IN THE LIFE

Sociologists study human society and social behavior through group formations and social, political, religious, and economic institutions. How individuals interact with one another within given contexts and the origin and development of social groups are important indices by which the sociologist conducts his or her research and draws conclusions. Because of the depth and scope of this field, sociologists usually specialize in one or more of a number of areas. Areas of specialty include education; family; racial and ethnic relations; revolution, war, and peace; social psychology; gender roles and relations; and urban, rural, political, and comparative sociology. Sociologists have keen senses of observation and analysis and abundant and natural curiosity.

{ impact on constituents }

Because they are engaged in observing, analyzing, defining, testing, and explaining human behavior, there is virtually no area of modern life in which a sociologist's research or conclusions are not valuable. For advertising, industry, criminology, medicine, and government, sociologists and the research they conduct can enhance sales, improve productivity, shape social policy, resolve social conflicts, promote political platforms, and influence lawmakers. Sociological researchers, with their evaluations of the relevance and effectiveness of social programs, have shaped and will continue to shape the direction and tone of political life as we know it. "Every political action committee, every group or organization with an agenda to introduce, extend, eliminate, or maintain legislative policies have or will at some time employ the services of sociologists," says one professor of sociology. "There are a vast number of social programs [that] are on the budget cutting block (such as funding for abortion clinics, AIDS research, welfare, and Medicaid). Sociological research is an invaluable tool in determining the impact these cuts will have on its constituents."

Sociologists must be meticulous and patient in carefully observing and gathering notes on a particular subject. Some results are measurably slow in manifesting themselves and could take months or years. Statistics and computers are central to a sociologist's work, but so too are qualitative methods such as focus-group-based research and social impact evaluations. Preconceived notions must give way to scientific methodology of data collection and objectivity, as sociologists must be open to new ideas and social and cultural situations. Strong analytical skills, statistics, data gathering and analysis, qualitative methods of research, survey methods, computer techniques, and counseling and interviewing skills are part of the course of sociology.

PAYING YOUR DUES

To bypass most entry-level positions in social services, marketing, management, or personnel, be prepared to keep studying. At best, a bachelor's degree in sociology with the requisite training in survey methods and statistics will land you a junior analyst post with a research company or a government agency. If you like the challenge of child care or juvenile counseling, then an undergraduate degree will also get you there. But if you have your sights set on applied research or teaching at a community college, then the minimum requirement is a master's degree in sociology. But keep studying: a PhD is the only route to most senior-level positions in corporations, research institutes, government agencies, and tenure at colleges and universities. If an extensive educational background is central to success in this career, then choosing the right graduate school is equally important. Applicants should look for schools that offer courses relevant to their areas of interest, adequate research facilities that provide practical experience, and placement services that find research and teaching assistantships for students.

ASSOCIATED CAREERS

Because the core requirement of sociology is an understanding of social institutions and behavior, the sociologist is not unlike other social scientists such as economists, psychologists, anthropologists, political scientists, and social workers in that their work also involves social impact assessment. Research methods crucial in sociology also form the basis of these other professions and thus ensure an easy transition to an alternate career.

PAST AND FUTURE

In the past, an undergraduate degree in sociology would ensure upward mobility in this profession. Today, advanced degrees and specialization are the norm. As society becomes more sophisticated and fragmented into special interest groups, there are no boundaries limiting the work that sociologists will be called on to do. The fast-paced growth of technology means that sociologists will have to keep current with computer techniques that make research easier. Sociologists will also need to be aware of changes to social institutions and be able to anticipate trends while constantly updating or reviewing research in particular areas.

QUALITY OF LIFE

2 YEARS The first two years are the groundbreaking years of this profession. A recent sociology graduate will probably find herself reading, researching, and writing reports, articles, and books. At any level of the educational ladder, and in any setting, private or public, the sociologist will experience the pressure of deadlines, possibly heavy workloads, and long hours. Individuals specializing in clinical or applied sociology should be certified by the Sociological Practice Association (SPA).

5 YEARS At this level, the sociologist has gained significant experience in the core elements of the profession and should be amassing a small bundle of published articles and reports. By this time, the professional should have risen up the ranks to a middle-management or senior-level position. If the sociologist has a PhD and is a college professor, then he or she should be seeking tenure.

10 YEARS At the 10-year level, the sociologist has made remarkable progress in his or her career. By now, he or she should have a few publication titles to his or her credit, should be abreast of the latest computer techniques, and should have returned to school for refresher courses and development seminars, workshops, and conferences.

MAJOR EMPLOYERS

Sociologists are employed by a wide variety of schools, businesses, research organizations, and government agencies.

MAJOR ASSOCIATIONS

AMERICAN SOCIOLOGICAL ASSOCIATION

1307 New York Avenue, NW, Suite 700
Washington, DC 20005
Tel: 202-383-9005
Fax: 202-638-0882
www.asanet.org

SPEECH-LANGUAGE PATHOLOGIST

BOOKS, FILMS, AND TV SHOWS
FEATURING THE PROFESSION
- **The Diving Bell and the Butterfly**
- **The Miracle Worker**

YOU'LL HAVE CONTACT WITH
- **Audiologists**
- **Occupational therapists**
- **Physicians**
- **Teachers**

PROFESSIONALS READ
- **American Journal of Speech-Language Pathology**
- **ASHA Leader**
- **Journal of Speech, Language, and Hearing Research**
- **Language, Speech, and Hearing Sciences in Schools**

A DAY IN THE LIFE

A speech-language pathologist is a specialist who evaluates, treats, and researches a variety of speech, voice, and language disorders. They work with people who are unable to make speech sounds or cannot make them clearly or people who stutter, have fluency and rhythm problems, inappropriate pitch issues, or harsh voice and speech-quality problems. Some of the conditions that speech-language pathologists treat include stuttering, dyslexia, and swallowing disorders (dysphagia). Other disorders may result from hearing loss, stroke, cerebral palsy, mental disability, or brain injury. Because speech disorders are usually related to neurological, psychological, and physical conditions, speech-language pathologists must be able to work as a member of a team, which may include { **understand and empathize** } other health care specialists such as a neurologist and psychiatrist; however, speech-language pathologists are autonomous and do not work under direct medical supervision.

An important part of a speech-language pathologist's work is the counseling and educating of individuals and their families about speech disorders. They also work with patients' families on treatment techniques to use at home and on how to modify behavior that impedes communication. Speech therapy is a painstaking process, but with patience and compassion, it can be as rewarding as it is frustrating. Tremendous attention to detail and a sharp focus are necessary in evaluating the patient's progress. Overall, speech-language pathologists must be able to understand and empathize with the emotional strains that such problems bring, both from the patient's and the patient's family member's point of view.

Speech-language pathologists, like other health care professionals, must carefully diagnose problems and, if necessary, call on the advice of other health specialists. The ability to distinguish the need for the professional input of specialists is critical for success in this field. Speech-language pathologists must also monitor the progress of patients, eliminate certain programs, and introduce others that are more effective. The ability to make informed decisions that may lead to the success and prevent the failure of any individual program is a skill that can only develop with years of experience.

PAYING YOUR DUES

An aspiring speech-language pathologist needs a master's degree in speech pathology, 375 hours of supervised clinical experience, a passing grade on a national examination, and at least nine months of post-graduate professional experience. Depending on the work setting and state, national certification, state licensure, or both may be required. With such a strong emphasis on education, practical experience, and licensure, entrants to this field must work long and hard.

ASSOCIATED CAREERS

Speech-language pathologists who wish to modify their careers have a range of choices open to them. Hearing loss is associated with speech disorders, and so the work of an audiologist is very closely connected. The speech-language pathologist seeking more and varied challenges may be able to find it in special education and private rehabilitation counseling services. Speech and language scientists research the underlying processes of normal communication, explore the impact of psychological, social, and physiological factors on communication disorders, and collaborate with related professionals like dentists, engineers, or educators to diagnose and treat individuals with communication disorders. High-level administrative positions in schools, hospitals, health departments, or clinics may offer significantly higher wages and more responsibilities. Other occupations requiring rehabilitation training include occupational therapy, physical therapy, and recreational therapy.

PAST AND FUTURE

As is the case for most areas of the health care profession, speech-language pathologists are expected to be in constant demand for years to come. Speech-language pathologists will be needed to service a rapidly aging population with significant growth in the seventy-five-years-and-over sector of the population. Hearing loss and its associated speech disorders are expected to be one of the major health concerns of an older population. The proliferation of health care agencies, nursing homes, residential retirement communities, and adult day care centers will assure employment opportunities for speech-language pathologists and other health specialists. With federal legislation guaranteeing the expansion of special education and related services in schools, more and younger students with disabilities will require the specialized training of speech-language pathologists.

QUALITY OF LIFE

2 YEARS At the two-year level, the speech-language pathologist will have completed nine months of supervised practice and can now practice independently. This is the stage at which the professional concentrates on making accurate diagnoses, knowing when to seek the opinion of other health specialists, and developing his or her "bedside manner," or way in which he or she relates to patients. Emphasis is on effectively communicating test results and clearly explaining proposed treatment to patients and family members. He or she is also careful in charting the evaluation, progress, and discharge of patients.

5 YEARS A speech-language pathologist with five years of experience should be involved in the developing and implementing of personalized treatment programs. He or she is now adept at working with physicians, psychiatric social workers, psychologists, and occasionally neurologists to create treatment programs that bring about effective results. At this stage the speech-language pathologist is wont to evaluate his or her own professional progress and advancement potential and can mentor graduate students and new clinicians.

10 YEARS Teaching and research and development at the college or university level will probably offer the most intellectual gratification. Writing books and articles for publication is an integral part of any professorship. Executive-level management positions, including a directorship, will offer lucrative salary scales and numerous responsibilities. Private practice offers more autonomy and flexible hours. The 10-year veteran has a number of ways to rise in his or her career.

MAJOR EMPLOYERS

Speech-language pathologists are employed by hospitals, schools, nursing homes, outpatient clinics, and private practices. Check for employment opportunities in your area.

MAJOR ASSOCIATIONS

AMERICAN SPEECH-LANGUAGE-HEARING ASSOCIATION

10801 Rockville Pike
Rockville, MD 20852
Tel: 800-638-8255 or 301-897-5700
Fax: 301-571-0457
www.asha.org

SUBSTANCE ABUSE COUNSELOR

A DAY IN THE LIFE

Substance abuse counseling is a demanding form of community outreach that requires patience, compassion, and a keen desire to help others in need. A good portion of the addict population is comprised of people who need help in many areas of their lives. Often these people are unaware of the kinds of assistance available, whether they are eligible, or how to go about finding help. Counselors refer patients to a variety of other services that may help provide a stable platform from which they can fight their drug addiction. The abuser may be directed to a family agency, food pantry, physician or psychiatrist, vocational training center, lawyer, welfare agent, or other professionals or agencies depending on the needs of the individual. One of the most frustrating aspects of the job, counselors report, is the bias that clients typically face when applying for other services. "People hold addicts more responsible for their problems," griped one interviewee. Many people who seek help do overcome their addiction—counselors estimate that 20 percent of the people in treatment programs can eventually return to work and function normally, and these successful cases are a source of unique job satisfaction among counselors. But staying clear of the dependent substances requires ongoing vigilance, and recidivism (or backsliding) among those with dependencies is a painful reality that can be a source of depression for counselors as well as the users themselves.

{ You see everything. }

Counselors see people in both group and private sessions. Each case varies according to the personality of the individual. In the words of one counselor, "You never know what will come up. I spend a lot of my time making referrals, but most of what I do is crisis intervention." Crisis intervention demands a sympathetic, nonjudgmental attitude and a supportive approach no matter what situation the addict is in, and, as one counselor put it, "You see everything." Many people who are drawn to this career have deep-seated personal or religious beliefs about its social value. Their commitment to the principle of helping others keeps them going through the setbacks they inevitably witness on the job. Probably the most difficult aspect of the job is seeing patients die. Between drug addiction and the range of other problems that often accompany it, such as homelessness, mental illness, and AIDS, death is unfortunately a common sight. One of the great challenges of this noble vocation is learning to control anger, frustration, and even the bonds of friendship that can undermine the counselor-patient relationship. Not surprisingly, the burnout rate for substance abuse counselors is very high.

PAYING YOUR DUES

Substance abuse counseling is considered one of the most challenging areas of human/social services. To become a counselor, you need a bachelor's degree plus two years of counseling in a related field or equivalent life experience. This could include other kinds of counseling, volunteer work, or experience as a former addict. Though certification is available from most states, it is not required. Some people believe this will change in the future as cutbacks are made and jobs become scarce.

ASSOCIATED CAREERS

Substance abuse counselors work closely with a variety of other health and human service professionals, including psychologists, social workers, family counselors, career counselors, lawyers, welfare agents, and other state employees. Because substance abuse counseling has a high rate of burnout, it's not unusual for people to turn to other forms of counseling as a career alternative.

PAST AND FUTURE

Though clergy members have always provided counseling to people in need of help, substance abuse counseling as a discrete profession evolved fairly recently. Its theory and practice have grown out of a synthesis of three older methodologies: the psychoanalytic/psychotherapeutic model of mental health treatment, Alcoholics Anonymous's 12-step recovery program, and the Therapeutic Community treatment model as used by such organizations as Synanon and Phoenix House. Promising pharmacological treatments currently in development may yet produce new breakthroughs in recovery programs.

The future of substance abuse counseling rests largely on the financial commitment of government. Most substance abuse programs are state and federally funded, and as a result, there is a lot of government supervision in most counseling clinics (and lots of paperwork). Cutbacks have already altered the landscape, and further reductions are possible in the future. Counselors report that the patients they see are showing increasingly ill effects from the economic downturn and resulting cutbacks in resources devoted to assisting them.

QUALITY OF LIFE

2 YEARS New counselors are typically handling at least 50 cases at any given time. Much of their day is spent in contact with other agencies during the referral process. A counselor is also responsible for clinical assessments, group and individual counseling sessions, urine monitoring, and charting. People often burn out at this stage and pursue another path within human services.

5 YEARS At five years, a counselor is performing many of the same daily tasks as before, but their caseload decreases as their administrative responsibilities increase. A midlevel professional has more experience and better judgment to handle the pressure of the job, and pay scales are increasing steadily, but there is a high burnout rate at this stage, too. Most counselors are constantly reassessing their commitment to the field.

10 YEARS Despite the high dropout rate in the field, a healthy segment of the profession serves a long career and retires with benefits, having worked at a single facility. Counselors in the field after 10 years are likely to be serving in an advisory capacity on a hospital staff or perhaps have taken on directorship of an agency at this point. Counselors at this level are responsible for the treatment of the most challenging patients, such as those individuals with severe mental illness.

MAJOR EMPLOYERS
CONTINUUM HEALTH PARTNERS, INC.
(includes Beth Israel, St. Luke's, Roosevelt, and Long Island College Hospitals)
www.wehealnewyork.org

FEDERAL BUREAU OF PRISONS
320 First Street, NW
Washington, DC 20534
Tel: 202-307-3198
E-mail: info@bop.gov
www.bop.gov

UNITED STATES DEPARTMENT OF HEALTH AND HUMAN SERVICES
200 Independence Avenue, SW
Washington, DC 20201
Tel: 202-619-0257 or 877-696-6775
www.samhsa.gov

State alcohol- and substance-abuse agencies also employ substance abuse counselors.

MAJOR ASSOCIATIONS
NATIONAL ALLIANCE OF METHADONE ADVOCATES
435 2nd Avenue
New York, NY 10010
Tel: 212-595-6262
www.methadone.org

NATIONAL ASSOCIATION OF ALCOHOLISM AND DRUG ABUSE COUNSELORS
901 North Washington Street, Suite 600
Arlington, VA 22314
Tel: 800-548-0497
Fax: 800-377-1136
www.naadac.org

TEACHER

BOOKS, FILMS, AND TV SHOWS
FEATURING THE PROFESSION
- Dangerous Minds
- Dead Poets Society
- Election
- In and Out
- Lean on Me

YOU'LL HAVE CONTACT WITH
- Coaches
- Fellow teachers
- Parents
- School administrators
- Students
- Tutors

PROFESSIONALS READ
- Independent School Bulletin
- Journals in area of specialty

A DAY IN THE LIFE

The majority of teachers are employed by primary or secondary schools. Their focus is a specific subject or grade level. Before arriving at the classroom, teachers create lesson plans tailored to their students' levels of ability. At school, usually beginning at 8:00 A.M., teachers must begin the difficult task of generating interest in their often sleepy students. A good sense of humor and the ability to think like their students help teachers captivate their students' attention. Teachers have to generate interest in subjects that students often find tedious. Rousing them from their apathy and watching their curiosity grow is a giant reward of teaching. One teacher said her favorite aspects of teaching are the creative challenges and the "iconoclastic opportunities."

{ iconoclastic opportunities }

Teachers must have high expectations of their students and also be able to empathize with their concerns. They must be comfortable dealing with a spectrum of personality types and ability levels and must be capable of treating their students fairly.

About a fifth of the teacher's workweek is devoted to their least favorite aspect of the profession—paperwork. Teachers have a block of time each day, called a professional period, to accomplish paper grading; however, all teachers report that this is not enough time. Teachers also perform administrative duties, such as spending one period assisting in the school library or monitoring students in the cafeteria. Teachers also need to be accessible to parents, as well. Some teachers meet with parents once per term; others send progress reports home each month. Most schools require teachers to participate in extracurricular activities with students. A teacher may be an advisor to the school yearbook, direct the school play, or coach the chess team. Often they receive a stipend for leading the more time-consuming extracurricular activities. Teachers may also be required to act as chaperones at a certain number of after-school functions, such as dances and chorus concerts.

All good teachers agree that the main reason for entering this profession should be a desire to impart knowledge. Teachers must want to make a difference in the lives and futures of their students.

PAYING YOUR DUES

A college degree is required in this profession. You can receive your bachelor's degree in elementary or secondary education in five years. Prospective teachers take 24–36 credits in an area of specialization and 18–24 credits in teaching courses. They spend the fifth year student teaching. Postgraduates can become teachers by returning to school for a master's degree in teaching. In addition, many states offer alternative teaching licenses (designed to help schools acquire a more diverse pool of applicants for teaching positions); the usual requirements are a bachelor's degree in the subject the candidate plans to teach, a passing score on state-required examinations, and completion of a teaching internship. Prospective teachers are also advised to gain skills in communications, organization, and time management. Teachers can apply for teaching positions through their college's placement office or directly to their chosen school district.

ASSOCIATED CAREERS

While part-time substitute teaching can offer a path of entry to a full-time teaching career, it is also a common way to remain involved in the community without experiencing the time pressures placed on full-time teachers. Teachers' aides assist teachers and administrators in all aspects of their job. Students meet with guidance counselors to discuss family or school dilemmas or their plans for the future. Teachers who have obtained postgraduate degrees may advance to the position of school principal or become a member of the Board of Education. A school principal organizes and manages the school's faculty and ensures that the school's goals are met; board members are elected or appointed officials who decide which courses schools will offer and which textbooks the school system will use.

PAST AND FUTURE

Benjamin Franklin revolutionized the American school system. He created an educational program in which students were taught many subjects, but initially such schools were attended only by wealthy patrons. Various types of children's schools began in different states in the early 1800s, but it was not until 1834 that schools began to be supported by public funds. In those days, students of various ages spent the day with one teacher in a one-room schoolhouse. Today, the trend is toward having teachers specialize in one or two areas. Some states are even passing laws limiting the number of subjects that an instructor may teach. There are shortages of qualified teachers in some urban areas and in some areas of specialization. The subjects that offer the most opportunity are English as a second language (ESL), mathematics, the sciences, and special education. ESL instruction has growing potential not only in areas of America with high concentrations of immigrants, but also in foreign countries, though language requirements limit the pool of qualified candidates.

QUALITY OF LIFE

2 YEARS Teachers just entering the profession generally say they plan to remain for at least 5 or 10 years, but in fact the burnout rate in the first two years is very high. New teachers are learning themselves as they discover ways to encourage student participation in class, generate homework assignments, and guide individual students in their work.

5 YEARS Satisfaction with the profession is above average, and those who survive the first five years are likely to enjoy a long career. Many teachers contemplate pursuing advanced degrees that will expand their teaching options and bring them higher salaries.

10 YEARS Dedicated teachers continue to find satisfaction even after 10 years on the job. While some have taken on additional administrative responsibilities, many find the work as rewarding as when they first entered the profession.

MAJOR EMPLOYERS
CHICAGO BOARD OF EDUCATION
125 South Clark Street, 2nd Floor
Chicago, IL 60603
Tel: 773-535-1000
www.cps.k12.il.us
Contact: Department of Human Relations

COLORADO DEPARTMENT OF EDUCATION
201 East Colfax Avenue
Denver, CO 80203-1799
Tel: 303-866-6600
Fax: 303-830-0793
www.cde.state.co.us

LOUISIANA DEPARTMENT OF EDUCATION
PO Box 94064
Baton Rouge, LA 70804-9064
www.doe.state.la.us
Contact: Personnel

MAJOR ASSOCIATIONS
AMERICAN FEDERATION OF TEACHERS, AFL-CIO
555 New Jersey Avenue, NW
Washington, DC 20001
Tel: 202-879-4400
www.aft.org

NATIONAL EDUCATION ASSOCIATION
1201 16th Street, NW
Washington, DC 20036-3290
Tel: 202-833-4000
Fax: 202-822-7974
www.nea.org

THEOLOGIAN

A DAY IN THE LIFE

If you'll turn to the letter "T" in *Webster's Dictionary*, you'll see that theology is defined as "the study of God and of God's relation to the world." A theologian concentrates on the rational study of religious history and modern-day religious issues. They are the professors of God. Most theologians are found in seminaries—religious schools—where they study religious texts and pass on what they learn to others. The theologian teaches the religious leader (e.g., priest and rabbi), and in turn, the religious leader teaches the lay person. Utilizing the tools and methods of biblical research, spend a great deal of their time reading and writing. A theologian is described as someone who studies diverse denominations from many cultures, is biblically and theologically responsible, professionally competent, intellectually astute, and spiritually mature. A theologian strives to raise his or her mind to the contemplation of God and one who seeks to understand what he or she believes. An Old Testament professor describes his school of theology this way: "We're a traditional seminary with a strong curriculum, doing traditional things well, but we're also sensitive to how the Spirit is leading the church into new forms and new areas of engagement and service in the world." Material gain isn't really on the mind of most theologians. The study of God is a lifelong pursuit with no guarantees in finding the answers until it's too late to act on them.

{ lifelong pursuit }

PAYING YOUR DUES

Most young theologians with teaching on their mind start off as associate professors. After a few years, they may become full professors, and eventually become deans of the religious studies department. In some settings, a theologian can move on to an administrative role, such as principals of private schools or presidents of seminaries.

ASSOCIATED CAREERS

Some theologians lead double lives. After receiving a degree from a seminary school, many theologians choose to become teachers themselves, be it in private schools, university religion departments, or other seminaries. Some students of theology become youth pastors or family ministers in churches; some even go on to become religious leaders—pastors, priests, or rabbis.

PAST AND FUTURE

As long as there have been religious texts, there have been theologians studying and writing about them. Saint Augustine and Thomas Aquinas are two of the most famous early theologians whose writings are still studied today. Theological study in America had its start in the early eighteenth century when individual pastors would take one or two students under their tutelage. In 1812, the Theological Seminary of the Presbyterian Church at Princeton in New Jersey was founded. This was the first institute to focus on the education of theology in a systematic way. Today, there are hundreds of seminary schools and university religious programs that focus on the study of God.

QUALITY OF LIFE

2 YEARS Assuming the theologian has taken the latter of two career tracks—that of college academia—the beginning years are dominated by research, writing, and teaching intro-level courses.

5 YEARS An academic career has begun to take shape at this point. The theologian has probably published a couple of books or major research projects and has established clear areas of expertise. In addition, he or she has been promoted to associate professor, the final step before tenure. Associate professors have more control over their teaching schedules; they are likely to be teaching fewer low-level classes and more classes and seminars in their areas of specialization with older undergraduates and graduate students. In addition, as academic marketability is determined by a university's specific needs for expertise, professors become more able to move around between institutions as they establish themselves in theology.

10 YEARS By now, theologians have either made tenure at the university where they started, found another university that will give them tenure, or left the profession altogether.

MAJOR EMPLOYERS
ASBURY THEOLOGICAL SEMINARY
204 North Lexington Avenue
Wilmore, KY 40390
Tel: 800-227-2871 or 859-858-3581
www.ats.wilmore.ky.us

DALLAS THEOLOGICAL SEMINARY
3909 Swiss Avenue
Dallas, TX 75024
Tel: 800-992-0998 or 214-824-3094
Fax: 214-841-3664
www.dts.edu

FULLER THEOLOGICAL SEMINARY
135 North Oakland Avenue
Pasadena, CA 91182
Tel: 626-584-5200
www.fuller.edu

PRINCETON THEOLOGICAL SEMINARY
PO Box 921
Princeton, NJ 08542-0803
Tel: 609-921-8300
www.ptsem.edu

UNION THEOLOGICAL SEMINARY
3041 Broadway
New York, NY 10027
Tel: 212-662-7100
E-mail: contactus@uts.columbia.edu
www.uts.columbia.edu

MAJOR ASSOCIATIONS
AMERICAN ACADEMY OF RELIGION
825 Houston Mill Road NE, Suite 300
Atlanta, GA 30329-4205
Tel: 404-727-3049
Fax: 404-727-7959
E-mail: aar@aarweb.org
www.aarweb.org

TRAVEL AGENT

SALARY

HOURS

EDUCATION

BOOKS, FILMS, AND TV SHOWS
FEATURING THE PROFESSION

- **The Accidental Tourist**
- **The Great Vacation**
- **Visa Revoked**

YOU'LL HAVE CONTACT WITH

- **Advertising executives**
- **Airline representatives**
- **Hotel managers**
- **Insurers**

PROFESSIONALS READ

- **Condé Nast Traveler**
- **Resort Review**
- **Travel**
- **Travel and Leisure Magazine**

A DAY IN THE LIFE

Travel agents help their clients figure out how to get the best value for their travel budgets. The agent does the legwork for his or her client, from making all the necessary airline, car rental, and hotel reservations to finding out about visa requirements or scouting weather forecasts. The travel agent is largely a salesperson, and so he or she must be familiar with his or her products and services. Once the customer settles on his or her travel plans, the agent makes all the arrangements using various computer sources, particularly the SABRE computer network. The agent then explains such practical matters as customs and currency exchange to the traveler and offers his or her advice on things like sightseeing and wardrobe. There is no margin for error in this career, since mistakes can leave clients stranded and frightened. This means the agent must always confirm every reservation. The need to repeat these tedious activities is the downside travel agents cite most often. Travel agents spend most of their time at their desks, and the majority of these hours are spent dealing with clients, whether in person or over the phone. The travel agency's hours accommodate its clientele, so most agents work more than 40 hours per week in a variety of shifts. Extensive travel at deep discounts is often cited as the biggest perk in this field. Many agents also spend time as tour guides to become familiar with not just the well-traveled areas of the world but also spots "off the beaten path."

{ off the beaten path }

PAYING YOUR DUES

Many travel agencies require that their agents hold a liberal arts or business degree from a four-year college or university. No one major is preferred, but some companies require specific degrees reflecting the focus of the agency. Along these lines, some specialized and international agencies require their agents to be fluent in the language of the area they work with. Since client service is the largest part of the travel agent's job, experience in other service occupations is a good idea. Potential travel agents must be able to work under the pressure of anxious customers; patience is a crucial quality. With foreign language skills and experience in service industries, a candidate stands a better chance of finding employment with the more competitive international agencies.

Even for individuals without a bachelor's degree, the field is not restricted. Another option is completing a 6–18-week travel course. This course offers the basic skills needed by a travel agent and is often the minimum requirement for agent status. Still others begin by working in a related field, such as at a ticket agency, and work their way up to a job as a travel agent. This route enables you to discover the perks and gain experience before making a commitment to the career. One agency owner surveyed says she is more likely to hire a well-traveled ticket agent than an unseasoned travel school graduate. Finally, many agents obtain the approval of agencies such as the Air Traffic Conference. All agents should be licensed by or registered with the state in which they practice.

ASSOCIATED CAREERS

There are a number of positions in the travel industry that do not require the training necessary for travel agents. Reservation, ticket, and car rental agents are responsible for providing these services to customers. There is often only a short on-the-job training period before these agents begin working. These jobs also offer discounts on travel services that make travel cheap and easy. Other travel fields require some specialized knowledge. For instance, an adventure travel guide must have extensive knowledge of the touring area and must be an expert in an activity, such as hiking. Vacation and location tour guides need not have the physical skills of the adventure travel guide, but must have intimate knowledge of their area. Entertainment and cruise directors plan events for travel groups and often attend the event, which gives them immediate customer response and lets them enjoy the results of their efforts.

PAST AND FUTURE

Thomas Cook began the first official travel agency in England in 1841. Every year he organized tours for thousands of travelers to "exotic" places. The first American travel agency was established in 1872. Since then, travel has become routine as a leisure activity and business standard. Travel and tourism has become one of the largest service industries in the United States. In the next 10 years, it is anticipated that the number of agents needed will grow substantially. The structure of the industry will probably change, though, as people change the duration and location of their trips. The travel industry is affected by political factors and the fluctuating dollar, but many regions depend on tourism as their primary source of revenue. This makes it highly likely that travel will remain a stable industry for many years to come.

QUALITY OF LIFE

2 YEARS At this point, new agents are often frustrated that they are viewed as novices. They are still struggling to build up a regular clientele. Nonetheless, they are enticed by the opportunities to travel, which provide them with the experience they need to get ahead in the field.

5 YEARS Agents report discovering that the travel industry is not as glamorous as they had thought. While they are happy with their promotions to managerial status, they are tired of the long hours.

10 YEARS Many travel agents change companies at this time to advance further, perhaps into managerial positions at large agencies, or they may put their years of experience to work by going into business for themselves.

MAJOR EMPLOYERS

EMPRESS TRAVEL
97 Post Avenue
Westbury, NY 11590
Tel: 516-333-6677

TRAVEL GEMS
381 Park Avenue South, Suite 1201
New York, NY 10016
Tel: 212-889-3131

MAJOR ASSOCIATIONS

AMERICAN SOCIETY OF TRAVEL AGENTS EDUCATION DEPARTMENT
1101 King Street, #200
Alexandria, VA 22314
Tel: 703-739-2782
Fax: 703-684-8319
E-mail: askasta@asthq.com
www.astanet.com

THE INSTITUTE FOR CERTIFIED TRAVEL AGENTS
148 Linden Street, Suite 305
Wellesley, MA 02482
Tel: 800-542-4282 or 781-237-2080
Fax: 781-237-3860
E-mail: info@thetravelinstitute.com
www.icta.com

TRIAL LAWYER

A DAY IN THE LIFE

Trial lawyers represent clients involved in civil and criminal litigation cases. Criminal lawyers may represent plaintiffs or defendants. Civil litigators take the side of a party in a dispute where no crime is involved. The trial lawyer's job is to persuade a jury of the facts in a case and to display them in a way that best supports their client's position. Each piece of evidence must be presented and disputed according to a complicated set of rules. On days out of court, trial lawyers review files and scheduling orders, contact witnesses, take depositions, and talk to clients. On court days, lawyers argue motions, meet with judges, prepare scheduling orders, select jurors, and argue cases. The preparation for a trial can take many months. Due to the tremendous cost of litigation, however, most cases settle before they ever { probable outcome } reach trial. Trial law requires excellent analytical skills. Litigators use their knowledge of legal precedents to analyze the probable outcome of a case.

PAYING YOUR DUES

After finishing law school and passing the bar exam, new litigators put in long hours assisting more experienced lawyers. Typical duties include fact gathering and legal research, "the nitty-gritty things" that are essential to a successful trial. The volume of records to sort through and organize can be daunting, but well-sorted documents make it easier for the principal lawyer to present a coherent case before a jury. Eventually, beginning lawyers sit in on trials as second or third chair. They may at this point participate in conferences with judges or even prepare evidentiary arguments. This mentoring process eventually leads to responsibility for an entire case. The starting salary and experience of trial lawyers can vary greatly depending on where they work. Generally, private practice is much more lucrative than public interest law, clerking, or working in the D.A.'s office. These positions are prestigious, however. In smaller towns and smaller firms, you have more responsibility and client contact early on, but the pay is much better in a large firm.

ASSOCIATED CAREERS

People often obtain a law degree as a stepping stone to another profession; many lawyers ultimately opt to enter business or finance. Trial lawyers sometimes become judges or seek public office—most senators and a number of presidents have had a legal background. Some people also teach law once they have an area of expertise. The competition is stiff, and the money is not as good as in a private practice in a large metropolitan area, but the hours are better.

PAST AND FUTURE

Early colonists were suspicious of lawyers; many of them had just escaped what they considered to be an unjust legal system. They also identified law with lay officers of the crown, such as tax collectors—unpopular characters in any society. In addition, the concerns of lawyers were frowned on as very "earthy" and "material" by the clergy in the colonies. Later, the profession of law grew more honorable as it became associated with the idealism of the founding fathers and the building of the nation. Law has been glamorized in recent years by television shows and highly televised trials. In truth, the practice of criminal law is fairly routine. The main difficulty with the modern-day litigation is its exorbitant cost. Even lawyers believe it is too expensive to maintain in its current form. We may also soon see legislation limiting the damages that may be awarded in civil litigation. (Read: No more $5 million settlements for spilling coffee in your lap.) In addition to being expensive, litigation is also time consuming. Society is exploring new methods of dispute resolutions to streamline the process.

QUALITY OF LIFE

2 YEARS New lawyers in a big firm spend much of their time doing legal research, gathering evidence, and administrating the cases their higher-ups are handling. Billable hours are a major concern. Most new associates are responsible for between 1,800–2,400 billable hours each year. This means working long hours and weekends. In a smaller firm, budding litigators have more exposure to the partners and are more likely to get feedback on their work. There's a chance that you'll have a wider variety of tasks and see more challenging work in the first few years in a small firm, but the salaries are not as high as salaries of individuals who work in larger firms.

5 YEARS The five-year mark brings increased responsibility. Litigators may be drafting their own documents by this time, taking depositions, arguing motions in court, and managing their own caseload. More client contact occurs at this stage. Associates work to develop a specialty and have usually decided whether to pursue a partner track. Individuals who decide not to dedicate their efforts to becoming a partner may opt for an in-house position with a company or pursue a different career track entirely. In-house counsel work fewer hours than do partner-track associates, but the pay is less as well.

10 YEARS By this time, attorneys should have made partner in their firm. With ownership in the firm comes responsibility. Good lawyers have a reputation in their specialty at this point, and they use it to bring in business. How much business they generate will help determine the cut of the profits they receive, and their continued success will depend on their ability to become a "rainmaker." Individuals who don't make partner usually move to another firm. Though in some situations, they stay on as an associate or are retained in a position known as "of counsel." The compensation is very good at the 10-year level.

MAJOR EMPLOYERS
UNITED STATES DEPARTMENT OF JUSTICE
950 Pennsylvania Avenue, NW
Washington, DC 20530-0001
Tel: 202-541-2000 or 202-353-1555
www.usdoj.gov

Trial lawyers may also work for state attorney generals' offices and in private firms.

MAJOR ASSOCIATIONS
AMERICAN BAR ASSOCIATION
321 North Clark Street
Chicago, IL 10610
Tel: 312-988-5000
www.abanet.org

AMERICAN BAR FOUNDATION
750 North Lake Shore Drive
Chicago, IL 60611-4403
Tel: 312-988-6500
www.abf-sociolegal.org

THE ASSOCIATION OF TRIAL LAWYERS FOR AMERICA
1050 31st Street, NW
Washington, DC 20007
Tel: 202-965-3500 or 800-424-2725
E-mail: info@atlahq.org
www.atla.org

NATIONAL ASSOCIATION OF CRIMINAL DEFENSE LAWYERS
1150 18th Street, NW, Suite 950
Washington, DC 20036
Tel: 202-872-8600
Fax: 202-872-8690
E-mail: assist@nacdl.org

VIDEO GAME DESIGNER

BOOKS, FILMS, AND TV SHOWS
FEATURING THE PROFESSION

- **The Last Starfighter**
- **Trigger Happy: Video Games and the Entertainment Revolution**
- **Tron**
- **War Games**

YOU'LL HAVE CONTACT WITH

- **Artists**
- **Marketers**
- **Producers**
- **Testers**

PROFESSIONALS READ

- **Gamsutra (Game Developer's Magazine)**
- **Introduction to Game Development**
- **The Journal of Computer Game Design**
- **Journal of Game Development**

A DAY IN THE LIFE

Ideas for the next big video game usually originate with designers—whether they're brilliant inspirations or the results of a licensing hook the company has obtained from a movie or television show (*Star Wars*, Tony Hawk, NFL games, etc.). Usually a designer is given an assignment to work on, and he or she is charged with fleshing out the details to pitch to the company execs for approval. After nailing down the concept, it's the designer's job to write a detailed description of the game. Detailed in this context means really detailed—that is, 50–200 pages outlining game characters and their personalities, describing the game world and how the game controller works, providing examples of sound effects and music, and outlining the objective

{ The designer is involved in every aspect of production. }

(whether that's to obtain as many points as possible or to rescue the princess from an evil, two-headed, fire-breathing, gigantic hamster). The designer is involved in every aspect of production and will work hand-in-hand with programmers to write code, artists to bring the characters to life, sound engineers to nail the effects, and a marketing team to pave the way for release. Game sales ultimately rest on the shoulders of the designer, since he or she has to be able to present the game to sales and marketing so that the best features can be highlighted.

The real genius of a game designer is not the ability to fashion good ideas into great designs, but rather the ability to survive the production process. The designer has to come up with ideas that pass muster with programmers, marketers, and executives alike. Someone who has a college degree, a demonstrable passion for games, and a proven desire to work hard just may have what it takes to land the job and launch what many consider to be a dream career. Since a video game publisher may invest millions of dollars in the development of a game, it is understandable that he or she would want to choose game designers carefully: One or two poor game concepts could end up costing millions of dollars of revenue and could even risk bankrupting the company. For this reason, game publishers usually choose game designers who have a proven track record with several hit games under their belts. Less seasoned designers may be assigned to lower-profile games that have budgets in the low tens of thousands.

PAYING YOUR DUES

The position of video game designer is not entry-level. If you don't have experience working with a video game company, you won't be hired to fill this spot off the bat. You'll also need a college degree, but not necessarily in design. Schools that offer programs in game design are few and far between, so when choosing a major, opt for something that interests you; but make sure you study drawing, writing, literature, computer science, marketing, even mythology—any subject that could help you get your foot in the door. The most obvious requirement for breaking into the field is lots and lots of experience playing games. Join internet message boards; apply to become a professional gamer; or start fan sites for your favorite games. You should also maintain a portfolio with samples of your artwork and writing, flyers or clippings of any game events in which you've been involved, game concepts, and even CD-ROMs with animations, audio, or programs you have created.

PAST AND FUTURE

In the beginning, there was pinball. There were robotic fortune tellers along the boardwalk that, for a quarter, would give you a glimpse into your future. In 1958, at a nuclear research facility, William Higinbotham developed an educational game using the computer technology available at the time—missile trajectory. Tennis for Two, simple yet infectious, debuted at the next open house exhibit that the laboratory hosted. In 1968, Ralph Baer applied for the first video game patent for his "Home TV Game," a system that allowed spots to be moved around a TV screen. The graphics were so rudimentary that the system actually came with a set of two sizes of color mylar overlays to put over the television screen; these represented the various playfields, including those of tennis and hockey. In 1980, a game designer decided to create a game that looked more like a cartoon, inspired by a Japanese folk hero; hence, "Puckman" was launched. The game was an incredible hit in Japan, and after a quick-fix of the name, Pacman was released in the United States.

Early in the history of video games, game designers were often the lead or sometimes the only programmers for their respective games. This was the case for such noted designers as Sid Meir, Chris Sawyer, and Will Wright. As games became more complex and computers and consoles became more powerful, the job of game designer evolved into its own separate job function. Today, with very complex games or a big-budget action or sports title, designers may number in the dozens for each game. Note, however, that an entire generation that grew up playing video games is entering the workplace—so it's especially important to set yourself apart from the outset.

QUALITY OF LIFE

2 YEARS Game designers generally start out in programming, marketing, customer support, or in product testing—just about any entry-level position with a production company. Through marketing, testing, or dealing with customers, you'll learn to answer questions about choices the game designers made, manufacturing, and "bugs" (viruses, graphic/audio problems, or functional errors). With a couple years of experience (and lots of overtime), these entry-level jobs provide the necessary experience to move onward and upward.

5 YEARS Most games need several designers. With five years of industry experience (not to mention an impeccable portfolio), an entry-level designer can expect assignments on background levels or team projects. To rise above the crowd of competitors trying to break into the field, it's necessary to go the extra mile or work the extra hour(s) to get noticed. After you've been working in design for several years, you are like to move up the design/production ladder.

10 YEARS A successful game designer can, at this point, move into a creative director role or a producer position, or even strike out and start a new game company. In these leadership roles, the game designer does less day-to-day coding and development spends more time building the greater vision of a game, and ultimately, of the company.

MAJOR EMPLOYERS
ELECTRONIC ARTS
Redwood City, CA
www.ea.com

NINTENDO OF AMERICA
PO Box 957
Redmond, WA 98073
www.nintendo.com

THQ
29903 Agoura Road
Agoura Hills, CA 91301
Tel: 818-871-5000
www.thq.com

MAJOR ASSOCIATIONS
DIGITAL GAMES RESEARCH ASSOCIATION
www.digra.org

INTERNATIONAL GAME DEVELOPERS ASSOCIATION
870 Market Street Suite 1181
San Francisco, CA 94102
Tel: 415-738-2104
www.igda.org

VIDEO JOCKEY

A DAY IN THE LIFE

Screening music videos, making idle chitchat with Madonna or Diddy, starring on a national TV show—yes, a career as a video jockey (or VJ for short) certainly earns the moniker "dream job." The televised equivalents of their radio DJ brethren, VJs are typically hired by music channels like MTV and VH1 to act as intermediaries among videos, musicians, and the audience. Witty and charismatic, VJs are called on to converse with star-struck adolescents and to conduct celebrity interviews. They are also expected to sustain viewer interest, infusing the time between videos with jokes, conversation, and pop culture anecdotes. While VJs should have extensive knowledge of all types of music, many end up specializing in a particular genre, such as rap, Top 40, or classic rock. Successful VJs often become public icons for particular musical subsets.

{ **witty and charismatic** }

The term VJ also refers to video performance artists. Although less famous than their MTV counterparts, these individuals create live visuals for all genres of music. Typically using an analog mixer, these artists blend and superimpose various sound inputs over visual clips. The industry has really grown over the last few years, and those in the technology and instrument design fields have responded with vigor; companies have recently begun marketing equipment designed specifically for VJs. Furthermore, the evolution of computers has provided motivation for producing VJ-specific programs, and thus has made the art form accessible to a broad spectrum of people. VJs of this latter type tend to work live-performance venues. Their work can be screened anywhere from dance clubs and raves to concerts and an assortment of other events. Some VJs have even retained corporate clients, for whom they generate content for product-specific presentations. Professional VJs work extremely hard; they typically arrange about one hundred clips for each hour of performance. Additionally, VJs generally require a computer with a fast external hard drive.

PAYING YOUR DUES

While there is no clear-cut path to becoming a VJ, many who pursue this profession hold bachelor's degrees in such subjects as communications, acting/drama, music, or media studies. They also tend to work at school stations and seek out internships with television production companies. Many are persistent, as landing a VJ position often entails working up from entry-level positions. Regardless of the route a VJ takes, one attribute that remains universal is a passion for music and pop culture.

For those interested in becoming video performance artists, it is critical that you spend time acquiring a deep understanding of the technology and computer programs the medium utilizes. Many VJs practice the art form for years, continually gaining insight as to how one effectively and creatively manipulates images. They also spend a great deal of time filming original content to incorporate into their art. Finally, it is imperative that VJ's have the skills necessary to both present in front of and connect with a live audience.

ASSOCIATED CAREERS

Many video jockeys ultimately opt to segue into other jobs within the music and entertainment industries. Some go on to achieve prominent careers as music journalists, both in print and on screen. Still others use industry knowledge and connections to become producers or music video directors.

PAST AND FUTURE

At midnight on August 1, 1981, both the music and television industries were forever altered when MTV first aired, screening the Buggles video for "Video Killed the Radio Star." The early format was modeled after Top 40 radio shows. The original videos lacked the artistic merit of those you'll see when you tune in today. They were initially crude promotional videos, cobbled together from concerts clips or whatever sources could be found. Cable channels like MTV and Fuse continue to gain momentum. They have become formidable players (yes, pun intended) within the entertainment industry, and are no doubt at the forefront of pop culture. Interest does not seem to be waning, and it appears as though VJs will populate the television landscape in the years to come.

Video performance art is a relatively new field. It has risen significantly over the past few years, with a growing number of venues hiring VJs. As technology improves and expands, VJs will likely evolve into new (and perhaps unexpected) roles.

QUALITY OF LIFE

2 YEARS The entertainment industry is highly competitive. After two years in the business, you probably have yet to land a job hosting TRL. Chances are, you're either working in an entry-level production job, or you've landed a VJ position on a smaller cable channel.

It typically takes longer than two years for performance video artists to make a name for themselves. At this point, VJs who specialize in performance art spend most of their time familiarizing themselves with essential equipment and experimenting with different sound and visual clips.

5 YEARS At the five-year mark in this industry—if they have lasted that long—VJs can consider themselves established. They are recognized television personalities and have most likely secured a daily hosting job. By now, most VJs have achieved comfort in front of the camera and in dealing with celebrities and fans alike.

Video performance artists with five years of experience are consistently landing jobs at smaller clubs or venues. They have amassed an impressive array of knowledge about existing VJ programs and know how to utilize the available technology to enhance their work

10 YEARS Longevity is not the first adjective that comes to mind when thinking about the VJ career. Despite the fact that it takes hard work and perseverance to attain this position, VJs rarely stay in the job for 10 years. (This may be partly attributable to the inherent "hip" factor of the position.) By now, many have climbed the proverbial ladder and parlayed their VJ success into prominent music journalist gigs or positions as network producers.

After 10 years, video performance artists have fully established themselves. Many have mastered the tools of the trade and have gained a thorough understanding of what audiences enjoy and expect. At this juncture one can certainly find jobs at some big-name clubs.

MAJOR EMPLOYERS
FUSE
www.fuse.tv

MTV
1515 Broadway
New York, NY 10036
Tel: 212-258-8000
Fax: 212-846-1804
www.mtv.com

VH1
1515 Broadway
New York, NY 10036
www.vh1.com

MAJOR ASSOCIATIONS
VJ CENTRAL
http://vjcentral.com

VOICE-OVER ARTIST

PROFESSIONAL PROFILE

# of people in profession	N/A
Avg. hours per week	25
Avg. starting salary	$27,000
Avg. salary after 5 years	$38,000
Avg. salary after 10 to15 years	$50,000

SALARY •
HOURS •
EDUCATION •

BOOKS, FILMS, AND TV SHOWS FEATURING THE PROFESSION
- **News Radio**
- **The Simpsons**
- **The Tonight Show**
- **Toy Story**

YOU'LL HAVE CONTACT WITH
- **Actors**
- **Agents**
- **Directors**
- **Editors**

PROFESSIONALS READ
- **The Art of Voice-Acting: The Craft and Business of Performing for Voice-Over**
- **Voice-Overs: Putting Your Mouth Where the Money Is**

A DAY IN THE LIFE

Voice actors do the off-screen voices you hear in commercials, trailers, and animations—and don't forget that automated robot from directory assistance you just spoke with to get the number of the pizza place down the street, that funny talking doll that all the kids wanted last Christmas, or that book-on-tape you listened to in college instead of reading the actual text. Anywhere a voice is needed, there's an actor who is ready to talk. Voice-over artists can even be movie or TV stars—think HAL from *2001: A Space Odyssey* and John Forsythe in *Charlie's Angels*. For most actors in the field, voice acting has all of the benefits of regular acting work without the hassle of the makeup, costumes, and lighting. Once you've broken in to

> { Anywhere a voice is needed, there's an actor who is ready to talk. }

the business and are getting called for readings, a day at the office can mean 30 minutes in a sound studio. Virtually every day brings brand new material—a car dealer spot to be aired in Georgia, a surly New Yorker voice for a radio promo, or a friendly animated handyman reminding warehouse employees to lift with their knees. Though many voice actors develop a signature persona to market, the particular aspects of the job and the character change from day to day. Acting assignments are typically short—they range from one day to perhaps a few months—and so actors frequently experience periods of employment between jobs.

In most cases, actors don't see the script for the reading until they arrive at the studio; they have to be prepared for anything. Competition can be fierce, but even the smallest local network station needs a promo, so opportunity abounds. The professional voice actor will rely on an agent to take care of the all the legwork, such as marketing and arranging auditions. Voice artists don't have to ensure that their physical appearances mesh with the characters they are playing. Often, the voices of young boys really come from women, like that of Bart Simpson (played by Nancy Cartwright). A voice actor may occasionally be credited under an alias for the purpose of attracting producers who aren't willing to pay the high costs of hiring members of unions. (Unionized actors are prohibited from taking nonunion jobs.) In such situations, it's especially important to remain heard and not seen.

PAYING YOUR DUES

Even though it's possible to break into the field with no experience, most professional voice artists have a background in communications, interning, or volunteering at their college radio stations and are accustomed to being in front of a microphone. Some voice agents even recommend that actors who are starting out train in production skills (editing and learning the computer software used in sound studios) and then seek out employment in radio production to immerse themselves in voice spots. To really get your name out there, it's almost a necessity to create a demo tape to submit to agencies containing various "reads": hyper voice, soothing voice, maybe even an accent or two. The truth is that most voice actors keep a day job on the side—until they get that big break.

PAST AND FUTURE

For much of the history of animation, voice actors kept a low profile and were seldom credited for their work. The Screen Actors Guild didn't recognize voice actors until a little more than a decade ago. The major exception to this rule was Mel Blanc, the voice of Bugs Bunny, Daffy Duck, Wile E. Coyote, Barney Rubble, and many other classic Hollywood animated characters. Over time, celebrities began performing voice-acting roles in movies, a transition made clear by the star power behind Disney's *Aladdin*, marketed with emphasis on Robin Williams's role. Oscar-winning celebrities are now lining up to guest star on animated television shows and feature films. Curious about the newest trend for voice actors? Voice-overs for video games. Games are a mainstay for the entertainment industry now, with some titles pulling in more revenue on release dates than major Hollywood film releases on opening night. SAG estimates that 1,900 of its members have worked in video game recording sessions and earn a set $556 per four hours in the studio.

QUALITY OF LIFE

2 YEARS If you've followed the voice actor track of first breaking into radio as a production assistant, intern, or spokesperson for local businesses, you've gained the experience necessary to start marketing your voice. Voicing local radio commercials is the best way to get noticed by local agencies looking for new talent. After learning the ups and downs of speaking into a microphone, it's time to create a demo tape of your various styles, reads, and personas.

5 YEARS Always adding to your demo, larger agencies have your name on file and know where to turn when looking for the perfect "mid-to-upper thirties, two-small-children-at-home, drinks-coffee-and-does-Pilates-every-Wednesday" voice to reach their target audience. With some persistence, at this point in your career you can potentially have landed a recurring commercial role—and an agent.

10 YEARS The professional voice artist's dream, a major film or television role, can only happen if he or she has attained enough of the right exposure. With a successful and savvy agent, years of experience under your belt, and a recognizable studio voice, that dream has the potential to become a reality. As a member of one of the two actors' unions (these add credibility to your resume), the minimum salary that you can be paid is predetermined, but the experienced and in-demand actor negotiates for more.

MAJOR EMPLOYERS
CESD VOICES
275 Park Avenue, Suite 900
New York, NY 10010
Tel: 212-477-1666
www.cesdvoices.com

CREATIVE ARTISTS AGENCY
9830 Wilshire Boulevard
Beverly Hills, CA 90212
Tel: 310-288-4545
www.caa.com

NAKED VOICES, INC.
865 North Sangamon, Suite 415
Chicago, IL 60622
Tel: 312-563-0136
www.nakedvoices.com

MAJOR ASSOCIATIONS
SCREEN ACTORS GUILD
5757 Wilshire Boulevard
Los Angeles, CA 90036
Tel: 323-954-1600
www.sag.org

AMERICAN FEDERATION OF TELEVISION AND RADIO ARTISTS
260 Madison Avenue
New York, NY 10016
212-532-0800
www.aftra.org

WEB ART DIRECTOR

BOOKS, FILMS, AND TV SHOWS
FEATURING THE PROFESSION
- **City of Golden Shadow**

YOU'LL HAVE CONTACT WITH
- **Creative directors**
- **Information architects**
- **Programmers**

PROFESSIONALS READ
- **Communication Arts**
- **ID magazine**
- **Industry Standard**

A DAY IN THE LIFE

A Web art director works with Internet websites and is responsible for translating the overall business objective of the website into a visual solution. The art director works closely with the creative team to figure out the best way to communicate the site's strategic goals and brand message in an online environment.

Websites contain very complex technical elements, so art directors in this industry need diverse experience. It's not enough to be a designer; you also need to understand the technical aspects of Web design. Whether or not you can write code, you need to comprehend what the code is capable of, otherwise you end up designing something that can't be built. The Internet's nonlinear nature allows for a variety of ways to navigate to a piece of information. Therefore, you need to understand the principles of information architecture, which deal with the flow of information and how effective the user finds it. "It's a lot more than deciding 'this is blue or red' or 'the button goes here or there,' but whether there needs to be a button, what the button will do, and how it will function," says one Web art director. "For instance, if it's a shopping site, what is the ideal e-commerce experience for the user? What information must consumers fill out and in what order if they want to purchase something?"

{ **principles of information architecture** }

During the actual design process, a Web art director can spend many hours on the computer designing the content and functionality according to plan. One Web art director sums up his work like this: "I sit in front of my computer 90 percent of the day, trying to figure out what stuff's going to look like and what the best interface is to create the best user experience." The job is very team-oriented, more so than other print design work. Because website development is so complex, one person can't be an expert in all the necessary disciplines of design, information architecture, and programming. Thus, a Web art director works closely with a variety of different people on a day-to-day basis, as well as throughout all phases of the project.

"Gain as much technical knowledge as you can without sacrificing basic design. If you have a choice between a technical class and a design class, go for the design," recommends one art director.

PAYING YOUR DUES

Five years ago, most art directors came from traditional print design backgrounds and had no interactive experience. Today, expectations have changed in the industry—if you are a good designer with good design sensibility, you need to build up your interactive knowledge. However, there is a big difference between designers with solid design skills and designers with interactive skills. "We get a lot of young designers who are technical wizards but don't have the design background, and a lot of really good designers who don't have the technical background," notes one art director. "More than technical experience, we're looking for solid design, which a lot of the people don't bring to the table. My advice is to focus on being a good designer and problem solver."

"Generally, we want to see a bachelor of fine arts degree in graphic design," says a Web art director. "But because so much of your [chances of being hired depend] on your portfolio, your degree is not that critical. We would hire someone who never took a design class, provided their portfolio shows fabulous designs."

ASSOCIATED CAREERS

If you're a good designer, you can apply your skills to any field. While a print designer can't jump to industrial design without further training, one could make the transition to packaging design. In school you generally choose a particular field of design, and there is unique training and knowledge for each field. In graphic design, which Web design is based on, you could also make the leap to book design or advertising design. A good designer is infinitely marketable.

PAST AND FUTURE

The structure of an art department and how an art director fits into the picture is pretty standard across industries. The model that exists in the interactive world is borrowed from traditional advertising, modifying the structure to encompass the complexity of new design. The history of Web design is brief, but it's evolving. The field initially focused only on content, as people simply threw information up onto the Internet. Now the Web is oriented toward advertising and sales, and it's important to have an understanding of these fields.

The Internet is changing so quickly that we can only imagine what the future will bring. As programming, entertainment, news, and commerce converge, the Web art director will take on new and varied roles, conceptualizing interactive flow and setting up the design that contextualizes chains of information.

QUALITY OF LIFE

2 YEARS Junior designers may be assigned smaller tasks of a larger project and work an hour or two less than the art director, who is juggling more work. However, during the actual design phase, anyone involved will put in long hours.

5 YEARS Some Web art directors are involved in the actual hands-on design while others manage a team of designers and focus on delineating tasks. In the design world, every company has a different title for their positions; an art director in one place may have the same responsibility that a senior designer has in another—there is no standard across the industry. Generally, moving from a junior position to a full-fledged art director requires three to five years of experience in either interactive or advertising work, and many people make the switch from print jobs into the interactive world.

The higher up the position, the more hats you wear and balls you juggle when dealing with collaborative teams. Being in a higher-level position does not mean your hours are reduced because other people are handling the work. In the Web environment, things happen all of the time, and you need to be there to manage the crisis.

10 YEARS As art directors continue to find new and inventive ways to manage design on the Web over the next decade, the more experienced staff will take on a bird's-eye role in managing projects in their conceptual stages—dealing with the design's requirements and strategic objectives and working through the methodology of a solution.

MAJOR EMPLOYERS

Most major companies with a Web presence require the services of a Web art director.

MAJOR ASSOCIATIONS

WORLD ORGANIZATION OF WEBMASTERS
9580 Oak Avenue Parkway, Suite 7-177
Folsom, CA 95630
Tel: 916-608-2933
Fax: 916-987-3022
E-mail: info@joinwow.org
www.joinwow.org

WEB EDITOR

A DAY IN THE LIFE

A Web editor develops the content or editorial plan of a website, working with a team that may include a creative director, a writer, a designer, and an information architect. Web editors at different types of companies have varying responsibilities. Someone at iVillage.com, for instance, deals with major amounts of content and updates the site on a daily basis. An editor at an online magazine could be brought in to match the site's particular style or to provide an original voice. But if you work for a Web developer that produces original content for different companies, your work will be more project-oriented. You will develop material for a range of clients, as well as ensure that the information is accurate and conveys the true voice and tone for the site. The editor's work encompasses a broad spectrum of writing and can run the gamut from writing a short article or product description copy to creating a script. Copyediting and proofreading may also be part of an editor's job.

{ **an editor as well as a writer** }

An editor in the Web world has a very different job than one in a traditional print position. The online world is one of interactivity, which may involve creating single-loop feedbacks such as real-time polls or developing community-oriented content—information that is taken from people responding to a site. While print media are geared toward the masses, interactive content relies on an understanding of the one-to-one nature of the Web. "In most traditional media, once you've written a piece, it's done," notes one writer. In contrast, many online writing projects are never really finished, especially as far as website content is concerned. "Expect to update, revise, expand, or tweak existing written materials not just occasionally, but continuously," she notes.

"Editing and project-management skills are helpful for any writer, but having a background as an editor or managing editor can prove especially lucrative. Many online publishing venues lack experienced editorial talent. Being an editor as well as a writer is likely to open more doors for you in online media than it would in print media," she further observes.

PAYING YOUR DUES

As an editor, it's important to familiarize yourself with HTML and a variety of page design programs. An editor should have an understanding of certain back-end technologies; for instance, if you are writing copy for an e-commerce site, it's helpful to understand the functionality of how an online store works and how it operates before you actually write material for it. Gaining some HTML knowledge will help you understand the possibilities and limitations of online media much better than someone who only writes, and you can easily teach yourself basic HTML and basic Web design from a good book.

Web editors require a combination of editorial common sense and good writing skills. They must also embrace the technology. "If someone is out to write his novel and wants to pick up some interesting work on the side, this is a harder road," cautions one Web editor. "People who really have a curiosity about the medium and are jazzed by learning about it tend to flourish more."

Junior writing and proofreading positions exist for recent college graduates who can also enter the field in a support role to gain some experience. "We're at the point now where we're looking for people with Web experience," says one senior editor, "but people who have had some copywriting or print work experience and who can demonstrate a penchant for the medium can earn a junior staff writing position." Strong original writing will open the door, along with the ability to write on a variety of topics in different styles.

ASSOCIATED CAREERS

A lot of people enter the field from a direct marketing background because that type of one-to-one interaction is the basis for online business. Web editors with strong conceptual skills can move up to associate and senior creative director positions. Others who want to leave the field can take their skills back into the print world to magazines, ad agencies, or any other arena in need of original writing.

PAST AND FUTURE

The Internet industry went through its infancy in which content was little more than online brochures. Today, it's in its adolescent phase, growing through e-commerce and broadband, which encompasses more robust content delivery.

Contextual shopping is the Internet's modus operandi. A user may read a piece on a female artist, download her MP3, watch her video, load a slide show of a storyboard, click on an outfit she's wearing, and purchase it directly from the site. Editors are the glue that will allow this to happen, conceptualizing the interactive flow and setting up the copy that contextualizes this chain of information.

In the future, writers and editors will have to be much more multifaceted. "Rather than having an original voice, I look for someone who is more chameleon-like, who can write in a different tone for a particular client," says one Web editor. "I also look for people who can adapt quickly."

QUALITY OF LIFE

2 YEARS A junior editorial position involves copyediting, proofreading, and perhaps some original writing. Learning the basics of interactive writing comes from experience in the medium. Entry-level writers and editors need to familiarize themselves with the nonsequential nature of online media and learn how to "write in chunks."

5 YEARS At this level, editors need to be able to conceptualize the final product. There is a lot more collaborative, team-oriented work, and editors are often helping writers to set up the interactive experience. The editor may have a variety of copy duties, from acting as a copywriter or scriptwriter to generating copy for a short, interactive movie. At this stage, Web editors can expect their salaries to vary, depending on the nature and responsibility of the job.

10 YEARS The Internet as we know it today is going to be a much different medium in 10 years as entertainment, information, television, and computers finally converge. Programming, commerce, research, and news-gathering agencies will develop new ways to feature content, as users may be able to buy various things (from a pizza to a sweater) directly from the sitcom they're watching.

MAJOR EMPLOYERS
Any company with a website needs a Web editor.

MAJOR ASSOCIATIONS
WORLD ORGANIZATION OF WEBMASTERS
9580 Oak Avenue Parkway, Suite 7-177
Folsom, CA 95630
Tel: 916-608-2933
Fax: 916-987-3022
E-mail: info@joinwow.org
www.joinwow.org

WEBSITE DESIGNER

SALARY   • •

HOURS   • •

EDUCATION   • •

BOOKS, FILMS, AND TV SHOWS
FEATURING THE PROFESSION

- Idoru
- The Net

YOU'LL HAVE CONTACT WITH

- Computer programmers
- Internet/intranet managers
- Marketing and sales managers
- Online technicians
- Webmasters

PROFESSIONALS READ

- Computerworld Magazine
- Network Computing Magazine
- Slashdot
- Wired

A DAY IN THE LIFE

The Internet is a major force in the marketplace. The need for companies to have an attractive and enticing Web presence has caused them to hire Webmasters and website designers in droves. Website designers are, in a sense, a breed of graphic designers and typesetters, whose medium is the Internet, and their audience is millions strong worldwide. It is no wonder companies want website designers who can capture the attention of that audience for brand awareness, advertising, and sales reasons.

Although Webmasters are generally accountable for the functionality of the final website, it is the website designers who are initially in the trenches, coming up with the look, layout, and overall impact the site will have. Some consulting website designers may also author the text that appears on the site, while most individuals who work for large corporations will most likely receive text and information intended to be published on the Web from copywriters, Webmasters, or marketing managers. The text that writers give to designers may also indicate where to place hypertext links in the finished product. From there, it is up to the designers to work all of these elements into a functional, intriguing, user-friendly design.

{ user-friendly design }

To accomplish the task, website designers need varied and numerous technical skills. Knowledge of a coding language (like HTML) is required. A website designer's knowledge should be exceptional as he or she is expected to be the HTML expert. Designers must also be competent in browser compatibility issues, extensions (tables, frames, server push/client pull, and server-side protocols), and Common Gateway Interface (CGI) scripting devices (Java, Perl, C, UNIX, and others). Skilled knowledge of TCP/IP and networking protocols is also necessary in such areas as service ports, names servers, USENET, HTTP, FTP, and, naturally, e-mail. But they are designers after all, and in addition to their technical know-how, they must have graphic design skills—and not just in the artistic sense. Full knowledge of the capabilities of graphics applications within their medium (i.e., Photoshop, Fractal Painter, and 3-D modeling among others) is crucial, or their designs, however nice, won't work. If all that isn't enough, a website designer must be a certified net geek, familiar with downloading time and bandwidth problems, content-driven pages, and a working knowledge of netiquette. Oh, and it doesn't hurt to have patience—as the hours can be long when meeting deadlines—and good interpersonal skills. You will be working with a lot of other people who are expecting you to translate their ideas into a functional thing of beauty, whether you work for a corporation or are a self-employed consultant.

PAYING YOUR DUES

A lot of creativity and knowledge is required to be a successful website designer. Knowledge of computer science, programming, advertising, graphics, and art and design is preferable. A bachelor's degree in computer science or design helps, although unlike most other technical professions, the level of education is not as much a factor in success as is design talent and hands-on technical skills.

ASSOCIATED CAREERS

The heavy emphasis on electronic layout and design creates many crossover opportunities for website designers. Graphic designers have much in common with website designers, using many of the same design applications and requiring the same talent for layout. Electronic typesetters who design and produce everything from books, magazines, and menus also share many job skills and traits. Computer programmers have less in common, but also share knowledge of computers and scripting languages. However, being a website designer provides great preparation for careers in all multimedia applications as well as a career as a Webmaster.

PAST AND FUTURE

Companies have become extremely savvy about multimedia and Web designs, expecting high-end results. Long gone are the days when you could get paid nicely for simply publishing a corporate logo, a paragraph of text, and a few links on the Web. Website designers are still well paid for their services, though, and a full-time, in-house staffer can make anywhere from $30,000–$70,000 per year. Companies still hire many freelance and consulting website designers, although the tendency to hire in-house is becoming more standard.

This profession will continue to grow. Web designers are sought in every field imaginable, from the entertainment industry to the health care industry, because every company that has something to sell or information to disseminate wants to be on the Web. This is good news for website designers, as there doesn't look to be any shortage of demand for them in the short run. Staying on top of changing technology and market needs is the key to staying on top in this profession for the foreseeable future.

QUALITY OF LIFE

2 YEARS Salaries are attractive, as are the working environments for a website designer at any level. Usually, in an in-house setting, a website designer's space is slightly more relaxed than the surrounding corporate culture, but work is sedentary and hours can still be long, especially when management wants a site up yesterday. Designers who are self-employed can naturally make their own hours, but handling several clients at once can make for long hours and tax personally owned equipment. Responsibilities tend to remain along the graphic and creative lines for in-house designers, whereas consulting designers may put together an entire package for a client, requiring copywriting, marketing strategies, and plans for updating the site after its initial implementation.

5 YEARS After five years, many designers move on to become Webmasters or Internet technology managers, increasing their responsibility, opting for more professional challenges, and, of course, making even higher earnings.

10 YEARS After 10 years, most website designers have moved onto IT or other fields; those website designers that haven't left to become IT managers contract their work out, commanding higher rates with a steadily growing portfolio.

MAJOR EMPLOYERS
Any company with an Intranet or website will need website designers.

MAJOR ASSOCIATIONS
GRAPHIC ARTISTS GUILD
90 John Street, Suite 403
New York, NY 10038-3202
Tel: 212-791-3400
Fax: 212-791-0333
www.gag.org

INFORMATION TECHNOLOGY ASSOCIATION OF AMERICA
1401 Wilson Boulevard, Suite 1100
Arlington, VA 22209
Tel: 703-522-5055
Fax: 703-525-2279
www.itaa.org

INSTITUTE FOR THE CERTIFICATION OF COMPUTER PROFESSIONALS
2350 East Devon Avenue, Suite 115
Des Plaines, IL 60018-4610
Tel: 800-843-8227 or 847-299-4280
Fax: 847-299-4280
www.iccp.org

WORLD ORGANIZATION OF WEBMASTERS
9580 Oak Avenue Parkway, Suite 7-177
Folsom, CA 95630
Tel: 916-608-2933
Fax: 916-987-3022
E-mail: info@joinwow.org
www.joinwow.org

WRITER

A DAY IN THE LIFE

Writers come in all shapes and sizes—film critics, novelists, editorial columnists, screenwriters, technical writers, and advertising copywriters. Many of them spend the beginnings of their careers practicing their skills as they await a big break. While all writers prefer to write on subjects of personal interest, most of them are assigned topics by their editors. The writer receiving this assignment is either freelance or on staff. Writers may work at home, in an office, or in a hectic newsroom, but wherever they set up their office, writers generally spend upwards of 40 hours a week hard at work—even if only a fraction of that time is spent actually tapping the keys of a word processor. If they are on staff, these writers enjoy a regular paycheck and benefits, while the freelancer { **big break** } must foster his or her clientele to pay for his or her own health insurance. However, the freelancer generally retains stronger copyright control of his or her work and enjoys the freedom that comes with not having an assigned beat.

Writers begin by asking questions and researching a subject. The process of writing may involve conducting interviews, reading up on a subject at the library, traveling to a far-off location, or even surfing the Internet for clues. A writer must be open to the possibility that new information will change the original angle of a piece. As he or she gathers the necessary information, he or she gradually develops a working outline from which he or she is then able to work up a draft. Then it may be time for an editor to review the material and suggest changes. A writer is usually required to send a completed draft manuscript to an editor, with book authors being the exception as they are often permitted to send the manuscript in "partials" (sections or chapters) to give the editor a chance to see the work in progress from an earlier stage. The editing process continues until the editor and writer feel the material is ready for publication.

Writers collaborate with other professionals involved in the media, such as photographers, graphic designers, and advertisers. Screenwriters and playwrights write original pieces or adapt existing books or stories for the screen or stage. Usually they attend readings or rehearsals to make revisions because problems may appear when the piece is performed that they had not anticipated when they wrote it. Copywriters generally work for advertising agencies, researching market trends to determine the best way to sell their clients' products. Technical writers take esoteric subjects and write about them in simpler terms so that readers can easily grasp the ideas and information.

PAYING YOUR DUES

The one point most employers agree on is that good writers combine a natural gift for language with an unwavering devotion to their craft. For a professional career, a bachelor's degree in journalism, English, or literature is all but essential. But most important of all is practice, practice, practice, regardless of the medium. In high school, potential writers can write for the school newspaper or the yearbook; in college, they should continue writing for school newspapers and apply for internships at publishing houses. Technical writers should be well-versed in their subject areas and perhaps have advanced degrees. Every writer should be a proficient typist with mastery of a word processor; nowadays many writers, especially journalists, are expected to deliver their copy electronically via e-mail. Writing experience is very important. Writers must be disciplined, focused, good at research, and able to work under deadlines. Writers should collect samples of their work to show to prospective employers. A writer's first job is often as an assistant to a writer or an editor. Beginning writers generally work hard at research and clerical tasks while awaiting recognition and opportunity from their bosses.

ASSOCIATED CAREERS

Editors review and edit manuscripts and give authors guidance and direction for clarifying and otherwise improving their pieces. (Many editors admit to being failed or aspiring writers; the reverse can also be the case.) Journalists, who are of course themselves writers (see separate entry), tend to work under the direction of an editor who sends them out into the field to dig up stories, follow leads, and interview people and submit their findings in the form of a readable article.

PAST AND FUTURE

The earliest known writings are papyrus rolls recovered by archaeologists in Egypt and Greece and dating back as far as 3,000 B.C. It was not until the fifteenth century, however, when Johannes Gutenberg developed the first printing press, that books became accessible to more than a privileged few. Newspapers were established by the eighteenth century, heralding the dawn of the modern publishing age. As the printing press became more sophisticated, writing flourished.

Writers are needed everywhere, but it seems that there are still more writers than there are assignments, a phenomenon that led John Steinbeck to comment, "The profession of writing makes horse racing seem like a solid, stable business." Most freelancers obtain their primary income from other sources for many years before "making it" as authors. Demand is expected to increase for writers in commercial areas, though, as the number of commercial venues continues to expand. The world of electronic publishing has increased the demand for writers as Web publishers seek out content; this bodes well for writers in the coming years.

QUALITY OF LIFE

2 YEARS Writers just starting out generally work as assistants, receiving bit assignments here and there. Most individuals spend a substantial amount of time perfecting these pieces because they know this work may be a step toward a bigger writing assignment or a promotion. Freelancers struggle to be heard, and some create websites to get their work seen and to receive more feedback than a form rejection letter. Competition remains fierce, and many writers prepare themselves for an alternate career and pursue writing on the side, especially at first. This way they can eat and pay the rent while they obtain the experience they need for technical writing or wait for the day they get a letter of interest from a literary agent.

5 YEARS Most writers have been published in one form or another by this time. They may still be working on the Great American Novel, but the most determined (and most fortunate) writers have begun to receive the occasional paycheck for their commercial or technical writing. Individuals with steady employment never find their workday dull, but instead enjoy its daily changes in pace and subject. They have learned to operate under strict deadlines.

10 YEARS After 10 years, writers are now able to obtain assignments with the publications they like. But many writers continue to write even without substantial pay, since writing is often something the writer needs, rather than just wants, to do. Many published writers continue for years to subsidize their writing careers with other jobs, but those fortunate few individuals who have found steady work in journalism or elsewhere report high satisfaction, despite moderate pay and often intense pressure.

MAJOR EMPLOYERS
CONDÉ NAST PUBLICATIONS INC.
7 Times Square, 17th Floor
New York, NY 10036
Tel: 212-286-2860
http://www.condenast.com

PENGUIN GROUP
375 Hudson Street
New York, NY 10014
E-mail: jobs@Penguingroup.com
www.penguingroup.com

RANDOM HOUSE
1745 Broadway
New York, NY 10019
Tel: 212-751-9000
E-mail: humanresources@randomhouse.com
www.randomhouse.com

SAATCHI & SAATCHI
375 Hudson Street
New York, NY 10014-3620
Tel: 212-463-2000
Fax: 212-463-9855
www.saatchiny.com

MAJOR ASSOCIATIONS
AMERICAN SOCIETY OF JOURNALISTS AND AUTHORS
1501 Broadway, Suite 302
New York, NY 10036
Tel: 212-997-0947
Fax: 212-937-2315
E-mail: info@asja.org
www.asja.org

NATIONAL CONFERENCE OF EDITORIAL WRITERS
3899 North Front Street
Harrisburg, PA 17110
Tel: 717-703-3015
Fax: 717-703-3014
E-mail: ncew@pa-news.org
www.ncew.org

NATIONAL WRITERS UNION
113 University Place, 6th Floor
New York, NY 10003
212-254-0279
212-254-0673
E-mail: nwu@nwu.org
www.nwu.org

ALPHABETICAL INDEX

BIBLIOGRAPHY

Birkman, Roger, PhD. True Colors. Nashville, TN, Thomas Nelson Publishers, 1995. An in-depth appli-cation of the Birkman Method in significant life arenas: career, personal relations and spiritual values. Dr. Birkman's clarity of mind and spiritual authenticity shine through.

Bolles, Richard Nelson. The 1996 What Color is Your Parachute? Ten Speed Press, Berkeley, 1996. This is the book for source ideas. Dick has pruned and artfully shaped his material over a quarter of a centu-ry and encourages you to discover self, society, career, and spirit. I owe a great personal and profession-al debt to this book, as does anyone writing in the field.

Goleman, Daniel. Emotional Intelligence. Bantam Books, New York, 1995. A good book for assessing personal ideas about intelligence (What is it really? How can we best motivate?). Dr. Goleman expands ideas about the meeting ground between thought and feeling, the individual and society, and the impli-cations for our education and career choices are significant.

Ormont, Louis R. The Group Therapy Experience. St. Martin's Press, New York, 1992. If you want to know why and how groups of people can function in creative ways, this book will give you the answers. Written by a master of the craft in clear, workmanlike prose.

Porot, Daniel. The PIE Method for Career Success. JIST Works, Indianapolis, 1996. Daniel has a master-ful grasp of the by-play between employer and job seekers. "How do we calm each other down enough so that you see me at my best and you feel free to hire me?" is the subtext of this irreverent and wonder-fully illustrated text.

U.S. Department of Labor. Bureau of Labor Statistics. Available on the Web at www.bls.gov.

Wendleton, Kate. Through the Brick Wall Job Finder. Five O'Clock Books, New York, 1994. This book bristles with energy and verve. Who could not use an employee armed with the dedication and zeal this text imparts to its readers? The specific sections on "Researching Your Job Targets" and "Research Resources for an Effective Job Search" (by Wendy Alfus Rothman) alone are a wonderful addition to a career explorer's library.

ABOUT THE AUTHOR

Alan Bernstein is a psychotherapist, author, and career counselor who has held faculty positions at New York Medical College, NYU Graduate School, and Rutgers University. His work focuses on a central question: how do we become active in choosing our lives? The answer to this question is pursued in print, TV, and public forums. He maintains a private practice in New York City.

Notes

Notes

Lower your monthly student loan payments by
up to 51%

Call The Graduate Loan Center to find out how

Federal student loan consolidation is a free, government-backed program created to save you money. Call now and you can:

- **Lower your monthly payments by up to 51%**
- **Make just one payment each month**
- **Choose your own repayment plan**

Call right now and you can lock in the lowest fixed interest rates in history.

The Graduate Loan Center   **Call 1-866-581-4GLC**
(5 8 1 - 4 4 5 2)

The Graduate Loan Center

MANAGE STUDENT LOAN DEBT LIKE A PRO

The day finally came. It was the moment you had been waiting for. The past four years melded into one huge blur of quirky professors and impossible exams. All of the seemingly endless headaches and the occasional heartaches that you experienced throughout your college career became part of an expansive collage of scrapbook memories. The day you thought would never come not only arrived, but now it's a distant memory.

Now that graduation has passed, it is time for you to face the "real" world and do things that you thought could never be accomplished. Many exciting journeys lay ahead such as getting your first job and moving away from home. However, combined with these exciting journeys, there are some pretty big obstacles like buying a home and paying off your student loans.

Many people find it exceptionally difficult, if not impossible, to pay their college tuition without taking out loans. Fortunately, the United States Federal Government recognized this problem several years ago and developed a program that helps ease the pain of repaying student loan debt.

In 1965, the Federal Government passed *The Higher Education Act*. This legislation was passed to strengthen the educational resources of our colleges and universities. It provides financial assistance to students who are enrolled in postsecondary and higher education programs; thereby encouraging more students to pursue their college dreams.

Average college tuition increases have outpaced the growth in personal and family income over the past two decades. For this reason, the need for private and federal aid has increased dramatically. As school has become more expensive to attend, students and parents have been required to increase the amount they need to borrow to finance their education. Consequently, the loan amount that students and parents have to pay on a monthly basis has also increased.

In order to ease the financial burden on student and parent borrowers, Congress passed the *Consolidation Loan Program* under the *Higher Education Act in 1986*. Through this program, student loan borrowers are able to benefit by combining all of their existing variable rate federal loans into one new loan, locking in a low fixed interest rate for the life of the loan and extending the term in which they need to repay the loan. By consolidating, in some cases, borrowers can lower their monthly payments by up to 51%.

The Federal Consolidation Loan Program

The Federal Consolidation Loan Program is a unique program offered by the Federal Government that provides student loan borrowers with the following benefits:

- Borrowers can lower monthly loan payments up to 51%.

- Borrowers have the ability to lock in a low fixed interest rate for the life of the loan.

- All existing federal loans are combined into one new loan, requiring you to make only one payment per month.

- All existing deferment options are maintained and there are no prepayment penalties. (Deferment is the postponement of payment on student loans. While in deferment, all subsidized loans will accrue zero interest).

- There are several types of payment plans to choose from. In some cases you can take up to 30 years to repay and you can change the plan annually without any penalties.

- Additional borrower benefits may be offered by the lender to reduce the interest rate even more substantially

- Borrowers can apply with no application fees or credit checks required.

The eligibility guidelines for this program are very simple. In order to be eligible for a consolidation loan:

- The borrower's loans must be in their repayment (including deferment and forbearance) or grace period.

- The borrower must not be in default on their loans.

- The borrower must have at least $10,000 in total outstanding loans. This minimum balance may vary, depending on the lender.

Qualifying Loans Under the Federal Consolidation Loan Program:

Several types of student loans are eligible for consolidation, including:

- Federal Family Education Loan Program (FFELP)
  - o Federal Subsidized and Unsubsidized Stafford Loans
  - o Federal PLUS Loans
  - o Federal Consolidation Loans
- Direct Loan Program
  - o Direct Subsidized and Unsubsidized Stafford Loans
  - o Direct PLUS loans
  - o Direct Consolidation Loans
- Perkins Loan Program
  - o Federal Perkins Loans
- Health Profession Student Loans (HPSL)

www.gradloancenter.com   *1-866-581-4GLC*

- Federal Education Assistance Loans (HEAL)

- Federal Nursing Student Loans (NSL)

The Six Month Grace Period = Opportunity for Big Savings

Most borrowers know that they do not have to start paying off student loans until six months after graduation. This six month period is called the 'Grace Period'. Recent graduates are awarded time to start planning for their future before they are required to make payments on their student loan debt.

Contrary to popular belief, the grace period is actually the best time to begin repaying student loans. During the grace period, student loan interest rates are actually over half of a percent lower than when the borrower is required to make payments six months later.

If student loans are consolidated while they are in their grace period, a borrower may be able to enjoy up to 51% additional savings each month on their loan payments. Depending on the total amount due on the borrower's loans, this savings could translate to hundreds of extra dollars in the borrower's pocket each month.

Student Loan Interest Rates

Not all student loan borrowers have - or lock-in - the same interest rate when they take advantage of the Federal Family Education Loan (FFEL) Consolidation Program. This is not due to the borrower's personal credit or the lender selected, but rather, it's due to rules mandated by the government. A borrower's interest rate is determined by several factors. For each of the following Stafford loan scenarios, we are at very low interest rates.

- Originated after 07/98 in grace period or any type of deferment—4.70%

- Originated before 07/98 in grace period or any type of deferment—5.50%

- Originated after 07/98 in repayment or forbearance—5.30%

- Originated before 07/98 in repayment or forbearance—6.10%

FFELP Consolidation is a federal program. The actual interest rate is determined by a set of rules defined by the U.S. Department of Education. The interest rate is determined by taking the weighted average of all of the loans being consolidated and rounding up to the nearest 1/8th of a point. This new interest rate is fixed, rather than variable, and locked-in for the life of the loan. For this reason, the maximum increase of 1/8th of a point, or 0.1249%, is minimal. And, this is the only cost associated with consolidation.

As of July 1, 2004, interest rates on Federal Stafford Loans, the most common type of education loan, have dropped to nearly their lowest point in years. The interest rate is 4.70% in school, grace or deferment status and 5.30% for loans in repayment. Parent PLUS loans have a rate of 6.10%. Rates are adjusted on July 1 of each year based on the final auction of the 91-Day T-Bill for loans disbursed after 7/1/98. The PLUS loan interest rate is equal to the weekly average of the one-year constant maturity Treasury yield for the last calendar week ending on or before June 26 of each year.

Many mailings and advertisements from consolidation lenders promote the lowest possible interest rates and favorable borrower benefits. It is standard practice for companies to offer a 0.25% interest rate reduction for making automatic payments from a checking account. Many lenders also offer a 1% interest rate reduction once a certain number of on-time payments have been received. The actual interest rate is mandated by the federal government and is the same for all companies.

Repayment Options

The Federal Consolidation Loan Program allows borrowers to get the best payoff terms without imposing penalties for early re-payment. All Stafford loans are initially based on a ten-year payoff plan and the borrower is able to opt for a non-payment status such as deferment or forbearance when experiencing a cash flow problem. Many borrowers want lower monthly payments and may choose to have the payoff term on their loans extended. Switching to a longer-term payoff plan provides an immediate increase in short-term cash flow. Since there is no pre-payment penalty in the program, a borrower can make aggressive payments toward the principal at any time.

Most lenders do not require a borrower to accept the extended terms associated with repayment plans. At the borrower's request, the servicer of his/her consolidation can adjust the payment plan to a ten-year payoff schedule. Borrowers are initially set up on the following terms based upon the balance of their Consolidation Loan:

Total Loan Balances	Maximum Repayment Period
$10,000 to $19,999	15 years
$20,000 to $39,999	20 years
$40,000 to $59,999	25 years
$60,000 or more	30 years

A borrower may choose among four types of repayment plans:

- **Level Repayment**
  The level repayment plan, which is by far the most common method selected, provides for a fixed monthly payment throughout the life of your loan. Many borrowers choose this plan because they like the security and simplicity of a fixed monthly payment. But, more important, the level repayment plan usually is the least expensive in terms of total interest charges. The latter plans cost more because they slow down the repayment of the principal.

www.gradloancenter.com   *1-866-581-4GLC*

- **Graduated Repayment**

  The Graduated Repayment Plan offers more affordable payments throughout the early years of repayment and increases gradually over the remaining period of the loan.. The payments increase no more than 4% every couple of years. The loan is repaid in the same timeframe as the Level Repayment program, but the total interest costs are slightly higher. The purpose of this payment plan is to provide the borrower with more disposable income immediately upon beginning repayment.

- **Extended Repayment**

  This plan allows the borrower to repay their Federal Consolidation Loans over a 25-year period under a level or graduated repayment schedule. In order to qualify for this plan, the oldest Federal Stafford (subsidized and unsubsidized), Federal PLUS and/or Federal Consolidation Loan must have been disbursed on or after October 7, 1998. In addition, the combined outstanding balance on all eligible loans must be between $30,000 and $40,000.

- **Income-sensitive repayment**

  The income-sensitive plan is targeted to those borrowers who have considerable financial difficulty. Under this plan, monthly payments rise and fall on an annual basis and are tied to the borrower's income. This is the most flexible plan, but it also could prove to be the most expensive in the long run. It's also important to note that the borrower must reapply for the plan annually.

Thirty years is the maximum length for a loan unless a borrower takes out another federal loan. For those who qualify, a new federal loan allows a borrower to consolidate again with new payment terms. While extending the repayment term may increase the overall amount of interest paid over the life of the loan, those who have higher interest debt often find the longer payoff schedule to be acceptable.

In addition to the choice of plans, the borrower can switch from one repayment plan to another once a year. There's no additional cost or penalty, but not everyone qualifies for this service.

Making the Right Decision

Now that all of the benefits of the Federal Consolidation Loan Program have been explained in their entirety, it is up to you, the borrower, to make the final decision. Find the company that offers the best explanation of terms, or find the one with the best incentives. Remember, the actual interest rate is the same everywhere. The decision simply becomes a matter of personal choice. So what are you waiting for? Consolidate your student loans today and save money tomorrow!

The Graduate Loan Center, based in Chicago, Illinois, helps borrowers manage paying for the high cost of education by offering the Federal Consolidation Loan Program and Private Loan Programs. The Graduate Loan Center works with some of the nation's leading financial institutions, which combined have consolidated well over $1 Billion in student loans. Call today to speak with one of our specially trained Financial Aid Advisors.

www.gradloancenter.com   *1-866-581-4GLC*

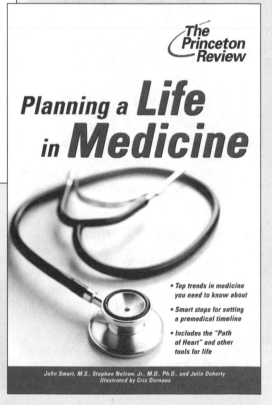